THE AMERICAN FOOTBALL TRILOGY

THE AMERICAN FOOTBALL TRILOGY

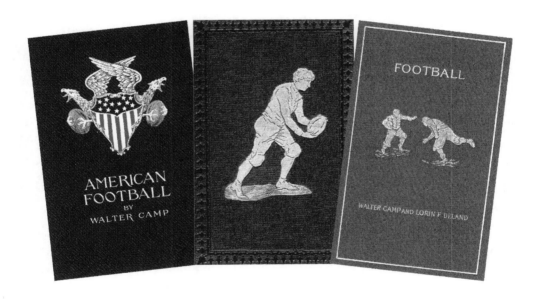

THE FOUNDING DOCUMENTS OF THE GRIDIRON GAME

Written by

WALTER CAMP & AMOS ALONZO STAGG

LORIN F. DELAND & HENRY L. WILLIAMS

THE LOST CENTURY OF SPORTS COLLECTION

This volume contains the complete text and illustrations from the following three books:

AMERICAN FOOTBALL
   By **Walter Camp**
      Harper & Brothers, Franklin Square
      New York
      1891

A Scientific and Practical Treatise on AMERICAN FOOTBALL for Schools and Colleges
   By **A. Alonzo Stagg** and **Henry L. Williams**
      Press of The Case, Lockwood & Brainard Company
      Hartford, Conn.
      1893

FOOTBALL
   By **Walter Camp** and **Lorin F. Deland**
      Houghton, Mifflin and Company
      The Riverside Press, Cambridge
      Boston and New York
      1896

ISBN: 9780982489123

Library of Congress Control Number: 2010931149

Printed in the United States of America

The Lost Century of ™
  Sports Collection

www.LostCentury.com

THE AUTHORS

WALTER CAMP (1859-1925) was the first football coach and literally wrote the football rule book. He was Yale's best player and captain in the 1870's when the sport was played under Rugby rules. As the most prominent member of the football rules committee in the 1880's, Camp introduced the line of scrimmage, the scoring system, the series of downs to retain the ball, and other fundamental features of the game. He was widely-known as "the Father of American Football" by the time these books were published. Many of his former players became pioneering coaches at colleges nationwide. Camp was a prolific writer and America's most admired sports authority.

AMOS ALONZO STAGG (1862-1965) was a famous player for Walter Camp at Yale and was named to the first All-American team in 1889. In 1892 the University of Chicago hired Stagg as the nation's first athletic director and football coach with faculty status. The diagrammed plays in his book became templates for innovative coaches to design their own plays. "The Grand Old Man of Football" was named Coach of the Year at age 81, and retired from coaching at age 97 with 314 career victories. Stagg was a standout pitcher in college and played in the first public basketball game in 1892. He is a member of both the football and basketball Hall of Fame.

HENRY L. WILLIAMS (1869-1931) was Stagg's teammate on Walter Camp's Yale squad. In 1891 he invented the "tackle-back" formation, coached West Point to its first victory against Annapolis, and set the world record in the 120 yard high hurdles. He later became the head football coach at the University of Minnesota for 22 years, during which he also maintained a medical practice. Dr. Williams was an influential member of the rules committee and an early proponent of the forward pass. Williams was inducted into the College Football Hall of Fame in the inaugural class of 1951, along with Camp and Stagg.

LORIN F. DELAND (1855-1917) was a military historian who never played football, or even attended a game, until he was in his mid-thirties. Within two years he was Harvard's head coach and recognized as a football genius. Deland analyzed the American sport as if it were a battlefield and devised plays based on military tactics, including the fabled "flying wedge," which he unveiled in a game against Walter Camp in 1892. The two rival coaches united in 1896 to write their comprehensive study of the sport. The diagrammed plays were drawn by Deland's wife, the novelist Margaret Deland.

THE GAME

DIFFERENCES:
- 110 yard field
- 3 downs to gain 5 yards
- No forward passing
- Ball was watermelon-shaped
- Same 11 played offense, defense, and special teams
- Full-back was also the defensive safety and kicker
- Substituted players could not reenter the game
- Scrimmage kicks could be recovered by either team
- Sideline coaching was not permitted during a game
- Scoring values: TD-4, PAT-2, FG-5, SAF-2
- Players were much smaller than today
- All wore pads but none wore helmets

FROM 1891 TO 1896:
- The sport was under attack for its brutality
- The Flying Wedge was invented, deployed, and prohibited
- Number of players moving at snap lowered from ten to one
- Officials blew whistles to end plays
- Unnecessary roughness and piling-on became penalties
- Stagg's Chicago team huddled versus Michigan in 1896

STREAMLINED SINCE:
- Point-After-Touchdown procedure
- Sideline inbounds, with hash marks
- Signals, with the huddle
- The shape of the ball, for passing

MODERN TRANSLATIONS:
- Rusher or forward = Lineman
- Rush line back = Linebacker
- In touch = Out of bounds
- Fair ("from a fair") = Put ball in play from out of bounds
- Interference = Run blocking, not the modern penalty
- Rules referred to "kicker" rather than "fullback" in 1914
- Eliminated: Punt-out in 1921 and kick-out in 1922
- Still legal but rare: drop-kick and free-kick
- Phrases defined on pages 185-190

CAUTION:
- The diets and training methods in these books are historical artifacts, not guidelines for modern players.

Page numbers in the original Contents and Index are conformed to this volume.
Original spelling forms are retained (e.g., inclosure, practise, reenforce).
The Trilogy Index on pages 387-390 encompasses all three books.

THE BOOKS

FOOTBALL
by Walter Camp and Lorin F. Deland, 1896

AMERICAN FOOTBALL

BY

WALTER CAMP

WITH THIRTY-ONE PORTRAITS

NEW YORK
HARPER & BROTHERS, FRANKLIN SQUARE
1891

PREFACE.

THE progress of the sport of football in this country, and a corresponding growth of inquiry as to the methods adopted by experienced teams, have prompted the publication of this book. Should any of the suggestions herein contained conduce to the further popularity of the game, the object of the writer will be attained.

CONTENTS.

ENGLISH AND AMERICAN RUGBY

Rugby football – for it is from the Rugby Union Rules that our American Intercollegiate game was derived – dates its present era of popularity from the formation in England, in 1871, of a union of some score of clubs. Nearly ten years before this there had been an attempt made to unite the various diverging football factions under a common set of laws; but this proved a failure, and the styles of play became farther and farther apart. Of the Association game one can say but little as regards its American following. It is quite extensively played in this country, but more by those who have themselves played it in Great Britain than by native-born Americans. Its popularity is extending, and at some day it will very likely become as well understood in this country as the derived Rugby is to-day. Its essential characteristic is, that it is played with the feet, in distinction from the Rugby, in which the ball may be carried in the hands.

To revert to the Rugby Union. Years before the formation of this association the game was played by sides almost unlimited in numbers. One of the favorite school matches was "Sixth form against all the rest of the school." Twenty on a side, however, became the ruling number; but this was, after a time, replaced by fifteens, as the days of twenties proved only shoving matches. With the reduction in numbers came increased running and an added interest. This change to fifteens was made in 1877, at the request of Scotland. At once there followed a more open style of play, and before long short passing became common. In 1882 the Oxford team instituted the long low pass to the open, and by the use of it remained undefeated for three seasons.

After the decrease to fifteen men the number of three-quarter-backs, who really represent our American half-backs, was increased from one to two, and two full-backs were played. A little later British captains put another full-back up into the three-quarter line, playing with only one full-back.

The Englishmen also play two men whom they call half-backs, but whose duties are like those of our quarter-back, for they seize the ball when it comes out of the scrimmage and pass it to a three-quarter for a run.

Nine men is the usual number for an English rush line, although a captain will sometimes take his ninth rusher back as a fourth three-quarter-back. There is much discussion as to when this should be done. The captain selects his men much as we do in America, and he is generally himself a player of some position behind the line, centre three-quarter being preferred. The opening play in an English Rugby game is, as a rule, a high kick well followed up. If one will bear in mind that the half backs are, like our quarter, the ones to seize the ball when it emerges from a scrimmage and pass it to the three-quarters, he will gain some idea of the character of the English method. He should understand, however, that the English half-back is obliged to look out sharply for the ball, because it comes out by chance and at random, and not directly as in our game, where the quarter can usually expect to receive the ball without trouble from the snap-back.

The forwards in an English match endeavor, when a scrimmage occurs, by kicking and pushing to drive the ball in the direction of their opponents' goal line, and they become extremely expert in the use of their feet. There are two umpires, whose duty it is to make claims (which they do by raising their flags), and a referee, who allows or disallows these claims. The penalty for fouls, which was at first only a down, is now in many cases a free kick.

The American game, it must be remembered, came from the Rugby Union in 1875, and not from the Rugby Union of to-day, although the changes in the English game have been by no manner of means commensurate with those made on this side of the water. Being bound by no traditions, and having seen no play, the American took the English rules for a starting-point, and almost immediately proceeded to add and subtract, according to what seemed his pressing needs. And they were many. A favored few, whose intercourse with Canadian players had given them some of the English ideas, were able to explain the knotty points to a small degree, but not enough to really assist the mass of uninitiated players to an understanding. Misinterpretations were so numerous as to render satisfactory rulings almost out of the question and explanatory legislation imperative. In the autumn of 1876 the first game under Rugby rules between American colleges was played at New Haven, and before another was attempted a convention had tried its hand at correcting the weak points, as they appeared to the minds of the legislators, in the Rugby Union Rules.

The feature of the American game in distinction from the English is, just as it was within a year from the time of adoption of the sport, the *outlet of the scrimmage.*

In this lies the backbone to which the entire body of American football is attached. The English half-backs stand outside the scrimmage, and when the ball pops out it is their duty to seize it and pass it out to a three-quarter, who runs with it. The American quarter-back stands behind the scrimmage and gives a signal, immediately after which he knows the ball will come directly into his hands to be passed for a run or a kick. What is, therefore, in the English game a matter of considerable chance is "cut-and-dried" in the American game; and the element of chance being eliminated, opportunity is given for the display in the latter game of far more skill in the development of brilliant plays and carefully planned maneuvers.

The Americans started with the English scrimmage, kicked at the ball, and pushed and scrambled for a season, until it was discovered that a very clever manifestation of the play was to let the opponents do the kicking – in fact, to leave an opening at the proper moment through which the ball would come, and a man a few feet behind this opening could always get the ball and pass it while the men who kicked it were still entangled in the scrimmage. After a little of this, no one was anxious to kick the ball through, and the rushers began to roll the ball sidewise along between the lines. Then almost immediately it was discovered that a man could snap the ball backwards with his toe, and the American outlet was installed.

At first the play was crude in the extreme, but even in its earliest stages it proved distinctly more satisfactory to both player and spectator than the kicking and shoving which marked the English method.

The same man did not always snap the ball back as he does now, but any one of the rushers would do it upon occasion. The men did not preserve their relative positions in the line, and any one of the men behind the line would act as a quarter-back. Such a condition of affairs could not, however, last long where intercollegiate rivalry proved such an incentive to the perfection of play, and the positions of centre-rush or snap-back and quarter-back became the most distinctive of any upon the field. The centre-rush at that time was selected more for his agility, strange to say, than for his weight and strength; but in case he was a light man he was always flanked by two heavy guards. One season's play convinced all captains that the centre section of the forward line must be heavy, and if any light-weights were to be used among the rushers they should be near the wings.

Quarter-back has, from the very outset, been a position in which a small man can be used to great advantage. The half-backs and backs have usually been men of speed coupled with skill as kickers.

The number originally adopted for matches in this country was eleven on a side. From some silly notion that it would increase the skill displayed, this number was changed to fifteen, although the Englishmen were moving in the other direction by reducing their numbers from twenties to fifteens. A year or two of fifteen on a side drove the American players back to elevens, and there the number has rested.

In the early days of the sport, while the players individually were courageous, the team play was cowardly; that is, the tacticians were so taken up with a study of the defence – how to protect the goal – that the attack was weak. The direct result of this was to place too few men in the forward line and too many behind it. If to-day we were to revert to fifteen on a side, there is little doubt that we should throw eleven of them up into the rush line, and upon occasion even twelve. We now realize that the best defence does not consist in planning how to stop a man after he has obtained a fair start towards the goal, but in throwing all available force up against him before he can get free of the forward line. The only way to effectively defeat this aggressive defence is by means of skilled kicking. It is possible with really good kickers to throw a team playing in this fashion into disorder by well-placed and long punting, followed up most sharply; but it requires nerve and an unfailing accuracy of aim and judgment.

It is only a few years ago that it required considerable argument to convince a captain that he could with safety send one of his halves up into the forward line when his opponents had the ball; but it will take better kicking than is exhibited in most of the championship matches to frighten that half-back out of the line now. Even the quarter was wont upon occasion to drop back among the halves and assist them rather than the rushers.

All the tendency for the last two years has been towards diminishing the number of men held in reserve, as it were, behind the line, and increasing by this means the crushing force by which the forwards might check either runner or kicker before his play could be executed.

Should the English ever adopt an outlet for their scrimmage, making the play as direct as is ours, their men would gravitate to the forward line as rapidly as have our players.

Next to the difference in scrimmage outlet between our game and that of the British stands a much more recent development, which we call interference. This is the assistance given to a runner by a companion or companions who go before him and break a path for him or shoulder off would-be tacklers. This, to the Englishman, would be the most detestable kind of off-side play, and not tolerated for an instant upon any field in the United Kingdom.

Even into this the Americans did not plunge suddenly, but rather little by little they stepped in, until it was necessary to do one of two things – either legalize what was being tacitly consented to, or penalize it heavily. The result was that it was legalized. With this concession, though, there went a certain condition which gained a measure of confidence for the new ruling.

To understand just how this state of affairs above mentioned came about one should know that, in the attempt to block opponents when the quarter-back was receiving and passing the ball, the forwards fell into the habit of extending their arms horizontally from the shoulder, as by this method each man could cover more space. For a number of years this went on without detriment to the sport in any way, but after a time there was more or less complaint of holding in the line, and it was ruled that a man must not change his position after the ball was snapped, nor bend his arms about an opponent at such a time. Unfortunately the referee (for at this stage of the game there was no umpire) could not watch the ball and the players with sufficient care to enforce this ruling, and the temper of the players suffered accordingly. It is always the case when a rule is not enforced unflinchingly, no matter from what cause, that both sides suffer, and the tendency always is towards devising additional infringements. The additional infringement in this instance was even worse than could have been foreseen; for, not content with simply blocking or even holding an opponent until the quarter should have passed the ball in safety, the players in the forward line saw an opportunity for going a step father, and actually began the practice of seizing an opponent long after the ball had been played, and dragging him out of the way of the running half-back. In the thick of the rush line this was frequently possible without risk of discovery by the referee; and, emboldened by successes of this kind, men would reach out even in the open, and drag back a struggling tackler just as he was about to lay his hands upon the runner. It was this state of affairs which brought up the question, "How much should a comrade be allowed to aid the runner?"

American football legislators answered this question satisfactorily, after long discussion, by determining that the runner might be assisted to any extent, provided the assistant did not use his hands or arms in performing this office. The first result of this was to lower the arms of the rushers when lined up, and, in spite of some forebodings, this proved really a benefit to the game. The second result has been to perfect a system of flanking a runner by companions who form almost an impassable barrier at times to the would-be tacklers.

At the same time with mention of the solution of this problem, one should also call attention to a menace which threatened American football far more seriously than did this; and that, too, at a time when the sport was by no means so strong in years or popularity as when this later difficulty arose. I refer to the "block game." This method of play, which consisted in a succession of "downs" without advance and without allowing the opponents any chance of securing possession of the ball, proved a means by which a weak team could avoid defeat. The whole object of the match was thus frustrated, the game resulting in no score.

To meet this difficulty a rule was introduced making it incumbent upon a side to advance the ball five yards, or retreat with it ten in three "downs." If this advance or retreat were not accomplished, the ball went at once into the possession of the opponents. Never did a rule in any sport work so immediate and satisfactory a reform as did this five-yard rule.

Within the last few years there has been no important change in the conduct of the American game, nor in the rules. Outside of the above-mentioned points of difference between it and the English game, there is only that of the methods of enforcing rules and determining differences. The English have a referee and two umpires, although the umpires are sometimes replaced by touch-judges. The umpires act, as did the judges in our game of ten years ago, as advocates for their respective sides, and it is this advocacy which is causing them to fall into disfavor there exactly as they did here. Touch-judges merely watch the lines of the field, and decide when and where the ball goes into touch. In cases where they are employed, the referee renders all decisions upon claim of the captains. In our method there is a division of labor, but along different lines. Our two officials, the umpire and referee, have their separate provinces, the former ruling upon the conduct of players as to off-side and other offences, while the latter determines questions of fact as to when the ball is held or goes into touch, also whether a goal is kicked or not. As the rule has it, the umpire is judge for the players, and the referee for the ball.

END RUSHER

The end rusher must get into condition early. Unless he does, he cannot handle the work that must fall to his share, and the effect of a poor performance by the end is to produce disorder at once in the proportion of work as well as the quality of the work of the tackles and half-backs. This is not well understood by captains and coaches, but it is easy to see if one follows the play. A tired end rusher, even one who has experience and a good idea of his place, will lope down the field under a kick, and by his lack of speed will allow a return; and, against a running game, while he will, it is true, force his man in, he will do it so slowly that the runner is enabled to pass the tackle. The first will surely result in his own halves shortening their kicks, and the second in drawing his own tackle too widely from the guard. Both these results seriously affect the value of the practice for halves and tackles; consequently, the end must be put in condition early. The finer points of his position can be worked up gradually, but his endurance must be good at the outset, in order that the others may become accustomed to rely upon him for regular work. But it sometimes happens that the captain or coach has no chance to make sure of this. His candidates may be raw, and only appear upon the first day of fall practice. In that case there is a method which he can adopt to advantage, and which answers the purpose. It is to play his candidates for that position one after the other in rotation, insisting upon hard playing even if it be for only five minutes at a time. In this way not only will the tackle receive the proper support, but the ends themselves will improve far more rapidly than under the usual method. Every player upon a team has to labor under two distinctly different sets of circumstances: one set arising from the possession of the ball by his opponents, and the other from the possession of the ball by his own side. Many an error in instruction or coaching arises from terming the tactics adopted under these two conditions defensive and offensive. It is no uncommon thing to see an end rusher, who has been told that such and such is his defensive play, so affected by the word *defensive*, as applied to his action, as to fail entirely to perform any aggressive work when his opponents have the ball. And a similarly undesirable state of affairs is brought about by the term *offensive* when his own side have the ball. In this latter case, he seems inspired to become aggressive in his conduct towards his opponent from the moment the men are lined up, and this very often leads him to make any interference of his so premature as to render it useless towards favoring his runner. One of the first things, therefore, for a coach to tell an end rusher is that the terms offensive and defensive, as applied to teamwork, have nothing to do with the aggressiveness of any individual. Then, as a matter of still better policy, let him avoid using these terms in individual coaching.

When the opponents have the ball, the end rusher must, in the case of a kick, do his utmost to prevent his *vis-à-vis* from getting down the field early under the ball. That is the cardinal point, and it is not necessary for him to do much thinking regarding anything else when he is facing a kicking game. When his opponents are about to make a run, the situation is much more involved. He must then consider himself as the sole guardian of that space of ground extending from his tackle to the edge of the field, and he must begin at the touch line and work in. That is, he must remember that, while on one side of him there is the tackle, who will do his utmost to help him out, there is on the side – that is, towards touch – no one to assist him, and a run around the end means a free run for many yards. "Force the man in" is always a good motto for an end, and one he will do well to follow conscientiously. To force the man in does not mean, however, to stand with one foot on the touch line, and then reach in as far as possible and watch the man go by, as nine out of every ten ends have been doing for two years. It means, go at the runner with the determination of getting him any way, but taking him always from the outside. An end cannot tackle as occasionally does a half-back or back, slowly and even waiting for his man, then meeting him low and strong. An end always has to face interference, and good interference will bowl over a waiting end with ease. An end must go up as far and fast as he dares to meet the runner, and when his moment comes – which must be a selected moment – he must shoot in at his man, reaching him, if possible, with his shoulder, and at the same time extending his arms as far around him as possible. Many times this reaching enables an end to grasp his man even though a clever interferer break the force of his tackle. And when his fingers touch the runner, he must grip with the tenacity of the bull-dog, and never let go.

It seems almost unnecessary to say that a high tackler has no chance whatever as an end rusher. He may play guard or centre, but before a man ever essays the end he must have passed through all the rudimentary schooling in tackling, and be such an adept that to pass him without the assistance of the most clever interference is an impossibility.

An end should be a good follower; that is, if the runner make in towards the tackle, the end should run him down from behind when interference cuts off the tackle. This is one of the best points for cultivation, because it effectually prevents any dodging by the runner. If he fail to take his opening cleanly, a following end is sure of him. This is not a safe point, however, to teach until the player has fairly mastered the ordinary end-work; for the tendency is to leave his own position too soon, giving the runner an opportunity to turn out behind him, and thus elude the tackle without difficulty.

A few years ago there was quite a fashion for the man putting the ball in from touch to run with it along the edge of the field. For some unknown reason this play seems to have been abandoned, but it is likely at any time to be revived, and the end rusher should therefore be posted upon the *modus operandi* of it, as well as the best method of preventing its success. The most popular execution of this maneuver was the simplest; that is, the man merely touched the ball to the ground and plunged ahead as far as he could until brought to earth or thrown out into touch. This was accompanied by more or less helpful interferences upon the part of his own end and tackle. There were more intricate methods, however; and surely, with the amount of interference allowed in these days, it is odd that the side line has not been more fancied by those who have generalled the great games. There was one team a few years ago whose captain used to deliberately place the ball just inside the line on the ground, as though only thoughtlessly leaving it there, and then spring in, crowding the end rusher three or four feet from the touch line, while a running half, who was well started, came tearing up the field, seized the ball, and usually made a long run before he was stopped by the astonished halves. Many also were the combination passes in which the ball was handed to the end rusher, who, turning suddenly with his back to the foes, would pass to his quarter or running half. Of these close double passes at the edge of the field the most effective were those wherein the runner darted by just inside the touch line, and the weakest the ones wherein the attempt was made to advance out into the field. For this reason there ought to be no particular necessity for coaching any but the end rusher and the tackle upon means to prevent advances of this nature. To the players in the centre of the line there is no apparent difference whether the ball be played from touch in any of these ways above mentioned, or through the more customary channel of the quarter-back. To the end and tackle, however, the difference is marked, because the runner comes so much sooner and the play is so greatly condensed and focused, as it were, directly upon them.

The instructions to the end are to handle the ball as much as possible while the opponent is endeavoring to get it in, and thus make the work of that individual as difficult as possible; and, secondly, to plant one foot close to the touch line and the other as far out into the field as is consistent with stability, and to maintain that position until the play is over. He must neither try to go forward nor around, but, braced well forward, hold his ground. If he does this, no runner can pass within three feet of the touch line, and outside of that the tackle can take care of him. This player, like the end, should, when the ball is played from a fair, be very loath to plunge forward until the play is located, because in the present stage of development of the game one can be quite sure that the opponents will not play the ball from touch unless they have some definite and usually deceptive line of action. Without such it is by far the better policy to walk out the fifteen paces and have it down. The quarter-back also has work to do upon side-line plays, in assisting at the edge as much as possible. But to return to the end. When his own side have possession of the ball, his play, like that of any other man, must be governed by the character of the intended move, and the knowledge of what this move will be is conveyed to him by the signal. The nearer the play is to his end, the greater is the assistance he can render. There is little need of coaching him to do his work when the run is along his line, nor, in fact, when it is upon his side of the centre. The knowledge of the proximity of the runner stirs him up sufficiently, if he have any football blood in him. The point towards which coaching should be directed and where it is needed is in starting instantly to render assistance when the play is upon the other side of the line. There is no limit to the amount of work an end may perform in this direction. A good end can toss his man back so that he cannot interfere with the play, and then cross over so quickly as to perform effective interference even upon end runs. In "bucking the centre" he can come from behind with valuable weight and pressure. A coach should remember, though, that it will not do to start an end into doing too much unless he is able to stand the work, for an end had better do the work well upon his own side than be only half way useful upon both ends. A tired-out end makes the opponents doubly strong.

THE TACKLE

Those teams upon which the work of end and tackle has been best developed have, for the last few years, been markedly superior in the opposition offered to plays of their opponents. This fact in itself is an excellent guide to the style of play one ought to expect from these two positions. The four men occupying them are the ones to meet nine tenths of the aggressive work of the opponents. The position of end has already been dwelt upon at length. That of tackle, a position much later to reach the full stage of development than the end, has nevertheless now attained almost an equal prominence. The tackle is an assistant to both end and guard, while he has also duties of his own demanding constant attention.

When the opponents have the ball and are about to kick, the tackle is one of the most active components of the line. He may not be moving until the ball is snapped, but upon the instant that it is played he is at work. He may himself go through to prevent the pass or kick, or still oftener he may make a chance for a line half-back to do this. By a line half-back is meant that one who, upon his opponents' plays, comes into the line and performs the duties of a rusher. This method has become so common of late that it is well understood. The play of this line half-back must dovetail into the work of the tackle so well as to make their system one of thoroughly mutual understanding. For this reason they should do plenty of talking and planning together off the field, and carry their plans into execution in daily practice until they become in company a veritable terror to opponents, particularly to kicking halves.

One of the very simple, yet clever and successful, combinations worked in this way has been for the line half to take his position outside the tackle, who immediately begins to edge out towards the end. This opens a gap between the opposing tackle and guard, for the tackle will naturally follow his man. This line half simply watches the centre, and as he sees the ball played goes sharply behind the tackle and through the opening. This play can be greatly aided by cleverness on the part of the tackle, who, to perform it to perfection, should edge out most cautiously, and with an evident intention of going to the outside of his man. He should also watch the centre play, and, most important of all, jump directly forward into his man when the ball is snapped. This will enable the half to take almost a direct line for the half, and with his flying start have more than a fair chance of spoiling the kick. The tackle must not be idle after his plunge, but should follow in sharply, because there will always be an opposing half protecting the kicker; and if the line half be checked by this man, as is not unlikely, the following tackle has an excellent opportunity by getting in rapidly. The tackle and half should alternate in their arrangement, neither one always going through first, and thus add to the anxiety and discomfort of the opponents.

When the opponents are about to run instead of kick, the same combination of line half and tackle can be put in operation, except that it will not do for these two to follow each other through with such freedom, as there is too much danger of both being shunted off by a clever turn coupled with well-timed interference. The cardinal point to be remembered is, to be far enough apart so that a single dodge and one interference cannot possibly throw off both men.

The tackle's duties towards the end have been partially described in dwelling upon the work of the latter, but there is plenty of detail to be studied. One of the first things to impress upon the tackle is, that he must watch the ball, not only upon the pass from the quarter, but also after it settles in the runner's arms, for the most successful double or combination passes are those which draw the tackle in towards the centre and give the second recipient of the ball only the end to pass. It has been too common a mistake of coaches to caution a tackle who has been deceived by this double pass against "going so hard." This is wrong. It soon results in making a slow man of the player, for he hangs back to see if the runner be not about to pass the ball, until he is too late to try for the man before he reaches the rush line; and, with the present system of interference and crowding a runner after he reaches the rush line, there is no chance to stop him short of three, and it may very likely be five yards. The proper coaching is to send him through on the jump, with his eyes open for tricks. Let him take a step or two towards the runner, so that, if no second pass be made, the tackle will be sure to meet him before he reaches the rush line, and not after it. This method of coaching makes not only sharp tackles, but quick and clever ones, with plenty of independence, which will be found a most excellent quality.

As regards the relations between the tackle and guard, they are best defined by saying that the guard expects to receive the assistance of the tackle in all cases requiring agility, while in cases requiring weight the guard is equally ready to lend assistance to the tackle.

When his own side has the ball, the tackle has far more than the end to do. In fact, the tackle has the most responsible work of any man along the line, having more openings to make, and at the same time the blocking he has to perform is more difficult. The earlier description of the work of a line half and the tackle in getting through is sufficient to indicate the difficulties which the opposing tackle must face in preventing this break through. While blocking may not be the most important duty, it is certainly the one which will bear the most cultivation in the tackles of the present day, for the ones who are really adept in it are marked exceptions to the general run. It is no exaggeration to say that more than two thirds of the breaking through that does real damage comes between the end and guard, and therefore in the space supposed to be under the care of the tackle. By successful blocking is meant, not unfair holding, which sooner or later will result in disaster, nor backing upon a runner or kicker as the charger advances, which is almost as bad as no blocking, but that clever and properly timed body-checking of the opponent which delays him just long enough to render his effort to reach his man futile every time. This kind of blocking looks so easy, and is so difficult, that it is found only in a man who is willing to make a study of it. Coaching can but give any one wishing to acquire this a few points; the real accomplishment depends upon the man's unflagging perseverance and study. The first thing to be noted is, that a really good forward cannot possibly be blocked every time in the same way. He soon becomes used to the method, and is able to avoid the attempt. Dashing violently against him just as he is starting may work once or twice, and then he will make a false start to draw this charge, and easily go by the man. Standing motionless, and then turning with a sharp swing back against him, will disconcert his charge once in a while. Shouldering him in the side as he passes will throw him off balance or against some other man, if well performed, occasionally. Falling down before him by a plunge will upset him even when he has quite a clear space apparently, but it will not work if played too often. By a preconcerted plan he may be coaxed through upon a pretended snap, and then the ball played while he is guarded and five yards gained by his off-side play, but he will not be taken in again by the same method. These are but a few of the strategies which engage the study of the tackle. How soon to let the man through is also an important question. When the ball is to be punted, the tackle upon the kicker's side must block long and hard, while the tackle upon the other end should block sharply, and then let his man through for the sake of getting down the field under the kick. When a drop is to be attempted, the blocking upon both sides must be close and long, much longer than for a punt. Moreover, it is by no means a bad policy to have the blocking last until the ball is actually seen in the air in front of the line, because then, if the kick be stopped, the tackles can go back to assist the backs in recovering the ball. The blocking for a kick, as a rule, should be close; that is, every opponent must be matched from the centre out, leaving the free man or men on the ends. This rule has its exceptions, but when there is any doubt about the play it is safest to block close, and take the chances from the ends rather than through breaks in the line. In blocking for a run the case is very different, and depends upon the point of assault. If the run is to be made around the right end, for instance, by the left half-back, the right tackle must block very slowly and long. That is, he must not dash up to his man the instant the ball is snapped and butt him aside, for the runner will not be near enough to derive any advantage from this, and the opponent will easily recover in time to tackle him. Rather should he avoid contact with his man until his runner makes headway, and then keep between the opponent and runner until the latter puts on steam to circle, when it is his duty to engage his man sharply, and thus let the runner pass. In blocking for an inside run upon his own side, he should turn his man out or in, as the case may be, just as the runner reaches the opening, being particularly careful not to make the break too early, lest the opponent reach the runner before he comes to the opening.

THE GUARD

The position of guard, while it requires less agility than that of tackle, can never be satisfactorily filled by a man who is slow. Many a coach makes this mistake and fails to see his error until too late to correct it. I remember once seeing upon a minor team a guard who weighed at least 190 pounds replaced by a man of 155, and the latter actually filled the position – greatly to my astonishment, I confess – in excellent fashion. This does not at all go to prove that weight is of no value in a guard. On the contrary, it is a quality especially to be desired, and if one can find a heavy man who is not slow he is the choice by all means. But weight must be given work to do, and that work demands practice, and slowness of execution cannot be tolerated. At the outset the coach must impress this fact upon the guards, and insist upon their doing their work quickly. It is really wonderful how much better the effect of that work will prove to be when performed with a snap and dash that are not difficult to acquire.

When the opponents have the ball and are about to kick, the guard should have in his mind one persistent thought, and that is, to reach the quarter before the ball is away from his hand, but not to stop there. It is only once in a great while that fortune favors sufficiently to crown this attempt with success. When it does, so much the better; but the guard should take in the quarter only in a general sweep, making on for the kicker, and at the same time getting his arms up in the air when he comes before him, so as to take every possible chance of stopping the ball. Just here it may be well to explain the confidence with which in these details of coaching the phrases are used "when the opponents are about to kick" and "when the opponents are about to run." It is true that one cannot tell infallibly every time whether the play will be a kick or a run, but experienced players are really so seldom at fault in their judgment upon this point that it is safe to coach as though there never existed any doubt about the matter.

To continue with the work of the guard when the opponents are about to attempt a run. One of the most important features of the play in this position is to guard against small wedges. If a guard simply stands still and straight he will be swept over like a wisp of straw by any well-executed wedge play directed at him. An experienced man knows this, and his chief thought is how to avoid it, and how, first, to prevent the formation; second, to alter the direction, and, finally, to stop the progress, of this terror of centre work, the small wedge. There are as many ways of accomplishing these results as of performing the duties of tackle or end, and it rests with the individual player to study them out. To prevent the formation of small wedges, the most successful method is that of sudden and, if possible, disconcerting movements. Jostling, so far as it is allowed, sudden change of position, a pretended charge – all these tend to break up the close formation. Once formed and started, the change of direction is usually the most disarranging play possible; but this should not be attempted by the player or players opposite the point of the wedge. At that spot the proper play is to check the advance, even temporarily; for the advance once checked, the wedge may be swung from the side so as to take off the pressure from behind. So it is the men at the side who must endeavor to turn the wedge and take off this pressure. Without the actual formation upon the field it is difficult to fully explain this turning of the wedge; but if the principle of the defence be borne in mind, it will not be found so hard to understand. Check the peak even for a moment, and get the weight off from behind as speedily as possible. The men who are pushing must necessarily act blindly; and if their force is not directly upon the men at the point of the V, they pass by the man with the ball and so become useless. Both guards must keep their weight down low, close to the ground, so that the wedge, if directed at either, cannot throw that one at once off his balance backward. If this occurs, the wedge will always make its distance, perhaps go many yards. Lying down before the wedge is a practice based upon this principle of keeping close to the ground, and is by no means an ineffectual way of stopping an advance, although it is not as strong a play as bringing about the same result without actually losing the power to straighten up if the wedge turns. Moreover, the men in the front of a wedge are becoming so accustomed to meeting this flat defence that they not infrequently succeed in getting over the prostrate man and regaining the headway on the other side. This, as one can readily see, must always yield a very considerable gain. When a run is attempted at some other point in the line, it is the duty of the guards to get through hard and follow the runner into his opening, even if they cannot reach him before he comes into the line. In this class of play a guard should remember that if he can lay a hand upon the runner before he reaches the line he can spoil the advance to a certainty, for no runner can drag a heavy guard up into and through an opening. It is like dragging a heavy and unwieldy anchor. A guard can afford to, and must sometimes, tackle high. Not that he should, in the open, ever go at the shoulders, but in close quarters he often has no time to get down low, and must make the best of taking his man anywhere that the opportunity offers. He must always, however, throw him towards the opponent's goal. Another point for guards to bear in mind is, that in close quarters it is often possible to deprive the runner of the ball before he says "down." A guard who always tries this will be surprised at the number of times he will find the referee giving him the ball. He will also be astonished at the way this attempt results in the runner saying "down" as soon as he finds someone tugging at the ball. A man gives up all thought of further advance the instant he finds the ball slipping at all in his grasp; and when his attention is distracted from the idea of running, as it is when he is fearful of losing the ball, he can never make use of his opportunities to good advantage. For this reason the coach should impress upon all the forwards the necessity of always trying to take away the ball; but the men in and near the centre are likely to have the best opportunity for this play, because it is there that the runner encounters a number of men at once rather than a single individual.

When his own side have the ball the guard must block sharply until the quarter has time for receiving the ball, and, at any rate, beginning the motion of the pass. It is safer, in the case of inexperienced guards, to tell them to block until the quarter has time to get rid of the ball. The distinction is this: that an experienced guard sometimes likes to gain just that second of time between the beginning of the pass and the completion of the swing, and utilize it in getting down the field or making an opening. So accustomed does he become to measuring the time correctly that he will let the opponent through just too late to reach the quarter, although it seems a very close call. It is not safe to let green guards attempt anything so close. They must be taught to block securely until the ball is on its way to the runner or kicker. The blocking of a guard is much less exacting in its requirements than that of the tackle. Not that he must not block with equal certainty, but the act requires no such covering of two men as often happens in the case of a tackle. The guard forms closely towards the centre, and then follows his man out if he moves out, but only as far as he can go, and still be absolutely certain that the opponent cannot pass between him and the snap-back. To be drawn or coaxed out far enough to admit of an opponent's going through the centre shows woeful ignorance in any guard.

When a kick is to be made the blocking must be prolonged a little, and on a drop-kick (as mentioned earlier) it should last until the ball goes from the foot. When blocking for a run, of course much depends upon where the opening is to be made, and a guard must be governed accordingly. The method itself is, again, different in the guard from that exhibited in the tackle. A guard may not move about so freely and must face his man more squarely than a tackle, for the guard must protect the quarter first, while the tackle considers the half only. If a guard allows his opponent to get a fair lunge with outstretched arm over or past his shoulder, he may reach the quarter's arm even though his body is checked, while such a reach at the point in the line occupied by the tackle would be of no value whatever. Previous to the snap-back's playing the ball it is the duty of the guards to see that their individual opponents do not succeed in either kicking the ball out from the snap-back's hand or otherwise interfering with his play. This is quite an important feature, and a centre should always feel that he has upon either hand a steady and wide-awake assistant, who will neither be caught napping nor allow any unfair advantage to be taken of him. The guard should bear in mind one fact, however, and that most clearly. It is that squabbling and general pushing about are far more liable to disconcert his own centre and quarter than to interfere with the work of the opponents.

THE CENTRE, OR SNAP-BACK

The man who may be selected to fill the important position of centre-rush must be a man of sense and strength. Brain and brawn are here at their highest premium. But there is another element of character without which both will be overthrown, and that is patience. Practical experience has taught football coaches that none but a thoroughly self-controlled man can make a success in football in any position, while in this particular one his disposition should be of the most equable nature. He will be called upon to face all kinds of petty annoyances, for his opponents will endeavor to make his play as difficult as possible; and never must he allow himself for one instant to lose sight of the fact that his entire attention must be devoted to his play, and none of it distracted by personal feeling. Moreover, while he must be able to play the ball quickly when called upon, he can never afford to be hurried by his opponents. With the present excellent rulings of umpires regarding interference with the ball before it is snapped, much of the most harassing kicking of the ball from under his hand has been stopped; but, for all that, he is indeed a lucky centre who does not feel the ball knocked out from under his grasp several times during a game. In addition to this, every man who breaks through gives him a rub. Sometimes these knocks are intentional, often they are given purely by accident, and the latter are by no means the lightest. Then, too, a man is pushed in to the snap-back just as the ball goes. It may be his own guard, but the blow hurts just as much; and a centre who is not amiable under such treatment soon loses his head and forgets that he should care for nothing except to accomplish gains for his own side. The object of placing so much stress upon this qualification is to impress upon a coach the almost inestimable value of the quality of patience in any men he may be trying for this position. He can never say too much about it.

As regards the duties of the place, they differ from those of any other position in the line on account of the constant presence at that spot of the ball. The centre is either playing the ball himself or watching his antagonist play the ball at every down; so that while he has all the other duties of a forward to execute, he has the special work besides. Here is the weakness of so many centres. They are snap-backs only or forwards only, the former being by all odds the more common. A good critical coach of experience will see nine out of every ten men whom he may watch in this position playing through day after day with no more idea of doing any forward work than if they were referees. Putting the ball in play at the right time, and properly, is a great achievement, but it does not free the centre-rush from all other obligations. He must protect his quarter; he must aid in making openings, and perform any interference that may be possible, as well as always assisting a runner of his own side with weight or protection. He must always get down the field under a kick, for it is by no means unusual for him to have the best opportunity in these days when end rushers are so carefully watched. When the opponents have the ball, he must not be content with seeing that the opponent does not roll it to a guard, but must also see that there is no short, tricky passing in the scrimmage. Then he must be as ready as either guard to meet, stop, or turn a wedge. He must make openings for his comrades to get through, even when he himself may be blocked, and always be ready to reach out or throw himself before a coming runner to check the advance.

The details of the special work of the centre are many, and thorough knowledge of them can only come from experience. During his early progress a new snap-back usually sends the ball against his own legs, or, if he manages to keep them out of the way, is upset by his opponent for his pains. It is no child's play to hold a ball out at arm's length on the ground in front of one and roll it back so that it passes between one's feet, and still preserve a good balance in spite of a sudden push of a hundred-and-eighty-pound opponent. But that is just what a centre has to do every time the ball is down and belongs to his side. The first thing to teach a centre is to stand on his feet against any amount of jostling. Then he must learn to keep possession of the ball until ready to play it. Both of these acquirements take practice. The most finished and experienced centres have a way of playing the ball just as they are half straightening as though to meet a charge from in front. This insures their not being pushed over on to the quarter, and yet does not cause them to lean so far forward as to be pitched on their noses by a little assistance from the opposing centre. When a man stands so as to prevent a push in the chest from upsetting him, he naturally puts one foot back some distance as a support. When a centre does this he is apt to put that foot and leg in the path of the ball. A second objection to this way of standing is, that the centre does not offer nearly as much opposition to any one attempting to pass as he does when he stands more squarely faced about with a good spread of the legs. As to holding the ball, some centres prefer to take it by the end, while others roll it on its side. It can be made to rise for the quarter if sent on end, whereas if played upon its side it lies closer to the ground. The quarter's preference has, therefore, something to do with it. It requires longer practice and more skill to play the ball on its end, but it permits an umpire to see more clearly whether the ball be actually put in play by the snap-back or played for him by the surreptitious kick of the opponent. It has also the advantage of sending the ball more narrowly upon a line, so that its course is less likely to be altered than when rolled upon its side. While the snap-back is seldom held to the very strictest conformity to the rule about being on side when he puts the ball in play, it is necessary for him to practice with a view to this particular, because he is liable to be obliged to conform every time if the opponents insist. The reason for carelessness in this respect is, there is no penalty for infringement except being obliged to return to the spot and put the ball in play properly. A certain laxity, therefore, is granted rather than to cause delays. But, as stated above, a center must be able to put the ball in play when fairly on side, and must live up to this with some moderate degree of regularity, or else the umpire will call an off side and bring him back. A centre ought to practice putting the ball in play with either hand until he is fairly proficient with his left as well as his right. Not that he should use his hands alternately in a game, but that an injury to his right hand need not necessarily throw him out of the game. It is by no means an unrecognized fact that the greater amount of experience possessed by the regular centre is so valuable as to make it policy to keep him in his place so long as his legs are good, even though a hand be injured, rather than to replace him by the substitute with whose methods the quarter-back is not so familiar.

A coach should see to it that his centre has a variety of men to face, some big, some tricky, some ugly. If any old players come back to help the team in the way of coaching, and among them are some centre rushers, they can do no better work than by donning a uniform and playing against the "Varsity" centre.

THE QUARTER-BACK

The quarter is, under the captain, the director of the game. With the exception of one or two uncommon and rare plays, there is not one of any kind, his side having the ball, in which it does not pass through his hands. The importance of his work it is therefore impossible to overrate. He must be, above all the qualifications of brains and agility usually attributed to that position, of a hopeful or sanguine disposition. He must have confidence in his centre himself, and, most of all, in the man to whom he passes the ball. He should always believe that the play will be a success. The coach can choose no more helpful course during the first few days, as far as the quarter is concerned, than that of persuading him to repose confidence in his men. Many promising half-backs are ruined by the quarter. There is nothing that makes halves fumble so badly, get into such awkward positions, start so slowly, and withal play so half-heartedly, as the feeling that the quarter does not think much of them, does not trust them, or believe in their abilities. Every half-back can tell the same story – how he is nerved up by the confidence of the quarter, and what an inspiration it is to good work to see that confident look in the eye of the man who is about to pass to him. But not alone in the work of the half does it make a great difference, but in that of the quarter himself. When he lacks confidence in his man, his passing is unsteady and erratic as well as slow. He allows the opponents a far better chance of reaching the man before he can get started, both by irregular and slow passing, and also by a nervous looking at him before the ball is played.

In practice, great stress should be laid on quick handling and sharp passing of the ball. A quarter can slow up in a game if advisable, but he can never do any faster work than that which he does in practice without throwing his men completely out. In order to make the play rapid, a quarter must be figuratively tied to the centre's coat, or rather jacket, tails. As soon as the centre reaches the ball after a down, he should know that the quarter is with him. Usually there is an understood signal between them, which not only shows the centre that the quarter is on hand, but also when he is ready to receive the ball. One of the most common of these signals has been placing the hand upon the centre's leg or back. A pinch would let him know when to snap the ball. In spite of this method's having been used by opponents to fool a centre, it has been, and still is, the most common. One of the best variations of it has been for the quarter to put his hand upon the centre and keep it there until he is ready for the ball, then take it off and let the center snap the ball, not instantly, but at his convenience. Should anything occur making it advisable, for some reason, to stop the play, the quarter puts his hand upon the centre again at once, and until it is once more removed the snap-back understands that the quarter is not ready to have the ball come. Almost any amount of variation can be made in the signal of the quarter to his centre; but in arranging this it should be constantly borne in mind that the signal should not be such as to give the opponents the exact instant of the play, because it gives them too close an idea of the moment when they may start.

The speed of a quarter's work depends upon his ability to take the ball close to the snap-back and in proper position for a pass. In merely handing the ball to a runner, one might suppose that there would be no particular position in which the ball should be held; but in that he would be in error, for a ball so handed to a passing runner as not to settle properly in his arms or hands means in many instances a disastrous fumble, or at best a slowing-up of the runner's speed. In giving the ball to a passing runner, it should be held free and clear of the quarter's body and slightly tilted, so that it can be taken against the body, and without the use of both hands for more than an instant, because the runner must almost immediately have use for his arm in going into the line. It is impossible to give in print the exact angle and method of holding the ball for this purpose, but practice and the wishes of the runners, if consulted, will soon show the quarter just what is meant. When the ball is to be passed any considerable distance, it should be taken so that the end is well placed against the hand of the quarter, while the ball itself lies against the forearm, the wrist being bent sharply. This will enable the quarter to send the ball swiftly and accurately almost any distance that it may be necessary to cover. Of course, in many cases the ball does not actually rest against the forearm of the quarter; but this is the best way of conveying the idea of the proper position of the hand upon the point of the ball, and by practicing in this way the correct motion for steady passing is speedily acquired. In receiving the ball, the right hand, or the hand with which the throw is made, should be placed upon the end of the ball, while the other hand stops its progress, and should be placed as nearly upon the opposite end of the ball as convenient. This is the theoretically proper way of receiving the ball; practically, the handling cannot be as accurately performed as this would indicate. If, however, the quarter will in practice be constantly aiming at receiving the ball so that his right hand grasps the end just as his left hand stops the ball, and settles it securely against his right, he will find that after a few weeks he can receive four out of five snap-backs in such a way as to make any great amount of arranging the ball for his pass, after it is in his hands, quite unnecessary. After the preliminary weeks of practice, and when in a game, he must bear in mind the fact that, in order of importance, his duties are, first, to secure the ball, no matter how; second, to convey it to his own man, no matter whether in good form or not. He must never pass the ball if he has fumbled it, unless he has a perfectly clear field in which to do it. He must always have it down in preference to taking the slightest risk of losing it. Even though he receive it without a fumble, there may be a way through in that part of the line towards which his pass is to be delivered; and here, again, he should hold the ball for another down rather than take any chance of the opponent's intercepting the pass. After letting the ball go, the quarter should follow his pass; in fact, he should be almost on the run as the ball leaves his hand. No matter whether the ball be caught or fumbled, he is then ready to lend assistance; whereas if he stand still after his pass, he is of no use to the rest of the play. When the play is a run, he can do excellent work in interfering; and when the play is a kick, he can take any opponent who gets through, and thus aid the half in protecting the kicker. In either case, if his own man muff or fumble he is close at hand to lend assistance in an emergency, which otherwise might prove most disastrous. When lining up the quarter should take a quick glance, not directly at the player he is to make the recipient of the ball, but covering the general position of all the men. In doing this he locates his individual without making it apparent to the opponents which man is to receive the ball. Any amount of disguise may be practiced in the way of taking a last glance at the wrong man, or calling out to some one who does not enter into the play. The chief point, nevertheless, is to avoid that tell-tale glance at the right man which is so difficult to omit.

When the opponents have the ball, the quarter makes an extra man in or near the forward line, and, as a rule, he can by his shrewdness make it very uncomfortable for any point in the line which he chooses to assail. No law can govern his tactics in this respect, but he should be a law unto himself, and show by his cleverness that he is more valuable than any man in the line whose position is fixed. One caution only is worth giving to the quarter in this line of play, and that is, to be less free of going forward sharply when the play is evidently to be a run than when a kick is to be attempted. In the latter case, a quarter can always be sent for his best.

THE HALF-BACK AND BACK

As the game is at present played, the back is more of a third half-back than a goal-tend, and so should be trained to half-back work. It has been well said that all that one can ask of the best rush line is to hold the ground their half-backs gain; and when one follows carefully the progress of the play, he sees that this is the proper division of the work. The half-backs, then, must be the ground-gainers of the team. Such work calls for dash and fire – that ability to suddenly concentrate all the bodily energy into an effort that must make way through anything. Every one has such half-backs in mind, but unfortunately many of those half-backs who possess this type of character have not the necessary weight and strength to stand the amount of work required. Although a light man be occasionally found who is particularly muscular and wiry, the constant shock of going into a heavy line of forwards usually proves too exhausting for any but those of middle weight before the end of a season be reached. It is not that the work of a single game proves too much for the light-weight half. It is that in both practice and games he is so overmatched by the weight of the forwards whom he must meet that every week finds him less strong than the preceding, until his playing falls off so markedly that the captain or coach is at last convinced that there is something wrong, and the man is replaced by some one else, often too late to bring the substitute up to anything like the mark he might have reached had he been tried earlier in the season. Such thoughts as these will suggest themselves to the experienced coach when at the outset of a season he has placed before him a number of candidates for the position of half-back, among whom very likely there may be two or three men of perhaps one hundred and forty pounds' weight. Likely enough, too, these men may be at that period easily superior to the middle or heavy weights. In such a case the very best advice that can be whispered in the ear of coach or captain is, to make quarters or ends of them, even though it be only substitute quarters and ends. It will leave the way open for the proper cultivation of half-backs better built to stand the wear and tear of a season.

Almost equally to be deprecated is the waste of time often devoted to making half-backs of slow heavy weights. Only a quick man can perform a half-back's duties successfully; and although much can be left to practice, there must be some natural quickness to build upon. Slow men can be improved far more rapidly in the forward line than among the halves. All this regarding the weight of half-backs applies not only to 'varsity teams, but school teams as well, if one will make the proper proportional changes in weight. That is, a 'varsity player will be called upon to face a forward line averaging one hundred and seventy-five or thereabouts, and men of less than one hundred and thirty-five to one hundred and forty are too light to meet that weight. In school teams the rush line will be some twenty pounds lighter, and the halves can therefore be selected from even one-hundred-and-twenty-five-pound men, if well built. In other words, a half-back ought not to face over twenty-five pounds' difference in weight; and the more that difference is reduced, supposing that speed and agility be retained, the more chance there is of turning out a thoroughly successful player. It is worth while to be thus particular upon the point of the early selection of candidates for the position of half-back, because, while no more work is demanded of them in a game than of others of their side, the quality of that work must be more uniformly good. When a half-back has to tackle, he must be as sure as a steel-trap; when a half-back has to catch, he must be a man to be relied upon; when a half-back is called upon for a kick, it must be no fluke; and, although no one expects a half-back to always make on his run the five yards, he must be a man who will not be denied when he is called upon for that last yard which will enable his side to retain the ball.

Almost the first thing to be critically noted by the coach is the way in which a half-back takes the ball from his quarter. The case in which he takes it directly from the hands of this player has been already dwelt upon at some length under the head of the quarter's passing; but when the ball is thrown or passed some little distance, it is just as important that it be properly received. Except when about to kick, the half-back should be moving when he receives the ball, and, more than that, the reception of it should have no perceptible effect upon his movements. In other words, he must take it as easily and as naturally as a batsman in a ball game drops his bat after he has hit the ball fairly. No batsman remembers that he has had the bat in his hands after the ball has been hit, and yet, when he is at first base, he has left his bat behind him at the plate. Thus a football half-back should so receive the ball as not to know the exact instant of taking it, but find that he has it as he comes up to the line. It will never do for a coach to suppose that an inexperienced half can be told that he must take the ball "without knowing it," but it is necessary to explain to a half that until he does take the ball naturally, and without having to stop and calculate about it, he can never come properly up to the line nor get his whole power on early. To acquire the habit of taking a pass easily, a half-back should spend a little time every day off the field in practicing taking a sharp pass when on the run. By a sharp pass is not meant hurling the ball with all possible force against a runner so that he is nearly knocked over by it, and cannot by any possibility catch it except at the expense of giving the catch his sole and undivided attention. Such passing in practice does far more harm than good. The ball should be passed with that easy swing which sends it rapidly, accurately, and evenly up to the runner without any great apparent force, for it is remarkable how much the appearance of force tends to rattle the runner, who easily handles fully as much speed properly delivered. Daily practice of this nature between the quarter and halves accustoms each to the other, so that the regular work of the team on the field is not disorganized by loose passing and looser catching. While this passing is progressing, the coach should stand by the side of the half, and watch him closely, correcting any careless tendencies of receiving or stopping, and paying particular attention to his going in a straight line – that is, not running up to meet the ball and then sheering off again. The best half-backs endeavor to receive the ball at approximately the same height relative to their bodies, no matter how it comes, and they will correct quite a variation in the quarter's throw by a little stoop or a slight jump. A half-back must be taught to be uniform in starting, and in reaching the spot where the ball is to meet him. The coach will have no great difficulty in teaching him this steady uniformity of pace, which will enable the quarter to throw the ball so as really to assist rather than retard his motion. There are two other things which the half-back must practice apart from his team-play. They are kicking and catching. The former is of sufficient importance to deserve a separate chapter, but a few hints under the half-back column will not be out of place. It is usually the case that of all three men behind the line, the two halves and the back, any one can do the kicking upon a pinch, but one of the three is, nine times out of ten, manifestly superior to the other two. In this state of affairs there is altogether too great a tendency to slight the practice of the two inferior kickers and rely almost entirely on the best man. It is quite proper to let the best man do all the kicking possible in an important game, but it is a very short-sighted policy to neglect the practice of the other two during the preliminary games. Not only should they have the advantage to be gained in the length of their kicks by daily practice, but they should also have the steadying experience to be acquired only in games, It may happen at any moment in a most important game that the kicking will devolve upon them on account of an accident to the third man, and it is, indeed, a foolhardy captain or coach who has not taken sufficient forethought for this contingency. The principal reason why we develop so few really good kickers is, that coaches, captains, and players have given so little attention to the detail of that part of the work. Fully nine tenths of the men who do the kicking upon American teams are more natural kickers than practiced ones. Let me explain this so as to be fully understood. As in boxing one often sees a man who, having taken no lessons, and being therefore unable to make the most of himself, can yet more than hold his own against a more finished opponent on account of his natural quickness, strength, and aptitude; so in football one sees here and there a man who is able to do some fair kicking without having devoted particular attention to it. In boxing, however, when a teacher takes the natural hitter in hand, he begins by putting him at work upon the rudiments of guarding, holding himself upon his feet, hitting straight, and moving firmly. He never undertakes to make a first-class man of him by merely encouraging him to go in harder, and increase his power without regard to the proper methods. In football, coaches rarely teach the kickers the first principles, but instead urge upon them only the necessity of constant practice in their own way. For this reason our kickers show all manner of styles, and the only wonder is that they kick so well in such wretchedly bad form.

While it is neither advisable nor necessary that a kicker be prevented from attempting to kick hard until he has mastered every detail of the swing and brought it to the same point of perfection that a finished oarsman does his stroke, it certainly is best, in his practice, to subordinate power to method until he acquire good form. The coach should take his man in hand by watching him make a half- dozen kicks in his own way. Then he should select the worst of his faults, and show him why it is a fault, and how to correct it. He should keep him upon this one point for a few days, until he is convinced that there will be no backsliding, and then begin upon the next. In this way a few weeks will serve to make a second-class man a good one, and open the way for his becoming something out of the ordinary run in another season.

In judging the faults of a kicker, the coach should note just where he gets his power on, what is the position of his leg and foot upon the swing, and what part of the foot strikes the ball. These are the principal points, and deserve the first attention. Regarding the first of these, his power should be put on just as his foot has passed the lowest part of the arc in which it swings, and it should meet the ball in the upward sweep very soon after passing this point. The position of his leg and foot is to be next noted, and the "snap the whip" phrase is as good a one to convey the idea as any that can be adopted. As the leg begins to swing the knee is bent and the body pitched a little forward, so that the weight of the kick seems to start from the hip and travel down the leg as it straightens, reaching the foot just as it meets the ball, as above mentioned. As for the third point, the ball, when punted, should be struck between the instep and the toe, impinging most upon the former. In a drop-kick and a place-kick the ball is met by the toe, and the sweep is made with "a longer leg," as the expression has it; that is, the foot swings nearer – in fact, almost along the ground.

All these three points can be most clearly illustrated by noting the effect of departures from them. If the power is not put on as above described the man will simply send the ball along the ground, or will hook it up, merely tossing it with his foot instead of driving it. These two are the extremes, of course; but they illustrate where the power is lost or wasted. If the leg be not swung in proper position, the ball will be simply spatted with the foot, the only force coming from the knee. Finally, if the ball be not met with the proper part of the foot it may snap downwards off the toe, or be merely bunted by the ankle. There is still another thing to be watched, which, while not the kick proper, really belongs to it as much as the swing of the leg. It is the way in which the ball is dropped to the foot from the hand or hands. The usual tendency of beginners, and many half-backs who could hardly be classed in that category, is to toss the ball from the hand; that is, to give it a motion up from the hand, which, however slight, causes much valuable time to be lost. The ball should always be dropped to the foot, the distance between the hand and foot being made as short as possible. The hand should be merely withdrawn just at the proper moment, and with practice it is not difficult to make the entire transfer from hand to foot so rapid as to almost eliminate any danger of having the ball stopped or struck during that part of the play. In drop-kicking the fall is necessarily greater, but it should never be a toss even then. There has been no little argument as to whether the ball should be held in one or both hands when about to kick, and such are the examples of good kickers arrayed on both sides that one cannot fairly say that either way is the only right way. If a player has become so accustomed to the two-hand method as to make him uncomfortable and inaccurate if forced to the one-hand way, it is hardly advisable to make the change. But any player who is taken early enough can be taught to drop the ball with one hand, to the great advantage of both his quickness and his ability to kick from tight quarters or around an opponent.

The entire series of motions, therefore, which go to make up a well-performed kick should be in the coach's mind just as the separate parts of an oarsman's stroke are in the boating-man's mind when coaching a crew. The ball dropped, not tossed; the leg well swung, the power coming from both leg and hip with all the advantage that the poise of the body may add; the foot meeting the ball with the forward part of the instep on a punt, with the toe on a drop, and in either case just after passing the lowest point of the arc of swing, rather later on a punt than a drop, because the ground helps the latter to rise, while the rise of the former must come entirely from the foot. The next step in the education of the kicker is the side swing. The ball cannot be kicked as far when met directly in front of the kicker – his leg swinging straight, as it would in taking a step in running – as it can be kicked by taking a side sweep with the leg and body, the hips acting as a sort of pivot.

One of the most common false ideas regarding this side kick is, that it is not performed with the same part of the foot as the straight punt, but that the ball is struck by the side of the foot. Of course, this is all wrong. The foot meets the ball as fairly and directly as it does in the ordinary straight kick, and the ball impinges upon the top of the instep and toe just as before, the word "side" referring to the swing of the leg and position of the body only.

All the suggestions thus far have been applicable to both half-backs and back, but before bringing the chapter to an end it is well to note a few of the special features of the full-back's position. The place originally was that of a goal-tend, but with the increase of the aggressive system of defence his duties have become more those of a third half-back. Other things being equal, it is eminently proper to select as a full-back an exceptionally strong tackler; but as for placing tackling ability above that of kicking, that is a mistake which might have been made six years ago, but of which no coach or captain would to-day be guilty.

The importance of the position is rapidly growing, and there is no doubt that the time will come in another year, if it be not already here, when the selection of the three men behind the line will be after this fashion – namely, picking out the three best half-backs, all things considered, then selecting that one of the three whose kicking is the best, and making him the third half or full back. After the man has been in this way chosen there will devolve upon him certain duties which do not commonly fall to the lot of the other two half-backs. Chiefest among these is the duty of making a running return of a kick. The opponents have sent a punt down towards him, which he secures while the opponents are still some yards away from him, although they are coming down rapidly. In this case, a thoroughly finished player will not only gain a few steps before he takes his kick, but he will take that kick on the run, sometimes dodging the first man before taking the kick. A full-back who can do this and never lose his kick is the greatest kind of a treasure for any team, and it is worth a captain's while to devote a good bit of attention to the full-back's perfecting this special feature of his play.

He will also be likely to have the long place-kicking to do. In fact, it is proper to practice him at this, because, if he be the best punter among the men behind the line, he can be made the longest place-kicker, and few realize the great advantage of these long place-kicks to a team upon occasion of fair catches.

Tackling, when it does fall to the lot of a full-back, comes with an importance the like of which no other player is ever called upon to face. It usually means a touch-down if he misses. For practice of this kind it is well to play the 'varsity back once in a while upon the scrub side. This is likely to improve the speed of his kicking also.

SIGNALS

When Rugby football was first adopted in this country, it was against a strong feeling that it would never make progress against what had been known as the American game. This old-fashioned game was much more like the British Association in a rather demoralized state. Not only was there no such thing as off-side, but one of the chief features consisted of batting the ball with the fist, at which many became sufficiently expert to drive the ball almost as far as the ordinary punter now kicks it. There was very little division of players by name, although they strung out along the field, and one (known as the "peanutter" — why, no one knows) played in the enemies' goal. Coming to players accustomed to this heterogeneous mingling, it is no great wonder that the first days of Rugby were characterized by even less system than that displayed in the old game.

The first division of players was into rushers, half-backs, and a goal-tend. The rushers had but little regard for their relative positions in the line; and as for their duties, one can easily imagine how little they corresponded with those of the rusher of to-day when it is said that it was by no means unusual for one of them to pick up the ball and punt it.

The snap-back and quarter-back play soon defined these two positions, and shortly after the individual rush-line positions became distinct, both as regards location and duties. All this was an era of development of general play with but a few particular combinations or marks of strategy. If a man made a run, he made it for the most part wherever he saw the best chance after receiving the ball, and he made it unaided to any degree by his comrades. If the ball was kicked, it was at the option of the man receiving it, and the forwards did not know whether he would kick or run.

It was at this point that the demand for signals first showed itself. The rushers began to insist upon it that they must be told in some way whether the play was to be a kick or a run. They maintained quite stoutly and correctly that there was no reason in their chasing down the field when the half-backs did not kick. As a matter of fact, the forwards even went so far as to contend that the running-game should be entirely dropped in favor of one based upon long kicks well followed up. Failing to establish this opinion, they nevertheless brought it about that they should be told by some signal what the play was to be, and so be spared useless running. This was probably the first of the present complicated system of signals, although at about the same time some teams took up the play of making a rather unsatisfactory opening for a runner in the line, and made use of a signal to indicate the occasions when this was to be done. The signaling of the quarter to the centre-rush as to when the ball should be played antedated this somewhat, but can hardly be classed with signals for the direction of the play itself.

To-day the teams which meet to decide the championship are brought up to the execution of at least twenty-five different plays, each of which is called for by a certain distinct signal of its own.

The first signals given were "word signals;" that is, a word or a sentence called out so that the entire team might hear it and understand whether a kick or a run was to be made. Then, when signals became more general, "sign signals" (that is, some motion of the hand or arm to indicate the play) were brought in and became for a time more popular than the word signals, particularly upon fields where the audience pressed close upon the lines, and their enthusiastic cheering at times interfered with hearing word signals. Of late years numerical combinations have become most popular, and as the crowd is kept at such a distance from the side lines as to make it possible for teams to hear those signals, they have proven highly satisfactory. The numerical system, while it can be readily understood by the side giving the signal, because they know the key, is far more difficult for the opponents to solve than either the old word signals or signs. Still, the ingenuity of captains is generally taxed to devise systems that shall so operate as never to confuse their own men and yet completely mystify the opponents throughout the game. Clever forwards almost always succeed in interpreting correctly one or two of the signals most frequently used, in spite of the difficulty apparent in the solution of such problems. The question as to who should give the signals is still a disputed one, although the general opinion is that the quarter-back should perform this duty. There is no question as to the propriety of the signals emanating from that point, but the discussion is as to whether the captain or the quarter should direct the play. Of course all is settled if the captain is himself a quarter-back, but even when he is not he ought to be able to so direct his quarter previous to the actual conflict as to make it perfectly satisfactory to have the signals come from the same place as the ball. It is in that direction that the eyes and attention of every player are more or less turned, and hence signals there given are far more certain to be observed. Moreover, it is sometimes, and by no means infrequently, necessary to change a play even after the signal has been given. This, if the quarter be giving the signals, is not at all difficult, but is decidedly confusing when coming from some other point in the line.

The important fact to be remembered in selecting a system of signals is that it is far more demoralizing to confuse your own team than to mystify your opponents. A captain must therefore choose such a set of signals as he can be sure of making his own team comprehend without difficulty and without mistake. When he is sure of that, he can think how far it is possible for him to disguise these from his opponents. Among the teams which contest for championship honors it is unusual to find any which are not prepared for emergencies by the possession either of two sets of signals, or of such changes in the manner of giving them as to make it amount to the same thing. Considering the way the game is played at the present time, this preparation is advisable, for one can hardly overestimate the demoralizing effect it would have upon any team to find their opponents in possession of a complete understanding of the signals which were directing the play against them.

While it is well for the captain or coach to arrange in his own mind early in the season such a basis for a code of signals as to render it adaptable to almost indefinite increase in the number of plays, it is by no means necessary to have the team at the outset understand this basis. In fact, it is just as well to start them off very modestly upon two or three signals which they should learn, and of which they should make use until the captain sees fit to advance them a peg.

If, for instance, the captain decides to make use of a numerical system, he cannot do better to accustom his men to listening and following instructions than to give them three signals, something like this: One-two-three, to indicate that the ball is to be passed to the right half-back, who will endeavor to run around the left end; four-five-six, that the left half will try to run around the right end; and seven-eight-nine, that the back will kick. The scrub side will probably "get on" to these signals in short order, and will make it pleasant at the ends for the half-backs; but this will be the best kind of practice in team work, and will do no harm. After a day or two of this it will be time to make changes in the combination of numbers, not only with an idea of deceiving the scrub side, but also to quicken the wits of the 'Varsity team. Taking the same signals as a basis, the first, or signal for the right half-back to try on the left end, was one-two-three – the sum of these numbers is six. Take that, then, as the key to this signal, and any numbers the sum of which equals six will be a signal for this play. For instance, three-three, or four-two, two-three-one – any of these would serve to designate this play. Similarly, as the signal for the left half at the right end was four-five-six, or a total of fifteen, any numbers which added make fifteen – as six-six-three, seven-eight, or five-four-six – would be interpreted in this way. Finally, the signal for a kick having been seven-eight-nine, or a sum of twenty-four, any numbers aggregating that total would answer equally well.

A few days of this practice will fit the men for any further developments upon the same lines, and accustom them to listening and thinking at the same time. The greatest difficulty experienced by both captains and coaches since the signals and plays became so complicated has been to teach green players not to stop playing while they listen to and think out a signal. By the end of the season players are so accustomed to the signals that all this hesitation disappears, and the signal is so familiar as to amount to a description of the play in so many words.

The other two methods of signaling by the use of words rather than numbers, and signs given by certain movements, although they have now given way in most teams to numbers, are still made use of, and have merit enough to deserve a line or two. The word-signal was usually given in the form of a sentence, the whole or any part of which would indicate the play. As, for instance, to indicate a kick, the sentence "Play up sharp, Charlie." If the quarter, or whoever gave the signals, should call out, "Play up," or "Play up sharp," or "Play," or "Charlie," he would in each instance be giving the signal for a kick. Sign-signals are more difficult to disguise, but are none the less very effective, especially where there is a great amount of noise close to the ropes. A good example of the sign-signal is the touching of some part of the body with the hand. For instance, half-back running would be denoted by placing the hand on the hip, the right hip for the left half, and the left hip for the right half. A kick would be indicated by placing the hand upon the neck. Particular care should be exercised when sign-signals are to be used that the ones selected, while similar to the acts performed naturally by the quarter in stooping over to receive the ball, are never exactly identical with these motions, else there will likely enough be confusion.

No matter what method of signaling be used, there is one important feature to be regarded, and that is, some means of altering the play after a signal has been given. This is, of course, a very simple thing, and the usual plan is to have some word which means that the signal already given is to be considered void, and a new signal will be given in its place. There should also be some way of advising the team of a change from one set of signals to another, should such a move become necessary. It is very unwise not to be prepared for such an emergency, because if a captain is obliged to have time called and personally advise his team one by one of such a change, the opponents are quite sure to see it and to gain confidence from the fact that they have been clever enough to make such a move necessary.

TRAINING

At the present advanced athletic era there are very few who do not understand that a certain amount of preparation is absolutely essential to success in any physical effort requiring strength and endurance. The matter of detail is, however, not faced until one actually becomes a captain or a coach, and, as such, responsible for the condition, not of himself alone, but of a team of fifteen or twenty men.

Experience regarding his own needs will have taught him the value of care and work in this line; but, unless he differs greatly from the ordinary captain upon first assuming the duties of that position, his knowledge of training will be confined to an understanding of his own requirements, coupled with the handed-down traditions of the preceding captains and teams. When he finds himself in this position and considers what lines of training he shall lay down for his team, unless he be an inordinately conceited man he will wish he had made more of a study of this art of preparation, especially in the direction most suited to the requirements of his own particular sport.

Many inquiries from men about to undertake the training of a team have led me to believe that, even at the expense of going over old ground, it will be well in this book to map out a few of the important features of a course of training. It should go without saying that there are infinite variations in systems of this kind; but if a man will carry in mind the reasons rather than the rules, he has always a test to apply which will enable him to make the most of whatever system he adopts.

He should remember that training ought to be a preparation by means of which his men will at a certain time arrive at the best limits of their muscular strength and activity, at the same time preserving that equilibrium most conducive to normal health. Such a preparation can be accomplished by the judicious use of the ordinary agents of well-being – exercise, diet, sleep, and cleanliness.

One can follow out the reasons for or against any particular point in a system rather better if he cares to see why these agents act towards health and strength.

Exercise is a prime requisite, because the human mechanism, unlike the inanimate machine, gains strength from use. Muscular movement causes disintegration and death of substance, but at the same time there is an increased flow of blood to the part, and that means an increased supply of nourishment and increased activity in rebuilding. As McLaren has expressed it, strength means newness of the muscle. The amount and quality of this exercise will be treated later in this chapter.

In considering the matter of Diet, a captain or coach should think of this question not according to the tradition of his club, nor according to his own idiosyncrasies. He should regard the general principle of not depriving a man of anything to which he is accustomed and which agrees with him. Of course, it is advisable to do without such articles of food as would be injurious to the majority of the men, even though there might be one or two to whom they would do no harm. Men should enjoy their food and it should be properly served. I remember once being asked my opinion regarding a certain team at the time in training, and I expressed the conviction that something was wrong with their diet. The team, as a whole, were not seriously affected, but some three or four were manifestly out of sorts. I heard the coach go over the bill of fare, and it sounded all right. I then decided to take dinner with them and see if I could discover the trouble. One meal was sufficient, for it was a meal! The beef – and an excellent roast it was, too – was literally served in junks, such as one might throw to a dog. The dishes were dirty, so was the cloth. Vegetables were dumped on to the plates in a mess, and each one grabbed for what he wanted. Some of the men might have been brought up to eat at such a table, still others were not sufficiently sensitive to have their appetites greatly impaired by anything, but the three or four who were "off" were boys whose home life had accustomed them to a different way of dining, and their natures revolted. So, too, did their appetites. As it was then too late to correct the manners of the mess, I simply advised sending these men elsewhere to board, and they speedily came into shape. I cannot too strongly advocate good service at a training table. The men should enjoy their dinners, should eat them slowly, and should be encouraged to be as long about it as they will. As food is to repair the waste, it should be generous in quantity and taken when the man will not, from being over-tired, have lost his appetite. Sometimes a team is not overworked, but worked too late in the day, so that the men rush to the table almost directly from the field, and fail to feel hungry, while within an hour they would have eaten with a zest. This course persevered in for several days will show its folly in a general falling-off in the strength as well as the weight of the men. To train a football team should be, in the matter of the diet at least, the simplest matter compared with training for other sports, because the season of the year is so favorable to good condition.

Crews and ball nines have oftentimes the trial of exceptionally hot and exhausting weather to face, while a football team, after the few warm days of September are passed, enjoy the very best of bracing weather – weather which will give almost any man who spends his time in out-door work a healthy, hearty appetite. In order that any captain or coach reading this book may feel that, while it offers several courses of diet, it would emphatically present the fact that there is no hard-and-fast system of diet that must be religiously followed, I submit a variety of tables, showing some old as well as new school diets. None of them are very hard, several are excellent; and I don't think that a captain or coach would be called upon to draw his pencil through very many of the items enumerated.

TORPID RACES.
A DAY'S TRAINING.

Rise about 7.30 A.M. . . . . Early rising not compulsory.

Exercise . . . . A short walk or run . . . . Not compulsory.

Breakfast, 9 . . . . As for summer races.

Exercise (forenoon) . . . . . . None.

Luncheon about 1 P.M. { Bread, or a sandwich.
{ Beer, half a pint.

Exercise . . . . { About 2 o'clock start for the river,
{ and row twice over the course.

Dinner, 5 . . . . { Meat, as for summer races.
{ Bread.
{ Vegetables, as for summer races.
{ Pudding (rice), or jelly.
{ Beer, half a pint.

Bed, 10.30.

THE OXFORD SYSTEM.—(Summer Races.)
A DAY'S TRAINING.*

Rise about 7 A.M. . . . . { So as to be in chapel; but early rising
{ not compulsory.

Exercise . . . . A short walk or run . . . . Not compulsory (walk only, and short).

Breakfast, 8.30 . . . . { Meat, beef or mutton.
{ Bread or toast, dry . . . . The crust only recommended.
{ Tea . . . . As little as possible recommended.

Exercise (forenoon) . . None . . . . { American football men should kick,
{ catch, and pass.

Dinner, 2 P.M. . . . . { Meat ; much the same as for
{ breakfast.
{ Bread . . . . Crust only recommended.
{ Vegetables, none allowed . . . A rule, however, not always adhered to.
{ Beer, one pint . . . . { This is what Americans call ale, and
{ not indulged in to any great extent
{ except after a hard game.

Exercise . . . . { About 5 o'clock start for the
{ river, and row twice over
{ the course, the speed in-
{ creasing with the strength
{ of the crew.

Supper, 8.30 or 9 . . { Meat, cold.
{ Bread ; perhaps a jelly or
{ watercresses.
{ Beer, one pint (see above).

Bed about 10.

*As has been stated elsewhere, improvements have been made in diet since this table was compiled. This will also apply to the Cambridge System, page 143.

THE CAMBRIDGE SYSTEM. Summer Races (1866).
A DAY'S TRAINING.

Rise at 7 A.M.

Exercise . . . . { Run 100 or 200 yards as
{ fast as possible.
{ "The old system of running a mile or
{ so before breakfast is fast going out,
{ except in the case of men who want
{ to get a good deal of flesh off."

Breakfast, 8.30 . . . . . { Meat, beef or mutton.
{ Toast, dry.
{ Tea, two cups, or towards the end of a training a
{ cup and a half only. Watercresses occasionally.

Exercise (forenoon) . . . None.

Dinner about 2 P.M. { Meat, beef or mutton.
{ Bread.
{ Vegetables—potatoes, greens { Some colleges have baked apples,
{ Beer, one pint. { or jellies, or rice puddings.
{ Dessert — oranges, or biscuits,
{ or figs; wine, two glasses.

Exercise . . . . { About 5.30 start for the river, { "Most men get out for a little time
{ and row to the starting- { before rowing back."
{ post and back . . . . }

Supper about 8.30 { Meat, cold.
or 9. { Bread.
{ Vegetables—lettuce or watercresses.
Bed at 10. { Beer, one pint.

C. WESTHALL'S SYSTEM. For Amateurs.
A DAY'S TRAINING.

Rise at 6 A.M., or earlier in the summer. } Cold bath and rub-down.

Exercise..................... {
Sharp walk about a mile out, and run home ; or a row of a couple of miles at three-parts speed.
A dry rub-down.
}

Breakfast (time not stated).... {
Meat, mutton-chop or steak (broiled).
Bread, stale or toast.
Tea, half a pint.
}

Exercise.....................(Not stated.)

Dinner, 2 P.M............... {
Meat (as at breakfast).
Vegetables, none; "except a mealy potato."
Bread, stale.
Beer, one pint.
}

Exercise (afternoon)...........Rowing.

If dinner be late, luncheon to be taken to consist of
Meat, beef or mutton, hot or cold. Bread. Beer, one glass.
(If dinner be early, "tea with viands and liquids as at breakfast" to be taken.)

Supper.......................Half a pint of thin gruel, or dry toast and a glass of ale.
Bed...........................Time not stated.

N.B.—It is added "that the above rules are of course open to alteration according to circumstances, and the diet varied successfully by the introduction of fowls, either roast or boiled—the latter preferred;" and "it must never be lost sight of that sharp work, regularity, and cleanliness are the chief if not the only rules to be followed to produce thorough good condition."

McLAREN'S SYSTEM.
A DAY'S TRAINING.

Rise at about 7 A.M..(Glass of cold water recommended.)

Exercise.......... {
The crew meet at 7, walk and run for four or five miles ; or, in later practice, quick run of two miles.
Wash and dress.
}

Breakfast, 9....... {
Meat (broiled); bread (brown) and butter; tea, two cups. "Cocoa made of the nibs boiled for four hours is better than tea for breakfast."
Smoking allowed (conditionally). "Smoking is barred, for, though here also a man's habits are to be taken into account, the subjects of training in match-boats are usually too young to have contracted a custom of smoking so inveterate as to have made tobacco indispensable to the body's internal functions, though it is not unfrequently so in older men. After breakfast is the only time allotted to the pipe."
}

Luncheon at 1..... {
Beef sandwich with half a pint of beer, or
Biscuit and glass of sherry, or egg in sherry.
}

Exercise.......... {
At 2.30 go out to row, and row over the whole course. "This altogether depends on the state of the crew."
Wash in tepid water.
}

Dinner at 6 P.M... {
Meat (roast, broiled, or boiled). "Any kind of wholesome meat thoroughly cooked."
Vegetables—"The green foods permissible contain in their list spinach—the very best of all; sea-kale, asparagus, but without melted butter; turnip-tops, young unhearted greens, but not solid cabbages; broccoli, carrots, parsnips, and cooked celery. Turnips are also favored, and pease condemned; also cucumbers, and all salad mixtures. But boiled beet-root is good, and Jerusalem artichokes; and French beans stand next to spinach in virtue." The course is varied daily, so that no two days together shall see the same articles on the table.
Pudding. ("Light puddings may be eaten.")
Bread. Beer, one pint.
Wine, two glasses of old port or sherry, or three of claret.
Biscuits and dried fruits, as cherries, figs, etc., allowed. ("All fresh fruits are avoided.")
Jellies. ("Plain jellies are innocuous.")
Water. ("As much spring water as they have a mind to.")
}

Supper, 9..........Oatmeal gruel if desired.
Bed at 10.   N. B.—On Sundays a brisk walk of three hours or so is taken.
SUMMARY.
Sleep, eight or nine hours.   Exercise, about three hours.   Diet, very varied.

H. CLASPER'S SYSTEM.
A DAY'S TRAINING.

Rise between 6 and 7 A.M.
Exercise.........A country walk of four or five miles.

Breakfast, 8....
- Meat, chop or
- Couple of eggs.
- Bread.
- Tea. ("We never drink coffee.")

Exercise.......Rest for half an hour, and then a brisk walk or run. If morning exercise has not been heavy, a row on the river, terminating about 11 A.M.

Dinner, 12 M..
- Meat, beef or mutton (broiled).
- Egg pudding, with currants in it if desired, or other light farinaceous pudding.
- Ale, one glass.
- Wine, one glass (port), or
- Ale, two glasses, without wine.

Exercise.......Rest for an hour, and then on the river again for a hard row. "Rowing exercise should be taken twice every day."

Tea..........."Tea, with toasted bread sparingly buttered, with one egg only—more has a tendency to choke the system."

Supper........Not recommended. When taken, to consist of new milk and bread, or gruel, with raisins and currants and a glass of port wine in it.

Bed about 10.

STONEHENGE'S SYSTEM.
A DAY'S TRAINING.

Rise at 8 A.M.....
- According to season and weather.
- Cold bath.

Exercise, 8.30 to 9...Walking or running. "Let all take a gentle run or smart walk."

Breakfast, 9 to 9.30
- Oatmeal porridge, with meat (beef or mutton, broiled) and bread.
- Tea or coffee, or table beer, one pint. "Tea is preferred to coffee. Cocoa is too greasy."

Exercise, 9.30 to 11.30, Billiards, skittles, quoits, or other light exercise.

11.30 to 1.30......Rowing.

1.30 to about 2.30.
- Running. "According to circumstances."
- Rubbed dry and linen changed.

Dinner, 2.30 to 3 or 3.30........
- Meat—beef (roast) or mutton (boiled mutton occasionally), roast fowl, partridges, or pheasants (allowed), or venison (nothing better). "It is generally directed that the steak or chop should be underdone ; this, I am sure, is a fallacy."— Bread (*ad lib.*). — Puddings occasionally, made of bread, eggs, and milk, and served with preserved fruits. — Vegetables—potatoes (one or two only), cauliflowers, and broccoli (only as an occasional change). If training is protracted, fish allowed (cod or soles).— Beer, from a pint to a pint and a half.— Wine, a glass or two, port or sherry.

After dinner, until 5 or 6..A gentle stroll or book.
Exercise, 6 to 7......Rowing.
Supper, 8..........Oatmeal porridge with dry toast or chop, with glass of port.
Bed at 9 or 10.

SYSTEM OF JACKSON AND GODBOLD

Breakfast. – Stale or whole-meal bread, or toast, a little butter, plenty of marmalade if you like, but not jam. Bacon and eggs, or chops or steaks, with watercress if obtainable. To those who like it, a basin of oatmeal porridge, *properly made*, taken with pure milk about an hour before breakfast, is an excellent thing, and has a very beneficial effect upon the stomach, but it should not be taken every day. It is better to miss it every third day, or to take it regularly for a fortnight and then omit it from the next week's diet, as the too frequent use of it is rather injurious to the skin of some persons. Tea – not too strong – is better than coffee. Good ripe fruit is a capital adjunct to the breakfast-table, and is an excellent article of food.

Dinner. - Lamb, mutton, beef, fowl (tender and boiled), varied by fish, of which haddock, whiting, and soles are the best, with potatoes (well boiled, and not much of them), and well-cooked vegetables, followed by a small allowance of light, farinaceous pudding or stewed fruit, will be a good, wholesome diet. If you want bread, have it stale. Never eat *new* bread. Avoid all sauces, or made dishes, and adhere to plain food only. One thing we would particularly impress upon the reader, and that is never to take his exercise immediately before or after meals, nothing is more injurious, or likely to produce indigestion, and its concomitant evils. Some authorities abjure the use of sugar, but taken in moderation it is not injurious. A well-known champion of our acquaintance, when in the pink of condition, was wont to amuse himself by eating the contents of a sugar basin, if one were inadvertently left near him, and without feeling any ill effects from so doing. Our readers need not follow his example, for although it might suit him, it probably would not agree with them. We have said, take sugar in *moderation.* Now, in the last word lies all the lectures one can give on the subject. Be moderate in all things, one might say, but above all things be moderate in the use of all edibles not actually necessary to support the increased exertion which a man in training is called upon to perform. No liquid shall be taken except with, or just after meals, but we would not advise stinting the quantity too much. In summer three or four pints, and in winter two or three pints per diem would be about the quantity. Never drink just before exercise, and it is better not to drink just before going to bed. In fact, the less one has to digest when retiring for sleep the better, and be sure not to drink tea late at night.

Tea, or Supper, should be taken at least two hours before bedtime, and we would allow a small chop, or some light fish, bread, and very little butter, with some ripe fruit. The best meal to take before a race, and which should be taken about two hours before starting-time, is the lean of mutton-chops and a little dry toast. We have said that no liquids should be taken except at meal-times; but we do not intend to state that if a man be very thirsty he may not touch them. If he does so, it must be a very small quantity. Thirst can often be assuaged by rinsing the mouth out with cold water, and this is by far the better plan if it is efficacious.

A COMMON-SENSE SYSTEM

One author says: "Rise at six; bathe; take about two ounces (a small cup) of coffee with milk: this is really a stimulating soup. Then light exercise, chiefly devoted to lungs; a little rest; the breakfast of meat, bread, or oatmeal, vegetables, with no coffee; an hour's rest. Then the heaviest exercise of the day. This is contrary to rule; but I believe the heaviest exercise should be taken before the heaviest meal; a rest before dinner. This meal, if breakfast be taken at seven or eight, should be at one or two, not leaving a longer interval than five hours between the meals. At dinner, again meat, vegetables, bread, perhaps a half-pint of malt liquor, no sweets. Then a longer rest; exercise till five. Supper light – bread, milk, perhaps with an egg. Half an hour later a cup of tea, and bed at nine."

J.B. O'REILLY

Seven o'clock is a good time for an athlete in training to rise. He ought to get a good dry-rubbing, and then sponge his body with cold water, or have a shower-bath, with a thorough rubbing afterwards. He will then go out to exercise before breakfast, not to run hard, as is commonly taught, but to walk briskly for an hour, while exercising his lungs in deep-breathing. Before this walk, an egg in a cup of tea, or something of the kind, should be taken.

The breakfast need not always consist of a broiled mutton-chop or cutlet; a broiled steak, broiled chicken, or broiled fish, or some of each, may be taken with tea or coffee.

Dinner may be far more varied than is usually allowed by the trainer's "system." Any kind of butcher's meat, plainly cooked, with a variety of fresh vegetables, may be taken, with ordinary light puddings, stewed fruit, but no pastry. A good time for dinner is one o'clock.

An American athlete, when thirsty, ought to have only one drink – water. The climate and the custom in England favor the drinking or beer or claret; but, beyond question, the best drink for a man in training is pure water. After dinner, rest, but no dozing or *siesta*. This sort of rest only spoils digestion, and makes men feel slack and "limp."

Supper, at six o'clock, should not be a second dinner; but neither should it consist of "slops" or gruel. The athlete ought to be in bed by ten o'clock, in a room with open window, and a draught through the room, if possible, though not across the bed.

The American football captain or coach should bear in mind, when reading these various systems, that the use of ale and port seems to be much better borne by those who live in the English climate than upon this side of the water.

Also, that stiff exercise before breakfast has not been proven advantageous to our athletes except as a flesh-reducer, and then only in exceptionally vigorous constitutions.

Also, that tea is not as popular with us as with the men who train in England.

SLEEP AND CLEANLINESS

To come to the third agent of health enumerated some pages back, Sleep. As a rule, it is not a difficult matter to see that members of a football team take the requisite amount of sleep. There are occasions, as in college, when some society event of unusual importance tempts the men to sit up late, but with such exceptions as these there is no great difficulty experienced in making the majority of the men keep good hours. And this is growing more and more simple as athletics become more general, for they take the place of much of the dissipation which was formerly the only outlet for the superabundant animal spirits of young men. In the case, however, of the occasional candidate for the team who comes under the captain's eye as inclined to late hours, there must be the strictest kind of discipline shown. Such a man is the very one whose stamina will be affected after a while by lack of sleep, and that too at a time when the rest of the men are nearing the perfection of condition. Thus he will be found falling off at the very time when it is a most serious matter very likely to fill his position with a new man. Eight or nine hours sleep should be insisted upon, and that sleep should be taken with regularity. In fact, not only the sleep, but the meals and the exercise, should all be made as nearly regular, regarding hours, as possible. Men should have separate rooms, and particularly when off upon trips they should not sleep together. Plenty of fresh air should be admitted to the sleeping-room, but draughts are to be avoided. This is not because every time the air blows upon a man he is liable to contract a severe cold, for the chances are against this, but because there are times when he is particularly prone to such an accident, and if he is in the habit of sleeping without regard to draughts it is not likely that he will take precautions then. If a man has, for instance, played an especially stiff game and upon a muggy exhausting day, he will undoubtedly turn in thoroughly tired out, and perhaps still somewhat heated. Now if he, when in that state, sleeps in a draught, he will probably find himself very lame in the morning, even though he escape other more serious consequences. Just one more word of caution regarding sleep, and that is in the matter of obtaining a good night's rest just before the important match of the season. To insure this is to do much towards securing the best work of which the men are capable from the team upon the following day.

First and foremost, they should not be allowed to talk about the game or the signals or anything connected with football during that evening. If possible, they should do something to entirely divert their minds from all thought of the game. Nor should they be hustled off to bed an hour or two earlier than usual. Rather ought it to be a half-hour later, for then the chances are that the men drop off to sleep immediately instead of tossing about, thinking of the exciting event of the morrow.

Finally, as to overtrained men, and that restlessness and inability to sleep that almost always comes with the worst cases of this kind. There is but one thing to do with a man when he "goes fine" to this extent, and that is to sever his connection with the team for a time. If it is early in the season, there is some chance of his recuperating rapidly enough to still become serviceable. If it is late, there is no hope of this. In either case he must neither play, eat, nor spend his time with the members of the team. He can do almost anything else; he can go and watch the crew row or the ball nine play; he can study or read; he can, and in fact should, do everything possible to disassociate himself from football and violent exercise for a time, and, unless the trouble has gone too far, it will only be a couple of weeks before he will find himself coming out of it all right, and among the first signs will be good, refreshing sleep.

To pass now to the fourth of our agents for health, Cleanliness. It is fortunately seldom necessary to argue the advantages of the "tub" or "sponge bath" to our football players, because they are usually accustomed to it. A daily splashing has been their ordinary habit. It is well to mention also that a fortnightly warm bath may be indulged in to advantage. But with the present understanding of all these advantages, the wisest remarks that can be made are cautions as to indiscretions in the use of baths. In the first place, one bath a day is enough, and any other should be a mere sponging and rubbing. Men who indulge in a tub in the morning and then spend another fifteen minutes in a plunge after practice in the afternoon get too much of it. Again, the habit of spending a long time under the shower every day is a mistake. It feels so refreshing after a hard practice that a man is tempted to stay too long, and it does him no good. The best and safest plan is to take a light, quick sponge bath in the morning immediately upon rising, and then, after practice in the afternoon, to take just a moment under the shower, and follow it by a good rubbing. This, with the fortnightly warm bath, will be all that a man may do to advantage.

A CHAPTER FOR SPECTATORS

To those who have never played the game of football, but who chance to open the covers of this book, a short explanation of the divisions and duties of the players will not be out of place. For these this chapter is added.

The game is played by two teams, of eleven men each, upon a field 330 feet long and 160 feet wide, at either end of which are goal-posts with a cross-bar.

The ball, which is like a large leather egg, is placed in the centre of this field, and each team endeavors to drive it in the direction of the opponents' goal-line, where any scoring must be done. Goals and touch-downs are the only points which count, and these can be made only as follows:

A goal can be obtained by kicking the ball in any way except a punt (a certain kind of kick where the ball is dropped by a player and kicked before touching the ground) over the cross-bar of the opponents' goal. A touch-down is obtained by touching the ball to the ground behind the line of the goal. So, in either case, the ball must cross the end of the field in some way to make any score. The sole object, then, of all the struggles which take place in the field is to advance the ball to a position such that scoring is possible. A firm grasp of this idea usually simplifies matters very much for the casual spectator.

The object of the white lines which cross the field at every five yards is merely to assist the referee in determining how far the ball moves at a time; for there is a rule which states that a team must advance the ball five yards in three attempts or retreat with it twenty. If they do not succeed in doing this, the other side take possession of the ball, and in their turn try to advance it.

There are certain rules which govern the methods of making these advances, any infringement of which constitutes what is called *a foul*, and entails a penalty upon the side making it.

Any player can run with the ball or kick it if, when he receives it, he is "on side" – that is, between the ball and his own goal line. He may not take the ball if he is "off side" – that is, between the ball and his opponents' goal-line – until an adversary has touched the ball.

Whenever a player running with the ball is held, he must cry "down," and a man of his side then places the ball on the ground and snaps it back. This puts it in play, and is called a scrimmage, and this scrimmage is the most commonly recurring feature of the game.

For the purposes of advancing the ball or repelling the attack of the opponents it has proved advisable for a captain to divide his eleven men into two general divisions: the forwards and backs. The forwards, of whom there are seven, are usually called rushers, and they make practically a straight line across the field when the ball is put in play on a "down." Next behind them is the quarter-back, who does the passing of the ball to one or another of the players, while just behind him are the two half-backs and the back, usually in something of a triangle in arrangement, with the last named nearest the goal which his team is defending.

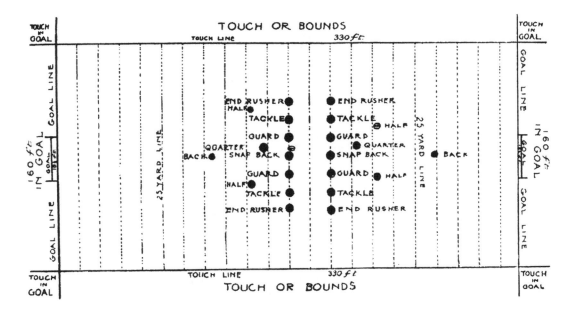

The following definitions will also aid the spectator in understanding many of the expressions used by the devotees of the sport:

A **drop-kick** is made by letting the ball fall from the hands, and kicking it at the very instant it rises.

A **place-kick** is made by kicking the ball after it has been placed on the ground.

A **punt** is made by letting the ball fall from the hands, and kicking it before it touches the ground.

Kick-off is a place-kick from the centre of the field of play.

Kick-out is a drop-kick, or place-kick, by a player of the side which has touched the ball down in their own goal, or into whose touch-in-goal the ball has gone.

In touch means out of bounds.

A **fair** is putting the ball in play, from touch.

A **foul** is any violation of a rule.

A **touch-down** is made when the ball is carried, kicked, or passed across the goal-line and there held, either in goal or touch-in-goal.

A **safety** is made when a player, guarding his goal, receives the ball from a player of his own side, and touches it down behind his goal-line, or carries the ball across his own goal-line and touches it down, or puts the ball into his own touch-in-goal.

A **touch-back** is made when a player touches the ball to the ground behind his own goal, the impetus which sent the ball across the line having been received from an opponent.

A **fair catch** is a catch made direct from a kick by one of the opponents, provided the catcher made a mark with his heel at the spot where he made the catch.

Interference is using the hands or arms in any way to obstruct or hold a player who has not the ball.

The **penalty** for fouls and violation of the rules, except otherwise provided, is a down for the other side; or, if the side making the foul has not the ball, five yards to the opponents.

The following is the value of each point in the scoring:
  Goal obtained by touch-down – 6
  Goal from field kick – 5
  Touch-down failing goal – 4
  Safety by opponents – 2

The rules which bear most directly upon the play are:

The time of a game is an hour and a half, each side playing forty-five minutes from each goal. There is ten minutes' intermission between the two halves, and the game is decided by the score of even halves.

The ball is kicked off at the beginning of each half; and whenever a goal has been obtained, the side which has lost it shall kick off.

A player may throw or pass the ball in any direction except towards opponents' goal. If the ball be batted or thrown forward, it shall go down on the spot to opponents.

If a player having the ball be tackled and the ball fairly held, the man so tackling shall cry "held," the one so tackled must cry "down," and some player of his side put it down for a scrimmage. If, in three consecutive fairs and downs, unless the ball cross the goal-line, a team shall not have advanced the ball five or taken in back twenty yards, it shall go to the opponents on spot of fourth.

If the ball goes into touch, whether it bounds back or not, a player on the side which touches it down must bring it to the spot where the line was crossed, and there either bound the ball in the field of play, or touch it in with both hands, at right angles to the touch-line, and then run with it, kick it, or throw it back; or throw it out at right angles to touch-line; or walk out with it at right angles to touch-line, any distance not less than five nor more than fifteen yards, and there put it down.

A side which has made a touch-down in their opponents' goal *must* try at goal.

HECTOR COWAN.
Princeton.

LIST OF PORTRAITS.

[P. stands for Princeton, Y. for Yale, and H. for Harvard.]

HECTOR COWAN, P
HARRY W. BEECHER, Y
HENRY C. LAMAR, P
D. S. DEAN, H
E. L. RICHARDS, JR., Y
W. A. BROOKS, H
R. S. CHANNING, P
L. K. HULL, Y
E. A. POE, P
EVERETT J. LAKE. H.
WYLLYS TERRY, Y
B. W. TRAFFORD, H
T. L. McCLUNG, Y
V. M. HARDING, H
JESSE RIGGS, P

W. H. CORBIN, Y
ALEXANDER MOFFATT, P
RALPH WARREN, P
JOHN CORBETT, H
W. BULL, Y
KNOWLTON L. AMES, P
W. C. RHODES, Y
P. D. TRAFFORD, H
R. HODGE, P
H. H. KNAPP, Y
A. J. CUMNOCK, H
JEREMIAH S. BLACK, P
C. O. GILL, Y
E. C. PEACE, P
W. HEFFELFINGER, Y
R. M. APPLETON, H

HARRY W. BEECHER.
Yale.

HENRY C. LAMAR.
Princeton.

D. S. DEAN.
Harvard.

E. L. RICHARDS.
Yale.

W. A. BROOKS.
Harvard.

R. S. CHANNING.
Princeton.

L. K. HULL.
Yale.

E. A. POE.
Princeton.

EVERETT J. LAKE.
Harvard.

WYLLYS TERRY.
Yale.

B. W. TRAFFORD.
Harvard.

T. L. McCLUNG.
Yale.

V. M. HARDING.
Harvard.

JESSE RIGGS.
Princeton.

W. H. CORBIN.
Yale.

ALEXANDER MOFFATT.
Princeton.

RALPH WARREN.
Princeton.

JOHN CORBETT.
Harvard.

W. BULL.
Yale.

KNOWLTON L. AMES.
Princeton.

W. C. RHODES.
Yale.

P. D. TRAFFORD.
Harvard.

R. HODGE.
Princeton.

H. H. KNAPP.
Yale.

A. J. CUMNOCK.
Harvard.

JEREMIAH S. BLACK.
Princeton.

C. O. GILL.
Yale.

E. C. PEACE.
Princeton.

W. HEFFELFINGER.
Yale.

R. M. APPLETON.
Harvard.

A

Scientific and Practical Treatise

ON

AMERICAN FOOTBALL

FOR

𝔖chools and 𝔆olleges

BY

A. ALONZO STAGG

AND

HENRY L. WILLIAMS

HARTFORD, CONN.
Press of The Case, Lockwood & Brainard Company
1893

PREFACE.

THE game of football is fast becoming the national fall sport of the American youth. Among the larger eastern colleges, where it has been fostered and developed, football has now been raised to a definite science, but in the west the game is, as yet, comparatively in its infancy

The demand has been rapidly increasing among the smaller colleges and large preparatory schools from year to year for competent coaches, and it is evident that there is felt a wide-spread want for some source of definite information which shall describe the manner of executing the various evolutions, the methods of interference, and the more difficult and complicated points of the game.

It is with the desire of meeting this want so far as is possible, and with the hope of stimulating a love for the game and of raising the standard of play among the school-boys of this country, to whom the colleges and universities must look for the material out of which to construct their future elevens, that the authors have prepared this volume.

The endeavor has been made to begin with simple steps in the early development of the game and advance by gradual stages to the most difficult evolutions and scientific tactics which have been mastered up to the present day. In working out this principle the aim throughout has been clearness and precision.

While it is the primary desire to furnish in this work a practical aid in the attainment of a higher standard of play among the preparatory schools and colleges, still it is hoped that the general public will find it an assistance to the better understanding of American football, which has come to hold such a prominent place in popular favor.   THE AUTHORS.

September 15, 1893.

CONTENTS.

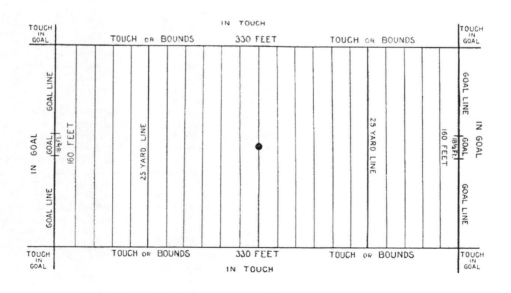

INTRODUCTORY CHAPTER
FOR
BEGINNERS AND SPECTATORS

American football is played on a rectangular field, three hundred and thirty feet long and one hundred and sixty feet wide, enclosed by heavy white lines marked in lime upon the ground. For the convenience of the referee in fulfilling his duties, the field is marked by additional lines five yards apart crossing from side to side, the fifth from either end being indicated by an especially heavy one known as the "twenty-five yard line." The "center of the field" is located at the middle point of the eleventh line.

At the center of the goal lines at each end of the field two goal posts, from fifteen to twenty feet high, are erected eighteen and one-half feet apart, and connected by a cross-bar ten feet from the ground. Two "teams" of eleven men each contest in the game. Seven of them, called the rushers, or forwards, stand opposing a corresponding seven of the opposing eleven, whenever the ball is down for a "scrimmage." The one in the middle is known as the center rusher, or center, and on either side of him are the right and left guards, the right and left tackles, and the right and left ends, respectively. The four remaining players are the quarter-back, right and left half-backs, and the full-back, who stand behind the line of rushers and occupy positions which vary according to whether they or their opponents have the ball. The positions which the players will occupy when about to execute the different movements of the game are shown by the diagrams in the chapter describing the various evolutions. At the beginning of the game the ball is placed at the center of the field. The side in possession of the ball constitutes the side of attack, and endeavors to carry it down the field by kicking or running with it, in order to place it on the ground behind the opponents' goal line. The other side, forced to act upon the defensive, are drawn up in opposition, and strive to check their advance and to get possession of the ball themselves, so that they may no longer act upon the defensive, but become, in turn, the attacking party.

The rules of the game (see final chapter), place certain restrictions upon the attacking side and upon the defense, and it is the attempt made in accordance with these rules by each side to retain the ball in their possession and carry it down the field through all opposition, in order to place it behind their opponents' goal, which furnishes in rough outline the essential features of the American game of football.

Before the game is to begin the captains of the respective teams decide by a toss of the coin which side shall first be given possession of the ball. The side having the ball then places it down upon the center of the field and arrange themselves in any formation which they desire, behind the line on which the ball is placed, in preparation to force it into the enemy's territory. The side acting on the defensive are obliged to withdraw ten yards toward their own goal, and are there drawn up in opposition to await the attack of their opponents until after the ball is put in play.

As the "center rusher" of the attacking side puts the ball in play by touching it with his foot and passing it back to some other player for a run, or a kick down the field, the rushers upon the defensive side are at liberty to charge forward to meet the attack. The clash following this charge constitutes the first actual encounter of the game.

When the runner with the ball is caught, or "tackled," thrown upon the ground, and there held so that he can advance no further, he calls "down," whereupon the ball is "dead" for the moment, and cannot be carried forward or kicked until the center rusher again puts it in play according to rule.

As soon as "down" is called, an imaginary line, crossing the field from side to side and passing through the center of the ball, immediately comes into existence. Each player must remain on the side of this line toward his own goal until after the ball is "put in play," and it is one of the duties of the umpire rigidly to enforce this regulation. Should any player cross this line and fail to return before the ball is "snapped back" it constitutes an "off side play," for which the rules provide a penalty.

To again put the ball in play, the center rusher places his hand upon it at the spot where "down" was called. The rushers then "line up" opposing one another, the line of attack being drawn closely together for a greater concentration of energy, while the defensive rushers are slightly spread apart to facilitate breaking through the line and stopping the advance, when the ball shall be put in play. The captain upon the attacking side then shouts some signal, understood only by his own men, which indicates the evolution that he wishes his eleven to execute; whereupon the center rusher puts the ball in play by "snapping it back," that is, by rolling it back between his legs.

Immediately behind the center rusher the quarter-back has taken his stand. He receives the ball as it is "snapped back" and instantly passes it to one of the half-backs or a man in the line, for a run, or to the full-back for a kick down the field. Thereupon the first "scrimmage" of the game takes place as the opposing team attempts to break through the line and stop the play.

One side is not allowed to retain indefinite possession of the ball without making gain or loss. The rules provide that if the side having possession of the ball shall fail to make an aggregate gain of five yards, or a loss of twenty yards, in three consecutive "scrimmages," the ball shall be forfeited to the other side at the spot where it was last down.

Advances by running are made by the player directing his course through one of the six openings in the rush line, or around the ends, according as the signal may direct. The signal also indicates the player who is to receive the ball. The runner is assisted in his course by the players who border on the opening through which he is to go. These seek to enlarge the space by pushing their opponents to one side. He is further assisted by others of his own players, some of whom precede, to "block off" the opponents from "tackling" him in front, while still others follow to push him further if he is checked. The players who are to precede and the players who are to follow change with the play according as each man is enabled by his position to adjust himself to it.

Four points are scored when one side carries the ball across the goal line and makes a "touch down." The side making the "touch down" is then allowed to carry the ball out into the field as far as they may desire in a line perpendicular to the goal line and passing through the point where it was "touched down," in order that one of their number may attempt to kick it between the goal posts above the cross-bar. The other side meanwhile are obliged to take their positions behind the goal line. Should the attempt be successful, it will constitute a "goal," and two additional points be added to the score. But whether the attempt be successful or not, the ball must be delivered to the other side, who will take it to the center of the field and put it in play in the same manner as at the beginning of the game.

If the ball can be kicked between the posts and above the cross-bar by a "drop-kick" or "place-kick" by any one of the players, without having been previously carried across the goal line, it will constitute a "goal from the field," and will count five points.

In case the ball is kicked or carried across the boundary line on either side it will be "out of bounds" and must be brought into the field at right angles to the line at the point where it crossed. This is done by the side which first secures it after it passes out of bounds.

It is usual to bring the ball into the field from ten to fifteen yards and then to place it upon the ground for a "scrimmage" as from a regular down; though the ball may be passed to any one of the players, in at the point where it went out, provided that it is thrown in at right angles to the side line; or it may be "touched in" at the same point.

The game is divided into two halves of three-quarters of an hour each, and the team succeeding in scoring the greatest number of points during that time are declared the winners.

The reader should thoroughly acquaint himself with the rules in detail, before passing on to a study of the book.

TRAINING

In the early days of college athletics and amateur sports the popular belief was universally accepted that a most rigorous diet must be entered upon if the young aspirant for college honors would fit himself properly to represent his alma mater in the boat, on the running track, or in individual contests. Many an alumnus who pulled an oar on the crew in the fifties and sixties will recall visions of raw beef, a limited bill of fare, and a prescribed daily amount of water that made the training of thirty years ago a hardship for which dim dreams of possible glory seemed a doubtful compensation.

These old ideas have now changed almost entirely, and the young collegian of to-day, who secures a position on any one of the college teams, and obtains a seat at the "training table," is an object of envy rather than of compassion to his classmates. The training table diet of to-day is almost sumptuous, and few men in college enjoy better living than the members of the university athletic organizations. Roast beef, lamb chops, beef steak, roast lamb, and broiled chicken, oatmeal, rice, mush, and the cereals, potatoes served in all styles but fried, stale bread, onions, garden vegetables in season, eggs, dry toast, apple sauce, baked apples, prunes, grapes, oranges, figs, dates, and fruits in season (with the exception of raw apples), rice and bread puddings, furnish an abundant variety from which to choose.

A few things only are put upon the proscribed list: Pies, cakes, salads, all forms of pork, veal, rich dressings, fried food, ice-cream, confectionery, soda water, so-called soft drinks, (and it is needless to say drinks of a stronger nature,) tea, coffee, and chocolate, should be cheerfully and absolutely given up. From the first day of training it should be rigidly enforced that all pipes, cigars, and cigarettes be laid aside, absolutely, until the contests are over.

Regularity in all the daily habits of life is of the greatest importance. The hours for rising, for meals, and for retiring should not vary from day to day; and in so far as it is practicable to do so, it would be advantageous to have the regular practice come at that portion of the day in which the important games of the season will take place.

That the football player should have long hours of restful sleep is a point too frequently overlooked. While it is impossible to state a definite time that shall apply to all cases, a sleep from ten o'clock in the evening until seven the next morning, and a short walk before an early breakfast, will be found to be of the greatest benefit in all instances. Probably a large proportion of the cases of over-training, that occur during the football season, are caused by late hours, irregularity of habits, and insufficient rest. Had these points been carefully attended to, the hard work upon the field would have produced no hurtful result. When the recreation period of the players makes it necessary that the daily practice shall come immediately after the noon meal, it will be found more healthful to have the practice hour preceded by a light lunch, and postpone the hearty dinner until night. But should the daily play come in the morning, or in the middle of the afternoon, it will be better to have the dinner hour at noon.

Over-training is something which is much easier to prevent than to remedy when once it is an accomplished fact. In preparatory schools, where a less violent and less tiring system of training is followed, no thought need be given to this point, but in the larger colleges one or more cases of over-training among the valuable men is apt to occur toward the end of a season of hard work.

Should any one of the players get into this condition, he should be given an absolute rest for several days, and then be allowed to play only part of the time during each remaining day of practice. An immediate change of diet with a removal of all training-table restrictions, will also be found of value.

When a faithful worker finds himself coming upon the field day after day with a worn and tired feeling, no longer able to play with his former dash and energy, and his speed gradually decreasing, he should at once suspect that his muscles are becoming over-tired, and so fatigued that they cannot recuperate between one day's work and the next.

The practice of drinking water during the game is exceedingly bad, and never should be permitted, though rinsing the mouth is admissible. The best results will be obtained if no water whatever is swallowed until more than an hour after the practice is over. The habit which some players have of chewing gum during the game is pernicious. After the first week or two has passed, the mouth will be found to be far less dry where no gum is used, than where a constant flow of saliva is kept up by the act of mastication.

During the season there undoubtedly will be a number of rainy days. These by no means should be lost. As a rule, it is best to practice upon the field as usual, since the most important game of the season may come in bad weather, and the experience of having frequently played in the mud with a wet and slippery ball will prove invaluable.

On special occasions light work in the gymnasium, tackling the bag, and practicing the signals indoors, may be substituted with advantage. Every team should be provided with a tackling-bag. This may be made of leather or canvas, and should be from four to five feet long, a foot in diameter and stuffed with hay, hair, or excelsior, to represent the body of a man. No better practice can be had for low hard tackling than to have such a bag suspended by a long rope from a rafter in the gymnasium over a number of floor mats, letting the men run half the length of the floor and spring for it from some ten feet away as it swings slowly backward and forward. But except on such special occasions when no out-door practice is taken for the day, indoor gymnasium work should be given up, as the exercise upon the field demands every energy.

During the last few weeks of the season, when the final eleven has practically been decided upon, and team play is being developed, an opportunity should be found each day to send the eleven up and down the field in their regular positions, upon short runs of from five to fifteen yards, with no opposing rush line drawn up against them, in order that the signals may be thoroughly drilled into each player and substitute, and all learn to work together as one man. It is of the highest importance to have a number of substitutes, each of whom is thoroughly acquainted with the signals, as the replacing of a player in case of accident by one in the slightest degree unfamiliar with the signals will destroy team play and cause the side a loss much greater than the value of the man who has left the field.

The number of regular games a week a team can play to advantage cannot definitely be stated. The condition of the men and their especial needs must determine this. As a rule, more than two match games a week cannot be played if the best results are to be obtained. A hard game should not be played within less than a week before one which is considered to be of great importance if it can be avoided, on account of the danger of having a valuable man disabled, and in order that there may be an abundance of stored-up energy upon the day of the important contest.

During the last few days before the final game, the practice should be short, but sharp while it lasts, with a considerable amount of time devoted to practicing the signals, falling upon the ball, and perfecting team play. On the day immediately preceding the game an absolute rest should be taken.

It is a mistake to attempt to play the full hour and a half on each day of practice throughout the season. About two half hours of sharp work, with a rest of five minutes between, will produce the best results, and in the earlier regular games each half should be limited to thirty minutes.

The daily practice of the team upon the field will not afford sufficient opportunity to the backs to become proficient in kicking and catching the ball. When it is possible, a half hour should be devoted by them at some other portion of each day throughout the entire season to punting, catching, and goal kicking. Numerous minor sprains and bruises will necessarily be received during the season, for which hot water and flannel bandages will be the best remedy.

In case of a sprained ankle or a serious bruise to one of the muscles of the leg, a long period of disability may result from continued playing, and the captain should insist that a player so hurt should leave the field at once. A thin leather anklet had better be worn inside the shoe by each player in the team as a safeguard and protection.

When a man has a bruised and sensitive knee, a moistened sponge, the size of a fist, placed just under the knee cap will afford relief and protection. Sprains and bruises of a serious nature are more liable to occur during the first few weeks of practice than at any other time in the season. This is due to the fact that many of the men have just returned from long vacations of ease and idleness, and their muscles are not ready to endure the sudden strains and wrenches to which they immediately find themselves subjected, The careful captain will see to it that the promising new candidates for his team and the old men are all gathered together from one to two weeks before the season of actual playing is to begin, and put through a series of light exercises, given short runs, made to pass, kick, and fall on the ball, and are given such general light work for wind and muscle as shall enable them to engage in the regular practice without danger. Thick sweaters and overcoats should always be in readiness to put on after playing, and proper care taken to guard against catching cold.

Cleanliness is a hygienic necessity during the football season, and every team should, if possible, have hot and cold water shower baths connected with their dressing rooms.

Long hot baths are weakening, and should be avoided; though upon special occasions, when a cold has settled in the muscles, a Turkish bath may prove of great value.

The captain's word upon the field is absolute law, and should be followed with unquestioning obedience.

THE CENTER-RUSHER

The prevailing idea in time past has been that the largest and heaviest man who could be procured should be used for the center-rusher, or snapback of the eleven. So universal has this idea become that it has long been a common joke to say of an especially large and stout person: "He would make a good center-rusher." Every new team formed, as a rule, selects the center according to this axiomatic fallacy. It is easy to see how this principle of selection became established under the old pushing style of game, and it still should hold sway, provided it brings with the selection certain qualities of mind, and certain physical capacities, which will enable the center to be one of the most active and effective agents on the field.

The center occupies a unique position on the eleven in that he starts the play after each down, and is the only member of the team who cannot run with the ball from a scrimmage, because it is impossible to make him a third man advantageously. His work, therefore, is limited in that particular. By reason, also, of his having to protect the quarter-back after he snaps the ball, and because he is invariably entangled with the opponents, it is impossible for him to become a valuable running interferer. What work in interference he is able to do is limited to blocking the opponents from breaking through the line, or running behind their own line to head off the runner with the ball at one side. Possibly, when very clever and swift, he may be able to cut across the field to interfere with a half-back or the full-back. The center should make a practice of doing this latter work on every play around the end, and on every play between the tackle and end. Perhaps he may not be able to get ahead of the runner, but he will be of valuable assistance by checking some of the opponents from running behind their line and tackling him. Now and then, also, he will be able to get ahead of the runner and go down the field with him.

From these statements it might appear that it did not matter especially whether the center rusher was a slow runner or not, and that emphasis should be laid on his possessing size and weight, which are understood as necessary to the proper filling of that position. The truth is, that while a slow runner, if he has cleverness for that position and is strong and weighty, will be able to do fairly well as a center, he cannot begin to be as serviceable to his team as if he were also a fast runner. Granting that a fast runner will not be able to do much interfering, or running with the ball, he will still be able to use his speed most helpfully in breaking through the line to tackle; in crossing over to one side to head off a runner; or in going down the field on a kick. Furthermore, his speed will be most helpful in playing a quick game, because he is thus able to follow the ball so closely that there will be no delay in putting it in play. This is a most important point in the center's play. He must be on hand to receive the ball the instant it is down.

It is impossible to play a quick game where the center lags, or to prevent one on the part of the opponents. When there are not many large men who are fast runners it is better, perhaps, to place the speedy man in the position of guard and take a slower man for center.

The ideal center will be one who is swift of foot in addition to his other powers. He should be a large man, not a ponderous man, unless he is quick and strong. He should be especially strong in his legs and back, for he must stand steadily on his feet against the continuous pushing and wrestling which he receives, directly from the opponents, and incidentally from the guards on either side of him. If he is easily moved, or toppled over, he will be likely now and then to snap the ball poorly, thus making the quarter-back uneasy and flurried in handling it. Steadiness is a most necessary part of the center's work and it cannot well be overlooked in the selection of a man to fill that position. Further, as in every position on the eleven endurance is a prime requisite, so is it in this. More of it is needed, however, than in most others, because the work is much harder. No short-winded, fat man can long stand the hard work of that position, if he does his duty. Not only is great physical labor required of the center, but he must also be constantly subjected to knocks and bruises from the plunging and tearing of the rushers and half-backs as they try to break through the line.

No man, therefore, can play in this position who is not physically courageous, and who is not able to rise to his work after each assault with new grit and determination. He should be a man who is cool and collected at all times; combative, but never losing control of his temper; one who endures worrying without being rattled by it; one who never gives up and is bound to conquer. Nowhere in the line is there need for such steadiness as in the center. From him every play starts, in a scrimmage, and a little unsteadiness on his part will be likely to make havoc with the quarter-back's work, and hence with the offensive play of the whole team. Nothing can be more fatal to quick and steady play, for it is sure to produce hesitancy in action in some of the players, with hurried action in others.

In assuming his position for a scrimmage, the center may follow either of two methods of standing, when snapping the ball: one, where one foot is placed back for a brace, the ball being snapped between the legs and a little to one side; the other, where both feet are widely spread to interfere with opponents, as they attempt to break through, and to avoid getting into the way of the ball which can be snapped straight back. Where the first position is followed, the center should be able to work equally well with either foot forward, in order to secure certain advantages in handling his opponent. The center-rusher should make a study of the best way of snapping the ball back, and then hold it the same way every time. He should confer with the quarter-back on this point, as the latter is to handle the ball, and it may be easier to take it when snapped in a particular way.

There are two methods followed in snapping the ball: one, in which the ball is held on the small end and sent back swiftly with little effort, in such a way that the quarter-back catches it in the air all ready to pass; the other, where the ball is laid on its side and rolled along the ground to the point where it is stopped by the quarter-back and then picked up in very good position for passing. This latter method is more generally used because it does not require as delicate work on the part of the center in giving the snap; but speed is sacrificed by it and there is greater liability that the ball shall be deflected from its course by touching the legs. It would be well for the center to learn to use either hand in snapping, for it will often prove an advantage. The center-rusher will do well to make a study of snapping the ball by both methods of standing, and by both ways of holding it until he settles on the one best suited to him. He should then practice this against an opponent until he is able to stand firmly on his feet and send the ball back accurately, at a uniform rate of speed each time. In case the ball is placed on end, it is better to have it lean toward the opposing center at an angle of about sixty degrees. It can be held more firmly in this position and can also be sent back more swiftly, with a bound into the air. Care must be taken not to send the ball *too* swiftly. While the center is practicing to secure steadiness, accuracy, and uniformity in snapping the ball, he should likewise practice getting his opponent out of the way.

In putting the ball in play, the center has the advantage of being able to select the time to snap and he can choose it to meet his own purpose. Besides, he knows the exact instant when he intends to send the ball back and can get the start of his opponent. The center, therefore, is master of the situation when he has the ball. It is for these reasons that he can frequently be down the field on a kick as soon as the ends, and yet not expose the full-back to great danger in having the ball stopped.

There are various ways for the center to handle his man and get him out of his way. He may plunge forward at the instant he snaps the ball, carrying his opponent before him; he may lift him to one side or the other, according to the play called for and the position of the opponent; he may fall on him if he is down too low; or he may get under him and lift him in the air, if his opponent reaches over him.

In any one of these methods, the opportune moment must be seized like a flash and the action be quick and powerful. A slow, strong movement will never succeed. Long and faithful practice is necessary before the center can acquire this quickness and power. In his eagerness to take advantage of his opponent, he must never fail to wait for the quarter-back's signal before snapping the ball. A little forgetfulness on this point might prove disastrous.

The center can be a most valuable man in defensive play if he understands his position. By giving his opponents a quick pull forward or to one side at the instant the latter snaps the ball; by lifting him suddenly backward; or by grasping his arm, the center can frequently break through more quickly than either guard or tackle. Whenever he succeeds in getting through he will be a strong obstacle to all dashes between himself and the guards, and he will sometimes be able to interfere with the quarter-back's pass. Another way in which the center may play on the defense is to spend all his energy for a moment in getting his opponent out of his way and then spring at the runner. In this case the center must throw off his opponent quickly, and not allow himself to be carried backward. At the same time he must not attempt to break through the line.

When the play is around the end, or even at the tackle, the center should move quickly from his position and pass around behind his own line to meet and tackle the runner. When the opposite side is about to kick, the center should do his utmost to break through the line and stop it; but sometimes it may be better instead to make an opening for the quarter-back. He is helped in doing this, by the opposite center himself, as he plunges forward to block him. In such a case a good opening can be made for the quarter-back, if the center will place himself in front of his opponent a little to one side, and then pull the latter forward to the right or left. The guard at the side on which the opening is made should know of this plan so that he may not spoil it, either by pushing his opponent in the path or by getting in the way himself. If there is danger of his doing this, it will be better for him to help enlarge the opening for the quarter-back.

On the defensive the center may play a little to one side or the other of his opponent, or directly in front, to suit the situation. It is most unwise for the center to assume the same position every time, for by so doing he gives the opposite center only one problem to work out and that one probably the same each time. Where the center takes an extreme side position, unless he does it just before the ball is snapped, he gives the captain of the other eleven a fine chance to call for a play which will take advantage of the situation.

There is abundant opportunity for the display of headwork in outwitting the opposing center in breaking through the line. The line is so compact at this point that it is not an easy task to slip by, especially as the opposing center is watching to take his man at a disadvantage. Various methods are resorted to in breaking through the line. Sometimes the center, acting on the defense, is thrown head foremost to the ground by a quick, hard pull, the attacking center stepping aside or over him as he falls. He may also be turned sidewise just enough to slip past him, or he may be lifted back perhaps into the face of the runner. The most common method employed by the center in getting through is to catch the arm of the opponent on the side on which it is desired to go through, give it a jerk, and dash into the opening.

The center in defense must insist on the ball being down where it belongs. Some center-rushers have a way of moving the ball forward several inches further than it should be. There is no occasion for generosity under such circumstances, and the center must feel that it is his duty to stand up for the rights of his team by constantly guarding against any infringement of this kind. On the other hand, a constant bickering over an inch or two of ground may be made of such importance that the game is interfered with and delayed to such an extent that a much greater gain would have resulted were the ball put in play the instant the signal called for it.

A good referee will see to it that the ball is snapped each time from the proper spot.

It is always the duty of the center-rusher to keep close to the opponent who brings the ball in from the side line, in order to protect the rights of his team. Likewise, it is well to "pace in" the opponent who brings the ball to the twenty-five yard line, in order to prevent a quick play being made when his own side are not in positions. The guards assist him in this.

THE GUARD

The main work of the guards may be summed up as blocking, that is, guarding: making openings for the passage of the runner whenever certain signals are given; running behind the line to interfere for the man with the ball; running with the ball occasionally; breaking through the opposing line to interfere with the quarter-back in passing the ball; and tackling the runner or stopping a kick. The guards and the center have the most laborious work on the eleven, if they do their duty, for they practically have no respite from hard work. They must bear the brunt of the heavy plunging of their opponents through the center, and at the same time struggle to break through the opposing line, which is doing its utmost to prevent them. They must do this without a let-up just as long as the other side has the ball, and, moreover, in that part of the line which is most compact. Then, when their own side has the ball, they are expected to use their strength and wits from the moment the ball is put in play until it is again down, in blocking, making openings, and in interfering for the player who is attempting to run. Further, they have little time to catch their wind, for almost the first point which should be drummed into them by the captain or coach is to be always on hand the moment the ball is down, to make or prevent a quick play. It can be truly said that no team is well trained until the center part of the eleven, as indeed the whole team, is prompt on this point. While the guards have all this hard work, they seldom have a chance to distinguish themselves, either by a run, a clean tackle, or a fine interference which is apparent to the untrained eye of the spectator. On the other hand, it does not take much yielding at the center to bring forth criticism that that part of the line is weak.

On account of the nature of their work, the guards should be large and powerful, like the center. It is even more necessary that they should be quick, agile, and swift, than the center, because the guards should always go through the line when the opponents have the ball. On their success in doing this largely depends the strength or weakness of the team's defense.

The chief point in defensive play is to tackle the runner before he reaches the line, and the guards are large factors in doing this. Unless this is done, the ball can be steadily carried down the field when not lost by a fumble, for any team is able to gain five yards in three consecutive trials when the runner is allowed to reach the line each time before being tackled. Any means, therefore, which the guards can employ to interfere with the quarter-back before he has passed the ball, or the runner before he has reached the line, should certainly be used. All the strategy and tricks known in wrestling which can be applied to the situation should be eagerly sought and practiced. The great point to remember is to apply the power quickly and hard, to summon all the strength for the initial effort, and to work desperately until free from interference. Only by doing this can the guards hope to break through and secure the quarter-back or runner behind the line. Slow pushing, however powerful, will accomplish little. If held in check until the runner and the pushers strike the line it is only a question of how many yards the runner will gain before the mass breaks and falls forward.

In applying his power the guard, as well as his companion rushers, has an immense advantage in being permitted to use his hands and arms freely in getting his opponent out of the way. This enables him to put into practice all the skill he possesses in handling an opponent who is allowed to block only with the body. The guard also has another advantage in being free to move whenever he pleases, but he must remember that the opening for the runner may be made on either side of him and be careful not to give his opponent help in making it. It assists the guard greatly in breaking through if the tackle draws out the opposing line as much as is wise in a good defense. This separation should be wide enough to allow the players in defense to break through easily without interfering with each other. It is also usually helpful in breaking through to be restless, but cautious at the same time, in order not to give the opponent an advantage.

The guards and the tackles especially should watch for signs which shall indicate what the play will be, and then go through the line as low as possible for a tackle. They should break through to the right or left of their opponents as seems best at the moment. In order to break through quickly they must have their eyes on the ball when it is snapped and spring forward the instant it is put in play. Quick glances may be cast at the opponents while still constantly watching the ball.

The guards, with the center, are usually called upon to meet the heavy charges in the opening plays from the center of the field. These, as a rule, come in the form of wedges. Two points should be carefully regarded by these center men in attacking a wedge: first, to approach the wedge with the body bent in a position for the greatest power and for meeting the wedge down low; second, to focus on the mass in such a way that it cannot break through between them without being separated, and so giving the guards a chance to tackle the runner. In doing this it should be the aim to focus as nearly as possible upon the point of the wedge, in order to check its advance and throw the forwards back on the runner. The runner will then be forced to come out, if he has not already become entangled in the mass. In making the attack the guards and center should run with dash and determination, at the same time watching closely for the runner and trying hard to tackle him.

Two successful ways of attacking a wedge have been originated. One member of the center trio will sometimes jump over the heads of the forwards and try to fall on the runner and thus secure him, or he will hurl himself headlong at the feet of the oncoming wedge and cause it to trip over him. To make either one of these attacks well the player must be perfectly fearless, and should also use good judgment. In the former case the player must time his jump and not land short of the runner, or he will be pushed quickly to the ground or carried along on the heads of the forwards; neither must he jump so far over that he will miss his man. If he throws himself in front of the wedge he should not do it too soon, lest the wedge will be able to avoid or step over him.

When a wedge is formed in the line on a scrimmage the guards and center must be sure to get low, or they will be carried along before it. The *point* of the wedge must be held in check. In resisting the attack of a revolving wedge the guards should separate slightly from the center and join with the tackle in trying to penetrate the mass to secure the runner. This should be done in such a way that the defense shall not be weakened. Care should also be taken by the side of the line away from which the wedge revolves not to add impetus to it by pushing too far.

The position of the guard varies slightly in defense and offense. In offense the first thought must be to protect the quarter-back until he has passed the ball; his next to block his man long enough to prevent him from reaching the runner. His third thought, which may also influence the way he stands while he attends to the former work, is to make the opening if the play is in his quarter. His fourth thought, which will be influenced by his first and second, is to get in his interference ahead of the runner when practicable, or follow him as closely as possible and do what he can to assist. In fulfilling all these duties he will be limited in his freedom of movement. He cannot stand too far from the center rusher, and he may be compelled to stand shoulder to shoulder with him.

Further, he will have to assume a position which best enables him to carry out his duties. It may be well for him to stand with both feet on a line, or it may be better to have one or the other foot behind, according to his purpose. It is nearly always better for him to bend forward, or even to get down very low if his opponent tries to get under him. The bent-over position is better for meeting attacks, because the weight is well forward and low down and the body is better braced and not so much exposed to effective handling. In this position, also, one can move forward better for making an opening.

In blocking the legs should usually be spread widely apart. They should not be spread so much, however, that the guard will not be able to move quickly whenever his opponent shifts his position. In blocking, as in breaking through the line, the guard should try hard to get his power into action before his opponent. This can be best done by a shoulder check.

The general position of the guard must be determined by the play in hand and the way the opponent stands. He may be forced to move out a little because his opponent does so, but he must be careful that the opening between him and the center is not occupied by the quarter-back or some other free player, in which case the tackle will sometimes be obliged to step in and take the opposing guard. Neither the guard nor any other rusher except the center should ever take a fixed position in standing.

On the defensive much depends on strong blocking by the guards, for weak blocking is fatal at the center of the line. The quarter-back, being so near to the guards, is in imminent danger in case of weak blocking, and he can little afford the loss of a fraction of a second in handling the ball, much less a fumble. Under these circumstances, if a fumble occurs, the quarter-back must always fall on the ball and not run any risks of losing it. Furthermore in weak blocking, the runner has little chance on a dash into the line, for in place of an opening he finds an opponent. "Block hard" has come to be one of the axioms of the game. Blocking for a kick is treated fully in the chapter on team play.

The guard has an advantage over the center in making an opening for the runner in only one particular, and that is that he is freer to move in his position. The center rusher is largely dependent on the position which his opponent takes in standing to help him out in this matter, since he cannot move his relative position from the opposing center more than the latter allows; but he can often influence that position to suit his own purpose. By clever generalship and strategy he may be able to induce his opponent to do the very thing he needs to help him out in his play. Some of the ways of handling an opponent are given in the description of the duties of the center rusher.

When the guard is going to run with the ball he should take a position which will enable him to get away from his opponent quickly, but he should not make his intentions evident. For this reason it is better for the guard, as well as for the tackle, not to take a set position until the signal is given; but if one is taken, let it be such that it would not make it necessary to change in order to run with the ball. The one who is to run with the ball should seek in every way to conceal the purpose of the play.

The guard is in the most difficult position from which to get under headway in order to run with the ball. As commonly played, the guard swings round the quarter-back and dives into an opening between the tackle and guard on the other side of the center. The very beginning of his run is the most difficult part. He cannot run fast from his position, for he has only a step or two to make before he must turn sharply around the quarter-back and run in almost an opposite direction. If he runs back too far he will be tackled before he reaches the line, and if he turns in closely, he is likely to run against his own men as they are struggling with their opponents. It needs, therefore, careful judgment and a great deal of practice to be able to run well from this position.

Long-legged guards, as a rule, find it easier to take a long step backward with the foot next the center, and use that as a purchase from which to circle around the quarter-back. Some guards prefer to take three or four short, quick steps in making the turn around the quarter-back. Any way which will enable the guard to get under headway most quickly is the method which should be used. It will be easy for the quarter-back to place the ball in the guard's hands, and it will probably be better for him to carry it under the arm away from the center.

When the guard runs around to interfere, he should place himself so that he can get away quickly and not "give the play away." If the guard is to run around in order to interfere by getting ahead of the runners, the quickest possible start is necessary. There must be no delay whatever, even when the guard is a fast runner, or else the runner with the ball will have to slow up so much that he cannot make the play. Whenever the guard runs around to interfere or to run with the ball, the tackle should keep the opposing guard from following him. The guard can sometimes do this himself by pushing his opponent back just as he starts, but it must be done in such a way that it will not delay him.

THE TACKLE

The tackle occupies the most important position on the rush line. It is possible to get along with a lumbering center and slow guards if they are able to block well and make good openings, but it is not possible to have slow tackles and play good football at the same time. The position which the tackle occupies in the line explains this, and it is best appreciated when it is understood that the tackles should take part in more than half the defensive work of the team.

The tackle occupies the most responsible position because he assists in checking two distinctly different styles of play. On the side toward the center he is to help the guard in blocking the heavy plunges which are frequently aimed at that point of the line, while on the other side he has to work with the end-rusher against all plays between them and on all plays around the end. To play this position properly on the defensive, therefore, requires a master mind and an equipment of physical capacity and skill unequaled by any position on the eleven.

Next to the half-back the tackle, from his position in the line, has the best opportunity for running with the ball. In fact, he can be used with telling effect, if a good runner, in supplementing and resting the half-backs. Again, he is the end-rusher's chief assistant in going down the field on all kicks, and he must be under the ball almost as soon as the end himself, in order to prevent the catcher from dodging inside the end men.

The points mentioned are sufficient to show that the tackle should be a man of considerable weight, because he has to bear a great deal of the heavy plunging into the line. The greater the weight the better, provided, of course, that the other requirements are met. As a rule, it is rare that a man weighing over one hundred and eighty pounds can meet these requirements, and it is more often that men weighing one hundred and sixty-five or seventy pounds are selected for this position on the best teams. The general build of the man also qualifies his usefulness. The one hundred and sixty-five pounds will be much more effective in a man from five feet six to five feet ten inches in height than in one above that height. In truth, the man of stocky build can usually fill this position much better, because his weight is nearer the ground and he is always in a position to make a low tackle. As a great deal of his tackling should be dashing and brilliant, right in the midst of interference where he must throw himself instantly, a tall man would be at a disadvantage. A thick-set, round-bodied man with large arms and legs would also be a much harder man to stop when running with the ball.

Of equal importance with weight, the points which should determine the selection of the tackle are agility, speed, and the ability to tackle in the face of interference. The name of the position indicates the work of the player. He is to *tackle*. Even speed can to a small degree be dispensed with if the man is quick and agile and is a sure tackler. Quickness in getting through the line, agility in avoiding interference, sure tackling, getting down the field on a kick, and running with the ball are essential qualifications to look for in selecting a man to fill the position of tackle.

The tackle must be endowed with more than the ordinary amount of shrewdness and judgment. To a certain extent this can be acquired by long practice, but the tackle must be of quick perception and good judgment naturally in order to play the position in the best manner.

When acting on the defensive the distance which he should stand from the guard and the manner of going through the line, either to the inside or outside of his opponent, should be determined by previous judgment as to where the play is to be made and influenced by an instantaneous perception as the play starts. The position, too, must be taken with the utmost caution and selected at just the right distance from the guard to best meet the play and still be able to defend his position on either side. There is need of the closest and quickest observation and cleverest judgment.

Moreover, as many of the plays cannot be determined beforehand, such a position must be taken as will best enable the tackle to check any play which can be made. He must then be on the alert for the very first indications of the play and act on them, and at the same time he must still keep the closest watch for later developments which change the direction in which the ball will finally be carried.

Playing up close to the guard is always dangerous unless it is necessary to do so in order to stop a wedge play, for the tackle could then be blocked in very easily from helping, if an attack were made on the space between himself and the end man, or in a play around the end. He therefore would cut himself off from defending two-thirds of his territory and the most defenseless part of the line. Playing far away from the guard is also dangerous, for he then leaves the part of his territory which is nearest the opposing half-backs too much exposed and gives his opponent a chance to block him off from defending it. Of course, if the tackle were free from the checking of an opponent, he could play some distance away from the guard and still defend the space between them; but the fact that there is a player opposite who is giving all his attention, wit, and energy to securing an advantage over him, gives a turn to the problem which he cannot ignore in making his calculations. The tackle takes a certain position; the opponent takes one also. It may be a little to the right or a little to the left of him, or it may be directly in front of him. The tackle may change his position a little and then the opponent perhaps change his, but their relative positions may, or may not, be changed; or possibly his opponent may remain in the same place. Just this action or inaction on the part of the opposing tackle is sufficient to help him determine how he should play in his defense, and is one of the signs to be considered in deciding upon his own position and action.

The tackle should usually play right up to the line, on the defense. Sometimes with a very quick opponent, it may be better to play a little back from the line. He should be restless, and on the alert for an opportunity to go through on the side of his opponent offering the best advantage. He should watch the ball closely and spring the instant it is snapped. His course of action in reference to his opponent must be to get him out of the way as quickly as possible. It may often be best for the tackle simply to drive his opponent back with hard, quick pushes. This might frequently be best when the play is between him and the guard, because the time for preparation to tackle is exceedingly short before the runner will be going past, and the whole attention must be given to securing a momentary freedom from interference, for a quick spring. The tackle has a great deal of this quick tackling to do because the runs are so frequently made in his region. Much of this also must be done right in the midst of interference, when the only chance to get the runner is by hurling himself headlong at him as he passes.

On end plays the tackle must break away from his opponent as quickly as possible. He will have no time then to carry his man before him except, perhaps for an instant, as he pushes him back to get by him. Yet he must make sure to knock his opponent sufficiently off his balance to prevent his following him and giving him a shove at a critical moment. In defense on an end play, everything depends on the tackle reaching the runner before he begins to turn in order to circle the end, and before he has swung in closely behind his interference. The runner then has not yet gotten under full speed and the interferers are somewhat scattered and looking toward the end. The tackle has the best chance for defeating end runs; in this he is ably seconded by the end man, the two working together, in fine team play.

The tackle must go through the line on the defense. The plan of waiting until it is seen where the run will be made and then running behind his line to help, if the play appears to be on the other side, is disastrous to a good defensive game. It not only is dangerous, because it leaves the way clear for a splendid run on a double pass, but it is also especially harmful because it gets the tackle into the habit of waiting for every play to become well started, and this is fatal to a strong defense. If the play is around the other end, the tackle should follow the runner around and try to overtake him. It is sometimes possible for a fast runner to do this when he breaks through quickly. In following the man with the ball, the tackle must be on the watch constantly for a double pass. If he suspects one is to be made, he must be sure not to be drawn in or blocked as he runs behind the line. It would be better, in that case, to go straight through. The tackle can do more to defeat a double pass than any other player, for, if he plays his position well, he will meet the runner when there is not more than one interferer to combat. If he then does not tackle the runner, he can force him to run so far back of the line that the rest of the team will be able to come to his assistance before he circles the end.

When the opponents are going to kick, the tackle has an especial burden resting on him because he is in a very advantageous position for breaking through quickly and stopping the ball. No other rusher should reach the full-back so quickly, unless, perhaps, the guard, because none other is so well placed and at the same time interfered with so little.

He should, therefore, go through with all his strength and speed, and jump high in the air to stop the ball. His hands should be raised at the same time in order to place as high an obstacle in the way of the ball as is possible. The tackle on the same side as the kicking foot has a better chance to stop the ball than his companion on the other side, and he must, therefore, put forth his utmost efforts. Frequently, the tackle, like the guards and center, can work some very clever team play in conjunction with an extra man, whereby one or the other can go through the line with little opposition.

There are a variety of tactics which can be employed in getting through the line, and every tackle should be able to use them at will. Those are best which enable the tackle to get through quickly and at the same time permit him to watch the runner closely. This is a point which ought to be deeply impressed on the minds of all the rushers. The situation changes so quickly when a run is being made that it is not safe to have the eyes off the runner for a second. The methods usually employed in breaking through the line are: striking the opponent in the chest quickly and hard, and following it up with a shove to one side when he is off his balance; whirling suddenly around him, using either foot as a pivot; ducking quickly to one side; making a feint to go one side and going the other; striking the opponent with the head or shoulder and lifting him aside; stepping a little to one side as the opponent comes forward and swinging him through behind him. The tackle can sometimes secure an advantage for breaking through by pushing his opponent back from the line just before the ball is snapped. He must be very free to move, and go through with a jump. It is better to keep as low down as possible in doing this.

The position which the tackle should take on the defense against mass plays from the center of the field is shown in the diagrams further on. He should move off from the guard sufficiently to protect the side of the field and at the same time be able to spring back close to him on any play directly forward. It is his special duty to tackle the runner if he comes out at the side of the formation. In case the runner does not come out before the opposing rushers meet, the tackle should dive in and secure him, if possible, but in doing this he must be careful not to leave too great a space between himself and the guard, as an opening through which to send the runner may be intended at that very point.

It is impossible to lay down rules of action for the tackle on wedge plays in the line. He must work according to his best judgment based on the situation; but an important factor in successful play will be to put in the work low down. If he is caught by the wedge in an upright, or nearly upright position, he will be rendered absolutely useless. For this reason, it is often best to dive in at the side of the wedge about knee high and try to tackle the runner, or cause him to fall over him. If the wedge is revolving, it is often best for the tackle to fall down in front of it. The tackle must consider it his first duty to assist the center and guards in checking the wedge, and leave the other players to attend to the runner if he comes out from behind or at the side.

On the offense, the tackle cannot leave any unprotected space between himself and the guard, if it be occupied by an opponent. He must therefore always take the inside man. This may require him to play close to the guard. From this position he must do all his running with the ball, all his blocking, all his interference for the runners, and make all his openings; varying his attitude toward his opponent to meet the special need of the moment. In making his opening the tackle has to outwit and combat a very free opponent, one who, as a rule, is constantly changing his position. This renders it difficult, sometimes, to make an opening because frequently it has to be done while the opponent is changing his position, and when, perhaps, the tackle himself is not in a favorable position for making that particular opening. Likewise, when trying to block his opponent, the tackle must follow him closely and keep in front of him, and must be all on tiptoe to dart forward to get in a body check before the opponent acts.

When the tackle runs with the ball or moves away from his position to accompany the runner, he is much more at liberty in choosing his place in the line. His great aim should be to take a position which should not be noticeable by its strong contrast to previous ones, and yet, at the same time, be one which he can use to the greatest advantage in the play in hand. Usually that position should be up in the line not more than two or three feet from the guard, but sometimes it is better to stand a little behind the line.

It is most important to the tackle when he runs with the ball that he get away from his opponent with the utmost quickness, and then, that he run with tremendous speed and power. The secret of successful running from any position lies in this. The practice given to improving in this particular should be faithful and constant. The run of the tackle cannot be successful until there is added to the quick start and strong headway, such training in taking his course that he will neither run too near the line, nor too far back from it; and the ability to circle around the quarter-back and take the ball from him without a diminution in speed, and then plunge into his opening with a force which cannot be stopped short of several yards. Much depends on the course taken. The tackle's failure in running often results from slowing up to turn into the right opening and thus losing his power. Instructions in running and holding the ball are given in the chapter on the half-back and full-back.

THE END-RUSHER

The end-rushers fill two of the most important positions on the eleven. In defense, their especial duty is to prevent the long runs of the game. It is an unusual thing for a long run to be made through the center part of the line on account of the support given the rushers by the quarter-back and half-backs. Let a runner once get around the end with one or two interferers ahead of him, as is usually the case when such runs are made, and he is likely to go a long distance down the field and not infrequently make a touchdown. In defending his territory against these runs the end stands at the most remote part of the field for assistance to be rendered him. He is at the extreme part of the rush line and has no one close to him to help him. His nearest neighbor, the tackle, must be depended on for most of the assistance, and when he cannot render it, the end is put to the test of tackling a runner preceded by a group of interferers. In such an emergency a deep responsibility rests upon the end-rusher, because he is probably the last man left to prevent a long run and perhaps a touchdown, producing a sensation akin to that of the full-back when he alone stands between the runner and the goal.

Moreover, the end-rusher has to meet the runner under most trying circumstances. The runner and the interferers have gotten well under way; they have passed the most dangerous spot in the line and are coming on at great speed. The interference is now more focused and effective in arrangement than it has yet been. There are more interferers and they are more closely bunched. At the same time, the end well knows that he is an especial mark on all sides. He realizes that a particular man is appointed to do his utmost to check his play and that if this man fails to do it, the work is to be attended to by other interferers who come immediately after. Under these difficulties in tackling and maneuvering, it is not strange that every captain is most careful in the selection and training of his end men.

The kind of man who could play a brilliant game at end, might not, perhaps, be able to fill any other position in the rush line, yet this is not necessarily true. His qualification would be questionable only as regards build and weight. There are most brilliant end players who only weigh about one hundred and fifty pounds, and sometimes a little less, but the tendency now is toward selecting slightly heavier players for that position in order to gain more weight with which to meet the tremendous on-rush of the interferers. But it is not infrequent that the light, agile, cat-like men are much more likely to tackle the runner, and so are selected in preference to those possessing plenty of weight but less skill. The tackling of these light, quick men is necessarily most brilliant, because they do not bore their way through to the runner but seize a momentary opening to put in their telling work. Such a man, as has been said, could not play in any other position in the rush line, for he would not be heavy enough to stand the hard pushing and plunging to which, for example, the tackle is subjected. With the exception of meeting the end plays and plays between the end and tackle, the end-rusher does not have the hard, wearing work of the other rushers. Not that he does not have plenty of work to do, but he is not constantly combating an opponent and struggling with might and main to get through the line, thus being subjected to the little knocks and bruises which the other rushers have to endure.

The end-rusher is at liberty to take any position he chooses on the offense. His one thought, however, should be to take that position from which he can best operate in helping out the play. Many end-rushers fail to do this. Some ends play up in the line and follow their opponents wherever they move, no matter how far out they go. Others take a stand a little back of the line, about a yard or two from the tackle, shifting this now and then as the play suggests and admits. This latter is generally the best position which can be taken for helping in the interference, and it is also a better position from which to start if the end-rusher is to run with the ball himself. Whenever the end-rusher is going to take the ball he should carelessly assume a position a little nearer the quarter-back – perhaps almost behind the tackle. Otherwise, the distance which he would be obliged to run before he reached his opening would be so great that the opponents would have enough time in which to intercept the play. On this play the quarter-back should give the ball to him by a short pass and then run ahead to interfere.

If the end-rusher plays up in the line he should always take the inside man when acting on the offensive. This is a point frequently forgotten, and oftentimes is the reason why end runs are stopped before the runner reaches the end. The end-rusher should also remember to help the tackle whenever the latter takes the ball. In this case, it may be necessary for the end-rusher to step in and block the opposing tackle, but if the tackle can break away from his opponent without assistance it is better that the end should follow the tackle right around. When the tackle is to go into the line the end can do no better than place his hands on his hips and steer him into the opening. If the end-rusher does this well he can be of great assistance to the tackle in running, and at the same time prevent him from being caught from the rear. The best way to play the end position in making the different evolutions is shown in the chapter containing diagrams.

On kicks into touch the end-rusher must cover the ball well and secure it the instant the full-back puts him on side. Whenever an opponent secures it the end-rusher on that side must be on the watch to prevent his quickly putting it in play at the point it crossed the line. He should also be on the watch for all side-line tricks. The other end man should return quickly to his position to guard his field against a throw in from the side or any quick play. The end-rushers must be sure to keep their eyes on any outlying men who might receive the ball on a pass.

"Be the first man down the field on a kick" is the motto early instilled in the would-be end-rusher, and to do that and be there in time to tackle the catcher before he starts is no small accomplishment. It means that with a good punter, who has perhaps the wind behind him to propel the ball, the end must be exceedingly quick in starting and very swift of foot. If the end fails to get down the field in time, the ball will be carried or kicked back, whereas a swift runner might be able to prevent this. Moreover, the full-back ought not to be compelled to limit his kick because of the slowness of the end-rusher.

It requires long practice and much careful study to determine just the direction the ball has taken almost at the moment it is kicked without wasting time in turning around or in looking over the head into the air. Likewise it requires practice to decide upon the best way of approaching the man to whom the ball is kicked. It is a common fault for end-rushers to run blindly down the field without knowing the exact direction which the ball has taken, when a little study of the faces and actions of the half-backs will indicate in a second whither the ball is going.

Another common fault with the end-rusher is the failure to tackle the man who gets the ball. This results largely from over running him. The player with the ball simply jumps to one side at the proper moment and lets the end go by in his headlong run, and then goes down the field. The one remedy is that he should slacken speed a little as he approaches and watch for a chance to tackle.

Care should be taken by the end-rusher as he runs down the field to approach the player who has received the ball so that he will be forced to run on the *inside* of him. Then, in case the end misses his tackle, he will fall into the hands of the other rushers, now near at hand. The position of the end-rusher when a kick is about to be made, should be such that he can protect the field. Usually he draws off well from the tackle. This must be done without fail when he has a large field to guard, that is, when the other end of the line is near the side of the field. The general form of the rush line as it advances when a kick is to be made, is described in the chapter on team play.

It may be said further, that usually the end-rusher should start his line of direction slightly towards the side lines until he gets the first inkling of the direction the ball has taken. He should then bear in or out still farther, according as seems best. This would not be good advice to the end-rusher who stands close to the side line. The reason for the end taking such a start is that he should protect the whole field against a run, and the least protected part should be attended to first. This suggestion has especial weight when there is a great deal of space between the end-rusher and the side line.

The end-rusher must be especially watchful at the start for signs of a short kick, or for one which goes to the side. Sometimes these are caused by inaccurate kicking, or by the partial stopping of the ball by an opposing rusher. In any event, he must be careful not to over-run the ball, and must secure it whenever an opponent puts him on side by touching the ball. If the end is in doubt where the ball is, he should glance around quickly and find out. The end-rushers must be especially careful when the ball is kicked from near the side of the field, for it often happens that only one end can be near the opponent when he catches.

The end-rusher should be under the ball when it falls, and if the opponent is a good catcher he should usually force him to make a fair catch. If, however, the end-rusher is where he is absolutely sure of securing the catcher if he should run, it may sometimes be better for him to give the opponent a slight chance to run for the sake of increasing his liability to drop the ball. This liability is further increased by a hard tackle just at the moment the catcher starts. The end should be on the watch to secure the ball at such times. He should also make sure that the catcher does not pass the ball to a companion near at hand.

There are many conditions to be met by the end as he goes down the field on a kick which cannot be described. He must note them as they come and act accordingly. One of the hardest of these is to know how to handle bounding and rolling balls. Observing the angle at which the ball descends, also the way it acts for two or three bounds after it strikes, will give some information on which to base action, but there is a constant uncertainty; and in those cases where the ball is revolving on an axis constantly shifting as it goes through the air, there is no certainty of its action after it strikes the ground. It therefore takes the most careful playing at such times on the part of the end-rusher, for one of the opponents may dart in opportunely and seize the ball and go sprinting up the field. If there is any chance for this, and he is not well supported with helpers, the end-rusher should immediately touch the ball and force a down for the other side. Furthermore, when a kicked ball is likely to go over the line in goal, the end-rusher should do his utmost to touch it just before it reaches the five-yard line so that it shall be down at that spot and shall not be brought out to the twenty-five yard line.

THE QUARTER-BACK

As popular opinion has always assigned the snap-back's position to the largest man on the eleven, so likewise it was given the quarter-back's position to the smallest man. There is less reason in having the smallest man quarter-back than the largest player at center. Indeed, there is no question that a swift, agile man of one hundred and sixty or one hundred and seventy pounds would be the most useful quarter-back, if his other qualifications are equal. The trouble is that the man of such a weight, who was qualified to fill the quarter-back's position, would be the man who would be most needed at tackle or end, or as a running-back. There is rarely more than one man with these qualifications on the best teams, while there are usually several men of sufficient speed and agility among the candidates, who perhaps could not be useful in any other position, and yet are too skillful players to lose. The result is that on university elevens the quarter-back is usually a man who weighs from one hundred and forty to one hundred and fifty-five pounds, is agile and swift, is a hard worker, with great endurance and unlimited pluck. Well does he need all of these qualities, for he must always be in the thick of the fight. No play can take place from a scrimmage without his being a medium in its execution, not only in the passing of the ball, but also, if he does his duty, in assisting the runner on his way up the field. Not that he runs ahead of the runner every time, for he is unable to go in front on some plays, but he can always get behind to push if the runner is stopped, or to block off those who try to tackle him from the rear.

The quarter-back's position demands a peculiarly heady player at the same time that it calls for agility and quickness. No other player on the eleven is forced to do as much thinking and planning while in the midst of most skillful and invaluable work. He has no chance to "soldier," either mentally or physically, as the rest of the eleven may do, to a limited extent, occasionally during the progress of the game if so disposed. His brain must be as clear as his muscles are quick and steady. He has to translate with absolute exactness every signal which is given, and as accurately carry it out by forwarding the ball in the most advantageous manner possible to the player who is to receive it. On no account, then, must a man be selected for this position who is inclined to become "rattled," for the position itself is enough to render unsteady the coolest man.

When the quarter-back is appointed to give the signals for the play a new duty emphasizes the importance of his being a heady player, for he then is made the general of the game. By having this duty to perform the chances for his making a mistake in giving the ball to the wrong player are perhaps slightly decreased, but the demand for clever judgment and shrewdness in field tactics more than offsets this.

The quarter-back must know no physical fear. He must be fearlessly unconscious that there are several opponents almost within reach of him who are doing their utmost to fall upon him. No nervousness must enter into his work; else he is not the man for the position.

In assuming his position on a down, the quarter-back is allowed considerable freedom. Some players prefer to receive the ball close up to the center-rusher and then move away as they pass it on to the runner; others take a position between the two, just as far away as is possible while still being able to reach the center conveniently for giving the signal.

The quarter-back who plays close up to the center renders himself liable to be interfered with in his pass by the opposite center and guards, who may reach over to check his play; at the same time he cannot so well take part in the interference on end plays. On the other hand, the quarter-back who takes his position far behind the center is limited in some of his plays. He can be of more assistance, perhaps, in helping on the end plays, but it will be impossible for any of the guards and tackles to run with the ball with any chance of gaining ground, because they will have to run so far behind the line to receive the ball that they will easily be tackled. When the quarter-back takes this position he will have to give the signal in some other way than that usually followed. It has been customary for the quarter-back to press the calf of the center rusher's leg, or some other part of his body, with his thumb when he is ready for the ball; but there are reasons why some other signal would be better at times, and the giving of the signal would be of little moment if there is to be a decided advantage gained by playing so far behind the center. It is accepted as the best way for the quarter-back, in playing his position, to stand bent over, at arms length from the center, with his eyes fixed on the ball.

He has already learned the position of the player who is about to receive the ball as he glanced around at his team when the signal for the play was given. The instant that he gives the signal for the ball to come back he turns quarter round, throwing his right or left foot well behind for a brace, according as he wishes to pass the ball to the right or left. The quarter-back must not take his final position for receiving the ball before the signal for the ball to come back is given; otherwise the opponents will have time to study out his method of passing for the different plays and can guess in what direction the run will be made. It is all done so quickly in the other case that there will be no time to anticipate the play.

The quarter-back should never give his private signal for the ball until the captain has given the signal for the play, and then only after he comprehends it himself. In a well drilled eleven the quarter-back understands the signal for a play the instant it is given, and yet it is not a rare occurrence in important games for signals to be mixed or the key numbers to be left out. In that case the quarter-back should not signal for the ball until the signal for the play is made plain or a new one given. It is now a common practice for the quarter-back to give the signals for the play himself, whether he is captain or not. This has grown out of the fact that he is in one of the best positions for observing the whole field, and also because he will no longer need to interpret the signal after it is given, but can call for the ball as soon as he thinks best. This facilitates the play somewhat and lessens the liability of making mistakes in translating the captain's signal.

There are three styles of passing a ball used by quarter-backs. Two of these make use of only one arm in forwarding the ball – one by an overhand and straight-arm movement especially valuable for passing long distances, but too slow for ordinary use; the other by an underhand pitch with an easy, natural swing of the arm. This latter style is the quickest of the three, for no time is lost in raising the arm into a position for delivering the ball. This pass supplements the movement of the ball along the ground most quickly and naturally. In the third style of passing both hands and arms are used and it is closely allied to the one-arm underhand pass. This insures accuracy, but places limitations on the distance the ball can be thrown. It is commonly used in all short passing. It would be of great advantage if a quarter-back could pass accurately with either hand.

In receiving the ball from the center the quarter-back should stop it with the hand which corresponds to the leg already placed behind for a brace and immediately adjust the other hand to it for a pass. This is done by placing one end squarely in the hand from which the pass is to be made and spreading out the fingers. The hand should then be bent at the wrist until the ball rests against the forearm. The ball is now in position for a pass. Care should be taken to have the hand squarely behind the ball, also to have the long axis of the ball parallel with the forearm. The easiest way to make a long pass is to swing the arm at full length just below the level of the shoulder.

The quarter-back must give considerable time to practicing all parts of his work in receiving, handling, and passing the ball. It is no easy matter to receive the ball as it comes bounding back from the center-rusher and adapt it to the hands for accurate passing while quickly turning into position to deliver it to the runner; but it is necessary for the quarter-back to do this in order not to be interfered with by the rushers who break through the line, and also not to delay the runner. It requires long practice, also, to be able to handle the ball and be off the instant the ball is in the hands, but it is an achievement which enables the quarter-back to be of great service in end interference. Unless, however, there is the most skillful handling of the ball it is impossible for the quarter-back to get ahead of the runner without delaying him. It requires much practice to be able to do quick and accurate passing – to be able to place the ball at just the right distance ahead of the runner at just the right height and at just the right speed, so that he shall not be delayed an instant, and can give his whole thought to running and dodging.

Too great stress cannot be laid upon quick work by the quarter-back. It means success or defeat to some of the plays. At the same time the quarter-back must be exceedingly careful in handling and passing the ball. It is better to be a little slow than to be quick and unsteady. He must never become excited and lose his self-control, for that would be disastrous to all careful work and also would be likely to cause him to make mistakes in signals.

On all dashes through the center it is better for the quarter-back to make short passes of the ball at the runner's waist. The ball must not be passed fast and must be most *accurately* placed, for the runner is bent over for a plunge and is not in a position to handle it, unless on a slow and accurate pass. These points are worthy of the most careful consideration, for much of the fumbling by the half-backs is due to poor passing. What would ordinarily be an excellent pass if the half-back were at some distance, would be a poor one when he is coming forward at full speed, with his body somewhat bent at the waist, and his attention partly on the ball and partly on the opening he is to take. In this case, also, a high pass is harder to catch than a low one, because the hands will have to be raised quickly from their position at the waist.

The quarter-back should also use the greatest care in his pass to the full-back for a kick, for a poor pass will most likely result in the opponents stopping the kick and securing the ball on four downs, if not on a fumble. The full-back can kick most quickly when the ball is passed at his waist.

Some quarter-backs prefer to *hand* the ball to the runner as he dashes by, whenever that is possible. This method, without doubt, is best when the guard or tackle runs around for a plunge through the line between center and guard, or guard and tackle, on the other side of the center. In this case the quarter-back will turn half around, with his back to the center-rusher, the ball being held by the ends between the extended hands. In most other cases an advantage is gained by *passing* the ball, because the quarter-back will not be in danger of being tackled by the opposing rushers or quarter-back, as they break through the line, and also because he will be free after his pass to give his whole attention to helping the runner. He may do this either by going through the opening and pulling the runner after him; by grasping him and going through with him; by shoving him hard when he strikes the line; or by jumping into an opponent who has broken through in the path of the runner. Occasionally it may be better to hand the ball to the runner when the quarter-back runs out to the side to interfere for him; but even in that case, a short pass usually facilitates the play because the quarter-back can run faster and do better interference when free from the ball. It is of great assistance in getting into the interference on end plays for the quarter-back to be able to pass the ball accurately on the run, for every fraction of a second counts in making a helpful connection.

On the defense the quarter-back usually hovers in the rear of the center and guards, watching his opportunity to go through and tackle the opposing quarter or half-backs.

A powerful style of defensive play has now, however, been largely adopted, in which the quarter-back takes a position behind one of the tackles, while a half-back is brought up to a corresponding position behind the other tackle. They there await the play without attempting to go through on the instant the ball is snapped, and as the line of their opponents separates for the play, the one on whose side of the center the opening is made dives into it to meet the runner before he can strike the line.

He must know just when to go through the line and when to wait in order to see where to meet the play; also through which opening in the line to go in order to best check the play. Some shrewd guessing can be done, which will help determine this by noting all the signs of the direction of the play spoken of in the chapter on team play. The center and guards, and sometimes the tackles, should help the quarter-back find his opening and assist him in getting through. The quarter-back should always be helped through when the opposing team is going to kick, since it will be much easier for *him* to go through quickly on account of his size and quickness in starting. If the rushers and the quarter-back work together on the defense the latter can be a most valuable adjunct to their play, because he is free to move anywhere. When a runner is checked or tackled, the quarter-back, as indeed all the eleven, should endeavor to pull the ball out of his hands before he calls "down." The quarter-back often has a good chance to do this when the runner is entangled in a mass.

THE HALF-BACKS AND FULL-BACK

The half-backs and the full-back, who is practically a third half-back, stand usually from two to four yards behind the center of the line. They group themselves at short distances from one another and in a way to best assist in carrying out the play which is about to be made. There is a difference in the latitude given the half-backs and full-back on different teams in arranging themselves for each play. Some captains require these men to occupy the same position on every play, claiming that it is of great advantage in obscuring the play to have a fixed arrangement. On other teams the half-backs and full-back are allowed to move about, and shift their places to the position in which they think they can best help out the play.

There is also a great difference among teams in the placing of the half-backs and full-back in reference to *each other* and also in reference to the rush line. In general, the full-back is stationed behind the center and usually about a yard or a yard and a half further from the line than the half-backs. On some teams, these three play close together, separated by not more than a yard or a yard and a half; on others, they are separated from two yards to three yards and a half. There is also a decided difference in the distance behind the line which the backs play. This varies from two to five yards.

The arrangement of the backs should, in a measure, depend on the style of game to be played; and the style of game should be determined by the composition of the team. That is to say, that if it is deemed wise to play a center game, it can best be done by bunching the backs; while, on the other hand, the combinations can be best made for an end game when the backs are more spread apart.

Captains who are limited in the selection of their players will find it well worth their while to consider the arrangement of the backs, both in regard to their relative distance from each other, and also in regard to the distance which they stand behind the line. Indeed, there is an opportunity for fine generalship in deciding upon the place for these ground gainers.

When the three men who are to occupy positions behind the line have been decided upon, there is also need of careful consideration in determining which position each one of the three shall fill. The full-back is usually selected for his ability to kick, and yet, it is sometimes better that the man occupying that position should act as a half-back until the signal for a kick is given, and then drop back; while a half-back sometimes could do more effective work in the middle position during the general play. If one of the backs is slow, his best position is usually at full-back, for there he receives the greatest protection and help. The light, quick men can succeed better at half-back than the slow, heavy men.

It frequently happens that one of the backs invariably carries the ball under the right arm and is able to use only the left effectively in blocking off, or *vice versa*. This fact should be considered in determining which position the men shall occupy.

It is unfortunate for a half-back to be so limited, but many of them are, and they do not practice with the other arm enough to train it. Some naturally run in one direction better than in another; or some are surer and stronger of foot, perhaps, when running around on a particular side. A player is sometimes put in the right or left position because the interference is stronger on that side; or possibly the arrangement is made to take advantage of a certain known strength or weakness in the team which they are to meet.

The half-backs and full-backs are largely the ground gainers for the team and most of the advances into the enemy's territory are made by them. For this reason, only men who possess special qualifications are selected to fill these positions. In quickness and agility they should equal the quarter-back; in point of speed, ability to dodge, courage, and dash, they should be unequaled by any man on the team. Again and again they must rush headlong into the line, oftentimes only to be hurled back by the opposing rushers who plunge through upon them. Yet, never losing courage, again and again they must come to the rally, now attacking the opponent's center by heavy plunging now trying to make a detour around the wings.

Too great emphasis can not be placed on quick starting. The inability to get under headway quickly is very often the difference between a first-rate half-back and a second-rate one. The second-rate half-back may be just as fast a runner, and may be just as hard to stop when once under way, but he does not get under headway nearly so often, because he loses so much time on his start that he is tackled before he passes the critical point in the run. On all plunges into the line the utmost speed must be used in conjunction with the quick start. The distance is very short in which to get under headway, and there is need of the greatest force to project the runner through the resistance, as well as need to reach that point of resistance in the shortest time. It is common with many elevens to have one heavy back to do the plunging into the line, but frequently this man is so slow in his start that he is not so effective for line-breaking, against a strong defense, as the lighter man would be. It very frequently happens that in choosing the half-backs, men have to be selected who have only part of the qualifications for the position; who perhaps can run fast, or, again, what are termed "fighters," but lack some of the other requisites. When such is the case, the captain should immediately take means to train these men in the other necessary qualifications for good half-back play. It is indispensable that a half-back should be able to run into a line *hard* time and again, and with no fear or hesitation. It is likewise most necessary that a half-back should be a powerful runner and not easily stopped; one who does not fall easily but keeps his feet well when tackled, and struggles on for the gain of a few feet. But he would be a much more useful man if, at the same time with this pluck, determination, and ability to stand on his feet under difficulties, and keep struggling forward, he also had the ability to dodge an opponent or ward him off with the extended arm, instead of running straight into him.

Dodging in running can be cultivated through the study and practice of its points of deception. The underlying principle is the quick movement of the body, or portion of the body, from a point where it would have been if it had continued in the same direction. In the most simple form of dodging the runner suddenly changes his direction. As usually practiced, the runner is obliged to slow up a great deal, in order to change his course. In all dodging, the runner, if at topmost speed, must slacken speed a little, just before he reaches the tackler, in order to reduce the size of his stride so that he may have a proper balance for projecting the body in another direction, or so that he may make certain preliminary body motions which cannot be made when at full speed.

There are several ways of dodging, but one man seldom possesses more than one or two. The zigzag dodge, which used to be so common when individual running and poor tackling were in vogue, is performed by a combination of leg and body feints. Its weakness is that it retards the runner too much. In another dodge the runner strides suddenly one side with a long step. This is a very effective method for long-legged runners. In another, the runner sways his body from one side to the other, the legs being planted wide apart as each step is taken in a zigzag course. The runner moves in the same general direction until the opponent is reached and then darts to one side. Still another dodge is made by drawing the hips away, and in this dodge a clever use of the arm is valuable. It is one of the most effective, since the hips are usually the part aimed at in tackling. Another way is to duck under a tackler by bending the body low at the waist. This is practiced most effectively by small men and is most valuable against high tackling. Another method is to turn the body completely around when about to be tackled, upon one foot as a pivot. This comes into splendid use when the tackler has been unable to grasp the runner with both hands. In another form of avoiding a tackler, the runner, on being approached from the side, slows up a little; whereupon the opponent delays just long enough to allow him to go around by putting on a burst of speed.

Good dodging is not complete unless there is added to it the power to use the arms well in warding off. The latter supplements the former most effectively when well done. When the tackling is high, or when the runner is well bent over, the arm should be extended against the face or chest of the opponent. Often, on a long dive or reach for the hips by the tackler, the runner can break the hold by striking down with his arm. All the above styles of dodging can be acquired by practice. It is better to practice them with only one or two men to act as opponents, after the movement has been learned.

There is another requisite needed by the half-back in addition to dodging, and that is the ability to follow an interferer or interferers well. Half-backs differ greatly in skill on this point. The work of escaping a tackler should not rest wholly in the interferers' hands, as it so often does. The half-back should supplement the latter's work by taking advantage of the protection given him to work every ruse and feint he knows. Where there are several interferers, there is a chance for the runner to move from one to the other as occasion suggests. It needs quick wit and agility to follow interferers well, but much can be learned by practice with or without opponents, and every half-back should devote himself to perfecting his play in this particular.

The half-backs must be good catchers, not only of kicked balls, but also, and especially, of balls passed from the quarter-back. Oftentimes, the fault of a muff or a fumble can be laid to a poor pass, but if the quarter-back is unsteady on his part, there is all the more reason that the half-backs and full-back be skillful catchers. If weak in catching, much practice should be given by the half-backs to perfecting themselves. They should work at this in conjunction with the quarter-back in order that they may get used to each other. In catching short passes, it is usually better to catch the ball with the hands. This is surer because the hands can adapt themselves much better than the arms to the position and shape of the ball when a man is running. In running sidewise to the pass, as it is necessary to do in so many plays, the arms could not be used without checking the speed; while there need be no diminution in speed when the ball is caught in the hands, provided the quarter-back does his work well.

There are three ways of carrying the ball, and each has its proper occasions for use. When the play is straight through the center the general order to the half-back is to put the head down on a level with the waist, gathering the ball up under the body with both arms, because there could be no use for an arm to ward off an opponent until the line has been penetrated, and there is great danger of losing the ball by the pulling and hauling to which the runner is subjected. After the runner is well through the line and has a chance to run freely, he should transfer the ball to the side of the body opposite the arm with which it is necessary to ward off. The runner should look for opponents as he emerges from the opening, and likewise for interferers. Where the play is through the more open part of the line the runner should usually carry the ball under the arm which is away from the opponents who are likely to meet him first, shifting it to the other arm when necessary. In this case, likewise, it is occasionally better to carry the ball in both hands until there is need for warding off an opponent, at which moment the ball can be easily shifted to whichever arm it is desired. This provides for any emergency. This way of carrying the ball is especially valuable in dodging, since the ball can be placed quickly under either arm and a better defense made; for if forced to dodge, the runner may transfer the ball to the arm away from his opponent and have the other free to ward off. By moving the ball from one side to the other in front of the body while running, the dodge will be made more effective.

In carrying the ball under the arm it should be held well forward, because it can be held more tightly in this position. The reason why the ball is often pulled out from under the arm is that it is held so far back that the strong muscles of the chest are of little assistance. When held in this position the ball is often forced out from under the arm when the runner is thrown to the ground. By testing these two positions it will be easily seen which is the safer way. If a runner is inclined to lose the ball he should practice squeezing it in the most approved manner until he has trained himself to hold it fast under all circumstances.

We have already spoken of the runner getting under headway quickly. It is also necessary that he should run with all his speed; whether he plunges into the center part of the line or follows the interference out to the wings (unless he is obliged to slow down in order to receive the ball, to let a runner in ahead of him, or to get by an opponent). No runner is so invincible in all his play as he who rushes with all his strength; who shows by his every movement the determination and power with which he is charged; who inspires in his opponents a hesitancy and dread of tackling him; who never gives up when tackled but keeps struggling on, twisting, squirming, and wriggling himself out of the grasp of one after another until he can no longer advance. Such a man is worth a dozen who hesitate.

The dashing runner is the one who usually makes the advances. If he goes through an opening he goes through on a jump. Such a man, when checked, will keep his feet and legs going like a treadmill and will bore his way through in spite of resistance. This sort of pushing accomplishes wonders. For effective application of power it is worth vastly more than the same amount of force applied slowly, for the attack is sudden and continuous. Its effectiveness, however, is altogether dependent on the head being well bent over, so that the whole weight and impetus of the body is forward, for the legs are then in a position to exert the greatest power.

Another reason for running into the line well bent over, is that it is much more difficult to tackle a runner when in that attitude. It is impossible to get under a short man in order to make a low tackle when he is coming straight toward one, and the result is that the tackler receives the runner's head in his stomach, or if he be good in the use of his arm, he will very likely have a hand thrust into his face or against his chest. At such times, the runner is very often able to slip past.

Again, running with the head down enables the runner always to fall forward when tackled. This usually means a further gain of two or three yards.

In running low care should always be taken not to lose the balance. After considerable practice the balance can be very well kept when running much bent over and still great speed be maintained. As soon as the line is cleared and there are no opponents very near, the runner should assume a more upright position so that he can run at his utmost speed, lowering his head whenever he thinks best.

In making the end plays, the runner need not put his head down except, perhaps, when it is necessary to duck under a tackler. He must now put on speed up to the full limit of the interferers, following them very closely, now using this one and now that, according as the danger shifts. He must constantly be on the alert for changing his position to take advantage of every little help, or to prevent being pocketed, at the same time being ready to break away from his interferers if he sees he can gain more by so doing. In general, the runner should keep behind his helpers until the last, but now and then an opportunity comes which he ought to accept.

The light-footed, agile man who can keep his balance well is physically best capacitated for running behind interferers. To do it well the runner should be able to change his stride to meet the emergencies which arise in passing from one interferer to another, or in following very close when a long stride would cause him to stumble over his interferers.

Another requirement which the backs, or at least one of them, presumably the full-back, should have, is the ability to kick. It would be well if all three possessed this ability, for there are times, now and then, when consternation could be brought to the opponents by the half-back returning a kick. But this could happen only occasionally, and it is much more important that the half-backs be especially strong in running with the ball, for that will be their main work. The full-back, however, should be a skillful kicker both in punting and drop-kicking.

It requires long practice to punt well. The oval shape of the ball precludes simply tossing or dropping it from the hands and then kicking it, to get the best results.

The mechanical construction and adjustment of the muscles of the leg and body in their relation to kicking require careful study. Long practice is necessary to be able to regulate the power, and at the same time determine the angle and direction which the ball shall take. All the practice which the full-back can get to acquire skill in punting will be well repaid, for it will make him of inestimable value to his eleven.

Where the full-back does not know how to punt, the following directions will be found helpful: Hold the ball between the hands, the ends pointing to and from the body, lacings up. Extend the arms horizontally in front and bend forward with the body until the ball is held just below the level of the waist. Take a short step forward with the foot not used in kicking, and at the same time drop the ball from the hands and bring the kicking leg quickly forward to meet the falling ball about knee high. Do not try to kick hard at first. Attend simply to dropping (not tossing) the ball without changing the relative position of the axis. This must be closely regarded or there will never be any certainty as to where the ball will go. The first point noticed by a novice will be that the ball reaches the ground before his foot meets it. This shows that the foot was not started forward soon enough. One way to obviate that difficulty is to drop the ball from a higher point; but the best point has already been selected and the tardy member must be trained to be on time. It will also be noticed that sometimes the ball will meet the leg above the ankle. The aim should be to have the ball fit into the concave of the extended foot, and it will probably be necessary to give the ball a slight toss forward in order to make the kick powerfully. Care should be taken when doing this that the ball is not turned, or tossed so far that power is lost. In practicing in this way it will at first be noticed that the whole force of the blow will be given by using the leg from the knee down. This, one can readily see, would weaken the blow because the leverage is short and the muscles which extend the lower leg not especially powerful, and at the same time it is very trying to the knee joint. The most powerful kick would be one which had the leverage of the full length of the leg, thus bringing into play the strong abdominal muscles to add speed and power. In making this kick, the leg should be extended at full length (with toes pointed) and should swing on the hips as an axis. After the forward kick has been learned so that it can be well executed, the side kick may be attempted. In this case the ball is dropped a little to the outside. The great advantage of the side kick is, that if not too much on one side, a very considerable increase in power can be gained, because a longer swing can be given to the leg, and because the swing is further assisted by some additional muscles which give increased power. Another advantage is that the full-back can take a step to the side and kick around an opponent.

In practicing, do not keep the leg rigid through all the swing. The muscles must be sufficiently lax to make the swing easy, the rigid contraction coming just before the foot reaches the ball.

The angle at which the ball is kicked can be regulated by elevating or lowering the point of the ball farthest away from the body, or by dropping the ball in such a way that the position of the foot in the arc described by it shall regulate the direction which the ball shall take. If the kicker wishes to make a high kick, he drops the ball so that the foot reaches it when knee high or above, and when he wishes to make a low kick he allows the ball to get closer to the ground before his foot meets it. By trial, it will be found that a point varying from about six inches above to six inches below the height of the knee is the place of greatest convenience and power.

After punting and drop kicking has once been learned, the whole practice should be centered on kicking quickly. The ball should be caught, adjusted, dropped, and kicked just as quickly as possible. In practicing this, it will be found expedient to have several balls for the quarter-back to pass. After practicing for a few weeks in this way the full-back will find that he can stand considerably nearer the rush line and still avoid having the ball blocked.

The drop kick is made by dropping the ball on one of the small ends and kicking it with the toe at the instant it rises from the ground. Some kickers prefer to have the ball lean toward them at a slight angle as it strikes, others to have the ball lean slightly toward the goal, and still others drop it with the long axis vertical. The latter style is most commonly used. Practice in all these will determine in which position the foot meets the ball most naturally. The ball should be kicked with a free and easy, though quick, swing of the leg. If close under the goal the kick may be made more quickly with a short half swing, whereas in punting the leg is swung from the hip and the large abdominal muscles of the body brought strongly into play. In drop kicking very accurate, rapid, and effective work can be accomplished when the swing is made almost altogether from the knee joint with only a slight swing from the hip. Beginners frequently make a great mistake in drawing the foot far back in preparation for a long drop kick. By extending the leg below the knee quickly and suddenly, so that the point of the toe will meet the ball at the instant it rises from the ground, great distance can be attained with little apparent outlay of force.

It requires a great deal of practice to be quick and accurate at the same time. The full-back should place himself a little farther from his rush line in attempting the drop kick than in punting, because the ball starts lower and it is not so easy to control the angle it takes.

In trying for a goal from a place kick the ball should be brought out to a spot from which the angle to the goal and the distance from it are most favorable for the trial. If the touchdown is made directly behind the goal, or near it, the ball should not be carried far out into the field. A point should be selected where there will be no danger of the opposing rushers stopping the ball and from which it will be easy to kick the goal. Some men prefer to make the trial from a point not more than ten yards away, while others carry the ball out fifteen or twenty yards. The former always make a quick half swing of the leg in kicking, lifting upward with the foot as they kick: the latter usually kick with the leg swinging full and free from the hip.

The ball should he held between the outstretched hands of the quarter-back or some other player as he lies extended flat on his stomach. The best way of holding the ball is to place the fingers of one hand behind it about three inches from the lower end, the fingers of the other hand being placed at a corresponding point at the top and slightly in front of the ball. The ball should be held in firm but easy balance, and the fingers should be so placed that it will be easy to turn it and least interfere with it when placing it down for a kick. Great care must be given to holding the ball steady.

When the spot has been selected from which the trial is to be made, and the player who is to hold the ball has prostrated himself in firm balance on the ground, at right angles to the line of direction, and on the right or left side of the kicker, according to the foot which he is to use, the ball being properly held between the fingers with the elbows resting on the ground, the kicker must proceed to sight the ball. He first asks the holder to turn the lacing of the ball toward him; next he tells him how he wishes the ball to point and at what angle, if any, using such expressions as "head forward" and "head up," meaning that the ball is to be tipped away from the kicker in the first instance and held vertically in the second. Other expressions like "head out" and "head in" indicate that the point of the ball is to be moved in or out in reference to the player holding it.

The sighting of the ball toward the goal can be done best by using the lacings as a guide, the holder being directed to twist the ball out or in, in reference to himself, by the expressions "lacings out," "lacings in." When the ball has been well aimed and everything is ready the kicker should tell the holder to "touch it down," at the same time moving forward to kick. In touching the ball down the holder must be very careful not to change the position. As the ball touches the ground the lower hand is removed in order not to interfere with its course. It is well to remove beforehand all pebbles or tufts of grass at the spot selected for placing the ball down, for a slight unevenness is often sufficient to prevent a goal.

The kicker should keep his eye on some point in the ball as he steps forward and aim to kick it in that spot. Practice beforehand will determine the best place to give the impetus. When the ball is vertical, this spot will be found by trial to be very near the ground; when the ball leans toward the kicker the best point for the kick is just below the lacing. The height of the point above the ground is nearly the same in both cases, but the point on the ball changes as the ball leans. If there is a wind blowing the kicker must take into consideration its force and direction in pointing the ball.

In catching kicked balls and long passes, it is usually better to catch them with the arms. Every effort should be made to take the ball when about waist high, for at that point the arms can be better adjusted to it. The body also, here much softer, can at this part be drawn in to form a sort of pocket, as it were, for the ball. Care must be taken not to have the ball strike high up on the chest, for it is then difficult to shape the arms well to receive it and the ball rebounds much quicker from its firm walls.

There are two ways of catching with the arms. In one, the arms work in conjunction with the body, the latter being used to stop the ball while the arms close around it. In this style, one hand and forearm should be held lower than the point of contact with the body, while the other hand and forearm should be held above that point. The arms should be bent and should not usually be extended far from the body. In the other case, the ball is caught entirely with the arms and hands. This can be done only when it is kicked well into the air. The arms are held parallel in front of the body about six inches apart, being half bent at the elbows and wrists. The instant the ball strikes, the hands are curled forward over it. The fault of catching in this way usually lies in the catcher failing to bring his elbows near enough together and so leaving a space for the ball to go through.

In nearly all plays the backs, from the nature of their duties, are among the first men to start. Their position behind the line renders their every motion conspicuous, and the watchful rushers upon the opposing team will be upon the constant lookout for some movement, glance, or position of the body that betrays the direction of the play which is about to be executed. On this account the backs should take the greatest precaution to conceal their intentions. It is of assistance sometimes in deceiving the opponents to assume a position as if being about to go in one direction when an entirely different move is intended, but if this is practiced too frequently it will defeat its own end.

EXPLANATION OF THE DIAGRAMS

Before passing on to consider the following plays, a few words of explanation will be necessary.

The side of attack in every instance, when in their regular positions, will be represented by the solid dots (● ● ●), and the side acting on the defensive by rings (O O O). When it is desired to represent a player in a position other than that which he originally occupies the ✲ ✲ ✲ figures will be used. The broken line (—·—·—·—) will represent the course of the ball in the pass and the direction taken by the runner who receives it.

A simple dotted line (- - - - - - - - -) will be used to indicate that a player is to *follow* the runner with the ball, while the solid line (————) indicates that the man shall pass in *front* to act as a line-breaker or interferer. The arrows indicate the direction which the players shall take.

The men represented by the letters given in the diagrams are as follows: C, indicates the center; QB, the quarter-back, RH, LH, RE, and LE, the right and left half-backs and right and left ends respectively; the right and left tackles are indicated by RT and LT; while FB represents the full-back.

It must be *distinctly understood* that the drawings are in a measure *diagrammatical* and do not in all instances represent accurately the *relative distance* between the players.

For example: in the diagrammatical representation, wide spaces are left between the individual men in the rush line, while as a matter of fact, when the game is in progress, the rushers stand so closely together that they can easily touch one another and are frequently placed shoulder to shoulder. This manner of representation has been decided upon as conducive to greater clearness in showing the relative positions and directions where a number of men are obliged to pass through one opening, and in case the beginner is misled by this in any way, his error will be readily corrected by careful study in other parts of the book.

In arranging the positions of the side acting upon the *defensive*, the quarter-back has been placed immediately behind one of the tackles while a half-back has been brought forward and stationed behind the other tackle. The abilities of the two half-backs should determine which position they shall occupy; the points to be considered being the ability to catch the ball when it is kicked, and the qualification for meeting the heavy tackling in the line.

Sometimes it is preferable upon the third down, or when the ball is to be kicked, that the half-back stationed behind the tackle should *immediately* return to his proper position. At all other times the quarter-back and half-back usually remain directly behind their respective tackles as indicated, after the ball is snapped, until it becomes clearly apparent through which one of the openings the opposing side is to make their attack, and then to spring forward directly into this breach and meet the oncoming rusher *in the line*.

This is considered a safer and more powerful defense than to have either one of these men attempt to break through, in the hope of meeting the runner behind his own line before he reaches the opening, and is the method adopted by the leading college football teams in the country. When opposed to a team using the running game almost altogether, *both* half-backs may be sent forward to support the line, the full-back alone remaining well behind the line for safety.

It will be noticed that the ends upon the side acting on the *offense* are placed near the tackles and are drawn slightly back from the line. We believe that the ends are in the strongest possible position for an attack in any direction when they stand about a yard and a half from the tackles, and about a yard back from the line. From this position they are of equal value in blocking, should the play be made around their end, while in plays through the center and around the opposite end, their position back from the line enables them to get into the play with far greater rapidity, and well-nigh doubles their efficiency. From a position *in* the line the running of the end, with the ball, which may be made a powerful play, would be extremely difficult.

Nearly every diagram represents *two* plays or more, and it should be borne in mind that, whereas in the diagram a play may be represented as made to the *left*, the same play may also be made to the *right* and *vice versa*.

In representing the arrangement of the men in the wedges and in the opening plays from the center of the field, the formation is given which in the majority of cases would seem to be most advantageous. But this arrangement need not be considered fixed and may be changed at the discretion of the captain.

For special reason, too, it may in some instances seem best to alter the arrangement of the interference so that the positions of the preceding and following runners shall be interchanged. When there is sufficient reason for doing so, there should be no hesitation in making the alteration. When nothing is said as to duties of a player in the description of the diagrams, it will be understood that the player blocks his man.

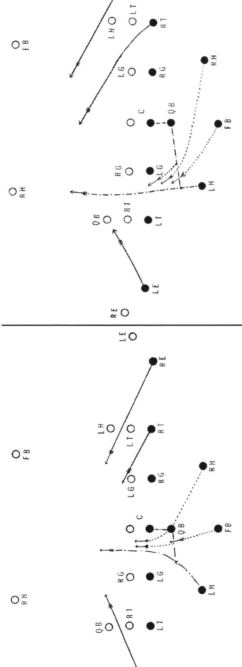

1. Half-back between guard and center on his own side.

To send LH between LG and C, the half-backs stand about *three** yards behind the rush line, directly in the rear of the opening between guard and tackle, RH stands directly behind center, about *four* yards from line, and the ends play *in* the line about *one and one-half* yards from tackles,* or as shown in diagram 5.

The *instant* the ball is snapped, LH, FB, and RH *dash* forward for the opening between LG and C; LH receives the ball from QB as he passes him on the run and strikes the line at *utmost speed* between LG and C, with *head down as low as the waist*, and the ball clasped tightly into his *stomach* with *both* arms. At the same instant the ball is snapped, LG lifts his man *back* and to the *left*, C lifts his man *back* and to the *right* to make an opening, while the ends and RT pass through the line at *full speed*, in the lines indicated, to be ahead of and interfere for LH in case he succeeds in getting through. FB and RH following directly behind LH at full speed, push him *with all their might* as he strikes the line. The instant QB has passed the ball he follows behind LH and helps push him.

NOTE. Many times when the runner is apparently blocked in the line he may be torn loose and carried on for long gains if all *plunge* and *tear* and *push* till the ball is "down." *Never let any man cease work until* "down"'s called.

*The positions of the backs behind the line may vary from 2 to 4 yards, dependent upon the quickness of the men in starting.

2. Half-back between guard and tackle on his own side.

To send LH between LG and LT, the backs and ends occupy *exactly* the same position as in play No. 1.

The *instant* the ball is put in play, LH, FB, and RH dash forward as before ; LH receives the ball at about x on a short pass from QB, and with *head down* and ball clasped at the stomach with both hands,* dashes into the opening between LT and LG, while FB, RH, and QB follow *directly behind* and push *with all their might* as he strikes the line.

LT lifts his man *back* and to the *left*, while LG lifts his man *back* and to the *right* the moment the ball is snapped, in order to open the line.

LE, RT, and RE also start the instant the ball is put in play ; LE dashes into the first man behind the opposing line, making sure at the same time that no one reaches LH from outside of LT before he strikes the line, while RE and RT take the directions indicated in the diagram, to arrive ahead of and interfere for LH as they go together down the field.

NOTE. It will be the duty of RE and RT to block the opposing RH and FB, and each should make for the point in front of LH where he can best interfere with and block his particular man.

*It will be a great advantage upon emerging from the line to shift the ball to one arm, in order to have the other to use in warding off.

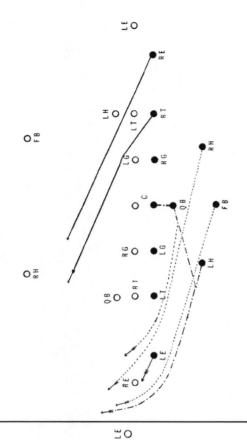

3.* Half-back between tackle and end on his own side.

To send LH between LT and LE, the backs and ends occupy the same position as in the preceding plays.

LH, FH, and RH start forward the *instant* the ball is snapped, as before, and LH receiving the ball at X on a pass from QB, dashes for the opening just to the *left* of LT, with his head down.

FB, and RH and QB follow directly behind, as in the preceding diagram, to throw their whole weight against LH when he strikes the line and push him through, in case he is blocked.

LT makes a supreme effort to carry his man *back* and in the *right*, while LE runs directly for the opposing end and endeavors to force him *out* to the left.

RT and RE, without stopping an instant to block their opponents, pass directly through the line and take the directions indicated in the diagram, to arrive in front of LHt at the left end and interfere for him in case he passes the line successfully.

* This play was made in the early stage of the development of the game, when the runner's ability to dodge was trusted to in order to make the play successful, but is now seldom if ever used.
† See NOTE, diagram 2.

4. Half-back around his own end.

To send LH around LE all the men occupy the same position as in the preceding plays of the series, * with the exception of LH, who shifts his position several yards to the left without attracting attention.

As before, LH, FH, and RH start forward at utmost speed the instant the ball is snapped, and LH, receiving the ball as he runs on a long pass from QB, sprints for the left side of the field in order to circle around and pass to the *outside* of the opposing end.

LE makes directly for his opponent, and endeavors to force him in toward the center, while FH, RH, and QB follow at utmost speed as before. FH and QB seek to over-take LH, running to the *inside* of him and interfering for him as they go together down the field, while RG follows as closely as possible behind LH to prevent his being caught from the rear.

RT and RE pass directly through the line and take the directions indicated as before,† to interfere for LH if he succeeds in circling the end.

* See explanation of diagram 1.
† See NOTE, diagram 2.

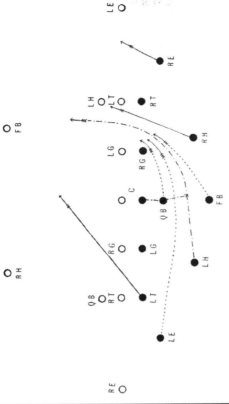

5. Half-back between guard and center on the opposite side.

To send LH between RG and C, the ends stand about *one* yard *back from the line* and a *yard* and a *half outside* of the tackles, the half-backs stand between two and three yards directly behind the *guards*, RH withdrawing slightly to RH², and the full-back stands between three and four yards behind the center.

The *instant* the ball is snapped FB, LH, RH, RE, and LE dash forward for the point between RG and C; RG lifts his man *back* and to the *right*, while C forces his man *back* and to the *left* to make an opening.

FB dashes straight into this space, passes directly through the line, breaking an opening, and jumps into the first man in his path behind the opposing line.

LH receives the ball from QB's hands as he passes on the run or by a short pass, and plunges into the opening directly behind FB with his *head down* and the ball tightly clasped at his *stomach* with *both hands*.*

RH, RE, LE, and QB dash in immediately *after* LH, throw their *entire* weight against him and push him through.†

LT, simply forcing his opponent to pass *outside* of him, dashes in the direction indicated the instant the ball is in play, to arrive ahead of and interfere for LH in case he succeeds in getting through the line. It may be best for LT to select a *particular* back, and make it his especial duty to take *him* each time.

NOTE. RH may go in advance of LH together with FB, if so desired.

---

* See NOTE, diagram 2.
† See NOTE, diagram 1.

6. Half-back between the guard and tackle on the opposite side.

To send LH between RG and RT the men occupy the same position as in the preceding diagram.*

The *instant* the ball is snapped RH, FB, LH, and LE start forward at utmost speed in direction of lines indicated. RG lifts his man *back* and to the *left*, while RT lifts his man *back* and to the *right*.

RH dashes straight through the opening and takes the extra man behind the *opposing* LT. LH follows immediately behind and dives into the opening so made with head down, the ball held as before.†

LE leaves his position the moment the ball is put in play and follows directly behind LH.

FB and QB also dash in and all throw their combined weight in behind him as he strikes the line, to push him through.

The play of LT is the same as in diagram 5.

RE takes his own man and endeavors to force him *out* toward the side.

NOTE. FB may be sent through the opening with RH *ahead* of LH, to break the line and interfere, instead of following and pushing from behind.

---

* See description of positions of diagram 5.
† See description in diagram 5.

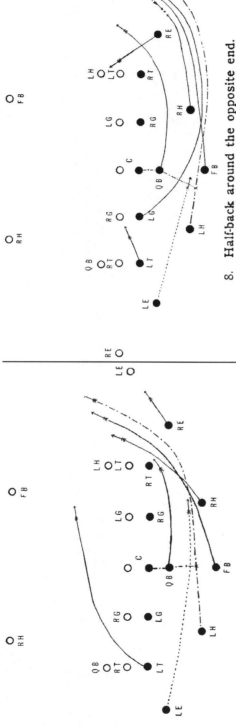

7. Half-back between tackle and end on the opposite side.

To send LH between RT and RE, the men take the same position as in the preceding play.*

As before, LH, FB, RH, and LE start in the direction indicated at *utmost speed* the instant the ball is snapped. RE takes his opposing man and forces him *out*. RH and FB dash for the opening to the right of RT ahead of LH, take the first men they meet after passing the line, and run in the direction indicated down the field to interfere for LH.

LH receives the ball on a pass from QB at x, makes for the opening at utmost speed, with *head up*, and as he turns down the field takes a line a little to the *outside* of RH and FB to have the benefit of their protecting interference.

QB should, if possible, seek to arrive at the opening *ahead of* and interfere for LH.

LE follows LH closely, to prevent him from being caught from behind.

LT, going through the line as before,* makes for the right side in the line indicated, to block the opposing backs.

NOTE. Care must be taken by RH and FB that they do not run so far ahead of LH as to diminish the value of their interference. They should precede him from one to three yards.

_____

8. Half-back around the opposite end.

To send LH around RE there is no change in the position of the men behind the line.* As before, RH, FB, LH, LG, and LE start forward for the right end the *instant* the ball is snapped, at *utmost speed.* RT blocks his man and forces him as far as possible to the *left*. RE jumps directly into the line and either helps RT block his man, or takes the first extra man. RG blocks his man hard. RH runs straight for the opposing end-rusher, whom RE has left entirely exposed, meets him at about x, jumps into him and knocks him over or forces him in. FB following at RH's elbow will, if necessary, assist in blocking off the opposing end, and pass on down the field in the line indicated, to interfere for LH. LH receives the ball on a pass from QB on the run, and encircles the opposing end at top speed and passes down the field, a little to the *outside* of the line taken by LG.

LG breaks away from his opponent as the ball is snapped, and cutting in either directly behind QB or between QB and C, dashes for the right end, a little ahead of LH, and between him and the line, in order to interfere for him. A slow and lumbering guard may not attempt this play. LH may be obliged to withhold his speed until nearly at the end, in order to allow LG to get ahead of him.

QB *must* succeed in arriving at the end before LH. LE and LT play as in the preceding diagram,† or in case LG runs, LT leaves his own man to be taken care of by LE, and blocks the guard whom LG has left. This play requires the perfection of co-operation at every point, and can only be made successfully with constant practice. The attempt to have the guard run should not be abandoned because of numerous failures.

NOTE. In case LE, on the opposing side, plays far out, RH may force him still farther out, and FB and LH pass *inside* of him. Judgment must determine each time whether to pass the end on the *inside* or *outside*.

_____

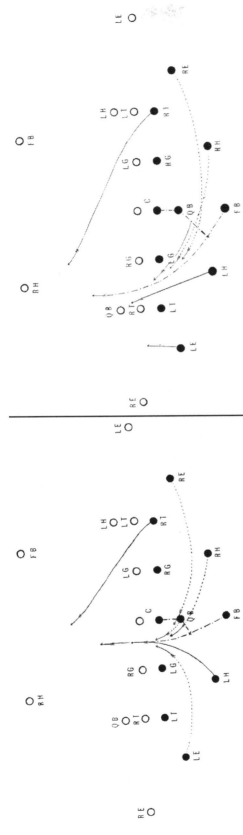

9. Full-back through the line between center and guard.

To send FB through the line, between LG and C, the men are placed as in the second series.*

The *instant* the ball is snapped, LH, FB, RH, LE, and RE dash forward for the opening between LG and C. At the same moment LG lifts his man *back* and to the *left*, while C carries his man *back* and to the *right* to widen the breach. LH rushes straight through the opening and down the field, making for the nearest back who opposes. FB, receiving the ball from QB as he passes on the run, plunges in directly behind LH, with his *head down*, and the ball clasped at his stomach with *both hands*.

LE, RH, RE, and QB rush in behind FB and throw their entire weight against him as he strikes the line, to push him through in case he meets with any resistance.†

RT slips through the line to the *inside* of the opposing tackle, without attempting to block him an instant, and takes the direction of the line indicated, to arrive ahead of and interfere for FB, in case he succeeds in passing the line.

LT and RG block their men.

NOTE. It may be well for RT to run directly for the opposing RH, and make sure that he is thoroughly blocked.

* See description, diagram 5.
† See NOTE, diagram 1.

10. Full-back between the guard and tackle.

To send the **full-back** between LG and LT, the men stand as before.* All three backs and RE dash for the point between LG and LT, the instant the ball is put in play. LT lifts his man *back* and to the *left*, while LG lifts his opponent *back* and to the *right*. LH rushes through the opening ahead and takes the extra man behind the tackle.

FB receives the ball at x, on a pass from QB, as he runs, and dashes into the opening, directly behind LH, with his head down and the ball held as before.

RH, QB, and RE follow immediately behind FB, and throw their entire weight in to help him as he strikes the line.

LE takes the first man in the line outside of the tackle, and prevents the opposing end from coming in.

RT, without holding his man an instant, plays as shown in the preceding diagram.†

* See description, diagram 5.
† See NOTE, diagram 9.

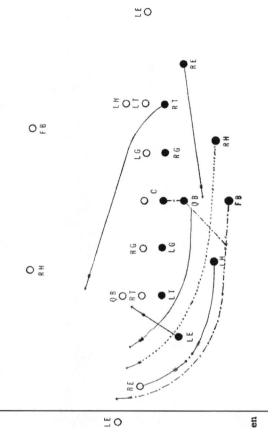

11. Full-back between the tackle and end.

To send the full-back between LT and LE, there is no change in the position taken by the men.*

The three backs and the ends dash forward in the lines indicated the instant the ball is snapped.

LE takes the tackle, the extra man behind the tackle, or the first man in the line outside of him.

LH runs directly for the opposing RE who has been left free, blocks him and endeavors to force him *out*.

FB receives the ball at x on a pass from QB and runs in the line indicated, at utmost speed, with head well up.

QB cuts in close behind LT and endeavors to get *ahead* of FB in order to give him interference.

RH and RE, running behind FB at utmost speed, seek to protect and assist him. RT plays as before.†

LT exerts every power to force the opposing tackle *back* and in toward the center.

NOTE. The ball should always be carried in the arm *away* from approaching tacklers, both as a protection, and that the free arm may be that nearest the opponent, to be of use in warding off. It is fine play to shift the ball from arm to arm as occasion requires.

* See description of diagram 5.   † See diagram 8 and NOTE.

12. Full-back around the end.

To send the full-back around the end there is no change in the position of the men. The play is made in almost identically the same way as shown in the preceding diagram, except that in the present case LH endeavors to force the opposing end toward the *inside*, while FB puts on utmost speed and rounds the end *outside* of him.

In all plays around the end circumstances may arise which offer an advantage in selecting the side of the opposing end other than that called for by the signal. While as a general rule it is best to follow the signal, for the interferers are working with that in mind, still, a skillful runner may secure long gains for his side by judiciously seizing an unexpected opening.

LE takes the first extra man in the line outside of tackle as before. (See diagram eleven.) Another play in which FB runs around the end is shown in diagram 63.

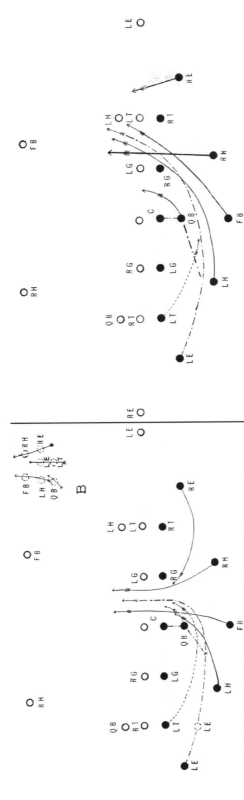

13. End between the center and opposite guard.

To send the LE between RG and C, the positions are the same as in the preceding series.*

The instant the ball is snapped the three backs and the ends dash forward for the point between RG and C, in the lines indicated.

C lifts his man *back* and to the *left*, while RG endeavors to force his man *back* and to the *right*.

FB and RH plunge through the opening abreast, and close together. LH follows directly behind FB and throws in his weight *as he strikes the line*, while RH is followed by RE in the *same manner*.

LE works in slightly to LE[2] before the ball is snapped and receives the ball from the hands of QB as he passes him; LE then turns in immediately behind and between LH and RE, carrying the ball in the same manner as shown for FB in play No. 1, diagram nine. A flying wedge is thus formed as the men strike the line at the point between C and RG. (See cut B.) QB falls in immediately behind LH and LE, while LT, who leaves his man almost instantly, follows directly in the rear of RE and pushes forward as the wedge strikes the line. (See cut B.)

NOTE. A vital point in the play is that LE be *close in behind* his interferers, and that the wedge, preserving its form as far as possible, strike the line with dash and force.

* See description in diagram 5.

14. End between the opposite guard and tackle.

To send LE between RG and RT, there is no change in the position of the men.

The instant the ball is snapped RH, FB, LH, and LE dash forward for the point between RG and RT. RG lifts his man *back* and to the *left*, while RT forces his man *back* and to the *right*.

RH passes directly through close to RG, and, butting the opposing guard with his shoulder if he blocks the way, proceeds down the field and interferes with the first man that he meets behind the line. FB rushes diagonally through and runs directly into the opposing LT or the extra man behind the line, while LH dashes straight through the center of the opening and rushes down the field to interfere.

LE receives the ball at x on a pass from QB, and with *head down* dives into the line *directly behind* LH.

LT plays as shown in diagram thirteen.

After making the pass the best play for QB is to block the opening between RG and C, to prevent the opposing guard or center from coming through and getting LE before he strikes the line.

RE takes the first man outside the tackle, and prevents any one from passing around RT and stopping LE before he reaches the opening.

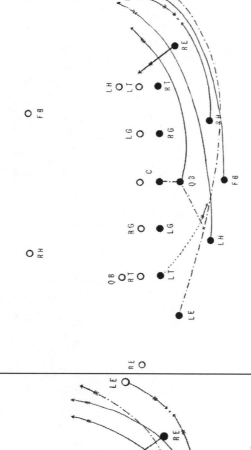

15. End between the opposite end and tackle.

To send the LE between RE and RT, preserve the same positions as in diagram fourteen.

RE plays as shown in diagram eight.

RH plays as LH in diagram eleven.

FB plays as shown in diagram seven.

QB plays as shown in diagram eight.

LH proceeds in the line indicated, at utmost speed, takes the first man on the opposing side as he rounds the tackle and continues on down the field to interfere. In case either the opposing LG or LT breaks through the line QB must tackle him in order to prevent LE from being stopped before he reaches the end.

LT, leaving the line as shown in diagram thirteen, follows directly behind LE to make the play safe and prevent him from being overtaken from behind.

RT plays as shown in diagram eight.

LE receives the ball at x from QB, and, passing inside the opposing LE, turns down the field in the line indicated at utmost speed, passing to the *outside* of his interferers.*

NOTE.—The end must be careful to run just far enough behind the line to clear the opposing rushers as they break through.

* See NOTE, diagram seven.

16. End around the opposite end.

To send the LE around the RE the play is made in identically the same manner as shown in diagram fifteen,* except that RH forces the opposing end-rusher *inside* instead of *out*, while FB and LE, after sprinting straight for the side line at utmost speed, turn down the field *outside* of the opposing end.† LG and LT might possibly play as shown in diagram eight, though there would be danger of having LE tackled from behind, as he would in this case have no protecting interferer behind and might be obliged to withhold his speed slightly in order to allow LG to get ahead of him.

NOTE.—This play, as nearly all end plays, depends for its success on the swiftness of the interferers and the man with the ball, and upon the *quickness* with which all *start*. Care must be taken that the interferers do not get too far in advance of the runner.‡

---

* See diagram fifteen.

† See NOTE, diagram eight.

‡ See NOTE, diagram seven.

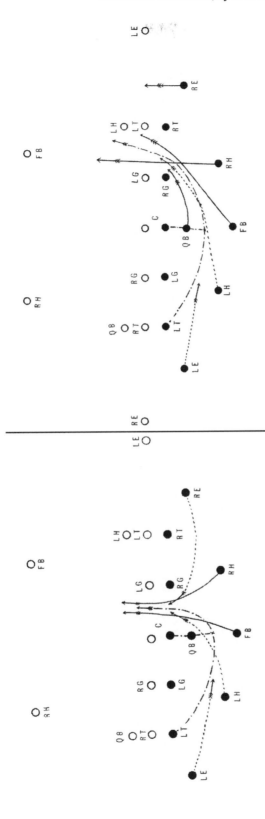

17. Tackle between the center and opposite guard.

To send the LT between C and RG, preserve the same position. C and RG play as shown in diagram five.

RH and FB dash into the opening ahead of LT and take the first men they meet behind the opposing line.

LT breaks away from his man the instant the ball is snapped and receiving the ball from QB, turns in sharp around him as a pivot and plunges in behind FB and RH, with head down and the ball clasped at the stomach with both hands.

LH follows LT and plays as does LT in diagram ten.

RE rushes in behind LT and plays as shown in diagram five.

In case LT finds difficulty in getting away clear from the line, LE jumps in and takes the opposing RT as the ball is snapped, if necessary.

If LT is able to break away from his opponent without assistance, LE may follow directly behind LT to prevent his being caught from the rear and to push him through as he strikes the line.

QB follows LT, playing as shown in diagram five.

Note. LH may precede LT if it is thought best.

18. Tackle between the opposite guard and tackle.

To send the LT between RG and RT, there is no change in position. RE, RH, and FB plays as shown in diagram fourteen.

RH is nearer the opening and should pass through first. FB will cut in directly behind him, but both must take great care that they break *through* the line and are not stopped so that they choke up the opening, and are thus rendered of greater hindrance than help to the runner.

LT leaves the line as shown in the preceding diagram and dashes into the opening between RH and FB, with *head down* and the ball tightly held under the *right*[*] arm, or clasped at the stomach with both hands.

RG and RT play as shown in diagram six.

QB and LE following LT immediately, and push as shown in diagram seventeen.

LH also follows[†] directly behind LT to throw in his entire weight and push him through as he strikes the line, in case he meets with any resistance.

[*] When RT runs he will carry the ball in the left arm. In this way the ball will be kept on the side farther from the opponents where it will be less liable to be torn away, while it leaves the arm toward the opposing tacklers free for use in warding off.

[†] See Note, diagram seventeen.

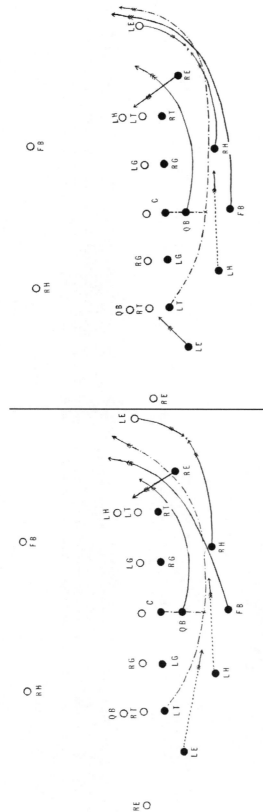

19. Tackle between the opposite tackle and end.

To send the LT around the RT, the RH and FB all play as shown in diagram fifteen.

RE jumps directly into the line and either helps RT block his man, or takes the first extra man in the line.

LG and RG hold their men and force them back.

RT blocks his man and forces him as far as possible to the left.

QB plays as shown in diagram eight, or takes the opposing LT in case he succeeds in breaking through the line.

LT leaves the line as shown in diagram seventeen and carrying the ball in his *right** arm plays as does LE in diagram fifteen.

LE jumps into the line and blocks the opposing tackle, if necessary, or follows LT and plays as shown in diagram seven.

LH follows close in the rear† of LT to prevent him from being tackled from behind and to assist him by interference as he rounds the end.

NOTE. In all plays around the right flank of the line, the rushers on that side must redouble their energy in order to make the play successful. When the play is on the left, the rushers upon that side will in turn block with their utmost power.

* See NOTE, diagram eighteen.

† See NOTE, diagram seventeen.

20. Tackle around the opposite end.

To send LT around the right end, there is no change in the positions taken.

RE jumps into the line and helps RT block his man.

RH starts the moment the ball is snapped and runs directly for the opposing end who has been left exposed, bowls him over, or forces him in toward the line.

FB also starts with the snapping of the ball, and following almost directly behind RH passes slightly outside of him, helping block the opposing end-rusher if necessary, and then passes on ahead of LT to interfere for him in his run down the field.

RT plays as shown in diagram eight.

QB plays as shown in diagram nineteen.

LT leaves the line as shown in diagram seventeen, and taking the direction indicated, encircles the right end at utmost speed and plays as does LE in diagram sixteen.

LH and LE play as shown in diagram nineteen.

LG, C, and RG block their men.

NOTE.—It may be necessary in this play for LE to jump in and take LT's man, as he leaves the line; otherwise he may follow and assist him as he rounds the end.

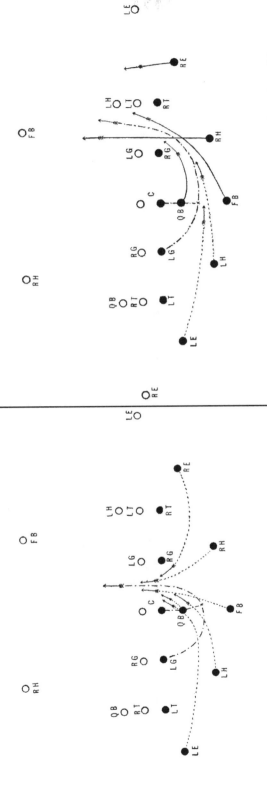

21. Guard between opposite guard and center.

To send the LG between RG and C, the instant the ball is snapped LG jumps straight back from the line, breaking away from the opposing guard. He whirls directly around QB as a pivot and, receiving the ball from his hands as he passes, plunges into the opening between C and RG, with the ball held as shown in diagram one.

C and RG play as shown in diagram five.

RE, RH, FB, LH, and LE all start instantly and throw their entire weight in behind LG as he strikes the line, and force him through.*

QB also follows immediately behind LG and plays as in diagram five.

LT and RT block their men.

NOTE.— Instead of following behind LG it is often better that RH should draw slightly nearer the line before the ball is snapped, dash into the opening ahead of LG, and play as does FB in diagram one.

* See NOTE, diagram one.

22. Guard between the opposite guard and tackle.

To send the LG around between RG and RT, LG breaks away from his opponent the instant the ball is snapped, as shown in diagram twenty-one, receives the ball from QB as before, and dashes into the opening with head down.

RG and RT play as shown in diagram six.

RH starts forward the instant the ball is snapped and, dashing into the opening between RG and RT, strikes the opposing LG with his shoulder with the greatest possible force as he passes through, and then proceeds on and takes the first man behind the line.

FB crosses behind RH and rushing into the same opening plunges into the opposing tackle or the man immediately behind him.

RE plays as shown in diagram fourteen.

QB, LH, and LE follow behind LG and play as shown in diagram eighteen.

LT plays as in the preceding diagram.

NOTE.— RH and FB must see to it that they break *through* the line and are not there blocked so that they fill up the opening through which LG, who is following immediately behind, is to pass.

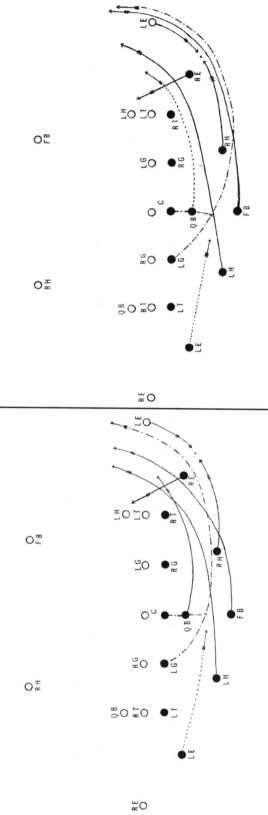

23. Guard between the opposite tackle and end.

To send LG around the opposite tackle, LG leaves the line as shown in diagram twenty-one, and receiving the ball from QB, plays as does LE in diagram fifteen.

RH, FB, and LH start for the right end at utmost speed the instant the ball is put in play. RH runs directly for the opposing LE, forces him out or bowls him over.

FB and LH cut in, in the lines indicated, and passing outside of RT interfere by taking the first opponents whom they meet on arriving at the end.

RE and RT play as shown in diagram fifteen.

QB having passed the ball, runs at utmost speed by the *side* of LG if possible, *between* him and the line, in order to give him protection and assist him from being overtaken from behind.

LE follows directly in the rear of LG to make the play safe and prevent him from being overtaken from behind.*

LT and RG block their opponents.

* See NOTE, diagram seven.

24. Guard around the opposite end.

To send LG around the right end, LG leaves the line as shown in diagram twenty-one; receives the ball at x from QB and passes around the right end at full speed, swing back several yards from the line.

RH, FB, and LH dash toward the right end the instant the ball is put in play, RH runs directly for the opposing end, who has been left exposed, and forces him in or blocks him off.

FB assists RH if necessary, and then passes on around the end ahead of LG to interfere. LH crosses in front of LG and cutting in close behind RT blocks the first free man on the opposing side.

RE and RT play as shown in diagram twenty.

LT and QB play as in diagram twenty-three.

LE follows LG to protect him from behind and to make the play safe.

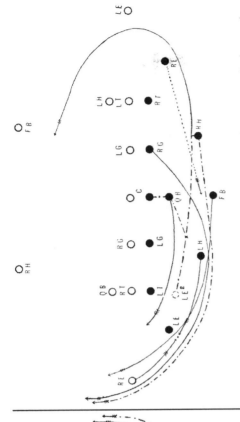

26. End criss-crosses with half-back in play around the end.

To send the RH around the left end on a pass play from LE to RH, and as the ball is snapped, dashes in slightly from his original position to LE⁹, and as the ball is snapped, dashes for the right end, receiving the ball at x, and carrying it at his right side, passes on close in *front* of RH, as indicated.

RH dashes still in his position until LE nearly reaches him. On receiving the ball RH dashes in the opposite direction and passes around the left end at utmost speed.

As RH receives the ball, FB, LH, QB, and RG, who have, until this moment, stood in their positions, dart for the left end, in order to precede RH and interfere for him.*

LT and LG block their men with the *greatest energy*.

LH makes directly for and blocks the opposing RE.

FB takes the direction indicated, helping LH block his man, if necessary, and then proceeds on down the field.

QB plays as shown in the preceding diagram, while RG, breaking away from his man, plays as does LT in diagram twenty-five.

RT also plays as does LT in diagram twenty-five.

RE follows immediately behind RH to protect him from the rear.

NOTE. LH may precede LE and take the first man in the line outside of RT, to aid in the deception ; in which case FB will take the opposing LE, while the others play as before.

_____
* See NOTE, diagram twenty-five.

25. Criss-cross half-back play around the end.

To send LH around the right end on a criss-cross between the half-backs, the men stand in their regular positions with the exception of LH, who works out nearer LE and slightly back, without attracting attention, to the second position as shown in the cut.

The instant the ball is snapped, RH starts in the direction indicated, receiving the ball at x, and passing close in front of LH, carries the ball at his left side, so that LH may receive it from him as he rushes by, and proceeds on in the line indicated; LH *stands in his tracks* until RH nearly reaches him, and upon securing the ball instantly starts in the opposite direction at utmost speed and passes around the right end.

RT, RG, and RE play as play as shown in diagram eight, FB works slightly to the left before the ball is snapped, and *stands still* until RH nearly reaches LH, and starting forward as indicated at the same instant with LH, makes directly for the opposing LE, and blocks him or forces him *in*.

LG breaks away from his man the moment that LH receives the ball and plays as in diagram eight. QB having passed the ball, stands still until LH has received it, and then plays as in diagram eight, or in case an opponent comes through the line between C and RT, it is the duty of QB to attend to him. LT blocks his man hard or blocks the opposing RG, left exposed by LG. LE follows LH and protects him from behind as shown in diagram eight.

NOTE. In all end and criss-cross plays, great care should be taken that the runners do not pass so close to the line that their own men will be pushed back upon them, or so far in the rear that time and space will be lost.

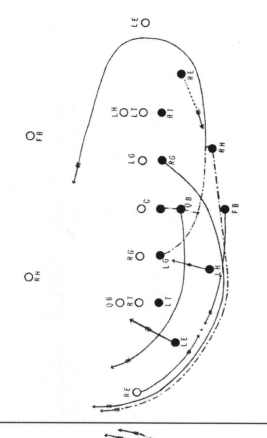

27. Tackle criss-crosses with half-back in play around the end.

To send the LH around the RE on a pass play from RT, RT leaves the line the instant the ball is snapped, and receiving it at x runs close in front of LH, passes him the ball as he goes by.

RE jumps in and takes the man left exposed by RT as he leaves the line. RG holds his man hard.

As LH receives the ball, QB, LG, LT, and LE all play exactly as shown in diagram twenty-five.

RH and FB stand still until the instant that LH receives the ball, and then play as shown in diagram eight.*

NOTE. To make the deception more complete, RH may start the instant the ball is snapped, and directly precede RT and take the first man he meets on the other side of LT; in that case FB will take the opposing LE.

*See NOTE, diagram twenty-five.

28. Guard criss-crosses with half-back in play around the end.

To send the RH around the left end on a pass from LG, LG leaves the line as the ball is snapped, as shown in diagram twenty-one, and passes directly in *front* of RH, giving him the ball as he rushes by.

As LG leaves the line, LH dashes in and takes the opposing RG, who has been left exposed.

At the moment that RH receives the ball, FB, QB, and RG start for the left end, in the lines indicated, in advance of RH, to interfere for him.

FB runs directly for the opposing RE and bowls him over or forces him in.

RE, RT, RG, QB, and LT play as shown in diagram twenty-six.

LE helps LT block the opposing tackle or takes the inside man in the line.

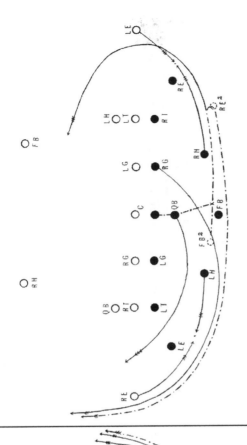

29. Half-back criss-crosses with the end in play around the opposite end.

To send LE around the RE on a pass from RH, LE draws slightly in and back to LE², nearly on a line with the half-backs, before the ball is snapped.

RH dashes forward as the ball is put in play, receives it at X, and passing close in *front* of LE gives him the ball, and then rushes directly into the opposing LE.

LE, having received the ball, starts for the right end in the line indicated, trusting altogether to his speed, as there is no one to protect him from behind.

RE may either jump into the line and help RT block his man, or take the first man that comes through on the right side of the rush line and force him in toward the center.

RT, RG, LG, LT, and FB play as shown in diagram twenty-five.

It may be necessary for QB to precede RH and take the first extra man in the line on the left end, in order to allow LE to get away with the ball without being caught from behind. Otherwise he will play as shown in diagram twenty-five.

In case a man comes through the rush line on the right of C, where QB is playing as shown in the cut, it is his duty to block him.

NOTE. FB may precede RH and play as LH in note on diagram twenty-six.

30. Full-back criss-crosses with the end in play around the opposite end.

To send RE around the left end on a pass from FB, RE works slightly in and on a line with RH, at RE², before the ball is snapped, while FB moves a little to the left to FB².

As the ball is put in play RH and FB dash toward the right, FB receiving the ball on a pass at X.

RH rushes directly for the opposing LE, or takes the first extra man in the line, while FB runs close in *front* of RE to whom he gives the ball as he passes.

Upon receiving the ball RE instantly starts in the opposite direction and encircles the left end at utmost speed.

RG and LH precede RE and play as shown in diagram twenty-six.

RT plays as does LT in diagram twenty-five.

LE and LT play as in diagram twenty-eight.

LG blocks his man hard.

In case anyone succeeds in breaking through the line to the left of center, QB immediately blocks him. He will otherwise play as in diagram twenty-eight.

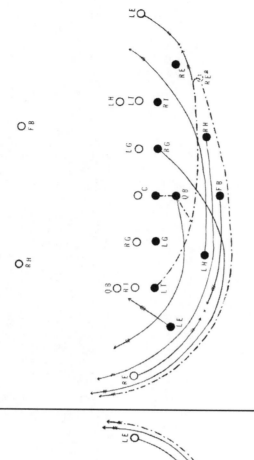

31. Ends criss-cross and play around the end.

To send LE around the right end on a pass from RE, LE and RE both play in slightly, while LE works back until he is nearly on a line with the half-backs.

RE and RH start toward the left the instant the ball is snapped, RH preceding and taking the first extra man in the line beyond the tackle.

RE receives the ball at X on a pass from QB, and running close in *front* of LE, passes him the ball and rushes on into the opposing RE.

As RE reaches LE, FB, LH, and LG dash toward the right in the lines indicated.

FB takes the first extra man in the line beyond RT, LH runs directly for the opposing LE, and LG, preceding LE, plays as shown in diagram twenty-five.

QB blocks the first man through on the right hand side of the center, if necessary, or plays as shown in diagram twenty-five.

LE, upon receiving the ball, starts toward the right at utmost speed, keeping just to the outside of LG.

LT, RG, and RT play as shown in diagram twenty-five.

32. Tackle criss-crosses with the end in play around the opposite end.

To send RE around the left end on a pass from LT, before the ball is snapped RE works in and slightly back to RE².

As the ball is put in play LT leaves the line as shown in diagram seventeen, receives the ball at X, runs close in front of RE, and gives him the ball as he passes. LT then blocks the opposing LE.

LH precedes LT and plays as does RH in diagram thirty-one.

FB plays as shown in diagram twenty-eight.

RG and RT play as shown in diagram twenty-six.

QB plays as shown in diagram thirty.

RE plays as does LE in diagram twenty-nine.[*]

As LT leaves the line, LE jumps in and takes the opposing tackle as in diagram seventeen.

LG plays as shown in diagram thirty.

RH starts forward in the line indicated as RE receives the ball, and precedes him around the left end, crossing in front of RG as the latter swings in behind the line.

[*] See NOTE, diagram twenty-five.

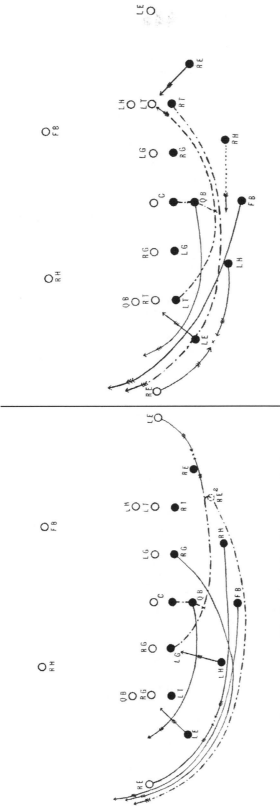

33. Guard criss-crosses with the end in play around the opposite end.

To send RE around the left end on a pass from LG, RE draws in and slightly back to RE².

As the ball is snapped LG breaks away from his man as in diagram twenty-one, receives the ball at x, passes close in front of RE and rushes directly into the opposing LE.

RE remains in his position until LG has almost reached him, receives the ball from LG as he runs by, and plays as in the preceding diagram.

LH plays as shown in diagram twenty-eight.

QB, RH, and FB remain standing in their positions until the instant that RE receives the ball. They then dash toward the left and precede RE at greatest speed to interfere for him.

FB runs directly for the opposing RE. RH follows FB and assists him to block the end if necessary or continues on around the end and takes the first free opponent.

RG leaves the line as LG reaches RE, and plays as shown in diagram thirty-two.

All the other men play as shown in diagram thirty-two.

34. Tackle criss-crosses with tackle in a play around the end.

To send RT around the left end on a pass from LT, the instant the ball is snapped LT plays as shown in diagram eighteen and runs directly for RT.

As LT reaches the line RT jumps suddenly back and receives the ball from LT as he passes, while LT rushes on directly into the arms of the *opposing* LT.

RE jumps in and helps block the opposing LT or takes the first extra man in the line.

LE blocks the opposing tackle as LT leaves the line. Upon receiving the ball RT instantly starts back in the opposite direction, taking the line indicated, and circles the left end with QB, LH, and FB in advance as interferers, and RH to follow and protect him from behind.

LH, FB, and RH stand still until RT receives the ball.

NOTE. RH may also run in advance of RT to interfere when the opposing LE has not come around the end of the line.

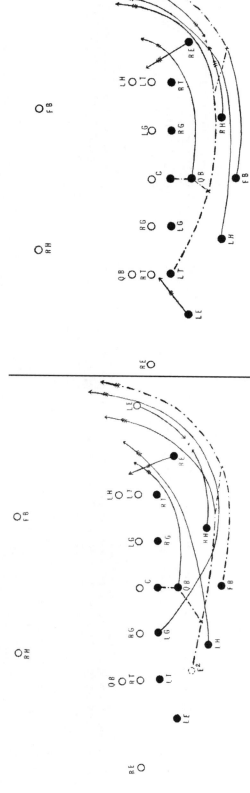

35.   Double pass from end to full-back in play around the end.

To send FB around the right end on a double pass from LE, LE should work in slightly before the ball is snapped to LE?, as in diagram twenty-six.

The instant the ball is put in play, RH, FB, LH, LG, and LE leave their positions and dash for the right end, in the lines indicated in the diagram.

QB, RE, RT, LG, LT, and RG play as in diagram eight.

LH cuts in close around RT, and blocks the first man he meets.

RH runs directly for the opposing LE, and blocks him off or forces him in.

LE receives the ball at x, on a pass from QB, and running at full speed in a course, about two yards nearer the line* than that taken by FB, throws the ball on ahead of him to the full-back, with a clean pass of from four to five yards, as FB reaches the point behind RT, and turns slightly sidewise, as he runs, to receive it. LE then cuts in, as shown, and blocks the first free man on the opposing end.

FB, upon receiving the ball, passes to the outside and encircles the end.

The play may sometimes be made to greater advantage by having LH take the line indicated for FB, and receive the ball on the pass, while FB runs on ahead. The guard will find great difficulty in getting in advance of the man with the ball, and may find that he can be of more service by cutting across close behind the line.

NOTE.   It may be necessary for FB to withhold his speed slightly until LE has passed him the ball. If it becomes necessary to block the opposing RG, LH may play as in diagram thirty-three, though LG should so time his action that his man will be unable to interfere with the play.

* See NOTE, diagram twenty-five.

36.   Double pass from tackle to full-back in play around the end.

To send FB around the right end, on a double pass from LT, there is no change from the regular formation in the primary arrangement.

The instant the ball is snapped, LT leaves the line, receives the ball at x from QB and starts for the right end, precisely as shown in diagram nineteen.

LE jumps into the line and takes LT's man as he leaves him.

RE, RT, RG, and LG play as shown in diagram eight.

QB also plays as shown in diagram eight.

LH, FB, and RH, all start for the right end the moment the ball is snapped.

RH runs directly for the opposing LE, and bowls him over or forces him in.

LH assists RH, if necessary, and then cuts in down the field, as indicated, to interfere.

As FB is about to round the end, he turns half around without slackening speed, and receives the ball at about x, on a clean pass from LT.   LT then turns in to interfere on the end, while FB passes on encircling the opposing LE.

NOTE.   The pass may be made with equal success to LH; in which case FB will assist RH in blocking his man, and then pass on down the field to interfere, while LH swings out in a course just outside of the opposing end-rusher.

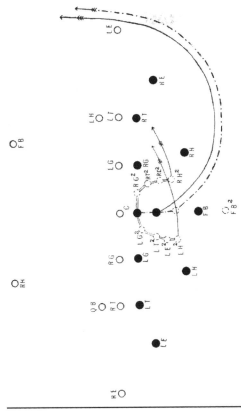

37. Double pass from guard to half-back in play around the end.

To send LH around the right end on a double pass from LG, there is no change in the arrangement.

LG leaves the line the instant the ball is put in play, as shown in diagram twenty-one, receives the ball at X, and takes a direction similar to that shown in diagram twenty-three.

RE, RT, RG, and LT play as shown in diagram eight.

RH, FB, and LH start for the right the instant the ball is snapped.

RH runs directly for the opposing LE, and disposes of him. FB assists RH, if necessary, and then proceeds on down the field to interfere.

LH runs somewhat back from the line taken by FB, and as he nears the end turns back and receives the ball, on a pass of four or five yards, from LG.

LH then puts on utmost speed as he swings out around the end, while LG continues on, cutting in slightly to interfere.

LE follows directly behind LH, to make the pass safe, and to protect him from behind.

38. Slow mass wedge from a down.

To send the slow pushing wedge through the center from a down, the men *spring* to their positions in the wedge formation, as shown in the cut, *the instant the signal is given.*

RG forces himself as close as possible to C's right, directly abreast of him, while LG holds himself firmly against C on the left and slightly back from the line.

The remaining rushers and half-backs take their positions behind the guards, as indicated, in a similar manner to that shown in diagram forty-one.

The men must be drilled until they can spring into their positions in the formation *instantly.* The ball should come back at the same moment and be passed to FB, who has come in to FB^1, and the whole wedge surge forward with the greatest possible force, as in diagram forty-one.

This play may be repeated several times for short gains until the tackles and ends on the opposing side are drawn well in to mass against it, when FB, accompanied by QB, will dart suddenly out from the rear for a long run around the end of the opposing team, as shown in the diagram; in which case RH and RE will cut across in the lines indicated to block the foremost men among the opponents. Should it be found that the opposing backs come up to help block the play FB may drop suddenly back to FB^2 and punt well down the field.

Note. On the play in which the FB is sent out from behind the wedge for a run around the end, there should be a little delay in snapping the ball, in order to give the opposing team more time to draw well in behind the center.

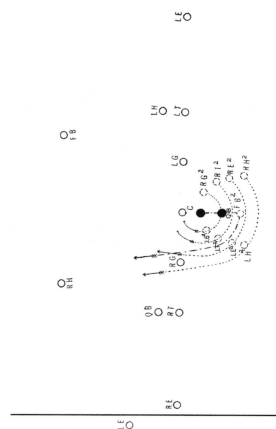

39. Feint run around the end from the wedge in the line.

The wedge in the line is formed at the given signal as shown in diagram thirty-eight. The men are closely drawn into a compact formation, so that the opposing side cannot see what goes on within the wedge.

The moment the ball is snapped QB slips it under the left arm of RE or RT, who receives it quietly, without making the slightest demonstration that the ball has been passed to him, and stands still in his position, bent over somewhat in the act of pushing, while the rest of the wedge plunges forward. As soon as QB has passed the ball to RE he instantly starts back from out the wedge, seizing FB by the arm as he goes. RH leaves his position at the same moment, and all three dash off to the left together, as shown in cut A, swinging in a long circle back from the line to attract attention and to give the opposing team more time to cut across the field in order to intercept them. As they pass into view LH and LE leave the wedge in the lines indicated, as if to block for them.

The opposing side at once supposes that the wedge has been simply a blind to permit the run around the end, and the entire team dash off to intercept FB, whom they suppose to have the ball. When FB and his interferers have arrived at about x in the lines indicated, RE darts out to the right unobserved.

NOTE. This play can be worked most successfully after sending the wedge straight ahead for several downs.

40. Revolving wedge from a down.

To send the revolving wedge through the line the arrangement shown in the cut is formed in precisely the same manner as explained in diagram thirty-eight.

The ball is put in play immediately, and the entire wedge plunges *straight forward*, as before, in a *closely compact body*.

After a few seconds, when the opposing side have massed themselves in front of the wedge so that its forward progress is nearly blocked, the entire formation throws its weight to one side, each man turning slightly in order to face the direction in which he wishes to proceed, and attempts to revolve around the opposing team, *turning upon c as a pivot*.

The very fact that the opponents are pushing with utmost force in a direction exactly contrary to the *original* line of advance of the wedge, is of great assistance in performing the evolution.

When the wedge has swung sufficiently around, the rear men may break away and dash down the field with the ball.

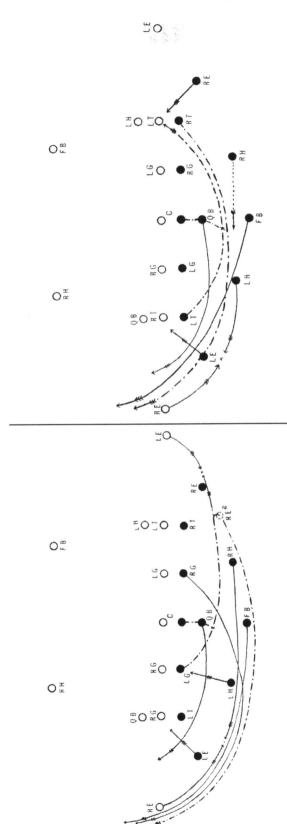

33. Guard criss-crosses with the end in play around the opposite end.

To send RE around the left end on a pass from LG, RE draws in and slightly back to RE².

As the ball is snapped LG breaks away from his man as in diagram twenty-one, receives the ball at X, passes close in front of RE and rushes directly into the opposing LE. RE remains in his position until LG has almost reached him, receives the ball from LG as he runs by, and plays as in the preceding diagram.

LH plays as shown in diagram twenty-eight.

QB, RH, and FB remain standing in their positions until the instant that RE receives the ball. They then dash toward the left and precede RE at greatest speed to interfere for him.

FB runs directly for the opposing RE. RH follows FB and assists him to block the end if necessary or continues on around the end and takes the first free opponent.

RG leaves the line as LG reaches RE, and plays as shown in diagram thirty-six.

All the other men play as shown in diagram thirty-two.

34. Tackle criss-crosses with tackle in a play around the end.

To send RT around the left end on a pass from LT, the instant the ball is snapped LT plays as shown in diagram eighteen and receives the ball directly for RT.

As LT reaches the line RT jumps suddenly back and receives the ball from LT as he passes, while LT rushes on directly into the arms of the *opposing* LT.

RE jumps in and helps block the opposing LT or takes the first extra man in the line.

LE blocks the opposing tackle as LT leaves the line.   Upon receiving the ball RT instantly starts back until RT receives the ball.   Upon receiving the ball RT instantly starts back in the opposite direction, taking the line indicated, and circles the left end with QB, LH, and FB in advance as interferers, and RH to follow and protect him from behind.

NOTE.   RH may also run in advance of RT to interfere when the opposing LE has not come around the end of the line.

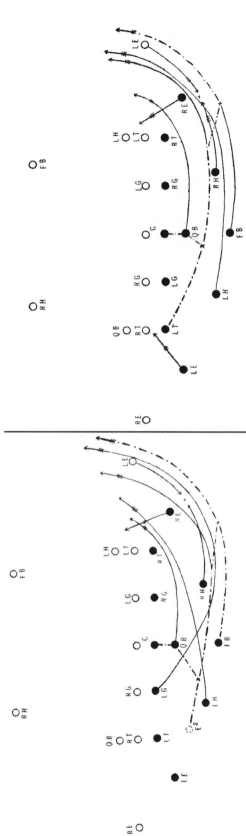

35. Double pass from end to full-back in play around the end.

To send FB around the right end on a double pass from LE, LE should work in slightly before the ball is snapped to LE², as in diagram twenty-six.

The instant the ball is put in play, RH, FB, LH, LG, and LE leave their positions and dash for the right end, in the lines indicated in the diagram.

QB, RE, RT, LG, LT, and RG play as in diagram eight.

LH cuts in close around RT, and blocks the first man he meets.

RH runs directly for the opposing LE, and blocks him off or forces him in.

LE receives the ball at x, on a pass from QB, and running at full speed in a course, about two yards nearer the line* than that taken by FB, throws the ball on ahead of him in to the full-back, with a clean pass of from four to five yards, as FB reaches the point behind RT, and turns sightly sidewise, as he runs, to receive it. LE then cuts in, as shown, and blocks the first free man on the opposing end.

FB, upon receiving the ball, passes to the outside and encircles the end.

The play may sometimes be made to greater advantage by having LH take the line indicated for FB, and receive the ball on the pass, while FB runs on ahead. The guard will find great difficulty in getting in advance of the man with the ball, and may find that he can be of more service by cutting across close behind the line.

NOTE. It may be necessary for FB to withhold his speed slightly until LE has passed him the ball. If it becomes necessary to block the opposing RG, LH may play as in diagram thirty-three, though LG should so time his action that his man will be unable to interfere with the play.

* See NOTE, diagram twenty-five.

36. Double pass from tackle to full-back in play around the end.

To send FB around the right end, on a double pass from LT, there is no change from the regular formation in the primary arrangement.

The instant the ball is snapped, LT leaves the line, receives the ball at x from QB and starts for the right end, precisely as shown in diagram nineteen.

LE jumps into the line and takes LT's man as he leaves him.

RE, RT, RG, and LG play as shown in diagram eight.

QB also plays as shown in diagram eight.

LH, FB, and RH, all start for the right end the moment the ball is snapped.

RH runs directly for the opposing LE, and bowls him over or forces him in.

LH assists RH, if necessary, and then cuts in down the field, as indicated, to interfere.

As FB is about to round the end, he turns half around without slackening speed, and receives the ball at about x, on a clean pass from LT. LT then turns in to interfere on the end, while FB passes on encircling the opposing LE.

NOTE. The pass may be made with equal success to LH; in which case FB will assist RH in blocking his man, and then pass on down the field to interfere, while LH swings out in a course just outside of the opposing end-rusher.

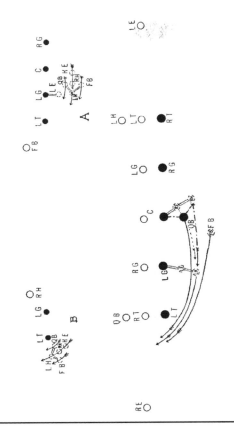

41. Lifting wedge through the center.

To send FB in a wedge through the line between LG and C, the play is peculiar in that it consists of two distinct parts. At a given signal to form the wedge, together with an additional signal which shall indicate whether the play is to go through the center or around the tackle, LE, RE, LH, and RH rush in and take the position shown in the large cut. LE stands behind LG whom he *grasps by the hips*, his arms only *slightly bent* at the elbows and his body held *well back* from LG, in the best position for pushing. LH occupies the same relative position *behind* and slightly to the *left* of LE.

RE jumps in and takes the position *behind* and a little to *one side* of C, giving QB just room enough in which to receive the ball, and places his hands on the hips of C with his body braced back at arm's length. RH takes a similar position behind him and a little to the right. FB comes in slightly closer, to FB².

As soon as possible after the wedge has been formed C puts the ball in play. FB dives *straight* into the vortex of the wedge, receiving the ball from QB as he rushes by him, and rams his head *low down* between the hips of C and LG, the ball held tightly at his stomach with both hands.

The *instant the ball is snapped* LG and C press *close together* and *do not allow themselves to be forced apart.* FB shouts lustily "now!" the instant before he strikes the line and all *lift straight ahead* for *three* or *four* seconds, FB pushing with his head. (See cut A.) Then LG and C burst apart, carrying their men with them and allow FB and QB to shoot through the opening. (See cut B.)

42. Wedge from the center around the tackle.

To send the wedge around the LT, a preliminary signal of "form the wedge" is given, together with the signal which is to indicate the direction of the plays, and the formation seen in the large cut is instantly made, in precisely the same manner as shown in the preceding diagram.

All the men in the wedge should have the appearance of being about to go through the center as before.

At the instant the ball comes into his hands QB whirls about, turning his *back* toward RE, and *places the ball in the hands of RH.* QB then instantly turns *back* and attaches himself to the side and a little *behind* LH, while FB, springing forward at the same moment, attaches himself in a like manner on the other side of LH, and all three dash away together in the lines indicated, around LT.* RH follows close *within* the vortex of the wedge so formed, while RE runs directly in the rear of RH and pushes with all his force as they round the tackle.† LE throws his entire weight in behind LG to help hold the line back, and LT forces his man back and to the *right.*

NOTE. LH must take *great care* not to leave his position until the *instant* that QB and FB reach him. The formation must be somewhat open and all endeavor to run at great speed.

NOTE. It must be borne in mind that the representation in the cut is diagramatical and that in reality the guards are drawn close in by the side of center, while the tackles are shoulder to shoulder with the guards in all plays with the above wedge formation.

---

* See cut A.
† See cut B.

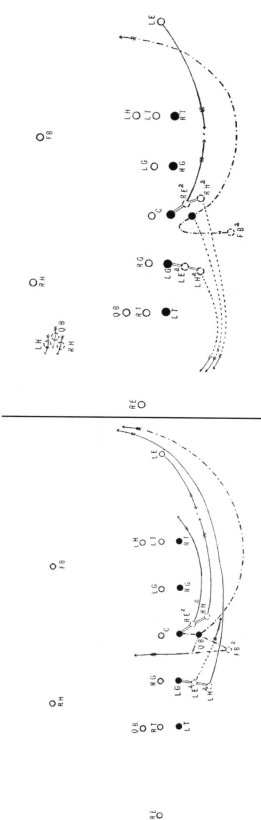

43. Quarter-back around the end from behind the wedge.

With the preliminary signal to form the wedge, a signal is given to indicate the direction of the play, and the formation as seen in the cut is taken in precisely the same manner as shown in diagram forty-one.

The instant the ball is snapped QB passes it straight back to FB, who dashes forward, hands the ball directly back to QB as he passes (being careful *not to make a forward pass*), and dives into the line between LG and C.

As QB receives the ball he instantly runs out from behind the wedge and makes for the right end at utmost speed in the line indicated.

At the moment the ball is returned to QB, RH, RE, and LH dash for the right end, LH crossing *behind* QB as he comes out from the wedge. RH runs directly for the opposing LE. RE takes the first man on the opposing side after he rounds the tackle, while LH runs on the inside of QB and interferes for him as they go together down the field.

LE follows in the rear of QB to protect him and prevent him from being caught from behind.

LT holds his man hard, and LG, RG, and RT play as shown in diagram nineteen.

44. Feint play from the wedge.

At the signal the wedge is instantly formed as shown in diagram forty-one.

As the ball is snapped FB rushes forward and, receiving it from QB at x, immediately crouches down behind C, shielded from view by the center, guards, and ends, who are *tightly massed together*.

QB then instantly darts out from behind the wedge to the left, accompanied by LH and RH, who swing well back from the line to attract attention, and hold closely together* to deceive the other side into the belief that they have the ball.

The opposing team immediately suppose that a play around the end from the wedge is being attempted and rush toward the side of the field to intercept it.

FB remains crouched behind C until QB, RH, and LH are well off toward the side of the field, as at x, and then suddenly springs up and circles the opposite end, accompanied by RE, who makes sure to block the opposing LE in case he has come around behind the line.

NOTE. Compare this play with that shown in diagram thirty-nine.

*See cut A.

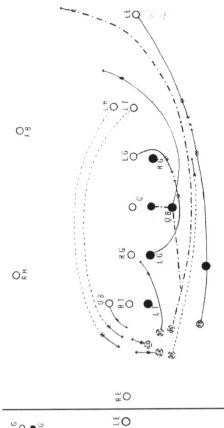

45.   Wedge on the end of the line.

To form a wedge on the left end, at the given signal LE comes up into the line, and RT, RE, LH, and RH rush on instantly and form the wedge directly behind him, while FB moves over to a position about two yards in the rear of RE, as shown in the large cut. C allows RT just sufficient time to reach the left end, by which time the wedge will be perfectly formed if the men are properly drilled, and then snaps the ball as soon as possible. As QB receives it he springs toward FB, passing him the ball as he does so, avoiding all possibility of being caught by the opposing LT. FB plunges forward at the same moment, receiving the ball at x (see cut A), and at the same time shouts "Now!" as he rushes in behind the wedge. At that same instant the whole wedge dashes forward *on a slight angle to the left*, LE jumps into the opposing RT, or the extra man in the line, while QB attaches himself to the rear of RE as the wedge rushes forward (see cut B). FB *must* succeed in getting well in between RH and RE, while all rush forward with utmost force, LH and RT *holding firmly together.*

NOTE.[1]   RH may leave the wedge to take the opposing RE if he attempts to break in from the side.

NOTE.[2]   In case the opposing side sends the backs up into the line to mass against the wedge and block it, FB may kick the ball down the field instead of rushing it, QB protecting him from the opposing LT as he does so. While not an especially strong position from which to kick, a short quick kick just over the heads of the opposing back will serve every purpose, as on all future similar formations it will compel the opposing side to retain at least one man well behind the line as a protection.

46.   Play around the opposite end from the wedge on the end.

After the wedge has been formed on the end, as shown in the preceding diagram, there may be some delay in snapping the ball, and the opposing LT, or in case of an inexperienced team, both LT and LE run around in order to mass against the wedge when it advances.

In that case the following modification may be made. Before the ball is snapped the captain, seeing that the opposing LT has run around, gives some key word which all understand as a signal to indicate that the play is to be changed to one around the opposite end.

QB makes the pass as shown in diagram forty-five, but passes to RE instead of FB, and then instantly turns and precedes RE around the right end.

FB and RE dash toward the right as the ball is passed, FB preceding and blocking the opposing LE.

RE attempts to lift his opponent back and force him in toward the center as far as possible.

As RE starts forward in the line indicated, LG breaks away from his man as shown in diagram eight, and preceding RE, dashes into the LG on the opposing side in case he succeeds in getting around RG, while RT jumps in and takes the man whom LG has left exposed. RH follows directly in the rear of RE to prevent him from being taken from behind, while LH and LE block the extra men in the line.

NOTE.   This maneuver will prevent the opposing team thereafter from drawing all their men from the opposite end to mass in front of the wedge.

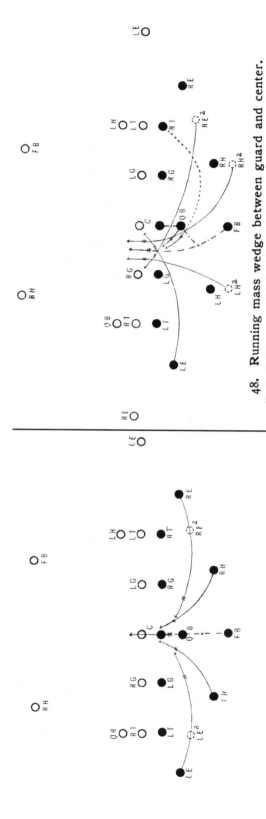

47. Running mass wedge through the center.

To send FB through the center on a running mass play directly behind C, the ends and backs start forward the instant the ball is snapped.

The guards lift their men *back* and *out from the center*, while C endeavors to force his man straight ahead of him.

LH and RH dash in and attach themselves behind C on each side of him.

FB springs forward at the same moment, and receiving the ball on a pass at X from QB, who slips to one side, dives in directly behind C with *head down*. At the same instant that FB reaches the line, the ends close in on either side of him directly behind the half-backs. QB throws himself in the rear of FB, and all push forward with the greatest possible force in a solid and tightly formed mass.

The vital point in the play is that all strike the line at as nearly as possible the same instant and form a *tightly massed wedge*, which is driven directly through the line.

NOTE. By drawing the ends in to LE[2] and RE[2], they may be enabled to strike the line ahead of the half-backs, in which case the latter will attach themselves on either side of FB as he rushes forward. The wedge must never cease pushing until the man with the ball is actually downed and absolutely held.

48. Running mass wedge between guard and center.

To send the running mass wedge through the line between LG and C, the half-backs draw back slightly before the ball is snapped to LH[2] and RH[2], in a line with FB, in order to give the ends more time to reach the opening ahead of them, and also to enable themselves to gain greater headway before striking the line.

RE also works over slightly to the left to RE[2].

At the instant the ball is snapped, all the men behind the line dash straight for the opening in the lines indicated.

C lifts his man back and to the *right*, and LG forces his man back and to the *left*.

LE passes through the opening ahead,* at an angle, and strikes the opposing C with his full force, while RE, crossing directly behind him strikes the opposing guard in a similar manner.

At the same moment, FB with his head down and the ball held as before, strikes the opening so made, immediately behind the ends, with the greatest possible force, the half-backs firmly attaching themselves to his flanks, as he receives the ball at X, and forcing him through. RT leaves the line as the ball is snapped, as shown for LT in diagram thirteen, and together with QB, closes in behind FB. All mass firmly together as before and drive directly through the line.

LT and RG hold their men and force them *out*.

---

* When the ends find difficulty in reaching the opening ahead, they may follow the half-backs as in the preceding play.

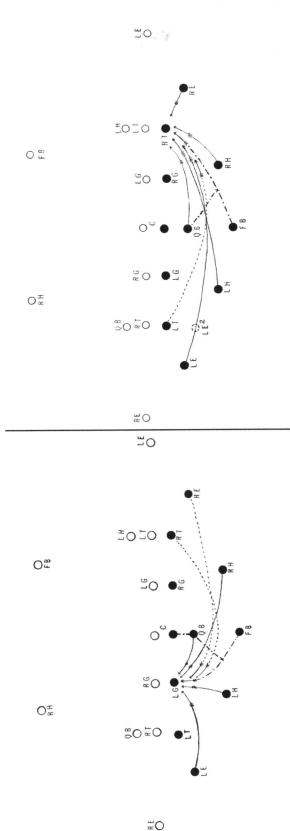

49. Running mass wedge directly at the guard.

To send the running mass wedge into the line directly behind LG, very little change is made from that shown in diagram forty-seven except that the play is directed at the guard instead of C.

C and LT force their men back to the right and left respectively, as the ball is snapped; the half-backs dash forward in the lines indicated, and attach themselves to the flanks of LG with the greatest possible force; the ends strike the formation so made, at that same instant, and each grasps FB from the side as he rushes in behind LG with his head down; while RT and QB throw their weight in behind FB as shown in diagram thirteen, and all plunge forward in a mass pressed firmly together.

The success of the play depends upon the formation of a compact mass which continues to hold firmly together after it strikes the line, and in which all push with their whole weight.

50. Running mass wedge directly at the tackle.

To send the running mass wedge into the line behind the tackle, the same principle is carried out as that shown in diagram forty-nine.

The instant the ball is snapped all the men behind the line start for RT in the directions indicated, at utmost speed, FB receiving the ball at x on a pass from QB. LH and RH strike the flanks of RT at full speed on either side, while the ends, QB and LT, mass on the sides and rear of FB as he strikes the line, as shown in diagram forty-seven.

The mass must continue its closely locked formation and push directly down the field.

LE works in slightly to LE[2] before the ball is put in play.

LT leaves the line the instant the ball is snapped, as if he himself were to run with the ball, follows directly behind FB and overtakes him if possible before he reaches the line, in order to push him as he strikes.

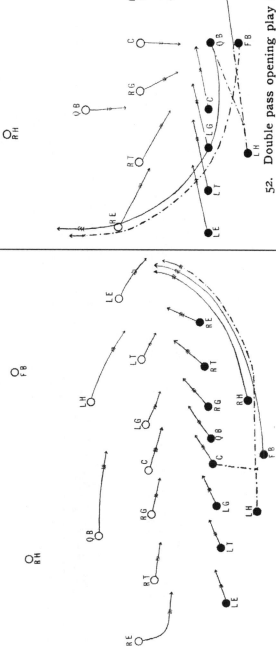

51. Free opening play from the center of the field.

The men are lined up at the center of the field as shown in the cut, from five to six feet apart.

A signal makes it understood around which end the play is to be made, and each player selects the man on the opposing side whom it has been prearranged that he shall block.

C puts the ball in play by kicking it while still retaining it in his hands, and passes it back to LH, in case the play is to be made around the right end. At the same instant the entire rush lines move diagonally toward the right as one man, and dash into the opposing rushers as they meet midway between the two lines.

RH and FB precede LH to interfere for him as they reach the end, and all sprint at topmost speed.

NOTE. The rushers must see to it that they do not betray by their looks, before the ball is put in play, the direction in which the run is to be made.

52. Double pass opening play from the center.

To make the double pass opening play around the left end, the rushers are placed as indicated, on the center line, about two yards apart, leaving an interval of about ten yards between C and QB, and five yards between QB and RG, while the backs are about three yards behind the line.

The instant that QB puts the ball in play* C, LG, LT, LE, and LH dash toward the center of the field in lines nearly parallel with the cross lines, preserving their distances from one another. QB makes a long pass to LH at X, as he advances toward him on the run.

The men to the right of QB start directly down the field, swinging in slightly toward the center to block the oncoming rushers. QB and FB stand still.

LH passes close in front of FB, carries the ball in his right arm, and passes it to FB, to take it as he rushes by.

FB and QB then instantly start in the opposite direction and sprint at utmost speed to encircle the opposing team which has been drawn in toward the center.

NOTE. From this same formation QB may pass the ball either to FB or RH for a kick, in which case the rushers will all run straight *down* the field instead of across in the lines indicated in the cut.

* See description, diagram fifty-four.

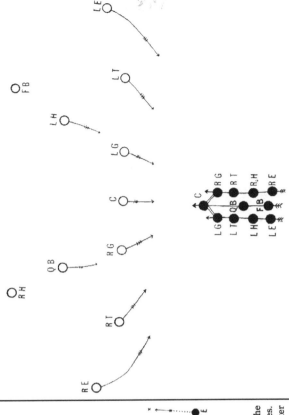

53. Opening play from the center with team divided.

The men are arranged as indicated in the diagram, on either side of the field, the rushers being about two yards apart and the ends about five yards from the side lines. FB is placed about two yards, and the half-backs about three yards, behind the center line.

QB looks to the one side and then to the other, in order to render the opposing team uncertain whether the ball is to be passed to the right or left, or to FB for a kick down the field. He then puts the ball in play as shown in diagram fifty-one, and makes a long pass to LH, who receives it on the run at x, following it immediately to make the play safe, in case of a wild pass.

The instant the ball is in play every player in the field will dash forward in the lines indicated, *except RE*, who stands still in his position or drops flat upon the ground close to the side lines, unobserved by his opponents as the other three men dash across the field.

It is of no consequence if only a small advance is made. All depends upon the quickness of the following play for success. Every man upon the team rushes to his position in the line, and without waiting for a signal the ball is immediately snapped and a long pass made by QB straight across the field to RE, who catches the ball upon the run and has the entire field before him.

NOTE. This play is only practical when QB can be relied upon for a long and accurate pass, and when the wind is not unfavorable.

54. *Princeton opening wedge from the center of the field.

To send the wedge straight down the field from the center, the men form in the positions shown in the cut, as closely and firmly bound together as possible.

At the signal, C puts the ball in play by touching it with his foot, and passes it back to QB, who is immediately behind him, ready to receive it. As the ball is put in play the entire wedge rushes forward in a compact mass, preserving its formation, and endeavors by mere force of weight and momentum to advance the ball as far as possible straight towards the opponent's goal.

QB upon receiving the ball places it at his stomach, clasps it tightly with both hands and charges forward with head down, while FB throws in his entire weight from behind.

NOTE. It is a vital point that all the men keep their feet and run in a compact mass, preserving the formation.

* The wedge formation at the center of the field originated at Princeton.

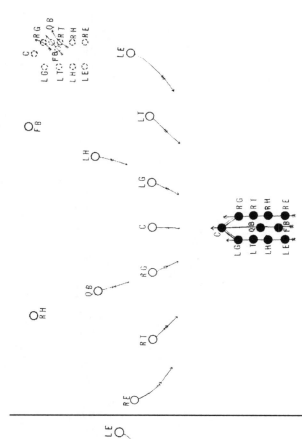

55. Yale modification of Princeton wedge.

This wedge differs in one very important respect from the preceding. Instead of being a part of the wedge formation the guards are placed *outside* of the wedge directly abreast of C.

The instant the ball is put in play, LG and RG spring forward in advance of the wedge, and meet the opposing guard and center *midway between* the wedge and the point from which their opponents start.

LG jumps directly into his man and attempts to throw him to the *left*, while RG, meeting the opposite C in the same manner, attempts to throw him to the *right*.

The wedge advancing immediately behind is thus saved the shock of being struck by the opposing guards under full headway.

The wedge may charge thus at an angle slightly to the right or left, the guards taking the opposing C and RG or C and LG, as the case may be.

NOTE. As it is highly desirable that the men without the wedge be swift and dashing, it may be found more advantageous to place the tackles, or two comparatively light men, in these positions, while the guards are retained within the wedge itself.

56. Princeton split wedge.

The formation is precisely the same as that shown in diagram fifty-four. The ball is put in play as before, and the wedge advances straight down the field.

As the on-coming rushers strike it, the wedge suddenly opens at some point previously agreed upon, and allows QB, who carries the ball, to break through and dart down the field.

The opening usually selected is that between guard and tackle, as shown in cut A ; in this case, the guard and tackle separate and force their opponents to the left and right, respectively, while QB, with his head down, and RB pushing him from behind, forces his way through, and breaks clear of the wedge.

This opening may be made either to the right or left, and at any point desired.

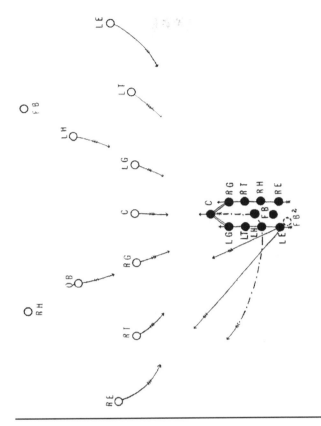

57. Yale split wedge.

The formation is very similar to that of diagram fifty-six, but the two lines are arranged so that the parallel sides are *nearer together.* The *half-backs and ends* brace themselves well back, at arm's length from the men directly ahead of them, precisely as shown in diagram forty-one.

QB stands well back between the half-backs, as shown in the cut. The guards, tackles, and half-backs stand with toes pointing *straight forward,* to leave a narrow unobstructed lane between the two lines, down which the ball is to be rolled *on its side.*

C places the ball on its side between his legs, and puts it in play by touching it with his toe (the ball the while firmly held under his hand), and rolling it back. At the same moment the entire wedge surges straight ahead. QB will have had just time to secure the ball, turn toward RH, when the charging rushers will be upon the apex of the wedge. LH then instantly turns *square to the right,* and seizing RH by the arm, knocks him directly out of the wedge on the opposite side. LE follows immediately behind LH, FB attaches himself to RE, and the *new* wedge, with RH as its apex, and QB directly in the center with the ball, dashes off at an angle of about 45° to the original direction. (See cut A.)

NOTE. The wedge may split either to the right or left. It is very important that the second wedge preserve a *loose,* yet firm, formation, so that all may run at utmost speed

58. Side play from wedge at the center.

The formation is precisely as shown in diagram fifty-four. C puts the ball in play as before, and passes it back to QB, and the entire wedge advances with a rush.

QB quietly transfers the ball to LH unperceived, under cover of the wedge formation; and as the on-coming rushers strike the apex, LE and FB, who has changed his position to FB², slip by on the side in the lines indicated, to block the opposing RT and RE, while LH darts suddenly to the left, passing *behind* LE and FB, and attempts to encircle the end, sprinting at utmost speed.

NOTE. The ball may be passed by QB to either of the half-backs or ends, and the play made as shown.

A play is sometimes made closely allied to this, in which QB remains in the wedge until after it has encountered the opposing rushers, and then suddenly darts out from behind, with a single interferer, trusting to his speed and the unexpectedness of his appearance to carry him safely around the opposing team.

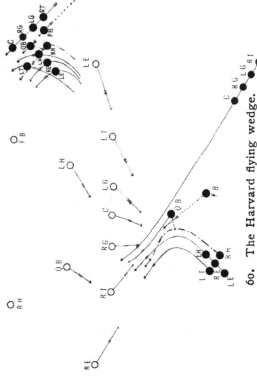

60. The Harvard flying wedge.

QB stands with the ball in the center of the field. FB stands from five to ten yards behind QB and a little to the right. The remainder of the team is divided in two sections.

Section No. 1 is composed of the heaviest men in the line and is drawn up from twenty to thirty yards from the center, back and to the right, facing QB.

Section No. 2 is composed of the lighter and swifter men, drawn up five or ten yards back and to the left of QB.

Section No. 1 has the "right of way," the others regulating their play to its speed.

At a signal from QB, section No. 1 dashes forward at *utmost speed* passing close in front of QB.

At the same moment FB and section No. 2 advance, timing their speed to No. 1. Just before the sections reach the line QB puts the ball in play, and as they come together in a flying wedge and aim at the opposing RT, or straight down the field, passes to RH and dashes forward with the wedge.

A slight opening is left in front of QB to draw in the opposing RT. (See small cut.)

As opposing RT dives into the wedge, LH and QB take him. RE and LE swing out to the left to block opposing RE. At the same moment RH puts on utmost speed and darts through opening between LH and RE.

NOTE. The arrangement of the men is arbitrary. The wedge may be directed against any point desired. Its strength lies in the fact that the men are under full headway before the ball is put in play.

59. Hard running wedge with loose formation.

The men are formed in a wedge shaped as above, from three to four feet apart, with the half-backs in the center.

C puts the ball in play by kicking it and passing it back to one of the half-backs, and the whole formation dashes forward at utmost speed without massing together, preserving the arrangement as far as possible.

Each man in the line dashes directly into the opposing rushers as they meet the wedge, while the half-back with the ball, assisted by his fellow, endeavors to slip through the most favorable opening which the open formation shall offer.

The play may be directed straight ahead, or to the right or left.

NOTE. If the entire formation, without changing its arrangement, withdraws ten yards behind C, and comes dashing forward on the run, C putting the ball in play just before it reaches him, the play may be made even more effective.

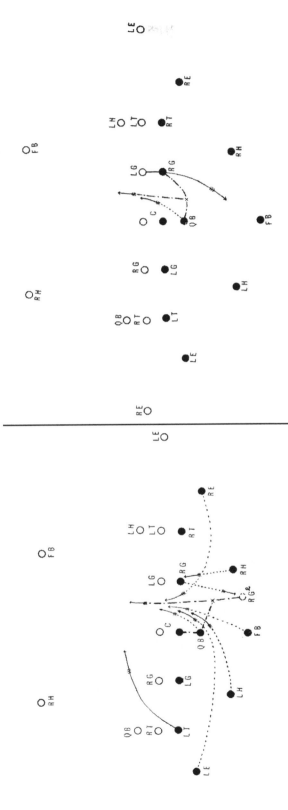

62. Guard through his own opening on the same side.

To send RG through his own opening to the right of C, the full-back and half-backs are placed back as if for a kick, as shown in the cut. FB assumes every appearance of being about to receive and kick the ball.

As the ball is snapped RG jumps slightly back and toward QB, allowing the opposing LG, who is eager to break through and stop the kick, to pass through the line *outside* of him. QB instantly hands the ball to RG, who plunges back into the line through the opening left vacant by the opposing guard, with QB directly behind him.

C endeavors to force his man well to the left as he snaps the ball.

A similar play is less successfully attempted at the tackle.

The old play of having the end lie well out and receive the ball on a long pass from QB is now almost absolutely discarded.

NOTE. Care must be taken by QB not to make a forward pass.

61. Guard drops back and bucks the center.

To send RG to buck the center, at a given signal RG runs back from the line and takes the position at RG², while RH jumps in and fills temporarily the position of RG.

As soon as RG is in his position the ball is snapped. RG dashes forward, receives it at x, and plunges into the opening to the right of C with his head down, striking the line *hard.* An opening in the line is made as shown in diagram five.

RE, FB, LH, LE, and QB all rush in behind RG, starting forward in the lines indicated as the ball is put in play and push, as in diagram twenty-one.*

LT, LG, and RT play as in diagram five.

NOTE. The above play is valuable for a light team if they happen to have a heavy and powerful guard.

After RG has been sent at the center once or twice it will be very effective to have QB pass the ball to LH, instead of RG, for a run around the right end, as shown in diagram eight. RG will then precede LH as does RH in diagram eight.

* See NOTE, diagram one.

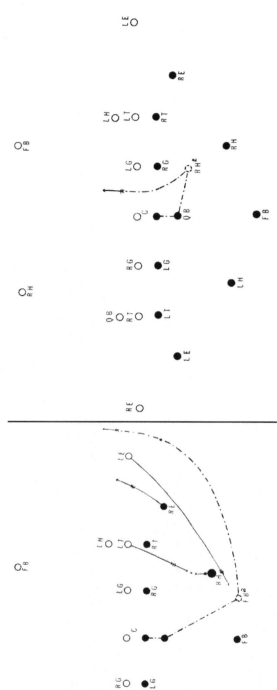

63. Full-back feints a kick and runs around the end.

To send FB around the end on a feint to kick, RH and LH draw from one to two yards behind their original positions, while FB moves over toward the right to FB², from two to three yards in the rear of RH.

When the ball is put in play QB passes carefully and accurately to FB, who, with coolness and *deliberation*, without betraying by the slightest glance or uneasy movement that he is about to run, goes through the preparatory movements of being about to kick.

All the men in the line block their opponents as usual, with the exception of RE. The latter allows his man unimpeded progress straight for FB, simply forcing him to run to the *inside* of him as he passes, or takes the first extra man in the line outside of RT.

As the opposing LE is *almost upon him*, coming forward at full speed, FB suddenly darts to the right in order to dodge LE, which is easily done, and dashes around the right end. The entire success of the play will depend upon the coolness and skill of FB in waiting until the last moment before dodging to the right and in not allowing his ultimate design to be prematurely discovered. In case the opposing tackle succeeds in breaking through the line RH must take him and force him to the *inside*.

64. Full-back feints a kick and half-back darts through the line.

To send RH through the line on a feint to kick, LH and FB drop back. RH remains in nearly his original position, while FB assumes every appearance of being about to receive and kick the ball. Just before the ball is snapped RH draws in slightly nearer to RH². Upon receiving the ball QB instantly passes it to RH, who is close to the line and plunges directly through the opening between C and RG with head down, and the ball held as shown in diagram five.

The opposing guards and center are all intent upon breaking through and stopping the kick, and are entirely unprepared for a dash into the line.

As the ball is put in play RG throws his man suddenly and violently to the *right*, while C throws his man in a similar manner to the *left*, and RH darts through the opening so made without assistance or interference.

NOTE. This play is also frequently made between guard and tackle.

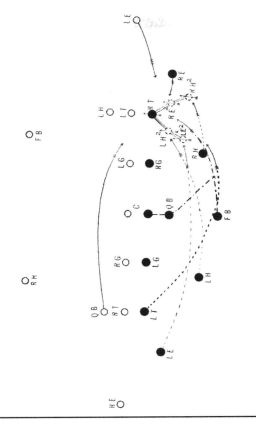

66. Harvard line wedge.

To form the line wedge upon the right side. At the given signal RH, RE, LH, and LE, dash toward the right and form a wedge directly behind RT, occupying the positions RH², RE², LH², and LE², and taking a formation similar to that shown for LE, LH, RE, and RH in diagram forty-one.

C puts the ball in play the instant the men reach their positions, and QB passes to FB, who receives the ball at x, on the run. LT leaves his position the instant the ball is snapped, and follows directly behind FB. Upon receiving the ball, FB dashes in behind the wedge with head down, and all plunge forward, preserving a compact mass. LG blocks his man hard, while C and LG block their men and endeavor to force them to the left.

As soon as QB has passed the ball, he should dash forward to throw his entire weight behind the wedge.

See NOTE, diagram sixty-eight.

65. Criss-cross play from the side line.

To perform the criss-cross play when the ball is out of bounds at the side line, C places the ball well within the field, keeping the other out of bounds, and faces the opponents' goal with the ball in his hands ready to put it in play by touching it to the ground and passing it back between his legs to QB. RG stands as near the side line as possible directly behind C, out of the way of QB.

FB stands about two yards behind QB, while LH occupies a position three or four yards behind the line and from ten to fifteen yards from the side of the field. The remainder of the men stand closely and solidly together in the line.

When the ball is put in play QB passes quickly to FB and both start at utmost speed for the center of the field in the lines indicated. FB runs close in front of LH and gives him the ball as he passes, upon which LH instantly starts back in the opposite direction.

Just before FB reaches LH, the guards and center swing around to the side and sweep their opponents a yard or two into the field, leaving a narrow lane by the side line down which LH may pass, as shown in cut A.

The play can be made with equal success when the ball is "down" within a yard or two of the side lines.

NOTE. LH must take the greatest care not to step over the boundary line as he runs.

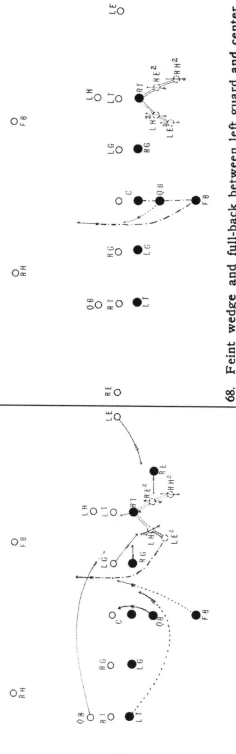

67. Left end between guard and center from the line wedge.

This play is a modification of the one shown in diagram sixty-six.

When the wedge has been sent forward several times in succession for short gains of from two to five yards, and the opposing LG has found the way to dive into it low down between RT and LH, to stop it; at the signal for the play, RG allows his opponent to break through to the right, as the ball is snapped, without resistance, and then forces him further to the right. C blocks his man and forces him hard to the left.

QB then instantly passes the ball to LE (instead of FB), who immediately darts through the opening between RG and C, followed by FB and LT.

QB helps C block his man and force him to the left.

The rest of the wedge plunges in behind RT when the ball is snapped, as before.

See NOTE on diagram sixty-eight.

68. Feint wedge and full-back between left guard and center.

After the plays shown in diagram sixty-six and diagram sixty-seven have been worked a few times in succession, RG and RT on the opposing side may find that they can accomplish nothing, as the wedge is upon the other side of the center, and run around in order to help block it. In that case the wedge will form at the signal, and immediately dash in behind RT as before. QB passes FB the ball the instant it is snapped. But FB, instead of plunging in with the ball behind the wedge (as shown in diagram sixty-six), darts through the line between C and LG.

C lifts his man back and to the *right*. LG forces the next opponent in the line to the *left*. QB follows directly behind FB.

NOTE. In case the opposing LG runs around to block the wedge, FB should pass through between LG and C. If RT goes, or RT and QB, he should pass between LG and LT.

NOTE. A strong sequence of movement in the series is as follows:

(1) Play as in diagram sixty-six; (2) If LH, RH, and QB mass in front of the wedge, play as in diagram sixty-seven; (3) If they mass close in behind the center play as shown in diagram sixty-nine; (4) If the opposing RG or RT runs around to block the wedge, play as in diagram sixty-eight; (5) At all other times play as shown in diagram sixty-six.

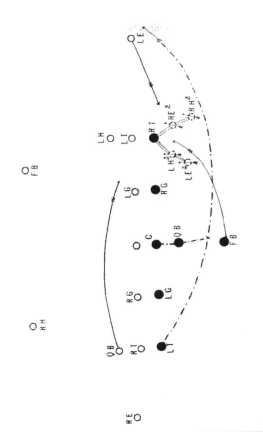

69. Feint wedge and tackle around the end.

At the signal the wedge is instantly formed as shown in diagram sixty-six, and as the men reach their formation, C snaps the ball. As the ball comes back, FB dashes in behind the wedge in the same manner as shown in diagram sixty-six, when carrying the ball, and the entire formation plunges forward behind RT.

LT leaves his position in the line the *instant* the ball is put in play, receives the ball at x from QB as he passes, but instead of following behind FB, as in diagram sixty-six, swings slightly out around the wedge, in the line indicated, at utmost speed.

The opposing LE may very likely be deceived into thinking the play shown in diagram sixty-six is being attempted, and dive into the wedge where he may be re-pinned by RH.

If the opposing LE does *not* dive into the wedge, RH and RE should dash away to the right ahead of LT the instant he reaches them, to interfere. RH should run directly for the opposing LE, while RE takes the first free man outside of RT.

See NOTE, diagram sixty-eight.

INDEX OF PLAYS

FIRST SERIES.

SECOND SERIES.

THIRD SERIES.

FOURTH SERIES.

(13) No. 1 and No. 2. End between center and opposite guard.
(14) No. 3 and No. 4. End between the opposite guard and tackle.
(15) No. 5 and No. 6. End between the opposite end and tackle.
(16) No. 7 and No. 8. End around the opposite end.

FIFTH SERIES.

(17) No. 1 and No. 2. Tackle between center and opposite guard.
(18) No. 3 and No. 4. Tackle between the opposite guard and tackle.
(19) No. 5 and No. 6. Tackle between the opposite tackle and end.
(20) No. 7 and No. 8. Tackle around the opposite end.

SIXTH SERIES.

(21) No. 1 and No. 2. Guard between the opposite guard and center.
(22) No. 3 and No. 4. Guard between the opposite guard and tackle.
(23) No. 5 and No. 6. Guard between the opposite tackle and end.
(24) No. 7 and No. 8. Guard around the opposite end.

SEVENTH SERIES.

(25) No. 1 and No. 2. Criss-cross half-back play around the end.
(26) No. 3 and No. 4. Ends criss-cross with half-back in play around the end.
(27) No. 5 and No. 6. Tackle criss-cross with half-back in play around the end.
(28) No. 7 and No. 8. Guard criss-cross with half-back in play around the end.

EIGHTH SERIES.

(29) No. 1 and No. 2. Half-back criss-cross with the end in play around the opposite end.
(30) No. 3 and No. 4. Full-back criss-cross with the end in play around the opposite end.
(31) No. 5 and No. 6. Ends criss-cross and play around the end.
(32) No. 7 and No. 8. Tackle criss-cross with the end in play around the opposite end.
(33) No. 9 and No. 10. Guard criss-cross with the end in play around the opposite end.
(34) No. 11 and No. 12. Tackle criss-cross with the tackle in play around the opposite end.

NINTH SERIES.

(35) No. 1 and No. 2. Double pass from end to full-back in play around the end.
(36) No. 3 and No. 4. Double pass from tackle to full-back in play around the end.
(37) No. 5 and No. 6. Double pass from guard to half-back in play around the end.

TENTH SERIES.

(38) No. 1. Slow mass wedge from a down.
(39) No. 2 and No. 3. Feint run around the end from wedge in the line.
(40) No. 4 and No. 5. Revolving wedge from a down.

ELEVENTH SERIES.

(41) No. 1 and No. 2. Lifting wedge through the center.
(42) No. 3 and No. 4. Wedge from the center around the tackle.
(43) No. 5 and No. 6. Quarter-back around the end from behind the wedge.
(44) No. 7 and No. 8. Feint play from the wedge.
(45) No. 9 and No. 10. Wedge at the end of the line.
(46) No. 11 and No. 12. Play around the opposite end from the wedge at the end.

TWELFTH SERIES.

(47) No. 1. Running mass wedge through the center.
(48) No. 2 and No. 3. Running mass wedge between guard and center.
(49) No. 4 and No. 5. Running mass wedge directly at the guard
(50) No. 6 and No. 7. Running mass wedge directly at the tackle.

THIRTEENTH SERIES.

(51) No. 1 and No. 2. Free opening play from the center.
(52) No. 3 and No. 4. Double pass opening play from the center.
(53) No. 5 and No. 6. Opening play from the center with team divided.

FOURTEENTH SERIES.

(54) No. 1. Princeton opening wedge from the center of the field.
(55) No. 2. Yale modification of Princeton wedge.
(56) No. 3. Princeton split wedge.
(57) No. 4. Yale split wedge.
(58) No. 5 and No. 6. Side play from wedge at center.

MISCELLANEOUS.

(59) No. 1. Hard running wedge with loose formation.
(60) No. 2. Harvard flying wedge.
(61) No. 3. Guard drops back and bucks the center.
(62) No. 4. Guard through his opening on the same side.
(63) No. 5. Full-back feints a kick and runs around the end.
(64) No. 6. Full-back feints a kick and half-back darts through the line.
(65) No. 7. Criss-cross play from the side line.

FIFTEENTH SERIES.

(66) No. 1 and No. 2. Harvard line wedge.
(67) No. 3 and No. 4. Feint wedge and end between guard and center.
(68) No. 5 and No. 6. Feint wedge and full-back between opposite guard and center.
(69) No. 7 and No. 8. Feint wedge and tackle around the end.

TEAM PLAY

American football is pre-eminently a game for the practice and display of what is known as "team play." No other game can compare with it in this particular. Not that the individual element in skill, in physical capacities, in strategy, and headwork are overlooked, but these are made subservient to the intent of the particular play in hand, and so adjusted to that play as shall best contribute to its success. To get eleven men to use their individual strength, agility, and speed, their wit, judgment, and courage, first in individual capacity, then working with one or two companion players, then as eleven men working as one, is a magnificent feat in organization and generalship.

The individual element, perhaps, is most prominently set forth in defensive play, although there is abundant opportunity in offensive play also for it to show itself; but individual and team play are so closely joined, as a rule, that the beauty of the latter is heightened as the individual efforts of each player are perceived. In defensive work the players have more reason to feel their individuality, because they are often compelled to combat alone one or more opponents before they can get an opportunity to tackle the runner. The defensive system, however, gives a splendid chance for clever team play in the placing of the players, in the general and particular understanding that certain men shall nearly always go through to tackle behind the line; that certain others shall wait to see where the attack will be made and there hurl themselves against it; that others shall go through the line, or not, just as it seems wisest at the time; and that still others shall never involve themselves in the scrimmage, but act only when the play has been carried into their territory. Furthermore, there is constant opportunity for the exercise of team play in the working together of certain players of the rush line in defense, and also in the working together of any two or three players at special times; for example, when one or two men sacrifice themselves to clearing away the interferers so that a companion can tackle the runner; when one follows hard after the runner to overtake him, if possible, even after having missed a tackle; or helps check him from further advance when tackled, or endeavors to secure the ball.

In the rush line the center and guards work together in defense, having an understanding with each other and with the player hovering in their rear, whenever it seems best to try to let him through on the opposing quarter-back or full-back, or whenever a special defense for certain plays seems best. Likewise the ends and tackles are closely joined in team play, in that they are the players relied on to stop the end plays and those between tackle and end. The most perfect adjustment and team work is needed in doing this, for they play into each other's hands while, at the same time, they seek to tackle the runner. Similarly, but less closely, do the guards and tackles work together in defense against certain plays.

It is an essential point in the working out of this team play between the different parts of the rush line, that the players study most carefully the positions they should occupy to meet the different kinds of play – how far from each other they should stand for this play, how far for that. In doing this, they must have regard for their own freedom to attack, not allowing themselves to take a position where they can easily be tangled up, nor one in which they can give their opponents an advantage in blocking them. Except on wedge and mass plays, the players in defense should draw their opponents apart sufficiently to give themselves space to break through on either side.

The backs supplement the work of the rushers in defensive play, arranging themselves behind the rush line at such distances from each other and from the forwards, as shall give the strongest defense. In that degree in which they make their work strong in team play, will they give the rushers encouragement and support in going through the line. The forwards will thus be enabled to play as a unit, because they know that there is a reserve force directly behind them to lend them assistance and make their play safe.

The backs work together in special defense on a kick, arranging themselves, either one or both, in front of the catcher to protect and encourage him, and to secure the ball, if muffed; or one stands behind to make the play safe, or to receive the ball on a pass from the catcher for a run or kick. The ends sometimes come back with their opponents at such times, to bother them all they can and to be in a position to interfere for the catcher, if he runs. The backs, also sometimes have a chance to help one another out by blocking off opponents, while one of their number makes sure of a rolling ball which, perhaps, has been kicked over the goal line or into touch.

When one side has the ball, it is often possible for the opponents to guess in which direction it will be carried, by the way the half-backs or quarter-back stand; by their unconscious glances in the direction they will take; by certain anticipative movements of the muscles; by false starts before the ball is put into play. Further information is often given by the rushers themselves – often by the rusher who is to carry the ball. Frequently the players who are to make the opening indicate by the way they stand, by shifting their positions after the signal is given, or by certain actions peculiar to them at such times, the general direction of the play, and perhaps, the exact place at which it is aimed. All this is most valuable information and ought to be imparted to the rest of the team whenever sufficiently positive to be of service. Indeed, the team play of the future will not be considered satisfactory without a set of signals being used to spread just such information.

At the same time that it is possible to gather much information of this character from the side with the ball, it must be remembered that shrewd players, knowing how they are watched for these tell-tale signs, have cultivated certain false motions, and are using them as points in strategy to deceive their opponents into expecting a different play from the one which is actually made.

From the foregoing, one draws the lesson to hide the intended play. At least, the play must not be indicated by any of these signs which the green player, and too often the experienced player, shows. Thoughtful self-control in every particular is what each player must cultivate, if he would do the greatest service for his team.

Now and then, also, in offensive play the maneuver resolves itself into a test of individual skill, speed, endurance, and headwork; but this is nearly always the outcome of team play in the first part of the movement. Occasionally a mishap furnishes a player a chance to make a run wholly through his own unaided efforts.

The history of the evolution of the hundred or more plays in American football is the history of the development of a "team" game. The perfecting of this has largely increased the number of combinations now possible and has given a wideness in variety of play, and at the same time a definiteness of action for each play, which makes it possible for every member of the eleven to assist powerfully in its execution. In fact, the execution of the play depends on every player doing his particular work for that play. Hence, the interdependence of the players is very close from the moment the ball is down until the run is made, or until a fair catch or a down by the opponents declares that the ball has been released. It is therefore exceedingly important that the adjustment of every factor in the play be made with perfect skill and in exact sequence, from the beginning till the end. It is most important, however, that the starting of the play be well made, for no amount of cleverness afterward can atone for a bungling start.

Team play from a scrimmage should begin the instant the center receives the ball from the hands of the runner (which should be immediately after he is stopped). Every rusher and back should be in position for the next play, and the signal be given before the runner has had hardly time to rise from the ground. The delay of one man in taking his place might be sufficient to spoil the play, whether that man be a rusher or a player behind the line.

As soon as the ball is in play the rushers must give their united support to the quarter-back and the runner, blocking their opponents, if necessary, long enough for the quarter to pass the ball and the runner to get well started. The center and guards especially must work together to protect the quarter while receiving the ball and passing it, and then all or part of them may move elsewhere to help out in the play, or may stay in their positions to make an opening for the runner. There must be the most united work in these preliminaries to the run. Irregular snapping of the ball, either in direction or in speed, which causes the quarter to fumble or to be delayed in getting it to the runner, a poor pass from the quarter, a muff or fumble by the runner, the letting of an opponent through too soon, are usually sufficient to spoil the play.

The rushers will do well in the preliminaries if the runner succeeds in getting up to the line without encountering an opponent, or in the end plays if he is able to get under good headway. They perhaps need only to make a strong blockade in those parts of the line where the particular play is in greatest danger of being checked, but in order to do this well they must regard each other's position as well as their own, touching elbows when necessary, or separating according to the line tactics deemed most effective at the time.

The work of a part of the rushers consists in preceding the runner whenever possible, working together by strategy and combination to make an opening for him and his interferers to go through. The others follow closely from behind to render what assistance they are able. This work comprises the hardest part of the whole play, for it must be executed in the face of the strongest part of the resistance. The rushers can block their men for a second or two, but to block them from three to six seconds is impossible against good players. It is here that the interferers come into especial prominence and value, for they are to clear the way of these free opponents. It is in anticipating the probable positions of the opponents in the vital stage of every maneuver, and in providing the cleverest team play to meet each contingency, that a team excels in advancing the ball by running.

Several things are especially necessary to produce skillful team play. First there should be a wise selection of players, and they should be placed in their final positions as early in the season as possible. There also should be such judgment in the arrangement of these players for each position as will produce the least friction in working out the plays, and that arrangement will usually be most effective in which there is the least delay and ill adjustment in making the plays quickly. There should be hard, systematic daily practice, backed by a close study of every play by each player in his particular position. The same players should be used together as much as possible, so that they can become thoroughly acquainted with each other's style of play and know each other's weak and strong points. In this way only can the fine adjustments and combinations which go to make up team play be brought about.

Team play in interference can only be the result of a carefully-planned system in which every player studies the general directions laid down for each play with a view to perfecting his particular work, varying his position on the field whenever necessary, starting like a flash in this play and delaying somewhat in that, blocking his man in one game perhaps in a certain way and in the next in one entirely different, because his opponent plays differently, sometimes taking another opponent instead of his own, when he sees that he can be of more assistance by so doing, and, in fact, doing whatever will more conduce to the furtherance of the particular play in hand.

In most plays the part which each player shall take in the interference can be laid out very definitely, but in the end play, and plays between end and tackle, only part of the interferers are to take particular men; the rest block off whatever opponents come in their path. It is in this free running that there are frequent chances for the display of fine team play in interference in striking the opponent at the nick of time, in pocketing him, in forcing him in or out as it seems best on the instant (the runner being on the watch for either), and in the runner sometimes slowing up to let an interferer who is close behind go ahead and take the man. Very often the reason that a play is not successful is because the interferer is too far in advance of the runner to be of any service to him. Interference must be timely to be effective. It must be the projecting of a helper at the moment a point of difficulty arises – the swinging into line of a series of helpers in timely sequence as the runner advances. Nor must the runner be delayed by the interferers except, perhaps, when the guard comes around on an end play where it is necessary to slow up a little at a certain point to let the guard in ahead.

The execution of nearly all the plays depends for its success on each player doing his duty at the right moment. Here and there in certain parts of the play one or more players must delay a particular work as much as possible, otherwise their action would be immature and so valueless; but for the most part, the movement of each player should be quick and definite, and those plays are most effectively made in which every player does his duty quickly.

Naturally, the end plays and the plays between end and tackle require more delicate adjustment of the players in the interference than do the center plays. In the latter, the interference nearly always must be done after the line has been reached and penetrated. Here the extra men, who rush to the opening as soon as they see where it is, will be encountered, while in the end runs an opponent is likely to show himself here and there and everywhere before the runner reaches the line.

In all mass and wedge plays where the pressure is brought to bear on one point in the line, the team play is not nearly so delicate and skillful. The virtue in the wedge play, be it quick or slow, lies in the power to project great weight and strength on a given point, while at the same time closely protecting the runner.

Every play should be made as safe as possible by having at least one player always in a position to get a fumbled ball, or in case an opponent secured the ball, to prevent him from making a run. Where there are so many parts to every play in snapping, handling, passing, and catching the ball, there is constant danger of a slip. The value of having one or more players behind the runner is frequently demonstrated also, when, by the aid of a timely push, the runner is able to break loose from the grasp of some tackler who has not secured a strong hold on him, and so adds several yards to his run.

In running down the field on a kick the rushers should run in parallel lines two or three yards apart, for most of the distance, converging as they approach the man with the ball, in order to pocket him. The ends approach the catcher in such a way that he will be forced to run in towards the approaching rushers, if he runs at all. All must be on the watch to thwart a pass to another man.

There is a nice point in judgment to be considered by the rushers in going down on a kick. The end men being so far away from where the full-back will stand when about to kick, can start instantly down the field, leaving the half-backs to block off their men if they come through too fast; for the ends' first duty is to be under the ball when it falls. Occasionally, when kicking from near the side line, it may be necessary for the end next to the side line to block his man or to push him back as he breaks through to go down the field. What the ends will do in this case, the tacklers should do nearly every time that a kick is made. Both tacklers should feel it their bounden duty to support the ends by going hard after them the instant they judge their opponents cannot reach the full-back in time to interfere with his kick. Hence, any tactics which they can put into practice which will enable them to block their opponents and, at the same time, not delay them in going down the field are the ones to be used. The tackles must bear in mind that the distance from their positions to the full-back is not very great, especially on the side on which the full-back kicks; but while this makes the duty of blocking on that side greater, the other tackle can afford to take an extra fraction of a second from blocking his opponent and use it in a quicker start.

On the guards and center rests the greatest burden in blocking their opponents on a kick; for while there is not that openness in the line, as at the tackle and end, which will let an opponent through quickly, the distance to the full-back is here the shortest and it is usually here that tricks are worked by which one or two men are let through, one usually being the quarter-back. They must, therefore, be very careful not to be over hurried in going down the field, remembering that it is their first duty to block, following the tackles and ends as soon as possible. If the guards and center are very skillful there need be no great delay in doing this, for it is necessary to check the opponents only long enough to enable the full-back to punt over their heads. Whenever it is possible for the guards and center to carry their men before them for a few feet, it is generally safe to leave them and go down the field at full speed. It is comparatively easy for the center to do this at the instant that he snaps the ball. Generally there is too much blocking done and too little "following the ball."

In this connection, as a help to the rushers, several points must be borne in mind by the full-back in kicking. It is not enough for him to kick the ball as hard as he can each time it is sent back for that purpose. That would be a poor performance of his duties. He must kick for his team's advantage always, and therefore must regulate the distance, and direct his kick with the utmost skill. Even long and puzzling kicks are dangerous unless closely followed up by the rushers; for, letting a good dodging half-back get free, with one or two interferers in a broken field of opponents, and he will be almost sure of a long run.

The full-back must take into account the ability of the rushers to get down the field in time to prevent a run or a return kick and punt accordingly. He may find it necessary to elevate the angle of his kick so that it will give his men time to get under it, or he may find it best to direct the ball straight ahead, in order to give his rushers the shortest distance to run, and at the same time be able to advance in the best formation for checking a run. At least, he must punt the ball where it shall be difficult for the backs to reach it quickly, and so give the rushers the advantage of a longer time to get under it. Especially must he be very careful not to kick the ball diagonally across the field without weighing well the risk involved, in comparison with the chances for increased advantage; for the risks are unusually large in such a kick. It would be well for the full-back to give the rushers a signal as to the direction he meant to kick. This should always be done when he intends to kick off to one side of the field, or when he purposes making a high kick or one outside of bound in order to put his men on side by running forward. The rushers would be able to work some splendid team-play on such occasions.

The question of when to make a fair catch and when to run is well worth the consideration of the backs, who are the ones almost always called upon to exercise their judgment on this point. It was formerly judged best, in handling a kicked ball, to make a fair catch on all occasions. To-day there is a division of opinion, some adhering to the old way, while others prefer to run whenever they get a chance.

There are two points to be considered in deciding this question: First, whether it is possible to kick a goal from the place where the ball will fall, or whether a punt from that point would be desirable; second, whether it will add much to the risk of not catching the ball, if the attempt is made to run. It is clear, that when near enough to the opponent's goal to try a place kick, every effort should be made to secure a fair catch.

When a goal from the field would be impossible, it is almost invariably best to run with the ball, unless this would add greatly to the danger of muffing it. Catching the ball necessitates a positive loss of ground before again putting it in play, and it is doubtful whether this loss is compensated by the advantage of putting it in play unmolested by opponents and behind the whole team under slight headway.

In attempting to run the player will at the worst be forced to make a down, which would furnish only slightly less advantage than a fair catch, while on the other hand it presents opportunities for gain.

FIELD TACTICS

Clever tactics on the football field depend first of all on the captain's possessing an accurate knowledge of the strength and weakness of his team, both in individual play and in team play. This can all be acquired during practice by carefully noting every play which is made, and giving thought to the strength of the individual men and the value of the play in its relation to the others, both in regard to the perfection of execution and in intrinsic merit from a strategic point of view. It also depends upon the captain's observing as soon as he enters the field and throughout the game, the incidents of the day; the direction and force of the wind; the position of the sun; and the condition of every part of the field. All these points are of great importance in good generalship. Lastly, it depends upon the study which he makes of the way the opponents arrange themselves on the defense, as well as the style of their play when in possession of the ball. He must also seek to find out by trial which of his plays can be used most effectively.

Having the knowledge of the first and second requisites for good generalship, the captain must immediately proceed to find out the weakness and strength of the opponent's defense, not by trying each play in turn and just noting its success, but by using the best tactics the occasion demands, and closely observing the result on each play. Every play known to be strong because of the ability to concentrate or mass the players at some part of the line, or for any other reason, should be tried at least two or three times early in the game in order to give it a fair test, that the captain may know which will be his most effective plays. It is a mistake to keep pounding away on two or three plays which give an advance of a few yards, just on that account, until after other reliable plays have been given a fair trial. In making this trial, the time should be well chosen, both as to position on the field and as to the number of the down, and the previous loss or gain, if it is the second or third down. It often happens that a powerful play is discarded because in one or two trials it did not work well. The difficulty may have been in its imperfect execution, or in a neglect of duty on the part of one man even, or it might result from the inability of one player to do his work because of circumstance or tactics on the part of his opponents which he could not overcome, but which, later on, he would discover a way to meet.

By confining tactics to a few plays which have proved successful for more or less gain, the captain limits his play very decidedly and clearly indicates his policy, thereby giving his opponents a knowledge which is invaluable in thwarting him. The result will be that all the available players upon the opposing team will be called from the appointed positions where they had been placed in order to meet the most varied style of plays, and stationed where they can render these particular plays most ineffective. The knowledge that the play will probably be one of a few, also gives every player on the defense a certainty of action which will make his opposition very much stronger. The uncertainty which comes from combating a variety of tactics weakens each man's defense considerably, and puts him at his wit's end to discover what the play will be and how to meet it. It also makes him more liable to be blocked off and pocketed.

Sometimes, to be sure, it is fine strategy to keep pounding away at some particular point or points in the line, in order to draw the attention wholly to this place and to draw the men away from other parts of the line in order to weaken it for a sudden attack; but this is quite different from the limited style of play so often used, and really, if well done, is a mark of clever generalship.

The captain sometimes uses all his plays in succession simply because he has been accustomed to run through them in practice. This is poor tactics. If it has once been clearly proven that a certain play cannot for any reason be made, every clear-headed captain will realize that it is very poor policy to waste downs in the effort.

A similar mistake sometimes grows out of giving the signals in practice. If the captain or quarter-back in giving the signal is not careful, he will get into the way of unconsciously arranging the plays according to the law of association of ideas, one play following another in unvarying sequence. The principle of sequence in plays would not be fatal, and, indeed, would sometimes be very effective, if the plays are well selected. But account should be taken of the physical capacity of the players; the duties which they have just been called on to perform; and the right time and place on the field, in reference to the side lines and nearness to the goal. The great advantage to be gained lies in having the sequence come in the form of a series which is perfectly learned, so that play after play shall be made in rapid succession. The series, however, should not consist of more than from four to six plays, as contingencies often arise which seriously injure their effectiveness. In any case the series ought to be stopped if for any reason it is unwise to make the next play, or if the conditions allow a much better move. A simple signal will indicate that the series is to be stopped. The great virtue in series plays lies in the fact that a certain signal starts the series and each play can be made in the quickest manner, because the players all know what is coming next and are ready the instant the ball is in the center-rusher's hands. Series plays are especially effective against a team which is slow in lining up. They are very valuable also in their moral effect, because of the rapidity and enthusiasm with which the plays are made.

Under a varied style of play where many movements are well executed, the opposing team must exercise the greatest headwork and caution in its defense. If the other team has not already indicated its policy by clearly defining its plays, every one on the opposing eleven will be conscious of so much uncertainty as to what the play will be, that his attack through the line is likely to be cautious and therefore not strong; or else it is likely to be sufficiently daring to give the opponents a decided advantage in making their plays. When undue caution is exercised on the defense, its effect often is to make the players hesitating. This, when extending throughout the rush line is fatal to a strong defensive game. A daring, reckless defense is far more effective than the cautious defense which makes a rush line hesitate, because of the moral effect on the other team, if for no other reason.

And this leads us to consider the moral effect of certain tactics. The three most effective styles of plays when successfully used are: a kicking game when there are weak catchers behind the opposing line (or when the latter are poorly positioned); end plays; and dashes through the center in mass or quick wedge plays. These three plays, in the order named, have the most disheartening effect on the opposing team, when the side having the ball has a long, accurate, and scientific kicker who is able to place his punts well, and also to regulate the height and twist which the ball shall take.

Every football player knows the chances for a fatal misplay which hang on a kicked ball: first, because of the difficulty of judging it accurately if it be twisting in certain ways; second, because of its exceeding susceptibility to currents of air which make its gyrations and deviations excessively perplexing; third, because of the nicety of final judgment required, even when the player is well under the ball, since its shape and elasticity make it necessary to allow for its full length and its smallest dimension at the same time, also for a quick rebound from the arm or hands. The catcher must attend to all this in the face of a fierce line of rushers coming down on him at full speed, eager to tackle him or to seize the ball if he muffs or fumbles it.

The moral effect of having uncertain catchers behind the line is very telling on the team. If all the hard, wearying work of the rushers and half-backs to advance the ball forty or fifty yards is to be spoiled over and over by muffed punts, even though the ball is not lost to the other side (as it is likely sometimes to be in such cases), there is sure to be a diminution in effort in a short time on the part of the whole team. This comes imperceptibly at first, but comes just as surely, and ere long evinces itself in the more determined and successful efforts of the other team.

Almost equally disheartening, if not fully so, is it to have runs made repeatedly around the ends; because the runs in that locality, if successful, are usually for long gains often resulting in touch-downs, and they arouse the greatest fears in the minds of all the players from a feeling of inability to stop them. The result is that every effort is centered on anticipating these end plays, and the rushers, instead of going through the line, wait to see if it is an end play, in which case they run out to the side to stop it. That very moment in which there is a hesitancy on the part of the guards and tackles in going through the line, is a moment of triumph for the team with the ball; for it immediately gives them a decided advantage, in that, while perhaps unable before to make progress through the center part of the line, they will now have two strong points of attack. The chances now are that the defense will grow weaker and weaker as the game advances, for unless the end runs are well stopped the players will decrease their efforts somewhat and the tackling will become less and less daring and effective.

It is hard to say which of these two styles of play really has the more discouraging effect on the opposite team. If the eleven which has the poor catchers back of their forwards are successful in making advance by rushing the ball, they have a vast deal to encourage them, even though now and then they lose it all through the muffing of their backs. The period in which they have the ball is one in which their minds are not conscious of the weakness of their own defense but are completely taken up with the good work they are doing, and they are unanimous and buoyant in it. That period of success does much to keep up their spirits during the time when the other side has the ball and their fears are so all-powerful.

When a team is able to make frequent runs around the opponent's end, there is perhaps less to actually dishearten them than in the preceding case, for there is less fear of losing the ball. It can be gotten only through a failure to advance the five yards in its three trials; through a fumble; through a penalty imposed by the umpire; or through a kick. The latter will be tried probably only under extreme conditions where there has been a loss of yards, while in the kicking game mentioned above, the side not in possession of the ball always has the hope of securing it.

That captain is not a good general who follows out the same tactics in each game; who, having perhaps worked out a system of plays which his men could best execute, attempts to apply this system in every game, regardless of the composition of the opposing eleven and their systems of defense and offense. The captain, in truth, has learned a good deal when he has learned what plays his team can best execute, and he has most valuable, though far from complete, information for conducting a wise campaign against the opposing eleven. He still has much need to exercise his generalship as to whether this point of attack should be assailed three or fifteen times; this place a few times; and this place not at all, or perhaps only once or twice for sake of trial or strategy.

Oftentimes, the rusher can give invaluable information to the captain as to his own ability to handle his opponent, where for example the opponent so places himself constantly as to render it an easy matter to get him out of the way for certain plays, although it is impossible to move him on other plays. This is especially true in handling a large man who stands constantly in the same way; as for instance, well over to the side of his opponent. It would be comparatively easy to block such a man for opening up a hole in one direction, but almost impossible to shove him in the opposite way. Such information would furnish the captain with valuable data on which to base certain tactics, and would inform him that he could doubtless make plays to one side of this man and seldom if ever to the other side.

It would be foolish, even if it were possible, to lay down a complete system of tactics which should be followed in a game. Indeed, the wonderful part of football is, that it is a game which cannot be worked out by rule and learned by note. One play does not follow another in sequence, but only as the captain or commander of the day directs.

What makes the game preeminently one requiring science and brains, is that to be well played the captain must use the utmost wisdom and strategy in directing the plays, and the players to a man must do their duty in executing them. Very many points of advantage and disadvantage must constantly be borne in mind, or else the best generalship and results cannot follow. It is far from true to say that the captain must simply take into account the strong and weak points of his opponent's play, together with the incidents of the day and field, such as the direction of the sun and condition of the grounds in each particular part of the field; he must also have regard for his men, selecting his plays with such wisdom as to secure the greatest economy of physical energy with the greatest result, so that no man nor men shall be overworked at any time of the game and thus be incapacitated.

No captain is a good general who does not know the limitations in strength of his ground-gainers, and who does not take this into account in directing the play. Men differ greatly in their power to repeat a performance quickly; essentially, then, in their powers of endurance. Some men can do effective work only when in first-class condition; that is, when they have had a certain length of time to recover after each effort, they can be relied on for a good gain, if not a brilliant run. Then, there is a vast difference in the kind of play as to the drain on a man's strength. End runs, and runs in which a considerable distance is covered, or runs in which there is a good deal of dodging and struggling to get loose from tacklers, are the most taxing on the wind and strength. Most men can stand two or more dashes through the line in quick succession, or two or more mass and wedge plays where the runner does not run fast for a long distance before being tackled. But when a run has been made which has called for a vast deal of energy the captain should not fail to notice it, and in calling the next two or three plays, choose such as do not ask for too much strength from this player. The star runner as a rule is the one who suffers most from overwork through injudicious leadership.

This does not preclude the fact that there are occasions in the game when some player or players must be forced to draw heavily on a reserve fund of energy in order to secure a permanent advantage or to prevent disaster. It sometimes seems necessary when nearing the opponent's goal, that some player be put to his supreme test of strength in order to secure points, and likewise, when it is necessary to carry the ball away from one's own goal, and there is only one man who is sure to meet the crisis; but these are in truth critical periods and are exceptions not to be mentioned in this connection.

We know that it is sometimes considered clever tactics, when there are strong, substitute players for certain positions, to work men in these positions to their utmost limit of service, and then "have them get hurt" in order to substitute a fresh man or men. If this be shrewd, it is at least not honest tactics.

If a team is not capable of playing an uphill game, or is one which is strongly affected by success and repulse; or, if the opposing eleven is one which is similarly influenced, the tactics should be those most likely to produce the exultation of success on the one hand, and the feeling of discouragement on the other. The plays should be those which can be executed quickly, and which have a certainty of gain with little risk of loss; which combine the efforts of every man in the eleven sufficiently to make him feel that he has an important part in them;

which bring the energies of the opposing eleven, particularly the rushers, to the severest test, taxing especially the wind and courage.

It must always be remembered, as a point in tactics, that the side in possession of the ball has a great advantage, especially if the other side is weak in defensive play, and that it requires a greater outlay in strength and wind to check plays than it does to make them. It is likewise true that the courage of a team may be measured by its promptness and determination in defense. If a team repeatedly and continuously comes up to the scrimmage, after being outwitted and outplayed, it has the true courage, the courage which would probably enable them to win if possessed of an equal degree of skill in team-play.

What style of game shall a team play? That depends on many contingencies. Setting aside for the time the incidents of the day, such as wind, rain, and sunlight; the soft, slippery, and rough places in the grounds; the up and down grades;—not even taking into account the strength and weakness of the opponents, and the contingencies which arise, let us consider solely the composition of the team, and see if we can deduce any style of play which applies to teams made up of certain types of men.

Without defining the make-up of the team, except on general terms, we see that when the rush line is strong and heavy, the chances are that they will be able to handle their opponents and make good openings for the dashes through the line. Plunges through the central part of the line will probably be the most effective, if the center, guards and tackles are large and strong men. If the backs are slow and heavy also, a center game will probably be the only kind they can play with success. And the result is that this will be the style of game adopted; not perhaps because the captain has analyzed the reasons for the ability of the backs to make advance in that place, and their inability to circle the ends, for example; but just because that is the part of the line in which they can make their gains every time. Perhaps it will occur to him that those same backs can be so quickened in starting and running, and then so well guarded, that they will be able now and then to try an end play, or a tackle and end play successfully, and by so doing, strengthen that very center play. The chance for making a successful end play is increased where a center game is being played, because the ends will be likely to draw in somewhat to help the center.

When the center men of the line are rather light, if the backs are heavy and slow, the advantage will still be in attacking the openings between the center and guards and between the guards and tackles; for, if the backs and ends mass on these places, as they can do quickly and powerfully, they can still force a few yards at a time, and now and then break through for considerable gain. When well massed, this can be played even against the strongest centers. All that the rush line will need to do is hold their men momentarily until the backs get under headway, and the combination of so much weight and power will be sure to make advance when well directed. If it be remembered that the advantage is always with the side which has the ball, and if the players, though checked now and then, go into each play with undaunted courage, advance will surely be made.

As a general rule, when a team has light, swift runners behind the line, they should lay the emphasis on plays around the end and between the ends and tackles. Not that they should confine themselves to those points of attack, but it would be foolish for a team composed of such material not to perfect the plays in these parts of the line, because of the ability of the backs to move quickly to these remoter places. Such men, too, are not so well built for the hard, plunging work in the center, and will probably stand less of it, and be less effective, than heavier backs. This of course depends in part on the build of the men, but in general it is true.

But even if the backs are equally good in plunging into the line, it would be better policy to keep the line spread out, for no runner can make much gain through a close line. Swift drives through the line can be made frequently, and are usually very telling when the line, being spread out, is opened up for these little backs to come darting through. But if the backs and central part of the rush line are both light, while those of the opponents are heavy, the end style of play must of necessity be depended on, or the opposing rushers will be able to resist the plunges. Furthermore, it will be exceedingly hard to make holes through the line, and, in fact, even to hold their opponents long enough for the backs to get up to the line.

The question of what shall be the proportion of end plays and plays between the ends and tackle, to the plays through the other four openings in the line depends, of course, very largely on the backs. The composition of the rush line as to strength and skill, especially the center, guards, and tackles, also affects the proportion.

On the ordinary college and preparatory school team, the relative effectiveness of an end game to a center game would be much smaller than where the teams are better trained, simply because the risks are larger; for, while the defense against well executed interference would be much weaker, the attack also is much weaker.

Every end play and play between the tackles and end is attempted with a much greater risk from actual loss of ground, or with a loss of a down with no gain, than are the plays in the center. The reason is that the rushers are given time to break through the line while the runner is moving out to the point of attack, and unless well protected he will not reach the opening.

Further, this movement for a considerable distance is almost entirely sidewise before an advance can be made, while in the plays in the central part of the line the rushes are made nearly straight forward, except when the rushers take the ball, and the runners scarcely ever fail to reach the line. The times when there is no gain whatever and when there is an actual loss are comparatively few, for the runner, catching the ball at full speed, is up to the line in an instant, and then it becomes a question how far he can advance beyond that point. Taking these elements of risk into account, it would seem that the proportion of plays at the end to plays through the line should not be larger than one to three, and oftentimes less, even where a team is able to use both styles effectively. The only occasion for a larger use of end plays than this would be when the runner seldom fails to reach the line, and is usually good for a gain. In that event the large element of risk has been taken away, and the proportion of these should then depend on the relative amount of gain which the trials have shown can be secured from each with the least expenditure of energy.

Right here it might be well to add that it requires more skillful generalship to know when to use an end play than when to make a play through the center. It is only occasionally that the ball is down so close to the side lines that all four openings in the center are not available on account of running outside the line, while it is frequently the case that the ball is down near enough to the side line to limit the end play to one side, that is, to two openings. Nor is this enlarged space on one side of the field sufficient compensation for the loss of the two points of attack, but it adds to the science of the game, as it requires more varied tactics and maneuvers.

It is poor tactics to keep trying end plays when it has been clearly proven that it is not possible to make them and that there is a likelihood of a loss in the trial. If it seems best to try the end for the sake of keeping the opposing line spread out so that the center plays can be made more successfully, the most propitious times should be selected. It should never be on the second or third down, because the risk of losing the ball by failure to gain the requisite five yards would be entirely too great.

There are times when an end play should not be used at all, or very rarely, on account of the risk involved; as, for example, when the ball is being carried out from under the goal where it has been forced by the opponents. Anywhere within the fifteen or twenty yard line it is much better to trust to bringing it slowly out a few yards or feet at time, sufficient, perhaps, to secure only the requisite five yards in three trials. Beyond the twenty-yard line and up to the thirty-five-yard an end play should be tried only on the first down, or, in rare instances, on the second down, unless the risk of losing ground, and subsequently the ball, is worth taking. In such cases the possession of a powerful punter behind the line, who could place the ball well out of dangerous territory if necessary, might be a sufficient reason for attempting a long kick down the field. It does not seem, however, that it is necessary to run any risk of losing the ball if there is good reason for not playing a kicking game, for there will be ample chance to try an end play on the first down. Mistakes in generalship are frequently made right along this line in nearly every game which is played, an end run being sometimes tried on the third down when there is less than a yard to gain. Better gain the yard or two by the surest ground-gaining play and then try an end run on the very next.

When inside the opponents' twenty-five-yard line the greatest skill must also be used, and the aim should be to get the requisite five yards by the most reliable tactics. Plays which risk the loss of ground and the ball should be sparingly used, and every caution and strategy be exercised to place the ball across the line. Nor should there be less prudence because a team has a good drop kicker. The proportion of goals secured from drop kicks is not more than one in every four or five attempts, with the best kickers in America, and the most certain way to score will be to strain every nerve to place the ball across the line by steadfastly holding the ball and using the drop kick only as a last resource.

Every now and then a point is lost unnecessarily when the ball is in possession of a team under its own goal. It is judged not wise to kick. Perhaps the wind is strong in the opposite direction and there is no reliable punter, or perhaps it would simply give the opponents a fair catch from which to make a try for goal if kicked. The captain also realizes that if the opponents secure the ball they will force it over. Two downs may already have been used up and ground lost in vain attempts to advance the ball by running. There seems to be no other alternative, and so another trial is made, but without avail, whereupon the ball goes to the other side. Under these circumstances it would be well for the captain to remember that by making a safety touchdown and allowing the opponents to score two, he could have brought the ball out to the twenty-five-yard line and prevented a probable six points.

The mistake is often made of frequently using end plays when the ground is slippery and soft from rain. Nothing can be more foolish, unless the aim is to get the ball on firmer ground, for with insecure footing it is impossible to start quickly, run fast, or turn and dodge quickly. This makes it easy, also, for the opposing eleven to stop the runner and nearly always with a loss of ground. The same is true, in a measure, when the ground is soft or very sandy. It is comparatively hard to make end plays even when there are no favorable conditions, when the ground is firm and level.

He is a wise general, therefore, who notes the field carefully, knowing where all the soft and slippery and rough places are, as well as where the good ground is, and then keeps them in mind throughout the game, and makes his moves wisely in reference to them. Few captains take the field sufficiently into account in directing the plays, so that the greatest advantage can be secured by avoiding the hindrances as much as possible. Again and again unsuccessful trials to advance have been made in muddy places, when, with one well-planned move, the ball could have been placed on solid ground with little or no sacrifice, and a vast advantage secured. It is usually worth the loss of two or three yards, and oftentimes more, to make an end play in order to give a better footing to the backs and the rushers for putting the ball into play, for handling it, for making holes, and for starting, running, and dodging.

When the ground is very slippery, all plays which cause the runner to move a considerable distance sideways and across the field before turning to advance, and all plays requiring a sudden change in direction, whether when under strong headway or not, are hard to gain ground on, and, therefore, must be used with great judgment. Equally hard to make are the plays in which the tackle and guard and end carry the ball around for a run through one of the openings on the opposite side of the line. There is not, however, the chance for so much loss of ground in these plays, as usually played, than there is in a run out to the end by the half-backs, because the former run closer to the line and the play is not so quickly perceived.

It naturally follows, then, from what has been said, that those plays which send the runner directly forward; those in which the impetus from the start is more forward than sidewise; those in which the runner does not have far to run before he strikes the opening; and those in which he can get the greatest protection and assistance quickly, are the plays to be relied on when the ground is soft, sandy, or slippery.

In bringing the ball in from the side lines, the privilege is given of having it down anywhere from five to fifteen yards from that line. This option of ten yards should be valuable in determining the tactics to be used next. Too often is it the habit for the captain to shout out "Bring it in fifteen," whether the "fifteen" would carry them into a mud hole, or whether there was a positive advantage in operating from a nearer point to the side line by avoiding the usual custom of an end run, and sending the runner through on the other side. Generally the fifteen yard point is the best place to have the ball down, but not always. The ten-yard point has decided advantages in making certain side-line plays, because the opponents will reason that the chances are in favor of an end play being attempted, and will draw one or two men away to strengthen their defense in that quarter. These they will feel that they can well spare from that side without very apparently weakening the defense, because they are protected from long runs by the side line.

The side line does not enter into the consideration in field tactics as much as it should. As a rule, it is considered a misfortune when the ball is down within less than ten yards of this boundary line, because it gives the opponents a good chance to anticipate the play, which is likely to be a run around the other end. The free men who are behind the rushers nearest the side line rarely fail to move over as far as the center-rusher. This leaves the defense of that part wholly to the rushers, supported by the side line, and is the best situation possible for making certain plays. Long runs, however, cannot be expected, and the captain must be contented to work steadily up the field by short gains. After several dashes into the line, of this kind, an end run suddenly carried into execution may have considerable chance for success.

This suggests the thought that it is possible to use the side line helpfully when the ball is down very near it and when it is impossible to make any strong plays because of the limitations which must be met in such a situation. At such a time, instead of attempting to make a run out toward the end, or tackle, which will be expected, the play should often be straight forward or on the side toward the boundary line, until the runner is finally pushed over the line and has the privilege of bringing the ball in to a more favorable position from which to operate.

Furthermore, the position near the side line can be made more useful in working tricks than a point nearer the center of the field, for reasons which are evident.

There is no question that kicking the ball has not entered into the tactics of football as largely as its possibilities would warrant. There are many reasons for this. First, there is only here and there a team which has a reliable kicker. Punting and drop kicking are practiced by a few only, and, for the most part, not intelligently and successfully. It is a science with several points of skill to be acquired. Second, many teams have an uncertain punter who does not himself know exactly where the ball will go, whether far down the field or just over the rush line, along the ground or to one side, and so place such little confidence in the value of kicking under so great a risk that they will usually trust to a run, even on the third down, if the distance which they have to gain is not too great. Third, in all but a few leading colleges when the teams are evenly matched, the question of points is largely a question of which side has the ball. The offensive game is much better developed than the defensive game, and it is not infrequent for one team to carry the ball from one end of the field to the other without losing it. Under these circumstances the necessity for kicking is seldom felt, and they would rather take the risk of not gaining the requisite number of yards, than release their right to the ball by an uncertain kick. Fourth, it is a fact that most punters can not kick accurately if forced to punt quickly. They are, therefore, compelled to stand so far back of the rush line that the value of their punt is decreased by several yards, or else they run the risk both of a poor punt and of having it stopped by the opposing rushers who break through the line.

No better proof of the value of a good punter behind the line is needed, than to see a game in which one side is visibly weaker than the other in its power to advance the ball by running, but which, possessing a strong punter, is able to keep its opponents in check. Frequent punts are doubly effective when the opposite side is without a good kicker, or is not accustomed to a kicking game.

The worth of an accurate kicker is magnified very much when there is a wind in his favor. Comparatively few games are played without a wind to help or interfere, according as it is favorable to one side or the other. When the wind is in the favor of one side, they should be able to use it to the greatest advantage. The captain should be alive to its value, and make it a powerful factor in his tactics. It would then be a question whether it would not be wise to kick the ball just as soon as it was secured, provided, of course, it was not so near the opponent's goal that it would be wiser to hold the ball and attempt to rush it over. Certain it is that a side should never fail to kick on the third down except on account of the liability of kicking the ball over the goal line when inside of the twenty-five yard line, or because so close to the goal line that it is worth taking the risk of losing the ball in making a supreme effort to get it over.

When there is danger of the ball being kicked across the goal line a clever punter will usually aim to kick the ball across the side line into the touch as near the goal line as possible. This is intentional and is quite different from the juvenile efforts which do not take the wind or position into account when punting from near the side line and send the ball outside, only a few yards away.

It is sometimes good tactics on the third down, when there is considerable doubt whether the required advance can be made, to have the full-back kick the ball across the side line with no intent perhaps of a gain in ground. While giving the opposing team technically an equal chance, it is wholly with the purpose off having the end-rusher secure the ball, which will be upon the first down. The kick must be well placed, of course, and must not be so much forward that there will be great risk of the opponents securing the ball, and also not so far ahead that the full-back cannot put his men on side easily. The end man on that side must also know of the full-back's intention, and place himself well over toward the side line. Such a kick cannot be attempted safely when the full-back is not able to place his punts with great accuracy. The occasions when the use of such tactics would be wise, might be when the side in possession of the ball was able to make good advances by running but had lost ground, perhaps through a misplay; or when they had the ball inside their opponents' twenty-five yard line and were not in a good position to try a drop kick; or when the risk of making the required gain by running would be too great.

Right here would come in the question of a drop kick on the third down when inside the twenty-five yard line, and in fair position to make the trial. It is safe to say that, in general on the third down, this should be the play called for. It is for the captain to decide whether the trial is worth the making; whether the nearness and angle to the goal, and the quickness and skill of the kicker warrant a drop kick in preference to the chances of making a further advance by running.

If a run is attempted without gain the ball will be down where it is for the other side. When the kick is made on the other hand, there will be a possibility of having the ball stopped by the opposing rushers, and a run made up the field; or, if the goal is missed, the opposing team will be allowed to bring the ball out to the twenty-five yard line.

The captain must weigh all these possibilities before making his decision.

The great advantage in the wind does not consist alone in the increased distance the ball can be propelled, but also in the increased likelihood that some one upon the side which kicked will again secure the ball on a muff or fumble. The wind has added to the problem of the player who attempts to catch the ball these points of difficulty: greater distance covered by the ball, an increased speed, and a greater probability that the ball will suddenly veer to one side or the other from the line of direction.

The increased advantage of a favoring wind is in direct proportion to the strength of the wind. If the wind is very strong, the side which does not have its assistance is severely handicapped, and for the time is not able to do any effective kicking. Even with the best punters, it is impossible to drive the ball far in the face of a strong wind, and then the kick must be low or the wind is likely to blow it back near the spot from which it was kicked. On the other hand, when kicking for distance with the wind, it is usually better to kick the ball high, in order that the wind may affect it more powerfully during the longer interval of time in rising and falling.

There is also an economic reason for kicking the ball whenever it can be wisely done. It is a good way to rest the backs in order to save them for the supreme effort of carrying the ball across the line; for, if the ball has been carried for a considerable distance, they will be likely to be somewhat fatigued as they approach the goal line, and they will be weakest where and when the opposing side always puts in their most determined and desperate resistance.

It is a severe test of a team's courage to bear up against a kicking game in the face of a strong wind; for, even if they are able to make good gains in return by running, the players are constantly fearing a slip or fumble, which will give the ball back to the other side only to have it returned with all the chances of a misplay, if not a gain in ground. The effect of the wind also is to make the side against it think that they are working very much harder than their opponents just to hold their own.

There is no question as to the value of having every member of the team able to run with the ball when it is possible and wise. The more varied the style of play, provided it is strong, or is likely to be successful because unlooked for, the more powerful would be the plan of attack and the less effective the defense. This is true for two reasons: first, it keeps the opposing team constantly guessing as to what the play will be and enables the side with the ball to secure advantages through the variety of its play; second, it distributes the labor and secures the advantage of fresh strength, while it rests the main ground-gainers. For these reasons, then, it is well worth the while to run the guards, tackles, and ends, although these are not in as advantageous positions for gaining ground as are the half-backs and full-back.

The most valuable of the three rush-line positions for ground gaining is the tackle, because from that position the runner can get under sufficient speed to carry him forward against opposition, and he can also secure the most protection and help. The run also can be made in the quickest time and without being immediately noticed.

The end position, when the end plays behind the line and near the tackle, comes next in value of the line positions for running with the ball, because of the large number of interferers ahead. If rightly played by a fast runner, the end will be able to make good advances between the tackle and end, and even around the end on the other side.

The guard is in the hardest rush-line position for advancing the ball, because it is impossible for him to get under speed when making a quick turn around the quarter-back, and on the other hand he cannot afford to run out to the end, because he would be sure to be tackled whether he ran close to the line with little interference, or ran farther back with better interference but with greater risk of loss of ground.

SIGNALS

In the modern game of football it is absolutely necessary that before each play a signal should be given, which will inform every man on the team of the movement about to be executed. Every player has a special duty to perform each time the ball is snapped, and unless he is informed beforehand of the evolution intended, it will be impossible to render the requisite assistance. It is of equal importance that the opposing team should be kept in absolute ignorance in regard to the intention of the play, so that they may not anticipate and thwart it.

That code of signals will be best, then, which will indicate the simplest manner the play intended, while at the same time being unintelligible to opponents. Too frequently such a complicated system of signals is adopted that the players themselves become confused, or at least are unable to comprehend the order upon the instant, and the momentary delay thus caused proves a great disadvantage. There is far less likelihood that the opposing team will be informed by the signal what play is intended, than that they shall discover its probable direction by the position assumed or nervousness betrayed by some one of the backs or rushers.

There are three systems of signals which have a practical value: Sign signals, word signals, and number signals. Sign signals possess one advantage which neither of the other two can claim. They can be understood with readiness amid the most deafening cheering from the side lines. It often happens that the cheering is so continuous at critical moments during the great matches, where many thousand people are assembled, that for several moments the play is almost paralyzed on account of the inability of the captain to make his orders heard. It is readily perceived what an advantage it would be to have a code of signals which would direct the play rapidly and unerringly at such a time.

On the other hand, there is, perhaps, more danger that the opposing team may notice and soon learn to understand signs than when spoken signals are used, for it is necessary that each man on the side shall look at the quarter-back or captain at the time when he gives the signal (usually this will be when the men are lining up) and this will of necessity attract more or less attention to what is expressly desired to cover up. Every team would do well, however, to have a complete system of sign signals, which they can use at critical times in case of emergency.

The following extract from a code once in operation will furnish suggestions which will enable any ingenious captain to devise a practical set: Pull up trousers on right side – RH between C and RG. Pull up trousers on left side – LH between C and LG. Right hand on right thigh – RH between RG and RT. Right hand on left thigh – RH between LG and LT. Right hand on right knee – RH between RT and RE. Right hand on left knee – RH between LT and LE. Right hand on collar on right side – RH around RE. Right hand on collar on left side – RH around LE. Right hand on chin – RT around between LG and LT. Right hand on right hip – RE around the LE. Pull on jacket lacings – kick down the field.

Similar motions with the left hand will direct corresponding plays in the opposite direction. The motions should be made so naturally that they will not attract attention, but in deciding upon movements care should be taken not to select those which will be used involuntarily, lest signals be given sometimes without intention.

In the system of word signals peculiar expressions, such as "Brace up now," "Now brace," "Hold your men hard," "Tear up this line," "We must do better now," and the like, introduced by the captain with a few offhand sentences before each play, direct the next movement. Again, speaking to the left tackle may indicate that the left half-back is to run around the right end, each man being made to indicate a different evolution; and a word of encouragement or blame thus be made the signal for the next play.

Perhaps the system of signaling by numbers is most simple and satisfactory, for it admits of a great variety of combinations, and the key will not be readily detected. Sometimes a long sequence of numbers are called out, the signal being conveyed by the first two or three, and the others being added merely to mystify the opposing side, but a combination of three numbers is rather preferable.

A very simple code may be arranged, in which each opening is given a number, and each player a number. The combination of two numbers, then, will indicate the man who is to receive the ball, and the opening through which he is to pass, while a third will be called for the sake of deception. For example: We will suppose that the openings in the line as they radiate from the center, have been numbered 4, 6, 8 and 10, respectively, upon the right, and 5, 7, 9 and 11 upon the left, the center-rusher will be No. 1, RG will be 2, RT will be 4, RE will be 6, and RH will be 8, while on the left LH will be 3, LT will be 5, LE will be 7, and LH will be 9, with FB 11. We will further suppose that but three numbers are to be given each time; that the first number called will mean nothing; the second number called will indicate the player who is to receive the ball; and the third number the opening through which he is to pass.

To illustrate: The captain calls "9, 5, 8!" The 9 means nothing. The second number indicates the player who is to receive the ball, which in the present instance is No. 5, the left tackle. The third number shows the opening through which he is to pass – in this case No. 8, and hence between RT and RE. The interpretation of the signal, then, is that LT is to receive the ball, pass around the center, and dash into the line between RT and RE (see diagram nineteen). Thus any combination desired may be effected.

If, after a time, the opposing team discovers the signal for one or more of the plays, the entire system may be changed by simply informing the team by a peculiar signal, previously arranged, that the first number will thereafter indicate the opening, while the third will indicate the player who is to take the ball. The three numbers admit of six different arrangements, and the team should be drilled upon at least three of them until they can execute the plays with equal readiness under each arrangement.

In more difficult systems each play is given a separate number, which number may be called out either first, second, or third, as determined. Again, letting each play be indicated by a particular number, as before, the *sum* of the last two numbers is taken to make the number desired. This latter system, though, perhaps, a little more difficult, will prove the most satisfactory.

If two numbers are to be added together, the captain will do well to make one of them quite small, and call the larger number of the two first, for the addition will be performed by all much quicker and with less effort. During the first of the season it will be well to use one particular number to represent a play, and when these have been thoroughly learned it will be but a comparatively easy matter to change to the sum of any two.

When the number for the play has reached twenty, it may make the signals easier to have all the numbers between twenty and thirty indicate a certain other play; all the numbers between thirty and forty, another; and so on.

As the kick is a frequent play, and as it is nearly always apparent, it may be well to have two numbers, either one of which will be the signal for a kick down the field.

Enough has now been said to suggest how a practical system of signals may be devised.

AXIOMS

Line up quickly the moment the ball is down and play a dashing game from start to finish.

Never under any circumstances talk about your hurts and bruises. If you are unable to play, or have a severe strain, tell the captain at once. He will always release you.

When thrown hard always get up as if not hurt in the slightest. You will be thrown twice as hard next time if you appear to be easily hurt by a fall.

When coached upon the field never under any circumstances answer back or make any excuses. Do as nearly as possible exactly what you are told

Always throw your man hard, and toward his own goal, when you tackle him.

Never converse with an opponent during the game, but wait until the game is over for the exchange of civilities.

If you miss a tackle turn right around and follow the man at utmost speed; some one else may block him just long enough for you to catch him from behind.

Never play a "slugging game"; it interferes with good football playing.

Try to make a touch-down during the first two minutes of the game, before the opponents have become fairly waked up.

Play a *fast* game; let one play come after the next in rapid succession without any waits or delays. The more rapidly you play, the more effective it will be. Therefore *line up quickly* and get back to your regular place instantly after making a run.

When thrown, allow yourself to fall limp, with legs straight, and then you will not get hurt. Do not try to save yourself by putting out a hand or arm; it may be sprained or broken. If you are flat on the ground you cannot be hurt, no matter how many pile on top of you.

Always tackle low. The region between the knees and waist is the place to be aimed at. When preparing to tackle, keep your eyes on the runner's hips, for they are the least changeable part of the body.

Lift the runner off his feet and throw him toward his own goal. When not near enough to do this, spring through the air and hit him as hard as possible with the shoulder; at the same time grip him with the arms and drag him down. Always put the head down in doing this and throw the weight forward quickly and hard. Crawl up on the runner when he falls and take the ball away if possible; at least prevent its being passed.

When the runner is in a mass, or wedge, drive in and lift his legs out from under him, or fall down in front of him.

If the runner's feet are held, push back on his chest and make him fall toward his own goal.

Don't wait for the runner to meet you; meet the runner.

Always have a hand in the tackle. Don't "think" the runner is stopped; make sure of it.

Follow your own runners hard; you may have a chance to assist him, or block off for him. Always be in readiness to receive the ball from the runner when he is tackled.

Fall on the ball always in a scrimmage or when surrounded by opponents. When the ball is kicked behind your own goal, or across the side line, do not fall on it until it stops unless there is danger of the opponents being put on side.

Put your head down when going through the line and dive in with your whole weight.

Call "down" loudly, but not until it is impossible to make further advances.

Squeeze the ball tightly when tackled, or when going through the line.

Never under any circumstances give up because the other side seems to be superior. They may weaken at any moment, or a valuable player be ruled off or temporarily disabled. Let each man encourage the others on the team by monosyllables and keep up a "team enthusiasm."

Be the first man down the field on a kick.

Block your men hard when the opponents have the ball.

Tear up the line, break through and stop every kick that is made.

Never take your eyes off the ball after the signal has been given, if you are a man behind the line.

Do not be contented with a superficial reading on football, but *study* it carefully, if you would master it.

RULES ADOPTED
By The
AMERICAN INTERCOLLEGIATE FOOTBALL
ASSOCIATION For 1893

(Copyrighted and printed by permission of A.G. Spaulding & Bros.)

Note: The ball adopted and used by the American Intercollegiate Association is the "Spaulding J." ball.

Rule 1. (a) A drop-kick is made by letting the ball fall from the hands and kicking it at the very instant it rises.

(b) A place-kick is made by kicking the ball after it has been placed on the ground.

(c) A punt is made by letting the ball fall from the hands and kicking it before it touches the ground.

(d) Kick-off is a place-kick from the center of the field of play, and cannot score a goal.

(e) Kick-out is a drop-kick, or place-kick, by a player of the side which has touched the ball down in their own goal, or into whose touch-in-goal the ball has gone, and cannot score a goal. (See Rules 32 and 34.)

(f) A free-kick is one where the opponents are restrained by rule.

Rule 2. (a) In touch means out of bounds.

(b) A fair is putting the ball in play from touch.

Rule 3. A foul is any violation of a rule.

Rule 4. (a) A touch-down is made when the ball is carried, kicked, or passed across the goal line and there held, either in goal or touch-in goal. The point where the touch-down scores, however, is not necessarily where the ball is carried across the line, but where the ball is fairly held or called "down."

(b) A safety is made when a player guarding his goal receives the ball from a player of his own side, either by a pass, kick, or a snap-back, and then touches it down behind his goal line, or when he himself carries the ball across his own goal line and touches it down, or when he puts the ball into his own touch-in goal, or when the ball, being kicked by one of his own side, bounds back from an opponent across the goal line and he then touches it down.

(c) A touch-back is made when a player touches the ball to the ground behind his own goal, the impetus which sent the ball across the line having been received from an opponent.

Rule 5. A punt-out is a punt made by a player of the side which has made a touch-down in their opponents' goal to another of his own side for a fair catch.

Rule 6. A goal may be obtained by kicking the ball in any way except a punt from the field of play (without touching the ground, or dress, or person of any player after the kick) over the cross-bar or post of opponents' goal.

Rule 7. A scrimmage takes place when the holder of the ball puts it down on the ground, and puts it in play by kicking or snapping it back.

Rule 8. A fair catch is made direct from a kick by one of the opponents, or from a punt-out by one of the same side, provided the catcher made a mark with his heel at the spot where he has made the catch, and no other of his side touch the ball. If the catcher, after making his mark, be deliberately thrown to the ground by an opponent, he shall be given five yards, unless this carries the ball across the goal line.

Rule 9. Charging is rushing forward to seize the ball or tackle a player.

Rule 10. Interference is using the hands or arms in any way to obstruct or hold a player who has not the ball. This does not apply to the man running with the ball.

Rule 11. The ball is dead:

I. When the holder has cried down, or when the referee has cried down, or when the umpire has called foul.

II. When a goal has been obtained.

III. When it has gone into touch, or touch-in-goal, except for punt-out.

IV. When a touch-down or safety has been made.

V. When a fair catch has been heeled. No play can be made while the ball is dead, except to put in play by rule.

Rule 12. The grounds must be 330 feet in length and 160 feet in width, with a goal place in the middle of each goal line, composed of two upright posts, exceeding 20 feet in height, and placed 18 feet 6 inches apart, with the cross-bar 10 feet from the ground.

Rule 13. The game shall be played by teams of eleven men each, and in case of a disqualified or injured player a substitute shall take his place. Nor shall the disqualified or injured player return to further participation in the game.

Amendment adopted at a special meeting of the Intercollegiate Association, 1893: "No member of a graduate department, nor a special student shall be allowed to play, nor any undergraduate who has registered or attended lectures or recitations at any other university or college nor by any undergraduate who is not pursuing a course requiring for a degree an attendance of at least three years."

Rule 14. There shall be an umpire and a referee. No man shall act as an umpire who is an alumnus of either of the competing colleges. The umpires shall be nominated and elected by the Advisory Committee. The referee shall be chosen by the two captains of the opposing teams in each game, except in case of disagreement, when the choice shall be referred to the Advisory Committee, whose decision shall be final. All the referees and umpires shall be permanently elected and assigned on or before the third Saturday in October in each year.

Rule 15. (a) The umpire is the judge for the players, and his decision is final regarding fouls and unfair tactics.

(b) The referee is the judge for the ball, and his decision is final in all points not covered by the umpire.

(c) Both umpire and referee shall use whistles to indicate cessation of play on fouls and downs. The referee shall use a stop-watch in timing the game.

(d) The umpire shall permit no coaching, either by substitutes, coaches, or any one inside the ropes. If such coaching occur he shall warn the offender, and upon the second offense must have him sent behind the ropes for the remainder of the game.

Rule 16. (a) The time of a game is an hour and a half, each side playing forty-five minutes from each goal. There shall be ten minutes' intermission between the two halves. The game shall be decided by the score of even halves. Either side refusing to play after ordered to by the referee, shall forfeit the game. This shall also apply to refusing to commence the game when ordered to by the referee. The referee shall notify the captains of the time remaining, not more than ten, nor less than five, minutes from the end of each half.

(b) Time shall not be called for the end of a three-quarter until the ball is dead; and in the case of try-at-goal from a touch-down the try shall be allowed. Time shall be taken out while the ball is being brought out, either for a try, kick-out, or kick-off.

Rule 17. No one wearing projecting nails or iron plates on his shoes, or any metal substance upon his person, shall be allowed to play in a match. No sticky or greasy substance shall be used on the person of players.

Rule 18. The ball goes into touch when it crosses the side line, or when the holder puts part of either foot across or on that line. The touch line is in touch, and the goal line in goal.

Rule 19. The captains shall toss up before the commencement of the match, and the winner of the toss shall have his choice of goal or of kick-off. The same side shall not kick off in two successive halves.

Rule 20. The ball shall be kicked off at the beginning of each half; and whenever a goal has been obtained, the side which has lost it shall kick off. (See Rules 32 and 34.)

Rule 21. A player who has made and claimed a fair catch shall take a drop-kick, or a punt, or place the ball for a place-kick. The opponents may come up to the catcher's mark, and the ball must be kicked from some spot behind that mark on a parallel to touch line.

Rule 22. The side which has a free-kick must be behind the ball when it is kicked. At kick-off the opposite side must stand at least ten yards in front of the ball until it is kicked.

Rule 23. Charging is lawful for opponents if a punter advances beyond his line, or in case of a place-kick, immediately the ball is put in play by touching the ground. In case of a punt-out, not till ball is kicked.

Rule 24. (a) A player is put off side, if, during a scrimmage he gets in front of the ball, or if the ball has been last touched by his own side behind him. It is impossible for a player to be off side in his own goal. No player when off side shall touch the ball, or interrupt, or obstruct opponent will his hands or arms until again on side.

(b) A player being off side is put on side when the ball has touched an opponent, or when one of his own side has run in front of him, either with the ball, or having touched it when behind him.

(c) If a player when off side touches the ball inside the opponents' five-yard line, the ball shall go as a touch-back to the opponents.

Rule 25. No player shall lay his hands upon, or interfere by use of hands or arms, with an opponent, unless he has the ball. The side which has the ball can only interfere with the body. The side which has not the ball can use the hands and arms, as heretofore.

Rule 26. (a) A foul shall be granted for intentional delay of game, off side play, or holding an opponent, unless he has the ball. No delay arising from any cause whatsoever shall continue more then five minutes.

(b) The penalty for fouls and violation of rules, except otherwise provided, shall be a down for the other side; or, if the side making the foul has not the ball, five yards to the opponents.

Rule 27. (a) A player shall be disqualified for unnecessary roughness, hacking or striking with closed fist.

(b) For the offenses of throttling, tripping up or intentional tackling below the knees, the opponents shall receive twenty-five yards, or a free-kick, at their option. In case, however, the twenty-five yards would carry the ball across the goal line they can have half the distance from the spot of the offense to the goal line, and shall not be allowed a free-kick.

Rule 28. A player may throw or pass the ball in any direction except towards opponents' goal. If the ball be batted in any direction or thrown forward it shall go down on the spot to opponents.

Rule 29. If a player when off side interferes with an opponent trying for a fair catch, by touching him or the ball, or waving his hat or hands, the opponent may have a free-kick, or down, where the interference occurred.

Rule 30. (a) If a player having the ball be tackled and the ball fairly held, the man so tackling shall cry "held," the one so tackled must cry "down," and some player of his side put it down for a scrimmage. The snapper back and the man opposite him cannot pick out the ball with the hand until it touch a third man; nor can the opponents interfere with the snapper-back by touching the ball until it is actually put in play. Infringement of this nature shall give the side having the ball five yards at every such offense. The snapper-back is entitled to full and undisturbed possession of the ball. If the snapper-back be off side in the act of snapping back, the ball must be snapped again; and if this occurs three times on the same down, the ball goes to opponents. The man who first receives the ball, when snapped back from a down, or thrown back from a fair, shall not carry the ball forward under any circumstances whatever. If, in three consecutive fairs and downs, unless the ball cross the goal line, a team shall not have advanced the ball five or taken it back twenty yards, if shall go to the opponents on spot of fourth. "Consecutive" means without leaving the hands of the side holding it, and by a kick giving opponents fair and equal chance of gaining possession of it. When the referee, or umpire, has given a side five yards, the following down shall be counted the first down.

(b) The man who puts the ball in play in a scrimmage cannot pick it up until it has touched some third man. "Third man" means any other player than the one putting the ball in play and the man opposite him.

Rule 31. If the ball goes into touch, whether it bounds back or not, a player on the side which touches it down must bring it to the spot where the line was crossed, and there either

I. Bound the ball in the field of play or touch it in with both hands at right angles to the touch line and then run with it, kick it, or throw it back; or

II. Throw it out at right angles to the touch line; or

III. Walk out with it at right angles to touch line any distance not less than five nor more than fifteen yards, and there put it down, first declaring how far he intends walking. The man who puts the ball in must face field or opponents' goal, and he alone can have his foot outside touch line. Any one except him who puts his hands or feet between the ball and his opponents' goal is off side. If it be not thrown out at right angles either side may claim it thrown over again, and if it fail to be put in fairly in three trials it shall go to the opponents.

Rule 32. A side which has made a touchdown in their opponents' goal *must* try at goal, either by a place-kick or a punt-out. If the goal be missed the ball shall go as a kick-off at the center of the field to the defenders of the goal.

Rule 33. (a) If the try be by place-kick, a player of the side which has touched the ball down shall bring it up to the goal line, and, making a mark opposite the spot where it was touched down, bring it out at right angles to the goal line such distance as he thinks proper, and there place it for another of his side to kick. The opponents must remain behind their goal line until the ball has been placed on the ground.

(b) The placer in a try-at-goal may be off side or in touch without vitiating the kick.

Rule 34. If the try be by a punt-out the punter shall bring the ball up to the goal line, and, making a mark opposite the spot where it was touched down, punt out from any spot behind line of goal and not nearer the goal post than such mark, to another of his side, all of whom must stand outside of goal line not less than fifteen feet. If the touchdown was made in touch-in-goal the punt-out shall be made from the intersection of the goal and touch lines. The opponents may line up anywhere on the goal line except space of five feet on each side of punter's mark, but cannot interfere with punter, nor can he touch the ball after kicking it until it touch some other player. If a fair catch be made from a punt-out the mark shall serve to determine positions as the mark of any fair catch. If a fair catch be not made on the first attempt the ball shall be punted over again, and if a fair catch be not made on the second attempt the ball shall go as a kick-off at the center of the field to the defenders of the goal.

Rule 35. A side which has made a touch back or a safety must kick out, except as otherwise provided (see rule 32), from not more than twenty-five yards outside the kicker's goal. If the ball go into touch before striking a player it must be kicked out again, and if this occurs three times in succession it shall be given to opponents as in touch on twenty-five-yard line on side where it went out. At kick-out opponents must be on twenty-five-yard line or nearer their own goal.

Rule 36. The following shall be the value of each point in the scoring:

Goal obtained by touchdown - 6
Goal from field kick - 5
Touchdown failing goal - 4
Safety by opponents - 2

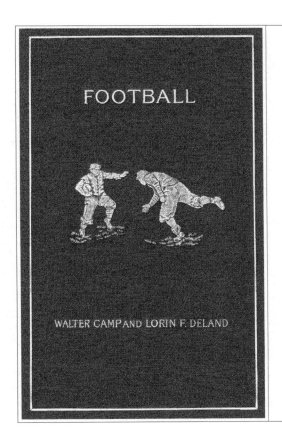

FOOTBALL

BY

WALTER CAMP AND LORIN F. DELAND

BOSTON AND NEW YORK
HOUGHTON, MIFFLIN AND COMPANY
The Riverside Press, Cambridge
1896

PREFACE

In the treatment of the many questions considered in these pages, it has not been possible to lay down arbitrary lines, or to give unqualified advice. The wider knowledge which has come with the development of the modern game has greatly multiplied the possibilities of every situation. Rarely can any question be now answered by the categorical imperative.

The difficulty is further increased in this volume by the constant necessity of discriminating between different grades of players. The conditions which exist with a 'Varsity team are not present in the team of a preparatory school. The argument for the one is not the argument for the other. The advice must be constantly qualified.

This volume is published in the hope that it may aid in the development of American football, and more especially that it may encourage a scientific study of the game. The great popularity of this sport is not without its reasonable warrant. It calls out not merely the qualities which make the soldier, — bravery, endurance, obedience, self-control, — but equally that mental acumen which makes the successful man in any of the affairs of life — perception, discrimination, and judgment.

To the casual observer, football doubtless presents merely the spectacle of vigorous physical exercise. But a deeper insight will discover the steady development of those other qualities which make the complete man — quick determination, instant obedience, self-reliance, physical bravery. The great lesson of the game may be put into a single line: *it teaches that brains will always win over muscle!*

It is no drawback to the game that its object is a simple one; when you tell the spectator that each side is trying to reach the opponent's goal, you have stated all that need be said. It is similarly no drawback to its popularity that professional football is unknown in America.

But the great merit of this sport is its practically unlimited field of tactical development. The fascinating study of new movements and combinations is never exhausted. It is this tactical possibility which has elevated football in popular esteem above all other sports. The cause of its attractiveness has its parallel in war. No pages of war history are so interesting to the student as the stirring descriptions of battles in which, by superior direction, a comparatively small body of soldiers has routed a force of twice its strength.

It is on these high lines that the American game of football may be developed. It is in the hope that they may aid that development that the authors print this volume.

September, 1896.

The Atlantic Monthly   *September, 1896*

FOOTBALL
By Walter Camp and Lorin F. Deland
Illustrated with more than fifty sketches and diagrams

Mr. Walter Camp has been since 1880 the football coach at Yale University, and Mr. Lorin F. Deland has been for the last four years the coach of the Harvard University football players.

The present work is the result of their joint collaboration, and is unquestionably the most thorough and important treatise on the subject which has yet been written. It represents a labor of over a year by each of its authors. It is the first attempt to combine in one volume the football methods of Yale and Harvard.

Part I. is football as it is seen from the spectators' seats, and represents the game as the public regard it.

Part II. is the players' section, and gives all the information needed by the beginner. It treats the fundamentals of the game, of the play of the various positions, of the relationships between positions, of team play, and of training. There are chapters on blocking, breaking through, interfering for the runner, opening holes in the line, kicking, etc.

Part III. is the advanced science of the game. In this section are considered the problems of generalship, of field tactics, of development and method in team coaching. It is addressed "To the Coach," and is undoubtedly the ablest exposition of scientific football ever made.

With the book are numerous diagrams: a diagram of the general coaching system for the season, a diagram of the ordering of the game upon the field, half a dozen training diagrams, and over fifty diagrams of plays.

The book is very comprehensive and really exhausts the subject of one of the most enjoyable of American sports which in addition to the element of skill in the player, has all the tactical possibilities of war.

The illustrations have been carefully drawn, and will be found a decided help both to the spectator and the player.

TABLE OF CONTENTS

PART I

CHAPTER I
THE HISTORY OF FOOTBALL,
WITH A BRIEF DESCRIPTION OF THE VARIOUS GAMES

CHAPTER II
EXPLANATION OF THE GAME AS NOW PLAYED

CHAPTER III
FINER POINTS OF THE PLAY LIKELY TO BE OVERLOOKED

CHAPTER IV
HOW TO WATCH A GAME

CHAPTER V
EFFECTS OF THE GAME ON THE PLAYERS

CHAPTER VI
EXPLANATION OF TECHNICAL WORDS AND PHRASES, SLANG TERMS AND COINED EXPRESSIONS OF COLLEGE FOOTBALL

CHAPTER VII
TWENTY YEARS OF FOOTBALL

CHAPTER VIII
TWENTY-FOUR HOURS WITH A 'VARSITY PLAYER

PART II

CHAPTER I
ORGANIZING A TEAM

CHAPTER II
TRAINING A TEAM WITHOUT A SECOND ELEVEN

CHAPTER III
INDIVIDUAL POSITIONS

CHAPTER IV
RELATIONSHIPS OF THE POSITIONS

CHAPTER V
BLOCKING

CHAPTER VI
BREAKING THROUGH

CHAPTER VII
OPENING HOLES IN THE LINE

CHAPTER VIII
INTERFERING FOR THE RUNNER

CHAPTER IX
KICKING

CHAPTER X
TEAM PLAY

CHAPTER XI
ON THE USE OF TRICKS IN FOOTBALL

CHAPTER XII
HOW TO CONSTRUCT PLAYS

CHAPTER XIII
FOOTBALL DON'TS

PART III

CHAPTER I
GENERAL SYSTEM OF COACHING

CHAPTER II
ACCESSORIES OF COACHING

CHAPTER III
CHOOSING THE TEAM

CHAPTER IV
THE POLICY FOR THE SEASON

CHAPTER V
TESTING THE DEVELOPMENT

CHAPTER VI
FIELD TACTICS

CHAPTER VII
ON THE EVE OF THE BATTLE

CHAPTER VIII
THE MORAL FACTORS IN AN IMPORTANT GAME

CHAPTER IX
IMPROVED SIGNALING

CHAPTER X
TRAINING

CHAPTER XI
SUGGESTIONS OF POSSIBLE FAKES AND BLUFFS:
HOW AND WHERE THEY MAY BE EMPLOYED

CHAPTER XII
WHEN ACTING AS AN OFFICIAL

CHAPTER XIII
DIAGRAMS OF PLAYS

CHAPTER XIV
RULES OF THE SEASON OF 1896

PART I

FOR THE SPECTATOR

CHAPTER I

THE HISTORY OF FOOTBALL,
WITH A BRIEF DESCRIPTION OF THE VARIOUS GAMES

Ancient Origin of the Game. It is impossible to state exactly at what time the game of football originated. Even the Greeks and Romans had a sport which consisted in kicking about some kind of an object under certain general rules, and this may be taken, in a wide sense, to have been the forerunner of the present game.

In English twelfth-century literature mention is made on several occasions of a sport which was known by the name of football, and was played with great enthusiasm by the lower classes. Shakespeare, in his writings, also speaks of football, classing it as a low form of amusement.

Crude Forms of the Early Sport. According to contemporaneous accounts of this game, the object of each side was to carry or kick a ball over a certain mark taken as the opponents' goal line, and at the same time prevent such a score from being made against themselves. The distances between these goals were generally very long, even reaching two or three miles at times, and extending from one village to another. A French writer who paid a visit to England in the seventeenth century describes the game as follows: — "*En hiver le football est un exercice utile et charmant. C'est un ballon de cuir, gros comme la tête et rempli de vent; cela se ballotte avec le pied dans les mes par celui qui le peut attraper; il n'y a point d'autre science.*" The description given in the last words of this extract is hardly in keeping with the statement that football was "charmant" and "utile." From the fact that it contained very little science and was played solely by the lower classes of the people, it is fair to assume that it was very rough, if not actually brutal. This supposition is further confirmed by the fact that numerous laws were passed, at intervals, imposing a heavy sentence upon any one who played or witnessed a game of football.

Growth and Popularity. In spite of these hindrances the game retained its popularity through several centuries, as a sport for the men rather than the boys, of the lower classes. The triumph of Puritanism was a serious check, however, and in the eighteenth century the enthusiasm waned considerably. When the sport was again taken up, it found favor among the younger rather than the older members of the community, and at the opening of the present century the public school boys were beginning to adopt it as a pastime in spite of considerable opposition from the parents of the better class, who did not like to have their boys engage in such a rough game at the peril of their clothes and limbs.

The Game in the Public Schools. Each of the public schools, in adopting this game, which as yet was governed by no fixed code of laws, was obliged to form its own rules and regulations, which to a large extent were demanded by the size and nature of the grounds and other local considerations. It was, for instance, at Rugby alone that the playground was large enough to allow the running and tackling game to be played. At Charterhouse and Westminster there were no places suitable for this style of play, so the "dribbling" game was introduced. The players were not allowed to touch the ball with their hands, but made progress through kicking alone. The art of rolling the ball along the ground by gentle kicks from the toe or shin as a player was running was called "dribbling," and it was in this way possible for experts to dodge opponents by quick turns to the right or left, and to gain much ground towards the desired goal without losing the ball. At Harrow the conditions were suitable for kicking and fair catching, but the players were not allowed to run with the ball or to collar each other. The Eton schoolboys introduced kicking to some extent on their rather limited field, and invented the "wall game," which is very unique and peculiar, adapted and confined to that school.

These various games developed gradually, each governed largely by the local requirements and resources; and in the beginning of the present century they could be divided roughly into two classes: the first of these was known as the "dribbling" game, and the latter as "Rugby," being the same that was played at that school. In the former it was not lawful to touch the ball with the hands, or to trip or tackle an opponent, but ground was gained in the proper direction by kicking and dribbling alone; while the principal feature of the latter, which was played at Rugby, was the "scrummage,"— which will be fully described later on, — and running with the ball and tackling were both allowed. Neither game was free from objectionable features, and players were always exposed to more or less serious injuries. The size of the field of play and the number of participants on the two sides were not defined in any respect. The readers of "Tom Brown at Rugby" will remember the vivid, though somewhat exaggerated, description of the Rugby game, as given by East to the new arrival at the school, and how it was a fixed custom for the sixth form boys to play against all the rest of the school. The methods of prohibiting rough play and of giving a high value to science and skill were discovered very slowly, and are not yet wholly attained.

Athletic Revival, 1850-1860. During the years 1850 to 1860 there was a decided revival of all athletic sports in the public schools of England, and football became the most popular game for the winter months. This was immediately followed by the formation of clubs through the efforts of old school players, in the universities and large towns, where the dribbling game was adopted more generally than the Rugby, but was played entirely under local rules. The first steps towards a joint football organization were taken in 1863, when a number of the London Rugby clubs attempted to draw up a uniform code of laws which should be acceptable to all parties. In the mean time, the more enthusiastic followers of the dribbling game had come to an agreement over their rules, and formed themselves into the "Football Association." A joint conference was next held between the Rugbeians and the Dribblers, for the purpose of effecting a compromise upon the points in which the two games differed. This step was, however, found to be impossible, as the principles of the two games were essentially different, and the Dribblers, though greater in numbers and advocating the more popular form of the game, were not strong enough to carry their points over the obstinate and persistent followers of the Rugby game.

During the next ten years the Rugby game greatly increased in popularity, and finally, in 1871, the principal London clubs united in forming the "Rugby

Football Union." Rules were adopted which tended to eliminate the more objectionable features of hacking and tripping, and to introduce more skill and science; otherwise the game remained essentially the same as had been played for a number of years at Rugby schools.

Association and Rugby Separation. From this point the two games, known as Association and Rugby, have drifted further and further apart, and have been adopted with more or less enthusiasm in all parts of Great Britain. There seems to be no danger of either one ever driving the other out of the country, and it is almost impossible to explain why their comparative popularity should vary as it does in the different sections of the country.

Development of Rugby. As the Rugby game is that from which our American Intercollegiate was derived, it is of interest to follow this branch closely and note the familiar points. In the original Rugby Union Rules, no provision was made for the size of the field or the number of men who should constitute a side. The fields probably varied very much in both length and breadth; but the most convenient dimensions were found to be 110 yards in length and 75 yards in breadth, while the number of players was usually twenty on a side. At each end of the field were erected goals, consisting of two upright posts 18 feet and 6 inches apart, joined together by a horizontal bar 10 feet from the ground. A goal could be obtained by either a "drop-kick," performed by letting the ball fall from the hands and kicking the instant it rose, or a "place-kick," when the ball was held in the proper position on the ground by one player, and then kicked by another. The only other form of kick was a "punt," in performing which the ball was kicked immediately after leaving the hands while still in the air.

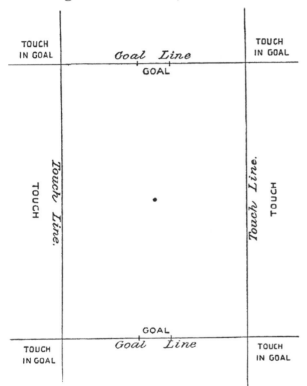

Diagram A. — Rugby Union Game.

The game was opened by a "kick-off," the captains having previously "tossed up" to see which side should have this privilege or the choice of goals. A man of the side choosing the kick-off then took a place-kick from the centre of the field, the members of his own side standing behind the ball, and of the opposing side at a distance of ten yards. Such a kick could not count as a goal. A player obtaining the ball after such a kick could kick or run, as he deemed most expedient, in order to make progress in the desired direction. If he chose the latter play his opponents were free to tackle him, and thus try to bring him to a standstill. When once fairly "held," the runner was obliged to cry "down," and place the ball on the ground for a scrummage. A scrummage was defined as taking place "when the holder of the ball, being in the field of play, puts it down on the ground in front of him, and all who have closed around on their respective sides endeavor to push their opponents back, and, by kicking the ball, to drive it in the direction of the opposite goal line." This was really the most prominent feature of the game, and was of very uncertain outcome. Not all the men of a side would take part, but a few stood behind on either side in order to capture the ball, if it should happen to roll or be kicked out, and then either make a pass to some other player, or try a run in person. At other times this mass of struggling, kicking players might move slowly down the field, or sway back and forth for several minutes before being broken up, or some lucky man might force his way through with the ball before him, and dribble it successfully for a considerable distance. If a player, in such ways as above described, could carry the ball at any point over his opponents' goal line, and there touch it down, his side was entitled to a "try" at goal, to be made by a place-kick from a point in the field of play either opposite to that point behind the goal where the ball was touched down, or at a point marked by a fair catch of a punt by a member of his own side from a point on the goal line opposite to the point at which the ball was touched down. A goal could also be obtained at any time in the game when a player had succeeded in approaching near enough to send the ball between the posts and over the bar by a quick drop-kick. This act was, however, very difficult to perform, as the opponents were very apt to block the kick, or interfere in such a way as to effectually spoil the kicker's aim. A quick and accurate drop kicker was a valuable man on any team, and the science of drop kicking was studied by all ambitious players.

Previous to the adoption of the Rugby Union rules, matches were decided by a majority of goals alone, tries being entirely disregarded; but after 1871, in case no goals were scored by either side, or an equal number by each side, the match was won by the team scoring the majority of tries, rather than count as a draw game. After a goal had been scored the game was recommenced by a kick-off at the centre of the field by the side losing the goal.

The Principal Rules. The principal features of the original Rugby Union game have thus been described. It now remains to speak of certain rules which, to a casual observer, would not seem to be of serious importance, but which are the key to the success of the game. If a player entered a scrummage from his opponents' side (i.e., facing the goal which he was defending), or got in front of the ball, either in a scrummage or in open play when the ball had been kicked, touched, or was being run with by any of his own side behind him (i.e., between himself and his goal), he was declared "off-side." No player when off-side could touch the ball or a player, or in any way interfere with the progress of the game. He was, however, put "on-side" again when one of his own side had run in front of him (i.e., had passed to a point between him and his opponents' goal), either with the ball, or having kicked it when behind him, or when the ball had touched the dress or person of any player on the opposite side. This rule appears at first very complicated and not altogether necessary; but when the principle was once mastered by a player, it was readily put into practice, and the referee of a game was obliged to enforce it strictly.

In case a player, while running with the ball, should allow any part of his person to pass out of bounds (or "into touch," as the technical expression has it), he must return to the spot where he crossed the line, and he himself or any player of his own side must put the ball in play (1) by bounding it on the ground; (2) by passing it out at right angles to the touch line; or (3) by carrying it out at right angles to the touch line any distance not less than five nor more than fifteen yards, and then putting it down for a scrummage, first stating how far he intended to walk out. If the ball rolled or was kicked out of bounds, the first player touching it down could put it in play in the manner just described.

A "fair catch" was made by a player who caught the ball from a kick, and in so doing made a mark on the ground with his heel. Such player was then privileged to make a drop-kick, punt, or to hold the ball for a place-kick, at a convenient point behind his mark, at which the opponents were allowed to take their position. As soon as the ball touched the ground, or was kicked, the opponents were free to "charge," i.e., rush forward to tackle the man with the ball, or stop the kick.

Furthermore, no player could deliberately hit the ball with his hand, or throw it forward (i.e., in the direction of his opponents' goal). No hacking or tripping was allowed, nor were players permitted to wear projecting nails, iron plates, or gutta-percha on any part of the boots or shoes. The time of the game was divided into two parts. During the intermission the two teams changed goals, and the kick-off at the opening of the second half was made by the side not having the kick-off at the commencement of the game.

The decision of disputes could be made by umpires chosen by the captains of the contesting teams, though the presence of these arbiters was not a fixed custom, but any question as to the interpretation of the rules was referred to the Rugby Union Committee.

Development to the Present Day. The development of the game from the adoption of the Rugby Union rules to the present day can be divided into three general periods: (1) tight scrummage and heavy forwards; (2) loose scrummage; (3) introduction of quick and frequent passing.

It will be noticed from the rules above described that the forwards were bound to become entangled in the scrummage and so not be ready, in the event of the ball rolling out, to follow up the play with much activity. On the contrary, the requisites of a forward were weight and force. He should be a good scrummager and nothing else. In entering a scrummage, he should keep his eye on the ball, and try to push it towards his opponents' goal, advancing it by gentle kicks from the toe or shins. The team whose forwards were best able to "shove" was thus at a premium. In case a side failed in shoving, it was evidently advantageous for them to allow the ball to be kicked out into the hands of one of their "behinds," who thus would have an opportunity to gain ground in a run. The principle of "heeling out" the ball by a gentle backward kick would here be expedient, but for some reason or other a strong prejudice has always been felt against this mode of play as being mean and tricky. It was, however, perfectly legitimate for a forward to open his legs, and allow the ball by accident to be kicked between them.

It was soon appreciated that much time and strength was uselessly spent by the forwards in these aimless shoving matches. The greater part of the tackling and defensive work as well as the offensive work in kicking and running fell upon the behinds. The play was entirely individual, and contained almost no science.

The first step towards an improvement was taken in 1877, when at the request of Scotland the number of men on a team was reduced from twenty to fifteen. The positions of the players were generally assigned as follows: ten forwards, two half-backs, and three backs. The half-backs were intended to hold a position close to the scrummage, and capture the ball if possible, when it rolled out, or to fall upon an opponent who might capture it, while the backs were the ground gainers and kickers. With this diminution in the numbers a more open style of game naturally followed, and the forwards were chosen for activity in leaving the scrummage and falling upon the opposing half-backs. For this reason these players were obliged to pick up the ball, and pass it with extreme quickness, and some of the best players were able to combine the two motions into one scoop. The advantages of dribbling were gradually felt to be important, and the forwards were required to be proficient in this respect also.

The Oxford Team and Short Passing. The Oxford team of 1882 was the first one to develop the art of passing to any great extent, and as a result were victorious over the best clubs in the country during three successive seasons. The behinds would station themselves at intervals across the field a short distance behind the scrummage, and by a series of quick short passes, the ball could be advanced to the end man, who then found a clear field for some distance before him. A few teams have since then successfully combined the two feats of passing and dribbling, and attained to a remarkable degree of skillfulness. These principles of the game are still discussed by captains, and the question has not yet been answered as to how far such tactics can be carried with expediency. The assignment of the fifteen players has undergone several changes. The position of three-quarter-back has been developed, and the number of forwards reduced to eight or nine men. Some teams play with three three-quarters, and others with four, while one full back is considered sufficient. He is a purely defensive player, and must be a sure tackler and accurate kicker. The three-quarter-backs have most of the active and prominent work to do, running, tackling, and kicking.

Rules, Ruling, and Scoring. With the gradual development of the Rugby game from a school pastime to the present stage of the sport, many rules have been adopted from year to year, calculated to remedy, as far as possible, all visible defects. In 1892 the code of Union laws became so confused and complicated, owing to these frequent amendments, that an entirely new set of rules was drawn up. According to this code the ball is required to be 11 to 11¼ inches in length, 30 to 31 inches in length circumference, 25½ to 26 inches in width circumference, and 13 to 14¼ ounces in weight. All games must be played with a referee and two touch judges, — the former to enforce the rules, the latter to render decisions regarding out of bounds. Matches are decided by a majority of points, the following being the mode of scoring: try, 2 points; penalty goal, given by referee owing to unfair play of opponents, 3 points; goal from a try (in which case the try does not count), 5 points; any other goal, 4 points. In regard to eligibility of players, the following rule has been enacted: "It is illegal for any member of any club in England in membership with this Union (a) to take part in any match or contest where gate money is taken, unless it is agreed that not less than fifteen players on each side take part in a match; (b) to play between May 1 and August 31, both dates inclusive, in any football contest, either for charity or otherwise, where gate money is taken."

The Association Game. The Association game, although not so important to students of the American game, is worthy of study as a contemporaneous sport. As already noted, it was established under regularly drawn up rules in 1863. It was not, however, more than a school pastime till 1872, when the international matches and cup ties were established. During its entire history the sport has demanded very skillful and careful playing, but the advantages of combined action and frequent passing were not appreciated till the middle of the seventies. The general method of play was for a certain number of the men to endeavor, by clever individual dribbling, to advance the ball down the field towards the opponents' goal, and then kick it through the posts. When combined action was introduced, the men were assigned to certain positions, and had certain duties to perform. The division of the eleven players at the present day is generally made as follows: five forwards, who engage themselves in the most active part of the play, and should be clever dribblers; three half-backs, one playing in the centre and one on either wing, who should always hold a position between their forwards and their goal; two backs, one on either wing, who are intended to receive any kicks beyond the half-backs, and return them; and one goal keeper. This player must remain close to the goal, and if possible prevent the ball from passing between the posts. He is the only player who is allowed to use his hands in stopping the ball, but may hold it only long enough to make his kick out of danger.

A peculiar knack which some players of this game have adopted is that of "heading" the ball as it descends from a high kick. In this way the sphere can be returned very quickly without taking the time of an ordinary kick.

As the forwards advance the ball towards the opponents' goal, they try to work it towards the centre of the field, so that the middle forward may kick it between the posts. Passing and combined action have been developed to a considerable degree by Association elevens, and form now the characteristics upon which the success of a team depends.

Rules regarding kick-off at commencement of the two halves and after a goal has been scored are the same as in the Rugby game, also those against intentional rough play, hacking, tripping, etc. When a ball goes out of

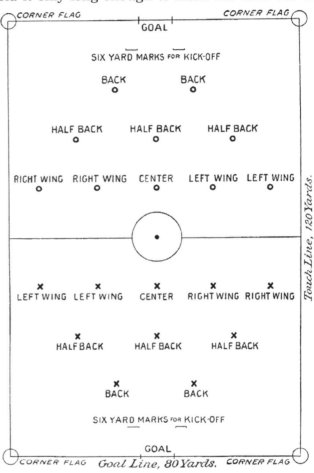

Diagram B. — Association Game.

bounds, it is thrown into the field of play by a player of the side which did not kick it out. This must be done with both hands, and can be in any direction.

The length of a field for the Association game should be between 100 and 200 yards, and the width between 50 and 100 yards. The goals are upright posts eight yards apart, with a bar across them eight feet from the ground. A goal is the only score that can be made, and is obtained when the ball is kicked between the posts and under the bar. The ball used is round, from twenty-seven to twenty-eight inches in circumference, and should weigh between thirteen and fifteen ounces.

Australian Football. In Australia, football is universally recognized as the national game, and at the present day the popularity of the sport is quite remarkable, single matches often attracting an audience of thirty thousand people.

A generation back the game was at the same stage of development as in England. Sydney and Melbourne were the leaders of this sport, as they are of everything else in Australia, and the former of these cities has always played the Rugby game, the necessary changes in the form of play being made in conjunction with those in England. But in Melbourne the general feeling has been that the English game was not fast enough, and as a result new rules were made and a very different form of sport, known as the "Victorian game," has been developed.

The field of play is from 150 to 200 yards long, and from 100 to 150 yards wide. The goal posts, being not less than 20 feet in height, are placed seven yards apart, and a goal is scored when the ball is kicked fairly between them at any height whatever. This is the only method of scoring, and hence constitutes the main object of the game. The ball is oval in shape, and 26 inches in circumference. The usual number of players composing a side is twenty, though more or less than this can be played if sufficient handicaps are allowed. The actual time of a match is one hour and forty minutes, and is divided into four parts, at the expiration of each of which the teams change goals. At the end of the second quarter the players rest ten minutes. These players have certain defined positions, and are supposed to remain in nearly the same locality during the entire game, the object being to advance the ball forward to the "goal sneak," who is an accurate kicker and should stand in front of the goal in order to accept any opportunity to score.

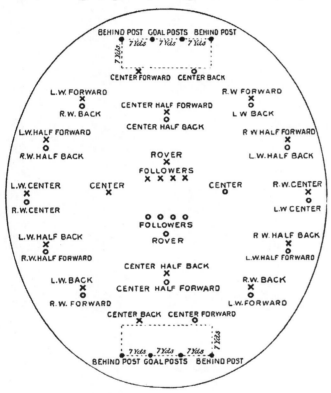

Diagram C. — Australian Game.

The ball can be advanced by kicking or running, provided in the latter case that the runner bounds it on the ground once in every seven yards. No tackling is allowed, but a runner is obliged to drop the ball as soon as he is touched by an opponent. "Shepherding," or protecting a player who is running with the ball from interference by opponents, is practiced to some extent, but if too many players thus are brought together into a tight mass the referee is bound to blow his whistle and stop the game. He then puts the ball in play by bounding it on the ground, this being also the method of opening a match and of bringing in the ball from out of bounds. The referee, in fact, has very wide privileges, and must follow the play very closely. He can at any moment, when he sees any unfair or even ungentlemanly conduct on the field, stop the game and again bound the ball into play. He also has opportunities to indulge in great partiality for either contesting side, but as no man can occupy this official position who is not licensed by the Football Association, he has, as it were, a reputation to uphold, if he desires to retain his office. The tendency in this game is to develop quick, open play, in which skill and science shall have more value than strength and weight.

In the development of this new game the example of Melbourne has been followed by all Victoria, South Australia, and Tasmania, while Queensland and New Zealand are loyal to the Rugby Union.

Canadian Football. Football is played to a considerable extent in Canada, where the various provinces play different games. For instance, in Halifax, Winnipeg, and Victoria, the English Rugby Union rules are adopted, while the Ontario, Quebec, and Canadian Unions play under their own rules.

The Canadian game is played by fifteen men on a side, on a field 110 yards long by 65 yards wide. The goals are the same as in the English Rugby game. At the kick-off, which opens a game, the ball must be kicked at least five yards and must not fall out of bounds. When a runner has been fairly tackled and held, the ball is placed dead upon the ground and the scrimmage[1] takes place. Any player of the side then having possession of the ball may put it in play by rolling it in any direction with his foot. In the mean time no opponent can interfere in this operation, which must take place immediately, or the side not offending may be awarded a free kick by the referee. This method of putting the ball in play is nothing but the unpopular custom in England of heeling out, which has been adopted as the simplest and quickest method of putting an end to the tiresome scrimmage. The ball when thus put in play may be picked up and passed to any other player for a run, kick, or any other play. It is unlawful to engage in any unnecessary rough play, or to knock or throw the ball forward (except when thrown in from touch) under penalty of disqualification or award of a free kick to the unoffending side.

The matches are decided by a majority of points which can be scored as follows: goal from a try, 6; from drop-kick, 5; from flying or free kick, by way of penalty, 2; from free kick, 4; a try without the goal, 4; safety touch, 2; and rouge, 1. "Safety touch" and "rouge" are the only points which need to be explained, the other terms having been already mentioned in descriptions of other games. Safety touch is similar to the American "safety," and a rouge is like the American "touch back," i.e., the former is a retreat from danger and performed by the side defending its goal, while the latter is merely the result of a kick by the opponents passing over the goal line without making a goal. The time of a regulation game is two halves of forty minutes each, an intermission of ten minutes being left between them.

Gaelic Football. Gaelic football, which has been played for several centuries as one of the most popular sports in Ireland, was known only traditionally to existing generations until November 1, 1884, when, as a result of the general revival of the national games, the Gaelic Athletic Association was formed at Thurles, County Tipperary. Four years later a delegation of athletes was sent to America, and in spite of setbacks at first, their efforts to establish clubs in the neighborhood of New York city were ultimately successful. Since then the game has penetrated to the west, and by 1893 the Gaelic Athletic Association of America included over a dozen clubs.

---

[1] The English word "scrummage" has been converted on this side of the ocean into "scrimmage."

This game is played on a comparatively large field, exceeding 140 yards in length and 84 yards in width. The goals, situated in the middle of the end boundary lines, consist of two upright posts twenty-one feet apart, joined by a cross-bar eight feet from the ground. On either side of these goals is erected another post at a distance of twenty-one feet. In order to score a goal, the ball, which is spherical in shape, must be kicked between the centre posts beneath the cross-bar. If it crosses the goal line between the outside posts, one point is counted, and in case the goals of a match are evenly scored by both contesting teams, a majority of these points decides the match.

The regular Gaelic football team of fifteen men is composed of the following players: one goal keeper; two full-backs; two half-backs; three centres; two wing centres; two forwards; two wing forwards; and one full forward. These men occupy relative positions on the field as indicated by their titles. The only allowable methods of advancing the ball are by kicking, striking, or "hopping." This latter trick is performed by a player who, as he runs, bounds the ball on the ground before him at least once in every three paces. The ball is put in play at the opening of the game and after the scoring of a goal, by the referee, who throws it in from the side, the men of the two sides having lined up opposite to each other, each one holding the hand of an opponent. When the ball strikes the ground, all drop hands and rush for it. From thence on there is no cessation in the play until a score is made, except when a foul occurs. If a player be detected in committing any unfair or unnecessarily rough action, the referee may either disqualify him or award a free kick to the other side, according to his own judgment.

A free kick is also awarded to a player making a fair catch, in which case the opponents are not allowed to approach nearer than fourteen yards to the

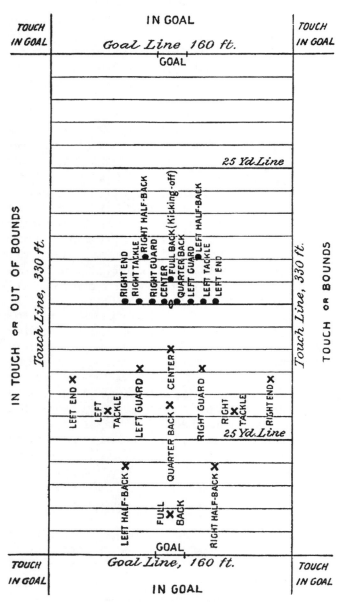

Diagram D. — American Intercollegiate Game.

"marked spot," and the kick can be made in any direction desired. When the ball passes over the goal line outside of all the posts, the goal keeper has a free kick, his opponents lining up at a distance of twenty-one yards from the line. When the ball goes out of bounds on the side of the field, it is thrown in any direction by the opposite side to that which last touched it in the field of play.

The play in a regular Gaelic match lasts during two half-hour halves, with an intermission of ten minutes, when the goals are changed, and is governed by two umpires and a referee. In case of disagreement between the former, the decision of the latter is final. The referee also keeps the time, and can call the game at any moment on account of darkness or unfair play. The validity of goals and points is decided by goal umpires, one at each end of the field.

This game as a whole is founded upon very simple principles, and is so full of action and life that it is very interesting, even to a spectator unacquainted with all the rules.

Thanksgiving Day Football of New England. The oldest phase of the game of football as known in the United States was when the inhabitants of New England, several generations ago, used to adjourn to the back yards of their houses, after the proper discussion of their Thanksgiving dinners, and the men of the party would amuse themselves by kicking about an inflated pig's bladder amid great joy and enthusiasm from their audiences. This innocent form of the game was, however, soon followed by the development of a crude and rough sport, which claimed some similarity to the English kicking or dribbling game. Rules, if they existed, were merely local, and knotty points had to be discussed and decisions made upon the field of play and at all times during the game. As such a pastime the game was played to some extent by the students at the various colleges.

Freshman-Sophomore Matches. At Yale an annual match between the Sophomores and Freshmen was a regularly instituted custom after 1840, the challenge and its acceptance being posted in a prominent place upon the door of Old Chapel. Such games, as described by eyewitnesses, were almost open riots, and resembled the more lately established annual rushes between these classes more than the modern form of football. The students fought with each other as much, if not more, than for the ball, which is described as "a round bladder ball inclosed in a leather case."

The challenge and acceptance for the last of these matches, between the classes of 1860 and 1861, read as follows: —

> "Sophomores, — The class of '61 hereby challenge the class of '60
> to a game of football, best two in three.
> In behalf of the   Class of '61."

The answer: —
> "Come!
> And like sacrifices in their trim,
> To the fire-eyed maid of smoky war,
> All hot and bleeding we will offer you."

> "To our youthful friends of the Class of '61, — We hereby accept
> your challenge to play the noble and time-honored game of football.
> In behalf of the   Class of '60."

After that year the faculty put a stop to these annual matches.

Quiescent Stage of American Game. During the following years, until 1870, football was practically dead at Yale. The class of '72, however, was very fond of all athletic sports, and participated especially in long hare and hound runs. The revival of football was due in a large measure to Mr. D.S. Schaff, formerly of Rugby School, who entered the class of '73, and succeeded in making the sport popular among his classmates, and eventually formed an association which sent challenges to the other classes. In 1871, four interclass matches were played upon a field at some distance from the college.

By this time other colleges had adopted the sport in the same crude manner, and some matches were played by them. In October, 1873, a convention was held at New York between Columbia, Princeton, Rutgers, and Yale, a set of rules was adopted, and thus was laid the foundation of the regular intercollegiate matches.

CHAPTER II

EXPLANATION OF THE GAME AS NOW PLAYED

Introduction. There are many persons unacquainted with the game of football who desire to so far comprehend the rules of the game as to be able to understand the general points of the play, and follow intelligently the operations on the field. They do not care to enter into a scientific study of the game, nor do they wish to be burdened with the minor details of the rules. They want merely to be told, as clearly and briefly as possible, the primary points of the play, leaving all technicalities to a later period, when their interest in the game may have advanced to the stage of enthusiasm.

There is, therefore, a legitimate demand for a brief, abridged explanation of the game as now played, which shall necessarily be inadequate, and in no way attempt to embody all features of the rules. The reader who wishes to gain a more complete knowledge upon the minor points in detail should refer to a later chapter, in which the rules of the present season are given.

The Field. Intercollegiate football, which this book will especially consider, is played on a field 330 feet long and 160 feet wide. The field is inclosed by a white border line, and whenever the ball goes outside of this boundary the play ceases until it is returned into the inclosure. The spectator will see, beside the boundary lines of the field, a large number of white lines crossing the field, each five yards apart. These lines are merely an aid to determine how far the ball is carried forward or backward.

The Ball. The ball is a rubber bladder, inclosed within a sack of pigskin; by means of a pump, the bladder is inflated with air up to the limit where it completely fills the pigskin sack, and when the pressure reaches a high point, the mouth of the bladder is securely tied, the pigskin tightly laced, and the ball is ready for use. It is then practically as hard as a block of wood, yet of almost no appreciable weight.

The Players. The game is played by two teams, of eleven men each. As the only object in the game is to advance the ball, these eleven men are placed in positions which experience has shown to best meet the varying needs of the situation, within the requirements of the rules. A forward line of seven men is made, and the ball is given to the centre man of this line. This line of seven men is called the rush line, and the centre man, to whom the ball is given, is called the centre rush, or the centre. The two men at the ends of the line are called the end rushers, or the ends. The two men located next the centre (one on each side) are called the guards, for the reason that they guard the centre each time the latter puts the ball in play. The two remaining men in the line, located respectively between each guard and each end, are called the tackles. The name is a purely arbitrary one, and not especially significant or well chosen, but it serves as a title by which the position may be designated. To the name guard, tackle, or end, we prefix the words "right" or "left," according as the man stands on the right or left of the centre-rush. The line, then, reading from left to right, would be as follows: left end, left tackle, left guard, centre, right guard, right tackle, right end. So much for the rush-line, or, as they are sometimes called, the forwards.

There are now four men of the eleven left, and they are assigned and named as follows: First, the man placed directly behind the centre is called the quarter-back. His business it is to receive the ball as the centre sends it back, and pass it to the player who is to attempt to carry or kick it forward. Behind the quarter-back, in a somewhat extended triangle, are three men known respectively as the left half-back, the right half-back, and the full-back. The full-back stands in the centre of the trio, and usually is the man who kicks the ball when a kick is desired.

The team occupies substantially these same relative positions, whether they are advancing the ball or opposing the advance of the other side. In the latter case, however, the full-back of the team, and possibly one other player, are located some distance behind the line, to secure the ball in case it should be suddenly kicked by the opposing team.

General Object in the Game. The object in the game is to advance the ball from the centre of the field, where it is started, until it can be touched to the ground beyond the boundary line at the end of the field. This is called a "touch-down."

The two teams line up for the game at the centre of the field; the captains of the teams have previously tossed a coin to see which captain shall have his choice between having the ball or deciding on which side of the field he prefers to play. The captain winning the toss may elect to take the side of the field which will bring his back to the sun, or give him the help of the wind; or he may elect to take first possession of the ball. Whichever he decides, the other team must take the alternative; if he chooses the field, they receive the ball; should he take the ball, they may choose either side of the field.

The game is divided into two periods of thirty-five minutes each, with a ten-minute interval for rest between the two periods. Whichever side takes the ball at the opening of the first half must yield it to the other side at the opening of the second half, and the two teams likewise change sides upon the field at the opening of the second half. This is in order to give each team the benefit of any wind that may be blowing, and divide the disadvantage of uneven ground, or any adverse conditions associated with either side of the field.

Divisions of the Field. Before beginning the actual movement of the game, let us explain here that the last boundary line behind each team is called their goal line. On the centre of each of these goal lines two posts are erected with a cross-bar of wood between the posts, at a height of ten feet from the ground. The posts themselves are 18½ feet apart. The white lines, which we have previously mentioned as being laid out across the field at intervals of five yards, may now be more clearly designated. The one five yards from either goal line is called the five-yard line of the team playing on that half of the field. The next is their ten-yard line; the next their fifteen-yard line; then comes their twenty-yard line, twenty-five-yard line, and so up to the centre of the field. It is not customary, however, to make use of this method of designation after we have passed the forty-yard line, and, indeed, the terms are rarely used to designate any distance more than twenty-five yards from the goal. Beyond twenty-five yards from either goal line, the space is generally designated as "A's territory," or "B's territory," or the centre of the field (A and B being here used to designate the names of the two respective teams).

The Game Opened. The game opens with the ball in the centre of the field. The side which has the ball brings its men up on a line with the ball; the opponents must retreat at least ten yards back from the ball. As the two teams stand in this position, the referee blows his whistle as a signal for the play to begin. The game must be opened by kicking the ball from the centre of the field, and the object in this case is only to kick it as far as possible. By the rules of the game, whenever a ball is kicked, it must be kicked at least a distance of ten yards into the opponents' territory, and it cannot then again be touched by the side which has kicked it until it has touched the person of some player on the opposing side or until the person who kicked the ball has gone down the field and reached a point on a line with the distance the ball has traveled. His action in going down the field in this manner puts his entire team in a position technically known as "on side," and they may then touch the ball before their opponents, if they are able to do so. The opponents, who have probably secured the ball themselves from this initial kick, are not required to kick it back, but may, if they prefer, attempt to rush or run the ball back by giving it to one of their own number to carry down the field. Their method of putting the ball in play will be by what is known as a "scrimmage," and as the ball is put in play at all times in this manner (with the single exception of the opening effort, which is repeated at the beginning of the second half, or whenever a score has been made), it may be well to describe the scrimmage.

A Scrimmage Described. The ball is placed in the hands of the centre-rush; he places it upon the ground, bending over it and holding it by one hand. The teams take their positions. The quarter-back, as the commanding general, issues his instructions, telling his men what particular movement or attack shall be made to advance the ball. These instructions are given by figure or hand signals (usually the former), and are always known as the "signals." The quarter-back calls the signal, and usually repeats it once or twice, that every member of the team may be familiar with it. Each team has its own signals, and they are, of course, unintelligible to opponents.

The ball is then snapped back by the centre into the hands of the quarter-back, who instantly passes it to the member of the team who is to run with it. The remainder of the players block their opponents in any effort they may make to reach the runner, and if this "blocking-off" of an opponent is done in the rush-line, it is called "blocking;" but if it is done immediately in front of the person of the runner, it is called "interfering for the runner," and the body of players who run with the runner, as a sort of bodyguard, are called his interferers, or the interference.

The other side, striving to check the advance of the ball, endeavor to get at the runner, to prevent his advancing. Their primary object is to secure the ball itself; but as this is usually impossible, the most that can be done is to check him by tackling him and throwing him to the ground, where he is then held; and the referee's whistle instantly blows to indicate that no further advance of the ball by this operation may be made.

First, Second, and Third Down. The referee's whistle always stops the play after each scrimmage, and the ball is not in play again until the two teams have been lined up and it has again been snapped back by the centre, as before described. Each of these efforts to advance the ball is called a "down;" and unless the side having the ball can advance it five yards in three consecutive downs, the possession of the ball must be given to the other side. It follows naturally, that if the first two efforts, or downs, are not productive of their full proportion of the five yards distance, the third effort will be a kick, which is a virtual relinquishment of the ball. If, however, the first two efforts have resulted in a good proportionate advance, the team will doubtless continue the rushing game, and avoid a kick as long as possible, in order to thereby retain possession of the ball, since no ground can be gained without possession of the ball, and to kick is to practically relinquish it.

As to the Runner. The handling of the ball by the quarter-back, between the centre-rush and the runner, is made necessary by a rule of the game, which provides that the ball must have touched a third player before any attempt can be made to advance it, and that until such time it shall not be carried or moved forward. Hence the quarter-back is unable to run with the ball himself, and the same prohibition applies to the centre-rush, although, if the ball were passed later to either of these players, this restriction would not be operative. It is also a rule of the game that the ball shall never be thrown or passed forward from one player to another, and any forward pass counts as a misplay, with penalty of loss of the ball.

Penalties of the Game. There are various minor restrictions in the rules, and some of these restrictions are protected by a penalty. The most important of these restrictions, and the penalties which attach to them, are as follows: —

(a) No player, when the ball is about to be put in play, shall advance beyond the line of the ball. If he so advances, he is designated by the umpire as off-side, and should the ball be put in play before he retires behind the line of the ball, his side must pay the penalty. This penalty is usually loss of the ball, if they have the ball in their possession at the time the offense occurs, or a loss of ten yards of distance if the ball is not in their possession. A liberal construction of this rule will often lead an official to avoid giving this penalty, if the player who is off-side, realizing his mistake, does not attempt to take any active part in the manoeuvre, and in no way participates in the play.

(b) The use of the hands or arms to hold or detain an opponent is prohibited to the side which has the ball, and the players of that side (the runner only excepted) can obstruct the progress of their opponents with the body only. But the players of the side which has not the ball can use their hands and arms to push their opponents out of the way in breaking through, though they are rigidly prevented by the rules from laying their hands upon, or using hands or arms to interfere with an opponent in any other way or at any other time, unless that opponent has the ball. The violation of any of this class of rules is generally designated as "holding," and is visited with the same punishment prescribed for off-side playing, namely, loss of the ball, or loss of ten yards of distance.

(c) Other general violations of rules are, intentional tackling of a player below the knees; striking with the closed fist; throttling, tripping up, or unnecessary roughness of any description. No player is allowed to wear projecting nails or iron plates on his shoes, or any metal or greasy substance on his person. No player, when off-side, is permitted to interfere with an opponent who is trying to catch the ball after a kick.

Methods of Scoring Points. There are four ways in which points may be scored: to carry the ball across the opponents' goal line, and touch it down on the ground is known as a touch-down, and scores four points for the side accomplishing the feat. Any touch-down gives the right to have what is commonly known as a "try-at-goal," which is effected by bringing the ball back into the field, on a line with the point where it was touched down, and making an effort to kick it from any point on this line, over the bar between the goal posts. If this kick is successfully accomplished, the touch-down is said to have been converted into a goal, and two more points are added to the score.

A goal may also be obtained by a kick direct from the field, provided this kick is not a punt. The usual method of making this attempt is by what is known as a drop-kick, which consists of dropping the ball to the ground and kicking it the instant that it rebounds. If the ball from such a kick passes over the bar between the goal posts, it is called a goal from the field, or a goal from a field kick, and counts five points to the side making it.

The only other method of scoring is a negative method, by which the side having the ball loses two points, and makes what is technically known as a "safety." This is accomplished when a player, having received the ball from a player of his own side, *touches it down behind his own goal line.* This counts two points against the side making it, and is only resorted to as a means of relieving the pressure of a fierce attack, and possibly preventing the opponent from making the larger score of four points by a touch-down. The result of a safety is that the side which has made it is given possession of the ball, and allowed to kick it from any point up to their own twenty-five-yard line. On this twenty-five-yard line the opponents line up, and the kick must be made at some point which will lift the ball over the heads of the opponents. The ball is, accordingly, kicked from about the fifteen-yard line, and if this kick is successful, the immediate threatening of the goal by the opponents is brought to an end.

The Ball out of Bounds. If at any time the ball is kicked or carried across either side boundary line time is immediately called by the referee, and the ball is then strictly out of play. It must be brought back by the side gaining possession of it, to the point where it first crossed the line, and there it is usually the custom for the team to take advantage of the rule permitting it to be brought back into the field a given number of yards, and the ball is so brought into the field, and placed down for a scrimmage.

Concluding Definitions. This brief explanation of the game may, perhaps, be best concluded by defining a few of the common expressions in the game:

A *fair catch* is made when a player, on catching the ball, advances either foot, and points his heel into the ground. He does this to signify that he will not make any attempt to run with the ball, and it protects him from being tackled and thrown. The making of a fair catch gives a team the privilege of putting the ball in play at that point, either by a scrimmage or a free kick. In the latter case, the side making the catch kicks the ball from that point, and the opponents cannot advance nearer that mark than ten yards.

A *punt* is an ordinary kick of the ball, made by letting the ball fall from the hands and kicking it before it touches the ground.

In touch means out of bounds over the side boundary line.

There are three officials: an umpire, who decides upon the conduct of the players; a referee, who decides all questions relating to the movements of the ball; and a linesman, who marks the distance gained or lost by each down. Substitutions of one player for another may only be made when a player is too seriously injured to continue the game.

A *line-up* is the grouping of the players for any play or movement. The side which has the ball is restricted by the rules from lining up too closely massed together, and the old form of wedge plays and the more recent momentum plays are not now permitted.

CHAPTER III

FINER POINTS OF THE PLAY
LIKELY TO BE OVERLOOKED

A Higher Appreciation. In another chapter we have described fully how to watch a game from the ordinary standpoint. There should, however, be some special hints given in order to enable the spectator to appreciate some of the finer points which are likely, otherwise, to escape observation.

Advantages of Present Uniforms and Accessories. Before taking up the points of the play, a few suggestions as to accessories may, perhaps, awaken additional interest.

In the first place, the uniforms, which would hardly attract attention save as rather soiled and badly fitting garments, are the product of considerable study. The original uniform consisted of tight-fitting jerseys, and tight, as well as rather thin, knickerbockers. There was no padding whatever, and nothing to break the force of falls. The first step in reform was the adoption of the canvas jacket worn over the jersey. The first team to adopt these had them greased as well, in order to make them more difficult to hold. The players who were obliged to tackle these men in canvas jackets thereupon put resin upon their hands, and later an especially sticky substance called Venetian turpentine. It was not long before a rule was passed forbidding the use of sticky or greasy substances on the person of the player.

The next reform in uniforms was in the line of padding, and the trousers or knickerbockers we see to-day are practically loose bags heavily padded at the knees and thighs. Padding is also being used more or less in the jackets and jerseys. There are also many appliances in the way of shin guards, nose guards, and other parts of armor, but there is a rule that forbids the use of any metal substance on the person of the player, so that such armor as is used is supposed to be of a material that will not injure the opponents. There are also individual appliances of all kinds, both as a prevention and as a cure of injuries, — ankle supporters, knee caps, and the like. The shoes have small blocks of leather fastened to them, taking the place of spikes, in order that the runner may not slip.

A leather uniform was brought out three years ago, and is undoubtedly a valuable help on a wet day, as the cloth uniforms absorb so much water as to be very heavy before the game is finished.

How to Judge the Preliminary Actions. To come to the play: If one watches the kickers and catchers on the field before the game commences, he sees that they are, both in catching and kicking, changing their positions, and are constantly watching with care the flight of the ball. These men are endeavoring to discover the force and direction of the wind, in order to make proper allowance for it, and also, in case of winning the toss, to tell which side to choose.

Watching these kickers and catchers, it is not a difficult matter to pick out the best of them by the ease with which they swing at the ball, and the way in which they handle it. A good man is apparently taking things very easy, but for all that his work is clean. When he kicks, as soon as his start is made, his swing increases in speed, and he drives the ball with a little side swing that adds many feet to its progress.

As soon as the game starts, the first point of interest to be noted is, as described in another chapter, the line-up of the side which is to receive the ball. The strategy of the opening play lies in the kicking side placing the ball in the most inconvenient spot for the opponents to return it either by a run or a kick. On the other hand, the side that receives the ball arranges its men so as to prevent the kicking side from landing the ball in any place where it cannot be returned a considerable distance.

What to Watch in a Scrimmage. A Stiff Line. The points to be noted in a scrimmage are many. Chief, perhaps, among them is the relative superiority of the two lines. Some idea of this can be gathered by the spectator from the relative "stiffness" of the two. This is a term which indicates the ability of one line to stand up against the other, and hold their own or even push the opponents back. If the spectator will glance along the line just as the ball is snapped, he will speedily learn to judge which of the two lines yields the most in the scrimmage. And almost without exception the team which is the stiffer in the line will prove the superiority of its forward play during the game.

The second point to be noted in a scrimmage is of similar character, and that is the ability of the men on the defense to break through and smash the interference or reach the runner before he gets up to the line upon which the ball is down. The line which can do this will make it very uncomfortable for both the interference and the runner before the game has ended.

Good Quarter Play. When one realizes that every instant gained between the time of putting the ball in play and the time of landing it in the hands of the runner is of the greatest value, he can and will watch with more interest the motions and playing of the little quarter-back. The sharper the play just behind the scrimmage in this respect, the better the game. Another point of superiority in the quarter-back is his ability to pass the ball and get into the interference as well. The spectator will see a good quarter receive the ball and actually get started on his run at the same moment that he passes it to the runner.

How to Predict a Kick. It is not always easy even for the umpire to be sure when a side is going to kick the ball. They may kick it on the first down, the second down, or the third down. Of course, a great many kicks are made on the third down, because that is the last chance, but it is now by no means unusual in good teams to see kicks made much earlier than that.

Probably the best way for the spectator to judge whether a kick is to be made is to watch the opposing full-back. Owing to the fact that it is almost imperative for him to know when a kick is to be made, one can rest assured that his powers of observation are probably the best of any one's on the field. If the spectator, therefore, will glance at him when the lines are drawn up, he will be greatly aided in judging this point, for he can make up his mind that as soon as the full-back commences to run back there is likely to be a kick by the opponents. Of course, there are other indications which foretell a kick, as the stepping back, and separating of the backs on the side holding the ball, and, in close formations, the hasty running back of the full-back on the side holding the ball. It is impossible for any one to tell certainly when a quarter-back kick is to be made, but an occasional glance at the end rushers is the best way to find out what the intention is. An end rusher will usually drop back farther for a quarter-back kick, and will go out toward the end on an ordinary kick.

What constitutes Good Play by End and Tackle. In watching the play of the line it should be observed that a good end will protect the side of the field carefully against any runs when he is on the defense, and will at the same time shoot in and seize the runner after the tackle has broken the interference. A poor end, on the other hand, is apt to hug the edge of the field and be undecided about the time when he should go in. In judging the quality of an end the spectator should also take into consideration the speed with which he gets down under kicks. An end ought to be always by the side of, or in front of, the man who catches the kick. That is his first duty, and clever men will almost always accomplish it, in spite of the attempts of the opponents to stop them.

A good tackle is one who breaks through his opponent and reaches the interference or the runner before either gets to the line. Good blocking is the kind that prevents just this breaking through of the tackle. A man is not allowed to use his arms or hands in blocking when his own side have the ball, and hence it is particularly interesting to see how he accomplishes the feat of holding his opponent back.

Good Interference. Good interference is the kind that moves rapidly ahead of the runner with the ball, so that he does not have to slow up to prevent his over-running it, and which yet holds its formation securely.

A Good Run. Never be deceived into thinking a good run has been made when the man merely goes across the field. Many an otherwise good player loses his chance to get on a 'Varsity team from the fact that he runs too far across the field, or even runs back. It is the advance that counts, and not the distance over which the runner passes, and the spectator should always bear this in mind, and he will not then make erroneous judgments about the quality of a man's playing.

Judicious Kicking. Good kicking is the kind which, while always high enough to enable the ends to get down under it, nevertheless gains a considerable distance for the side making the kick. In playing against the wind, kicks must necessarily be low and strong. In playing with the wind they should be high in order that the wind may get its full effect upon the ball. When the side is so near the opponents' goal that a kick will drive the ball across the goal line, either a drop-kick should be tried, or else a punt should be made over toward the side of the field, crossing the touch line before it does the goal line. For, if it crosses the goal line the opponents can bring it out twenty-five yards, whereas, crossing the side line, they must put it in play where it crosses the line, and it may result in their being obliged to make a safety. There is a good deal of skill displayed in this kicking, and the quality of a full-back or a kicking back should be judged considerably on his ability to do this.

A Punt-Out. The punt-out is a rather delicate proceeding and not often resorted to. To punt-out well a man should be able to land the ball so that the man catching it is considerably nearer, and in a more direct line with the goal. That is the only test of a good punt-out.

CHAPTER IV

How to Watch a Game

Watching the Practice if possible. Any one desirous of enjoying to the full, as a spectator, a football match should arrange to watch the practice of some team for a few days preparatory to viewing one of the important games. It is surprising how readily, in this way, the main points of the play impress themselves upon the on-looker.

But it is by no means always possible, and seldom practicable, for the average spectator to go through this preliminary preparation. For this reason the following chapter is offered for the benefit of the spectator who plans to see, as a very first experience, one of the big match games in the fall.

Preparing for the Game: Getting a Seat. The first thing to do is to secure a seat. Here there is but one advice to give, and that is, *get the best*. By the "best" is meant a seat near the middle of the field, preferably rather high up on the stands, in order that people running along the side lines will not obstruct the view, and back to the sun. Avoid the top seat, however, because there is likely to be a cold wind that chills one to the marrow, and a good deal of this is escaped by sitting farther down. Dress warmly, and above all things wear easy, comfortable shoes, because even in moderate weather, sitting out in the late fall is cold work, and the feet are the first to feel the discomfort.

These may seem small matters of detail, but if you are going to watch a football game, the only way to get real enjoyment out of it is to be perfectly comfortable, or as nearly so as possible in your surroundings. Then you can give your undivided attention to the game.

Difficulty of appreciating the Skill exhibited. Without doubt, the spectator watching his first football match feels a pleasurable excitement born of the very evident and easily appreciated struggle for supremacy going on between the two parties, but, so far as seeing any indications of special skill or design, it is likely enough that, unless his attention were called to it, he would not believe there was the least method in the apparently mad tumbling and pushing of the contestants. Football suffers, or rather has suffered, very much from the fact that it requires a knowledge of the game in order to be able to appreciate its real worth, both as a sport for sport's sake, and as a means of developing character.

We have already described the preparations that should be made in order to see a game. In the matter that follows we presuppose that the spectator has come prepared for enjoyment, and is comfortably seated, ready for the game to begin.

Why the Field is a Gridiron. The first things that attract the eye on entering the field are the white lines which divide it into spaces. The time was, and that only a dozen years ago, when there were no such markings, the centre of the field and two lines twenty-five yards from each goal being the only marks inside the field of play. But the game was beginning to suffer because there was too little progress of the ball, and it became necessary to enact a rule that a side must do something with the ball which should produce tangible results, or else give it up to the other side. The rule took the shape that a side must advance the ball five yards in three attempts or take it back twenty yards. Failing to do either, they must surrender possession of it to their opponents. In order to readily determine these distances, the field is now marked with white lines every five yards.

Preliminary Practice. As the players come out upon this "gridiron" field, as it is called, they begin to practice, some kicking and catching, others passing and rolling the ball about, one after another dropping suddenly to the ground and clasping the ball in his arms. The men who are kicking and catching are probably the half-backs and backs of the team, for that is one part of their work when the actual play begins. Those who are "falling on the ball" are for the most part the big fellows of the team, and make up the rush-line, or forwards. They fall on the ball in order to limber up, and because occasions to do this will offer in a game; and to secure possession of the ball and retain that possession is one of the chief factors in winning a match.

The Toss of the Coin. The two gentlemen in citizen's attire just coming upon the field are the referee and umpire, and the former calls the two captains of the opposing teams up to him; they then toss for choice of position, as described in the preceding chapter.

The Line-up. As soon as the choice is settled, and the referee has given the word to line up, you can tell which side is to kick, because that side will line up at the centre of the field, while the others will spread themselves generously over the other half, no one being nearer the ball than a line ten yards in front of it. They spread out thus, in order to thoroughly cover the entire territory where the opponent is likely to kick the ball, for they must have a man wherever it can possibly come, to the end that the opponents may secure no immediate advantage. With a very strong kicker and against but little wind, the side having the kick-off will most probably try to drive the ball across the goal line on the first kick. It is of no avail to kick it over the cross-bar at kick-off, because the rules provide that on this occasion it would not score a goal, even if it did so cross the bar. But if there be a strong wind, or if the kicker be not sufficiently powerful to be reasonably sure of sending the ball over the line, the side having the kick-off will probably not attempt to send the ball as far as possible, but instead will kick it only a moderate distance — perhaps to the twenty-five-yard line — endeavoring to make rather a high kick of it. The reason for this is that they thus enable their own men to get down under it (for they cannot start ahead of the ball), and thus prevent the receiving opponents from running the ball back a considerable distance. This the opponents are sure to try to do; so at the kick-off it is especially interesting to note what disposition the captain of the opponents has made of his men.

Interference. He will endeavor to so arrange them that they shall not only be able to reach the ball quickly no matter where it be kicked, but also so that the player thus taking it may be very speedily protected by two or three others of his side who will interpose between him and the oncoming men of the side which has kicked the ball. This act of interposing to protect the man with the ball is called interference, and there is much of it performed during the progress of a game. It assists the runner by preventing the opponents from tackling him, and is legitimate so long as those who interfere do not use their hands or arms in performing this office for their runner.

When the kick-off is made, it is not considered good play by the recipient to let the ball fall to the ground, and take it on the bound, if it can be avoided, because more time is consumed than if it be taken on the fly, and so the opponents will have more chance to collect about the man taking the ball, and probably prevent the run. More than this, it is impossible to tell in what direction the oval-shaped ball will bound, so that to catch the ball on the bound is a very difficult operation. Each side will avoid it whenever possible.

What the Recipient of the Ball May Do. A Fair Catch. The man who receives the ball may, if he chooses, make a fair catch, and take a free kick. If he does this, he will make a mark with his heel while in the act of catching the ball. It is not always good policy on taking the kick-off to thus "heel it," because the player can often gain more ground by running with the ball. Usually, therefore, we see the run with interference, as mentioned above. But the runner does not often make many yards before the opponents break through the interference, using their hands freely to do this, and bring down the runner.

A Down and Scrimmage. When this is accomplished, and the runner brought to a standstill, or thrown upon the ground, so that further progress of the ball is prevented, the referee blows his whistle, and a down occurs, that is, the ball is put down for a scrimmage, and the ball is put in play again, as described in the previous chapter.

Attack and Defense. The snap-back sends the ball back with his hand, and at the same time he and his companions in the line will guard and protect the runner from the attack of the opponents, who, at the moment the ball is snapped, endeavor to break through and reach the runner. The real theory of defense lies nowadays in a very bold repulse; that is, in so precipitately breaking through the opponent's line as to prevent the runner from reaching it with a fair start, and with his interferers well arranged. For if the runner succeeds in getting this protected start into the line, he is reasonably sure to gain two yards or more, which means that in three downs or tries he will have advanced the necessary five yards, and can retain the ball for three more attempts. Hence the most frequently repeated feature of the game is the onslaught of the rushers, one side endeavoring to break through, and having the right to use the hands and arms in so doing; the other side resisting with all its power this fierce attack, and obliged to refrain from the use of hands or arms in repelling. Behind these rushers come, with swift advance, the interferers and the runner with the ball, making for a preconcerted opening which the rushers are trying to prepare for them in the line.

Kicks and Fake Kicks. Again the runner is finally brought to earth, and another scrimmage is formed, and so the play goes on until, either from inability to advance the ball, or because a kick seems advisable, the man who receives the ball from the quarter (or it may be directly from the snap-back), punts it, that is, drops it from his hand, and kicks it before it strikes the ground, sending it usually high in the air and well down the field, while his end rushers, and perhaps one or two others in the line, charge down the field, and endeavor to be upon the man who receives the ball in time to prevent his returning the kick, or running with the ball.

But it may be only a "fake" kick, that is, all the arrangements are apparently made for a kick, and then, just as the ball is snapped back, it is quickly passed to a man who stands close behind the line, and who endeavors to plunge through. Or it may be passed properly to the man who is evidently about to make the kick, and he himself then tries a run around the end of the line.

Drop-Kick. So the game proceeds in a succession of downs or scrimmages, resulting in runs or kicks, until one side or the other succeeds in getting the ball within kicking distance of their opponents' goal. They may decide to try a drop-kick. The line forms exactly as above described, except that the half-backs go up into the line, too, it may be. Then the man who is to kick receives the ball and drops it to the ground in front of him; just as it rises, he kicks it. To the inexperienced spectator it is almost impossible to tell whether he kicked it just after it touched the ground, or at the same moment as the impact. If he succeed in kicking it over the goal bar by this kind of a kick, it counts his side five points, and the opponents take the ball back to the centre of the field, and kick off again.

Kick-Out. If he miss the goal, the game proceeds as before, save that, if the ball goes over the goal line, the opponents may bring it out, and from some point inside the twenty-five-yard line kick out, that is, kick it as far away from their goal as possible, keeping it, however, within the bounds of the field. There is one exception to this, and that is, if the side threatening the goal try a drop-kick on a "first down" inside the twenty-five-yard line, the defenders can only kick out from behind the ten-yard line. This rule was made in order to put a premium upon drop-kicks, which are always popular and usually rare. But the temptations of the running game are still too strong, and drop-kicks are not more used than formerly.

A Touch-Down. If the players do not try the drop-kick, as above described, but persist in running with the ball, and at last are able to carry it across the goal line, they have scored a touch-down which counts them four points, and also gives them the privilege of an undisturbed try-at-goal, and this try, if successful, adds two more points to their score.

Try-at-Goal. Having secured the touch-down, the try-at-goal is made in one of two ways. The simpler is that in which a man of the side that has made the touch-down brings the ball out in his arms, making a mark on the goal line as he crosses it, and, after bringing the ball out, in a straight line, to such distance as he thinks proper, holds it for another of his side to take a place-kick at goal. The holder does not put the ball on the ground until the kicker is all ready to kick it, and has secured his aim, because the defenders of the goal are obliged to keep behind their goal line until the ball touches the ground; then they can charge at once.

Try by a Punt-Out. The second and more complicated method of trying for goal from a touch-down is by means of what is called a punt-out. This in reality is only a way of getting the ball more nearly in front of the goal posts for a kick, and is, therefore, seldom used, except when a touch-down is made quite well over toward the side line. When this is the case, a player of the side which has made the touch-down brings the ball in a straight line up to the goal line, and there makes a mark with his heel, but he does not cross the line. Instead, he retires back from the line a step and a little distance away from the goal. His own men form not less than five yards out from the goal line, and it is to some one of them that he punts the ball for a fair catch.

The player who is to thus catch the ball stands as nearly over in front of the goal as he can go and yet render the kick and catch reasonably safe. The defenders of the goal may line up on either side of the punter's mark at a distance of not less than five feet from that mark, but behind their goal line, and they cannot interfere with the punter until he actually kicks the ball. The man who catches the ball makes a mark with his heel while in the act of catching it, and that mark serves in determining the position of both sides exactly as any fair-catch mark. The rest of the kick at goal is the same as in an ordinary try.

Time of Game and Scoring. After a touch-down and try-at-goal, whether the goal be kicked or not, the ball goes back to the centre of the field, and is kicked off by the side against whom the touch-down has been scored. Thus the game proceeds for thirty-five minutes of actual play, time being taken out for delays of any nature, and also while the tries-at-goal are made, as well as at kick-out, kick-off, and free kicks. After this period of play, there follows an intermission of ten minutes, and then play is resumed for another thirty-five minutes. When the play is thus resumed, the side which did not have the kick-off at the beginning of the match kicks off from the centre of the field. At the end of the second period of play, the side that has scored the most points (a goal from a touch-down counting six; from a field kick, five; a touch-down failing goal counting four) wins the match.

Officials and Fouls. In conclusion, a word about officials. There are three officials on the field. The referee, whom we have already mentioned as the one who tosses the coin for the choice of sides. He is "judge of the ball," as the expression goes; that is, he decides all questions of fact as far as the position and the progress of the ball are concerned. He also rules regarding interference with the snap-back, forward passing, and the quarter-back's running with the ball without first passing it, all of which are forbidden acts.

The umpire is the judge of the conduct of the players, and he calls all fouls with the exception of interference with the man who is to put the ball in play in the centre, forward passing, and running with the ball by the quarter-back, as before mentioned. The most common of these fouls or forbidden points are, interfering by use of the hands or arms, as already described, getting between the ball and the opponents' goal, piling up on the runner when he is down, interfering, when off-side, with the man about to make a catch, and all unnecessary roughness and brutality.

The third official is the linesman, who marks out the distances gained or lost. He usually walks along the side lines of the field, and it is customary for him to have an assistant.

All points not covered by the umpire, the referee has absolute power to decide.

CHAPTER V

EFFECTS OF THE GAME ON THE PLAYERS

Divisions of the Subject. The effects of football upon its players may be classed under two heads, physical and moral. We will take up briefly the benefits and detriments to the player, under each of these heads; restricting the discussion, however, to those factors which really belong to football, and not including the unquestioned evils and abuses which have connected themselves with the game as outside excrescences, nor the equally unquestioned advantages to the general public of a healthy interest in athletics.

Limitations of the Argument. As outside evils, the selection of a holiday, like Thanksgiving Day, for the date of a great match, to be played in a leading city; the gambling which inevitably precedes the game, and the rowdyism which too frequently follows it, are not arguments against the game of football *per se*. They do not concern the player who plays the game on the campus of his academy or college, in a quiet country town. In the limits of this chapter, as defined by its title, we shall only discuss the personal effect of football, and not refer to outside or collateral effects.

Physical Advantages. It has been claimed that football lays undue emphasis on physical prowess; yet the benefit to the player from a physical standpoint will be found to be inferior to the benefits from a moral or mental standpoint.

The physical benefits, however, are very real and very important. No game develops so many muscles in a given time as does the game of football. No game so thoroughly develops the man, when it is properly played. The running, dragging, pushing, dodging, vigorous struggle, up and down the field, is as well calculated to bring into activity the physical powers of the player as any exercise that has ever been invented. It has been repeatedly demonstrated by the physical directors at our leading colleges, that a large majority of the students who play football finish the season with greatly improved physiques. (See Note A at end of chapter.)

Official Proscription and the Strength Test. It would seem as though, in the face of this testimony, the case might fairly be rested without argument. It may be claimed, however, that the violent exercise of football is too great a strain upon many young men who attempt to play it. It must not be forgotten that the strength and vigor of young men varies greatly in proportion to their age and bodily measurements. Consequently, in view of the possible injury to a student from playing the game before he is strong enough for its demands, the authorities of nearly all the colleges and schools have for years insisted upon a physical examination of every candidate who desires to play football, and have prescribed by strict regulation the strength and capacity which a student must attain before he can be permitted to play.

This precautionary measure is of the greatest value, for it is true in football, as in many other things, that what is one man's meat is another's poison; and the sport which healthy young men may play with comparatively little danger, and with every prospect of deriving benefit therefrom, cannot be undertaken by weaklings or invalids, whose courage and zeal are often in excess of their bodily ability.

A Common Error. We must not make the error of judging the strain upon the football player by a comparison with our own physical abilities, unless we keep constantly in mind the great difference in strength and endurance between a person undergoing a course of football training and one of the same size, age, and weight who is not accustomed to vigorous exercise. This difference may be fairly represented by the ratio of 3½ to 1. In other words, the player in training has 3½ times the strength and endurance of the student who does not take vigorous bodily exercise. (See Note D at end of chapter.)

Physical Disadvantages. The physical disadvantage of football is the liability to injury, resulting partly from accident, and partly from injudicious methods of training.

Injuries from Accidents. Accidents in football are of much less frequent occurrence than is popularly supposed, for only those who follow the subject closely have any realization of the large number of students at all our schools and colleges who are playing football, and the relatively small number of accidents. If we take a single college like Harvard or Yale, we shall find that the 'Varsity squad alone is composed, in the earlier weeks of the season, of as many as four separate elevens, and will nearly always number as many as forty players. Added to these are four class teams, each composed of two elevens, making eighty-eight more players, or a total of one hundred and thirty-two. Yet even this falls short of the number who are playing the game at any one of the larger colleges. Harvard alone grants from 175 to 200 permits to play football every fall.

Considering the thousands of young men in our schools and colleges, as well as in the many athletic associations, and those in all our country towns who are playing football, it is not surprising that some injuries are received. But the fact that the serious injuries are so few, considering the violence of the exercise and the number of chances for accidents, is itself an evidence of the strong physique which the game bestows upon the player.

A Comparison with Other Sports. It must be conceded that the maxim of "nothing venture, nothing have" applies to football, as to all other sports. The increased bodily vigor must be purchased by bodily activity, and this involves a certain degree of bodily risk. Yet the injuries in football have been greatly overestimated by the newspapers, and are much misunderstood by the public. It can be proved that there is an equal element of danger in most sports and pastimes, just as there is a chance of injury in many of the simplest daily duties and occupations. There have been serious injuries from the feminine games of croquet and tennis; while the accidents from such legitimate amusements as bowling, sailing, baseball, cricket, rowing, horseback riding, coasting, shooting, swimming, lacrosse, and golf are in quite large proportion to the numbers of those engaged in them. What man is there who has not, as a boy, suffered accidents in such amusements? To prove that football is a dangerous pastime, it is first necessary to prove that not only is the proportion of accidents in football in excess of those in other sports, but that such accidents are necessarily incidental to football as it is played at the leading colleges of the country. (See Note C at end of chapter.)

The Real Source of Danger. It must be borne in mind that the liability to injury in football increases in proportion to the youth of the player, his inexperience, and the lack of intelligent precautions, with the absence of proper methods of training. Just as the driving accidents in Central Park are in large proportion confined to persons who do not know how a horse should be harnessed or driven, so the great majority of injuries in football are scarcely accidents, but the natural occurrences among those who have never prepared for the game by proper training. No young man is fit to play football until he has been thoroughly coached, and knows how to attempt the various movements he may be called upon to perform, in a way which shall not be harmful to him. When properly coached, he may, without the slightest risk, do many things which would be distinctly dangerous for one who had not had the benefit of this instruction.

An Exaggeration. One other point must not be overlooked. Football has been prominently before the public eye; it has been a bone of contention, and has aroused exaggerated feeling in both parties to the conflict. In all this dispute the law of proportion has been as much violated as in the public discussion of certain rare and exceptional diseases (as hydrophobia), which have both here and abroad led to most extraordinary legislation, with many remarkable schemes and propositions for relief, although the disease itself has been so rare that it does not figure as a cause of death in the statistics of any great city of the world.

Possible Injuries to the Nervous System. There is, however, a form of injury to the nervous system which may be occasioned by violent physical or nervous shock; and it is proper that we should look closely at football and determine whether the player is liable to such injury from the severe blow occasioned by the collision of two players, or the violent throwing of a player to the ground. This attitude of the question has been quite carefully examined by Dr. Morton Prince, of Boston, and the result of his investigations is here communicated, under date of May 8, 1896, as follows:

I am very glad, in response to your request, to give you the results of my inquiries into possible injuries to the nervous system from football playing. My inquiries have been directed into a special class of injuries. You must know that persons who are subjected to violent concussions, physical and nervous shocks (whether the shock be slight or severe) are liable to suffer from certain nervous accidents which are technically known as traumatic neuroses; they used to be called spinal concussion and "railway spine," the latter term being derived from the fact that such injuries are very common after railroad accidents. They may follow almost any accident in which there has been a severe physical or psychical shock. For example, they frequently are caused by falling from a height, or tumbling down steps, or indeed simply slipping and tumbling backward on to the ground; they are not uncommon as a result of carriage accidents, collision, etc., etc.

So common are these accidents that the courts are full of cases which are the subject of litigation in the matter of damages.

The symptoms which are most commonly met with in such cases are: paralysis of the arms and legs, or both; loss of sensation in different parts of the body; impairment or loss of sight; severe pains, generally located in the region which was the seat of the blow; general prostration; and various mental disturbances of different kinds, such as inability to apply the mind, irritability, loss of mental control and emotion. There are numerous other symptoms of this disease, but it is unnecessary to detail them further here.

These injuries to the nervous system may be very severe, completely disabling the injured person, and may last for many years. It occurred to me that if the generally accepted view regarding the exciting cause of these accidents be true, they should be common among football players. Any one who has watched a game must have been struck with the great momentum with which players frequently strike the ground or come together, and the severe blows that, in consequence, are inflicted on all parts of the body. The physical blow resulting from a man weighing 160 pounds being thrown to the ground when running at full speed, or when two such players collide, must be tremendous. It must far exceed the shock inflicted in many railway accidents, where, for example, a passenger may be simply thrown out of his seat, without any external injury being inflicted upon him; and yet that passenger may afterwards suffer from extreme nervous injuries of the kind I have above described.

With a view to determining whether such injuries may result from football accidents, I wrote the attending surgeons, or those in charge of the principal football teams of the country, asking whether they had ever known a player to suffer from a traumatic neurosis as a result of a football accident.

All my correspondents stated that they had never seen any injury of the kind I have described result from football accidents. I may further state that, while I myself have seen a great many injuries of the kind resulting from all sorts of accidents, I have never seen a single case which was due to football playing. From this evidence I think there is little doubt that whatever may result from football playing, traumatic neuroses are not caused by the game.

Yours truly,

Morton Prince, M. D.

This would seem to dispose of the hypothesis that there might be injury to the nervous system from the violent exercises of the game.

Injuries from Imperfect Training. Added to accidents, there is injury done to the player through injudicious methods of training, or the lack of all training. It is a deplorable fact that there is wide-spread ignorance on the general subject of training. Perhaps it seems singular to the casual observer that a young man with a fine natural physique should necessarily change the diet that has given him this exceptional vigor, now that he has most need for that vigor. In training for football, however, his diet, habits, hours, and method of life should be subjects of special care and oversight, to the end that his physical condition may successfully withstand the increased exercise which he is about to undertake. There is also need of care that, in the zeal for the game and the spirit of emulation, he should not overwork. Training is necessary, and it should be wisely directed. There is one training for speed, a different training for endurance or wind, and another training for strength. The intelligent trainer, knowing that all these are required in football, will study his players, treating them as individuals, rather than as a team, noting the effect of the game upon each man, and regulating individual exercise and diet in accordance with the clear indication of condition.

The Balance in the Argument. In considering the physical disadvantages possible to the player by reason of injury or injudicious training, let it be remembered, in conclusion, that no permanent injury from football has resulted to any player in the last ten years at any of the five leading colleges of the country. The injuries have been mainly of a minor nature, confined to ankles, knees, and noses. On the other hand, who shall estimate the advantages of the physical up-building of the thousands of players who have gone out from these five colleges in the last decade? As one of the leading surgeons of Boston said upon this subject recently, "Football may twist a few joints, but it is building up a new race of men."

Moral Advantages. Intellectual Activity. Great as are the physical benefits to the football player, there are advantages of a mental or ethical nature which outweigh them.

For football is essentially a game of severe moral and mental standards. The superiority of the thoroughbred over the ordinary "grade" animal is a mental rather than a physical superiority; and similarly the great lesson which the game of football teaches is that brains will triumph over mere strength always and everywhere in this world. It is the head that wins in football, and not the muscles. No dullard can play the game successfully, however great may be his physical development. Similarly, no inattentive player can ever succeed at football. To excel in the game demands of the player watchfulness and mental concentration.

The football player is taught, first of all, to think rapidly; he must use his mind on the instant; he must carry three or four thoughts at the same time, — the signals, his part in the play, the individual work of the man opposite him, and the intention of the opponents. He must train himself to meet emergencies, where momentary hesitation will mean certain defeat, and he must decide the issues for himself. Early in his career there will be developed in him a degree of self-reliance which probably no other sport in the world would inculcate. Only in a general way is his work laid out for him. There is no one to help him, and he enters the game with an urgent and realizing sense of responsibility, which is of unquestionable value. He knows that larger interests than he can possibly realize now depend on his complete performance of his duty.

Self-Control. With this self-reliance he is unconsciously acquiring in the highest degree another and an even more valuable quality, — self-control. By severe training he is made to realize that there is no place for him in football until he has schooled himself in self-restraint. Whatever the provocation, whatever the disconcerting incident, he must never lose his temper, he must never let his attention be drawn from the play. And no game so tries the temper as football. No set of players in any American sport receives such severe drill in self-control as do football players, and the lessons learned on the football field can never be wholly forgotten. The single ability to take hard blows and not retaliate is a lesson not too dearly bought at the cost of a few incidental sprains and bruises.

Moral and Physical Courage. A third ethical advantage follows closely upon the other two; with promptness of decision, good judgment, and self-restraint, he must now add courage. The distinction between physical and moral courage is by no means clear. Our civil war taught the lesson that the two are, to some extent identical, for the men of best morals were the best fighters. Both physical and moral courage are certainly needed in football. The player must have courage to start with; but he will find that he has much more of both courage and spirit as the season advances. The necessity for courage in the football player is too patent to need argument, and the opportunity the game affords to develop this admirable quality will doubtless be admitted by its severest critics.

Discipline. After courage comes the lesson of obedience. The world has never underestimated the value of a military or naval training in teaching implicit, unquestioned obedience and a fine sense of readiness to accept discipline. Football demands obedience. An army poorly officered becomes a mob; a football team would be even worse off without strict discipline. The biting sarcasm of the coaches must be borne without a thought of rebellion; the unmerited blame must be accepted without even an excuse; every order must be instantly and unquestioningly obeyed.

Negative Ethical Advantages. With these positive advantages to the player, there are other and almost equally great negative advantages. As the President of Lafayette College has stated, college athletics, and especially football, have done more to purify, dignify, and elevate college life than any other single influence in the last quarter of a century. No one will question this who is conversant with the inside history of the schools, academies, and colleges of this country and England. With this new systematic outlet for the animal spirits in young men, the old forms of disorder have almost disappeared. "Stacking rooms," "barring out," hazing, the stealing of signs and shutters, and all the old activities of the past, have been wholly laid aside. Vices of an even more vicious and dangerous nature, which exist wherever men are brought together in large numbers, have been greatly checked. Let any man compare the college escapades of his own day with those of the present time, and he will confess that the cause of good morals has been vastly advanced by systematic athletics, and that clean living, regularity of life, and their resulting vigorous manhood, have been insisted upon by football and other college sports.

The disorders to which we have referred are not charges chargeable to college life. Group young men together, with human appetites, large vitality, and the love of freedom, and whether in the city or country, in college or out of it, neither parental nor collegiate restraint has ever prevented, or ever will prevent, either folly or vice. A stronger attraction must take the place of the attraction to evil, and it is this important argument which is so often wholly overlooked by those who decry intercollegiate sports.

Increased Power of the Will. Other minor advantages to the player must be passed over with a few words. The game requires and teaches coolness; it leads to a study of the dispositions of men, and just as it subjugates strength to thought, so does it also teach the subordination of strength to the will. There is an element in human nature which finds a powerful attraction in personal contest between man and man. We cannot suppress this element, but we may wisely direct it. It shows in all the competitions of life, and while in some sports it leads to envy or cheating, it has quite an opposite effect in football. The man who loses his temper will be outplayed; the man who plays an unfair game loses more for his side than he can possibly gain.

Moral Disadvantages. A careful consideration of the evil influences engendered by football will, we believe, reveal the fact that every one of the so-called evils of the game is not properly a part of the sport, but rather an association of it. The playing of important games in great cities has led to all forms of disorder; the high price asked and readily paid for tickets to such games has brought an income from a single game greater than the total annual expenditure for the support of twenty-five instructors. With this exaggerated income there has been an objectionable extravagance in expenses. These vices are not a part of the game, but they are connected with it, and are often used as an argument against the sport by those who believe that not construction but destruction is the lesson of the hour, and that the manly features should be abandoned rather than that the vices should be reformed.

On the other hand, there is apparently no reason why our great games should not be converted into functions similar to the Eton-Harrow cricket match in England. As one writer says, it would be as reasonable to abandon our democratic form of government because it has produced a Tammany Hall, as to abandon football because its directors have not been wisely guided in their admittedly difficult task.

Attention Drawn from Study. One moral disadvantage which can properly be laid to the door of football is the fact that the excitement of the game draws the minds of the players from their studies. This is not a fault of the sport *per se*, but may, nevertheless, be so identified with it that it must be regarded as a drawback to the game. Let it be borne in mind, however, that this evil is not confined to football, but belongs equally to boat-racing and to baseball. It only becomes more obvious in football, in proportion as this sport is more popular than the others. The issue is really one which affects all competitive athletic exercises in colleges or academies.

The question is a deep one, for it involves a discussion of the objects for which a young man goes to college. He can never become a great scholar by four years of undergraduate life, but he may imbibe a spirit and learn methods which may fit him for the field he is to occupy. The college will have done its full duty to the young man if it puts him in a position from which he may become a learned man, a good business man, a sound scientist, an accomplished jurist, an able statesman, or an important factor in any walk of life. As one of the leading college presidents has pointed out: "The functions of the undergraduate college must not be confounded with the post-graduate and university training. The undergraduate is really a boy, — a large boy, to be sure, but still a boy, — and he needs physical as well as mental training. There is a danger in omitting from his curriculum of study that most important item of open-air amusement. With this left out, there will come the inevitable dangers which rise from the repression of a natural physical excitement. When the growth of the body has come to a standstill, and not until that time, can the great need of outdoor exercise safely remain unsatisfied." (See Note B at end of chapter.)

The Evils of Notoriety. One other evil influence stands in much the same class as the one of which we have just spoken; for, while it is not inseparably associated with football, it is so much a part of it in all leading colleges, that it must be considered here as a distinct drawback to the moral benefits derived from the sport. We mean the notoriety which attaches to the player by reason of the extensive publicity given to college games in the daily newspapers.

We must admit that this is not only a disadvantage to the young man, but that it is one which has so far resisted all attempts at correction. Undoubtedly some method may be devised for reforming the evils of notoriety, which are capable of working so much harm to any one, be he young or old, unless he is endowed with a strong head and an abundance of practical common-sense. We will not enter upon the discussion of the injury which the newspapers are inflicting to-day by their gross exaggerations of the importance of individual and topical affairs; it is enough to say that the cessation of newspaper notoriety, which the fickleness of journalism always renders inevitable, is a sore test to the unlucky beneficiary, who finds it difficult to preserve his balance in the midst of such bestowal and withdrawal of public attention.

But harmful notoriety is not confined to football; it is assiduously cultivated by that unfortunately large class of persons who are never more pleased than when they are mentioned in the society columns of the daily papers. Let us candidly admit the evil; but, while admitting it, let us confess that it is in no way associated with the game: it is rather a penalty paid for success in any public walk in life.

The Charge of Brutality. Perhaps the most serious charge brought against the sport of football is that it is brutal, and engenders brutality in its participants.

There is but one way to put this charge to the test, and that is to examine the character of our football players as shown by their conduct in private life, when not on the football field. The difficulty of judging their character by their football play lies in the fact that roughness is not brutality, although many critics refuse to recognize a distinction between them. That football is a rough game no one will deny. That it is a brutal pastime, or that it creates or fosters brutality, no one will affirm who will take the trouble to test the question by such a personal analysis as we have suggested. As a class, football players are the most gentle and warm-hearted men in college. Individual exceptions may readily be noted, but the average can easily be found by diligent inquiry among the friends, teachers, and associates of any dozen players.

Surely this is the true way by which alone we can measure the effect of the game upon the player. The test of an institution is the men that it produces, and football will splendidly abide this test.

NOTE A.

A great argument for football is the all-round physical effect on the player. It brings into active exercise not merely the muscles of the trunk, but of both extremities. Baseball and tennis are preeminently sports of agility, but football develops both agility and strength. As one well-known writer has pointed out, it is the old Greek Pentathlon revived and combined into one sport, — the running, the jumping, the wrestling, the boxing, and the throwing, all united in a single game. It is true that the tendency of the game is toward roughness, but this tendency may be quickly checked with competent officials.

NOTE B.

In regard to the time consumed by athletic exercises, it is a matter of record that this loss of time is in no way detrimental to the athlete's standing. On an earlier occasion, when the subject was under discussion, the faculties of Yale and Harvard consulted their books and found that, taken as a class, athletes stood a trifle higher in their studies than non-athletes. These results have since been substantiated by researches at other institutions.

It may be argued by those who favor the combination of dyspepsia with the midnight oil, that these men without their athletics would stand still higher. But let us not forget that the work of the modern university is not merely to make scholars of her young men, but to prepare them in all respects to combat the vice and ignorance and disease in this world. A few points more or less in scholarship-marks is not too great a sacrifice to make for self-restraint, presence of mind, courage, and obedience, taught on the football field.

NOTE C.

The danger to life and limb is, fortunately, a matter of record. In a recent number of the "Century Magazine," Mr. W. C. Church, drawing his facts from "reports in my possession from sixty-seven institutions of learning, scattered over thirty-seven States," says that there are abundant reports of minor mishaps among the thousands of football players from whom he has heard, but few permanent injuries are reported. He says that a California student had his neck broken, but he adds that he has heard of similar accidents in the families of his friends, which resulted from gymnastic practice. Mr. Church adds, "It is doubtful whether the percentage of accidents among undergraduates would lessen were football forbidden. Nature will exact her tribute in physical injuries for her bestowal of surplus energy upon the young."

To Mr. Church's facts we may add one more: A member of the Harvard faculty recently compiled statistics showing that injuries from football are fewer proportionately than those from the seemingly innocent sport of tobogganing. He might have added, with equal truth, that they are fewer, proportionally, than the accidents to skaters, to mountain-climbers, or to horseback-riders. It is not far from the fact to say that as many and as serious accidents have occurred to students from slippery sidewalks between lecture-halls and dormitories as from football.

NOTE D.

It is not necessary to claim for football that it is the best form of bodily exercise. It is certainly superior to the athletics of the gymnasium, but perhaps of less value in some respects than field-sports. Horsemanship, shooting, and fishing bring man into a closer relation to Nature than does football; in so far as they do this, they broaden and deepen his nature while developing his body and keeping him in the open air. But field-sports are largely out of the question with the young men in our schools and colleges, who have neither the time, the money, nor the location in which to indulge them. Football belongs with baseball, lacrosse, cricket, and boating. The weak point in tennis and track athletics is the comparatively private character of the sport, which fails to draw out the *esprit de corps* which team sports develop.

CHAPTER VI

EXPLANATION OF TECHNICAL WORDS AND PHRASES, SLANG TERMS, AND COINED EXPRESSIONS OF COLLEGE FOOTBALL

Back. A term used for either full-back or half-back, usually the former.

Backs. All the men behind the rush-line. More generally applied to the two half-backs and the full-back; that is, the three men farthest back from the rush-line.

Blocking. Interposing the body in front of a man to prevent his getting through the line.

Blocking-Off. Interposing the body between the runner and the would-be tacklers.

Block Hard, Block Long, Block Close, Block Low, Block High. Terms applied to the blocking: *hard* means with a forward push; *long* means to prevent the opponent for a considerable time from getting free; *low* means when the blocker crouches down; *high* means when he stands up; *close* means when the line blocks the inside men, that is, leaving any unblocked man or men at the ends of the line rather than at any other place.

Butting. Striking a man with the shoulder or head.

Canvas. A term applied to the jackets of the players.

Centre. A term applied to the snap-back, or the middle man of the rush-line, and also the middle spot of the field from whence a kick-off is made.

Centre Trio. Applied to the snap-back and his two guards.

Charging. Rushing forward to seize the ball or tackle a player.

Cleats. The small pieces of leather on the bottoms of the players' shoes.

Cocking the Ball up. Tilting it up, so that the point is higher from the ground.

Cork-Screw. A kick of a similar kind as a twister; also applied to a revolving wedge.

Cross-Bar. A stick that goes across the two uprights in the goal.

Dash. A term used to indicate spirited play; also the sudden run of a player breaking away from the rest.

Dead. A term used to signify "out of play." The ball is dead whenever the umpire or referee blows his whistle; when a goal has been obtained; when a touch-down, safety, or touch-back has been made; when a fair catch has been heeled, or the ball has been downed, having gone out of bounds.

Down. When the runner with the ball is tackled and held.

Drop-Kick. A kick made by letting the ball fall from the hands, and kicking it the very instant it rises from the ground.

Egg. A term applied to the leather ball.

End Rusher. The last man on-either end of the forward line.

Fair. (Used as a noun.) Putting the ball in play when it has gone out of bounds.

Fair Catch. A catch made direct from a kick by an opponent, or from a punt-out by one of the same side, provided the man making the catch makes a mark with his heel, when the ball is caught, to signify instantly that he does not intend to run with it.

Fake. A pretense; a bluff; an endeavor to make the opponents believe that a different play is to be made than the one actually used. Thus, a fake kick is always a run.

Falling on the Ball. The action of dropping quickly to the ground, and covering the ball with the body, in order to secure it more certainly than by attempting to pick it up.

Field-Kick. Technically, a goal kicked either from a place-kick, a drop-kick, or from a bounding kick, — in fact from any kind of a kick except a punt.

Field Tactics. An expression intended to cover the general direction or management of the play.

First Down, Second Down, and Third Down. (See *Down.*) These are terms used to indicate the number of attempts made to advance the ball. The first down is the one following an advance of the necessary distance, which must be a total of five yards in three consecutive downs. The second down is when one attempt has been made without succeeding in advancing it five yards. The third down is when two attempts have been made without securing a total gain of the necessary five yards. On the fourth down, which comes at the end of the third attempt, if the necessary five yards have not been gained, the ball goes to the other side. As soon as five yards have been gained, it is the first down again.

First Half. The first thirty-five minutes of the game.

Flying Wedge. A wedge that is in motion before the ball is put in play. (Now prohibited by the rules.)

Forwards. The seven men occupying the positions of end, tackle guard, and centre. (See *Rushers.*)

Foul. Any violation of a rule.

Free Kick. Any kick where the opponents are restrained by rule from advancing beyond a certain point.

Full-Back. The man nearest the goal, and the man who usually performs most of the kicking.

Fumble. To handle the ball with uncertainty; to drop it when it is in play.

Generalship. Used in contradistinction to field tactics, as meaning a broader consideration of the general methods to be adopted.

Getting Down, or Getting Down the Field. Going forward under a kick so as to be at the spot where the ball falls.

Getting Through. Breaking through the opponents' line on a scrimmage.

Ginger. Life and dash. A man has ginger when he plays very spiritedly.

Gridiron. A term applied to the football field on account of the white lines across it.

Ground-Gainer. A term applied to a man who, when running with the ball, is usually successful at making his required distance.

Goal. The sticks which are set up in the middle of the goal line over which the ball must be kicked. Also the act of kicking a goal; also, the territory behind the goal line.

Goal Line. The line running through the goal posts and at right angles to the side lines.

Goal Tend. Another term for full-back.

Guard. The player in the line next to the centre.

Hacking. Kicking a player in the shins.

Half-Backs. The two men standing next behind the quarter when the team is in possession of the ball and lines up to play. Half-backs are usually the men who do the greater part of the running. Designated also as right half and left half.

Held. Applied to a player when his progress is stopped, and the movement of the ball checked.

Heeling. The act of marking a fair catch by pointing the heel into the ground.

Heeling Out. A term applied in the Canadian game when the ball is put in play by being drawn back with the foot.

Holding. In general, unfair interference in the rush-line. Applied usually to detention of an opponent by use of the hands or arms.

In Goal. Over the goal line.

Interference. Interposing the person between any man and the object of his attack. It is usually applied to the assistance rendered a runner by his allies. It is fair interference when they do not use their hands or arms; it is unfair (or foul) when they do.

Intermission. An interval for rest; a period of ten minutes between the first and second half of a match.

In Touch. Out of bounds.

Kick-Off. A place-kick from the centre of the field of play; it is used to open each half of the game, and also whenever a goal has been obtained.

Kick-Out. A drop-kick, place-kick, or punt made by the player of a side which has touched the ball down in its own goal.

Lacing. A term applied to the leather thong which fastens up the ball; also, the string which fastens the canvas jacket.

Lacing Out and Lacing In. Terms used by the place kicker to indicate to the man holding the ball in what direction to turn the centre seam.

Leather. A slang term for the ball.

Line Breaking. Advancing into the line with the ball, and passing through an opening made usually by the assistance of the line men.

Line Bucking. Dashing straight into the line with the ball.

Line Men. Forwards or rushers.

Linesman. The man who marks the distance gained and lost.

Line-Up. The taking of positions by the team after each scrimmage.

Making the Play Safe. To closely follow the passing of the ball, so that if it be dropped the enemy may not secure it.

Muff. Missing a catch.

Nose Guard. A rubber protection for the nose.

Number Signals. Numbers used to indicate plays so that the opponents shall not recognize them.

Off-Side. In front of the ball; that is, between the ball and the opponents' goal. (The opposite of "on-side.")

On-Side. Generally speaking, behind the ball; that is, between the ball and one's own goal line.

Pacing the Distance. Pacing by the referee of the required number of yards when the ball is being brought in from touch.

Pass. Throwing or handing the ball from one player to another. More specifically, the movement of the ball from the quarter to the runner. The movement of the ball from the centre to the quarter is called the snap.

Penalty. Any forfeit inflicted by the umpire or referee.

Phase. (Slang.) Has a similar meaning to that of *rattle*, which see.

Piling Up. Falling upon the runner in a heap after the referee's whistle has blown.

Place-Kick. A kick made by kicking the ball after it has been placed upon the ground.

Play. A call of the referee to continue the game; also any single operation for the advance of the ball; also the manner in which an individual performs his part.

Point Out, Point In. Terms used by the kicker to indicate whether the holder is to swing the point of the ball out from him or toward him.

Points. The value of certain acts as expressed in the score.

Punt. A kick made by letting the ball fall from the hands and kicking it before it touches the ground.

Punt-On. A punt made in a similar fashion to a punt-out, only from within the field of play. (No longer used in the American game.)

Punt-Out. A kick made from behind the opponents' goal line to another player of the same side who stands out in the field to catch the ball.

Push Plays. Plays which depend for their success upon a body of men grouped behind the runner to force him through the line by sheer strength.

Quarter-Back or Quarter. The man behind the centre, who takes the ball when it is snapped back, and passes it to the runner.

Rattle. Slang expression, meaning to disconcert.

Referee. The judge of the position and progress of the ball.

Revolving Wedge. A form of attack in which the players group in the shape of a wedge, and after the first forward impact turn their course partially or wholly, so that the entire wedge rolls, as it were, around the obstacle.

Run. An advance made by the player carrying the ball.

Rushers or Forwards. The seven men who form the first or forward line when a team lines up. The rushers are two ends, two tackles, two guards, and the centre or snap-back. Their positions are not now so accurately defined as formerly.

Rush-Line Half. A back who, on the defense, plays up behind the line.

Safety. A point of scoring made against a team when one of its players, guarding his goal, receives the ball in some way from one of his own side, and touches it down behind his goal line; or when he himself takes the ball back and touches it down; or when the ball, kicked by one of his own side, bounds back across his own goal line and he then touches it down. The term "safety" is applied because this gives him the privilege of taking the ball out for a kick, and thus relieving the pressure against his goal. A safety scores two points for the other side.

Sailer. A kick where the ball takes advantage of the wind, and stays up a long time.

Score. Used either as a verb or a noun. To score is to make points against the opponent; the score is the number of points made.

Scrapping. Rough tussling in the line.

Scrimmage. A scrimmage takes place when the holder of the ball places it upon the ground and puts it in play by kicking it forward or snapping it back.

Second Half. The second thirty-five minutes of the game.

Series. Any number of different plays which are executed from the same formation or line-up. Also, any number of plays following one another in a predetermined order, without separate signals.

Shin Guard. A protection for the front of the leg.

Side Lines. The boundary lines running along the side of the field.

Signals. The method used by the quarter to indicate to the team what the play is to be.

Sign Signals. Those given by means of some motion of the hand, foot, head, or body.

Slugging. Striking with the closed fist.

Small Wedge. A group of two or three men, usually hastily formed for an attack.

Snap-Back. The act of sending the ball back to the quarter-back, usually performed by the centre man in the rush-line. The term is also used to indicate the player who does the snapping back.

Soldier. To shirk or play listlessly.

Spiral. A kick similar to the twister, in which the ball maintains a true course, while revolving on its long axis.

Split Wedge. A wedge which, after being started, divides into parts.

Spread Out. To stretch out the rush-line, separating the men one from another.

Tackle. Used both as a verb and a noun. To tackle is to seize the runner. A tackle is the act of seizing the runner, and is also applied to the man who plays between the end rush and the guard in the forward line.

Tandem. A method of grouping the players whereby a runner is preceded or followed by an interferer in direct line of his body; also used to designate a play in which the attack is by a grouping of this sort.

Team Play. A systematic cooperation of effort by each man on a team towards a common end.

Ten-Yard Line. A line drawn ten yards from the centre of the field parallel to the goal lines, in front of which the opponents cannot advance until the ball is kicked off. (Also used to designate a ten-yard distance from either goal.)

Throttling. Tackling which prevents an opponent from breathing; sometimes wrongly applied to any tackle around the neck.

Time. A call of the referee that stops the game.

Time Out. Time taken out by the referee when play is not actually in progress.

Touch-Back. The act of touching the ball to the ground behind one's own goal line, the impetus which sent the ball across having been received from an opponent.

Touch-Down. Touching the ball to the ground behind the opponents' goal line. A touch-down scores four points.

Touch-in-Goal. Out of bounds and past the goal line.

Tossing. The chance turning of a coin, by which the captains determine the choice of goal.

Tripping. Tackling below the knees, or in any way holding or stopping the runner by the feet or lower part of the leg when he is running.

Try-at-Goal. An attempt to kick the ball over the cross-bar of the opponents' goal. A touch-down entitles a side to a try-at-goal.

Twenty-five-Yard Line. A line drawn twenty-five yards from each goal, and parallel to the goal line. It is the limit of kick-off.

Twister. A kick which either temporarily or permanently rocks or sways the ball rapidly on its short axis as it moves ahead.

Umpire. The official who judges the conduct of the players.

Using the Arm. Similar to the use of the hands, only that the arm is used instead.

Using the Hands. Applied to both a fair use of the hands and an unfair use. A fair use is where the runner, having the ball, pushes out with his hand and thus wards off the men attempting to tackle him. Another fair use of the hands is in the case of the would-be tacklers pushing the interference aside in order to reach the runner.

Walking In. Bringing the ball in from the side line when it has gone out of bounds.

Warding Off. The same as using the hands or arm by the runner.

Wedge. A group of men formed about the runner to assist him in his advance.

Wedge on a Down. A wedge that is formed when the ball is in a scrimmage.

Word Signals. Various forms of expression (either sentences or single words), used by any player to convey information to his allies without its being intelligible to the opponents.

CHAPTER VII

TWENTY YEARS OF FOOTBALL

Difficulty of Assimilating English Rugby in America. When the game of football was taken up by the College Associations, and an attempt was made, by the aid of rules, to develop the former "rush" into a rational and well-regulated game, recourse was had to the English Rugby Rules. The American players found in this code many uncertain and knotty points which caused much trouble in their game, especially as they had no traditions, or older and more experienced players, to whom they could turn for the necessary explanations. The Harvard men, who had learned the game chiefly from the Canadians, were able to obtain information to some extent from this source, but even then satisfactory explanations were not always forthcoming. After struggling a year or two with these difficulties, the college players naturally began to think for themselves, and to plan how suitable rules could be made for their own game. In this way was brought about the commencement of a series of changes in the rules which has lasted to the present day, and even now for some time in the future bids fair to be a matter of discussion involving long sessions of committees, before all points can be satisfactorily settled.

Special Instances. The first rules to be changed in the Rugby Union Code were numbers 8 and 9, which were so ambiguous as to cause endless trouble in their correct interpretation. Rule 9 was as follows: —

"A touch-down is when a player, putting his hand on the ball in touch or in goal, stops it so that it remains dead, or fairly so."

Rule 8 defined the ball as being dead "when it rests absolutely motionless upon the ground." The idea of awarding a touch-down when the ball is "dead or fairly so" carried too great uncertainty for American minds. Every one who has played the game at all knows how easy and endless a proceeding it is for half a dozen men to follow a bounding ball across the goal line, and there tumble about and wrestle with each other in the endeavor to make it "dead or fairly so." When was the referee to discriminate and say that the touch-down had been made? The result was that the clause "or fairly so" was stricken out of the rules at the close of the first season.

The Scrimmage and its Development. The next change was in regard to the scrummage, or scrimmage, as American phraseology has it. This feature of the English game has already been described at considerable length in a preceding chapter. The Americans at first adopted this same method of putting the ball in play, but in a very short time the advantages of heeling out the ball from the scrummage, a custom not then tolerated in England or Canada, were keenly appreciated, and no prejudice was felt against the practice. The clever scrummagers, therefore, taught themselves to perform this feat quickly and accurately, with the result that the half-backs knew where and when to expect the ball, and so could be more efficient in passing it to the runner.

Heeling Out. From this point it was but a short step to assign a particular player to this duty of heeling out or snapping back the ball from the scrimmage to one of the halves. It was then no longer necessary for the other forwards to bunch close together about the ball and try to advance it along the ground, but it was found much more advantageous for them to line up across the field, taking care to be on-side when the ball was snapped, and each one on the lookout for a chance to break through at the proper moment and down the runner with as slight a gain as possible.

The Quarter-Back. The next point was the development of the quarter-back, who replaced the half-backs and held a position directly behind the snap-back or centre-rush, and received the ball directly from the latter's foot. This second man was at first allowed to run forward with the ball, but later this was forbidden, the quarter-back always passing the ball to some one else for a run or kick. This development of the scrummage into a more open style of play is the chief point of difference between the English and American games. The two divergent methods of putting the ball in play produce sports of an entirely distinct character, and it is at this point that the Americans broke entirely away from their predecessors and formed a new game of their own.

Solution of Further Difficulties. Attendant upon this very important change in the form of the game came the necessity of altering regulations which bore directly upon the scrummage in the English code of rules. This was especially the case in Rule 14, which forbade any player touching the ball with the hands when it was in a scrummage. It was impossible to determine when the scrummage began and when it ended, or how many men were engaged in it. The solution of this difficulty was reached by enacting that only the snap-back and the opponent directly opposite to him were participants in the scrummage, and that these two could not take up the ball from the ground until it had touched a third man.

Rules 12 and 13 in the Rugby code provided that no player should take up the ball when it was dead, but only when rolling or bounding. Players tried to dodge this rule by kicking the ball slightly as it lay motionless upon the ground, and then picking it up in the hands. In actual practice this was found to be of no great value, because of the small variety of cases when it would be applicable. The players were too quick in seizing the ball when free and rolling about, and would be upon it before it had time to come to a standstill. It thus never became dead except in the hands of a player or in touch. These regulations, therefore, were soon discarded.

Maul in Goal. The "maul in goal" was a feature in the original Rugby game which was a source of unending trouble to the Americans. Rules 19 and 20 provided that when a runner was tackled behind the goal line the ball should remain in possession of the side having it when it crossed the line, unless the players of the other side gained entire possession of it by force. In this way every one was instigated to join in the "maul" and form a lawless, struggling mass, which might grow rough at times, and in any case had no limit either in time or character. The referee could with difficulty tell where the ball was or when a touch-down was made, so that, after combating this feature for several seasons, and trying vainly to obtain a correct and satisfactory interpretation of the rules, all football players alike agreed that every rule containing the words "maul in goal" should be dropped. It was enacted instead that as soon as the runner was held after crossing the goal line, the ball should be put upon the ground and a touch-down counted at that point.

Block Games. Rules regarding "touch-in-goal" and scoring of "safety touch-downs" became necessary at the time of the "block game," which for a time threatened to actually kill American football. This style of game was adopted by a losing team, or by one which had made a few points and then desired only to prevent the opponents from scoring, not being desirous of adding to its own score. The idea was to keep possession of the ball, and by a number of short rushes backwards or forwards to use up the time till the half was over. Thus nothing was gained for either side and the game proved uninteresting and aimless to an extreme degree. If a team, using these tactics, should be forced behind its own goal line, the ball was taken out to the twenty-five-yard line and the same style of play resumed. This game could thus be prolonged indefinitely, and was used quite extensively during two or three seasons, after which two steps were taken to check it.

The Five-Yard Rule. The first of these was to make a safety count two points against the side making it, and the second was to adopt the so-called "five-yard rule." The latter provided that a team holding the ball must, in three successive fairs or downs, advance it five yards or retreat with it twenty, and, failing to do this, must deliver it over to the other side. By this rule was remedied the greatest fault that has ever been found in the American game, and its safety for the immediate future was assured.

English Off and On Side. The English rules regarding "off-side" and "on-side" seemed rather obscure to the Americans, and also appeared to contain a discrepancy. According to Rule 24 (as has been explained in the first chapter), a man off-side was put on-side as soon as the ball touched the dress or person of an opponent, while Rule 25 stated that the opponent may run five yards before those off-side are free to commence or attempt to run or tackle. The one restriction seemed to make the other unnecessary. Ultimately the latter was cut out of the American rules, and a man off-side was declared on-side again as soon as an opponent had touched the ball.

Punting Out and Punting On. The English method of punting the ball "out" or "on," in order that a team scoring a try in the corner of the field might have a better opportunity for kicking a goal, was used to advantage for several years. When touch-downs were made to count in the score, however, a serious trouble arose. After some practice it was possible for a player on the team so scoring a try to punt the ball with his shin, or even his knee, into the arms of another man on his own side, who stood only a yard or two from the goal line, and immediately after making his catch rushed across the goal line, thus scoring another touch-down. This proceeding was made easier by placing two of the heaviest men on a team in front of the catcher, so as to aid him in advancing the necessary short distance against the opponents' opposition. Upon one occasion a team at St. George's Ground, Hoboken, made in this way eleven successive touch-downs from an original one at the corner of the field, gradually working the ball nearer to the goal posts with every effort. Finally they grew tired of this method of play, and took the ball out in front of the posts, whence they kicked an easy goal. Legislation against such tactics has been adopted, and an effectual stop put to their use. As a matter of fact the practice of "punting on" is no longer of any value at the present day.

In Touch. The rules regarding playing the ball in from touch have been slightly altered in the American rules from those in the original Rugby code, and the style of making the play has undergone a marked change. The most common method in the old days of the game was to throw the ball in at right angles to the touch line, but now teams usually let the centre-rush walk in with it and put it down for a scrimmage, the distance varying between five and fifteen yards.

Tie Games and Time of Game. A long struggle has been carried on all through the history of American football in regard to provisions against tie games. For a time the several captains tried to make a satisfactory agreement before each match, the one of the stronger team being naturally the most urgent. The legislation on this point has been in two principal directions: (1) the time of game, and (2) the methods of scoring.

At the outset, matches lasted generally an hour and a half, this time being divided into three intervals. This arrangement gave one team the advantage of the wind or any peculiarity of the field during two thirds of the whole game, and hence was declared unfair. Next, the time was divided into two halves of forty-five minutes each, and two halves of fifteen minutes each were added in case of a tie. These extra halves were finally found unnecessary, as the very exact method of scoring in vogue during the last few years has greatly lessened the probability of tie games. At a much more recent period the time of game was still further reduced to two thirty-five minute halves, which regulation remains to the present day.

Scoring. The mode of scoring has been even more perplexing, and has undergone severe changes. Primarily, as in England, only goals were scored, but later, in case of a tie by goals, "tries" or touch-downs were made to count. Next, the wording of the rule was changed to read: "A match shall be decided by a majority of goals only," and only a year later the decision was made by touch-downs, a goal counting as four touch-downs. Furthermore, in case of a tie, a goal kicked from a touch-down was given precedence over a field-kick goal. The scoring of safeties became necessary in order to partially check the block game, and caused a struggle in which the weaker teams strongly opposed the idea of attaching any importance to the scoring of safeties. It was finally agreed that in games where no other score was made, — neither by touch-downs or goals, — a team making four or more safeties less than the opponents should win the game. At the same time the safety was defined as being made only when the ball was actually carried or passed by a team across its own goal line, and not kicked over by opponents. Later on, exact values were given to the various forms of score, and the matches came to be decided by points. Slightly more value was given to touch-downs than previously. The count for such scores was then arranged, and is now as follows: touch-down from which no goal is kicked, 4 points; touch-down and goal, 6 points; goal by proper kick from field of play without a touch-down, 5 points; safety scored by opponents, 2 points.

Other Discarded and Altered Rules. Various other rules of the Rugby Union Code have been found superfluous, the necessary points being otherwise covered, or considered unnecessary for the better development of the game. Rule 35, saying that a catch made when the ball is thrown out from touch is not a fair catch; and Rule 45, allowing a player to touch the ball down in his own goal, shared this fate; and Rule 48, forbidding the bringing out of the ball between the posts after a touch-down, was also discarded, as it really was of no particular significance. Rule 51 debarred players from making a fair catch in touch; and Rule 52 prevented opponents from interfering with the ball after a touch-down. These were both found unnecessary, and dropped.

Rule 54, relating to "charging," was somewhat complicated, but worked well enough, except that the question often arose whether the ball was put in play after a fair catch by the charging of opponents or not. The kicker could step forward, thus provoking the charge, but if he then drew back, were the opponents obliged to retire behind their line? If this were not so, and the ball was put in play by the charge, then the kicker was free to run forward or to pass the ball to another man of his own side for a run, and thus gain quite an advantage. It was finally decided that the charge did not put the ball in play.

Regarding rough play, Rule 57 in the original Rugby code read, "No hacking, or hacking over, or tripping up shall be allowed under any circumstances." This rule has been changed slightly and made more explicit. "Tripping up" was made to include tackling below the knees as well as throwing a runner by the foot, and is forbidden by a rule against foul tackling. "Butting" was also thought to be productive of injuries, and hence has been prohibited. The present reading of the rule forbids "all unnecessary roughness and striking," and seems to cover the ground very satisfactorily.

Uniforms. Rule 58 of the Rugby code forbids the wearing of projecting nails, iron plates, or gutta-percha on any part of the boots or shoes. These restrictions still exist in the American rules, with the additional provision that "no sticky or greasy substance shall be used on the person of players." This last clause was rendered necessary by a peculiar episode which took place in New Haven immediately after the canvas jacket had first made its appearance. A team, dressed in this new garb, came to play against the Yale men. In addition, its players had smeared lard all over their clothes, and in the game they greatly astonished the conservative New Haven men by the way in which their runners slipped through the latter's fingers. It was only by filling their hands with sand that the Yale men were able to retard their opponents' rushes. The players during these years also became accustomed to apply turpentine to their hands in order to counteract the effect of the lard on the dress of their opponents. As a result the ball soon became very sticky and difficult to pass accurately, and the best interests of the game demanded that the present rule be adopted, although this use of lard would never be so effective at the present time, since the science of low, hard tackling has been reduced to such a fine point. Tackling, which was in the early days not allowed below the hips, is now permitted down to the knees.

Officials. The question of referees or judges has given rise to considerable discussion, and alterations from the English rules have been many. The Rugby rule said that unless officials were appointed by the two captains, these two men should decide all disputes, and that questions regarding the correct interpretation of rules could be appealed to the Rugby Union Committee. The evidence of judges was found to be necessary, and for a time two men were employed in this capacity. Then a referee was added to decide in case the judges disagreed on any point. Three men made too large a number, and the two judges were all the time tempted to badger the referee, each one arguing his own case. The judges were therefore abolished, and all games were for a time regulated by one referee. This arrangement gave place only a few years ago to the adoption of two officials, a referee and an umpire, the former to pass judgment concerning the ball, the latter concerning the men. It was at first feared that it would be difficult to make a satisfactory distinction between the two fields of their respective jurisdiction, but in practice this arrangement has been found to work very well indeed. In recent years two more officials have been added. They are called linesmen, and have the duty of watching the downs. They stand on the side of the field holding canes fastened by a cord at a distance of five yards apart, and at each "first down" they mark in this way both the spot of this down and the point to be gained in three rushes. These men have proved of invaluable service to the referee in determining "first downs."

American Rule-making. It can easily be seen from the foregoing review of the most important changes made in the football rules since the introduction of the game into America, that much time and thought has been spent by all those interested in the sport in an endeavor to further its interests as much as possible. These energies have been directed chiefly towards perfecting the rules of the game, in order to prevent brutality and slugging, to make science and skill count for more in winning a match than brute force and weight, and to make the game fast and interesting to both player and spectator.

Rule-making in the early days of the sport lay chiefly in the hands of the various captains, who met together before a match, and decided in what manner certain points of discussion should be settled. Later on it was deemed wise to call a meeting of delegates from the various institutions which were supporting teams in the field, and allow them to draw up a code of rules for the ensuing season. The result of this plan was that each university was tempted to send a man to the convention with instructions to put through certain rules, which would be most beneficial for their own team in that particular season. Thus temporary circumstances were at times given more consideration than the best interests of the sport, and the tendency in this direction was very strong, however earnest and well-intentioned the individual delegates might be. It was not long before this danger was appreciated, and fear began to be felt that the rules were becoming worse rather than better. The matter was a subject of serious discussion for some time among graduates, captains, and certain members of the college faculties.

Advisory Committee. At last definite action was taken by these persons, and through the adoption of a new constitution by the football association it was provided that all changes in the rules should be made by a permanent Advisory Committee of graduates. This committee held meetings, adopted each year whatever changes seemed expedient, and submitted them for ratification to the Intercollegiate Association, which has in every case accepted the proposals thus made. In case the Association should not ratify, then the proposed rules could still be carried by a majority vote of the Advisory Committee. This plan of rule-making worked perfectly, no cause arising for any friction between the different parties as long as the Intercollegiate Association existed as a strong body.

University Athletic Club. In the fall of 1894 the Intercollegiate Association, after the withdrawal of Wesleyan and the University of Pennsylvania, consisted of only two universities, Princeton and Yale. The two representatives of these institutions felt that the year was a critical one for the success of football, and that rules formed by only two universities would not carry sufficient weight. Their gravest fears were caused by the greatly exaggerated development of mass plays, which had come into use during the last two or three years, and were regarded as an increasing evil. The University Athletic Club, of New York, was appealed to and was requested to invite a number of representative football men to a convention for the discussion of rule-making. Such a meeting was held, and the suggestions thus made were later accepted unconditionally, both by the University Athletic Club, the Advisory Committee, and the Intercollegiate Association.

The situation at the end of another year was still more complex. Two of the larger universities had a quarrel, resulting in a complete rupture of athletic relations between them, and a formation of two distinct sets of rules. The other college teams adopted one code or the other with slight variations, and before almost every match it was necessary for the two elevens to come to an understanding over all points of disagreement. The University Athletic Club was again requested to call together a convention of experts, but declined because one of the two universities mentioned above did not join in this appeal. The better sense of all football enthusiasts showed itself in the end, and a universal appeal was made before another year. The committee consisted of six men, each, with one exception, being empowered by his university to act as its representative. The sixth gentleman was invited as and considered a delegate at large. It was voted by this convention that no rule should be adopted without the unanimous consent of the members, and a thorough revision of the code was undertaken.

Rules — Committee's Work. The results of the work of this convention were published in June, 1896, and contain some few changes. The deliberations of the greatest importance bore on momentum and mass plays, while slight alterations were made regarding "fair catch," the duties of the umpire and referee, the more effective elimination of brutality and unnecessary roughness, "charging" and putting the ball in play.

Regarding the first of these points, it was enacted that before the ball is put in play in a scrimmage, no player of the side having the ball shall take more than one step in the direction of the opponents' goal, and that, when the ball is put in play, at least five players must be on the line of scrimmage. Also if more than five players, not including the quarter-back, be behind the line of scrimmage, two of them must stand more than five yards behind said line, or must stand outside of the end men on said line. These regulations prevent the players from massing together behind the line, or from gaining any momentum by moving forward before the ball is snapped.

The player making a "fair catch" is protected by a rule stating that unless the catcher advances beyond his mark no off-side man shall interfere with him under penalty of fifteen yards loss.

The referee has the final decision on all points not covered by the umpire, and he may appeal to the umpire and linesmen for testimony upon all points within his jurisdiction. The referee shall also determine the time for a down by blowing his whistle, and he can give fifteen yards to the opponents of any player who then "piles upon" the runner.

The snapper-back is given entire possession of the ball. If opponents interfere with his putting the ball in play, his side gains five yards for every such offense. The old rules used to allow the opposing centre partial possession of the ball, so that he could delay the game unnecessarily by preventing the ball from being snapped.

"Charging" by opponents is lawful if the punter advances beyond his line, or as soon as the ball touches the ground. If the opponents charge before the ball is thus put in play, they shall be put back five yards for every such offense.

Division of Labor in the American Game. As the American game has been developed by this series of changes in the rules, the idea of a division of labor by the assignment of particular duties to each individual player has been greatly emphasized. In a general way the eleven men of a team may be divided into two groups, the seven forwards and the four backs. In the early days the work of the former was best described as a steady, hard rush from the beginning to the end of the game, each one of the seven having the same duties. As the scrimmage developed into the more open rush-line, it was found that the men could be advantageously assigned to positions according to their weight, quickness, cleverness, etc. For instance, three heavy men, the snapper-back, with a "guard" on either side, would be placed in the centre, so as to protect the quarter-back till he should make his pass, and the play was thus under way. The men of moderate weight, quick in their movements and hard tacklers, were stationed next in the line, and acquired the name of "tackles." The two end rushers completed the line. These must be sure tacklers, fast runners, and clever players, for it is their duty to bring down a runner coming around their end, and to get down the field under a kick soon enough to stop their opponent the very moment he has the ball, or to take advantage of a muff or fumble. These line men have innumerable other duties, which gradually devolve upon them, and which vary in different teams, as every captain is very likely to have his own idea as to how his men should play together.

The four backs are the quarter-back, whose duties have already been somewhat explained, two half-backs, and the full-back. These positions result from those of the old Rugby backs, the number of men in each capacity being changed to suit the general development of the game. The half-back must be a player of considerable versatility. His chief function is to run and kick when on the offensive, and to tackle with judgment and certainty when on the defensive. These have always been the fundamental requirements of the English three-quarter-back, but the manner in which they are put into practice has undergone considerable change in America. The kicking is now left more to the full-back, though it is considered an advantage to have three good kicking backs. The running of the half is not as much dependent upon the player's individual merits, since now he has two or three other men to go before him, and block off the opposing tacklers, and the clever half is the man who knows how to follow his interference well, to make use of it as long as it is advantageous, and then to know when to break away from it, and make his own way. The duties of the full-back have developed into much the same as those of the half-back. He is chosen perhaps more as a good kicker and sure tackler, but is still expected to do a good share of the running and blocking. He corresponds to the English back, but is brought much more actively into the game. The duties of the backs vary considerably with the ideas of the various captains. Very often, when a team is playing on the defensive, it is thought advisable to bring one or both of the halves up into the rush-line, so as to overpower the opponents more easily, and at other times they play back a few yards to catch the runner immediately upon his passing the forwards.

The vital element in coaching a team lies nowadays in this problem of the division of labor. The greater part of the practice, during the latter part of the season especially, consists of constant drilling in the different plays, and of inventing means to stop the opponents' rushes. The captain and coaches of each team attend the games played by their opponents, and study their plays, in order to discern their weakest points, and plan how their own team can best meet them. It is so arranged that each man in the line knows what his play is, whatever may be the tactics adopted by the opponents. In offensive work each team has various plays, chosen as those best suited to advance the ball, taking advantage of any weakness of their opponents. In each of these plays every man in the eleven has a special duty assigned to him, and every one is informed beforehand what the play is going to be by means of a code of signals, sometimes very complex, which are usually given by the quarter-back.

CHAPTER VIII

TWENTY-FOUR HOURS WITH A 'VARSITY PLAYER

A Popular Error. There are many mistaken ideas in regard to the daily routine of a 'Varsity football player who is in training. Even persons ordinarily well informed about college sports go far astray upon this subject.

The popular impression seems to be that the football player rises at five in the morning, runs from four to ten miles across country, just to stretch his muscles, before breakfast; eats at all three meals a prodigious amount of nearly raw beef, washed down with a plentiful supply of ale; does little or no studying; plays football morning and afternoon; and finally presents to the coaches in the evening the serious problem of how to give him exercise enough to keep him in decent condition.

With this general conception are united visions of a still more lurid nature. Stories are told of players who, after eating several huge chunks of raw beef, forget that they have taken their meat course, and, under the impression that they have not dined, tackle the entire menu, and eat a second dinner. Other visions rise of the football player injured on the field during the afternoon play, and resting while a broken arm or a fractured rib is temporarily bandaged, in order that nothing need interfere with the practice.

Unfortunately, perhaps, for the football player, many of these visions are far from the truth. Too often, instead of having a voracious appetite, he has what is popularly known as a "skittish" one; and, so far from furnishing a problem to the coaches of how to give him work enough to keep him in condition, he is a source of no little anxiety by reason of his steady decline in weight.

What this Chapter will Offer. It is certainly due to the player that these exaggerated ideas should be corrected and the true condition of affairs stated. Perhaps there is no better way of doing this than to give, briefly, the routine of a 'Varsity player in a single day of the season. By reason of the varying arrangements at the different universities, a universal routine does not exist. A certain general outline, however, can be given, which at least shall not be exaggerated or fanciful. In its minor details, and in the relative order of the events of the day, the picture may need to be changed to fit the player at one or another of the leading colleges, but, generally speaking, it will be found to be a fair description of a single day as it is passed in the height of the season by a player on any one of our 'Varsity teams. We shall begin at the beginning of the day.

Rising and Breakfasting. From a sleep which, however disturbed it may have been by excitement or anxiety, in the earlier hours of the night, is abnormally sound in the early hours of the morning, the player is aroused by a sharp knock upon his door at seven o'clock. He is given three quarters of an hour in which to dress and report himself at the training quarters. These quarters are usually centrally located, and there the members of the team eat their meals together. The ideal training quarters are those at Princeton, where a perfectly arranged clubhouse is maintained, with reading-room, assembly-room, a large dining-room, and every comfort. At few of the other universities, however, are such arrangements as yet possible; and all that the "training-table" usually means to the player is a large dining-room in some boarding-house, where one or two tables run diagonally across the room, and twenty-five or thirty players crowd and jostle against each other in the endeavor to provide seats for all their number at one time. Sometimes there is a small assembly-room, in which the men gather before going in to the table, and here, if there is a piano, there is sure to be music and singing.

Into this room we go with the player. One by one the men straggle in; that they have dressed in a hurry is amusingly apparent; but they are not troubled with self consciousness, and are quite indifferent to their looks. Far from being the ferocious beings of popular conception, which believes that roughness on the field implies roughness off of it, they are, ordinarily, a very good-natured, decent set of fellows. As they enter they follow, with singular unanimity, a long established custom, and shy their caps into some faraway corner, or at some imaginary hat-peg on the wall. It is seldom that the cap of a football player is found in the position where it might naturally be expected to be.

When the men have nearly all reported for breakfast, the captain enters, with the air of having a vigorous sense of responsibility. There are half a dozen sharp interrogatories to different men on different subjects. This man is asked if he slept better than the night before; another is questioned as to the condition of his ankle or knee, and he is made to show his paces, with a view to determining how soon he can be counted upon for the work of the game. Another is told that he must secure the services of a masseuse, and be well rubbed during the morning. Thus the condition of the cripples is hurriedly noted, and dismissed with a word of direction. The men then either go into the breakfast-room, or, if it is late in the season, they are apt to be put through some signal practice on the lawn behind the house. By eight o'clock they are all at table. The menu is much the same as it would be at the ordinary American breakfast table: there is oatmeal, or some other cereal, followed by chops or steak in liberal quantities, with potatoes, and perhaps a bit of bacon. Eggs cooked in any style are always on call; there is no tea or coffee, but generally milk, with plenty of pure drinking-water or oat-meal water, served always without ice.

The Morning's Work. Breakfast over, the men separate for classes and lecture-rooms, not to meet again as a team until the hour of lunch, which is at one o'clock. During the morning there is but little football work prescribed or undertaken, unless it is within ten days of the close of the season, and the important match of the year is close at hand. But some of the backs will be out for an hour of kicking practice. This morning squad may include the centre and quarter back, with the other backs. The work will be almost exclusively devoted to passing, kicking, and catching. It will be supervised by the coach who has this department of the work in charge, and the captain will rarely be present, the only spectators being a few specimens of the genus "small boy," who will freely criticise and encourage the players. Sometimes the morning practice may be extended, for the development of some new form of interference, or for the correction of some fault which has shown itself in the team, and which needs to be remedied without delay. But morning practice very rarely amounts to anything more than an hour's work for a few individuals.

Lunch. At one o'clock the men assemble again at the training-table, where lunch is served. The meal is not a very popular one; it lacks the enthusiasm of breakfast. Taking place, as it does, before the hard work of the day, there is more or less earnestness, and even anxiety, among the men, and there is little jollity at the table. They seat themselves as they arrive, with no courtesy in waiting for late comers, the meal being eaten on the go-as-you-please order, with a not too attractive and elaborate menu. Soup, possibly; sometimes fish; but always a liberal supply of meat, with three or four vegetables, and vast quantities of dry toast. Tea and coffee are strictly barred, but a substitute in the shape of claret is allowed to some of the men in small quantities.

The Afternoon Practice. After lunch, at some hour between three and half past three, the men must betake themselves to the field, and be ready to report to the captain, dressed for the practice, at four o'clock sharp. At Yale the hours are somewhat different, the afternoon practice taking place at an early hour, leaving the balance of the afternoon for study; but in the majority of colleges the practice comes after the other work of the day, and begins about four o'clock.

The operation of dressing is pursued in a manner peculiar to the football player. It seems to be a part of his nature to scatter his limited clothing about in every direction, so that the work of dressing is undertaken in the most disjointed and generally irresponsible manner. Part of his clothing has been left in the drying-room; a stocking is found at a remote distance from its mate; his belt has strayed no one knows where; there is a broken lacing on his canvas, which he neglects to replace, preferring to fasten it in a few clumsy knots. He does not dress; he throws his clothes on, and loosely fastens them wherever they happen to hang. It takes the constant vigilance of manager, captain, and coach to see that he does not neglect the precaution of suitable padding, and that his shoes are properly cleated, and his clothes decently tacked together.

Promptly at four o'clock comes the call of the captain, and the men trot out upon the field. The description of the practice belongs to another chapter, and we need not refer to it here. Briefly, it consists of individual practice, followed by team practice without an opponent, followed in its turn by what is technically known as "stiff" practice, or hard practice, against a college eleven, and finally ending with the correction of personal faults in a short aftermath of individual practice.

Weighing and Rubbing Down. When it is over, back to the quarters, just at dusk, goes the tired player; tired in body, but refreshed in spirit; the work of the day is done, and he has a right to the rest he has earned; it would be idle to deny that a part of the work has been severe, and some of it drudgery. The dirty clothing is stripped off, and the delight of a shower bath is followed by a brisk rubbing down by the trainer or attendant, one of whom is regularly employed for this work by every college team.

After the bath, and before the rubbing down, comes the important operation of weighing-in. The player steps upon the scales, not apparently interested in his weight, but rather giving it up in a perfunctory and half satisfied manner to the manager, who stands on guard at the exit of the bath-room to prevent the escape of any player without having his weight duly recorded. Later in the season the weights of the players will often not be given to them to know, but they are carefully reported to the trainer, and the captain will himself give not a few anxious moments to the variations of this or that player upon the scales from day to day.

After rubbing down comes the leisurely dressing. The men talk about the incidents of the day's practice, and give a running comment on the work of the afternoon. The coaches are moving about among the players with words of criticism or approval, which the players take in equally good part, showing a marked willingness to learn their faults and profit by instruction.

The Evening Dinner. Dinner is served at the football training-table at 6.30 o'clock. It is the most enjoyable meal of the day, and altogether the most delightful period of the twenty-four hours. At the head of the table sits the captain, with the doctor or trainer at the foot. Most of the coaches are present at the festive board, and often there is, besides, some old graduate whose interest in the team has been great enough to induce him to pay a visit to the quarters, that he might meet the men personally and hear the latest news of their progress.

Bread Fights and Practical Joking. Spirits usually run high at the evening meal. There is a good deal of practical joking and story-telling. If the team is not depressed by some very recent defeat, the chances are strongly in favor of a bread fight. It always begins about the same way. Some unlucky fellow is pitched upon, and every effort is put forth to guy him. He is made the victim of innumerable jokes; his playing, or some incident in his behavior, or, perhaps, some trifling peculiarity in his dress or speech, is seized upon as the pretext for a general discussion of his qualities by the entire table. One word of remonstrance, or one attempt to answer back, is the signal for bread throwing.

In a moment the air is full of flying missiles, toast, crackers, potatoes, oranges, — anything, — go flying through the air in every direction! There is only one door of escape, and that is to drop under the table. One by one the quieter members disappear in this direction, and the final issues of the fight, which has now broadened and developed into half a dozen side quarrels, are concluded by the few remaining participants. It may be that an unlucky dodge upsets a pitcher of milk, or a good-natured struggle ends in an upheaval of one end of the table, while three or four dishes go clattering to the floor, and this unexpected *denouement* is apt to conclude the fight.

Spirits are never depressed, nor tempers ruffled in these combats. The only long faces are worn by the waiters, or possibly by the proprietor, as the former gaze upon the dirty floor, and the latter surveys the ruined wall-paper. When comparative order is restored, the players slip back into their seats, although the combat is apt to be renewed along side lines during all the rest of the meal, and half a dozen feuds are settled before the dinner is ended.

The menu for this meal is of most generous proportions; soup, a choice between two kinds of meat, four or five dishes of vegetables, cranberry or apple sauce, dry toast, and a light pudding or ice cream, make up a good list of eatables; while ale, claret, milk, and water furnish a fair choice of liquid refreshments.

Evening Work. With dinner the work of the day is not always complete. Very often there is signal practice, or the members of the first eleven are summoned to meet to learn a new play, or perfect the development of some new form of interference. Perhaps, in place of either of these, there is a brief blackboard talk by one of the coaches, or some graduate official talks to the men on the interpretation of certain rules and penalties.

In no case, however, are these meetings protracted beyond the hour of 9.30, for at ten o'clock the player must pack himself off to bed. The consoling evening pipe, or longed for cigarette, is of course denied him, but walking along in the darkness to his room, he is hailed by half a dozen of his college mates, and as he listens to their exultant tone of approval of the team, or their congratulations upon his splendid personal work in the last game, he tastes the intoxicating cup of popular favor, and is repaid liberally for all the trouble and exactions of the day.

PART II

FOR THE PLAYER

CHAPTER I

ORGANIZING A TEAM

Three Cardinal Points. In the organization of a football team, as in everything else, there is a right way and a wrong way to begin, and if a school or a college or a university begins in the wrong way, they will probably experience a succession of reverses, and will not have an equal chance until, after a term of years, they learn their mistakes by experience, and a reformation takes place. On the other hand, those who have begun in the right way find things easy to their hand. With reasonable effort, success comes at least in a fair proportion of years, and many of the evils attendant upon an unfortunate policy not only do not trouble them, but are absolutely unknown. There are three cardinal points to be observed in arranging for college athletics, and those are to secure the support of the faculty, to insist upon a clean record of candidates in the matter of pure athletics, and to obtain the sympathetic backing of the college or school.

Where no Team has Existed. In organizing a football team in a school where there has never been a team, the first thing to be done is to approach the head master and obtain his consent and support. This can usually best be done through influential graduates of the school, for their opinion in affairs is naturally of far more weight than are the desires of the boys themselves, and it is better form for the request to come through them as intermediates. The plans should be thoroughly set forth, and, if consent be obtained, as, barring some unusual reason, it is pretty sure to be, a school meeting should be held, and these graduates should address the boys there assembled. They should explain in detail the value of the sport as a means both of developing the individual who takes part, and also as a factor in stimulating loyalty to the school and binding together all the members in a stronger sympathy. Love of country in a man is only a growth of the feeling that makes him loyal to his college and loyal to his school, and competitive interscholastic and intercollegiate sport is a very strong factor in developing this side of character.

Committee in Charge. It is well at this first meeting to elect a committee consisting, say, of one graduate, one member of the faculty, and one representative of the school, to act as an advisory committee. This committee should report at a later meeting, formulating a plan of action which may properly consist of the election of a manager, and an assistant manager, from the school. These two, with the aid of the advisory committee, should have charge of the laying out of the field and the securing of candidates for the eleven. After a few days of practice they should appoint a temporary field captain, who should have charge of the men, and under whose directions the practice should be carried on. He will appoint a captain of the second eleven, and for perhaps two weeks be in sole control of the field practice. At the end of that time the advisory committee, the manager, and the field captain should hold a meeting and select some twenty players, who should then, subject to the approval of the advisory committee, elect a permanent captain.

Policy for Further Management. After this establishment of the sport, the manager and assistant manager of succeeding years should be annually elected by a mass meeting of the school, the assistant manager always being supposed to succeed the manager unless there is some stringent reason for breaking the line of succession. The captain in following years should be elected by the team, those members only having a vote who have played in part or the whole of the match that is classed as the important contest of the year.

Permanent Advisory Committee. In subsequent years the advisory committee may well be increased, and may consist of two graduates elected by the graduates of the school, two members of the faculty, appointed by the trustees or named by the head master, and the captain and manager *ex officio.* This committee may or may not have executive power, but, if it seem best to vest them with more than advisory powers, such powers should be conveyed to them through a vote of the school at a mass meeting.

Formation of the Association. A constitution should be drawn up, covering all points, both as to the powers of the various officers and also as to the right to vote. It may be best to give every member of the school the right to vote; or, it may seem better to qualify this right by the formation of an association, every member of the school who subscribes a certain sum being a member of this association, and so possessing the right to vote. The sum need not be large — merely sufficient to show an interest in the project. The subscriptions may be annual, or simply a certain sum paid in bulk, making the subscriber a member during his school course.

Practical Management. To return to the practical work. As soon as a team is organized it is time to consider the question of a coach. In the large universities there are naturally many graduates of the schools, and it is, therefore, not difficult to secure in this line the occasional services of some alumnus. It would be well, were it possible, to have a regular coach, — one who could be on hand every day, — but next best to this is to arrange for a succession of coaches coming each for a short time. The captain must then do most of the daily coaching himself. Fortunately, in almost every properly regulated school to-day there is upon the faculty some man who is thoroughly posted upon college and school athletics, and who is capable of giving the boys all they require in the way of special coaching. Under his charge should be placed the general direction of the team's progress.

University or College Organization. As the work of organizing a team in a college or university is along almost similar lines to those here laid down for a school, it is not necessary to cover it again in detail. An association should be formed, constitution adopted, manager, assistant manager, and advisory committees elected, as described for school organizations

Building up of a School of Coaching. In the matter of coaching and the selection of coach, the situation is somewhat more complex, for it is almost imperative for the eventual success of the sport at a college or university that the work be begun under the supervision of a thoroughly competent coach, who then may educate a body of coaches to assist him in the work, and eventually establish a strong system. If this be properly accomplished at the outset, the continuance of it, even in the absence of the original coach, will not be a matter of difficulty, and, in the end, the college or university will have a number of graduates who can, by working together, carry the team on from year to year. To organize such a body of coaches and to get the system in working order is only a matter of care and willingness on the part of the graduates. They should devote all the time possible to the matter, and be present, not only on the field, but also at the meetings off the field, to discuss the whys and wherefores of the proceedings. It is well that while the first appointed coach is with the team, some one of these graduates be selected as the one who shall afterward hold the position of head coach. If possible, a man should be chosen for this position whose business or profession is likely to keep him permanently in the university town. If this is not possible, try and find some graduate with leisure and a strong inclination towards clean sport who will accept this responsible charge. Although at first he may be no better posted than his companions, he will from an earnest study of the sport, coupled with his permanency of position, become the actual as well as the acknowledged head of the coaching staff. He in turn should do all in his power to build up a school of coaches, and use all efforts to have the desirable ones return year after year. By such a method of organization, and the establishment of a sound system, that will be carried on season after season, the very best results will be obtained, not only in point of deriving all the possible benefit from the sport, but also, what appeals more promptly and directly to the undergraduates' desire, in the greatest number of victories won.

CHAPTER II

TRAINING A TEAM WITHOUT A SECOND ELEVEN

First Decide whether there is a Second Eleven. The first thing a captain or coach should do upon taking charge of a team is to find out whether he is to have a second eleven or not. A great many teams presumably practise against a second eleven, whereas in fact there is no second eleven, and a frank confession of this at the outset would save a great deal of wasted time, and the result in the form of a finished team would be much more satisfactory.

There is no second eleven if the captain cannot rely upon having over twenty-two men at least out every day. To have twenty-five men out one day, and nineteen the next, almost invariably results in a long wait on the second day in the hope that the three extra men which are necessary to complete the second eleven will show up. Many a day is wasted from delays of a like nature, which a frank confession of the inability to have on hand a second eleven would turn into a satisfactory practice, for it is possible to get fairly good work and a moderately able team without the presence of a second eleven. In fact, it is almost easier to get a well-drilled team without a second eleven than with one.

Practice Possible without a Second Eleven. There are many teams in this country, representing colleges and schools, as well as athletic clubs, where the presence of a second eleven for daily practice is out of the question. It is always a study with the captain in such a condition of affairs as to what he can make out of his men, and how he shall go to work to develop the team. Let us take up first the points in which he simply follows the established precedent of teams that play against a second eleven. The second eleven is not used in the morning when practice in kicking, catching, and passing takes place. The second eleven is not used to any great extent when the first eleven are walking through their plays and practising the formation of interference. The second eleven is not used to assist in signal practice. In all these points, then, a team is as well off without a second eleven as the team which possesses enough men to make an actual game possible. We thus see that a team may practise kicking, catching, running, forming interference, and getting through signals without the aid of a second eleven.

How to Split a Team. But a team cannot practise blocking, breaking through, breaking interference, or practical tackling without opponents. The simplest way to secure these opponents, therefore, is to split a regular team in two. It is always practicable to, as it were, bend the line over, and with one extra man for the centre, play the guard opposite guard, the tackle opposite tackle, and the end opposite end, thus giving both sides of the line practice, and answering all the purpose of an ordinary opposition. Then, with four or five other men, the coach may have half-backs, quarter-back, and full-back on the opposing side. Thus with sixteen men it is possible to have a regular practice with the exception that it is directed on one side of the field, and criss-crosses are not available. But all the detail of blocking, breaking through, interfering, and breaking interference can be practised in this way with almost as good effect as in the regular line-up of university teams.

Drilling and Explaining. Beyond this the men can be much more carefully coached, and it is an acknowledged fact that the teams which have the least chance of playing with a second eleven are usually the best drilled in their formations. This is probably owing to the fact that the same amount of time is spent by these teams in going through their formations as the other teams pass in regular play. It is also easier to explain to and coach fifteen men than thirty, and when a coach is instructing a university team in the midst of a line-up, it is generally necessary to explain to a great many more men than the first eleven.

Less Chance of Injury. Another advantage of practising without a second eleven is that there is less chance of injury, and fewer men will be required to last through the season. A great many of the injuries that are received in the university teams come during practice, and here a team without a second eleven has a double advantage in that it preserves its men intact, and also that it is possible for such a team to practice with the same men day after day, until each one has his own part to perfection and they all move together like clock-work.

Daily Discussions. Another valuable feature that should be seized upon by the coach or captain who is without a second eleven, is that of daily talk and discussion on the points likely to arise. Some of these talks should occur on the field during intermission, while others should be held in the evening, so that there may be plenty of discussion and plenty of actual practice. It is possible, also, to take the men in small divisions, where the numbers are light, and practise, if the hours are short, sometimes both morning and afternoon, taking, for instance, six rushes at a time, and teaching them to block and break through, make openings, lift the line back, and do the other thousand and one things that there are for the expert forward of to-day.

Special Rules for Practice. The ingenious captain or coach can also devise many methods that will insure him as much line-up practice as is good for the men by simply making certain rules, in force for the time being. For instance, as mentioned above, playing entirely on one side of the field without criss-crosses or any plays that involve running on both sides of the centre. Then he can bar out kicking, or he can play a kicking game only on one side of the field, so that but one end has the opportunity of going down. He may also take an occasion when double passes alone are used, and with his extra five men put them all up into the line instead of using half-backs and backs. On the whole, no captain should be greatly grieved over the fact that he has but fifteen or twenty men, for it is better to have fifteen or twenty men that will work hard and practise with regularity than to have thirty men, only ten of whom can be relied upon to be on hand every day.

Strict Rulings. The practice when without a second eleven should be as much like a game as possible. By this is meant that each man should do his level best, and there should be strict ruling regarding fouls and unfair tactics of all descriptions. There is nothing that causes the practice to degenerate so rapidly as to allow holding in the line or unfair work of any kind. It is as necessary for the practice of a team that has no second eleven that there should be an umpire as it is for regular university practice. Then, too, the performance of the men should be thoroughly conscientious. Each man should go through his part of the play whether there is an opponent against him or not, exactly as he would in a match. There is nothing to drive him to do this save his own conscience, and that must be occasionally stimulated by the captain and coach.

Lack of Interest. How to Overcome. The greatest difficulty in playing without a second eleven arises from lack of interest, and this may be surmounted in a measure by special encouragement given to each man when he performs his work well, and by establishing a firm conviction that in order to play on a winning team each man must put his whole heart and soul into the work while on the practice field.

Outside Games Necessary. In order to carry out the ideas above expressed, it is advisable that as many practice games as possible with outside teams be arranged. These practice games should serve two purposes. First, they should provide for that part of the hard work which is necessary toward making a man able to endure; and secondly, they should be used as tests to find out wherein the plays that are being practised are weak, and what special parts of them need alteration. The captain and coach should also secure considerable valuable information from these practice matches as to the pluck or "sand" of the men on the team. It is very easy for a man when playing against his friends to exhibit plenty of courage, but when he faces a determined opponent, who is a stranger to him, he may show the white feather, and it is for this reason that the men should be closely watched in practice games, and action taken on any hint of shirking

Tests. To conclude briefly, the great difficulties which assail the captain and coach when so short of men as to make a second eleven impossible are those of lack of interest and lack of satisfactory tests. All the other difficulties can be overcome with a little ingenuity, but these two main ones must be always on the captain's mind, and he must work hard to stimulate interest, and watch closely the practice games, which must be to him the tests that ordinarily come through the aid of the second eleven's work.

CHAPTER III

INDIVIDUAL POSITIONS

End Rush. *Experience and Physical Characteristics*. The position of end rush is one capable of the highest development of any along the line. For here a man can be at the same time a part of the rush-line and also a part of the half-back division. It requires cleverness in the highest degree, and experience is one of the most necessary qualifications, although it sometimes happens that a man with a natural instinct for the game will make such progress as to really entitle him to the position at the end of a single season. This is the rare exception, however, and usually the ends are men who have served a long apprenticeship in preparatory schools as well as on the second eleven. The end needs the greatest attention of the coach. Personally, a man for this position will probably be a lively, dashing player of wiry build, with no superfluous weight to carry, but muscular and quite capable of making every pound of that weight tell. For this very reason he must not be worked to death, and yet he must be kept up to the best performance always.

Condition a Prime Factor. For the good of the rest of the team in making their plays what they should be, the end must be put in condition early, and kept in good shape all the time. Hence, as noted in another chapter in this book, the coach must provide himself with a good supply of end material, and work the candidates alternately, so as to keep them all fast and active.

His Defensive Play. On the defense, outside of his relation to the tackle, the end has to be prepared always for short kicks, and for quarter-back or "on-side" kicks. He should be ever ready to warn his line if he sees from his position of greater vantage any unusual formations being made, or any unaccountable preliminary move on the part of the enemy. He must also be ready to come back and assist his full-back when that player is handling a kick, and he must be quick to see and form an interference should his catcher have the opportunity for a run. The really clever end may often be made the director of this play, and may call out to the catcher the instructions as to running or heeling the ball, although this is preferably the work of the backs. The end is also the man to be ready for a bad pass by the opponents, that goes past the intended recipient toward the edge of the field. A fumbled pass is usually too far in toward the centre for the end to venture, and the tackle should lunge after that kind of a pass; but high passes, or passes too far in front of the runner, will come the end's way, and quickness to seize upon such an opportunity may mean a touchdown and perhaps a game.

Meeting Interference. As to the end's duties in meeting interference, one might almost fill up another chapter with this one phase of his play, for it is all important. But it is "a life that must be lived" to be appreciated. Calm, coldblooded directions may help a man to learn to kick, or to run, or to block, but they seem almost tame when applied to that part of football known as breaking up interference. The best description one can give of an ideal end in this respect is that he appears to be standing before an advancing wave of men as a swimmer about to plunge through the surf. As that wave strikes him he seems to cleave it apart, and, without apparent effort, appears standing behind the wave in the same expectant, waiting attitude as when it struck him.

Reaching the Runner. There are ends, and there have been ends, who apparently accomplished this, and, if one can get close enough to watch the eyes of such an end, he sees them fastened upon the man with the ball, and, whatever motion he may make with arms or shoulders in breaking the interference, he never takes his eyes off the runner, and hardly winks even as he is struck. All this seems too strong to be true, and of course even the best end cannot always thus make way through and reach the runner. When the runner, for instance, is hugging his interferers very tightly, the end has to keep beating at the interferers with his hands and arms, pushing them, and backing away toward touch, leading the play out across the field, and slowing it up so that while he, by keeping comparatively clear of the mass, forbids the outlet of the runner, some one, say the far tackle, coming from behind, reaches the man with the ball; and no ground, or but very little, results from the play. Again the mass may be moving too rapidly for such tactics, and yet too close to the runner to make it safe for the end to cut in. Then it may be necessary for him to go down against it, and bring it over him, taking a last chance on his knees of seizing the runner as the pile passes over him.

The layman, reading of such possibilities of end play, may be inclined to disbelieve in the willingness of a player to take such chances. It does look hard in cold type, but there are a dozen ends on every 'Varsity field ready to do far more dashing and plucky things than merely meet a formed interference.

On the Offensive. The duties of an end on offense are equally arduous. With the rapid advance in the science of the game in the last few years, he has become both a line man and a running half-back, — in fact, a good end may be used, on a pinch, as a half-back, either from his regular place at end, or he can actually substitute if there be a shortage in halves. As a runner from his own position he receives better interference than does the half or full back. Then, on the other hand, when the far half on his opposite end runs, he makes a most important part of the early interference by boxing the tackle or rush-line half.

On Kicks. Finally, on kicks, he swings out well in the line, clearing his obstacle, and goes down madly upon the receiving back, ready for a fumble, or springing like a cat upon the man who attempts a run. On a quarter-back kick he gets on-side, and, with perfect confidence, dashes forward and catches the ball on fly or bound, and may even get in a run at the end.

The Tackle. *Strength and Dash. Saves the End and Rush-Line Back.* After all this work by the end there is still left a little something for his more moderate-moving comrade — the "tackle" — to do. He, the tackle, has the pounds and the strength, and must take good care of his end and his rush-line back. He will not let them pound themselves to pieces against the heavy packed oncoming mass. He knows that they are both good men, and will not hesitate a moment, when it becomes necessary, to smash anything that comes, and for that very reason he appreciates the unsoundness of any play by him that shall leave heavy mass-meeting for these lighter and more high-strung bundles of nerves that flank him and pick the runner with an almost unerring certainty. He, the tackle, therefore, throws himself in on the instant of the snap-back, and if he does not hit the runner he strikes the interference hard, and smashes as much of it back on the runner as he can; he stays with it as long as he can, and when he goes down and it goes over him he grabs what seems to be the tail end of it, and which usually is the man with the ball. But if he gets nothing, he knows from his feelings that he has opened up a hole in it, and that one of his two tried friends is probably through that hole and anchored on the runner.

Play on the Offensive. On the offense he blocks, and blocks hard. When the run is coming his way he blocks long; when it is going on the other side, he comes away quickly and follows close. He may make runs himself. In that case he plans various methods of getting away free and cleanly from his vis-à-vis; he hugs the ball tightly as he takes it from the quarter, and, keeping his head down low to escape observation, he plunges into the line, never stopping as long as he can make his feet go.

Play on Kicks. On kicks, if he be on the kicker's side, he blocks close and hard, and when he hears that thump of the leather that tells the kick is made, he gets down the field. If he be on the other side of the line from the kicker, he only blocks short and sharp and moves down.

The Guard. *Steady and Powerful.* The guard is a peculiar type of man. He is apt to carry with his added pounds an amount of laziness and good-natured carelessness that requires all the coaching possible to eradicate. He ought to be a powerful fellow in legs, body, and arms. The more quickness he has with these the better; but he must, to play the modern game, be heavy. His duties on defense lie in assisting the tackle, and in protecting the opening between himself and tackle, as well as between himself and centre. He ought to plow through hard and low, but with enough swing to insure stopping any man trying to come through outside him.

A Block to Masses. When he meets the interference he should never be lifted up by the push, but must settle down, and, if he finds it crowding him back, go quite down on to the ground before it, and bring it to a standstill. He cannot, in the close quarters of the centre, always tackle low, but he should always bend back anything he gets hold of, and should be no gentle weight when he hangs himself upon the man with the ball.

A Protection on Offense. On the offense, that is, when his side has possession of the ball, it is his duty to see that the quarter-back is thoroughly protected. That is his first duty, and until he has accomplished that he should attempt nothing else. There is no more fatal blunder than that of allowing the quarter to be interfered with. But after that duty is performed, he has, in the running game, to make openings for plays on his own side the line, and to get out into the interference in plays over on the far side. Like the tackle, he may also be used to run with the ball, both from his position and by dropping back.

The Centre. *More General Activity.* Having thus covered the places on both sides, we should complete the discussion of the duties of the linesmen by a description of the work of the centre. He, like the guard, is a man of weight. But, while in the case of the guard we need, or rather expect, more general activity in breaking through, in the case of the centre we require more steadiness. For it is indispensable to the success of any play that the ball be snapped back properly to the quarter, and that uniformity of movement be preserved at this point in the play.

How to Stand. A centre must be strong on his legs, and must devote a great deal of practice to securing a good poise. The method of standing with both feet nearly on a line is preferable to placing one foot back farther than the other for a brace, although a centre who can stand in the former way may occasionally rest himself or bother his opponents by a change.

Defensive Play. In defensive work, that is, when the opponents have the ball, he should endeavor, while protecting the centre openings, to throw his opposing snap-back over on to his quarter at times, and he should also keep him very nervous about the openings. He, the centre, may go through himself, or he may help a guard through, or he may make an opening for his quarter to get through. Like all line men, he should have a variety of methods for accomplishing his object, and should seldom do the thing twice in the same way.

The Quarter-Back. Coming now to the men behind the line. The quarter-back forms the connecting link between the forwards and the half-backs. He is the man through whom must come almost every play that is made, and upon whom, therefore, rests more responsibility than falls to the lot of any other one of the eleven men. No position can be so constantly important as this.

Practically Captain. We find in him the practical captain of the team, so far as the direction of rapid play is concerned. It is possible for the captain to give signals from some other position, and thus run the team instead of permitting the quarter to do it; but thus far such a method has not proved so generally successful as has the plan of allowing the quarter to give the signals upon his own responsibility, the captain countermanding any play of which he disapproves. There is little doubt that with a fairly good quarter-back this works more satisfactorily than any other plan. We need, therefore, in this position, not merely a clever player of the game, but a general as well.

Clever and a General. Select Brains. Select then, for your quarter-back material, as much brains as can be found in any of your candidates. Then re-select again, taking the coolest of the lot, and finally pick out from these the men whom you class as the most capable in judgment and the most reliable in emergencies, — the chosen few who would never give up, no matter what the odds, — and you have the men upon whom you can afford to expend your energies in teaching the art of quarter-back play.

Size of Quarters. As a rule, quarters are not big men. There are several reasons for this: first, the cunning and strategy that the position demands seem inconsistent with large frames. Then, too, the amount of bending over and quick movement necessary in a quarter is cruelly hard on a big man, and he usually gets very slow after a half hour of it. Nor can the big man, as a rule, succeed in getting off quickly enough to lead the interference. Barring these exceptions, however, there is little reason why a large man should not play quarter.

Cheerful, Alert, and Confident. A quarter must keep up a cheery disposition; he should be absolutely above discouragement (save in his own playing), should always have confidence in his men, and should stimulate them by his very presence to do their best. He should never forget that every time his team lines up, his backs look at him, and they should always see him alert, ready, and confident.

Handling the Ball and Steadying the Line. In handling the ball he should learn to pass from either side, and to either side; he should learn to get off at the same time. He should practice holding the ball for the runner to take from him on short line bucking, and should swing himself in behind the runner on plays of this nature with all the pounds of push he can add. It is his duty to "jolly up" the guards to their work, to keep the centre steady, and on the defense to be ever ready for an opening, while never making the blunder of being drawn into a preconcerted trap-opening by the opponents. He must not only do more than any other man on the team, but he must think more.

The Three Backs. *Becoming All Alike.* The duties of the three backs on the offense, that is, when their side has possession of the ball, are comparatively the same, even though two of them are called halves and the third the full-back. One of the three runs, and the other two assist. For the variety of the play the reader is referred to the chapter giving diagrams. But there is something to be said regarding these players, aside from giving each his exact position for any running play. There are no men on the field who need so much confidence in each other, so much thorough reliance, one upon the other, as these three.

Confidence in Each Other. They should be essentially *en rapport.* When our full-back takes the ball and goes up with it, there should be two men with him who will fight like demons to help him gain an inch, who will strike the line with him as though it were but a yielding hedge, and who will drag him along somehow for his distance. And when the half goes up, he knows that the other half and the full-back will do the same for him. On this account backs should never be overworked. They need the fire and dash, and their game depends upon it. Don't take it out of them by sending them too much. They are of finer material than the line men, and must be kept fit by less work and more encouragement.

Build and Character. Backs should be, in physical build, not necessarily large, but well put together, and should be men who possess that art of control over all their muscles which is commonly termed "having the knack of doing things."

They should never be clumsy fellows, because such men inevitably lay up either themselves or their comrades. Many prefer short, thick-set runners, but the success of taller and more slender men in line bucking has demonstrated the fact that it is legs rather than body that help a man through a line. Besides, the taller men can usually out-punt the shorter ones, and hence, as a kicker (and two of the three should be good kickers), the long leg has the advantage.

One a Leader. One of the three men back of the line should act as a sort of leader, and give all commands regarding who should catch a kick, whether to run or not (this latter to be only *advice*, for the catcher himself has the final right of judgment here), and also general orders as to which opponent to take when protecting a catcher. Not only should these three men have, beside the daily practice at the lineup, kicking practice, but they should be especially drilled upon catching punts, the quarter being included in the practice, until, in the last two weeks, it may be determined which two of the four are the most certain catchers.

CHAPTER IV

RELATIONSHIPS OF THE POSITIONS

Theory of Line Defense. If one could imagine that the arms of the players in the rush-line were as long as their possible tackling distance, the theory of the rush-line defense would be to have each man's finger-tips touch those of his neighbor, while the outer arms of the end rushers reached the touch line. Some teams of the past have been so nearly perfect in defensive play and tactics as to reach very close to this stage of the theoretical ideal. Beginning, then, at the outside, we say to the end and the tackle that the space from the farthest reach of the guard, out to the touch line, is in their care. They have a rush-line half-back to aid them, and thus can count upon a certain greater freedom of action than in the old style of play, when the half-backs were kept more in the reserve. To limit the responsibility, it is fair to say that the end is solely responsible for the protection of the side line; that is, no matter what the excuse or provocation or temptation may be to draw in toward the field itself to help out the tackle, there is but one law for him that must not be broken, and that is "guard the edge." Here again the addition of the rush-line back has made it possible, by the style of team play spoken of in the chapter on that branch, for the end to go in and help the tackle under certain circumstances.

Triangular Relation between the End, Tackle, and Rush-Line Back. The relation is almost a triangular one of tackle, rush-line back, and end, and any two of them may, at a pinch, "go in," but three never should go in. Suppose the play is directed exactly at the tackle. Some rush-line backs play on the line with the tackle. In that case the tackle or line-back goes through, according as one or the other has the better opportunity. Whichever it is, he meets the interference, and endeavors to break it up, while his partner comes on behind, and takes the second turn at it, the end, meantime, covering the outside, but coming in as far as he can with safety, so that, if the interference actually engages the two, tackle and half-back, the end may take the runner as he comes free.

A Safe Stop for a Well-Protected End Run. Suppose, now, the run comes for the end. The inside man of the three is likely to be blocked or so tangled up in the interference that getting through in time to be in front of the runner is practicably impossible. Hence he can then be regarded as the safest man to help out the end by immediately going out, and as he goes out the end can come in, and with the tackle (or the second man, whether it be the tackle or half-back) smash the interference.

Having thus clearly defined the relationship of the end and the tackle in their defensive play, we make it possible for a coach to describe the duties and qualifications of both players with far greater directness than when merely handling each position by itself.

The Tackle's Inside Assistant. But the tackle has, like the end, some other good friends who are ever ready to back him up, so that he need never feel alone in his position. We have already spoken of the end and the rush-line back, and how, with the tackle, they make up a trio that on the defense should be a hard crowd to pass or put out of the way. On the inside the tackle has still another helper, and one, too, of a different character. In the case of the end and half-back, the tackle has two indefatigably active workers, who can either of them move with greater agility than he; but, as we have already noted, the tackle knows that he must never rely upon these two for heavy work save in the direst extremity. In the guard, however, he has a helper of quite another type. Here is a man not only the tackle's equal, but usually his superior, in the way of strength and weight, a big fellow who can plow into the heaviest mass like a bull, and who can always be relied upon to lift, and lift hard, when the attack is jammed up into the centre. For this reason the tackle always tries to turn the heavy plays in toward the centre where the guard and centre will be met, and where, if weight be required, it is always to be found.

Guard and Tackle on Fake Plays. In mentioning the tackle's intimate relation with his guard, we should say that this relation is not of such great importance as are the duties of the tackle toward the end, and his play with the rush-line back, save in mass plays and fake plays. In these two the guard-tackle play becomes vitally important. We will take up the fake plays first.

Suppose that the full-back pretends that he is about to kick, but the play is for the quarter to make a short pass to the half, who jumps straight ahead and tries to go through on his own side of the line. Although this play is frequently attempted outside the tackle, it is not a showy play, and seldom a successful one when sent outside. The trouble is that the necessary pause or length of pass is too great, and one of the three, tackle, rush-line back, or end, "nails" the man before he can get through.

The play — if it be properly worked as a "fake" — is far more likely to be a good one when directed inside the tackle. Here, then, comes the relation of guard to tackle. The guard is big, and not as lively as end or tackle or rush-line back. But he can project himself with a plunge a long distance on account of his size, and it is his duty to do just this in the case alluded to. He throws himself sidewise at the breach which he is likely to see just as the man lunges forward at the opening. He usually barely reaches him, but comes near enough to get his hands or shoulder on the runner as he shoots through.

Relation of Centre Trio and Quarter. The relation of the centre trio and the quarter complicates the position of guard, for, in addition to the above-mentioned duty toward the tackles, the two guards, on defensive play, work with the centre and quarter. The principle, as will be seen in the chapter upon team play, is that of always getting some one man through on every play. It is not always that the man is the quarter. The guard and centre may open up for him. But the two guards may also, on occasion, open up for the centre to go through, or the centre, quarter, and one guard make it so lively that there is an open space for the other guard to get through. All this can be planned and be in the hands of some one man of the four, who, as they are lining up, gives the signal indicating which method is to be used. Still again, it is sometimes played by the centre trio "stretching" the opposing line out as far as they can. Here the tackles also assist, and the quarter may even come up into the line himself. This is not a safe method to be played too often, but is a very disconcerting one to the opponents when used judiciously.

Relations on Kicks and Offensive Play. This covers practically all the relations between the line men and their attendant backs on defense. In cases of kicks by the opponents, the relations are more properly a separation of one or more of these backs from the rush-line and the attendance upon the receiving full-back. The quarter may be the man to go back, or the half-back. In either event the duties of the rush-line are, first, to attempt to spoil the kick or the pass, and then to assist either in interference for a run in, or, if the kick be returned, to get down the field. The ends get back as rapidly as possible to the aid of the catcher, interfering as much as possible with the opposing ends, and, in case of a run back, acting as the primary interferers.

Relationships between the various positions in offensive play are so unlike those on defensive play that no general rules can be laid clown. We have noted a few, but each play forms a rule by itself, the first merit of many plays consisting in the fact that a different method is followed when the initial part of two or more plays may be exactly alike.

CHAPTER V

BLOCKING

When to Teach It. Blocking is the first principle in offensive playing. There can be no successful offensive work without good blocking. Hence it is the first rudiment which a line man must master, and too much attention cannot be given by the coach to this branch of rush-line work.

It is a well-established maxim that successful blocking must be taught in the first three weeks of the season. In order that there may be no mistake about the thoroughness of the instruction in blocking during this early period, it is well to require of the rush-line that they shall play at this time without interdependence or any relationship between man and man. In other words, compel the team to win games from their earlier and weaker opponents of the season with the excellence of individual blocking only. Let there be no "theories of the defense" given to the line men until they are almost able to do without them; in other words, until they are able to meet strong opponents, and maintain their position by individual, unrelated efforts at blocking.

Two Divisions of the Subject. The rules for blocking may be divided into two parts: Instructions covering the general ground of blocking for any position in the line, and instructions which apply especially to the individual position and work of the player. We will take up the two divisions in their order, and give first, as briefly as possible, a few instructions for general blocking, under any circumstances and in any position.

Position in Blocking. As a rule, it is wise to get as close as possible to the man you wish to block. Take your position squarely in front of him, with legs and feet so placed that, while you can readily move in any direction, you are, nevertheless, so firmly planted upon your feet, and so squarely braced, that your opponent cannot push or pull you off your pins, or so far unsteady you that he can get free before you can recover.

As to the Feet and Legs. The position of the feet varies for different players; for the centre trio, the feet should be almost on a line latitudinally with the body; that is, neither foot should project to any appreciable extent ahead of the other. For a tackle, however, one foot should be slightly behind the other, so that the toe of the rear foot will be about upon a line with the heel of the forward foot. This is about as wide an opening latitudinally as should ever exist between the two feet in successful blocking. A wider opening may give a better brace against a backward push, but it will make a man's movements much slower.

Before deciding just where your feet should be placed in blocking, make several tests and ascertain the exact position which you can best assume, and in which these two essentials may be provided for, — namely, that you can get away quickly; and that you cannot be knocked off your pins in any direction by the most savage onslaught of your opponent. A little experimenting will quickly determine the weak and strong points of any position you may assume. Above all, do not straddle, and stand on your toes, rather than on your heels or on the flat foot. The heels should be used as secondary supports, against which you come back for a firmer brace, while your position on your toes will tend to extreme agility, and enable you to follow every movement of your opponent without loss of time. Keep your feet under you in any case, so that you can be firm upon them; and then vary your position with every movement of your opponent. Keep the legs bent, and apply your power rightly. One pound of force rightly applied in blocking is better than five pounds applied at a disadvantage.

General Movement in Blocking. Keep as close to your opponent as possible. Watch every movement that he makes; wherever he goes you are to follow; especially watch his eyes as a cat would watch a mouse. Do not look at his canvas, his belt, or, worse still, his feet. If his eyes cannot be readily seen in the position which you have taken look at his head. Keep your own head up. The ideal position for your body is to get low, well under your opponent, so that you can lift him up and run him back, if possible, the instant the play starts. Furthermore, by getting very low, you do not expose your chest to a straight blow. Keep the body high enough to prevent your opponent from seizing you by the head as he goes through, as this would speedily put you in a position where you would be of no possible help in checking the play. Concentrate your mind upon the problem of how to plunge into him at the moment that the ball starts. His eyes will probably be upon the ball; your eyes should be upon his eyes. The moment that you plunge into him, run him back out of the way, if possible, and make as large a hole as you can. If, by any mischance, your man should get by you, follow him, and run into him, or give him a running blocking-off before he can tackle.

Comparison with Sparring. The best general idea of blocking may, perhaps, be gained by comparing it to sparring. In the latter sport your opponent is trying to hit you on some part of your body. In the present instance the same thing is true, if qualified by the fact that he is only doing this to aid himself in getting you out of his way; in order to parry his attack you must watch him, and if possible jump into him before he can plunge into you. Go into him hard enough, if possible, to keep him out of the play, and then yourself instantly join the general interference. Strive always for the ideal position, which is to get your body directly across the path of your opponent in breaking through, so that your two bodies would form the shape of the letter X. Finally, listen closely for the signal, and let your blocking go with the play.

What is Body-Checking? Body-checking is a term which is generally synonymous with blocking, but in reality it is blocking in its highest development, for all blocking, properly, should be done with the body. The player should understand that the arms alone are never strong enough to block a man successfully; only to reenforce and supplement the action of the body, should the upper arms be employed.

A Common Fault with Young Players. A general error with inexperienced players is to try and reach too far with the body, and this weakens its resisting force. Wherever the body goes, the legs and arms should go with it. Keep the legs well bent under the body, until you are ready for the final movement of straightening up and putting all your force against your opponent as the ball starts in play. You can scarcely go into your opponent too strongly at this last decisive moment. The old expression, often used by coaches, "pile into him like a ton of bricks," is not so far wrong after all.

Other General Hints on Blocking. When you are blocking an opponent close to the line, do not yield an inch. Be careful not to let him get a grip on your outside arm, for it would be of immense assistance to him in going through the line.

Remember that your brace must not be merely against a backward push, but equally against a forward pull, or a sideways plunge. In other words, it must stiffen you against a throw in any direction.

Always block your man away from the play. It is fair to assume that you can successfully check his onslaught for a brief interval of time; and your blocking should be so directed as to prevent him from reaching the runner at the point at which the runner will be after this first interval has elapsed. In other words, if you are blocking a tackle for a run around the end, you would naturally block him on the outside, for it would be reasonable to assume that if you force him to go inside of you he would scarcely get clear from you until the runner had reached a point from which your opponent could not check him, except from behind.

Be careful in your blocking not to give away the direction of the play. This is a fatal error, into which, the inexperienced player will fall unless he watches himself.

Different Kinds of Blocking. Certain special occasions call for slight differences in the method of blocking, and it may be well to say here a word on three of these variations. We will classify them as "body-checking," "blocking hard," and "blocking long."

Body-checking. Body-checking implies temporarily checking the progress of an opponent, rather than preventing his final movements. It is well illustrated in the work of an end going down the field under a punt; while not lingering to block before he starts, he is, nevertheless, expected to slightly body-check an opponent in the rush-line, with a view to giving more complete protection to his own kicker.

Blocking Hard. Blocking hard is a term used to designate the kind of blocking which a man must do who is stationed on either side of the hole through which the runner is to pass. When we tell a man to "block hard" it means that the exigencies of this particular play require of him a special effort or spurt. He is to play his strongest card; he is to sharpen every faculty and redouble every energy. The whole success of the impending movement depends upon him. His blocking for this one encounter must be absolutely sure. This is all summed up in the brief instruction, "Block hard."

Blocking Long. Blocking long is a term used to cover those exigencies which require that the resistance to the opponents' movements shall be maintained during a considerable interval of time. When a player "blocks hard" he concentrates all his energy, and expends it in the briefest interval, during which he has his opponent completely at his mercy. If, on the other hand, he "blocks long," he so husbands his resources and his strength that he keeps his opponent from interfering with the play for a period of time nearly twice as long as the usual period covered by ordinary blocking.

"Long blocking" is, perhaps, the most difficult of any for the average player to acquire. It is not easy to lay down special rules for his guidance. It is, rather, a faculty which will come to him intuitively, as he studies different opponents and learns more of the principles of primary blocking. He will find that there are certain methods by which he can block one opponent for a considerable interval of time, which will be wholly useless when he tries them upon another opponent. Different men have different styles of play, which must be met by different tactics. In general, the position we have described, in which the bodies of the two men take the form of the letter X, is a sure position for long blocking.

Special Instructions for Blocking by the Centre-Rush. The problem of the centre-rush on the offense has been rendered much simpler by the recent legislation which forbids the opposing centre from interfering with the ball until it is put in play. Before this law was enacted, the blocking of the centre-rush was one of the most important features in the play of the line; but having now the exclusive control of the ball until it is snapped, his difficulties are greatly lessened.

There are various ways for the centre to block his man after he has put the ball in play. Of course, he knows the exact instant when the ball is to go back, and in this respect he has a great advantage over any other man in the rush-line. He can plunge forward into his opponent on the instant that he snaps the ball, gaining a foot or more by the very force of his plunge; or, if his opponent is down too low, he may fall on him. Beside this, he can frequently lift him to one side or the other, and in any event he has little difficulty in protecting the quarter, so far as interference from the opposing centre is concerned.

As for the position of his feet, it is a great advantage if he can keep his feet on a line, neither foot being in advance of the other. It is possible to take such a position, and be firmly braced in all directions. If, however, the centre finds it difficult to thus brace himself, let him take the position which the tackle would assume. This might be described as almost identical with the position of a sprinter "on the mark." The body bends at the knees and hips; and the support being on the toes, with the joints very springy, the position is altogether a very comfortable one to maintain; although it can easily be proved that the position first recommended for the centre is by far the better one to adopt.

Special Instructions for Blocking by a Guard. A guard in blocking has several duties to perform, and we will mention these duties in the order of their importance, for this is the order in which they should be in his mind, and in which they should receive his attention.

His first duty is to protect his centre in making the snap, and his quarter in securing the ball and making the pass; his second is the necessity of blocking his opponent long enough to prevent him from reaching the runner; next, the making an opening on either side of his position in the line; and lastly comes the necessity of getting into the interference himself as quickly and as strongly as possible.

It follows, naturally, that in performing all these various duties he will be somewhat limited in his freedom of movement, and his position must necessarily be more or less controlled by the exigencies of the occasion. In general, the guard should stand with his feet well spread apart. It is a safe rule to keep the legs as far apart as possible, up to the limit of not hindering his quickness and activity. The advantage is always with the man who can earliest put his power into action.

A very effective method of blocking for a guard is what is commonly known as the shoulder-check, which consists in meeting an opponent strongly on the upper part of his hips with the outside shoulder. It must be borne in mind that the blocking of the guard is of greater importance than the work of any other man in the line, for his close proximity to the quarter-back makes weak blocking here a serious menace to the safety of the pass. The guard should be careful not to allow his opponent to draw him too far from his own centre. He may follow his opponent out a little, but the limit of safety in this direction is quickly reached.

The guard of all other players must learn long blocking, for this is the method which he must always employ when a kick is ordered. In general, no set rules need be laid down for the guard as to the placing of his feet; the better position, if he can take it, is to stand with both feet on a line; this will be hard to acquire and somewhat painful at first, but the advantages of such a position repay his efforts. All his blocking should be done with his body very low bent fairly well forward. In this position he can be better braced, and not so much exposed to the rough handling of an opponent.

The guard's position in blocking will, of course, be different if he is himself to run with the ball. For this, it is necessary that he should get away free and clear from his opponent the instant the snap is made. He can sometimes contrive to strike his opponent in the chest, and then let the very force of his push or blow be his own impetus in the opposite direction. In any case, there must not be a moment's delay in getting clear. Whatever method will get the guard under headway in the shortest order will be the proper method to use.

Special Instructions for Blocking by a Tackle. Blocking by the tackle is but little less in importance than blocking by the guard. In certain plays the guard's position makes his blocking of greater relative value, but there are many operations in which the tackle bears a heavy load of responsibility for his blocking.

First of all, let it be understood that if the space between himself and his adjoining guard is occupied by any opponent, it is the tackle's duty to leave his own tackle and block this opponent instead. To use the language of the coaches, he must always "take the inside man." Thus, as a rule, the tackle will find that his blocking must be done in close proximity to the guard.

The position of the body differs somewhat from that assumed by the guard, for the tackle is a man whose activity must be much greater, and it will be better for him to take such a position as will make it possible for him to follow his opponent's every movement with lightning quickness. It will be better for the tackle to keep one foot slightly in advance of the other, letting the toe of the rear foot be about on a line with the heel of the forward foot. Keep well up on the toes, and avoid any tendency toward inertia. The tackle, in blocking, should be in almost continual motion. Follow the opponent closely, keeping well in front of him, and always on tip-toe, ready to start forward the instant the opponent attempts to go through. Expose no part of the body as a handle which the opponent may grasp. Keep the head high enough to prevent his seizing it; keep the arms close to the body, to prevent him from seizing them; keep the chest in a position where it is not exposed to a blow.

Finally, keep yourself squarely in front of the man opposed to you, and as close to him as possible. Watch him sharply; listen for the signal, and try and get away with it; remember that agility is the first requisite, and never allow your body to rest upon your heels or flat foot when you are in action.

A Few Words to the End Rush. Nothing need be added to the instructions already given, as the bulk of the blocking in the line is done by the three men playing respectively at centre, guard, and tackle. With the advance of the modern game the end rush is called upon to do almost no blocking whatever. In fact, he rarely plays in the line opposite to his opponent, and the blocking he is occasionally called upon to do is to assist the tackle to pocket his opponent. This blocking is of a different class from that which we have been considering. It is rather more in the nature of running blocking, and corresponds to "riding off" in the game of polo. From his position in the line, the end plunges forward, meeting the opposing tackle with his shoulder, striking him as low as the hip, and endeavoring to reach him before he has come clear of his immediate engagement with his own opponent.

CHAPTER VI

BREAKING THROUGH

Importance of It. The complement of blocking is breaking through. Of the same importance that blocking is to the side acting on the offense, breaking through is to the side acting on the defense. Of the two, it may fairly be claimed that breaking through is perhaps the more important, for in its highest development it is sufficient, barring accident, to prevent the opposing team from scoring, without which, of course, no game can ever be won.

Reason for This. On the other hand, weakness in breaking through is one of the surest signs of the inferiority of a team. The whole object in defensive play is to tackle the runner *behind his own line*, and this demands that the line of the opponent shall be broken through in less time than the ball can be advanced. It is not enough that the runner shall be stopped at the line. It may sound paradoxical, but if he can reach the line, he can always gain a certain distance beyond it. It is an old adage that when the runner is allowed to reach the line before being tackled, he can always gain his five yards in three downs.

An Indication of Spirit. Perhaps there is no single feature in football which calls for a truer courage and stoutheartedness than breaking through the opponents' line. It is the carrying of the war into Africa; it is the invasion of the enemy's country; it shows the courage of the player in the indication which it gives of his spirit. The player who repeatedly tackles behind his opponents' line is the one who cannot wait for the opponent to come to him in his eagerness to get at his opponent. He is the player who plays from a love of the game, rather than from any desire for personal distinction.

It has often been advanced as one of the arguments against football, that a comparatively small number of players on a team really play from love of the game *per se*. It has been claimed that in a majority of cases there is some other motive at work, — love of college, desire for notoriety, pride, etc. However true or false this accusation may be, there are men who play football from love of the game, and they will be found tearing through the opponents' line the instant the ball is put in play.

Instructions to Guard and Tackle. The rules for breaking through are the same for any position or any player. It is true that a different importance attaches to the breaking through of different players, and that a greater responsibility for breaking through rests upon certain players, but the methods employed are substantially the same in every case.

If any player could be immediately pushed through the opponents' line, it is probable that the guard would be, of all men, the most destructive, for he might, by his prompt arrival, interfere with the passing of the quarter, which would be the instant jeopardizing of the enemy's entire movement, with the loss of at least a yard, and possibly the loss of the ball. It is to the tackle, however, and not to the guard, that we look for the greatest amount of breaking through the line. He should be rigidly required to go through the line on the defense. Any tendency on his part to wait until he can see where the run is to be made should be instantly suppressed. When he is through the line he will be called upon to do one of two things, according as the play is directed toward his side of the line, or toward the opposite side. In the former case, his duty is to break up the interference, and if possible to secure the runner. In the latter case, his duty is to follow the runner, and bring him down from behind.

When not to go Through. Before beginning the explanation of the methods of breaking through, it may be well to point out the only case in which a green player, if he is a line man, should ever be coached *not* to break through, but to follow the play out behind his own line.

This one case is where he finds himself the third man from the end of the line, and some one of the opponents is stationed outside of that end rush. In such a case as this, upon being notified by the end rush that an opponent has gone outside of his position (or whether notified or not, in case he perceives the situation himself), he should, after retaining his position long enough to repel any attempt to pierce the line at that point, instantly go out behind his own line, and beyond his own end rush, and prepare to act as the end rush on any second pass of the ball to the man located on the outside of that end.

He must understand that the location of an opponent outside of his own end is always a menace, and, being the third man in the line, when any opponent has been placed beyond the limit of the end rush, responsibility for checking a play around that end devolves upon him. With this responsibility he is not freed, however, from a responsibility for his own position in the line; but with the placing of an opponent so far out from the centre, the probabilities strongly point to a double pass or a long pass, and the third man from the end of the line must be the man to get the runner, and not the end rush, whose duty it is to go straight for the first runner.

Discrimination between Players. With this single exception there is never a time when an inexperienced line man should be permitted to run back of his own line when acting on the defensive. It may be permitted sometimes to a veteran who thoroughly understands the game, and in whom this method of checking the advance of the opponents is not a careless tendency into which he has fallen through error. There are times in every game when a guard can most advantageously enter the defense by running back of his own line; but never should a guard be permitted to do this until he has demonstrated his ability to be trusted to act upon his own judgment, and to know instinctively when such times arrive.

Keep the Ball in Sight. From this slight digression we may now return to the subject proper, and discuss the different methods of breaking through the line. There are a variety of tactics which may be employed in breaking through. That one is always best which will work the quickest, and at the same time make it possible not to lose sight of the movement of the ball or the runner. It is of much less advantage to be through the line, if in going through the player has lost sight of the movement or passing of the ball, and is, for the instant, uncertain which opponent is the runner. That instant's hesitation required to locate the ball is fatal for the success of his operations, for the situation changes so quickly that it is not safe to lose sight of the ball for a second.

Two Foundation Principles. The first rule, then, is to watch the ball, and go through the line with the ball. The second rule is to keep yourself entirely free from the man opposite to you when going through, and prevent at all hazards any attempt on his part to hold or detain you. These two maxims are always to be borne in mind when attempting to break through the opponents' line.

Best Position for the Body. The best position for breaking through is to keep about arm's length from your opponent. Make no movements unless they are made with some distinct intention. Remember that any motion on your part in any direction will naturally produce a similar motion on the part of your opponent; keep this thought in mind, and take advantage of it at every opportunity.

Importance of Quickness. In enumerating the methods of breaking through, let us first say that quickness is necessary for all of them. The position of the feet and the general inclination of the body should be the same as in blocking; but much more than in the case of blocking should the player be at all times "on the edge." Watch the ball; try to detect, by any slightest indication, when and where it is going; break through with it if possible, and not a second later.

Attention to an Opponent. It is a safe rule to lay down that you can afford to almost ignore the man in front of you. With a little practice you can while watching the ball and never for a moment taking your eyes off it still see your opponent out of the corner of your eye. In other words, it is easily possible to bring your opponent and the ball both into the field of your vision at the same time. We have already said that you should keep at about arm's distance from your opponent, but if possible this arm's distance should be in his territory, and not in yours. Finally, go through with the arms well extended, so that they may be powerfully employed, to the end that you may not be bowled over by an interferer; and lastly, go through, circling on as small an arc as possible, to the end that your own line shall not be opened up too much.

Ten Methods of Breaking Through, (a) Strike your opponent on one side, as if making a feint to pass on that side, and dart quickly through on the other.

(b) Play for the outside arm of your opponent. You can sometimes catch this arm by a spring to one side. Your opponent, in the very attempt to free himself, may pull you through.

(c) Spring into your opponent with your arms extended, striking his chest a blow with both hands. The blow should be hard enough to start him back off his pins, or unsteady him, and you can then pass him on either side.

(d) The last method assumes that your opponent shall expose his chest. If he plays too low for this, see if it is not possible to take him by the head and pull him to one side or the other.

(e) Play very low yourself, with the body swung lightly backward, so that one hip is nearer the opponent than the other; let the arms be extended, and the hands opened out and together, nearly reaching the ground. The instant the ball is in play, with a sweeping upward stroke of the extended arms let your hands meet your opponent at about the height of his head. The force of the upward sweep will make the stroke strong enough to unsteady him, and perhaps make it possible for you to dart through.

(f) Catch your opponent by the shoulders and twist him around, taking care not to retain your hold upon him for more than an instant.

(g) Strike your opponent on the lower arm with both of your arms, imitating the swing of a sabre.

(h) With both hands and extended arms strike your opponent on either shoulder. That shoulder will either give way or push forward towards you. If it gives way, its righting power is instantly weakened, and you have the narrow side of his body opposing you, instead of the broad side. If, on the contrary, it advances to you, you will find that he has exposed his outer arm.

(i) Spring to one side, and with a sharp blow strike your opponent's arm down, and get through in that way.

(j) Decide which way you wish to go, then make any movement which will cause your opponent to move in the opposite direction to the one you have already decided upon. Let the feint be made the instant the ball goes, and your dodge will usually be successful.

Comments upon Them. We have given ten different methods of breaking through. All combined, however, they are not as valuable as is the method of studying the man in front of you, noting his faults, and adapting your breaking through in such a way as to take advantage of them.

Vary your methods continually. Work out for yourself original methods of breaking through, and have a good number of them, for all occasions and different opponents. Above all, watch the ball, and never take your eyes off it for a moment.

Dangers of Scrapping when on the Defense. If your opponent takes trifling liberties with you, such as slapping your face, or undertaking to "play horse" with you in any way, remember that these digressions are merely made with a view to induce you to take your eyes off the ball and give your attention to him. Let all such actions merely determine you to a closer watch upon the ball. Your opportunity for repaying such attentions — if, indeed, they ever need to be repaid — will come when your positions are reversed. But make up your mind early in the season that no shouldering, scrapping, or horse-play of your opponent shall ever induce you to ignore or relax that keen attention upon the ball which is absolutely indispensable to the success of defensive work.

Breaking Through on a Kick. The time when the opponents are about to kick is one of those critical moments when, by a single master stroke, the game may be won or lost. It is of the utmost importance that the kick should be blocked, or the kicker forced to have it down at the spot where he is standing. One such successful check will discourage your opponents more than a little, and the loss of the ground will be almost doubled in value by the loss of heart and spirit through the recognition of their own weakness at this vital stage.

For such occasions, therefore, you should reserve your very best efforts. If you have detected a certain weakness in your opponent which will permit you to break through him with comparative ease, hold it in reserve for the moment when the full-back retires for a kick. To break through at such a time is worth any three successful attempts in ordinary scrimmage plays. Apply your power quick and hard; summon all your strength for the crucial effort, and reach the kicker in the shortest possible space of time, springing high in the air, with uplifted arms, the moment you see that you arrive too late, and the kick is about to be effected. It is often possible, by thus leaping in the air, to intercept the ball, and do even greater injury to the opponents than if the kicker had been reached before he had the chance to get in his kick. For the blocked ball will probably rebound beyond the kicker, and your own side, charging forward, may easily gain possession of it and carry it down the field for a touch-down.

Formations which it is Unsafe to Break Through. In the old days, when heavy mass wedges were sometimes formed at a particular point in the line, the wisdom of breaking through was restricted, so far as the player was concerned at whose position the apex of the wedge was pointed. It was manifestly absurd to attempt to counteract by an onward plunge the combined force of the opposing mass. The player was, accordingly, coached to get as low as possible, even going down on his knees upon the ground, and to dive headlong between the feet of the oncoming players, and cause them to fall over his extended body. This was called "piling up the wedge;" and although it required a fearless player to make such an attack, it was one of the most common sights on the football field.

Of late years the use of such a heavy wedge has been effectually prevented by legislation, but the rules are still sufficiently elastic to make it possible for the formation of a body of men near a point in the line in such a manner that the attack may easily resolve itself into a solid wedge of a nature which it would be unwise to attempt to stop by permitting the player to go through the line in the ordinary way. It would be well for the player to study this point, and watch for every appearance of such a formation. If the indications are strong for a mass play at his point in the line, his cue will be to get lower, and at all hazards prevent his opponent from lifting him up as a preliminary to pushing him back. The instant the ball is snapped, the play will resolve itself sufficiently for him to ascertain whether his premises were correct. Should it prove to be a wedge or mass attack at his position, let him throw himself on the ground directly in front of it, and inclose in his outstretched arms all the feet and legs that he can seize; let him be especially careful, however, not to throw himself on the ground too soon, as, in that case, the wedge may easily avoid or step over him. Above all, he must get very low to the ground, or he will surely be lifted up and carried along with the first onslaught of the impending mass.

Conclusion. It is impossible to close this chapter without emphasizing once more the vital importance of aggressiveness in this feature of defensive play. No more disheartening criticism can be made upon a team than to call attention to the fact that they invariably make their tackles after the opponents have reached and pierced the line. A courageous and aggressive policy of breaking through is one of the most hopeful indications in a team. It is the more difficult to inculcate this style of play, because the excuse is always ready that the play may be coming at the exact point in the line at which the player is standing. There is, of course, in all such cases, a double responsibility, — the responsibility of protecting his own hole, and of breaking through and meeting the runner.

But while these are two separate responsibilities, they can never be separated in their consideration. They really belong together. Each one is the true accompaniment of the other. Let the player never hesitate or hold back from any notion that the play may be coming at his place in the line. Rather let him be encouraged to go through "on the jump," with his eyes wide open, with attention never for a moment distracted from the ball, and with his arms sufficiently extended to enable him to meet and resist an oncoming interference. By such tactics he may at times overrun his man; but this is a hopeful fault, compared with the weakness or laxity which holds him back and permits him to meet the runner at the line rather than tackle him in his own territory.

CHAPTER VII

OPENING HOLES IN THE LINE

Interference and Shepherding. American Intercollegiate football has a monopoly of the interference principle as applied to the breaking of a rush-line. In Australian football there is such a thing as assisting the runner, but this "shepherding," as it is called, is in no sense like our methods, and it is performed almost entirely in the open. In fact, in the Australian game, as soon as a mass of players get together the referee immediately blows his whistle, and the ball is put down.

Our interference is the product of the growth of many years. With our original adoption of the Rugby Union Laws we took over the principle of "on" and "off" side, and for several years lived fairly close to the traditions.

Heeling Out. The first step of variation from these traditions we took in the heeling out of the scrimmage. In this we are by no means alone, for the Canadians have also adopted heeling out, and it is the only natural outcome and relief from the monotony of the old tight scrimmage, with its stupid pushing. But with the heeling out was involved the question of the rights of the rush-line after the ball had been heeled back. Theoretically, every one of the side which had heeled back the ball was "off-side," for he was in a scrimmage, and had placed himself, or rather been placed, between the ball and his opponents' goal. There was no escape from the conclusion that he was infringing the rule.

But this was also true in almost any scrimmage, even if played in tighter fashion, for an absolute line drawn through the ball could hardly fail to cut off men here and there during the pushing. Besides, it was impossible in the tight scrimmage to be sure where the ball was at any moment, and frequently, as it popped out, the men were still pushing, so that, on the whole, it did not seem that the infringement would be much more heinous in the case of heeling out than in the older tight scrimmage.

The Development of the Use of the Arm by Forwards. The men in the line could not, of course, vanish into thin air the moment the ball was sent behind them, but at first they did the next most appropriate thing. They stood still where they were, or tried to run down the field in case they expected a kick. But it was not long before they found how serviceable an occasional extended arm was in cutting off an opponent who was going through to tackle the runner. From this it became the custom for the rushers to extend their arms as far as they could when lined up for the scrimmage, and thus give all the protection possible to their runner.

It was, however, traditionally improper to bend the arm at all in order to hold the opponent. Strange as it may seem, this tradition was lived up to for several seasons with a fair measure of propriety, but at last the temptation became too great, as the end to be secured seemed more important, and there came a year when our rush-lines reached out and held their opponents whenever the opportunity offered. This would naturally, unless corrected, have speedily put an end to the sport, for there could be no satisfactory tackling under such license.

Legislation against Holding. The players were themselves quick to see this, and at once began to consider legislation directed towards the abuse of holding. Two or three informal meetings between players of prominence at the universities finally led to a formal meeting and a very excited debate upon the matter. The result was, however, satisfactory. The convention took the bull by the horns, and enacted that the forwards of the side which had the ball should not use their hands or arms to block the opponents.

This was the first actual recognition of the distinction made between the side having the ball and the side trying to get through, and it was eminently proper that if we were to drift away from the strict "on" and "off" principles of Rugby Union, we should have some idea where we were eventually to arrive, and, until this distinction was made, the future of the sport looked problematical.

Saving the Game. The adoption of the five-yard advance rule had already saved the sport once from utter extinction when the block game threatened it so seriously, and now in another emergency the rule makers had found a satisfactory solution of a hard problem.

It was in this way that the making of holes in the line came to be a recognized part of American Intercollegiate football, and any one becoming a student of the game should bear in mind the origin of this part of the play, as it accounts for and reconciles many apparently arbitrary distinctions. The principle that the men between the ball and their opponents' goal have lost their right of way is the one that explains the underlying thought of the laws. But we do not hold, as was indicated and foreshadowed when we recognized interference, that the loss of the right of way means as much as the Englishman takes it to mean. He would view our interference as atrocious off-side play, and quite properly so under his rules. But we, after making it legitimate to obstruct an opponent so long as the hands and arms were not made use of in the act, have gone on developing our plays along that line until recent momentum and mass plays have made it necessary to call a halt.

This brief history shows how we have arrived at "opening holes in the line," and also how far such breaking a path for the runner is recognized as legitimate.

The Hole should fit the Play. The cardinal point for the men making a hole in the line to bear in mind is, "What is the object of the hole?" A hole may be opened merely to deceptively draw the quarter and a half-back over to that side of the line. Such a hole should be opened early, and as widely and with as much demonstration of force as possible. The men who, like the quarter and half, are behind the line are seldom able to closely follow the course of the ball, and they depend more upon the appearance of the line to tell where the attack is being made than upon any ability to actually see the man with the ball. Here demonstrations like that mentioned above are often wonderfully effective in drawing these protecting and defensive players over to the wrong side of the line.

Then, too, a hole may be opened for the purpose of distracting the attention of the opponents from a projected kick. Such a hole should have plenty of openers about it, and in this latter case it is also practicable to make it large and long, because the men engaged in making it are not needed later in any interference, as is sometimes the case in a criss-cross run or double pass.

Opening for a Plunge, and Opening for Long Interference. Coming now to legitimate openings, there are different varieties of openings necessary for different runs. The opening for a plunge through the line on a fake kick, where the half dashes through on his own side of the line, should be not much more than merely keeping the opponents in their tracks and preventing their falling or throwing themselves down across the opening. It is a very small hole that is wanted, and that only for an instant of time.

Farthest removed from that style of opening is that required for a "round the end" run (that is, practically, between the end and tackle), with the swinging interference that such a run entails. This opening is usually effected by the end and tackle boxing in the tackle while a part of the interference forces the end out. The opening must be a wide one, for anything less is likely to be choked up before the runner can get by.

Time of the Opening. It is this kind of an opening that requires long blocking, for the runner must follow his interference, and should not be forced to cut loose from it too early in the usually vain attempt to go through alone. How early such an opening should be made depends upon the starting speed of the runner and his interference, but it is safe to say that the later the real opening comes, so long as it comes before the main interferers reach the turn, the better; for it then enables the men to hem in the rush-line half, whereas, if the opening be made early, he will extricate himself in time to smash the interference before it gets well into the line.

What Happens when a Hole is Made at the Wrong Time. Interference met behind the line almost invariably loses half its dash through lack of confidence, and goes back against the runner, taking the pluck out of him as well. On the other hand, if the interferers once fairly reach the opening, they are confident as well as strong, and the feeling that they have already partly gained their end often enables them to carry the runner well past the difficult spot. The runner himself seldom gets on his real swing and dash until he actually feels that he has reached the striking point — then he has every muscle tense and he makes his supreme effort. For all these reasons, therefore, the opening should be rather a trifle late than too soon.

Opening for Tackle Run. An opening for a tackle coming around should be of a different character from that made for a running back. The inside man around whom he is to circle should crowd his opponent back as well as to the inside, while the man outside his opening may, if he be clever, even let his opponent through after a momentary blocking, provided he make him go on the outside and give him a little push onward with the shoulder as he goes by. The same is also true of the opening for a guard when performing a similar run.

Opening for Mass Play. Openings for mass plays striking the line at guard or centre are wholly different again from any thus mentioned. These openings are not made until the push part of the play has practically lost its force. As long as the mass is moving forward, it is utterly bad football to make any opening. Progress is all that is wanted, and the line men in front of the mass should stick together shoulder to shoulder until they find themselves brought almost to a standstill; then, with a final effort, they tear themselves apart, carrying a break into the opposing wall through which the runner, with the added push he is receiving from behind and from the sides, slips, and, should he come clear, steps out for himself.

An opening made before the mass has done its work almost invariably means an alley way for the opponents to reach the runner and stop him before he has gained a foot, and sometimes with actual loss of ground.

Don't Open the Door for the Enemy to Come In. *Don't open the door for the enemy to come in, but for the sortie to go out.* And this leads us to another maxim that the line men should always bear in mind. In all mass or push plays the door must always open outwards. In runs by the tackle and guard, the door may open in, but the hinges must be on the outside. A door opens outward when the runner's men who line the opening are in opponents' territory; it opens inward when the opponents have broken through the line, but are pocketed or blocked off to either side. When a team has thoroughly possessed itself of the idea that there must be no double hinge in these doors, that under no circumstances must the door slam back into the faces of the bunch of runners, then that team has reached a time of high development — the time when its greatest game should be played.

To carry out the idea of the door in the line, let us take up an ordinary push play between guard and centre. Here imagine that the door is a double one, its two sides formed by the guard and centre. The play starts, the pushing mass crowding directly upon these two men, with the runner in a straight line behind the crack that will eventually become an opening between these two line men. Everything moves ahead a step or two, then, as progress becomes checked, the guard swings himself forward and out toward the tackle, the centre swings himself forward and out toward his other guard, and the mass of tightly packed players with the runner, and possibly the quarter at its peak, goes through the opening doors as they sweep aside the attacking party.

How the Door Opens for a Tackle Run. Next, take the run by a tackle between the tackle and end. At the instant that the ball is put in play, the tackle on the side toward which the run is coming, manages to get squarely in front of his opponent. The chances are that that opponent does not desire to go inside, but has been instructed to go outside his man. This the tackle will have been able to discover with a fair measure of certainty some time earlier in the game. If he is sure of this he can take a decided step outward just as the ball is put in play, protecting the inside course slightly by keeping his leg and thigh still in front of his man. At the same moment the half jumps boldly forward, and to the outside of the tackle. On some teams the end also closes in quickly. The far half and the full-back make straight for the space well out, but still inside the opposing end.

The door that is now opening may be imagined again as a double door, but it does not swing as in the push play. On the contrary, the outside half of it is opening in; that is, the man farthest from the runner reaches the line first, and the man just behind him is the inside man, and between them they should pin the end, who at the last moment sees that he must come in to reach the runner. The inside half of the door, formed by the tackle, half, and end, is opening out, the end being the farthest toward the opponents' goal, the half next, and the tackle at the hinge. This half of the door should pin behind it the opposing tackle and rush-line half as the runner himself goes through, aiming in a diagonal line for the edge of the field, and only turning in after he passes his own end.

We speak of this door opening in, with the hinge on the outside, because, as the tackle comes, the inner half of the door formed by the tackle, half, and end is much less movable and performs its duty satisfactorily if it merely holds its own, while the outer half, having only the end against it, appears to him as the real door, and toward that he runs, almost rubbing his shoulder along it as he goes through. It must open in, of necessity, since the end has probably so far advanced that he will be met inside the runner's territory.

Classification of Openings under this Head. Almost all openings may be classed under one or the other of these two heads. Straight runs into the line are after the fashion of push plays, except that the door opens sharply, and before the runner quite reaches it. "Around the end" runs are usually made inside the end, and the door is like that for the run of a tackle or guard.

Detail of Individual Work in Making Openings. As for the individual work in opening holes, there is a chance for a great variety of detail. A player may not use his hands or arms, but he can use his shoulders, his head, his neck, his hips, and his thighs, and it is only necessary for a skeptic to line up against a first-class guard or tackle to see how thoroughly an accomplished man can perform his work, and still make no use of hands or arms. Some men will fairly wind themselves about an opponent like a huge snake, while others will obtrude such a variety of obstacles in the shape of shoulders and knees as to make an insurmountable barrier at the proper moment.

The usual fault and the tendency to be combated in most line men is that of opening the holes too early and getting their weight too high at the outset. The player should try to straighten up as he opens the hole so as to prevent the opponent from reaching or lunging over him, and getting at the runner; to this end he should begin at a low point, and *stiffen up* rather than *settle down*.

After the Runner has Gone Through. As soon as the opening has let the runner through, those who have made it should abandon it, and push from behind forward into the mass, or follow the runner if he has gone through singly.

CHAPTER VIII

INTERFERING FOR THE RUNNER

English and American Right of Way. In the chapter upon opening holes in the line we have already given something of the history of the growth of interference in the American game. In that section will be found an explanation of the "right of way," as observed in the American traditions. In English Rugby there is no such thing as interfering for the runner, and such an act would meet with the strongest disapproval of any one grounded in British beliefs as to off-side play.

Aid to the Runner. In order to appreciate the American methods one must begin with the premise now admitted in all our rulings, that it is perfectly proper, under certain restrictions, for a comrade to aid one of his side to get through the line, and to evade the attempts of the would-be tacklers. This assistance is usually rendered by the interposition of his body between the runner and his opponent or opponents. This assistance, as given by the line men in opening holes through which the runner may quickly pass, has already been dwelt upon at length. But it is not in the line that the art of interference reaches its perfection. It is rather in the long swinging runs out toward the end, or in the more closely formed mass plays hurled against a yielding spot in the opponents' front, that one sees interference in its highest development.

Theoretical Perfection. Its greatest possibilities can be best conceived when one realizes that, after the ball has been placed in the runner's hands, there are ten of his comrades who have no part to play save to assist him in making as long a run as possible; also, that there are but eleven opponents to stop him, one at least of whom (the full-back) is deterred by caution from entering into the attempt to catch the runner until that individual shall at least have come past the line of forwards, and started for the goal. And so, in an ideally perfect interference, each man of the runner's side should take a man. This would leave only the full-back to stop the runner, and it is notorious that not the best tackler in the world can stop a thoroughly expert runner and dodger, save by overtaking him from behind. So, in a perfectly organized interference, touch-downs should be the ordinary results of possession of the ball.

Man-to-Man Interference *vs.* Line Interference. No such perfection has been reached, and yet, with the development of new and original plays, we are advancing toward the attainment of a degree of skill in this line that makes the study of defense indeed a hard one. Before legislation was passed rendering it obligatory upon a side to actually kick the ball into the opponents' territory at kick-off, — thus practically surrendering possession of it, — it was by no means out of the range of possibility to steadily advance the ball by successive methods of interference from the middle of the field to a touch-down. At times this was accomplished by a succession of short advances, again by two or three long runs out toward the end. Many have been the plays based upon the supposition that the attainment of a man-to-man interference mentioned at the outset of this chapter was a practical possibility. Probably there has never been a coach who has not been at times carried away with the belief that such an interference can be arranged. It is not for us to say that it cannot. But the evidence of the games of the past is against it. Occasional plays partaking of this method may be used, and used to advantage, but there is too large an element of chance about it to make it a good base plan for general development of successful interference. There are better foundations to be laid in other theories, and the best of these theories is that one which depends upon the principle of dividing the opponents.

This principle can best be illustrated by supposing that a line of men is running across the field in a diagonal direction between the opponents and the man with the ball. If these men could preserve just the right distance between each other, it is easy to see that it would be almost impossible for the opponent to reach the runner. While there are many off-shoots of the theory of individual man-for-man interference, and while it is undeniably true that there are a number of minor plays that can and should be executed under an interference based upon this principle, the theory of line interference offers so much more possibility of practical field development that we set it down unquestionably as the one to be adopted as a basis for the general expansion of all plays.

Method of Line Interference. The first step in studying this method, in order to arrive at a thorough understanding of it and its application, is to consider the interference line as cutting off a certain section of the opponents' team from participation in the play. This is wholly different from the man-to-man cutting off, and it is not directed at certain individuals *wherever they stand*, but at a certain section of the field, and it affects, therefore, the men who chance to be in that section. If they stay out of that section, they will not be disturbed until the second movement of the play — the cutting off of another section of the field — commences.

Example of Line Interference. By way of illustration, let us take a simple run by a full-back through a space lying between the positions occupied by the opposing tackle and end. We arrange that a line of two or three men shall run diagonally, so that, just as the runner reaches the line, they may interpose between the path of that runner and the main body of the opponents. On the other side of him we may arrange for two or three other men to interpose between his pathway and the end rusher of the opposing line. That puts the case with the greatest degree of simplicity possible, and yet shows the entire theory of the first step in forming effective interference.

Second Step. The next step is after the same order. We have a runner moving between two converging lines of men. At a certain point this protection must cease because the runner and his interference must move with rapidity, or else the opponents, with their additional weight, will push through or crowd the interference against the runner. If both the interference and the runner are moving at high speed, the runner will eventually outstrip his interference. In fact, that is what he is expected to do in line interference. The passage through which he eventually emerges is called the outlet. If he goes clear to the end of the alley formed by his two lines of interferers, the play is simple, and, though effective, there is nothing in it to deceive the opponents, and the chances are that, though the runner will gain such distance as his interference is able to cut off for him, he will be met at the outlet, and there his run will come to an end.

Final Outcome. But now let us imagine the lines of interference considerably prolonged, and that when the runner has gone half way down the alley the interference is turned at almost a right angle, and the opening thus altered to another point. Such a move would deceive the opponents, and might add another chance of the runner's emerging at an unexpected point, and thus adding a long run. It is hardly practicable to actually turn the entire line of interference sharply, but it is possible to effect the same result by sending the runner through the side of it, and by making use of an extra man or men on the outside, practically forming a new interference as the old breaks up, and aiming that new interference in another direction.

Funnel-Shaped Alleys. In all this there must be borne in mind the advisability of having the alleys funnel-shaped, that is, in both primary and secondary interference, the end at which the runner is expected to enter the alley should be broad and well-opened, narrowing down from that to a small point at which he eventually emerges. This not only enables him to run straight for the most unprotected point of his opponents' line, but also makes it more difficult for more than one of his opponents to follow him from behind and thus prevent his escape if he be slowed up.

Combination of Primary and Secondary with Man-to-Man Interference. The most effective, but the most complicated in appearance of all interference, is that which, following out these two moves (that is, first a primary interference, which resolves itself into a secondary line), terminates in an outlet at which the runner is joined by a single interferer who has reached that point in time to precede him on down the field. Of course, with this may be combined a man-to-man interference performed by the one or two who could not get into the primary or secondary interference, against the man or men most likely to reach the final outlet or to get in the later path of the runner after he emerges. The possible expansion of interference carried on along these lines is almost unlimited.

Walking Through the Interference. To come now to the detail of it. With a team of veterans fairly proficient in the general practice of interference, new plays may sometimes be added without going through the drudgery of slow and careful performance. Unfortunately, however, for the work of the coach, there is seldom a team composed of all veterans, and so it is almost invariably necessary to walk through the plays and take up the interference gradually, accustoming each man to his position and his duty, and accommodating the speed little by little to the exigencies of the performers. In walking through plays especial attention should be paid to the precise point at which the runner receives the ball, and the exact position of each player at that moment. It will be found that that is the moment of time about and by which to regulate the play.

Three Points of Measurement. There are three positions at which a measurement can be taken to define the relative places of the men who act as interferers with the runner. The first is when the ball is put in play; the second, when the runner receives it; and the third, when the runner makes his break, — that is, attempts to go through the outlet. At the first of these three periods of the play there are three points for consideration: the protection of the quarter during his pass, the deception of the opponents regarding the direction, and the quick starting of the entire body of men used in the play. At the second period —

when the runner receives the ball — there are two principal considerations: first, to render its reception secure, and with that is involved the question as to which side of the quarter or the half back certain interferers should pass; and, secondly, to protect the runner for a moment from behind in case a man shall have broken through too rapidly, and with this goes, naturally, protection in case of a poor pass or a fumble by the runner when attempting to take the ball. At the third period — that is, when the runner makes his break on his own account — there are two great considerations to be observed: first, how to make his opening as safe from obstruction by either friend or enemy as possible; and, secondly, how to push or drag him along in case he fails to come free.

Addition of Double Passes. Having reached this stage in the analysis of the method of interference, we have placed in the coach's hands the material from which to build up all the necessary walls about his runner. Every play may be, and should be, studied by this process.

We now come to the still more complicated problem offered by the addition of double or even triple passes. By this term "double pass" we here mean either criss-cross or double pass, for it is general among players to distinguish these two by using the term "double pass" with the meaning that the ball be passed on in the same general direction; while by "criss-cross" is meant a pass whereby the ball is then carried by the second runner in the opposite direction, across the field. We have already noted that it is not practicable to alter suddenly the direction of a moving mass of men, and that to alter the course of interference to good effect requires the addition of one or more interferers not involved in the first line. But in the fact that the ball may be passed, and thus the position of the man with the ball be suddenly altered, we have an opportunity of accomplishing almost an equivalent to a sudden change in the direction of interference. And herein, as will be shown by some of the diagrams of plays in this book, we have possibilities thus far only partially appreciated and little understood. An ordinary double pass or a criss-cross is crude when compared with the same play elaborated by secondary interference, the primary being used not only to protect the first runner, but also to thoroughly involve the enemy at a point which suddenly becomes an unassailed point; while, at the same time, the whole force of perfected interference is sent at the spot which is left comparatively unprotected. Add to this the simplicity of using the same play with a variety of outlets, so that the very energy of the opponents will prove their own undoing, and one can gather something of the importance of these new movements.

Final Perfection of Interference, with Double Pass and Kick. Still beyond this may be placed the hitherto utterly neglected feature of play involved in altering by a kick all the momentarily existing conditions, and we come to a stage of perfected assault (consisting of a combination of primary and secondary interference rendered still more menacing by a double pass, and with a finally altered situation due to the placing of the ball by means of a kick far in advance of the actual runner) that may well give those on the other side, in whose charge lies the problem of defense, some bad hours of consideration. When a runner breaks with, let us say, but three men to pass, and deliberately punts the ball over the head of the full-back, after approaching as near as he can with safety, he and his companions who are going down the field prepared for this final manoeuvre will, in many cases, have a far better chance than the opponents of regaining possession of the ball, and with that possession the coveted touch-down.

This chapter, however, is not intended to deal with specific plays, but rather to lead up to the development of such theories of interference as shall make captains and coaches able to plan out, not a few plays that are already public property, but absolutely new plays which emanate from their own study, and which depend for success merely upon their perfected execution.

CHAPTER IX

KICKING

Decline of Kicking and its Present Return to Importance. The history of American football would show, if followed closely, the early importance and the gradually increasing attention devoted to kicking, followed by a period in which the running game so eclipsed that branch of the sport and so perverted the minds of captains and players, that the art of punting was almost lost, followed again in recent years by the steady rise once more into its proper place of what is known as the kicking game. To-day no team is a really strong one that has not a thorough knowledge and practical ability to play a game that combines both running and kicking in their highest development. Kicking is as essential to the success of a football team as batting is to a baseball nine. But, fortunately, the problem of development is greatly simplified in the case of the former by the fact that a football team can almost always permit one of their number to do all the kicking, while a ball nine must let each man take his turn at the bat.

Laxity in Educating a Team. This seeming advantage brings with it, however, a dangerous laxity in educating a team; for, in order to play a game to its proper limit, the knowledge of the kicking principles should be instilled into the whole eleven, and this is usually ignored except in the case of the ends and the full-back. Even here there is often a deal of inexcusable ignorance. For instance, many a full-back will, when his line has held well and his opponents are slow in getting through, exert himself to kick quickly and hurry his kick, when he ought to know that for every second he can hold back his drive, and still be sure of getting it in, his ends are making yards, and his opposing backs getting less chance to handle the ball. There is nothing so disconcerting to the opponents as this unexpected change in time, and a full-back who can not only kick quickly when necessary, but who has also the ability to hold his kick safely and then let it go with a hard, clean, well-placed drive, will so save his ends and rattle the opposing backs that he will add twenty-five, or even fifty, per cent, to his team's chances of success.

Blocking for a Kick. The forwards often lose sight of this point, and the coaches encourage them to lose sight of it by indiscriminate urging to "block first a second, and then go down the field." The best coaches do not want a slow, heavy centre and "ice wagon" guards shaking themselves to pieces and jarring their strength out, in hurrying to try to play the game of an end. If a team has a guard who is fast on his feet, by all means give him a chance to go down under a kick, and let the quarter block his man for him; but if a tackle, even, is too ponderous to be down quickly, let him block long instead of making a futile attempt to follow the example of tackles "who beat the ends" down the field. The far side can go down and the near side block; even an end on the near side may block, if the game is properly played by the other side of the line, and the play is sufficiently practised; but this is a part of the kicking development that will be better understood as coaches realize its value.

Who shall do the Punting? To return to the full-back and his specialty of punting. Of course it is understood that in speaking of the full-back as the kicker of the team it is not meant that the man playing the middle position of the three backs is the only kicker on the team. The practice of lining up is proverbially slow, and as no actual restriction is placed upon the length of time that a centre may wait while his team takes up their positions, any man may be used to do the punting. In fact, on, one very good team, that made a most enviable record, it was one of the tackles who did all the punting. True, the team was not first-class, because no team could be that was obliged always to indicate their intention of kicking, but the fact will serve to show that certainly any one of the three backs may do the punting, and it is often by no means a mistake to mystify the opponents somewhat on this point.

How to Learn to Kick. As stated elsewhere in this book, it is supposed that by the time any man reaches the point of trying for a full-back position on a 'Varsity team, he has had a year or two of kicking practice. But in this chapter we propose to begin at the very beginning of the subject, in order that any man who has never hit a football with his foot may learn to kick by a reasonable attention to instructions, — provided he possess ordinary capacity and has his muscular system under control. The first step in the instruction of a candidate for kicking, however, is to give him a ball and tell him to put it on the ground and then kick it around the field. He should do this for a considerable time, as often as twice a day for a week, before he undertakes a punt. The object of this is to let him find out where his foot is, before giving him a chance to hurt himself by kicking at the ball and missing it. The reason why many men fail absolutely in kicking is because they are not natural kickers; they have grown up with no experience of this kind, and at the outset are allowed to try punting without preliminary practice of locating the foot and ball. The result is that all the man's awkwardness in his first attempts becomes crystallized into hopelessly bad form, and, while by sheer brute force and persistency he may in time be able to kick thirty-five or forty yards, he is erratic in performance, unsteady in aim, and, if he be called upon in a game, a source of demoralizing anxiety to the rest of the team.

After the First Week. Having passed a week in chasing the ball about, and kicking it, the beginner may for the first time take the leather egg up into his hands. Now let him for a few days stand out from the goal posts, or a similar mark, a distance of not more than fifteen yards, and punt at the mark, never kicking the ball hard, but trying to hit it squarely with the instep upon the point of the ball. The ball may be dropped with both hands, and with one hand, alternately, in order that later the kicker may adopt either style. But the chief point to be observed is to acquire the ability to hit the ball with the instep of the foot squarely on its point, and in the line of its axis. The kicker must not leave this simple easy practice until he can thus strike the ball every time, and that, too, with accuracy of aim.

Kicking on the Run. Then he may begin a new exercise. Up to this point he has kicked the ball while standing still. Now he may take a run and kick it while on the run, tossing it a little to the side and not directly in front of him. At first he will almost stop or else hit the ball inaccurately, but soon he will find that his eye and foot understand each other, and he can reach the ball and hit it squarely, although he may have thrown it a little too far out or a little too near.

Increasing Distance and Improving Direction. By a few weeks' careful preparation along these lines we have a man broken in to an easy assurance of aim in swinging his foot before he begins to make those hard and violent efforts to drive the ball that will result in fixing permanently any clumsy motions and bad faults. He has not yet tried to kick over fifteen or twenty yards, but he may now begin to increase the distance. With this extension, however, the coach should include practice to acquire a better idea of elevation. Placing the man at the twenty-yard line, let him punt first between the bar and the ground. That is, let the ball pass under the bar and strike the ground behind the goal line. Then let him send the ball over the bar but below the tops of the posts, and finally let him punt the ball well up in the air, making it fall as nearly on the goal bar as possible. After two days at the twenty-yard line, place him at the twenty-five-yard line for a similar series of kicks. Then, instead of placing him at the thirty-yard line, put him on the fifteen-yard line again, but half way out toward touch. Then let him take the twenty and twenty-five-yard lines at a similar distance out, and after that place him once more at fifteen, but on the extreme edge of the field. From this take him once more to twenty and twenty-five yards.

Accuracy and Trick Kicks. By this time the coach will find that his punter, although he has never kicked any greater distance than from the junction of the twenty-five-yard and touch line over the goal, is yet able to put the ball within these limits with tolerable accuracy, and, what is more, he does not make any slip kicks. It would not be a bad thing for any man who has the time before him to keep at this point during his entire first year of punting. Naturally the development from this stage into regular distance punting is perfectly simple, and needs no especial attention, but a man will do it all the better if he takes more time to it. Then there comes the higher stages of kicking skill, the drop-kick, the twister, the cork-screw, the sailing kick, and the shoot, as well as place kicking. The place-kick and drop-kick deserve especial paragraphs, but the others are merely tricks to be acquired by practice, and, while very serviceable at times, are never to be too greatly relied upon in close quarters or with a wet ball or slippery field.

Place Kicking and Goal Kicking. The gradual practice advocated for the beginner in punting can be advantageously followed up with drop kicking and place kicking. The time at which to begin these two is not until the player reaches the stage of comparative facility in punting from any point along the twenty-yard line. Then he may begin place kicking and use it as a kind of relaxation from his punting. At the outset he should merely make a little nick in the ground with his heel, and by setting the point of the ball in this depression it can be placed securely at any angle desired. He should begin with the ball well "cocked up," that is, standing nearly on end, with the farther end tipping slightly toward the goal. In kicking he should take a couple of steps, and coming squarely upon the standing foot (that is, the one upon which he stands in delivering the kick, — the left, in the case of a right-footed kicker, the right in the case of a left-footed kicker), give an easy swing with the other leg, meeting the ball with the toe a couple of inches from the ground, taking care that the ball and foot are in line with the centre of the goal. After some practice in this manner he may tilt the ball the other way, that is, toward him instead of toward the goal. Later, in his long-distance kicking, he may place the ball almost level on the ground when a kick of half the length of the field is to be made. Hickok, of Yale, could easily kick the ball over half the length of the field from this position.

Close Kicks. The nearer the ball is to the goal, the more it should be "cocked up" for the kick, that it may go up into the air more rapidly from this angle. One of the most certain methods of goal kicking is to stand upon the left foot, with that foot by the side of the ball and almost even with it, then with a simple swing of the other leg the ball is lifted over the goal. This kick is not available for distance kicking, but is a very certain method when used by a man who has practised it for converting touch-downs made behind the goal into goals.

It is safer not to have the same man do all kinds of place kicking for the team, although in developing the men practice in all lines is distinctly advisable. Let one or two men be taught this short kick, and if a touch-down be secured directly behind the goal, call upon the short kicker to convert it. On the other hand, if the touch-down be at the side, or if any place-kick of distance be indicated, the short kicker should give place to the man who is trained especially for the longer drive.

Holding the Ball. Thus far, we have said nothing about the man who holds the ball for a place-kick. Probably four out of five missed goals are missed by the lack of coordination between the man who holds the ball and the kicker, and three out of five are the fault of the placer. It is by no means an easy task to place the ball on the ground quickly and lightly and without any variation in its aim or its position. It must be done at the word of the kicker, and above all without apparent motion. The ball is held in the hands of the placer, or rather by his finger-tips, and within the smallest possible safe distance from the ground. The most approved method is to place the forefinger and second finger of the hand on the top of the ball at the upper part of the end of the lacing. The other hand holds the ball in the fingers the same distance from the middle point (but back toward the kicker) as the upper hand is from the middle. That is, one hand is a little nearer the point of the ball than a median line, and the other hand a little nearer the butt or end that is to be placed on the ground than the median line.

The ball is then aimed under the direction of the kicker by such verbal instructions as "lacing away from you," "lacing toward you," "point away from you," "point toward you," "cock it up," "don't cock it up so much," and the like, until it points directly in the desired manner — allowance being made for the wind and the condition of the ball. Then the kicker says very quickly, "Steady," and follows it instantly with "down," as he takes his step, — or, in case of the short kick, he watches the ball as he says "down," and kicks instantly when he sees it placed, — and meeting it confidently with a straight foot he drives it over. The placer in putting the ball on the ground rests its point, and, withdrawing his under hand, steadies the ball with the fingers of the upper hand, never taking them off, but allowing the ball to be kicked out from under them.

Ball Affected by Weather Conditions. There are many variations of holding the ball, and some placers find changes from the above more convenient for their individual peculiarities. Place kicking should be especially practised in all conditions of wind and weather, in order that the kicker may acquire accuracy as well as confidence. He will discover that a wet and soggy ball must be cocked up more than a dry one — that a new ball should also be well pointed up as it travels low and fast, and the wind does not lift it as much as it does a ball that has grown round and old. He will also learn that it is best to do his practising with two different balls, — one practically new, and the other a ball that has been used through one day of practice. He should never waste his time upon a really old ball, as he will never be called upon in a game to kick such a ball. Should a touch-down be secured in the first five minutes, for instance, the ball is as new as when the referee blew his whistle, but a touch-down during the last five, minutes gives him a ball that has altered in shape not a little, and which does not travel so sharply into the wind. The points to be noted, and which the kicker will be the better for learning, are that he must establish a thorough sympathy with his placer, and that he should never become impatient or hurried in giving his instructions. Moreover, if he sees that the placer is nervous or shaky in his hands, he should stop and tell him to take the ball up and wait until he steadies down. There is no need of haste, as the time is taken out. The placer himself should also feel at liberty to stop and take a rest if he finds his hands becoming unsteady.

If ever there is a time when dependence must be placed upon calm, collected steadiness, it is when a touch-down is being converted into a goal, and the frequent failures to kick goals that we see every season are, many of them, inexcusable. One of the most common errors that is seen in place kicking is that of endeavoring to allow for the wind by the aim of either the foot or the ball alone. The ball is, for example, aimed well off toward the side from which the wind is coming, but the kicker kicks straight at the goal. This is the usual fault. Less common, but still not infrequently witnessed, is the mistake of aiming the ball at the goal and then kicking off toward the wind. The only way to kick a goal properly when allowing for a wind is to bear in mind that the foot must hit the ball in a line with the long axis; in other words, a line drawn from the heel of the kicker's foot straight through the middle of the sole of his shoe should, when continued, pass directly through the middle of the ball, so far as any side to side variation is concerned.

Another thing to be borne in mind, when kicking in a hard wind, is that there should be more force put into the kick. The harder the ball is driven, the less the wind will swing it, and a light kick will not only be swerved from its direction more easily, but will often, on account of meeting with that resistance, sail off and fall short of the goal. This, of course, applies to side winds as well as to head winds. When the wind is a following one, pains must be taken to cock the ball up well, especially on short kicks, for a new ball with a wind behind it goes low — unexpectedly low at times.

Punting Out. As to punting out to gain better position, it is not worth while to do this unless the touch-down be well over on the side. A good place kicker can readily enough convert all other touch-downs into goals without the interposition of the punter out. When the touch-down is unsatisfactory, however, either from its position near the edge or because the wind makes the kick a difficult one, the punt-out is demanded. If properly practised there never should be a failure in this part of the programme. The punter has every privilege allowed him, and has only to punt the ball with moderate accuracy and the catcher does the rest. For a short punt-out he may find it advisable to hold the ball with both hands by the ends and kick it on the side. This is, however, the only time when a ball should be kicked in this way. In fact, even here an expert punter will send the ball quite as accurately with the ordinary end kick. The rushers of the catcher's side should line up in front of him so as to protect him from the charge of the opponents, while his quarter and remaining back should take up positions by the side of and behind him in order to catch the ball if the kicker sends it wide.

Drop Kicking. To come to the drop-kick, that prettiest of all kicks, and the most fascinating to the man who once acquires skill in it, the kicker will find that beside it the place-kick, and especially the punt, become drudgery; and that is one reason why it is necessary to keep the backs at work on punting rather than drop kicking. Drop kicking is rarely employed. In the ordinary kicks of the game the full-back has no time for a drop-kick unless he stands back so far as to materially shorten the distance gained, and so lose the value of the kick. Thus drop-kicks are only employed when near enough to the opponents' goal to render scoring possible. The practice of drop kicking should, as stated above, not begin until a fair mastering of punting has been acquired. Then let the kicker try drop kicking.

Handling the Ball. To begin, the ball is held either in one or both hands, and it is well here, too, to practise at the start both methods. If the ball be held in one hand, let the point of the ball rest easily in that hand, which is made into a sort of cup for it. Let it be dropped by taking the hand gently but quickly out from under it, so that the ball falls without turning and strikes the ground in exactly the same position in which it was resting on the extended hand. At the very instant it rises from the ground — in fact, just as its spring is coming — it is met with the toe of the foot, and the drop-kick is accomplished. In holding the ball with both hands, it is held by the sides with the point toward the ground. The ball may be dropped in any one of three ways, and yet be driven exactly the same by the foot. It may be dropped with the long axis vertical, or with the upper point of the ball inclined slightly toward the goal, or with that point inclined toward the kicker. It seems to make little difference in the matter of strength or accuracy of the kick, although it is true that there are fewer slip kicks made by those who incline the ball toward themselves.

Kicking as in a Game. In all kinds of punting and drop kicking much of the practice should consist of kicking after receiving the ball from the quarter, and while one or more men rush forward and endeavor to block the kick. As a boy cannot learn to swim without going into the water, so no man learns to kick properly, in a manner to be of service in the game, unless he kicks under the conditions that prevail during an actual match. We have too many men who can kick fifty yards when they have everything in their favor and no opponent, and altogether too few who can punt forty-five when an opposing line is coming through on them. Especially should attention be devoted to the side swing, for with it a full-back is almost always sure to get in his kick unless two men together get through on him, while with the ordinary straight ahead kick he cannot dodge the first man, if one gets through.

CHAPTER X

TEAM PLAY

Breadth of the Term. In discussion of team play, it has almost invariably been assumed that the maximum development of that characteristic of the game is attained when eleven men play together as a unit. Unfortunately for captain and coach, this assumption fails to cover the case adequately. Primarily, such attainment presupposes the presence of the same eleven men through many days and weeks of practice. This not the most lucky coach can ever hope for, or, if he hopes for it, he is doomed to disappointment, and by a succession of such disappointments he becomes wise enough to admit, at least to himself, that he must plan beyond the point laid down in the books. He must make twenty men play as a unit, or rather fit twenty or more men so that any eleven of them, selected by himself or by the hand of a stern Fate, may show signs of having acted in concert upon former occasions.

When Team Play Begins. To reach, then, the real bottom of team play, one must begin at the selection of the candidates at the very outset of the season. The usual formula recited by the uninitiate is that team play does not begin until late in the season. Strictly the "play" part does not. or at least it does not come into prominence or even evidence until then. But the coach who is responsible for it must take up that branch of the play when the crowd of motley candidates first appears upon the field in the early fall.

The reason for this is not a far-fetched one, but after a few seasons appears too real. It is that the positions vary greatly in their demand for material. To state the ideal numbers for each position is, perhaps, to set too arbitrary a requirement before the coach, but it may serve as a pattern or guide which will aid him materially. There should be four centres, six guards, six tackles, eight ends, four quarters, and twelve backs, of whom six should be punters. That gives us the quota of forty men who represent a serviceable football squad. In the larger colleges and universities the number is usually doubled during the first quarter of the season, and sometimes during more than half the season, but if team play is to be successful the time when the candidates reach forty should see them approximately thus divided.

Actual Numbers for Each Position. Perhaps the importance of this plan cannot be better brought out than by a brief illustration. Take, for instance, the statement that there should be eight ends in the early part of the season. Why more ends than tackles, and what has the actual number of candidates for any one position to do with team play? Aside from any question of the number likely to be injured during the season, which is more or less guesswork, there is a most solid and convincing argument to show that eight ends are required. Primarily, there are two wanted for the first, and two for the second eleven to fill up the regular numbers. The four extra men are made use of to *teach the backs how to kick*, or rather to keep them up to form in punting, and also to *make the tackles properly perform their work*.

The Ends. It is all simple enough when one considers what the faults are that backs and tackles surely pick up, and that hurt the team play most seriously. The back has been practising punting more or less during the late summer, and from the very fact that he is a candidate for the position, one can conclude that he is a fair kicker. The first days of practice come, and the ends are not, of course, in really first-class condition, so that, naturally, after running down the field a few times under the punting of the back, they "go slow." The back sees this and does not kick so far, because he fears the opposing full will run the ball back behind interference, and make a good gain. Within a short time the full-back has actually reduced his kicking in point of distance to correspond to the inferior work of tired ends. To prevent this, we put in the first set of ends and tell them that they must get down under the kick, if it takes all their wind out of them in five minutes, and just as soon as a man goes a bit slow we put in one of the fresh ends. With four of them we can keep constantly changing, and the back has to keep his kicking extended, and cannot use as an excuse for a short kick the fact that the ends did not get down under his former one.

Effect on Tackles. As to the way the same fault affects the tackles. With the work of getting down the field under kicks and general play, an end is kept busy enough so that, if tired, he begins to let the tackle do work out toward the end which spoils the tackle for his proper play. For instance, a tackle breaks through sharply, and the runner goes by him out toward the end, but not very wide; that is, the runner swings in sharply after passing the tackle. A tired or lazy end, moving slowly, is caught by the interference, and the runner gets a good gain before being brought down by the half-back. This disgusts the tackle, as he knows that every one thinks it was his fault that the man got by, and after a few such plays — where really the tackle is doing exactly what he should, and the whole fault lies in the end being too slow, lazy, or tired — the tackle does not go through hard and fast, but moves out as he sees the interference going, and really becomes a second end instead of a tackle. Reasoning, then, upon this basis, we make the end play his position up to its limit every moment that he stays in the game, and as soon as he slows up we replace him with a fresh man. In this way we establish a strict standard of work for the full-back and tackle to live up to, instead of allowing them to deteriorate or take on bad habits on account of the weakness early in the season of that important player, the end.

This particular position, and its effects upon two at least of the other positions, has been discussed at length in order that a clear idea might be gained of the points involved at the very outset, in bringing about eventual team play of a high grade. It is unnecessary to do more than note briefly in passing the reason for the other numbers given above.

Tackles and Guards. While the tackles must be fresh and active always, the distances they travel upon kicks are shortened by the necessity of temporarily blocking their men, so that their wind is not quite so fiercely taxed as is an end's. Still more, they are in this respect secondary men at the best, and the fact that a tackle failed to get down quickly under a kick would never lead to a full-back's shortening his distance or waiting. The same may be said of a guard, except that the increased opportunity of quietly loafing that is extended to men cramped up in the centre makes it imperative that the competition for the places should be very keen. Were it not for this, four guards would be enough. The centre is in proportion better supplied with four men than the guards or tackles with six, for it takes but one centre to two guards or two tackles to form a team. But the centre man must learn to get out into the play, and that, for a heavy man, takes wind and endurance, and when the heavy man gets tired, he stops and stands around, letting his quarter and guards do too much, and thus altering what should be a normal proportion of work.

The Quarter in Team Play. Four quarters are the equivalent of eight ends, and are necessary on account of the importance of getting the quarter out into the interference. This is exhausting, and as soon as the quarter slows up, he should, like the end, be replaced by a fresh man. If he is not, then the interference slows up to let him get in his place, the runner slows up to let his interference reach the line, and there is not a man in the whole combination who does not begin to retrograde. And yet in late season, when the team is meeting strong opponents, no one can tell what is the matter with the interference!

The Number of Backs Necessary. Finally, the reason for the twelve backs is easily apparent to any one who has tried to take a team through a season. It is not necessary that more than half of the number should be punters, as one can generally count upon using two running backs to one kicking back. But the running backs get far more to do on the defensive, and hence are more liable to injury.

Team Play Begins with the Guard's Position. After, then, making an attempt, in the very earliest selection of candidates, to secure approximately the above proportions (and if the first quota varies greatly from this, to adapt and shift the men about early, so as to conform in as short a space of time as practicable to these numbers), the coach is ready to consider what may be done toward team play, while the real work is still largely individual. At the risk of exciting some controversy, perhaps, but with a thorough conviction that in the long run the statement will be found correct, let it be said that team work on the offensive should start with the guard's position. The general method has been to begin offensive team play with a number of interferers massing out for a run at the tackle hole or around the end. The effect of this beginning is always to delay the practice of genuine team play until after the ordinary straight runs have been used for some days and weeks; then the interference must all be begun by really a retrograde movement in point of speed. That is, in order to get the interference into form, the plays are almost walked through, or at best gone through at but half speed.

Proper Sequences. But with the proper beginning and a proper sequence of work, this element of slowness can be largely avoided, and, best of all, team play, though not of a marked character, may be initiated at the very outset of the season. It may reasonably be demanded of a properly trained guard that he shall be the first man to get off for the point to be assaulted. His earlier duty is that of blocking his man and getting away. He must block long enough to save his quarter, but that occupies an almost infinitesimal moment of time. His next study is on which side of the quarter to pass, and this depends wholly upon the immediate play. In a majority of cases he goes between the centre-rush and the quarter, but there are many plays upon the making of which he should go behind the quarter.

This play of the guard is the initial step toward offensive team play, and should be drilled into the candidates from the very start. There is a notion prevalent that to have the guard begin early to learn to get out into the interference hurts his blocking. This is erroneous, even in its theory; still more in its practice. The guards who make the real successes of the year are not only strong in interference, but never let their quarters suffer by the breaking through of an opponent. The very fact of the necessity of getting clear of his opponent rapidly spurs the guard to increased study of the possibilities of ingenious methods for keeping the opponent safe and out of reach of the play.

Second Step in Team Offense. The next step in team offense is to get the quarter out into the interference, or, in the cases where he is to follow later, to render him serviceable to the play in either making it safe, or adding the necessary push. This is not such a task as teaching the guard, but it should be begun early in the season, or a team will find that when the quarter endeavors to take it up he has become accustomed to passing from a standstill, and is therefore "off" in his passing because he has a new and additional duty to think of. At first the quarter may make bad work of the attempt to do two things at once, but he must be encouraged and judiciously criticised until he can land the ball with accuracy every time while he starts off "on the jump" himself for his proper position in the play.

The Farther Out the Attack, the Stronger it is. Having thus attended to the guard and quarter, it will be found that the nucleus around which is to be built a strong, speedy interference has come almost of itself. There is no great amount of hurry about adding to this pair until the general play has progressed for ten days or two weeks. Then it is time to find out the relative speeds of the men behind the line, and this first pair of interferers. By various trials of different plays it will be learned that the farther out is the assaulted point the greater is the possibility of really serious attack, and if a coach has the good fortune to bring into a final game his very pick of fast men working well together, a single long interference at the end may give him a commanding gain, even perhaps a touch-down. For this reason he must be satisfied to work slowly, steadily, and patiently toward bringing off a formed interference that shall grow more and more severe as it swings into shape at the end of the line and circles for the critical point.

Men in a Complete Interference. Such an interference, to be perfect, should carry a guard, quarter, and one back, with the runner, around the peak. One of these three goes over or out in making sure that the last man of the enemy's extended line dies without a chance of following. The extra men who, beside the above, assist in the long interference may be the far end and the third back. Thus we shall have in a complete interference the quarter, guard, two backs, and an end. (This chapter will not deal with the plays themselves, but a reference to other chapters of the work will show the exact position of the individual players in the execution of various kinds of interference.)

How Line Men should Work. The next step in the general training for offensive team play is the blocking of the line men. Naturally, this is a part of the individual department as well, but it is so necessary to the development of team play that it requires a few words under this head.

Ordinary blocking consists of merely preventing the opponent from getting through and spoiling the play. Blocking in the team sense adds the feature of getting the opponent into the most unfortunate position possible, so far as his hopes of taking any part in the subsequent stopping of the runner is concerned. For example, it is far better to get an opponent moving in the opposite direction from that he eventually finds he should have taken, than to merely hold him in his position, for in the first case he also interferes with his own men, who may have diagnosed the play better than himself. This is the underlying principle of team play in blocking — to make the opponent actually help in the interference.

Next, the forwards should be ever ready in case of emergency to take hold of their own runner and drag him forward. In almost all line plays there comes a moment when, before the runner has gone down, he is so situated with regard to one of his own rushers as to make it possible for that rusher to give him a pull of several feet, perhaps even yards. It has often happened, on account of this unexpected variety of assistance, that a runner is not only helped along, but even shaken free and put securely on his feet again for a run. Aside from this added gain, it is the part of the forwards to always give their backs physical assistance in getting on their feet when the play has to be particularly continuous in point of repeated plunges by these three men. With this help, and the moral force of such encouragement, three good backs can smash a stout line for fifteen minutes at a stretch, before they lose their dash.

Final Aid to the Runner. The assistance to be rendered by pushing a runner after he strikes the line is of late years well understood, and almost all teams put it in active practice. There is no reason why this should not be inculcated early in the season, for it does not in any way interfere with individual development. It is a matter of skill, too, more largely than is generally supposed. A runner, for instance, pushed from the hips and in a line with his direction, keeps his feet well, gains greatly in momentum, and can keep his eyes open for chances. A runner pushed above the hips, or not in the line in which he is going, is likely to be upset, and may, in trying to save himself, fumble the ball. The strangeness of being pushed often causes a runner at first to object, to say that it bothers him, and that he can do better without it, but after becoming accustomed to it he always finds the value of it. The most successful example of this added force is usually exhibited in the case of a good end and tackle working together on a tackle run. The drive of this pair when they come swinging at a line low and hard is a bad thing to face.

Importance of Rapid Lining Up for Successful Team Play. While it is hopeless to attempt rapid play during the first few days, the coach who expects to develop team play must not let more than a week or ten days go by before he begins work upon the subject of lining up quickly. There can be no team play on the offense or defense if there be a laggard on the line. Every man must jump for his place as soon as the referee has called the ball down; in fact, as will be seen later, on sequences of plays, when the ball is in possession of his own side, there may be times when a man must get in place when he sees his runner coming down.

How to Hurry the Play. One of the best methods of hurrying the play early in the season is to take the centre men aside before beginning the practice, and tell them privately that you want them to see how fast they can drive the team, and that for the first ten minutes you want them to jump for the ball the moment it is down. Then tell the quarters the same thing, only in addition, that they shall give the signal on the run for the line-up, no matter whether it is a good play or not. If the ends are slow, let the quarter work in a kick on the first down several times. If the guards are slow in lining up, let him give straight line bucking by a half.

Defensive Team Play. Defensive team play should be begun by instructing some pair of men to help each other out in word and act. For example, take the guard and tackle. Tell each separately the strength and weakness of the other, and then explain how they must aid one another by supplemental work. If they have good heads they will take it up readily. There should be no loud calling out of what the opponents are likely to do. That sort of work often does more harm than good. But a general caution, such as "Look out for a fake!" or something of that kind, is all right. Especially should the two men learn that they are responsible for *results*, — not merely for their acts, but what comes from those acts! This brings about unselfish team play and does away with the host of excuses. The relations of the various positions, one toward the other, are described in another chapter.

Backs on Defense. Defensive play by the backs in team work should be practised on the regular field of play and also in the kicking practice. One of the best theories is that of the formation of a triangle by three men whenever a kick is to be caught. This triangle is, of course, a very loose arrangement and subject to much modification, but whenever the kick is high enough, or there is time, two men should eventually reach the proximity of the man catching the ball in time to be of service to him in interfering or in saving a muff or fumble.

Field Divisible into Two Halves. The various arrangements for defensive team play are treated of in other chapters. Here it is enough to say that team play demands a defense that depends as little as possible upon any fixed formations of the opponents. Eleven men are too cumbersome a body to be handled in a minute and rearranged by a word, while the opponents are ready for action. The most that should be attempted are the changes incident to a probable kick and the few minor movements in the line-up, such as a line man crossing over when the play is crowded against the edge of the field. Each line man in defense should, in his mind, divide the field into two halves by a line drawn through the ball, and should think of his half as either *facing the runner while the other half pursue him*, or *pursuing him while the other half front him*. Many an up-to-that-point unsatisfactory line man has become a good one when he once had this picture clearly in mind. The half of the line before the runner —

end, tackle, and guard — slow up the play by their assaults upon it, while the half of the line behind the runner chase him and take advantage of that slowing-up by their comrades in front to overtake the play.

Working a Man Through. For the three centre men, and occasionally the quarter, there is a special line of team play on the defense based upon the principle of getting one man at least through absolutely unobstructed. Sometimes the two guards help the centre through, sometimes a centre and a guard open up for the quarter, sometimes all stretch the opposing line as far out as it will stand and every one takes his chance. No matter how it is done, it should be distinctly understood by each man just which one of the methods is to be used. For this reason one man of this body of four who has the best judgment should always give the signal as to which method to use.

Mutual Assistance without Sacrifice of Individual Skill. Generally, team play should be taken to include also all the smaller, finer points of mutual assistance, and this may be best developed by frequent meetings, talks, and free discussions. In fact, the great backbone of team play can be formed only by such methods. In conclusion let us say, however, that there is no fault that will so surely defeat a team as the sacrifice of individual understanding and execution to that part of team play that is known by the term "tricks." The first thing a team asks of a new coach who comes with a reputation for skill in tactics and successful team play is, "Teach us some tricks." There is only one trick that will win, and that is work. There is no royal road to victory. Every team must go through the dust and dirt and the hard daily practice to master the individual detail of each position. When that has been done, then team play will come without blunders, and a trick, though seldom very successful, is not attended by certain disaster.

CHAPTER XI

ON THE USE OF TRICKS IN FOOTBALL

The Player's Idea. The value and place of tricks in football is very generally misunderstood. To the players themselves tricks have an abnormal fascination. They seem to offer a short road to success. Deep down in the average player's mind there exists the feeling that tricks are the side-door to victory. The main entrance is through the hard daily toil, the well-grounded, consistent policy, and the long weeks of daily drill. But the side-door, although it offers a narrow entrance, seems, nevertheless, to offer a quick one. Given a reasonable amount of proficiency in the fundamentals of the game, and a strong defense, it often seems to the player as if one or two successful tricks would bridge the wide chasm which exists between the mediocre work of his team and the well-drilled but familiar interference of his opponents.

The Spectator's Misapprehension. With the public there is, perhaps, an even greater misapprehension in regard to tricks. The fickle public, with its constant tendency towards exaggeration, magnifies the importance of the successful trick, and bestows upon its author a degree of praise of which he is, in great part, unworthy. But the laws of compensation work here as elsewhere; to the same extent that its praise is exaggerated is its blame magnified when the attack fails, or when, through its misuse, the trick works disastrously; too much blame cannot then be heaped upon its author. In fact, the coach who supplies one or two startling tricks to a team, stands a fair chance of confusion because of over-praise or over-blame.

The True Conception. This state of affairs is, perhaps, as clear an evidence as is needed of the general misinterpretation of the place and value of tricks. A trick is a good thing if it is rightly constructed and rightly used. In its very nature it presupposes that certain opponents shall be misled, or shall follow their instinct as against their training. Therefore the success of even the best trick is doubtful. It is nothing but a hazard, more or less uncertain, and it finds its best warrant for existence when it is used in an emergency, as in the last three or four minutes of a game, when the score is slightly against the team; in other words, when there is everything to gain and nothing to lose by its operation.

Value of Tricks to a Team. Every team is the better for having two or three trick plays, provided only that the captain and quarter-back understand when and how they should be employed. This last point is important, for even the best trick may be so misused that its possession becomes a positive disadvantage to the team, while its reasonable use would have been of material value. But it is not difficult for the quarter-back of a team to gain a correct estimate of the needs and uses of tricks, and it may, therefore, be safely laid down that each team should employ one or two of them in the critical games of the season.

How They should be Made Up. A trick, to be of any real value, must be one movement in a series of plays from a common line-up. The reason for this is clear: if no other play is worked from the line-up, the success of the trick is limited to a single trial, for after once being used it will be tolerably familiar to the opponents, and on a second trial the method of stopping it (if it is a trick, pure and simple) will be discovered. Furthermore, the deceptive feature of a trick, which is its only element of value, is strengthened by an earlier introduction of some other play from the same alignment, so that the opponents are not simply attempting to diagnose the probable outcome of a new line-up, but are actually led to believe that they already know the plan of attack, and are only waiting for the ball to be put in play to take the same steps to check it which they employed before.

The old Greek tutor charged a double price to instruct those pupils who had been taught by any other master, explaining that they had both to learn what he had to teach, and to unlearn what they had been taught before. This story illustrates the condition of a team when first meeting a trick which is one of a series of movements from a common line-up; they have not only to learn the peculiar characteristics of the trick, but they are at the disadvantage of having to unlearn, or disburden themselves, of the instinctive tendency which has come with the earlier plays in the same series.

Each Play in a Series should be Judged by Itself. In proportion as there are a greater number of movements from the same line-up, the trick, when it is played, will be all the stronger, and if it is possible in a series of four or five plays to have two or three tricks, the series will be, if properly used, one of the strongest weapons that a team could employ.

The question naturally arises, how much can be conceded to a weak play, in order to help out a strong trick play from the same line-up. As a general rule, the concession must be very slight. Unless every play of the series is reasonably strong, the trick, although a good one, should not be attempted. Each play of the series must have sufficient intrinsic worth to warrant the reasonable assurance that, against strong opposition, the team can at least gain its distance in the trial. With this assured, the trick will be all the stronger when it is tried, for the very fact that the first effort resulted in the gain of the required distance will naturally compel the opponents to rush to its defense with even greater energy than before; and in proportion as they are instant on the defense are they hurrying to their own undoing. Thus the strength of each play in a series is contagious, and increases the strength of every other play in a first trial.

When and Where Tricks should be Employed. The first and most important place where a trick should be employed is in the last three minutes of a match, with a slightly adverse score. This is an emergency when everything may wisely be staked upon the issue of even the most hazardous trick; if it fails, the conditions are unchanged, and there is still at least a chance. It is a time for the application of the motto, "Nothing venture, nothing have."

The trick used at such a time may be of a different nature from that which would be employed at an ordinary stage of the game. In other words, it may be one of a most hazardous class of plays, such as a long double pass, or a difficult criss-cross, in which the effort itself is not only extremely difficult, but in which there may be a large risk of the loss of the ball. On the other hand, such plays, if successful, are usually abnormally successful. It seems as if the very hazard of the undertaking brought with it an additional measure of reward, and a touch-down is often the result of the successful execution of a play of this description.

A Side-Line Stratagem. Another opportunity where a trick may be wisely employed is offered when the ball is close to the side line. The possibilities of strategic operations in such a situation are very great, and any team which takes to tricks readily, and handles them skillfully, will do well to have in its repertoire at least one side-line trick. It is nearly always a play which makes every appearance of starting for the long side of the field, but by a dodge or criss-cross sends the runner with or without a single interferer, down the short side of the field, close to the side line. It is usually not a difficult play to bring off, but the runner should be cautioned against allowing himself to swerve over the line at any point in his run.

After a Loss on First Down. Another place where a trick may often be employed is on a second down, where the first down has resulted in a loss, and there is consequently over five yards to gain. The chance of gaining this increased distance in a single attempt by a direct attack is generally so small that it is a good time to employ a trick.

The relative value of a straight play and a trick may perhaps here be stated in such a manner as to make the whole subject easier of comprehension to the student; let it be understood, then, that a straight play is more certain to gain its distance than a trick play. It is less certain to gain an exaggerated distance. A trick which will gain one yard is almost equally certain to gain five or six yards. But a legitimate play is much more certain to gain a yard and a half than a trick play is of gaining at all. If a correct count was kept of the distance gained by each legitimate play and each trick, it would be found that the average of distance gained on tricks was undoubtedly greater than on legitimate plays, but the relative number of failures to gain any distance would also be greater in the trick list than in the legitimate list.

This teaches an important lesson, that trick plays are hazards, and that they are only to be used in situations which peculiarly adapt themselves to the acceptance of a hazard. This might be given as the formula or ground principle, upon which all tricks should be used: let the quarter-back once thoroughly grasp this, and there will be less danger of the misuse of tricks.

How Tricks should be Tested. Every trick, before it is incorporated into the team's list of plays, should be thoroughly tested against at least two or three different elevens.

A football team is like a baseball nine in certain respects. It has "off days," when it plays poorly; it has men in important positions who are exceptionally weak in certain single features of play, betraying in these a weakness far below the average ability of the team, — a weakness which cannot be counted upon in other teams of relatively equal strength. Furthermore, a trick, depending, as it does, upon the misleading of an opponent, can only be correctly gauged as to its value by the average of its workings upon a number of occasions. It is planned in uncertainty, and operated in uncertainty, and its value will be uncertain, if judged by any single trial against a single team. Only by records, carefully kept and averaged, can its true merit be known; and such records should always be secured by the captain.

Individual Opinions are of Little Value. It may be set down as a safe rule that the opinion of no man, be he player or expert, is of great value in regard to the probable success of a trick before it is tried. In no single point in the whole game of football does a man write himself down a greater blunderer than in daring to predicate the success of a movement before it is tried upon the field. Over and over again has the experiment been tried of showing a play upon paper to each one of half a dozen coaches, in private, with the result of half a dozen different opinions in regard to it.

In one such instance, four coaches were asked the probable man who would be dangerous to the working of a certain trick, or, in other words, the man who would check the play or bring down the runner. In each case a different man was named, and the result of these interviews was that four different objections were established to the play, because four different men in the defending team were singled out as "sure to stop the runner." When the play was tried, not one of these men was able to stop the runner until the play had gained such substantial distances as made its value assured for the entire season.

Therefore, take the opinion of no individual, however expert he may be, or however good may be his judgment, as to the value of any trick play, until he has seen it tried against opponents who are not familiar with it. Remember that every play looks differently on paper from what it does upon the field, and when the basis of a play is the deception of the opponent, it is impossible to predict the result with any degree of accuracy.

How many Tricks should be Employed. The number of tricks which should be employed by a team is an important matter. By this is meant, not the number which should be tested or tried, but the number which should be carried by the team into its final matches. This number must depend wholly upon the character of the team, as a team. If it is composed of heavy men, good at sledge-hammer ground-gaining, but not light and shifty upon their feet, one or two tricks are all that can probably be used to advantage. If, on the other hand, the team is composed of exceptionally light men, quick on their feet, good dodgers, clever at picking their holes in the line, and ready in expedients, the number of tricks may be increased up to a limit of five or six, beyond which number it is very rarely wise to go.

Hints upon Selection. Let the tricks be selected with great care, and in estimating their value do not forget that a less showy trick, if placed in a strong series of four plays, is worth as much as a more brilliant trick played with only one other play in the complement. Test every trick before it is used, and test it against different elevens. If this is impossible, endeavor to arrange for the change of the immediate defenders in your opposing team, and substitute in their positions green men who do not know the play. This will afford an opportunity of seeing how different men, who have been coached differently, will meet the conditions by which you have surrounded them.

Final Hints as to Tricks. Never forget that a trick is, after all, nothing but a trick. It is not football *per se*, but rather an offshoot of the game, born of the wonderful tactical possibility of the game, which is one of its greatest charms. A good trick is no disgrace to the sport. The odium which attaches to it is a case of "give a dog a bad name." If we call it a stratagem, it is dignified at once into a piece of headwork, by which brains may triumph over brawn.

But remember that it is not enough for the trick itself to be successful; it must also be used successfully, and by this is meant that it must be used sparingly, and only when the conditions clearly call for its use.

Finally, in giving tricks to a team, let them be surrounded by a reasonable degree of mystery, and let them be taught and rehearsed in private, if possible. Encourage the team to believe that they have in their list one or two trick points of decided advantage, about which their opponents are in entire ignorance. Encourage them to take a hopeful view of the result of such movements. They will then play them when they are called for with a much greater dash and spirit, because of their belief that the mine which they are about to explode will be all the more destructive because it is unsuspected.

CHAPTER XII

How to Construct Plays

Expert Knowledge not Required. The opinion prevails to a large extent that, in order to construct successful movements or plays for a football team, it is necessary to have a very thorough knowledge of the game, or to be specially gifted by nature with an inventive mind. As a matter of fact, neither of these is essential, and any one who has interest enough in the subject to give the time needed may construct very successful plays, although not in any way himself an expert in the game of football.

Nor is it necessary that one should have actually played the game, although it is essential that he should have a very thorough knowledge of the rules, and be reasonably familiar with the game itself, as it is played. This knowledge would naturally be the property of any one who wished to construct football plays, since interest in the subject might fairly be assumed to presuppose a knowledge of the game, and at least a superficial knowledge of the rules. It is only necessary to strengthen this superficial knowledge by constant reference as the work progresses.

At the very start it is a good plan to cut loose from old traditions, which are often false or misleading, and from all impressions of existing plays. In other words, do not try to improve the old-time plays, but strike out for yourself into new fields, and endeavor to open up undiscovered channels along which operations may be successfully begun. Remember that the game itself changes from year to year, and that the football player of half a dozen years ago, if he has not continued his study and interest, is quite behind the modern game of to-day.

Let us, in this chapter, speak directly to the reader who may wish to enter this interesting field, and in order to make what we have to say more explicit and perhaps more interesting, let us address him in the second person, as if we were face to face.

The only idea which you need to have in your mind is the single question of how to carry the ball through the opposing line, under the necessary restrictions of the playing rules. Drop every other thought from your calculations, and go ahead on this broad basis, and you may be surprised at the success of even your first crude efforts.

Two Different Methods of Work. You have your choice of two different methods of work. Neither can be claimed to be superior, and both may well be tried, with a view to adopting that method which proves most successful for you. One method is to use merely pencil and paper; the other method is to have small blocks, dice, or counters, representing the players themselves, and group them or move them about upon a table or slate, on which is drawn the plan of a football field.

If this latter method is employed, be sure that the spaces upon the field are in the same relative scale as the size of your counters or men. In other words, the size of the whole working equipment of diagram and players should be in correct relative proportion throughout. This is important, and it will greatly handicap your efforts unless you start with this one point accurately determined. Make the width of the field in the same scale as the five-yard distances. Then calculate how many men are needed to stretch across the five-yard spaces, if they stand at the customary distance at which football players are separated. This will determine for you the proper size of your counter or block which represents a player.

In the use of these two different methods, it is a good plan to use them alternately on the same play. In other words, having first constructed the play on paper, test its practicability by placing it on the field according to your second method of work. A play will frequently not look on the correctly-scaled field as it does on the roughly-drawn sheet.

Errors to be Avoided. Now that you have selected your method of work, let us say a few words on the errors which you should avoid. Your first efforts will very likely be wasteful of men. There are only eleven of them, as you will soon learn to your sorrow, for many a clever move will fail you for the lack of a twelfth man. At an early stage of your work you will discover that it is an unwise policy to make "bluffs" without the ball. In other words, the operation of sending two or three men on a "fake" dash toward the side lines, even though they make every appearance of having the ball, is expensive fooling. It *may* draw an end rusher down, but it probably will not. You must make your bluffs *with* the ball; that is, generally speaking, let the ball go with the play. A great deal of time may be spared by avoiding that fascinating but fruitless line of operations which always tempts the novice, and in which a great demonstration is made in one direction, while the ball, in the hands of a single runner, with perhaps one interferer, or often with no interferers, is started in exactly the opposite direction. Very rarely can such attempts be made without loss.

A second tendency of your earlier efforts, against which you should guard yourself, will be to subdivide the work. For example, if four men have separately to do two or three different things, and it seems possible for you to unite the four into one body, and let that body do the different things together, it will always be wise to so unite them. It is a safe rule to lay down, that individual labors should be united wherever it is possible. *Bunch your interference around the ball.*

Securing the First Idea. The first thing to secure in constructing a football play is an idea or conception of the movement, which, let us hope, will be an original one. The best ideas will not probably come to you when bending over your desk. They are far more likely to occur to you when walking in the street or riding on the cars, provided your thought is upon the development of the game. The instant you have the idea, take pencil and paper and go to work upon it without delay. Develop it fully, and do this at the earliest possible moment, before the train of thought has passed from your mind. If you have under consideration what you think is a correct new principle of attack, do not lose patience when you find it exceedingly difficult to work out your exact line of play from this principle. Remember that the principle is the important thing, and persistent thought upon it will nearly always prove fruitful in the end; the right play will surely suggest itself.

The Paper Upside Down. Right here there comes in a curious feature: *you must work out your problems upside down!* In other words, let the centre of your paper represent the defending line of your opponents, and bring your lines of attack from the top of the sheet down into the plan or diagram. To put it still more clearly, let your own team occupy a position at the top of the sheet, facing you, while you, in imagination, are occupying a position behind your opponents' rush-line, and not behind your own. Let the assault be directed at you, and you will be more quick to detect its weaknesses as you stand in the position of defending it.

New Principles from Old Ones. A new principle may often be built up on the improvement of an older principle. Thus, for example, the criss-cross may be perfected to a point which shall eliminate every dangerous feature (such as loss of the ball in the double pass, etc.), and make the confusion of the opponents doubly disastrous by compelling them to criss-cross their own forces as they follow the criss-cross of the ball. If you can devise a series of operations which shall bring two groups of your opponents moving against each other in exactly opposite directions, you have accomplished a master stroke, and one which will repay a generous expenditure of time in its development.

A Method of Working Backward. When, after much study, no new method of attack suggests itself to your mind, it is possible to proceed by a different method, and often attain a most successful result. This method is to "force a situation" by grouping your men in the most advantageous positions for them to effect a break through the opponents' line; then, working backward from this group, trace the path of each, man from his place in the group to his position in the original line-up. Choose your men with a view to effecting the line-up with the least possible confusion, and make your assignments in the interference correspond with the distance at which the player is located from the immediate spot of attack, to the end that the men who join the attack at the latest moment shall be naturally the ones who have the longest distance to travel. It is astonishing to discover what really good plays can be developed by this method.

Still Another Method. Another method of originating plays is to proceed along the following lines: Provide yourself with a collection of thin sticks or whittlings of some soft wood which will bear bending in various curves, and to different angles. With these sticks you can obtain a good idea of the possible concentration of men for an attack at any point along the line. By laying the sticks down, — a single stick accurately designating each man's course or path, letting each stick start from his position in the line-up, and terminate at his position in the final movement, — these sticks will then give you a graphic picture of the appearance of the movement at all stages. They will show you the route which each man travels and enable you to correct any possible interference of one man with another. They will give you a clear idea of the original line-up, and another comprehensive view of the interference when it is fully formed around the runner. They will further help you to effect the right assignments of men for the different labors of the play, since the length of the sticks shows the ground each man must cover to join the interference. In a word, the use of these sticks materially assists in the proper "timing" of the play, and time is the most important factor in football operations. No man can be a successful football general who does not realize the value of the fraction of a second in all operations. The use of the sticks which we have just described will reveal the possible danger which often arises from two players crossing each other's tracks in reaching the interference.

It is no drawback to a play, but rather a distinct advantage, to have the interference so carefully timed that the men shall cross each other's tracks in what might appear to the casual observer as a most reckless manner, but which practice will easily demonstrate to be an entirely safe movement if accurately timed at every point. It is such a movement which most confuses an opponent, for it is the perfection of accurate timing. Few mistakes can be made in constructing football plays if the student will but insist upon the vital element of duration of time in every movement.

Assigning the Men. When the play has been successfully conceived, a very important feature in the work of developing it is the assignment of the men for the particular labors of the play. These assignments will often be suggested by the peculiar ability of a certain player to do a certain part of the work. All care should be exercised, especially if the line-up is of a novel or unusual nature, to make the assignments so that the line-up may be taken in the quickest possible time, and with the least confusion.. It is always a drawback, and sometimes a sufficient condemnation of a play, if any appreciable moment of time is needed to take the lineup. Delays of this nature inevitably slow down the attack, and this is always a disadvantage to the side which has the ball.

Value of Detail Sketches. It is a very common practice, in illustrating points in football, to make a random sketch on a slip of paper (often the back of an old envelope), and as soon as the consideration of the point is concluded, or the paper is covered with the drawing, it is carelessly destroyed. This is a great mistake. It is impossible to foresee how much advantage may come to you through the ability to refer to a previous sketch, which, perhaps, at the time you made it, seemed wholly impracticable, but which, in the light of more recent developments, takes on a new value, and is now of the greatest service to you. To insure the preservation in compact form of all these random sketches and studies, it is a good plan to keep a scribbling book, in which shall be kept all studies of plays, detail drawings, random sketches, and casual memoranda of every sort concerning football. Never use odd scraps of paper! Let everything be entered in the book. A very cheap blank book will answer all needs, so long as you adhere to the rule that every sketch or drawing shall be thus preserved, *whether it seems of any value at the time or not.*

Sequences from One Line-Up. It is a safe rule that plays are doubly valuable when more than one play is constructed from a single line-up. It is, therefore, an excellent plan to always build a second play, which may act as a foil to the first movement, both movements starting from the same line-up. If the first movement is a deceptive one, the second movement may be the correspondingly natural tendency of operations. If both are played with equal skill, each helps the other. Until they are both fairly familiar, the opponents will have great difficulty in knowing which movement is coming. These two movements taken together constitute what is known as a series of plays. Series of plays of this nature (each play starting from the same lineup) are used by every college team. The average number of plays in a series is four, but many have six or seven plays, and some have been known which had as many as twelve. One especially good series was once used which had sixteen different outlets. An added value in the use of series plays is found in the fact that the team avoid the necessity of learning new line-ups. This is an important point, especially where substitutes are called upon during a game. It is a good plan, therefore, in building plays to group them, as far as possible, into series. If two separate plays have been invented, it is often possible to harmonize the two so that they may both be brought off from a common line-up.

It is difficult to lay too much emphasis upon the disadvantage to the opponents when the second play of a series is tried, the first play having already become tolerably familiar through repeated use. It is probable that the first play will be the natural tendency or operation of the line-up, while the second play will be the strategic or deceptive operation. When this second play transpires, it is a strong temptation to the average player who is opposing the play to "play for the trick." By this phrase is meant to play in a purely mechanical way upon the assumed familiarity with the earlier operations of the opponents. This tendency of a football player to go against his training, and rely too much on his judgment, is always strong, and it is this weakness which is taken advantage of when plays are grouped in one series with a universal line-up. In proportion as football players are taught to follow the ball, this dangerous tendency is less apparent.

Important Questions that Arise. Several interesting questions will suggest themselves at an early stage of the work — questions as to the easiest and hardest points in the line to assail; as to the value of an extra man in the interference, who may tend to slow it down, or to prevent its forming and getting away as quickly as it might do if he were not of its number; questions as to the relative merits of a play constructed with an evenly balanced line-up on each side of the centre, as opposed to a play, with a one-sided line-up, which leaves no reasonable doubt in the minds of the opponents as to which side of the centre is to be attacked; and many questions of a similar nature. In general, it may be said that the easiest point in the line to assail is the tackle-guard hole; the most difficult is a run around the end. In developing a round-the-end play, bear in mind that the first and most vital matter is that the runner shall get away quickly. It is not too much to say that a play which gets the runner started instantly, with comparatively small interference, is always preferable to a play which carries a much more formidable interference, but wastes an appreciable interval of time in its formation.

Where Balanced Line-Ups may be Most Effectively Employed. We have already mentioned that the easiest point in the line to assail is the tackle-guard hole. It is also, in many respects, the most profitable; it is certainly the point at which the majority of plays is directed. When assailing this hole, it is best to build plays with a balanced line-up; or, in other words, with a distribution of men which shall leave an equal number on each side of the centre, so that the opponents will find it impossible to determine in advance, from the appearance of the line-up, on which side of the centre the runner is to be met. This prevents their effecting a concentration of the backs on either side of the centre, and leaves only one rush-line back for the immediate supplementary defense.

The Wisdom of Exchanges when on the Offensive. In the construction of all plays, it may be set down as a safe rule, that *exchanges on the offensive are always wise.* For example, if by sending one of your men twelve yards back, with the evident intention of ordering a punt, you can induce your opponents to send an extra back up the field to receive the expected kick, it is always a wise exchange to make. Your own back can then, by starting quickly, be of some possible use in the play, and certainly join the secondary interference, while your opponent, who has gone up the field, will be of absolutely no service in the defense until the line has been pierced, and valuable ground has been gained.

On the same principle, if it were possible for an end acting on the offensive to draw his opponent out across the field and away from the immediate scene of action, it would be good policy for him to do this, since the value of men, numerically, is greater on the defensive than on the offensive. This point will be found more fully discussed in another chapter.

Plays with a One-Sided Line-Up. When a play has a one-sided line-up, or, in other words, when your men are massed in large numbers on one side of the centre, it follows, as a matter of course, that you will take an entirely different attitude towards such a play, and that your work will be less hampered, since it is perfectly clear to the opponents on which side of the centre the attack is to be made. There is much to be said in favor of one-sided line-ups, for however great the concentration of the attack may be on one side of the centre, it is unusual for an opposing captain to call over an end or a tackle from one side of the line to the other, to meet an unexpected concentration. Of course, if the line-up is in close proximity to the side line, the opposing captain would be justified in transferring a man from the short side to the long side of the field, in view of the limited width of territory to be covered in one direction, and the great danger of operations in the other direction, by reason of the wide stretch of territory in which those operations may be conducted. But at all other times, the line will practically remain the same, however great the concentration may be upon one side, and this is a great advantage in favor of the one-sided line-up. Naturally the rush-line backs will move over a trifle toward the stronger side, but this is only the secondary line of defense, and it is much more than compensated for by the requisitions which you have made from the deserted side of the centre.

Value of an Unexpected Kick. In developing any series of plays, it is well to remember that a quick, unexpected kick is most valuable at certain stages of the game, and one such play should, if possible, be included in every series. The addition of a quick kick is especially desirable in a criss-cross series. *Vice versa,* if the line-up is plainly for a punt, and the position of the full-back has induced the opponents to send an extra back up the field, the conditions are then most favorable for a criss-cross.

Operating a Fake Kick. It is an excellent plan to include in your series one play of the style known as a "fake kick," or a sharp dash through the side of the line from which the rush-line half has just been withdrawn and sent up the field, as the extra man to receive the expected punt. Fake kicks are a most powerful method of attack, and they have this added advantage, that they may be worked more rapidly than any other style of trick play. It is no unusual sight to see repeated gains of fifteen to twenty yards made against opponents who have not been sufficiently coached on the true protection against fake kicks.

Another Form of Strategy. One other profitable direction for strategy is to make use of a familiar procedure in an unfamiliar way. For example, the calling back of a guard to head a heavy interference is a familiar form of procedure, in connection with a round-the-end play, or a mass attack at the tackle-guard hole. In either case the guard heads the group, and in some cases takes the ball himself. Now it is easily possible, after a play has been made up, to introduce this familiar procedure of calling back the guard, but without, in this case, having any object in view except the very slight suggestion which it may give to the opponents that the play is to be one of these two familiar forms of attack. In reality the guard has been called back for no special purpose, but the simple change of work between two players, trifling and unimportant as it is, may yet be valuable from its mere suggestion of operations along the familiar lines suggested by the coming back of the guard.

Conclusion. Much more might be said on the subject of the construction of plays, but it is only possible, in the brief limits of this chapter, to assure the reader that any effort on his part to construct plays will be productive of much pleasure, and to again emphasize the fact that interest in the sport itself is all that is needed as an equipment for the work. The neophyte should never be deterred by the suggestion that he is not familiar with football. Successful plays have been repeatedly designed by men who knew comparatively little of the game. With the few brief hints contained in this chapter to guide him, and with a warm interest in the sport to serve both as a stimulus to his thought and a practical help in his work, he may devote his time to the attempt with every reasonable assurance of success.

CHAPTER XIII

FOOTBALL DON'TS

What is Football Instinct? This little collection of the faults to be carefully avoided in football should be thoroughly instilled into the mind of every player; he should commit them to memory, and keep them constantly in mind, until the thoughts which they embody have become a matter of instinct with him.

One often hears the expression, "football instinct." Perhaps there is no better definition of instinct in football than the emergency ability or proficiency to which a player has attained, who has so far mastered certain principles that in his playing he is rarely guilty of any of the errors pointed out in this chapter. It is not too much to say that the student whose game is up to the level of the tenets here laid down may be classed as a really great player.

What this Chapter Includes. It is not intended to present here a complete collection of the "Don'ts" of football, but rather to name a few of the more important ones, and with them to include some of less importance which, by a singular fate, seem always to be overlooked. The player should add to this list any special suggestions which may cover the weakness of his individual play. The list which we here give, and which is rather to be regarded as a collection of general faults, is as follows: —

Forty Cautions to the Player.

Don't fail to play a fast game. Line up instantly after each down. Your game is twice as effective if there are no delays.

Don't slug. Scrapping is not football. More than this, it prevents good playing.

Don't wait for the opposing runner in the line. Break through and stop him before he reaches the line.

Don't tackle above the waist or below the knees, but always at the hips. When about to tackle, keep your eyes on the runner's hips, and he cannot so readily deceive you in his movements.

Don't let any player whom you tackle gain an inch afterward. Never let him gain his length by falling forward. Lift him off his feet and throw him back toward his goal.

Don't fail to try and take the ball away from an opponent when he is tackled. Make a feature of this, and you will succeed oftener than you anticipate.

Don't let any thought take precedence of the ball itself. Keep your mind on the ball. Follow its every motion as far as possible. Always be ready to drop on it after any fumble or misplay.

Don't be satisfied with a superficial knowledge of the rules. Master every detail.

Don't let your opponents know when or where you are hurt.

Don't make excuses, however good they may be. There is no room in football for excuses.

Don't answer back to a coach upon the field, even if you know him to be wrong. Do exactly what he tells you to do, so far as you are able, and remember that strict obedience is the first requirement of a player.

Don't lose your temper. The man who cannot control his temper has no business on the football field.

Don't be one minute late to practice. The hour named is the hour for you to be on hand. If you have not interest enough to be prompt, resign from the game at once, for you have not the proper spirit for victory.

Don't rest contented after a misplay. Redouble every energy till it is redeemed by some exceptionally brilliant stroke.

Don't stop if you miss a tackle. Turn instantly and follow the runner at your highest speed. He is your man now more than ever. This is important.

Don't weaken or slow down when about to be tackled.

Don't forget that a touch-down is twice as valuable and only half as difficult to make in the first three minutes of a game. The opponents are often not completely waked up, and the moral effect of such an immediate score is very great.

Don't try, if you are tackled, to break the force of your fall by stretching out either arm or hand. It is dangerous.

Don't exchange civilities with your opposite in the line, no matter how much the score may be in your favor. It is better to delay conversation until after the game.

Don't "drop your sand" when the score goes against you, or when the ball is under your own goal. Then is the time of all others to show your pluck.

Don't magnify your bruises or let them frighten you. When hurt, make up your mind as quickly as possible as to your condition. You either can or cannot play. If the former, waste as little of your friends' sympathy as possible. If the latter, tell the captain at once, without any false pride, and get your release.

Don't let an opponent know when he irritates you, unless you want more of the same treatment.

Don't let an opponent ever see you weaken. It will simply redouble the attack at your position.

Don't rise from the ground rubbing yourself when you have been thrown unusually hard. You will be thrown twice as hard next time, if your opponent sees you mind a fall.

Don't give an inch in your blocking. If there is to be any space between you and your opponent, let it be on his side of the line.

Don't forget your instructions to "always block the inside man."

Don't give away the play by your attitude or movements in lining up. Watch yourself constantly in this regard.

Don't let half the players of your team be in their positions on any line-up before you have taken yours.

Don't forget the vital principle of team play, which cannot be too often impressed upon the mind. It is this: *Team play begins the instant the centre receives the ball from the hands of the runner.* In other words, it is a part of team play, and the most important part, to line up more quickly than your opponents. This is the very truest sort of team play, yet the delay of one single man in taking his place will ruin it completely.

Don't be an automaton. Thoroughly master each principle, and then vary your play as emergencies arise.

Don't let any man be ahead of you in dropping on the ball when it is fumbled.

Don't fail to try to be in every interference before it is finally stopped. Follow each runner, and watch for a chance to push him or receive the ball from him when he is tackled.

Don't play high if you are checking an interference or running as a part of the interference. When you drop out of an interference, meet your opponent as low as possible.

Don't fail to go down the field under every kick.

Don't forget the rule that your own runner must never be alone when he is tackled.

Don't shirk any required study or work for football. Earn the right to play football, or don't attempt it.

Don't be discouraged with your ability or progress. The right spirit in football is worth more than anything. Be sure you have that, and your chances of success are good.

Don't whine about decisions which seem unfair. Accept only honest, fearless officials, and then leave the game in their hands.

Don't do anything to undermine discipline, or you are putting the axe at the very root of the tree.

Don't be careless about guards, protectors, or padding, over any weak, injured, or exposed part of the body. One negligence may cost you the season's playing.

PART III

FOR THE COACH

CHAPTER I

GENERAL SYSTEM OF COACHING

Different Branches of the Work. It is one of the peculiarities of football that the coaching of a team calls for the ability to instruct in many wholly different branches which have little connection with each other. It is well for the coach to have these various branches clearly distinguished in his own mind, for it is necessary to take constant account of them in the development of a team.

In the training of a leading 'Varsity Eleven these different branches are usually assigned to different coaches, each coach taking that in which he is best fitted to instruct, and being responsible to the head coach for the faithfulness of his teaching and the successful development of the team along this particular line. The theory of his work is sometimes left to him to prepare, but more often it is decided by the council of coaches, or by the best expert talent at hand. But whether it is evolved by the coaches, head coach, or captain, the theory along which the work is elaborated is of great importance, and should not be left unhesitatingly in the hands of the individual coach who is to superintend the instruction and development of the team along the lines which the theory lays down.

In the development of a minor team, where only one, or possibly two coaches are available, this subdivision of the work and its assignment to different parties is manifestly impossible; but it then becomes all the more necessary that the single coach should keep in mind the various branches of the coaching, and the order in which they should receive attention.

These various individual branches may be set down as follows: —

(1) Coaching Individual Positions. This would include the careful instruction to the entire team in the details of their several positions. A large part of this coaching can be done off the field, or at least outside the hours of practice. The best method for such coaching, where it is practicable, is for the coach to put on his football togs and be prepared to illustrate practically every point of instruction which he gives. The coaching of individual positions should have almost entire sway during the first weeks of the season.

There will come a time when the season is a little less than half concluded, when individual coaching must be sidetracked, and the team handled as a unit. This is the period when team play is being developed, when the relationship between different players is being taught, and when precision, accuracy, and the "getting together" of the team need paramount attention. The coaching of individual positions need not entirely cease at this time, but it should be done in a way which will not interfere in the slightest degree with the handling of the team as a unit. It may be found necessary then to have no individual coaching during the practice, but insist that it shall all be done after the practice, when the players may be taken one at a time, and their individual faults explained and corrected.

(2) Kicking. It is imperative that some one man shall be responsible for coaching the kickers and catchers. It goes without saying, that the kicking ability of the team should not be concentrated in one player. Every one of the backs should be diligently trained in kicking and catching, not only to the end that the best kicker may be developed, but also because, through injury or unforeseen occurrence, any one of the backs may be called upon to undertake this feature of the work.

The particular style of kick which shall be taught is a question which can be settled by the captain and coach or coaches, but care should be taken not to alter the coaching policy in this direction when it has once been started. It may be found advantageous to coach one man for straight kicking, and another man for the side kick, but the most important element of all should be a watchfulness to see that all the kicking is done in the shortest possible space of time, and that the kicker understands clearly how to receive the ball, and how to handle it to the best effect. His particular stride in making the kick should be carefully rehearsed, and the time required for the pass and the long-distance punt should be constantly timed in practice. The limit of speed which must be attained in this particular has been well established by experience, and it is not difficult to determine arbitrarily whether a kicker is relatively slow or fast. All the various branches of kicking should be taught, and especial attention should be given to place kicking of goals. The points which are earned in this way are very important, since two place-kicks of goal are equal to a touch-down, and it is one of the maxims of football that a coach should strenuously insist upon the recognition of the full value of accurate place kicking.

Kicking practice, calling as it does for only two or three men upon the field, need not be undertaken in the regular hours of team practice, as time can always be found for this individual work.

(3) The Offensive Game. Under this head would come the planning of all the various plays which the team will employ, including the kick-off, the defense of the kick-off, and the protection for a punt. While the responsibility for preparing these plays, and making the various dispositions of men in each play, must positively be assumed by some person or persons, it is not necessary, of course, that the plays themselves should all be planned by this person. As a detail of the general system of coaching, this division of the subject deserves the special study of some competent head.

(4) The Defensive Play. Defensive team play has not reached, in this country, the great development which offensive play has attained. The defense of most teams is characterized by much purely individual play, and the establishment of a scientific theory of team defense has not yet been attained, even by some leading college teams.

As a general statement, it may be said that the defensive play of a team, as a team, should be daring and almost reckless. The moral value of such a defense is very great. It often happens in the development of a team that where the individual play of the line is very courageous, the team play of the line in defense is cowardly, and the result is almost invariably the spectacle of an opponent's charging forward without meeting any serious opposition *until reaching the line!* This is equivalent to a tacit yielding to the opponents of one yard on almost every play. The rule should be, *"Break up the play before it is started, and always tackle behind the opponents' line."* Hence the best theory of defense which can be elaborated must be one which demands of certain players that they shall go "tearing" through the line the instant the ball is snapped, with a view to tackling the runner before he has fairly started, and it may be, in some cases, before even the pass has been made.

Team Defense *vs.* Individual Blocking. A detailed explanation of a proper theory of defense is not given in this chapter for two reasons: first, it is impossible to formulate, arbitrarily, any system of defense which, in all its details, could properly be recommended to every team, or even to a large majority of college and school teams. Secondly, the various points in the establishment of a correct theory of defense for any team are elaborated in the chapters on relationships of one player to another in the second part of this book.

Some of these theories so far commend themselves that they are given here an entire and unqualified indorsement which is intended to imply that they are sufficiently practical for them to be recommended to any team. One such point, for example, is the relative playing of the tackle and rush-line back, where both half-backs are brought up to reenforce the line. In this case, the most acceptable theory of relationship between the tackle and line back would be that which has been described somewhat as follows: The tackle moves out until he reaches a position where he can clearly go through quickly outside of his opponent; if his opponent undertakes to follow him out, the rush-line back steps up into the tackle's place. The opposing tackle will naturally obey his coaching, and "take the inside man," moving in so as to give his whole attention to the rush-line back. The moment he does this, the rush-line back drops back a yard or more, which immediately takes him out of the line, and he becomes no longer properly an inside man. Following his coaching, the tackle would then move out slightly in order to block his opponent, and the instant he does this, the rush-line back steps forward again into the line. This constant see-sawing of the rush-line back and the opposing tackle is maintained up to the point where the ball is put in play. In whatever position the opposing tackle finds himself, the chances are good that both the tackle and rush-line back will get through the line. One of them will certainly succeed in going straight through to reach the runner.

The failure here of the opposing tackle is the old proverbial case of the man who falls between two stools. In trying to take care of both men at once, he is very apt to lose both. This supplementary work of the tackle and rush-line back on the defense should be practised by both tackles.

Preparing a Defensive System. These various details of defensive team play may easily be united into a system from a careful reading of the "Relationship" chapters in the second part, and a selection of those details which best commend themselves to the coach for the development of the particular team which he has in hand. Such a course will build up a stronger defense than were an arbitrary plan here offered for his guidance. His own theory, when thus prepared and carefully explained to the man who is to have charge of the defensive work of the team, should never be departed from in the later work of the season. The defense for a punt and for a drop-kick would not properly be covered by the theory here described, but should be made the subject of special preparation.

Delay in Starting Team Defense. One fact in this connection should be emphasized, for it is an important one, and may come as a decided innovation to some coaches: *The theory of the defense should not be given to the team until the close of the third week of the season*, not forgetting that there are teams to whom, as a team, this theory should never be given.

The reason for such a delay is the danger, which clearly exists, that the team may win its minor and unimportant victories in the early part of the season on its theory of defense, rather than on the primary virtue of good blocking. It is better for the team that its early victories should be secured on nothing but straight, simple, individual blocking in the line, with no relationship taught between the players, and no wise theories of defense to aid them. This method may result in keeping the score down in the earlier games of the season, but its value will surely be manifested later in the season, and the course of the coach in this particular will be fully justified by the final results.

When the theory of the defense is at last given to the team, there need be no fears that the line men have not been thoroughly grounded in the primary principles of blocking and breaking through. The higher science, when it comes, will be all the more prized because it will come as a powerful auxiliary to the early training, and, being new, there will be no danger of its being lightly esteemed by reason of over familiarity before the season closes. The average football player attaches an inordinate value to anything new, and the chances are strongly in favor of his thinking more and making more of the theory of the defense if it is not given to him until the season is half completed.

(5) Generalship. This is practically a matter which has to do with only three men, the captain, the substitute captain (in case of injury), and the quarter-back.

These three men should know the best tactics to employ in every game and in any position or contingency which may arise. More than this, they should not only understand what to do, but the reason for it, and this clear comprehension of the cause for each action will furnish a groundwork of football instinct which may carry the team safely through many unforeseen emergencies. It may be well, before any important game, to briefly summarize to the entire team the information which has been given to these three men, relative to the especial tactics to be employed in this particular game, and the reason why these tactics have been laid down. This feature of the matter has been more completely discussed in another chapter.

(6) Spirit. Quite apart from the training of the team, it is necessary that some attention should be given to the spirit which must be infused into the players. Football is a game which well tests the mettle of the man. Proficiency in the playing of a position in minor games against comparatively weak teams, or on the field of practice, is not sufficient assurance in itself that the player can repeat this proficiency when he meets a team of greater strength. The elements of personal bravery and a dauntless spirit must not be overlooked, and inasmuch as it is clearly possible to infuse a great deal of this "do or die" spirit into a team, so that its play shall be greatly benefited thereby, it is eminently proper to regard this feature as a separate branch of training.

(7) Conditioning. Under this head comes the work of the trainer. The team must be systematically developed, and their physical condition, entirely apart from the question of personal injuries, should be constantly watched over and developed. With the teams of the larger colleges, this physical conditioning should be done upon a carefully prepared method, which gradually develops the power of the team until it reaches its maximum at the date of the most important game. In the case of these more important teams, where a trainer is employed, this process of development does not properly consider the question of physical injuries, which may, therefore, be treated of under a separate classification.

(8) Physical Injuries. This is a department of the work which must, of necessity, be intrusted to other hands than the football coach. If the services of a doctor have not been secured, some provision should be made whereby an injured player can receive medical treatment promptly.

Head Coach. All of these various departments of the work will naturally be in the charge of one man, or possibly two men, in the case of school teams and the various minor league teams. But in college teams, where the services of graduate players may be requisitioned to assist in the development of the team, it follows, naturally, that there may be quite a number of coaches, and that the various departments of the work should be assigned to different men. With this elaboration of the system, there arises the necessity of a head coach.

There is great value, and equally great danger, in the creation of one-man power in any situation, and this value and this danger are both present in the establishment of a head coach for a football team. The thoughtful man who finds himself appointed to such a position will make his influence felt in all important matters, but he will himself be rarely seen. His power is well-nigh paramount, but the public display of his exercise of that power might easily become intolerable; on the other hand, the quiet guiding of the various conflicting questions, so that they shall all settle themselves along lines which wisdom dictates, need raise no antagonism, and will accomplish successfully all desired results.

It is the duty of the head coach to see that the various coaches attend strictly to the work to which they have been assigned, and that they conduct their coaching along the lines laid down as the proper policy for the development of the team. If any coach, from any cause, fails in the performance of his work, it is the duty of the head coach to see that the work is taken up by other hands, and carried forward. He should especially attend to all questions of discipline; he should make it his business to see that the attitude of the players toward their coaches is the proper attitude, and he should instantly suppress any breach of discipline, exhibition of bad temper, or insolence, from any player to any coach. He should advise with the captain on the laying out of the schedule of games, on the selections of officials, on ground rules, and on all the various questions of management which may arise during the season.

Development of the Team. With these various branches of the coaching work now fairly in mind, it is possible to proceed to a consideration of the proper order of work throughout the various weeks of the season. This order of work may be summarized as follows: —

(1) Primary and Conditioning Work: such as exercising on pulley weights in a gymnasium for a general strengthening of the muscles of the body; short and long runs for improving the wind, etc.

(2) General Individual Work. Under this head would come, for the rush-line, such preliminaries as blocking, breaking through, interfering for the runner, sprint starts, bowling over the end rush, breaking up an interference, dodging, going down the field under punts, long blocking, opening holes, etc. For the backs there would be constant training in kicking, catching, passing, interfering for the runner, quick starting, pushing the runner by shoulder and by arm, etc. Practice in such essentials as falling on the ball or tackling would be required for both rush-line and backs.

(3) Primary Offense. Under this head would come the simpler forms of attack.

(4) General Relationship between the Players. Or, in other words, what is vaguely known as "team play," including the theory of defense. This point in the general development should properly be reached when the season is half completed. The preliminary games, which have been played up to this point, must, of necessity, have been played with insufficient preparation, but it is fair to suppose that the preparation of the opponents has been similarly insufficient, by reason of the contracted limit of the football season, and the fact that the various colleges and schools of the country assemble their pupils within a very few days of the same date.

(5) Secondary Offense. This would embrace the "tricks" and special plays prepared for emergencies and for effective use on one or two important occasions in any game, when the presence of the team close to an opponent's goal has redoubled the efforts of the opponents, and made the gaining of ground exceedingly difficult. In this position, the value of a kick on the third down being very slight (owing to the proximity to the goal line), some special play may be tried. At such times, and at many other decisive situations in a game, the use of a special play is sufficiently important to warrant the spending of a few days at this stage of the season in the preparation of such secondary adjuncts to the offense.

(6) Precision. This may be more fully described as the shaping up of the interference, the clock-like accuracy of the various individual movements, the establishment of close sympathy between adjacent players, and the general oversight of all the details of play, to the end that greater speed and accuracy of movement may be attained. This last work might not inaptly be called "putting the finishing touches to the team."

(7) Ginger. It would hardly do to call it "spirit," for there is a slight shade of difference in the meaning of the two terms. "Spirit" the team, both individually and collectively, is supposed to possess, but "ginger" involves spirit and something more besides.

It is an established fact that, however hard a team is playing, it is always possible to call upon the men for an extra spurt at critical times. The infusion of ginger into a team is the arousing in it of a spirit which will keenly appreciate the importance of these extra spurts, and be ready to employ them when demanded. It is the putting into the team, as individuals, that "do or die" determination which experience has shown to be so valuable in close football contests. Whoever may be the members of the team, and whatever college they may represent, it will not be found safe to ignore this department of the coaching.

The Progress of the Work. To give the complete detail of the way in which this routine of coaching works itself out in actual practice would require too much space for the limits of this book. A running glimpse of the season's work as it unfolds itself will be sufficient for the needs of the average coach.

The school or college calls its pupils together, as a rule, about the 25th of September, and this event determines the opening of the football season. In the colleges it is the custom for a few of the more enthusiastic players to assemble from one to two weeks before the opening of the term, and even in the preparatory school such advance practising is eagerly entered into by the students, who have a keen realization of the close proximity of the first game of the season, and are anxious to "make the team early."

Let us assume that the college or school opens late in September, and that the first game of the season is to be played on the following Saturday. Many candidates for the team would undoubtedly be assembled at least one week before the opening of the school, so that systematic practice might be said to be possible at least ten days before the first contest of the season. It must be remembered that during this time the students have no work whatever upon their studies. It is a part of the vacation term, and their entire time is at the disposal of the coach, who can well employ a part of it in getting the men into first-rate physical condition.

First Three Days. To this end the first few days should be spent in the merest rudiments of football, with a great deal of time given to outside exercises not connected with the sport; expanding work to gently stretch the muscles, and short runs to improve the wind, should be the order for these first days. A part of the time can be profitably employed in the rudiments of the game, such, for example, as practice in falling on the ball, kicking, catching, sprint starting, etc. By the third or fourth day especial stress should be given to teaching all the candidates for the line the simplest fundamental principles. They should now make their first attempts at blocking, breaking through, and opening up holes. These three things might properly be called the A, B, and C of rush-line work, and it is upon the thoroughness with which these are taught that the later success of the team will, in large measure, depend.

While the line men are learning these general fundamentals of their position, the backs should be employed at kicking, catching, passing, sprint starting, interfering, tackling, blocking off, etc. The work of the backs in these directions corresponds to the work of the line on the fundamentals previously enumerated.

Coaching Individual Positions. After two or three days of hard and faithful work on these foundation principles, the time has come to begin the instruction of the various candidates in their special positions. The tackles must be taught the proper play of tackles, the ends must be taught the work of an end, the guards and centre must be faithfully instructed in the primary requisites of their positions, and so with the candidates for places back of the line.

This work will be going forward necessarily in connection with a few of the simpler forms of plays. No theories of offense or defense will as yet have been presented to the team. They will have advanced only to the point where they have begun to grasp the details of their position, and to have learned a few of the simplest plays, when the first ten days will have expired, and they will be called upon to play their first contest of the season.

Progress up to the First Game. Briefly running over their stock in trade for this first contest, it will be found that they have so far exercised and developed their muscles that the first stiffness will have passed away, and a sufficient amount of wind power will have been acquired to carry them through the very short playing intervals which mark the games in this early part of the season. They will have had a certain amount of practice in falling on the ball, and the other general exercises of a similar nature which mark the contest. The backs will be fairly proficient in kicking and catching. They have already begun to apprehend the meaning of interference; they know something about tackling, but very little. The line men will have a general idea of the proper play of their respective positions; they have been taught the first principles of blocking, breaking through, and opening up holes, although in the last-mentioned requisite they will for some time be very deficient. But it will be seen that in a general way the team has reached a point where it is possible to bring off, without discredit, a contest of two ten-minute intervals, with an opponent of about equal strength.

The Succeeding Three Weeks. During the next three weeks, which may stand for the first half of an average season, the individual work of each player should have close attention. The line men should be carefully coached upon the various details of their position play, and many helpful suggestions may be gained by them from the various books upon football which give prominence to this preliminary individual training. It will be wise to pay especial attention to the work of the quarter-back, to the end that he may handle the ball surely and swiftly in every play. The value of such extra work at this point is easily understood when it is remembered that nearly every play is affected by his quick or slow speed.

These first few weeks of the season are an excellent time for a captain to study his men. Changes in the make-up of the team may be made at this stage of the season with comparatively no harmful results, and many traits of the different applicants will be revealed to the coach, which will serve him at a later date, when the time comes to make the necessary discriminations between the ability of the competing players.

The practice on the field during these first three weeks must necessarily be very much interrupted by the coaching. Care should be taken, however, not to have the interruptions more frequent than is absolutely necessary. A very large amount of coaching can be done without any interruption to the practice. Standing behind a player and quietly talking to him, pointing out his defects, and showing him wherein he can improve, need not interfere in any way with the continuity of the play. The coach should not hesitate, however, to interrupt the practice at any moment when the importance of the instruction or its applicability to every man on the team makes it wise to speak publicly.

An Important Decision: Individual Defense *vs*. Team Defense. At the expiration of the first three weeks of the season, or thereabouts (the time depending upon the progress which has been made; the team having played its games thus far depending for defense solely upon the individual blocking of the men in the line), an important decision must be made by the coach. Shall the team, as a team, be taught any special theory of defense; that is, shall a system of relationships between different adjoining players when on the defensive be laid down? With some teams it is a serious question whether such a system should be taught to the team *as a whole*. For the establishment of a theory of defense for the entire team is not without its disadvantages. It makes the men inferior always as individual performers. But failing instruction in a theory of team defense, it may still be possible, during the rest of the season, to insist upon such a cooperation between the different players as shall make the defensive team play of the same high character and undaunted nature as the offensive team play.

The eleven is now approaching a time when it must be handled as a unit. Some one man must undertake to stand behind the eleven and see that its various movements are executed in such a manner that each man's efforts "dovetail" in with those of his neighbor. It will be found that one man is not blocking his opponent properly in a certain play; some runner is not clearly realizing the exact location of his hole or outlet in the line; some interferences are clumsily formed; some plays are being executed in a way which shows that the players do not realize that these movements are wholly dependent upon the dispatch with which they are worked; and thus, in one way and another, a great deal of faulty and defective work awaits correction. For the larger part of the balance of the season team play must have the "right of way" in all the coaching. Individual work must be wholly secondary, and when not actually done off the field or after the hours of practice, it must be done in intervals of rest, or when time has been called in the practice.

Supplementary Offense. The moment that team play has been brought to a fair stage of development, it will be the proper time to supplement the simple offensive game with the specially prepared movements and tricks. The amount of time required for the team to learn these supplementary manoeuvres has always been greatly exaggerated. Really surprising results may be accomplished through the spending of only half an hour on each play. Instances might be quoted where effective plays have been brought off in important games, which had actually not been rehearsed a dozen times in practice, and which had not probably consumed, in actual time, more than forty-five minutes throughout the season.

GENERAL COACHING PLAN FOR THE SEASON.

Period.	WORK ON THE FIELD.		Evening Conferences.
	Team Practice.	Individual work.	
First week.	Begin getting the guard out into the interference. Insist that quarter shall pass on the run.	More important than team play at this stage. Studying the condition, adaptability, quality, etc., coaching only the more common and glaring faults.	Rules and interpretation. (Attendance not obligatory except for coaches.)
Second week.	Quicken play slightly; bring the quarter out into the interference with the guard. Work them into the proper lines with the runner. Less confusion should be noticeable.	Coaching the blocking and breaking through. Ends down under kicks. More rapid line-up. Tackling. Check listlessness; watch especially for insubordination at this period.	Coaching:— what it means; the need of attention to it. (Attendance required for short talks only.)
Third week.	Begin to time the plays more closely. Still on the simpler forms of interference, but bringing the end in and drawing more men into the plays. Kicking game.	Coaching interference individually. How to take a man. How to cut out a tackler. Teach the making of holes. Playing low in the line.	Theories of Interference: where slow and where fast; speed and timing of it; keeping it off the runner. How holes in line should open.
Fourth week.	Starting upon the more complicated plays. Making them safer. Quarter-back and trick kicks introduced. (Watch for and resist strongly the great tendency to retrograde on work already learned.)	Ends and tackles on breaking interference. Receiving quarter-back kicks. Getting the jump on the opponents. (From this stage no interruption to team practice for individual coaching.)	Relationships between the positions, and theory of team defense.
Fifth week.	Having no man by himself when he comes down with the ball. Pushing and dragging. Getting the interference faster. Hurrying the runner. Practise trick plays.	Taking the ball away. Use of hand and arm when breaking through. Stopping mass plays. Regular umpiring daily.	Field tactics: especial discussions with quarter and field captain. Learn final signals.
Sixth week.	Testing plays for elimination. Reception of kick-off and kick-out with interference for run in on kick-off. Kick-out and punt-out. Practising sequences without signal. Fast play and long day.	Trying the individual endurance. Teaching quick start to catcher. Preventing overrunning the man. Converging lines toward opponent catching a punt. Close umpiring.	Objections to plays. Get a thorough open discussion of them. Spirit and dash. Review of field tactics.
Seventh week.	Smoothing out the plays. Continue kick-off and kick-out. Trick plays gone over carefully and made safe.	Getting life into each man. Short play but sharp. Making examples of mistakes. Strict umpiring.	Comparison with opponents, and need of every moment. Final warnings.

[DIAGRAM E.]

The Last Fortnight. As the last fortnight of the season is reached, the moments of practice become correspondingly valuable. It will now be well to examine carefully, in the light of the severer tests which it is receiving, the line-up for the defense of the punter, the line-up for the reception of the kick-off (and the eventuating play therefrom), and the form of attack upon the opposing full-back, when it is reasonably clear that the opponents intend to punt. These are three crucial points in every game, and it is wise not to leave them until the last moment, when the pressure of other matters may prevent their having that careful attention which they require.

Precision is now the important desideratum in the offensive work. The interferences must be formed quickly and accurately; the passes must be made in a manner which does not jeopardize the safety of the ball; the players must be watched, to the end that they do not, by their attitudes and movements, unconsciously reveal the nature of the impending play to the opponents; the team must be made to have confidence in each other, and a close sympathy must be established between all adjoining players.

The backs should be encouraged to take their correct positions, not by turning their heads to look in all directions, but by reaching out and measuring with their hands their distances from adjacent players, and if they give evidence of undue excitement they should be encouraged to talk quietly to each other, with a running undertone of conversation, during the whole time of practice. This conversation is easily possible in the excitement of the game, without being overheard by the opponents, and many an overanxious player has been reassured by feeling the hand of his companion upon his waist, and hearing his voice by his side. Such a player takes the ball and goes into the line with greater dash and confidence from his knowledge that he is being supported by his various interferers and pushers, who are close at hand. He has heard their voices and felt their touch, and he knows they are there. It is often this assurance of mutual support, this confidence in the supporting players, which carries a runner through the line for a good gain.

For the many details which the coach should emphasize while developing the team play of the eleven, reference should be made to other chapters.

Rousing the Right Spirit. One detail of the coaching still remains to be done. The proper spirit must be infused into the team. It is difficult to lay down any precise line by which this should be accomplished, nor is it necessary; for the knowledge of his players which the coach possesses, or will possess at this stage of the season, will suggest to his mind which one of various methods he may employ. The men should in these last few days before their final game be kept apart as much as possible from their more or less excited associates. The team should eat together; so far as possible they should live together. They should become excellently well acquainted with each other.

It will also be found wise to take the team to some extent into the confidence of the coach and captain, but not too unreservedly if you wish to win. Let them understand clearly all the various preparations which have been made for the ordering of the game; let them understand the authority which is to be exercised upon the field, and who is to exercise it. Tell them clearly all the arrangements for the delegation of that authority in the event of injury or disqualification. Explain any possibly cloudy points in the rules; as each point is elaborated, give the reason for that point. For example, if instructing the team to return the kick-off, without attempting to rush the ball, explain why this course has been adopted. This should not be delayed until the day of the game.

The Last Appeals. A very good time to have a quiet talk with the men, and endeavor to give them a realizing sense of the importance of the issue, is on the evening of the day before an important game. In a quiet meeting, without any attempt to transact exciting business, go over calmly the probable events of the morrow. So far as possible make it perfectly evident to the team that the question of victory or defeat lies entirely in their hands. Tell them that their best efforts are reasonably sure to result in victory. Picture to them exactly what defeat must inevitably mean. Give them a realizing sense of the important fact that the game cannot be played over again, but that the defeat must be final, and will stand as a record for all time to come.

So far as possible, make the appeals to the men, not only from one standpoint, but from several standpoints. Remember that the players are different in their nature and character, and that what will appeal to one man will not appeal to another. Some of the men may be moved by love for their school or college; others will be moved more by the vision of the disastrous results of defeat; others may be moved by the suggestion, skillfully made, of what victory will mean to the team if they win. This last appeal is nearly always a wise one to make to the average team. It is a fitting accompaniment to the portrayal of the significance of defeat. After showing the players the unfortunate side, by all means let them see the glory into which this misfortune can be converted by their united efforts. Instill into their minds the conviction that there are certain critical times in every game when a spurt must be made, when redoubled energy must be put into the play, and assure them that it is always possible to do this.

Without going further into the character of these last appeals, and the various arguments which may be skillfully presented with the methods by which the proper spirit may be inculcated in the players, let us once more emphasize the necessity of not leaving this part of the work to be done wholly in the few moments before the game. The last appeals which are always made at such a time are rather in the nature of a reminder of all that has been said before, and a final, stinging incentive to play the first five minutes of the game with a realization of their especial value. It is too late, in these last appeals, to expect to reach the thoughtful or deliberative mind. That must be done earlier, or not at all.

For more complete suggestions, and a fuller analysis of this part of the work, the reader is referred to chapters VI, VII, and VIII of this part.

CHAPTER II

ACCESSORIES OF COACHING

Utilizing Outside Friends as Coaches. It often happens that the development of a football team must be effected with only one coach. It rarely happens, however, that outside the players themselves there are not a great many interested individuals who are ready and willing to cooperate in the development of the team, and who would gladly attend the various practices and assist the work by any means in their power.

Whom to Select. The object of this chapter is to explain to the coach the various methods by which he can utilize the services of these interested outsiders, who have not themselves the ability or knowledge to take a coach's part in the coaching. It is safe to say that the services of two such persons can be constantly employed. In making the selection, care should be taken to secure those who will be faithful in their attendance, and who can be relied upon to execute the work intrusted to them with the least interference with the work on the field.

How to Employ Them. The work on which these two assistants will be employed is in the nature of keeping records or "tabs" upon the individual work of the men; and these records, extended over the entire season, form a mass of testimony from which very valuable conclusions may often be drawn. These assistants should keep entirely out of the immediate field of operations; following the team at a distance near enough to have a clear observation of everything which transpires, but far enough away not to hamper the work of the players or the coach. The result of their observations for the afternoon, carefully written out, should be turned in to the coach each day; and it will be well for the coach to see that he has them immediately at the close of the practice, when his own impressions and these actual results can best be compared. As has been previously stated, there are various channels in which this work may be pursued. We will take them up in their order.

(1) Who Brings Down the Runner? Let the coach delegate one of these outside assistants to make a careful note of the name of the player who brings down the runner in every attempt of the opponents to advance the ball. Where such an attempt is made by a mass play in the centre, and the movement is checked by the piling up of the interference in a confused heap, it will often be impossible to designate any one man and credit him with stopping the play. In all such cases of doubt, let the record be merely entered as "scrimmage." It will also happen, in some cases, that the credit of bringing down the runner may fairly be shared between two different men, one man temporarily checking the runner, while some follower, taking advantage of this momentary check, tackles and holds him. In such cases, where the credit belongs clearly to both men, their names should be entered together, and in reckoning up the total of the day, they should each be credited with one half a tackle, or a whole tackle, as the coach may prefer. The instructions given to the assistants should cover this point, as it will save a long explanation at some future critical time on the field.

Tabulated Report. At the close of the afternoon practice the results thus gained should be hastily tabulated, and when given to the coach they will appear in something like this form: —

Jones	17 tackles.
Smith	14 "
Brown	13 "
Robinson	7 "
Etc., etc., etc.	

A very little practice of this sort will make it possible for an assistant, later, to render more important services to the team, by making this same record in each game, even although his presence upon the field may not be permissible beyond the limit of the side lines. Proficiency will come with the daily practice, and he will be able to record his data from a longer range of observation.

Other Information. The coach will find, moreover, that as the season advances he can often gain from these assistants some very valuable information in regard to the method by which various forms of plays are stopped. This information will be of material value. For example, the coach will find it of profit to be informed by this assistant that a great many plays, directed at a certain point in the line, are stopped by a certain man. Some very significant pointers will undoubtedly be obtained from these records; it may be found that one man (the quarter-back, for example) is actually tackling the runner twice as often as any other man on the field.

The record of "missed tackles," which can very well be kept in this same connection, will also be full of interesting information, and will serve as useful corroborative testimony, indorsing, or perhaps upsetting the opinions formed by the coach from his hasty and necessarily divided attention.

(2) Gains Each Time of Each Play. Here is another set of records, the nature of which is sufficiently explained by this brief description of them. The object is to show the relative value of the different plays which the team is employing.

The keeping of this record is somewhat more difficult than the records last described, but it is not in any way work which cannot be successfully performed by outside assistants. The best method of keeping it is to number or letter each play, and commit this set of numbers or letters so completely to memory that it will be possible to immediately note down a play by a single character. The number of yards gained or lost should then be entered beside the play. Another form in which this record may be kept will be by the means of long columns, each column reserved for one particular form of play, and the columns lettered over the top with the names of the plays. The objection to this method is that it does not furnish to the coach the further data, which is quite as desirable, as to the order in which the plays were given. By keeping these records in the first-mentioned way, a double service is really performed, for beside noting the gain or loss by each play, the ordering of every afternoon's practice by the quarter-back is also made a matter of record.

These records may also, with comparative ease, be made in every game, even at the distance of the side lines. They must necessarily be frequently inaccurate when kept from such a long range of observation, but the results are sufficiently valuable to make the keeping of them in each game well worth the small labor involved.

(3) Where Gains are Made Through Your Line. This class of records will be just the reverse of the class mentioned in the previous section, and their object will be to show the weak points in the defensive play of different men, with a view to correcting their weakness by special instructions during later practice, or off the field. This record of gains may be sometimes joined with the second set of records, and both kept by one man; but it is better to have them kept separately, if the presence of an extra man can be commanded. In the absence of an assistant upon any afternoon, the double records may, however, be undertaken by any one who has attained a fair degree of proficiency in record keeping.

(4) Timing Passes and Punts. This should be done with a stop watch, and the information obtained can be utilized by the coach to good advantage. The fact that only two men (quarter and full back) are practically engaged in this particular play makes it easily possible to locate any tardiness or slowness on their part, and the best record of speed which they are able to attain in practice should be rigidly held up as the standard, below which they must never fall in a game.

(5) Photographs of Plays. This is an accessory of coaching which has at times been employed with excellent results, but the conditions are often of such a nature that the method is of little value. It goes without saying that some one must be found expert in the use of the small camera. The views taken must be instantaneous exposures, and it will be found that frequently the most desired exposure is impossible through the inability of the operator to be present at the exact spot from which the exposure can best be made. Practice taking place in the afternoon, the exposures must, of course, all be made away from the sun, and this further limits the efficacy of the method as an accessory in the work. On the other hand, while frequently impossible, and oftentimes of little value compared with the labor it involves, the results, when they are obtained, are of the highest importance.

If this method is undertaken it will be found best to make arrangements for the developing and printing of the films as quickly as possible after the practice is concluded, for the pictures will have an added value if the occurrence can be easily recalled, and a play accurately located, with all the details verified.

(6) How many Ways a Man has of Blocking. This is an accessory of coaching not connected with the keeping of records, and one which cannot possibly be left in the hands of any unskilled assistant. It is rather offered as a suggestion to the coach, of a way in which he may profitably utilize some evening when, assembling the line men about him, he may draw out from them all the information they may be able to give him under this head, and discover, as a result of the evening's talk, how much fertility of invention the players have, and how much they are reasoning and working out their own problems without his assistance. Suggestions from him should, of course, conclude the evening's talk.

(7) Notes on Defense and Offense Made by Each Man in Each Play. In the earlier part of the season, when the men are not being worked to an extent which deprives them of leisure time, it is an excellent plan, after some particular game, to ask the players to write off and hand in to the coach on the following day a short report on the results which they noticed in the game, in regard to some particular play, which may be a part of the offensive game. Just what they should write in these reports may be briefly indicated under three heads: —

(1) What difficulty, if any, did you have in doing the work which you were instructed to perform?

(2) Was the complete success of the play prevented by any man whom you were told to obstruct?

(3) What suggestions, if any, can you make whereby the play may be improved?

In any game, after some play which seems to be especially strong has been put against a team, it is often possible, by calling for reports from the various players who were opposed to the play, to get valuable information for the defensive coaching. It will be found, as a general rule, that the writing of a report upon any one of the offensive plays of the team sharpens the wits of the player, and gives him a better insight into his particular duties in the play, and the relation of those duties to the success of the movement.

(8) The Tackling Dummy. This is such a well-known accessory of coaching that only a word need here be given to the coach regarding it. While necessarily a part of the foundation work of the earlier days of the season, it will often be found necessary to revert to the dummy work whenever the tackling of the team retrogrades, and there is reason to believe that the players are losing a little of their skill in this direction.

It must not be forgotten that tackling the dummy is individual work, and may be done by the men at any time during the day, outside of the practice hours. It is also work of such a nature as may be prescribed for certain members of the team, while others may, very properly, be exempted from it by reason of more important work in other directions.

(9) Quarter-Back Examinations. It is absolutely essential that the quarter-back should have instruction in the generalship of the game. The most important part of his position is the ordering of the plays. Where this work is intrusted to his charge he must study the whole question of field tactics and football generalship. No book will successfully impart all the necessary information, for this information must be adjusted to, and tempered by, the peculiar characteristics of the team itself.

The instruction must be given the quarter-back by the coach or captain in conversations, from time to time, and when a certain amount of this instruction has been given to the quarter-back, it will be a good plan, on some disengaged evening, to give him a half-hour examination, covering various points which may arise, and on which, in the game, he must pass an almost instantaneous judgment.

It will be well to have two or three of these quarter-back examinations during the latter part of the season. In the first one, and perhaps in the second one, the quarter-back may be given all the time necessary to write out his answer to each question, but in the last examination it is imperative that he should be required to give his answer instantly, since all his decisions upon the field must be made in this manner. The experience of the coach or captain will suggest many questions for a quarter-back examination, but as a possible guide the following may be suggested for the first examination: —

1. Ball on your own eight-yard line; first down; what will you do?

2. Ball on opponents' thirty-five-yard line; third down; two yards to gain; what will you do?

3. Ball on your own fifteen-yard line; second down; six yards to gain; what will you do?

4. Ball in centre of field; second down; ten yards to gain; what will you do?

5. Ball on your own twenty-five-yard line; third down; one yard to gain; what will you do?

6. Ball on opponents' twenty-four-yard line; first down; what will you do?

7. Ball on your own twenty-yard line; third down; half a yard to gain; what will you do?

8. Ball on opponents' thirty-yard line; third down; four yards to gain; what will you do?

9. Ball on your own thirty-five-yard line; first down; score six to four in your favor; seven minutes more to play to end the second half; no wind; what will you do?

10. What do you consider the value of ball at opening of first half, in yards?

11. What do you regard as most important to know, — the weak spot in opponents' line, or the value of your different plays?

12. If you are able to arrange to send off one play on a quick line-up, starting it without signal, would you send it round the end, or through the centre, or at the tackles?

13. If you win the toss, and take a strong wind, are there any conditions which would operate to induce you to kick regularly at first down? If so, what?

14. Within what extreme distance from your own goal should you deem it expedient to sacrifice all attempts at rushing the ball and kick on first down?

15. If your first down failed to gain, at what distance from your goal should you deem it unwise to defer kicking until the third down?

16. A long run lands ball on opponents' eight-yard line, in touch; if all your plays were equally strong, how far would you bring ball in, and what would you play?

17. If you unexpectedly lost twenty yards, then fifteen yards, and so found yourself suddenly on your own fifteen-yard line, with the team somewhat rattled by the rapidity of these movements, does it occur to you that anything beside talking could be done by you to pull your men together? If so, what?

18. The score is four to nothing against you. You are within one minute of the close of the second half; the ball is in your possession on the opponents' forty-yard line; the first down has resulted in no gain; what will you order for the second down?

(10) Locating Men at the Hole in the Line to show where Runner is to go, and Practise Making Opening. A great deal of the practice of any team toward the close of the season is that which is generally known by the title of "running through signals." Where this signal work is done upon the field, it is usually conducted in a more systematic and thorough manner than when in the gymnasium in the evening. In the latter case the practice is mainly for instant recalling of the meaning of the signal itself, but signal practice on the field is usually undertaken for a different end. It is then intended by such practice to subserve the more important work of "shapening up" the plays, getting the different members accustomed to their positions, uniting the interferences quickly and correctly, and generally combining precision with speed in all offensive movements.

It is at such times that it is an excellent plan to locate men as supposed opponents (say two line men and one at the part of the line where the hole is to be made, back) and call upon your forwards to actually make the hole in every case. Of course the opponents are required to move from point to point in the line as the signal is called, and they, of course, know exactly where the play is to be. It is not required of them that they will stop the play, but that they will make such a demonstration (resembling the probable efforts of the opponents) as will give your own forwards practice in opening up a hole, and to reveal to your runner exactly where the opening is likely to be in the line.

Every coach realizes that a good game is often lost by the runner repeatedly striking the line a little to one or the other side of the exact spot where he ought to have pierced the line, and this error in locating the exact spot of opening will, unless it is corrected, continue through the entire season. Thus the results of a particular play may be very unsatisfactory, and the play itself may be subjected to much condemnation, when the whole difficulty lies merely in the runner not realizing that his hole lies a little farther out than the spot where he usually strikes the line.

It will be interesting to the coach who has not before made such an observation to notice how constantly a runner moves over exactly the same track in a particular play, and we have, in our experience, seen many cases in which the whole character of the play, so far as its results were concerned, was materially changed by the help which a coach has received from this simple accessory to his work.

Of course, the men who are acting as opponents need never throw the runner to the ground. It is enough that they simply tackle him. The runner, in this method of practice, should go a trifle farther than merely through the line, in order to be sure that he is not going to be stopped from behind by one of the opponents turning and overtaking him.

(11) General Examinations on Rules. This, although a very simple thing, is quite a necessary adjunct to the regular coaching upon the field. Frequent talks with the players would accomplish the same end as a set examination, but inasmuch as whatever is worth doing is worth doing well, and since conversations, which can always be indulged in, are usually rarely indulged in, it is well to have these examinations rather more frequently, and devote to them a specially appointed time. Members of the team should be supplied with pencil and paper, and they should be called upon to answer in writing from half a dozen to ten questions covering the various points in the rules. One or two of these examinations, if the questions are carefully prepared, will show whether any further work along this line is needed.

(12) Signal Rehearsals. It is to be assumed that every coach will insist upon a certain amount of signal rehearsing, at odd times, especially toward the close of the season, and immediately before important games. All the various plays have then been properly inventoried and filed away in the quarter-back's mind. It is for the coach to make sure that the team so thoroughly knows the various movements that no amount of confusion, excitement, or noise upon the field can so far distract their attention, that the mental process of instantly determining what play has been called for shall not go on without hindrance or accident. Signals must be so continually rehearsed by the team that the calling of any signal is almost like the actual explanation by the quarter-back of the play which he wishes to have made. In other words the interpretation of the meaning of the signal must be as quick as a flash.

In some of the largest college teams it is not impossible that great advantage may accrue from having a test made upon the various players, to the end of ascertaining the quickness with which each man acts upon impressions made upon his mind. The director of the psychological department of any one of the leading colleges, where the necessary apparatus is available, can fully explain to the coach the method by which this test can be made, and provide the means of making it.

Need of Strict Officials in Late Practice. The scope of this chapter may fairly justify a few words upon the necessity of securing capable and strict officials during the last fortnight of practice. For obvious reasons, the work of the officials during the practice in the earlier part of the season is necessarily lax. It would be too much of an interruption to the work of the coach if, in the short intervals of practice, the penalties of the referee or umpire were continually enforced.

But inasmuch as this portion of the work is slighted in the early part of the season, it is quite necessary that the coach should not forget its importance in the latter part. The team, then, is playing together more continuously; in practice there are fewer interruptions, and there is practically only one coach upon the field who is handling the team. In other words, there is only one man who is stopping the play to issue directions or impart instruction. It is proper and altogether advisable that the work of the officials should, at this point, be emphasized. Let the regular penalties be imposed, and let a second penalty for the same offense be always accompanied by a severe reprimand to the offending player.

At the end of the afternoon's practice a little consultation between the officials and the coach will be wise. The officials can then give to the coach the consensus of their observations during the afternoon, and he can speak the few words to the various players in private, after the practice is over, in regard to the faults for which penalties have been inflicted. The coach should insist that the rulings of the officials in this late practice shall be of the very strictest sort. To enter an important game and find that the rulings are less strict than the players have been accustomed to is no serious obstacle to their work; but many a team has been discouraged and disheartened in the first fifteen minutes of an important game by the repeated penalizing of some player for an offense which, whether real or fancied, has the same disastrous result. By all means let this point be covered in the late practice.

CHAPTER III

CHOOSING THE TEAM

Secret of Success. One of the best coaches of singularly successful teams said once, in a moment of confidence, that the eventual result of the season's work depended almost entirely upon the ability to select in the first two weeks the fifteen best men in the university. He added, furthermore, that of the fifteen thus selected the chances would be that five of them had never played on a 'Varsity team before.

He followed this up with this statement: that, although no one save the coach would know who those fifteen were, it was upon them that every ounce of energy should be thereafter concentrated by the head coach or his assistants, so that the men who finally went into the game were certain, with few rare exceptions, to have had every possible advantage given them for the entire season.

This man was especially a coach of rush-line men, and never failed to produce what is technically known as a "stiff line." There is little doubt that, had he been called upon to bring out the backs, he would have been equally successful, for he has a grasp upon this fundamental fact: that a football player cannot be made in a day or a week, and that, at the pace set to-day among the first-class elevens, that team which has had all its men well coached from the first of the season to the last practice will surely pull out ahead of the team of whom only two thirds have had the full amount of proper attention. In no sport do bad habits so persistently crop out if not daily corrected, and in no sport do these mistakes seem so trifling up to mid-season, or so painfully marked in the final games. In a crew, serious faults must be handled early; a later recurrence of them in mid-season in individuals is then at once pronounced; in fact, the whole swing is so affected that the matter is at once apparent to the eye of the practical coach. But in football there is so much more individuality that the faults may escape almost unnoticed until emphasized in the strain of an important match. Then it is too late to do more than regret the result.

Qualifications of a Good Man. What qualifications should a good man have? These have been rehearsed over and over again, but it is always well to hear them just once more. Courage— "sand," as the slang term has it — is the first. And by this is not meant unreasoning recklessness, nor mere toughness of nerve, but that kind of courage which, while recognizing the danger, feeling the hurt, or seeing the impending defeat, is none the less ready to face the chance, to ignore the pain, and to carry a good heart to believe that the defeat may be turned into victory. There are some men who refuse to be beaten, who come up smiling every time, but grow more and more determined after every mishap. A captain and coach can usually tell with fair judgment about the men who have played under their eyes for a season or so, but the new men and some of the old substitutes may be more of an unknown quantity.

Diagnosing. A good coach can be of the greatest service in the first day or two in diagnosing this quality of courage, and the more good men who watch the team during the first week, the better. Then, at a meeting of the advisers held at the end of the first week, the characters of the candidates should receive a very thorough sifting upon this cardinal point. It is well to become possessed of the earlier history of any of these men, where that is possible, because from this much can be determined. The old saying, "Blood will tell," is true here as in other football characteristics. Such names as the Traffords, the Riggs, the Poes, and the Blisses come at once to one's memory as examples. To-day many of our players come from preparatory schools, where their records are easily obtainable. So far as the skill of their playing is concerned, these records are not, perhaps, of great value, since the conditions are very different from those of 'Varsity work, but upon this one point of courage, the boy will have shown at the "prep" school what his rating ought to be in that respect. It may seem like taking infinite trouble to look up all this matter, but taking pains often proves the turning-point in the scales when the final day comes; and surely it is wisdom to expend the coaching upon men who, when they learn to play, will play their hearts out rather than quit, instead of wasting months upon a man who funks at the critical moment. Some men are born cowards, and cannot face grief; such men may prove showy players in practice when facing men they know, but in a game against strangers, when every play is in deadly earnest, may lose their nerve completely.

Inventiveness a Necessity. The next most important qualification of the player, and one that must be looked for in the early days of practice, is inventiveness or adaptability to changing circumstances. This is especially true of forwards. A man who, during the first week, is continually fooled by the same stratagem, a man who always blocks in just one way, and who goes through with such unvarying regularity of method that the opponents know exactly what he is going to do, and at what point in the line to expect him each time, is wanting in a characteristic that the successful rusher must naturally possess. Men may be coached to perform their work in a variety of ways, but, unless they possess some inventiveness of their own, they will never rise above the mediocre. It is a study in itself to watch the line men during the first week of a season. Two thirds of them go about their work in a set way, push hard, grunt, and struggle, but accomplish little. Here and there, however, stands out one who becomes a veritable terror to his opponents, who is always doing something new — something almost untraditional in the limited view of his fellows. He doesn't always run straight into his opponent and try to push him over. He tries strange jumps, he is abnormally quiet for a moment, but, just as his vis-à-vis is drawing a long sigh of relief, his erratic friend has bumped him unexpectedly, and goes clean through at the runner. "Who let that man through?" groans out the captain, and the offender hangs his head.

Strength and Ability. After these two points, strength and ability should be noted. The former is easily discoverable in line men from the way they hold themselves after some minutes of hard work. The strong man is as able to assume a stooping position, after ten minutes of hard work, as at the start, while the man who is weak will be straightening up to rest himself sometimes, even almost at the moment when the ball is put in play. The man who has good legs will be pushing with them every time, while the man whose legs are a bit shaky will be manifestly sparing himself. The man with the good back will be tossing his weaker opponent as the play goes on.

Agility. As to agility, the tests for this are less marked, because, while a line man ought always to be exerting his strength at every down, there are times when not to move quickly is an advantage, and so, although able to do this, he will simply block "solid," and be almost stationary in his tracks. Continued watching will soon convince the coach, however, whether the man is using judgment in this respect or is only naturally slow and ponderous. (From all this talk of line men the ends are to be excepted. They class rather with the half-backs, and a different set of tests should be applied to their work.) The rushers should also be watched separately for their blocking and breaking through.

How to Watch a Team. An excellent way of passing judgment upon these points is to stand in line with the rush line on every down and begin by watching the men who come through. Note which man comes through most quickly and reaches the farthest point before the runner strikes him or the line. Then reverse the observation and see which man is generally blocked. Then take up the blocking and see whose man comes through most quickly and whose man is effectively blocked. Two men should watch these points and take notes throughout two or three days, and then summarize these notes. After these questions of strength and agility comes the one of ability to learn. In the first week every man should receive some (even if only a little) coaching; not so much for the good it will do him as to see how much of it he can digest and make use of. It is folly to take up a man who shows in the first week that he cannot learn. Some men are slow, but not stupid. Such men may readily adapt themselves, but let them once grasp a point and they never forget it. It is better to have such a man than the stupid one who forgets what he has been told as soon as he is left alone. Later in the season the coaches have no time to waste in beginning over with the men.

Judging Men Behind the Line. In passing judgment upon men behind the line the problems are not so simple, but for all that there is seldom any candidate who cannot be fairly gauged in a week or ten days. In the first place, a quarter-back is even more liable to expose his lack of muscular strength than the line men, if one watches his position in getting the ball. Here the strength of back and legs count greatly. It is a rather remarkable fact that candidates for quarter almost invariably possess plenty of "sand." Probably it is because, if they didn't, every one — even the casual spectator — would discover it in a half hour. Agility they are also likely to possess. But strength and inventiveness and adaptability are not so common, and are the features of their play, therefore, to be especially watched. Observe whether the quarter knows what to do when his line is weak, and whether he can extricate himself from the annoyances of having a guard shoved over upon him or another reaching him through some break in the line. Note if he can help hold a line after the ball is passed when such a thing is rendered necessary by the rapid breaking through of a strong centre or guard. See if he can change his pass when its speed or slowness bothers the recipient.

Shiftiness in Backs. In the backs we must look for courage, strength, and something that perhaps had best be called "shiftiness," that is, the ability to act under suddenly altered conditions, — to decide on the instant, and to follow the decision immediately with the action. The things that will indicate these points may be grouped as follows. Under strength, note the ability to keep the feet, the play of the body and shoulders in throwing off men, and the strength of back in forcing ahead when tackled and falling always forward. "Sand" can readily be seen in the way a man takes his opening and his willingness to take it again even if the hole was a poor one. Shiftiness is distinguishable in backing up fumbles, in dodging after getting through clean, and in finding his interferers, even though they run wild all over the field. While it may happen that a good man may not be sure of his catch in the early part of the season, it is a pretty sound rule that if a back or half-back cannot get squarely under a ball in the first days of practice, he will make but an indifferent catcher always. It may be that his judgment of distance is at fault, and in that case it will be a hard matter to conquer. On the other hand, a man who gets squarely under the ball and allows it to bound from his arms can usually be made a sure catcher later. This is worth remembering in the early judgment of players.

General Observations of First Week. There are a few other general observations which should be made in the first week in order to determine upon the fifteen or twenty men who should have special attention. First among these is the question as to liability to injury. Here, again, previous records should be consulted. A strange instance of the value of this was exhibited in the case of two brothers, both excellent general athletes, who were candidates for a football team in one of the universities. The elder brother made the team his first year and played during the season, but in the final game received a slight fracture of the clavicle. The younger brother fractured a clavicle early in the season. Both were exceptionally plucky fellows — the former, after the accident, actually playing out the game, as his injury was not diagnosed until after the match was over. The next year the younger brother was almost outstripping the elder, and was certain of a place, when a week before the final match he fractured the other clavicle by a fall upon his shoulder. There is little question but that both boys were peculiarly liable to this injury, for, while otherwise very strongly built, the clavicle in each was not as strong proportionately as the muscular development would have led one to expect. In none of the three cases of injury was the fall or blow a severe one. There was no other tendency to injury noticeable in either of the boys.

Fragile Men Dangerous to Rely Upon. But to return. Some players, while not apparently fragile, are in some unaccountable way awkward in taking falls, or the ligaments about the joints are not sufficiently tense, or for some unknown reason they are continually on the cripple list. Such men are dangerous to depend upon, and if selected it should be owing to the fact that their play is very much above the average — sufficiently so to run the risk. Another point to be noted here is the effect of the early work. If a man, outside of an incapacitating injury, stands the work of the first week well, is on hand every day, and is markedly eager to be playing, it is an indication that his general condition and his muscular system are both good. The reverse of this is, however, not always to be reckoned upon as true, for a man may be a promising candidate, and yet stand the first few days badly. The light-weight candidates should be weighed after the first day's practice, and again at the end of a week. A man who, already light, goes off rapidly, is pretty sure to prove a highly strung player, with a decided tendency to overtraining, and, if he be selected, especial attention should be paid to this danger.

Love of the Game a Good Quality. Another thing worth noting is the enjoyment of the sport as a game. Old players may not exhibit this, but a new player who is likely to become a good man likes to have his side win, or make good ground, even in practice, and when he gets near a goal he plays with more dash and abandon, and is a fighter for every inch. Such spirit should not be overlooked, for oftentimes it happens that a team of old players are woefully lacking in that regard, and many a final game is lost because there is not enough of this kind of spirit in the eleven to carry it over the tight spots where experience and skill fail to make the necessary distance.

Making Up the List. Having passed the first week or ten days, and having carefully considered all these points, the coach should make up his list of fifteen or twenty players, and, while not giving out who they are, he should see to it that each one of them has especial coaching continually — that not a day goes by when any of these men passes an afternoon on the field without careful attention from himself or from one of his coaching staff. Of course this does not mean a neglect of the other candidates. He will need many more before his season is completed, but let him never lose sight of one of these first-choice men until that man is laid by for good. About mid-season it is time for him to take another inventory of his stock. He should then, with the added light he has gained, be able to make a selection of fifteen or twenty, which will include some new material, perhaps through the dropping out of some of his first list. About three weeks before the final game he can determine the ones to take into the great match. There is much divergence of opinion as to whether the men should be told directly. Generally it is sufficient indication to play them together as much as possible, and it avoids the difficulty of overconfidence of some and discouragement of others, to have it understood that the team will not be finally selected until the last moment. That, however, is no reason for not playing the pick of the men regularly. Good discipline sometimes requires a change upon the field during practice if a first eleven man is playing poorly and his opponent unusually well.

Final Selection. Coming now to the question of final selection. In another chapter we have treated of the points to be considered on the eve of the battle, but this selection is supposed to be prior to that. The cardinal principle to be observed is that of elimination. Take no man into the game who is slow for his position. This question is usually as to ends and halves. An end may be a wonder in all other points, but, if he lack speed, there may come a time when he is circled and then he cannot overtake his man. The same is true of the halves. It does not require a ten second man for an end or a half; but it does need a man who can overtake any ordinary runner who has the ball. Don't take any man in who cannot control his temper. He will fail you at the critical moment by not obeying orders. A writer upon cycling themes says regarding tandem riding: "Do not take any novice out on a tandem unless he understands the Yale football principle of not trying to run the machine." A man who loses his temper will try to run the machine when it means a smash-up surely. Do not take any man in who, aside from injuries either old or prospective, is not physically good to last out the two halves. You may want to use him the most when he has "bellows to mend." No matter what it costs in the way of the loss of otherwise good men, take but two men in back of the line who are not dead sure catchers. Of the four, two must be absolutely certain, so far as you are able to judge, of holding a fly. Do not take a centre in who is erratic in his snapping, nor a quarter who cannot hold the ball when the opponents are through. Finally, take no man in at any position who is not thoroughly unselfish in his play, who has any thought of grand-stand work. If you do he will lose you a touch-down by trying to pick up the ball when he ought to fall on it.

CHAPTER IV

THE POLICY FOR THE SEASON

What a Policy should Mean. The ability to direct an intelligent and consistent policy during an entire season is one of the most important qualities of the successful coach.

As in a business requiring a broad grasp of the constantly changing situation, success can only be attained through the vigorous and fearless yet prudent course of the manager or head, so in the case of a team, the coach must be mentally a strong enough man to keep a firm hold of his lines, and direct all men and acts towards his one preconceived end. A vacillating policy will wreck the strongest team, even more certainly than an ill-judged one, because, in the case of the latter, with the abundance of material usually at hand, and the infinite variety of tactics possible, a policy firmly adhered to will, nine times out of ten, bring forth, not perhaps a brilliant, yet a rugged and determined team. On the other hand, a vacillating, constantly altering plan of campaign produces a team that has neither knowledge nor confidence, and one that is as good as beaten before the kick-off.

Self-Reliance of Coach. A coach cannot always, in the matter of policy, depend upon his assistants. He must stand alone in many respects. He cannot trust his advisers, because there are usually several of them whose backbones are of the jellyfish order, and who cannot endure criticism. Such men should certainly not be informed regarding the full intent of the head coach at critical times, because they will hamper, rather than assist his actions. A coach may, after a careful study of the situation, decide that he must, in order to attain satisfactory results, overthrow many of the methods formerly in force, upset many, perhaps, of the most honored traditions, and likely enough drop off one or two of the most revered players. It is seldom the part of wisdom to do all this at once. Such a step might end in so great a difference of opinion as to split up the team and the university into factions, and so the season would prove a failure. It is the duty of the coach to accomplish his end with discretion; he should understand thoroughly what he has in view, and his reasons for it, and then quietly proceed to bring about the result. When accomplished, it will frequently meet with the full approval of even those whom it has robbed of an opportunity to take active parts.

Spare Weak-Kneed Friends. The fact that we use this rather extreme illustration need not alarm the intending coach. The situation is seldom as serious as this. But it is well for him to keep his own counsel as to questions of policy that are likely to be too heavy for weak-kneed friends to carry even in their minds, while he may freely discuss any minor point, the settlement of which requires only ordinary judgment and football experience. Furthermore, there is an open part of his counsel and direction that is very important, and that should be thoroughly understood and carried out by every member of his coaching staff, and by his captain. This has been, by general acceptance, designated as the policy of the season.

General Lay-Out of Coaching Lines. Under this head comes first: *The laying out of coaching lines.* Here he must make himself familiar, if he be not already so, with the distinguishing abilities of every man whom he can secure as an assistant. The trainer and medical adviser are two people of great importance to him. He must determine where their duties are likely to clash, and settle at the outset the question of precedence. It is hardly necessary to state that the medical adviser's word should be paramount in all cases requiring expert knowledge, while it is probable that the trainer can supplement the regular practitioner's skill by various ingenious devices for hastening the recovery in minor sprains and bruises. The physician, for instance, especially if he has had little practical experience with football men, will usually err on the safe side of recommending rest. Rest is probably the surest cure, but the man may be wanted. Then the physician should be willing to concede a point and cooperate with the trainer in hastening a partial state of recovery sufficient to make it possible to use the man, provided, of course, no serious results are likely to follow. There ought never to be, under a judicious coach, any trouble in reconciling the opinions of the two, and making the most of the services of both.

Coaches for Specialties. Among his other coaches he will find that he has men who are capital teachers of some one or two points, but who are, unfortunately, firmly of the opinion that they know all about the various other departments of the play. He must judiciously apportion the duties so that each man may perform those for which he is especially fitted. He ought to be able to secure three line coaches at least, — one for the centre and guards, one for the tackles, and one for the ends. He should also have two men for the backs, one of whom should be able to coach the quarter and the general running game, while the other should be a kicking coach.

Size of Staff. A staff of five men is by no means a large one, and is usually supplemented by several others. In that case there can advantageously be a division of duties as follows: One man shall be responsible for the defensive work of the team; another for the offensive. If further division is practicable, it may be almost infinitely multiplied along the lines of blocking, interfering, getting through, tackling, and the like. If the staff be small, the men may be handled in some such way as this: with three men, let one look after the individual work of the line, including the tackling, blocking, and getting through; let another look after the backs, the interferers, and offensive tactics; and let the third attend solely to the defense.

Each Day Lay Out Work for Following Day. The coach should, with his advisers, lay out each day the work that is to be performed upon the following day, so that there may be no wasted time on the field, and no discussion of plans there. The schedule should be arranged the evening before, and each man of the coaching staff should know exactly what is expected of him. In the early part of the season this is simple enough, but it becomes more complicated as the weeks go by, and when the time comes for the development of special team play, and the exploitation of intricate plays, it requires all the time the coach can put on it merely to lay out the work for his staff.

Discipline. Secondly comes discipline. Discipline should receive the very earliest consideration. If there be not an established tradition strong enough to absolutely prevent anything like "talking back" to the coaches, such a rule should be put in effect, and with sufficient severity to kill once for all any such tendency. It may be necessary to make an example by summarily dropping one such offender, in order to insure instant and unquestioning obedience. A man should not be permitted even to make excuses. If he has anything to say, it should be said to the coach in private off the field, and any inquiries that partake of even the appearance of questioning a coach's decision should be asked when off, rather than on the field.

Extension and Scope. The discipline should extend much farther than this. It should insure the prompt appearance on the field daily of every candidate properly dressed. If there be any reason why the man should not play, he should so inform the coach the evening before, or if that be rendered impossible for any reason, he should — even if the reason be illness or accident — be on the field in uniform, and thus convince the coach of his good intentions by his presence until excused. There is no greater element of danger than that found in a team where a man can stay away or wait until the time comes for play, without putting the coach in full possession of the reasons for his delinquency. And habitual tardiness at practice is equally bad.

A team should also be required from the very earliest days to line up instantly on the call of the coach, and always to take their positions on the run after a try-at-goal, a touchback, a safety, or any call of time. The men should be so educated and disciplined that it becomes second nature to them to get in position on the jump, and to be alert and active every moment while the line-up lasts. After the first two weeks the play must always be fast. It is better on this account not to stop the play for trivial faults, but to coach while the play is going on, or make such notes as will render it possible to coach the individual between the calls of play, or after the practice ends. To be continually waiting for coaching spoils a team in many ways other than that of slowing up their game. It makes them dependent and lacking in decisiveness of play. They constantly show a hesitancy of execution even after they are lined up and ready to begin.

Period of Progress. And this leads us to the subject, thirdly, of the development of the team, and how a wise policy should carefully map out the various periods of progress and see that the team is kept up to these lines. For fast play a team should be tested occasionally by the dropping of all coaching and the keeping up of a steady drive for five minutes. This will break them up a bit, if tried when the practice is only two weeks advanced, but at four weeks it ought not to affect the accuracy of their play in the least. Allowance must always be made, however, in case there is a new man on the team, or if there exists any other reason for inaccuracy aside from the mere speed of the play.

Tackling, Blocking, and Breaking Through. As to tackling, there should be no high tackling noticeable after the third week, and a case of really bad play in this respect should be made an occasion for something more than passing mention. It will be well to make an example of such a case for the good of the team.

In blocking and breaking through, as the second eleven improves equally, the apparent progress is slow, and it may not be until well into November that the first eleven will show a steady and constant superiority in this respect. During the first week or ten days they are noticeably in advance of the second eleven, but this is followed by a period when the two teams become fairly well matched, — perhaps on account of the greater effort exhibited at this stage by the second eleven men. After a time, however the first should once more show their advance and keep it up until the end.

Relation of Defensive to Offensive at Different Periods. Defensive play should be outstripped by the offensive play for the first two or three weeks. Then the defensive should become the better of the two, followed again by an advance of the offensive when the final plays are adopted and perfected. We mention these peculiarities of improvement and apparent retrograding, in order that the coach may not take them too seriously when they arrive. There is a good reason behind each advance or retreat of this nature, and it is not one which need cause any alarm.

Indeed, this state of affairs is by no means remarkable when one considers the conditions. Take the case just cited as an illustration. During the first part of the season there is much more enthusiasm put into the offensive play; each man is then trying to make a record for himself, and naturally feels that there is much more chance for display in the offensive than defensive part of the work. Then coaching begins to tell, and by mid-season the defense has been so built up and strengthened that that part of the play is strongly accented. And then, finally, comes the perfection of team attack, which crushes the defense down by sheer systematic pressure and makes way over or through the defenders.

Mid-Season Period of Depression. In commenting upon the policy for a season one ought not to omit to warn the coach against a certain period which seems to come at some time in the season, usually about November first, when the team seems "going to the dogs," when the whole season's coaching has apparently been wasted, and when both captain and players feel that they are simply useless. There is a reason for this state of affairs, and a good reason, too. It is by no means as bad as it looks, and is brought about in a way quite easy to understand. It is really nothing to be alarmed at, so long as it does not last too many days. The situation is simply this: During the first part of the season the men have a lot of enthusiasm; the eager struggle to improve and to win a place on the team stirs even the most sluggish. By the end of October, however, the men are beginning to realize who have the best chances; some are even ready to rest on their already won laurels; upon others the pursuit has palled; and altogether there is no especial stimulus left. This state of affairs usually comes before the coaching has really had a fair chance to exhibit results, and the men are, therefore, just between two stages. The first stage is that of fairly good play, as brought about by enthusiasm and life and dash; the second is the stage to which they have not yet attained, of really good play on a basis of knowledge and skill. It is not necessary to do more than tell the coach that inside of a week the men will probably be in the second stage, and his short period of despair will be at an end.

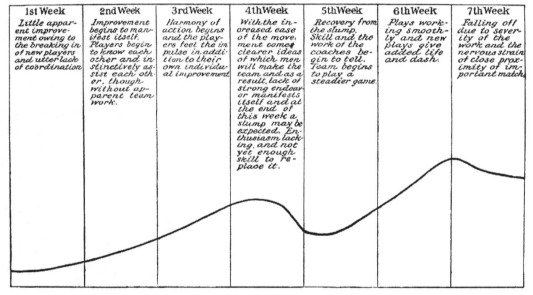

1st Week	2nd Week	3rd Week	4th Week	5th Week	6th Week	7th Week
Little apparent improvement owing to the breaking in of new players and utter lack of coördination	*Improvement begins to manifest itself. Players begin to know each other and instinctively assist each other, though without apparent team work.*	*Harmony of action begins and the players feel the impulse in addition to their own individual improvement*	*With the increased ease of the movement comes clearer ideas of which men will make the team and as a result, lack of strong endeavor manifests itself and at the end of this week a slump may be expected. Enthusiasm lacking, and not yet enough skill to replace it.*	*Recovery from the slump. Skill and the work of the coaches begin to tell. Team begins to play a steadier game.*	*Plays working smoothly and new plays give added life and dash.*	*Falling off due to severity of the nervous strain of close proximity of important match*

Diagram F. — Usual progress of the season.

Time of Line-Ups. In determining the amount of time the line-ups should last each day, the coach must remember that it is out of the question to expect the best work from the men in two consecutive days of hard long practice. It is occasionally advisable — in fact, necessary — to give the men a "trying out," as it were, by a long practice of fully an hour. There may be some good reason why, in mid-season, this should be repeated on the following day. But if there be such a reason, there is at least no ground for a coach to expect to get good work out of the team on the second day, and his criticism and fault-finding should be judicious, and tempered by reason and mercy.

New Coaches and New Judgments. The coach should so arrange his system that he may have, about once in two weeks, the addition of one or more new coaches. One of the strongest reasons for this is that the men may have become accustomed to the voices and ways of the familiar coaches, and the effect of their criticism is, therefore, lessened. Often a new voice and new manner of coaching will stir them up to better performance. The coach should also have a man or two in reserve who does not see the team frequently, who may be a fair judge of the actual progress made, and who will often discover some fault that has crept in. unknown and unnoticed by those who are with the team every day.

Order of Games. Fourthly, in arranging the dates of the matches, especial attention should be paid to the order in which they follow each other. The best arrangement possible is a progressive one, meeting the weak teams first, and gradually working up to the strongest with an interval containing but one game, and that with a weak team, between the last hard game and final match. Where such an arrangement is impracticable, the alternation of a hard and a light game should be sought for.

Selection of Plays and Control of Score. In playing these matches the team, or rather the team through the captain and quarter, should be given a schedule of what plays are to be tried in each game, and how far to go in methods. A team should never be allowed to "play off," no matter what the reason. If it be desirable — and this is seldom the case — to keep the score down, it should be done by confining the number and variety of plays they are to attempt, and in no other way. A team once allowed to "play off" is not to be trusted, and is a good team to play against. Nor should men be put on and told to "play easy." A man may be saved by telling him what plays not to attempt, and he may also be taken absolutely out of all interference if that seem advisable. He may be put in to kick, and that only. But whatever he does must be done with all his might, and what he is told to avoid must be entirely dropped. Otherwise you retard his advancement, and will probably have him laid up into the bargain.

Practice under Umpire. All practice should be done under an umpire, who may act also as referee. From the early part of the season he should always call fouls, and his word should be as much undisputed law as it would be in a match. For the last two weeks it is well to have two different umpires, — a referee is hardly necessary, — who shall keep as close a watch as possible for every indication of holding and off-side play.

Quarrels. Should any difference of opinion arise at any time in practice or off the field between the players, consideration should be given to it at once by the head coach and the matter adjusted. It should not be permitted to gather force. There is no greater element of success than a thorough and hearty sympathy between the players, and a coach should exercise his ingenuity to the utmost to secure this.

The same is true regarding differences among the coaches, save that in that event it may be necessary to let one of the coaches go. It is seldom so serious among the players. But with the coaches there may be a rupture of such a nature as to make such a step advisable. Harmony at all hazards must be the rule.

Personal Exhortation. There is one thing that we have not thus far touched upon in the policy of the head coach, and that is the element of personal and private exhortation. The head coach must do some of this himself, but his assistants should also perform a great deal of missionary work, both directly and indirectly. Some players must be talked with almost daily; some must be approached in addition through their friends and acquaintances. A man often reaches the point when he believes that the coach only talks to him from force of habit; that his play is as good as the next man's; and he loses all respect for the criticism of the coach. It is hardly a case for discipline, but rather for personal intervention by intimate friends. Often the man is a good man, means well and all that, but he has grown careless, and his friends can show him this without offense and more forcibly even than the coach. In a word, the head coach must make use of all means to point out to the players their weaknesses, and must then see that the information as to how to reconstruct their play is conveyed in the most effective way, and often in a variety of ways.

CHAPTER V

TESTING THE DEVELOPMENT

The Need of Such Tests. It is quite necessary that, at various times during the season, the coach should obtain an accurate idea of the development of the team, that he may see just where he ought to apply his immediate efforts. His own observations will teach him more than anything else; but there is, inevitably, much which he will overlook, partly from inability to give attention at all points, and partly because he is of necessity so close to the work of the team from day to day that he is unable to get a correct general estimate, which those who only see the team occasionally will often readily make.

As a help to his own observations, the criticisms of these casual visitors are always to be desired; but, beyond this, it is possible for the coach himself to apply certain tests to the development of the team from week to week which will show him latent weaknesses, or give him the welcome assurance that his efforts are proving successful.

With the aim of helping the coach, we will suggest certain salient features which should be carefully watched, outlining a dozen or more different tests which may be applied to the work of the team at stated intervals during the season; tests which will reveal much regarding its development along different lines.

(1) Test of a Weak Centre. It very often happens that, in the hurry of preparation for the earlier games of the season, the groundwork and fundamentals are not thoroughly imparted to the players. In other words, the elementary coaching has not been well grounded, and serious faults may be lurking below the surface of the play. One of the most serious of these faults, which sometimes, by a curious obstinacy, refuses to show itself until the season is well advanced (and then appears with positive malignity), is a weakness in the centre.

The first indications of this weakness are often evident to the practised observer before the coach detects its existence, by reasoning backward from their unfortunate results. For example: some play which is being tried will fail to work successfully; the coach knows that this play has been thoroughly tested by other elevens, and worked well, and he is naturally at a loss to understand why it does not work now. Following rapidly upon his perplexity, as if to add to the troubles of the situation, other plays which the team has been working with fair success now begin to show no gains; the runner is tackled time after time, without any advances. Apparently there is no explanation of the cause of this trouble, but its real cause lies in the weakness of the centre, and the first indications of this weakness might have been noticed by the expert coach days and weeks before, by noting carefully the result of the first impact between the two opposing lines of forwards, whenever the ball was put in play, the coach standing a little beyond the end of the line, and watching the three centre men closely. From this position he ought properly to see nothing more remarkable than the immediate engagement of the centre men with their opponents, with no yielding of the line for an appreciable interval after the ball has been put in play. Strictly speaking, neither side should be driven back (unless the play is an attack upon the centre), but both lines at this point should maintain the integrity of their position, without being forced, for at least an interval of from one and a half to two seconds after the ball has been snapped. The weakness in the centre, which develops in the middle or latter part of the season, will rarely occur without having given constant indications of its existence to the coach who has noted the effect of the first impact of the three centre men with their opponents when the ball is put in play. He will see that there is — not once only, but continually repeated — a "giving way" on the part of his centre. Their retreat may be only a very slight one; they may yield so little that the successful movement of the play is not seemingly embarrassed; their yielding may, indeed, only be evidenced by the bending or half turning of their bodies toward the quarter-back, but in each case these indications point to the conclusion that the centre men should be put through an immediate and severe coaching in low, hard blocking. Unless immediate attention is given to these instructions, the later results will be disastrous.

(2) **Following the Ball or Playing for the Trick.** It is imperative that your team, when acting on the defensive, should follow closely every movement of the ball, and not be deceived by possible fakes or bluffs on the part of the opponents. It is a very good plan to teach the second eleven (if there is a second eleven) some clever tricks which they can try upon your team. If you have no second eleven, see if it is not possible to secure for your practice the services of some clever and bright, even though greatly inferior, team; such a team will very likely have some especial forms of tricks in the nature of double passes, criss-crosses, fake kicks, etc., which will materially sharpen the wits of your men, when acting on the defensive.

The coach should then notice especially when any one of his team disobeys the instructions he has been given in the certainty of his belief that he knows the outlet of the play. Some coaches have had hard experience along this line. They have seen their favorite forwards, who have been constantly coached to go through the opposing line and follow up the play when it is moving away from them — they have seen these men, when facing an inferior team, disregard their instructions, and in their presumed certainty of the nature of the play try and get into the scrimmage by "running back of their own line."

This, of course, is a direct violation of coaching instructions, and would not often occur with a well-trained eleven; but there are other equally dangerous and more subtle ways in which the very best players are led into following their instinct as against their coaching, or, as it is often expressed, "playing for the trick instead of following the ball."

(3) **Criss-Crosses and Double Passes. (Calling out.)** Do not overlook the important lessons to be gained whenever your team faces an opponent who makes use of criss-crosses, and plays with a second passing of the ball. Your end rushers are the men most likely to detect first the second passing of the ball, and they should be instructed to instantly give the alarm by calling out in a loud voice that a criss-cross has been made.

A criss-cross is always a more or less dangerous type of play to meet, and the valuable practice which your team secures whenever it meets such a play is one which you should surely turn to advantage. Notice just what men are deceptively drawn away from the immediate field of action. The players who are usually the culprits in not rightly apprehending and performing their full duty in plays of this sort are the tackles, ends, and rush-line backs. They should be closely watched, and if one of these players has been fooled by a criss-cross in any game he should be given instructions which will enable him to successfully meet plays of this character in the future.

(4) Whether Backs or Forwards Give Away, by their Attitude, the Location of the Trick. This is an important test, and it should constantly be applied. Many members of the team, unless diligently coached to the contrary, will reveal to a clever opponent the general direction of the impending attack, by the attitude which they assume. If the player is in the rush line he will perhaps, by drawing back from his opponent, reveal the fact that he is to be the runner with the ball; or he will, by the very extra precautions and exertions which he takes, discover to his watchful opponent that the signal has called upon him to make the hole, and that the attack is, therefore, to be at that exact point in the line. Sometimes a forward, in his anxiety to get quickly into the interference, will assume almost the position for a sprint start, and his attitude clearly explains to the other side that the interference is to be directed at the very end of the line.

Oftener, however, it is the backs who give away the direction of the play; and for this reason they are the men who should be most closely watched. Especial attention should be given to their feet. A back who will be careful not to reveal in any other way, by his attitude, the direction in which the play is to move, will often be quite unable to prevent his feet from indicating clearly the course which he is about to take. The feet are great tell-tales in this matter. The backs should be continually coached to stand with their feet so placed that they not only do not reveal the direction in which the play is to go, but that they confuse the opponents by indicating a false direction. Thus, if the back is to move rapidly toward the end of the line, he should be taught to take an attitude indicative of an immediate plunge into the centre. With a little practice it will be found that he can easily become accustomed to this style of "take-off" for a round-the-end run. An exactly reverse attitude may then be assumed for a centre run.

(5) Starting by the Ball or by the Opponents. This is a point which will bear close watching. The penalties for off-side play are too great to take any risk of being drawn into a preliminary onslaught by some movement of the opponents. The invariable rule should be, when on the defensive, to *watch the ball*, and never to start until the ball starts, whatever movement the opponents may make. The instant, however, that the ball is put in play, every man should be in motion. Severe coaching should be given to the forward who neglects to watch the ball, or is deliberately induced to anticipate its movement by some bluff of the opponents.

(6) Punting for Distance and Location. It is not too much to insist as the standard of excellence for a full-back on a leading 'Varsity team, that he shall be able, in the majority of occasions, to drop his punt within the limits of a circle having a radius of ten yards. This accuracy of location in kicking punts is almost as important as the mere punting for distance. Certain emergencies arise when the ball must be punted into touch at or near a given point.

For example, when punting on a third down, on the opponents' twenty-yard line, it might enable the team to put the ball into touch inside the five-yard line, thus avoiding the danger of a kick-over. A full-back should be rigidly held up to the attainment of a high proficiency in the matter of both distance and location punting.

(7) Test of Blocking for Punts. This is too important not to receive constant attention, and repeated tests should be made of the efficacy of the defense for a kick. A very simple plan is to add to the opposing team an extra man in the line, and possibly one extra man behind the line. When making the test let it be known that the play is to be a kick, in order that every possible advantage may be taken by the opponents against whom you are practising. If the punt is blocked, do not fail to ascertain the exact method in which it was stopped, and the man who stopped it. Question the men who are deputed to obstruct the efforts of this man as to the reasons for their failure to so obstruct him at this time. Let the same effort be repeated again and again, until ten minutes' practice has been consumed upon this one test. Even if the result is entirely satisfactory, it will be necessary to make the same test as often as once or twice a week, for this is a most vital point in the development of the team, and the men individually must be coached to the best of your ability; there must be no doubt in your mind that they fully comprehend what is required of them.

In the event of the repeated failure of the full-back to get the ball away in time, it is necessary to ascertain the exact causes by which such failure is brought about. It may be that the punter is too slow in his motions; it may be that he is standing too close to his line; it may be that the blocking of some one or two men in the line is poor; it may be that the quarter is slow in the pass, or that the ball does not come back accurately and sharply from the centre. In any of these cases, unless the proper corrective is found, it will be necessary to force an answer to the problem and correct the error, even at the risk of jeopardy to some other part of the play. It may be found necessary to call the ends in from their outposts, and insist that they shall do a slight amount of body-checking before going down the field under the kick. If no other plan is successful, it would be good tactics to call the ends in altogether from their work of going down the field, and have them assist in the immediate blocking. The ball, however, should in that case be punted into touch, or so far over toward the short side of the field as to make it reasonably sure that no considerable run resulted.

When punting out from behind one's own goal line, if punts have previously been blocked, it is a question whether it would not be wise to bring back the ends for supplementary defense, in order that the kick at this critical time should surely be made without slip or accident. On such a play every man should exert himself to the utmost to go down the field as rapidly as possible after a moment's blocking of his opponent. In this connection the coach will do well to study the possible special formations for defending a punter. One of these is given in another part of this book; and others may be prepared by a little study and experiment.

(8) Test of Location of Hole (by Watching) and whether Back knows its Exact Spot and takes it clearly. This test can best be made by selecting three opponents, and lining up the team against them for signal practice. Let the three supposed opponents know the signals, and move rapidly from point to point in the line where the runner is to appear, or where the hole is to be made. Require your forwards to actually make the opening, and instruct the runner to go through the hole every time exactly as if in a regular play. The results of this test will reveal to the coach whether the back knows the exact point where the opening is made, and is not running wildly for a certain supposed part of the line between two men.

It is a very natural error into which the backs may fall, to locate the hole a foot or two away from the exact spot where it occurs. Sufficient allowance is not made by the average coach for the actual stretch of the line as it moves outward from the centre, and it is not enough, in an important play, to tell the runner that his hole is "between tackle and guard." The proper instruction should be that his hole is "exactly over the tackle's position," or "just inside the tackle's position." It must be borne in mind that in the average line-up the distance from guard to tackle would probably be five feet; between tackle and end, eight feet. These distances are too great to make it possible for a runner's opening to extend across the entire distance. It is, therefore, quite essential that the runner should be coached in signal practice as to the exact part of the distance between two men at which his opening occurs. The more that the careful coach studies this particular problem, the clearer it will grow, and the more convinced he will be of the importance of this test.

(9) A Given-Away Signal. It frequently happens that, after the calling out of a signal, a false start is made, and this slight accident is sufficient to give a momentary "rattling" to the team which may go far toward making their attempt to advance the ball an abortive one. Some method or course of action should be decided upon for all occasions where the signal is given away. There should not be the slightest embarrassment on the part of the quarter, and the correction of the signal should be immediate and unhesitating.

(10) The Line no Stronger than its Weakest Point. It is a good maxim for the coach to remember that, just as the excellence of the team as a whole can never rise as high as the excellence of its best player, so it will rarely fall as low as the inferiority of its poorest player. But it is this poorest player who must be borne in mind in all important operations and arrangements. It may be found necessary, at critical times, to reenforce his position, and at other times he will be entirely adequate for the needs of the situation. The watchful coach should never forget, however, the limitations which, by this single weak spot in the line, are drawn upon all his operations. The well-known method of "hammering" at one point in the rush line will reduce even a strong player to a weak one in the course of a single game, and there are very few teams who are not able, by the close of the first half of a game, to discover and report a weak spot in their opponents' line, if such a spot exists.

While there will usually, of necessity, be one man in the line who is less capable than the rest, the difference should not be a marked one, nor should the coach ever be satisfied by the easy assumption that the rush-line back or quarter-back can reenforce this weak player. Such reenforcement is seldom successful.

(11) Sympathy between Backs: of Backs with Quarter: of Backs with Line. The degree of sympathy between adjoining players is a very important element in team play. A back should never go into the line doubtful as to the presence of his interferers in their accustomed places about him. Naturally he has no time to look about him and make sure of their presence in their proper position; *he must have confidence in them!* He must also have confidence in the quarter-back, and feel assured that he is to receive the ball at a certain place and in the customary way. Without this confidence his play will inevitably be slowed down, and the whole effect of the intended movement will be weakened.

Sympathy between the three backs who carry the ball can best be established by coaching them, when they take their places, to extend their arms at full length, and for a moment grasp the arm or waist of their adjoining companions on either side. This actual touch or contact often imparts that "shoulder to shoulder" courage which marks the spirited attack. Confidence and sympathy are born in that immediate touch. The back no longer "thinks" that his interference is about him; *he knows it.*

In the same way the backs should be encouraged to converse freely at all times, in a low tone, regarding the intended manoeuvre, mentioning, perhaps, who is to carry the ball, and each assuring the other, in half whispers, that he understands the exact nature of the coming movement.

The sympathy of the backs with the quarter, while just as vital a matter, is more difficult to bring about. Close acquaintance, and the intimate knowledge of each other's thoughts and attitudes which comes with that acquaintance, will materially assist in establishing this sympathy. The coach can supplement this by endeavoring, in his own way, to instill into the minds of the backs a confidence in the work of the quarter. Let the coach himself make sure that the backs appreciate the fact that the best available quarter has been chosen; that his coolness can be relied upon; that he is being carefully instructed in the employment of the best tactics upon the field, and that he is generally a more capable and trustworthy player than appearances might, perhaps, indicate.

Yet another point is the sympathy between the backs and the line. One often sees a team in which the development has advanced to a point where the team is composed of two units, the backs and the line. The last and highest degree of development has not been reached, and there is a perceptible break in nearly every play where the work of one of these units does not immediately connect itself with the work of the other. It is, perhaps, unnecessary to take the space here to instruct the coach as to the best method to be pursued in each case, for the reason that the fault, which may lie in one of several directions, is usually easily discernible, and the remedy may as easily be applied. The line may be needlessly slow in their movements after the ball has been snapped; or the backs may have fallen into a style of play in which they are anticipating the movement of the ball, through their great familiarity with the actions of the quarter. The emphasis which has been placed upon the coaching of the backs may have resulted in speeding them up ahead of the point at which the line is starting; or, conversely, the line may have been so successfully developed that they are actually ahead of the work of the backs, and it is the latter who need attention. In either case the problem is not a difficult one, but it is important and should have the immediate attention of the coach.

(12) Test of Place Kicking of Goals. It is a safe maxim that a goal from a place-kick should never be missed. The coach should know, however, that the fault, when any exists, may have one of several causes, all equally liable to occur. It may lie in the holder of the ball; in the lack of confidence of the kicker; or in the bad form in which he has been taught to kick. It is well to have at least two kickers and two holders in every team, and the work of the holders should be more or less interchangeable, so that either holder may officiate for either kicker. It will be an advantage if one of the kickers is a rusher.

The errors through a lack of confidence on the part of the kicker should be carefully watched for during the season. No man who is uncertain in his moods, and whose play is marked by great variations in its excellence, should be intrusted with the kicking of goals. It needs, rather, a man of good judgment and extreme coolness.

It is always a mooted point in every close game, when a kicker has missed one goal, to decide whether he should be intrusted with the kicking of another goal if a second touch-down is made. If a strong wind is blowing, it may easily be that the kicker misjudged the wind, and, having seen the result of his error, will not again misjudge it, and is, therefore, better fitted to kick the second goal than any other man on the field. On the other hand, if his error arose from a nervousness in this particular game, it will be a mistake to allow him to try again. On the whole it is, perhaps, a safe plan to follow the course laid down by certain trans-Atlantic steamship lines, and punish the accident regardless of an investigation into its causes. Let the rule be, that if the kicker misses one goal he is not allowed to try for the second.

The matter of errors in the form of the kicker is too often overlooked. One constantly sees goal kickers who, after the ball has been touched to the ground, advance two or three steps and kick with much unnecessary force. The ball should not be brought out more than ten to fifteen yards, and with the present rules regarding punt-outs the angle of the kick need not be a difficult one. For this short distance let the kicker stand quite close to the ball, and in moving forward to make the kick let him not bend his body back as the leg is thrown forward, for this withdraws his eye from his intent observation of the ball, and on this intentness of observation his success largely depends. Let him rather make one step forward, and, bending over the ball, instead of bending backward, let him make an easy, light kick over the cross-bar.

(13) Test of Spirit by Driving. Every experienced coach will realize the necessity for this test, and little need be said about it here. In a group of eleven men, it is inevitable that there will be different degrees of spirit, and as a result of the weeks of training it is not unlikely that there may be short limits to the patience and discipline of the team. Under the spur of sharp censure and constant driving, if there is such a limit, the coach will surely discover it, and he may never know of its existence until, on some selected afternoon, he tests the temper of his team by the hardest kind of a coaching "drive." Later he may be able to credit to the account of such an afternoon some of the most important lessons of the fall practice.

(14) Test of Condition by Sending Full Length. This is a matter which concerns only the department of training, but as this department is the very foundation upon which the coach is working, it is proper that it should be subjected to a severe test. From time to time during the season, the development of the physical condition of the men should be ascertained by giving them an entire afternoon of the severest practice. At such times they should be played for the full limits of a game. Let the halves be long enough to allow a reasonable margin for time taken out, and still keep the actual playing halves of thirty-five minutes duration. The probable loss of time may be approximated as ten minutes in each half, and the team should then be played for two halves of forty-five minutes. As the best practice usually comes late in the season, it presupposes the selection of some day when the work may begin at an early hour. The coach should by no means overlook this important test of the endurance of his team.

CHAPTER VI

FIELD TACTICS

Generalship. Critical Moment in Every Game. In the progress of a game where much is at stake, there always comes a time when the two teams have fairly measured their strength with each other, have tried their best plays, have exhibited their methods, and betrayed their weaknesses. In nine tenths of our season's final matches, whether between school teams, small college teams, or crack exponents of the highest perfection of the game, — in nine tenths of these matches, we repeat, there is usually not a great deal to choose between the two contesting elevens, either in point of individual physical condition, or ability to execute plays. The contest, therefore, would be a tie if it were not for some other factor that enters into the equation and eventually shows one of the teams frequently markedly the superior of the other. The factor is generalship; and by this we mean the handling of the team in the immediate progress of the match. This entails, or rather is the result of a proper course of education through a season, for no effective generalship in a game is possible, save through a long study of its problems during the entire season. In the game itself, the captain and quarter carry out the lessons learned from the coach through the preliminary practice and lesser games. Later in this chapter we give the results of the study of many coaches through many seasons, and in doing this we hope to place the coaches and captains in a position to save themselves a great deal of labor over problems that can only be solved by experiment in big matches, and at times when an experiment, though its resulting knowledge may be valuable, may be of itself very costly.

Selection of Good Coach. The first thing to be considered by a team in the question of generalship for the season is the selection of a good coach. In most of the larger universities, and in many of the schools, there are nowadays not only two or three available men, but a little army of coaches, no one of whom is capable of assuming, or desires to be given, full charge of the entire season's work. Hence when we say good coach, we mean good head coach — that is, a man who takes entire charge, and is responsible for the final product of the season's work.

A Leader and General. Such a man must be by nature both a leader and a general. He must be of high character, and thoroughly deserving of the full confidence and respect of all with whom he may come in contact. It goes without saying, that he must know the game with something more than the merely superficial knowledge of the player. The coach must have studied its deeper problems, and apprehended its tactical possibilities. He should be *persona grata*, not only to the team and the rest of the coaches, but also to the faculty. With all this, he must not be a man who is swayed by any desire for individual popularity. He must not be influenced by considerations of what people he may offend, or whom he may please by certain selections of men or methods. He must have no weaknesses of this nature. He must not only know when he is right, but must also have to the full the courage of his convictions; and once set out upon the road that he believes is the right one, no amount of opposition should turn him. Still again, he must be willing to hear the opinions of others, anxious to accept such suggestions as are of value, and too unselfish not to be ready to give credit to another man's assistance. He must deserve, and, deserving, command respect. Then will he be able to produce a team that shall win against great odds, or, if losing, be defeated only at the hands of rivals who, through better material and greater experience, have an advantage at the outset which has proved too great for even the ablest coach to overcome. As this is a chapter to the coach himself, he should practise sufficient self-examination to learn whether he has these necessary attributes, and if he be not possessed of them, and feels that he cannot acquire them, our advice to him is to hand in his resignation at once, before he starts upon a campaign which can result only in distress and eventual disgrace to himself and to the team he endeavors to handle.

Relations of the Captain and Coach. As the captain is usually elected before the coach is chosen, it devolves upon the latter to realize at the outset that he must work in harmony with the captain, or be of sufficient power and standing to effect an immediate resignation of the captain and the elevation of another man. This should never be deferred to mid-season, or brought about by a system of undermining, too common in college politics. Face the situation at once, and if the captain be unsuitable, act openly, honestly, and straightforwardly, and if the captain is to stay, then send in your own resignation, and give the team the benefit of a coach and captain who are in accord.

But if the captain be a fit man for the place, see to it that you keep his position a thoroughly honorable one before his men. Treat his opinions with respect, and especially so before the players. If there be points in which you think him wrong, it will not be difficult in private to convince him of his error, and then you can both work together to correct any mistakes. You must remember that when it comes to the actual game itself, the captain must carry with him all the power, and have behind him all the obedience of his team. After the ball is kicked off, you, the coach, become but a spectator — one of a thousand others, while he has the carrying on of the battle and the encouragement of the troops. So make sure that you do nothing to weaken, but rather everything to strengthen his position with his men. Make a man of him by belief in him. It is not necessary that you believe in his theories. He may have foolish ones. But believe that he will make an ideal captain, and you will find it not at all difficult, if he is a man of good sense and personal courage, to teach him to be the mainstay of the team. This seems like a long digression from the subject of field tactics, but it is a part of the generalship, and a most important part too.

Selection of Substitute Field Captain. The next important point to receive attention, in order that the generalship of the great match be properly provided for, is the selection of a substitute field captain — a man who, in case of accident, can step into the place and handle the team. The selection of this man should also be made a matter of great care and consideration, and effected as early in the season as possible. Some trials may, if advisable, be made in this matter, and different men be given the opportunity of trying their hand at leading in some of the minor matches. The one caution that is worth giving in this selection is not to allow any man to be chosen who is likely to become so vain over the little brief authority as to set up an opposition to the captain. There are such men, and it is just as well not to place them where they can do harm.

Running the Team by the Quarter-Back. After the selection of these field captains comes the question of the interdependence between them and the quarter-back, as well as the substitute quarter-back, for provision must be made here also for accident. The captain should have the final voice during the game whenever he cares to avail himself of that privilege, but it is usually more convenient to have the quarter give the signals. In case the captain is a half or full back, he may be able to give the signals satisfactorily, but hardly when he is a line man. At any rate, in the final discussions and arrangements between the captain and coach, it is well to call in the substitute captain and the two quarters, in order that the general plan of the play may be thoroughly understood by all four.

Acquaint the Quarter and Captain with your Plans. Don't wait until the night before the game to acquaint these men with your views as to how the big match is to be conducted, what your designs are, and how you expect to see them executed. Begin some two weeks before to let these men share your considerations, and make them a part of your counsels. Many coaches put off the final planning of the game until the last few days, and then have so many little things to think of that they have no time to instruct substitutes. The result is that in the middle of the game the captain is laid up, and the team then goes to pieces because it has lost its head. In another chapter will be given in detail a *résumé* of the many points to be considered on the eve of the match.

Elimination of Unsatisfactory Plays. Two weeks, then, before the match, call the captain, substitute captain, and the two quarters together, and begin the consideration of the elimination of such plays, at that time being used, as are likely to prove *dangerous* in respect of losing the ball; *risky* in regard to the opening left for a long run on a fumble; *exhausting* to the men you wish to keep in the best shape; or *irritating* to the general spirit of the team.

Conditions Affecting Field Tactics. What to Consider. Outside of any consideration of the strength or weakness of the opponents beyond the question of the relative ability of the two teams, or of their individual comparison, there are conditions which the wise general must take into especial consideration. These are such factors as the wind, ground, rain, sun, seats, and crowd. Taking these in order, the effect of the wind is one that is thoroughly appreciated, though not perhaps perfectly understood by almost every football player.

Value and Effect of the Wind. It is hardly necessary to do more than to state that when the wind blows freshly down a field in a direction parallel to, the side lines, the side which has the assistance of the wind gains a great advantage over their opponents upon the occasion of every kick made by either side. But it is advisable to go into further detail regarding the possibility of increasing or decreasing this advantage. Let us consider, first, the side that has the wind: In the case of a really strong wind, this side should do almost no running with the ball until the last ten minutes of the half, or until they secure possession of it within twenty-five yards of their opponents' goal, or at least have it on a first down in close proximity to that line. This will seem to many a strong statement; for, it is argued, with a strong wind a punt from the forty-yard line will go over the goal line. Yes, but in that case it ought always to be a drop-kick, and then it may net five points. Again, if it be a punt, it should be placed across the side line well down toward its intersection with the goal line. Still further, even if kicking when at the twenty or forty yard line does result in simple touchbacks, the following kick-out may often result in its turn in a fair catch, which may be converted into a field-kick goal. Lastly, beside all this, it is killing to the opponents to be driven into playing a risky game of catching balls in front of their own line, or kicking out in the teeth of a strong wind, and by the time of the last ten minutes of the half, the team that with the wind has been constantly kicking will be sufficiently superior in wind and dash to be several yards to the good in their running game.

Style of Kick With the Wind. Next, as to the style of kick to be used by the side with the wind. When kicking from your own territory, and when you desire to make all the distance possible, lift the ball well up above the top seats of the bleachers so that it may have the full sweep of the wind, and not merely what little gusts get down into the amphitheatre. Take plenty of room for a hard swing, and give the ball all the drive you can. As you near the opponents' goal, the kicks may be lower and faster, making twisters that are hard to catch unless you wish to put your men on-side. Then, of course, the ball must go up more to give longer time for the descent. If the wind is not directly down the field, always work over for the kick so that you will get as much benefit as possible, even though you are thus obliged to kick across the field. Don't be afraid to try drop-kicks or place-kicks at goal from almost any point in reason. But be very careful to take plenty of room for these kicks, as they rise less quickly with the wind, and the loss of a blocked kick is greater in proportion to the distance that kick might have traveled had it not been blocked.

Duty of Ends when With the Wind. It is necessary to add a word or two here upon the important duty devolving upon the ends in playing with the wind. They must make almost superhuman efforts at times to get down the field in season, because the wind will carry the ball along at a tremendous rate, and their pace must, therefore, be correspondingly accelerated. This is important, not so much to prevent running the ball back, as because a muff is far more likely under these conditions than on a still day. In fact, a mere touch is all a rattled full-back may get at the ball which then goes on over the goal line. No touch-down is so easily secured, or does more damage morally to the losing side, than one resulting from a muff or a blocked kick.

Against the Wind. Turning now to the consideration of the side that is playing against these odds, with the wind in their faces; if the breeze be a strong one, it is indeed a difficult task, and one that will try the temper and patience of the leader and his men to the utmost. The first thing to consider is whether the wind is so strong as to make a kick wholly out of the question, save when actually forced to it. Fortunately we have had few such winds on the days of our great matches, but once or twice such conditions have prevailed, and have found leaders unprepared for them. A captain should keep close watch of the wind, even after he has entered a half convinced that it is too strong to kick against, for there may be lulls when he can get in an effective punt, and relieve his tired men for at least a few moments. He may also work in quarter-back kicking, and "on-side" kicks to some effect.

Style of Play. As to his running game, he should distribute it as much as possible, so as to enable his team to last out the half. He should play with deliberation, and bring off trick plays whenever there is a promising opportunity. In style of punting, when attempted, he should remember that nothing but a low, hard drive stands any chance of traveling against a wind, and his kickers should always aim just over the heads of the rushers, and put all the force they can into the kick. Try to work off to the side from which the wind comes, if it be not straight down the field. Bring your kicker up as close to the quarter as you dare have him, and block tight in the line. Every yard counts, and you cannot afford to throw distance away by letting your punter stand well back, as you can when you have the wind with you.

Style of Kick Against the Wind. Let your kicker get the ball pretty well up on the instep to drive it, a toe kick has less "go" in it, and is more apt to slip off against a big wind. Don't be afraid to make a safety unless it is late in the game, and the score so close that the safety would settle it. Coax your opponents to punt over, however, all you can, because touch-backs are a great deal better for you than safeties, but don't feel that the game is all over if you have to make two, or even three safeties in the first half with the wind against you. One good touch-down goal in the next half will tie the three safeties. Nevertheless, keep it two if you can, because the touch-down goal, or even a field-kick goal will then be a win for you, instead of a tie or too little. Before you go into the half, tell your forwards how much it means to secure the ball on a kick, — let them remember, also, how hard to handle these low kicks just over the heads of the rushers are for the other side, — how the wind holds the ball back, and a good, dashing forward will often receive the ball on a fumble by the opponents. They must fight for this hard, for even once or twice saves your team a load of hard work, and encourages them wonderfully in a trying time.

Rain. The story is told of two teams meeting in a rainstorm, and the captain of the defeated team saying, after the game, to his rival, "I don't see how your men handled the ball so much better than we did. We used to soak the ball all night, and then play with it the next day, just to prepare for such a time as this." The winning captain asked, "Didn't you practise when it rained?" "Why, no," said his rival, "we were afraid of getting men laid up. Did you play in the rain?" "Yes, we practised, rain or shine, just as we play a game, rain or shine."

What Plays to Use, and what to Discard, on a Rainy Day. That was some years ago, and nearly every team now knows that practice in the rain is necessary to a proper understanding of such conditions, and that they may prevail on the day of the big match. It is by this practice, also, that a captain learns what plays must be discarded, and what ones used on a wet day in a sodden field, and with a greasy ball. There are conditions peculiar to individual teams in this respect that can only be determined by practice and observation, but there are certain general rules that may be laid down without reference to the idiosyncrasies of any team. Primarily, most plays that involve quick, sharp turns or dodges must be discarded on a wet field. Then plays depending solely upon men from two different points meeting at a common point at an absolutely fixed moment can hardly be brought off successfully. All plays involving a double handling of the ball are hazardous at a time when the ball is wet and the footing insecure. Long end runs are impossible (except on a trick play, which makes the opponents the ones who must turn and retrace their steps). Much may be gained by constantly looking for favorable spots in the field both for runner and especially for kicker on a rainy day. There are always spots less bad than others, and the halves, quarter, and full back should keep this in mind continually.

Clothes and Shoes for a Rainy Day. Attention should be paid to each man's cross-pieces before he gets on the field, and extra pairs of shoes kept in readiness at intermission. If the rain be a heavy one, it is well to have a complete change of suit for each man at intermission, because the clothes become so heavy as to interfere with speed and kicks, and to actually tire out the wearers from their weight.

Handling the Ball when Wet. A wet, heavy ball must be handled with the arms and body more than a dry one. It will not do to try to take it on a pass in the hands only. Moreover, it must be kicked while the muscles of the leg are very tense, and must be met squarely. In catching it, on long kicks, the body and even upper leg should be kept well under it, forming almost a pocket in which, with the help of the arms, the ball may be securely held.

Sun. When to Choose It. As most of the games of football played in this country are not finished much before half past four or five o'clock in the afternoon, it follows that where the grounds run east and west the sun plays an important part on cloudless days. When there is no other element entering into the selection of goal, and a captain is debating upon the choice, he should always remember that the sun is far more disconcerting to the backs as it approaches the horizon, and he should, therefore, elect to face it preferably during the first half. But he may not have the choice, or there may be a wind or other reasons for a different selection.

How to Neutralize its Effects. The coach should, therefore, have provided against this contingency by having equipped the backs with the long-vizored cap. In addition to this, also, the backs should have been well trained in the practice of using the left hand as a shade, holding it out at arm's length as the ball is descending, and drawing the arm in as the ball settles. It is an easily acquired art, and is very serviceable. After a week or two of practice it does not in the least interfere with the catch, and renders trouble from the sun (unless it is very low in the horizon) comparatively harmless.

How to Make Use of the Advantage. To take every advantage of this factor of the sun in a match, the side having it at their backs should make a practice of sending kicks at a moderate height, and with a hard drive, kicking what are technically known as "sailers," that is, kicks that cause the ball to turn over and over very little, while it swerves from a true course, and comes swiftly, dropping very sharply toward the end of its flight. This is by all odds the most difficult punt for a back to handle when he has the sun in his eyes.

But all fields are not laid out running directly east and west, and it often happens that the sun is at the side rather than at the end of the field. Then such advantage is lessened, but with it comes another phase of the question that should receive constant consideration. With the sun very low, and on a field that is upon comparatively high ground, some long passes must be given up, and it is well to recognize this before a neglect results in a fumble.

Ground. Consideration of Snow and Irregularities. We have already treated the question of the condition of the ground in the preceding paragraphs, where that condition was dependent upon the effect of rain. Snow has a similar effect, save that it is apt to pack on the shoes even more than mud, and it is sometimes well to rub a little stove polish on the soles of the shoes before going into a game. Besides the weather conditions, the general lay of the land should be considered, and the ground thoroughly gone over, if it be a strange one. There may be paths crossing it. It may be that there is a decided pitch in some portion. There may be sandy spots. There may be a baseball diamond. All these things affect the play in a variety of ways, and should be known and allowed for. Especially should the ground inside the twenty-five-yard lines be examined, as in this section of the field most of the kicking for goals, both place-kicks and drops, is performed. Then the ground near the side lines, and just outside of bounds, should be examined. The proximity of a fence deserves attention, and ground rules should be made dependent upon these conditions. Note if there be a barrier or obstacle behind either goal, within such distance as might render a punt by a full-back, when the ball is down within, say, a foot or two of the goal line, difficult. If so, there should be an agreement entered into allowing a certain distance out in such a case. If the provisions for keeping the crowd back are inadequate, rules should be made such as will leave no room for argument after the game has once commenced.

Proximity of Crowd or Seats. Beyond all this the coach and captain should view with careful eye the provisions made for the seating of the crowd, also the portion of the field where reporters, substitutes, and others inside the ropes are to be allowed to stand. The seats of the main body of spectators are often so near the side line that the cheering will absolutely prevent the team from hearing the signals when the ball is near that line, and the coach must arrange that the team either collect to receive the signals, or that signs be used in place of the usual words.

Dividing the Field into Spaces. Scoring Distances. The question arises at once, when the coach begins to divide the field up into spaces, as to what is "scoring distance." A touch-down can, of course, be made from any part of the field. A fumble followed by a run (such as Suter's, in a Princeton-Harvard game) might result in carrying the ball the entire length of the field. But such plays as that must not be taken into consideration by the coach. He must be arbitrary in his divisions of the field, and, to be arbitrary, he must calculate upon probabilities, not possibilities. In laying out scoring territory, then, it is proper to reason in this way: How near should a team be when they always try for a score with some probability of attainment? Taking all the vicissitudes of the game and play into consideration, we conclude that the twenty-five-yard line is a fair spot, but we do not tell the coach or captain that he is never to try for score at twenty-six or twenty-seven yards out. We only first broadly lay down the law and consider the quarter a responsible and withal reasonable being, who will be properly balanced in making decisions.

Kicking Territory. From one twenty-five-yard line to the other is the kicking territory. Here the greater part of the punting should be done. The exchange of kicks is likely to take place largely in this division of the field, and it is a kind of common ground in which neither side is placed in that position of terrible anxiety which is apt to arise when the ball actually comes into what we have called scoring distance of one or the other of the goals. In kicking territory, therefore, it is possible to count upon fairly steady play, — to consider that even a blocked kick or a fumbled fly may be redeemed, and will not of itself mean a lost goal.

Danger Territory. As for the third division, — the danger territory, — it is the scoring territory of the opponents. Here come in the many problems of defense with increased importance and with added significance. Here, a mistake becomes serious, a bad blunder fatal. There are two or three general rules to be observed here that can be briefly stated as follows: First, in this territory it is dangerous to delay kicking after the ball is secured. If the centre and quarter are practically steady in emergencies, and the backs cool and reliable, the kick may be put off one down. But if the team be a nervous one, or if they are in a state of panic on account of the near

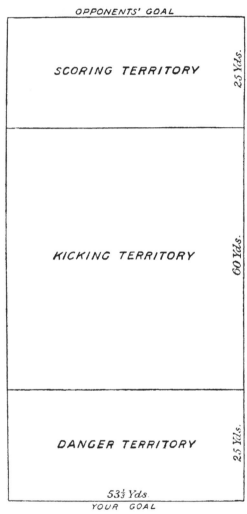

Diagram G. — The transverse divisions of the field.

approach of the enemy, the ball should be punted out of danger as soon as it is secured. Second: No pass should be made of any length when in this territory, and never across in front of the goal posts. Third: The kicker should always take enough room to make absolutely sure of getting in his kick, erring on the side of safety here always. Fourth: He should kick down the line rather than across.

Longitudinal Divisions. So much for a brief suggestion as to the three main transverse divisions noted in the first diagram. Next as to the longitudinal main divisions of the field. It has not been very apparent in the games, even the big games, of the past that any regard is paid to this very important point in field tactics. Plays are used indiscriminately, at the whim of the quarter or the caprice of the captain, rather than with any well-considered plan, or from any thoroughly understood reasoning. Even the teams that have played under some system in this regard have not themselves been possessed of the key to their play, but have simply followed orders, the coach alone understanding why his directions have been given. Beyond working the ball over in front of the goal when approaching that hallowed ground, their knowledge has not carried them. But there is almost as much to be considered in these longitudinal divisions as in the transverse ones, — more, in fact, as relating to the use of plays. Let us take the middle belt first.

The Middle Belt. It is in this belt that a variety of plays should be used, not only because it is practicable from this section to assault either side of the enemies' line, but because there are some plays which are absolutely excluded from the other two divisions on account of the side-line proximity. If, therefore, such plays are not freely used in the centre division, they are practically cut from the *repertoire* of the team. Criss-crosses are more effective in this section because neither side of the line is packed, and as both move freely the opponents are far more likely to overrun the second recipient of the ball as he goes up on the double. It is hardly necessary to say that drop-kicks for goal should always come from this division.

The Side Belts. As to the side belts, here all kicking is most efficacious when desirable to relieve a menaced goal, but the kicker should stand well out from the actual side line, so as to run no risk of sending the ball out too early in its flight. All double passes, as distinguished from criss-crosses, should start from the side belt, because this gives a long open for the second man to circle in, when he tries to go around the end. Trick plays on the centre are also best worked from the side spaces, because here the closely packed men on one side are handicapped, while those on the far side are too much spread out to be quickly of service, as they must guard carefully the open territory.

Diagram H. — The longitudinal divisions of the field.

Further Subdivision. Let us turn now to a more careful division of the field. In this, for the sake of making the deductions clearer, we once more make arbitrary lines which, in this discussion, we will assume are admitted, not as absolute, but as indicating in a general way the spaces for consideration. Of course, no captain or quarter can tell to a hair's breadth, when in actual contest, how many feet or inches he may be from the side line or the twenty-five-yard line. He must make always more or less rough calculations. But he is far better off with distinct ideas as to this division of the field than if he regard it, as do most of our teams, merely as one great pasture, in which to browse away at all sorts of plays.

Plays for Numbers 16, 17, and 18. With the ball in possession, and beginning at your own goal, in sections 16, 17, and 18, always kick on first down, and preferably down the side line. The best position for the kick is in section 16, at a point fifteen yards out from the side line. This is for a right-footed kicker. For a left-footed kicker, section 18 is preferable at the same relative distance from the side. If by chance the ball is in section 17, the kicker may so take up his position usually as to bring the kick out into either 16 or 18, as suits his pleasure.

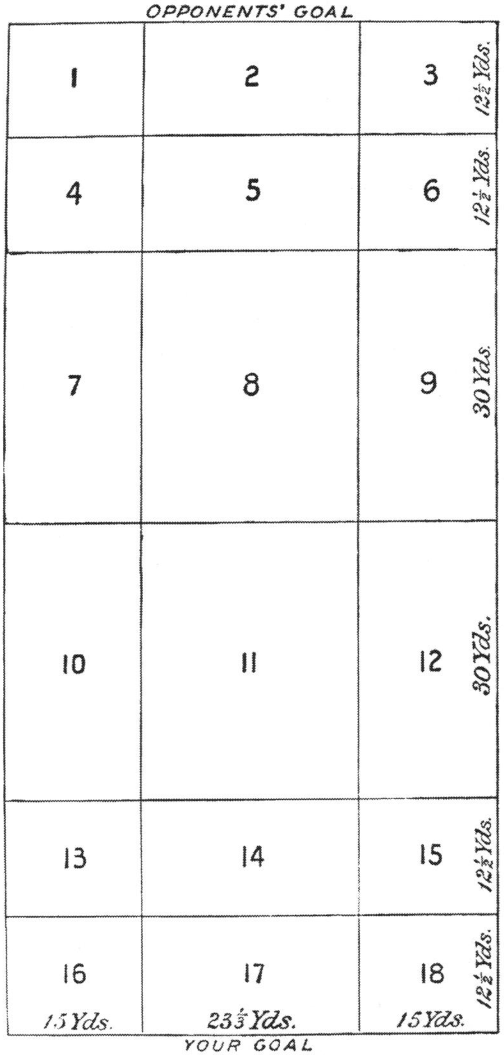

Plays for Numbers 13, 14, and 15. With the ball in 13, 14, or 15 of your own goal, always kick on second down, and usually upon the first down. Kicks to be made in a similar fashion as in sections 16, 17, and 18. Never pass the ball or kick the ball across the field when in 16, 17, or 18, or 13, 14, or 15.

Plays for Numbers 10, 11, and 12. With the ball in your possession, and in section 10, 11, or 12 of your own territory, you may play a running game, occasionally up to a third down, especially if on a generally rapid advance; that is, if you have made your five yards or more at a single try, not in two downs. Never continue the running game in this section when it becomes slow of progress. Kick then, and preferably land the ball at the end of the kick out of bounds, unless your opponents' backs are known to be fumblers or green men. In that case, give them a chance to muff the ball. In playing the running game use in section 10 and 12 double passes, long passes, and runs around end or around tackle. In section 11, use tackle attack, criss-cross, and variety play; that is, preferably plays that

OPPONENTS' GOAL

1	2	3	12½ Yds.
4	5	6	12½ Yds.
7	8	9	30 Yds.
10	11	12	30 Yds.
13	14	15	12½ Yds.
16	17	18	12½ Yds.

15 Yds.   23⅓ Yds.   15 Yds.

YOUR GOAL

Diagram I. — The field in sections.

would be impossible on the side of the field. It is a safe rule to lay down that straight attacks upon the centre should rarely be made in the middle belt, unless close to opponents' goal. Advancing still farther up the field, after you have passed the fifty-five-yard line, and are in opponents' territory, it is well (except for a disconcerting play) to defer the kick always to the second and often to the third down.

Plays for Numbers 7, 8, and 9. From section 8 a fair catch may often be turned into a close try for goal from a place-kick. A drop-kick may also be attempted on a third down, or even on a second down in this section. In punting from sections 7 and 9 it is well to land the ball out of bounds down near the corners. In running plays use an occasional trick that has a safe outlet, and otherwise follow instructions for 10 and 12 in 7 and 9, and 11 in 8.

Plays for Numbers 4, 5, and 6. As we go up the field we now cross the twenty-five-yard line, and come into scoring territory. Here never kick (except a drop-kick on first down) until you come at your third down, and don't kick then unless you have at least two yards to go, or possess a first-class drop kicker. If you have more than two yards to go, a quarter-back kick, or any "on-side" kick, is a good thing here. As for plays to use in sections 4, 5, and 6, use your best ones. Keep jamming the same thing at them as long as it is gaining, and then on a first down let them have a trick play, which, if it succeed, may give you a touch-down. Don't spare any man. Use your best man, and use him until he drops, so long as he gains ground.

Plays for Numbers 1, 2, and 3. This may bring you over the five-yard line into section 1, 2, or 3. When you have landed the ball within this space there is no excuse for not scoring. Daily you should have practised your plays in this section until your team thoroughly grasps the meaning of having the ball within five yards of the enemies' line. You should have a series, in fact two or three series, of plays for use at this juncture, and your quarter or captain should have decided, by use of the parts of these series in the earlier play, just which of the two or three series will prove most effective against the opponents. Bear in mind that if you are in sections 1 or 3, plays should be used that will tend to bring you into 2 before the line is crossed, but don't waste a play in order merely to carry the ball across the field. In selecting the series, give preference to those plays in which your men are best able to hold their feet. This is a case often of individual custom or peculiarity, and only to be determined in the days of practice. There should be no play tried in sections 1, 2, or 3 (except on a third down after loss) that gives an individual a long, circling run, because in spite of his ability a player under these conditions is liable to run back or be crowded back when alone at the moment he is tackled, so that in that instant of being tackled, having no support from his comrades, he is swept back sometimes several yards, and the ball landed outside the five-yard line. The only exception to this rule regarding long runs is upon a third down after losing ground, so that any ordinary line play is hopeless. Then it is best to risk a long run, or even a long pass, or sometimes a quarter kick, because the only chance left is to make a play that shall net more than the distance between the ball and the goal line, and it does not make any especial difference whether the opponents secure the ball on their five-yard line or on their one-yard line. They will kick it in any event, and the four yards on the end of a kick that lands the ball forty yards out into the field is immaterial. If you must lose the ball on opponents' five or ten yard line, try to leave it as near the centre as possible, and if you can force the opposing full-back to kick out from behind his goal posts, it is much gained. As you approach opponents' goal direct all punts at the goal posts.

Defensive Plays in Cross-Sections. If we stopped here in our study of the division of the field for the better understanding of field tactics, it might be said that we had done our duty, and that the case had been satisfactorily covered. But there is more to be considered. Almost every team has theories of defense, but these theories are behind the theories of offense by some three years. Just as a few years ago our theories of offense bore little relation to the portion of the field where the play was located, so now the most advanced theories of defense have little to do with field division, but are generally applied upon all occasions. But the division of the field into sections, and the study of these sections, is quite as important upon defense as it is upon offense, and the consideration of the subject will prove fully as important to the coach and captain.

Inside the Twenty-Five-Yard Line. Beginning, as we did before, with the three general transverse divisions of the field, we assume that the team is on the defense,—that is, the ball is in the possession of their opponents, and within twenty-five yards of the goal line. As this chapter does not deal with the specialized forms of defense any more than it does with the methods of offense, except so far as they are affected by the position of the play, we do not give the exact distribution of the teams, but we call attention to the results to be accomplished. The first point to be observed within these lines is the necessity of preventing repeated small but steady gains. Out in the middle of the field a gain of twenty-five yards in fifteen downs is not a serious matter, and, in fact, rather to be encouraged, if the opponents are thereby exhausting themselves, for it requires greater strength and wind, as a rule, to make such plays than to check their progress. But here it means a touch-down, and hence it must be especially guarded against and stopped. This is best done by accentuating the push of the line of forwards. That is, while in the middle of the field a long run is to be feared, within the twenty-five-yard line it is the steady gain of short distance that becomes alarming, and to check the latter the "lift" of the line, that is, its pushing power, must be increased even at the expense of other features. The opponents must not be allowed to push ahead after the runner strikes the line. They must be reached early by those going through, and the interference smashed, if possible, before the impact comes upon the line itself. Every man should here meet his opponent from below up. That is, whether he be free of the line or in it at the time of striking his opponent or the interference, he should be bent low down, and as he strikes should straighten up and lift to force the opponent backward. Some will argue that this is a good thing to do at any point in the field. It is; but, unfortunately, it cannot be kept up successfully for the entire game, and, for the same reason that a rushing game should not be played all the time, as too exhausting, so, too, the defense must be regulated according to the possibilities of physical endurance and the necessities of the situation. Again, inside the twenty-five-yard line, and particularly as the defense is forced nearer its own goal, the general order should be less loose than in mid-field. The full-back comes up close, the half-backs come in a little, the ends take less room, but put themselves where they can cover an outside run, and yet jump in after the play is diagnosed, and give assistance. The guards do not play as wide as in open field, for fear of centre pushing, and the general effect is that of far greater compactness. From the very fact that the opponents, if properly posted in even the rudiments of field tactics, will play a running game as soon as they reach what they consider scoring distance, the side on the defense is enabled to relax much of its vigilance against a kick, and thus concentrate its energy as mentioned above.

Defensive in Middle Section. When the play is outside the twenty-five-yard line, that is, in the middle section of the three transverse divisions, or the section known as "kicking territory," the formation should be more open, the full-back more prepared for quick kicks, the ends on the lookout for quarter-back or short on-side kicks, and they and the rush-line half-back swinging out wider on account of the greater danger of a long run. The guards and tackles can open up the line with less risk now, giving the quarter greater latitude, and harassing the opponents more in the execution of the first part of the play. This is possible, because short centre-smashing is far less serious here than near the goal, and may be risked as amounting to little so far as practically affecting the result of the game goes.

Defense when in Scoring Territory. In the third division, that is, in the opponents' goal (your "scoring territory"), the side not having possession of the ball should send its men through at the probable kickers with almost unlimited freedom, only the reserve of two men being back to receive the kick until it is actually made. One man, and one man only, on each side the line should watch for fake kicks, and the rest be sent through regardless of conditions. These two watchers for fake kicks, as soon as the actual kick is assured, come back to assist the two recipients of the punt. The probabilities of a run should be almost entirely disregarded in favor of stopping the kick, for here a blocked kick means a touch-down in all likelihood, either upon the immediate play, or upon securing the ball and crowding it over in short order.

Defensive Play in Longitudinal Belts. Coming now to the longitudinal division of the field: as upon the offense, we cut the field into three parts, the middle belt and the two side-line belts. Here again the defense, that is, the side not having the ball, is fully as much affected by position longitudinally as in the offense.

In the Middle Belt. In the middle belt the defense must be well extended, and well balanced in order that both sides may be covered with security. Always bear the wind in mind, and crowd your opponents to the leeward. This will usually mean less distance for them when they do determine to kick. In the middle belt, force your guards through sharply, and have them follow a play wherever it goes. Let your quarter be freely movable in this belt, except when otherwise governed by the rules regarding the transverse divisions. Let your full-back keep fairly in line with the ball, working a little off to his own right hand, however, as that is the probable dropping-place of the ball if kicked. In the two side belts the defense may be much less arbitrary, especially when the ball is so close to the side line that there is not room for both the end and tackle on that side of the line. Probably the most logical formation in this event is to swing the tackle over on the other side, because with the close proximity of the heavy guard to the end rusher, the latter will have no difficulty in checking any sudden push play. A clever move in this position is also the opening for the quarter and rush-line half to go through close to the centre, one on each side, the guards making the opening. This is practicable, because there is no danger of a long run on the cramped side of the field, and the rush-line half may then take unusual chances, as may also the quarter. In charging a kicker in the side belts, always crowd him on his kicking side, as that will tend to make him kick out of bounds early in his swing.

Defensive Plays in Sections 16, 17, and 18. Taking now the extreme division of the field, as in the diagram, into eighteen sections, the problems of the defense may be simplified by following these rules: In section 17, always pack your centre close, and crowd the play out to the side as much as possible. If you must get off-side, don't do it on a third down when your opponents have not succeeded in making their distance. Get your men in the line down low, and make them lift while your full-back and quarter and half keep their eyes open and heads up, ready to jump for the assaulted point, and crowd the runner over backwards while the low-lying line checks him. In sections 16 and 18, and especially when play is near the side line, place your strength out at centre and beyond, and then do your best with the whole force of that formation to pen the opponents in so that their advance must be tried on the short side of centre. If you can crowd them tight enough here, you can pen them up for three downs, and at best they will have a difficult punt-out if they do get across the line. If the score stands six to nothing in your favor, and the second half is two thirds over, fight hard for this, because they may fail to convert it, and thus leave you the winners after all. While always working yourself to make every score a six point, you should always try to force your opponents into fours or fives.

Defensive Plays in Sections 13, 14, and 15. Almost the same rules apply to sections 13, 14, and 15, as to 16, 17, and 18, except that you cannot throw up your men quite so freely into and over the line. A little more care must be observed to prevent an end run, and on third downs quarter kicks may be expected. In all six of these sections especial efforts should be made to knock the ball out of the runner's hands, if possible.

Defensive Plays in Sections 10, 11, and 12. As soon as the defense gets out into 10, 11, and 12, care should be taken, especially if the opponents have the wind, to watch for drop-kicks, or indications rather that such a kick is coming. In section 11, on a third down by the opponents, you can take great chances on the likelihood of a drop, letting only two men watch for a fake, while the rest go boldly through on the kicker. Let the two who are watching for a fake remember, however, the great possibility of a quarter-kick here also. In sections 10 and 11, the danger of a drop, while not great, is considerable, but a run around the free end or against that tackle is also to be feared. For this reason, as the play approaches the side line, the defenders should not hesitate to swing over a man, generally the tackle, as soon as the play becomes close on the side line end.

Defensive Plays in Sections 7, 8, and 9. In sections 7, 8, and 9, play with more abandon, and let the action of the line be freer, especially in the attempt to stop kicks. Occasionally an unusual play by the quarter, or even by the rush-line back, may be made here in the attempt to catch the opponents unprepared, and make them lose the ball, or so much ground as to be unable to recover it.

Defensive Plays in Sections 4, 5, and 6. With the entrance into 4, 5, and 6, screw up your line into desperate attempts to block a kick. When in either 4 or 6, and on a third down, send everybody through except the two who are getting back to receive the kick. Crowd the intending kicker down against the side line as hard as possible. Give the quarter a good chance to go straight through on him.

Defensive Plays in Sections 1, 2, and 3. In 1,2, and 3, try to keep the opponents penned up in number 2, that their full-back may be forced to kick out from between the posts, if possible. This will bother him, and may make him hit the bar or a post. As soon as the ball is as close to the opponents' goal as sections 1, 2, and 3, it is well to keep up a pretty active motion in the rush-line, not getting off-side, but rapidly shifting position in order to embarrass the play of the holders of the ball. As they are in such dangerous ground, they will naturally desire to get things rather steady, and you, being in your opponents' goal, become quite of another opinion. You should give them no chance to select a hole in your line, and no quiet in which to steady down for the kick.

CHAPTER VII

ON THE EVE OF THE BATTLE

State of Mind of Players. Whatever may be said of the ethics of it, there is no question in the mind of any man familiar with American intercollegiate rivalry, as to the willingness of the men on the contesting teams to sacrifice themselves in the contest for supremacy. There is really no hyperbole in the heading of this chapter, so far as the feelings of the men are concerned, except that, on the eve of the football match, they are thinking only of the victory or defeat, while before a real battle their thoughts might revert to the personal peril in the undertaking.

Each man is wrought up to the highest pitch. The test of skill for which he has trained for months — perhaps for more than one season — is about to be made. He is to stand before the eyes of his college, bearing its colors, and fight for them with all his skill and all his courage until the final call of time puts an end to the struggle, and leaves him — victor or vanquished? The captain has, perhaps, the most at stake, for he has his own game to play, as well as being responsible for the work of the others. We say nothing of the coach, who, with no outlet in actual play for his feelings, must endure in silence through two hours. There are the last instructions to give and the final decisions to be made, and this chapter is intended to make this a simpler and a more complete matter for captain and coach than are the usual hurried final thoughts that crowd into the mind in the rush of the last twenty-four hours.

Last Day of Practice and What Should Follow. When the team comes off the field from the last day of actual practice, the coaches and captain should assemble, and, calling the trainer and medical adviser before them, make a final decision as to the men who can be relied upon as fit, physically, to play. The days of carefully nursing — here a bad ankle, there a sprained knee — are over; there can be no more "playing him easy."

Injured Men. The men who are to go into the contest within forty-eight hours will be sent to their utmost if they once line up, and you want the best eleven, all things considered, that you can get. It may be you have to tell the captain that he isn't fit to go in. It is too bad, but such a thing must sometimes be said. The tears roll down his cheeks, perhaps, when he hears the decision, but he is a better man for the feeling that prompts them, and it is one of those cases of hard luck that come sometimes to the best of us. If it is hard to tell him, just mark these lines in this book and show them to him. He will not be the first captain who has had to bear this severe decision. As to injuries, it lies with the medical adviser and the trainer to give you the best information they can. A recent sprain may be very tightly bandaged, and a man, especially a line man, who does not need speed, can get through all right. An old sprain is less likely to be made good in this way, because from rest or further injury the limb is more or less weakened. A medical adviser must do his best for you in the sense of putting aside any question of the sensation of pain that the victim might have, while yet not jeopardizing health or a limb. The doctor, if his connection with football has been a very close one, ought to know that the patient will not feel much of anything during the game anyway. He has other things to think of, and if he himself be asked he will surely say that he is well enough to play.

Over-Trained Men. A more delicate matter comes up when there is no injury, but a player has been over-trained, and it is doubtful what he will be worth in the fever of a game. Here the decision must be governed somewhat by the exigencies of the case. If the substitute is greatly inferior, it is worth while to take some decided chances. If the coach and his advisers decide to play such a man, it is, perhaps, just as well, if he has supposed that he would not play, to let him remain in that conviction until the morning of the game. It may give him a good night's rest that he otherwise would have missed.

Possible Players. It is necessary to go over the entire list of the possible players in order that, in the later discussion as to what men shall be used, the coach and captain shall know exactly the physical fitness of every man. Lists should be made giving the sound men, the possible men, and those who are out of the question entirely. Then the last two lists should be carefully gone over once more before a final decision is rendered.

Captain at the Conference. It is a question whether the captain is absolutely needed at this meeting. Usually the captain is a man of sufficient force of character to prefer to have a voice in everything that concerns his team. But he may be over-trained himself, or, for some other reason, not be in condition to be worried with the details of this discussion. The coaches can take this off his shoulders if he so prefer. Should it be necessary, as noted above, to put the captain himself among the list of "out of the question," then the substitute field captain may attend these meetings so that he may know the condition of his men.

Second Meeting. Consideration of the Line-Up. This meeting finished, the next one — and it may be attended by the same men, though the medical adviser may leave at his option, but usually the quarter-back should be summoned to attend — is held to determine the exact line-up of the game. The lists of men as submitted by the medical adviser and trainer are read over, and the question is opened. The points to be considered that might possibly be overlooked are the question of the ground (that is, whether home grounds or not; for some players are better at home, and others when away), the probability of good or bad weather, for some players are "mud horses," while others are entirely at sea in sloppy weather and with a greasy ball, and finally, the style of play likely to be met. It is possible that the opponents have a remarkable punter who can always send the ball a long distance, and who is so much relied upon that the whole game has, perhaps, been arranged with especial regard to his work. In that case you must put in some punter who can fairly match his kicks, whether your man be a very good man otherwise or not. Whereas, if you know your opponents have only an ordinary kicker you can get along with an inferior punter, and rely upon doing more in a running game.

What Plays will be Used and When. Having then settled upon your line-up you take up the consideration of your style of game. Here get out your diagram of the field, and go carefully over the problems, discussing the chances and changes dependent upon wind, weather, or conditions of your men or of your opponents. If the last day's practice has been held at a sufficiently early hour, it may be that you have finished these discussions before bed-time in the evening. If so, it may be well to take the team into your discussion of plays. But usually it is so late that the following morning is the time for that. It will not be necessary to advise the team of the seriousness of the condition of some good player who has been counted upon, but put upon the list of "out of the question." Some teams, however, are mature enough and strong enough to face the situation, and may be told the exact condition of affairs. No matter how much there may be to discuss in these points of the line-up and the policy of play to be adopted, the whole should be settled before noon of the next day, save, perhaps, such few points as the coaches themselves decide to settle at the last moment. This will leave a good twenty-four hours of rest for the team, with their minds at ease, knowing that everything has been carefully considered and is determined upon according to the best judgment of all their advisers.

Ground Rules. Ground rules are best arranged several days before the match, if possible, for then they may enter into the calculations of the advisers in the final arrangement of plays. If, however, these rules have not been agreed upon, the officials and the captains should meet the night before the game and decide upon them, as well as the interpretation of doubtful rules. These agreements should be all drawn up in writing and signed by the umpire, and referee, and both captains. The list should be read over to the assembled team and substitutes the morning of the game, and if there be any unusual or especially important rulings these should be again read to the team when in their suits ready for the game. This duty should not be left to anybody,—coach, captain, or somebody or other. The coach should appoint some man whose sole duty it shall be to perform this office. Then it will not be forgotten. Many a good team has lost a match on a neglected, or rather forgotten, ground rule. Another man of the coaches should be appointed to see that everything concerning the uniforms is looked to and in complete repair and readiness. Not that he should personally take the shoes to the bootmaker to have the cleats renewed, or go to the tailor to have the elastic band properly fitted in the jacket and trousers, but it should be his duty to see that it is all done, and that, before ten o'clock of the morning of the game, there is not a missing part in the way of proper uniforms for all players and substitutes. It is just as well to have it understood that he report the fact to the head coach at that hour. A team upon which there is a half-back with worn-off cross-pieces may be beaten on that account, and many a team has been handicapped by some such piece of carelessness.

Selection of Officials. The officials have already been spoken of in this chapter as though they had been selected some weeks before the game, and so they are usually, and it indicates a bad state of affairs if such a matter has not been settled well in advance. Unfortunately, through disputes or disagreements, or the attempt by each side to obtain some advantage in this respect, it sometimes happens that the umpire and referee are not chosen until the very last minute. This may mean a too hasty selection, and subsequent dissatisfaction. The home team usually has something the better of it on late selections, as there is a greater chance of incompetent men deciding in favor of the home team on doubtful points; but this is by no means always the case, and a team that reckons on such an advantage is served properly if they lose the game by their own folly. Officials ought never to be picked up from the side lines on the day of a game. It hurts football and spoils sport. It is a wise plan for the coach of a team, if occasion offers, to see the umpire and referee acting in some other matches before the day of the game, because he can then instruct his team as to their methods and rulings.

Morning of the Game and Final Touches. On the morning of the game the team should be put through the signals, and the succession of substitutes not only settled, but the substitutes themselves put through the signals, and full instructions given them as to their calls in order that they may spend their time while on the side lines to the greatest advantage in watching the play of their probable opponent or opponents. A substitute tackle, for instance, when called upon in the second half, ought to be as familiar with the play of the man he is to face as is the player who is just leaving the field.

CHAPTER VIII

THE MORAL FACTORS IN AN IMPORTANT GAME

Comparison between War and Football. A comparison has often been made between the tactics of football and the theory of war. Looked at from one standpoint, the difference between the two is radical. A close study of both subjects, however, will reveal a very remarkable and interesting likeness between the theories which underlie great battles and the miniature contests on the gridiron.

It is not strictly within the scope of this book to follow out this comparison, though it might be interesting and profitable to the football coach. But in considering the moral factors in the game of football, there is much to be gained by a reference to the moral agents in war, and the value placed upon these agents by great commanders and tacticians.

Napoleon's "Three to One" Ratio. It was a maxim of Napoleon's that in war the "moral" is to the "physical" in the ratio of three to one. This ratio of the moral and the physical is doubtless equally great in the game of football. It remains to be discovered just what these moral agents in football are, and this discovery cannot be made in any better way than by continuing the analogy a little farther, and briefly enumerating the moral agents in war. McPherson, in his "Theory of War," clearly points out these moral forces, and we cannot do better than adopt his classification, referring at the same time to the parallels in the sport of football.

The Moral Agents in War. The moral agencies in war might be classed under four heads: —

(1) The Personal Qualities of the Commander-in-Chief. His knowledge of human nature; his power of influencing men through their hopes, fears, passions, interests, or prejudices; his ability to gain the love and confidence of his troops; his coolness, self-reliance, and readiness of resource in emergencies; with other qualities of a similar nature.

Coming now to the game of football, we find the correlative of these qualities in quarter-back generalship; in the influence of the captain over his men; in his reputation for coolness; in the comprehension of field tactics; in his self-reliance, and readiness of resource in all emergencies; and in the power of his last appeals to his team. These are all properly moral agents. If the captain does not possess them, the coach must do all he can to supply the deficiency both to the captain and to the team. It is better, of course, that they should be possessed by the captain himself, but in no case should they be overlooked, or their value underestimated.

The Qualifications of Generalship. On this subject let us quote the exact words of Napoleon: —

"The first quality of a general-in-chief is to have a cool head, which receives only a just impression of objects. He should not allow himself to be dazzled either by good or bad news. The sensations which he receives, successively or simultaneously, in the course of a day, should be classed in his memory so as to only occupy the just place due to each; for reason and judgment are the resultant of the correct comparison of many sensations. There are some men who, on account of their physical and moral constitution, make a single picture for themselves out of every event; whatever knowledge, wit, courage, and other qualities they may possess, nature has not called them to the command of armies, and the direction of great military operations."

Detecting the Critical Moment. Famous generals have all shared this opinion of Napoleon's. It must not be forgotten that in every battle there is a decisive point, and a decisive moment (which, once let slip, never returns), on which, and at which, every disposable horse, man, and gun should be brought into action. The problem is to correctly appreciate that point and time, and know when it arrives. The commander who anticipates the decisive moment, and brings forward his reserves too soon, is lost. The personal qualities before enumerated are manifested in their highest degree by the faculty of correctly determining this decisive moment. The knowledge of when, where, and how to make an attack is the critical thing which distinguishes great generalship, whether in war or football.

(2) Stratagems. The object of a stratagem in war is to deceive the enemy as to your designs. To illustrate this in its simplest form, if a commander desired a general action, he would spread reports of the weakness of his army, and appear to avoid one. If, on the contrary, he did not desire a general action, he would put on a bold face and appear desirous to engage.

Strategy in war finds its parallel in football in the various plays and formations designed and employed by the team. It is not enough that a team should depend upon the simple formations already so familiar to the average opponent that he can tell, with reasonable certainty, the nature of the attack, and where it is to be made in the line. With equal certainty he has probably been coached on exactly how to repel that form of attack. To depend upon this simple form of offense is to voluntarily ignore one of the most valuable weapons in football — namely, strategy. [1]

Force of Strategy in Football. It is a great thing in football to keep your opponents guessing. Properly, they ought never to be permitted to so successfully "size up" the impending play that they are able to move headlong into the defense of their own position, without a doubt of the nature of the attack. You should always work upon your opponents, not merely with muscle, but with brain. Your operations should demand of them that, at one and the same time, they exercise equally their minds and their bodies.

How difficult this may become, at critical moments, many of our readers can realize by experience. With your own players thoroughly skilled in their attack, and not needing to enter upon it with any doubt or uncertainty, but with, a concentration of mind and body both upon the one desired result, they are, theoretically, in a position of distinct advantage over the opponents, whose physical movements must wait upon their mental processes. The moment that you present to your opponents a form of play so simple as to ignore the necessity of a mental impression after the attack is begun, — in other words, so simple as to make it possible for them to readily predicate what the movement is to be, — you lose the advantage just mentioned, and their defense may, without extreme risk, be fully as precipitate as your attack.

---

[1] The use of the word "strategy" in connection with football operations is never technically correct. Strategy can only be applied to the movements which are made when no enemy is in sight. The moment that the enemy is in sight, the proper term for such operations is "tactics." However, inasmuch as, in football, the opponents are always in sight, the use of the word "strategy" is technically impossible. It is only used in this connection by virtue of the license which it has obtained from repeated use, by other writers, in the last two or three years.

(3) The Elation or Depression of the Soldiers. This may arise from any cause — from former defeats or victories; from the health or sickness of the troops; from confidence or distrust in the commander, etc.

The correspondent of this in football is the prestige of the team, or the college which the team represents; the spirit which is infused into the players by a realization of the issue; most important of all, the attainment of a right degree of confidence which never distrusts itself or the final result, yet stops just short of that over confidence which is so harmful.

(4) Information, and the Means of Obtaining It. This would mean in war the knowledge of the country, its topography and resources, its roads and turnpikes, its rivers and railways, its storehouses and factories, its people and their temper, etc. It would also involve accurate intelligence of the enemy's movements, without which the greatest military talent is useless. The faculty of organizing a system of intelligence is a prominent quality of a great commander in war.

One may draw the parallel between this intelligence and the intelligence required in football, by pointing out to the experienced coach the necessity of a thorough apprehension of the rules by every one of his players, and the ability to act instinctively upon this information, which will only come to the player when his information is well-grounded and thoroughly assimilated by him. His knowledge of the rules must be more than skin deep. If it is a "cramming" of the last few weeks, it can profit him little in the direction which we are indicating. It is not football knowledge which is so valuable to the player as football instinct, and by this is meant the certain ability to act intuitively and automatically upon the knowledge he possesses, doing the right thing at the right time, regardless of any previous specific coaching upon the point in question. No two games of football can ever be quite alike. The situations which constantly arise cannot be entirely apprehended and provided for by the coach in his instructions. The players must meet many emergencies, armed with no other weapon than their football instinct, and this can only come by an absorption of the rules and foundation principles of the playing game.

Explanation of Many Defeats. It is these qualities, then, combined together, which represent the moral factors in football, and it is, perhaps, not conceding too much to admit that the ratio between the moral and the physical in war, as determined by Napoleon, may also be established between these moral factors in football and the mere physical factor of force or strength.

Too often the public forms its estimates of probable results from the physical factors which are visible rather than from the moral factors which are invisible. They do not see the moral forces which are being employed by the master-hand behind the scenes. This "three to one" power is responsible for many seemingly inexplicable defeats. Correspondents of the press, and the unreasoning partisans of a defeated team raise the cry of "luck" in football. Obviously there is a percentage of luck in the game, just as there is luck in any of the situations of life. But football games are not won or lost by luck, except in very rare instances. What appears to be luck is inevitably some one of the moral qualities here enumerated, which, carefully nurtured by one coach, and perhaps unapprehended or unappreciated by the opponents, proves to be the turning-point in the contest.

The two teams may have been developed along exactly similar lines; to the ordinary observer, and by the tests of ordinary comparison, they are developed to an approximately equal state of efficiency. Yet these two teams play together through a series of years with the result of one of the two teams continually winning, and the other continually losing. The public, naturally anxious to know the reason for this, is full of inquiries: *"Are they not practically the same young men, brought from the same schools? Are they not of the same age, and is it not a matter of mere chance whether they attend one college or the other?"* The answer to this question may be read between the lines of this chapter. It is not the difference in strength or the difference in skill. Neither is it by a preponderance of instruction given to one team. Frequently we find, upon examination, that the eleven best players would comprise five from one team and six from the other. It is not always the increased knowledge of the principles of team play. The difficulty lies, too often, in the moral forces here enumerated. It is for this reason that the subject has been given the importance of a separate chapter.

CHAPTER IX

IMPROVED SIGNALING

The Use of Signals in Football. Every attempt to advance the ball is ordered by a private signal called, usually, by the quarter-back, and consisting of numbers or letters. It is, of course, understood only by the team itself which is making the play. A team which is on the defensive uses no signals.

Recent Changes in Signals. Signals are a very important part of football operations, as they are carried on in the present game. With each successive year there is a tendency on the part of the leading teams to simplify and abridge the signals used, and in the important contests of to-day the spectator seldom hears the long string of numbers which were deemed a necessary accompaniment of the game half a dozen years ago. At the same time the work covered by the signals is being increased, and great benefits have been gained recently by extending the operation of the signals so that they cover, not merely the ordering of the play, but the speed with which it shall start, or the moment when the ball shall be snapped.

Use of Two Codes. Two codes of signals are properly required for the work of a college team during a season: the first should be the practice code, to be used in practice and in minor games; the second, the final code, to be used in the important contests.

In the first set the need is principally for signals which can be, with very little difficulty, altered from day to day, so that the college eleven may not become familiar with them. Every coach will testify that an afternoon's practice is twice as valuable if the second eleven is unacquainted with the signals. It is not necessary that the system should be changed, but only that the key or pass-word which unlocks the system shall be altered from day to day, and it is possible to so arrange such a system of signals that they may be perfectly confusing to the opponents, and yet readily explained, with scarcely a moment's delay, to any substitute who may be called upon to fill a vacant place during the afternoon's practice.

Choice of Many Styles. In adopting a set of signals a choice may be made between a great many different styles. There may be word signals, phrase signals, letter or number signals. The latter may be still further subdivided into number signals based on addition, on odd or even terminals, on subtraction, and on combinations of different digits.

It is not the purpose of this book to prescribe any one series of signals. The very publicity given to a set of signals by their publication in book form would compel certain changes before they could be adopted in an important match. It is rather the object of this chapter to suggest the lines along which signals may be worked out; first stating clearly the advantages and disadvantages of different sets of signals, the possibilities of extreme simplicity in the combinations, and the methods of conveying added information, without multiplying numbers.

What is Really Needed. The important point in any set of signals is that they shall be as clear to the team which uses them as they are unintelligible to its opponents. To these two necessities there may be added a few other desirable qualifications. The signals should be capable of being quickly and surely handled by the quarter-back; they should be as short as possible, to the end that they may not slow down the play. Single digits are always better, other things being equal, than double numbers, since the single digit can be called with a snap and vim which communicates a certain quickness to the action of the team.

Two Sets in One Game. One often hears the advice given that no team should go into a match without a reserve set of signals to be used in the event of the regular signals being discovered by the opponents. As a matter of fact, very few teams could prepare two sets of signals for any important match without finding the remedy to be more hazardous than the original danger. A better system is for the team to have recourse, in such a case, to the regular set of signals which it has used in its practice during the season, and which can always be fallen back upon with a reasonable degree of security.

As previously stated, the tendency in the modern game is toward a simplification of the signals; and it is not too much to expect that we shall, within a very few years, find our leading teams playing with no spoken signals except at rare intervals, the play being directed by signs, and the use of sequences of plays previously committed to memory, and played very rapidly, without signal of any sort after the first call has been given.

We shall later refer to the advisability of employing one such sequence of plays at certain critical stages in the game. Before touching upon this, however, let us take up the subject of signals proper, and show a few codes which may suggest the possibilities of lines along which signals may be framed.

A Good Method of Numbering the Holes. Starting, then, with a simple set of signals for the use of a school team, let us suppose the various holes in the line to be numbered as follows: —

No. 1 hole, — Around your own right end.
No. 2 hole, — The first hole inside your right end.
No. 3 hole, — The second hole inside your right end.
No. 4 hole, — The second hole on the right of your centre rush.
No. 5 hole, — The first hole on the right of your centre rush.
No. 6 hole, — The first hole on the left of your centre rush.
No. 7 hole, — The second hole on the left of your centre rush.
No. 8 hole, — The second hole inside your left end.
No. 9 hole, — The first hole inside your left end.
No. 10 hole, — Around your left end.

The object of this elaborate enumeration is to prevent a possible misunderstanding in the event of a rush-line back playing in the line beside the tackle, or a quarter-back moving in between the guard and centre, while the guard moves out. Unless some provision has been made for such a contingency, there will be a doubt in the minds of some of your team whether the hole is to be on the outside or the inside of the extra man, or, in other words, whether the extra man is to be thrown out or in. This little uncertainty may suffice to ruin the success of the play. By employing such a system of hole numbering as is here shown, the error is guarded against. For example, if no extra man has stepped into the line, and the hole number is indicated by the signal 3, it will be between guard and tackle; if it is indicated by 4, it will also be between guard and tackle. If, on the other hand, the quarter-back has stepped up into the line between the centre and guard, and the guard has moved out, hole No. 4 would be between the quarter-back and the guard, while hole No. 5 would be between the centre and the quarter.

The Signal Completed. With this system of hole numbering committed to memory, the signal itself is very easily supplied. It may be the first or second digit of the first or second number in the signal, and the signal may consist of three sets of double numbers (or three sets of numbers each having two digits). In such a set of signals the quarter-back should use finger signals to indicate the runner, and a kick may be indicated by a double number of the same digits at the finish of the signal (as 22, 33, 44, etc.). Do not put the kick signal where the hole number is indicated in a simple set of this nature.

Arranging to Add a Starting Number. A very easy addition to this set of signals for an emergency would be to suddenly increase the number of numbers, and instead of using three sets only of two digits each, to use eight or nine double numbers, and let the play start instantly upon the calling of the first double number over sixty. The intermediate numbers after the calling of the signal and before the calling of the first double number over sixty, may be either single or double numbers. Thus, for example, suppose the second digit of the first number to be the hole number, and that the play started on the calling of the first number over sixty, the signal might be as follows: "27, 36, 33, 9, 5, 6, 7, 49, 65," — and the play would be off with a rush.

Another Set Illustrated. Another simple set of signals might be based upon a different numbering of the holes, and would be arranged as follows: —

No. 1 hole, — Outside end.
No. 2 hole, — First hole outside tackle.
No. 3 hole, — First hole outside guard.
No. 4 hole, — First hole outside centre.

If the key number at the end of the signal was an odd number, it would mean that the right side of the line was referred to, but if it was an even number, it would mean that the hole was on the left side of the centre. The set of signals might be composed of four single digits; the difference between the first and second digits would be the hole number. The third digit would have no meaning whatever, and the fourth digit, if it was odd, would mean that the hole was on the right side of the centre, in the position as signaled, and if it was even, that the hole was on the left side of the centre in the position as signaled.

Thus the signal 2, 5, 8, 1, would mean that the play was in hole 5 less 2, or hole 3, which is the hole first outside of your guard's position, and the last number being an odd number, you would understand that it was the right guard.

With this set of signals it would still be necessary to employ finger signals for the runner. A kick would be signaled by the fact that there was no difference between the first and second numbers, as 6, 6, 3, 1. It may be argued for such a simple series that the signal for the kick was too transparent, and indeed it would be. It will not be difficult, however, to devise some additional means of signaling for a kick, which shall make it impossible for the opponents to decide with any accuracy how the kick is ordered.

A Combination on One Double Number only. A good set of signals of a very simple sort, composed of only one double number, with suitable additions to screen it from the opponents, may be made up as follows (using the same numbering of the holes as described in the last set of signals). Let the first digit be the hole number, and the second digit designate the side of the line on which the play is to be ordered. If the second digit is odd, it is on the right side of the line; if even, on the left side of the line. A double number of the same digits would be the signal for a kick; finger signal for the runner. In all the sets we have thus far considered, the formation of the line-up must be separately announced before calling the signal.

With this last set of signals it would be possible to confine the signal to three sets of double numbers, of which the first and last would mean nothing; the middle, to be composed of two digits, would indicate by the first digit the number of the hole, and by the second digit whether the hole was on the right or left of the line. If this second digit was a double number it would mean a kick. Thus 47, 39, 12, would mean that the play was just outside your right guard. So simple a set as this could never be used against experienced players.

A Combination on One Letter only. A set which is not difficult, but may yet be very confusing to the opponents, can be composed of letters in such a way that one single letter alone is needed to convey the signal. The set is based upon the visualization of the lower-case letters of the alphabet, as they appear in writing (*not printing*), and the designation of the hole would be conveyed as follows: Any vowel stands for a play around the end. A consonant with no extension above or below the line (as c, m, n, r, s, v, w, z) would mean the hole between end and tackle; any consonant having an upward loop (as b, d, h, 1, t) would mean the hole between tackle and guard; any consonant having a downward loop (as g, q, y) would mean the hole between guard and centre; any consonant having both an upward and downward loop (as f, j, p), would indicate a kick. The formation would be called by the quarter-back before the signal, and there would be a finger signal for the runner.

The right or left hand side of the line might be indicated in a variety of ways; a second letter might be called which, if it was further along in the alphabet than the first letter, would indicate a play on the right side of the line, but if it was nearer the head of the alphabet than the first letter, or, in other words, if the letters were given reading backwards from their usual order, the play would be on the left side of the line.

A Well-Concealed System Illustrated. Another set of signals, which lacks a little the element of brevity, but is cleverly covered up from the comprehension of the opponents, would be based on a numbering of the holes as explained in the first set of signals here given, where the openings are numbered from 1 to 10, and provision is made for ten different openings in the line. One digit only is needed to designate the hole in such a system, and this would be the first digit of the first number following any number under 20. Thus, for example, 67, 83, 55, 19, 27, 4, 6, 5, would indicate that the play was the first hole inside your own right end. The same play might have been indicated by the signal 1, 2. By this set of signals a kick would be indicated in the signal by the absence of any number under 20. Thus, 65, 47, 23, 84, 71, would call for a kick.

Example of Practice Signals with a Changeable Key. We have already mentioned the advisability of a set of signals based upon a certain key or countersign, which may be changed from day to day, while the system remains the same. Such a set of signals is an excellent one for use in the earlier practice of the season, for by changing the countersign or key-number each day, it is possible to successfully mystify the opponents during the short interval of practice.

A very good set of this nature can be made up as follows: — the quarter-back calling the formation before the signal is given, and indicating by his fingers who the runner is to be. Let the hole be the first digit of the first number following any number in the twenties. Thus, for example, 53, 96, 17, 28, 45, 6, 9, 3, would signal for hole 4, since it was the first digit of the first number following the first number in the twenties. With such a series it would be well to employ the numbering of the holes which provides for ten holes for the runner, and includes both sides of the line, leaving it unnecessary to signal that the play is to go on the right or left of the centre.

If such a set was used as here given on the first afternoon of practice, it might be changed, on the second afternoon, by establishing the key, as any number in the fifties, or any number under twenty, or any number in the thirties over 34, but not under 34; on the next afternoon it might be shifted by making the hole number not the first digit, but the second digit, of the first number following the key number. If the key was any number in the forties, for example, and the hole number was the second digit of the first number following any number in the forties, hole No. 1 might be signaled for as follows: 13, 6, 89, 49, 31, 77.

The changes of the key number and the number of the digit which designates the hole, may be so endlessly continued that a single set of signals of this nature is all that is needed by both elevens during the early weeks of the season. When the use of double numbers has been so far employed as to exhaust the seeming resources, triple numbers may be employed, or the key number may be located as between two other numbers; for example, instead of saying that the key number was any number in the thirties, let it be put as any number between 35 and 45, and thus further complicate the system when it has become too familiar.

Example of an Advanced Set for an Important Contest. We have so far given only those signals which provide for the calling of the formation in advance of the signal, and the giving of a separate finger signal to the runner. Let us now study one elaborate set of signals, showing how much may be conveyed by the calling of three or four single digits. We will use for this set the enumeration of the holes as first given, with allowances for ten places in the line at which the runner may emerge.

We now number each formation from one to twelve, beyond which number it is not best to go, and, indeed there are few teams who ought to enter an important game with as many as twelve different line-ups.

(The advantage of not going beyond twelve is that we are endeavoring to confine this set of signals to three numbers which can be pronounced with the greatest speed, and we must avoid extra syllables. Eleven and twelve are each pronounced hurriedly as one syllable. But the moment we enter upon thirteen we have a number which must be called as two syllables, and which is, therefore, somewhat clumsy to use in signaling. This objection applies to all the numbers between twelve and twenty; it is, therefore, best to limit the line-up number to twelve, if possible.)

We will compose the signal of three single numbers, none of them over twelve; each signal is to be called at least twice. Each different line-up or initial formation is to be designated by a number, and this number is to be the first of the three numbers in the signal.

The second number indicates the hole, if a regular formation is used, or the number of the outlet, if the formation is a "special" formation, radically different from the customary line-up. This change of the second number by means of which we use it at one time to designate the hole in the regular notation, and again to designate the number of a play in a special series or line-up, is adopted in order to prevent the opponents from singling out any number in the simple series of three digits, which shall always be the hole number. It would manifestly be the most serious of all mishaps if the opponents were able to detect the scheme of the hole number. Where a single set of three digits is employed, the hole number must clearly be one of these three, and it would not require much effort on the part of a bright man to pick it out. On the other hand, the use of this second number, alternately as the hole number and as the number of a play in a particular series of plays from the same line-up, is just sufficient to confuse the opponents and prove conclusively to them that they do not know the system by which the hole is designated.

The third figure in the signal is to be a "speeder," or a signal to indicate the rapidity with which the play is to be executed. If this third figure is 3, 6, 9, or 12, the play is to be made instantly upon the beginning of the second calling of the signal. If it is any other figure under twelve, the play is to start when the ball goes, and not before, and the ball is to go back in the ordinary way.

The calling of the hole number, as 10, 11, or 12, would indicate a kick, and if the play was a drop-kick, it would doubtless have a special formation for its protection, and would be called, not as the hole number of a regular formation, but as the series number of a special formation. No formation need be called, and the opponents lose the advantage of hearing the formation designated.

A few examples of this set of signals will make their working clearer. Let us suppose that we have a series of formations as follows: —

Nos. 1, 2, 3, 4, Simpler formations, to be signaled by hole numbers.

No. 5 - Ends back.

No. 6 - Left end over.

No. 7 - Tandem formation at tackle.

No. 8 - Trick play for side line.

No. 9 - Trick play, long pass.

No. 10 - Special formation for criss-cross.

No. 11 - Special formation for protection of drop-kick.

Formations Nos. 1, 2, 3, and 4 would indicate by their second number the hole in the line, according to the regular system of numbering. The other formations would indicate by their second number the number of the play in the series having that especial line-up. Thus 3, 9, 6, the formation would be a regular formation; the play would be just inside the left end, and the play would be made instantly on the conclusion of the second calling of the signal. 5, 2, 4, the formation would be ends back; the play would be the second play in the series from that formation, and it would not start until the ball came in the regular way. 10, 1, 3, the formation would be the special formation for a criss-cross; the play would be the first play of that series, and it would be made instantly on the finishing of the second calling of the signal.

Individual Preferences of Players. Enough has been given here on the subject of signals to indicate the possibilities of the situation. One last point: adapt the signals to the team. Some teams will take more readily to one set of signals than to another. There are teams which cannot seem to handle a signal that requires subtraction; there are other teams which will positively rebel at the use of any letters in a signal. Yet these teams will find not the slightest difficulty with a more complicated set of signals based on numbers alone. As a rule, teams do not like signals based on both numbers and letters, and they are very apt to give numbers the preference over any other form of signal.

Quick Sequences without Signal. Before closing this chapter we want to revert to the subject of sequences of plays, where different movements are executed without signal, the order of the movements having previously been committed to memory. The use of the word "sequences" is here meant to cover any plays, not necessarily from the same line-up. A team which has had no previous experience in sequences had better limit their use to a single sequence of three plays. They should be three of the strongest plays which the team can employ, and the object of the sequence is to play them without signals, to the end that they may be sent away with the greatest speed, and without waiting for special information by signal after the usual method.

If the sequence is composed of three plays, the first one may be a dash around the end, the second may be between tackle and guard, and the third between tackle and guard on the other side of the line. Whatever they are, they should be constantly practised as a series of three movements, without any intermission or pause, and without any instructions from the quarter-back between the different movements. It goes without saying that the team must be able to line up before their opponents in every one of these manoeuvres. In fact, quickness in lining up is the vital necessity in all sequences. It is of little use to employ a sequence, or to waste time in committing to memory the order of any plays, unless the team, to a man, shall line up almost before the runner is off the ground.

The Signaling for a Sequence. The best method of signaling a sequence varies according to the nature of the system of signals which may be employed. One method would be to let the first number be a separate number entirely apart from the signal itself, letting it be a single digit under 10, and always followed by a decided pause before the rest of the signal is given. If the signal proper was 9, 5, 2, and it was desired to signal for a special sequence, it might be called as follows: 12— 9, 5, 2. In this case 9, 5, 2 would, of necessity, be the first play in the arranged sequence, and the calling of the figure 12—with a pause — would signify that three plays were to be played, following each other in the most rapid manner, and without any further signal.

It is well to construct a sequence for use inside the opponents' twenty-five-yard line, and in the making up of a set of signals it will be necessary to provide for it in their construction.

CHAPTER X

TRAINING

Training a Systematic Preparation. Training is a preparation. If the captain and coach can keep this fully in mind far fewer mistakes will be made and the tales of teams going to pieces in the middle of a season will be much less frequent. As a rule, a team has but one or two great games, toward which the management looks as the real end of all the striving. These matches come at the last of the season, usually within a week or ten days of one another. In many instances there is but one really great game. It may be argued that this is unfortunate from a theoretical standpoint, and that, as football is only a sport, the interest should be to get as much amusement out of the season as possible, and from this view every game should be an occasion for simple enjoyment. In this book it is not our purpose to dwell upon the ethics of college sport, but to treat the game of football exactly as it is, rather than as it might be in Arcadia.

To Produce the Best Play of which the Team is Capable. The preparation, then, with us is directed toward placing a team in the field upon the occasion of final contest in such a physical condition as shall insure their playing the best game of which, as individuals and as a team, they can be made capable. With broken-down pugilists of the past the methods were severe. It was believed that in severity of training lay the safety of condition. Possibly there was some truth in this, but probably even in these cases and in the old days more would have been accomplished by less heroic measures. However that may be, the case of the average collegian is not one for violent initial overturning of ordinary customs.

Gradual and Temperate. The more gradual the preparation, the safer and the more certain the final result. But there is much to be considered in this connection. It will not do to begin the preparation of football candidates in June, and work them gradually but steadily through July, August, September, and October. If that plan be pursued, it will be found that the mental effect of such prolonged preparatory labor has been to make the players tired of the game, and, of all sports, football needs the most fire and dash. Physically, if the preparation has been very temperate, the players may be all right, but they are sick of the game mentally. The first thought, then, to engage the attention of the coach, is when to begin the training. Some contend for a little preparatory work in the spring, followed by a long summer's rest, with occasional work on specialties, and this is, undoubtedly, a good plan for the kickers of a team. But outside of this, and in the case of the general run of men, it is best to wait until September before engaging in anything like the work of training.

Age a Factor. The age, too, of the candidates is an important feature, young players being especially liable to overtraining, and requiring much attention even in a short period of practice. A team in one of our big universities is almost always sure to have one or two men of but seventeen or eighteen, and these should be watched with especial care. Even at the outset, such men should be played only every other day, and generally handled in a far different manner from the hardened veteran of twenty-four or twenty-five.

Work of the Kickers. The early work of the kickers is treated in a separate chapter, but it is right to say here, that practice in punting and drop kicking should be short in hours and extended over a longer season than any of the rest of the work. The kickers of a team, or rather the candidates for positions likely to require kicking ability, should be men who have already had practice of a preliminary nature either at a preparatory school, or, at any rate, before becoming probable 'Varsity men. A one-season kicker is seldom satisfactory, either in point of length of kick, ability to "get in" his kick under trying circumstances, or accuracy of performance. We must suppose, then, as we do usually in the case of candidates for battery positions on a 'Varsity nine, that of the kickers the men we expect to handle have already placed themselves above the level of mere beginners. They should then be given some spring practice, and it is not a bad idea to stimulate this by the offer of prizes for superiority. At nearly all the universities this plan has been tried with more or less success. We say "more or less" advisedly, because the usual winner of such competitions is not the most serviceable kicker for a team, and is frequently a man who may fail utterly to make a place for himself. The difficulty of devising methods of scoring in this kicking competition has something to do with this. A combination of distance, accuracy, and quickness should be the desired achievement and the winning one.

Preliminary Practice. After the spring work there will be some few men who, perhaps, have no other athletic interest than football. These men may continue occasional practice. But the majority of men, with the varied interests now furnished in the athletic line, are apt to be taking up something on the track, or the diamond, or in the boats. For this reason, any concerted practice may just as well be dispensed with. The men should, however, be called together before the beginning of the long summer vacation, and each man should receive a ball. Nor is this enough to insure the proper amount of kicking practice during the summer. Each man should be urged to make certain promises regarding the work he will do. The average man will mean well, and will, on the first day that he thinks of it, and can get some one to chase the ball or take an interest in his punting, kick himself lame and tire out his muscles, and then drop it all for some weeks, only to do the same thing when, a month later, the sight of the ball pricks his conscience. There is no use in making drudgery of it, but a man ought to kick twice or three times a week during the summer, and only a short time, but with attention to good form and accuracy. By the latter part of August the kickers should kick every day, and spend a week together at some rendezvous before assembling once more at college for the fall work. The centres and quarters may be included in this meeting to good advantage, the quarters especially for practice, and the centres because they are apt to be soft and fat, and need the additional work. At this week of practice, the kickers can get work of especial value, in that their punting can be done from a pass from the quarter, and also because in the presence of so many kickers there is plenty of practice in catching. During this week, one or more coaches should be on hand — not the general coach, but the man or men who have charge of the kicking, and the work of the backs. As for the rest of the team, unless some revolution in methods of play may be necessary, there is no need of summer practice. It may be the case that a team, owing to lack of coaching or mistaken ideas, may have dropped entirely out of its class and only discovered the blunder in the final games of a season. Then a revolution is necessary, and in such a case it may happen that summer practice, while in itself really an evil in the case of a properly drilled team, may be, in their case, a practical necessity, owing to the immense amount of work involved in assimilating new methods.

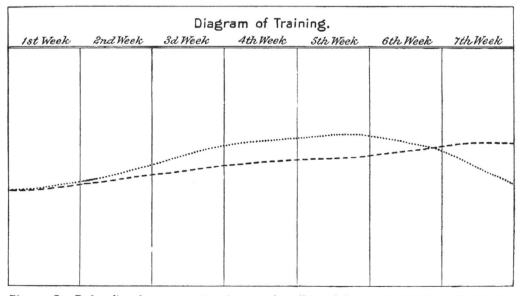

Diagram J. — Broken line shows course that the general condition of the men should follow. Dotted line indicates the usual course.

Opening Fall Campaign and Safeguards Against Accidents. This brings us to the opening of the fall season proper, with the assembling of the players on the field after the term begins. Here, no matter how much general training may have been practised by the individual during the late summer, there is the greatest need of caution. In spite of all the care that may be taken, there are almost sure to be some injuries in the early days of practice. This is due to a variety of causes; to the bad condition of the grounds, to the impact with green men, in a measure, as well as to the incentive to unusual endeavor in the excitement of making a good showing. Every man feels that he is on trial, as he may be a candidate for the 'Varsity team, and only those who have been through it realize how a boy's heart may be set on achieving this honor. But a coach can do no more than to take every precaution, and then the chances are that he will get through these trying days with nothing worse than sprains that will mend before a month is over. His first precaution should be to see that the ground is in good condition, that it is well rolled and free from holes and hummocks. He should then see that every one of his promising men have their leather ankle supporters on. Finally, he should use three men behind the 'Varsity line who understand each other, and the simple signals, or else use no one of his best men there. On the first day or two the playing of a green man and two old men may result in accident to one of the good players through mistaken signals.

Duration of Practice. The actual duration of the lineup playing on the first few days should be hardly over five minutes twice repeated. We will assume that this is the last week in September. The time should be kept at five minute line-ups for a week, and then be extended to one ten minute, and one, or on cool days two five-minute periods. After another week, two ten-minute line-ups may be indulged in, and by the end of October stretched out to fifteen or twenty. Match practice games at this time in a season should be limited to two fifteen-minute halves, or a twenty and a fifteen, if the day is cool. By November, if the weather is at all seasonable, the players should be able to stand once or twice a week a second half of twenty-five minutes, after a short first half of ten minutes.

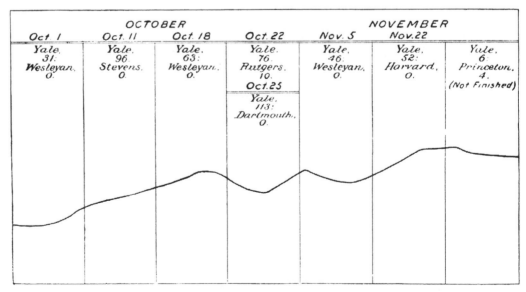

Diagram K. — Yale Team of 1884. Very irregular ; too early development followed by a " slump " in mid-season, with partial recovery. This was comparatively a veteran team.

It is well to bear in mind the fact that two days of hard playing ought not to come together, unless purely for the sake of discipline, as, for instance, in the case of a team that has been "babyed" too much and needs a lesson to show them that hard work doesn't kill anybody.

Detail of Training. We have briefly outlined the course to be followed with the average football team, so far as the amount of work that may be expected of them is concerned. Now, as to general condition; the four agents that effect that equilibrium which we call health may be grouped as exercise, diet, sleep, and cleanliness. So far as the limits of this chapter are concerned, we may say that the first of these agents has been discussed sufficiently in the directions as to the limits of practice.

Diet. The next agent, diet, brings us to a question of more or less personal idiosyncrasy, but fortunately, in the case of the candidates for a football team, we have in the main a set of men of normal stomach, and whose physical peculiarities, if at all pronounced, lie in an almost abnormal ability to eat and digest anything. Naturally there will be, here and there, an exception, but the majority are in that happy condition of not knowing that they have stomachs or livers, or any of those possessions that many find, later in life and under violations of the laws of health, are of such importance.

Hours for Meals. In spite, however, of the fact that little goes amiss with our candidates in the way of food, it is well to be on the safe side, and to consider what foods are most conducive to satisfactory assimilation, and, what is fully as important, the best time for taking these foods into the system. Briefly, breakfast should be from seven to eight; the midday meal preferably about one o'clock, and surely not later than that, and the evening repast should be soon after six. Under these conditions, the practice should be from ten to eleven in the forenoon, and at some interval between three and five in the afternoon. Much variation of these hours for practice should be followed by a similar change in the hours of meals, two to three hours elapsing after eating before the violent effort, and an hour of rest succeeding before sitting down to the table. In certain

OCTOBER				NOVEMBER		
Oct. 10	Oct. 14	Oct. 28	Oct. 31	Nov. 14	Nov. 21	Nov. 25
Yale, 55: Stevens. 0.	Yale, 18: Wesleyan, 0.	Yale, 71: Wesleyan, 0.	Yale, 51: Technology. 0.	Yale. 53: Penn. 5	Yale, 5: Princeton, 6.	Yale: 61: Wesleyan, 0.

Diagram L. — Team of 1885 at Yale. A green team, composed of new men almost without exception. (Peters' team.) Most consistent progress. Met a veteran Princeton team, and although supposably out-classed, played a remarkable game, losing by one point.

cases the hours of recitation or lecture in a university are such as to make some changes in this arrangement necessary. In that event, make the best of it, but conform as nearly as possible. Under no circumstances venture the experiment of permitting hard play too near a hearty meal. We have seen one of the strongest men incapacitated temporarily, and for a time it was feared quite seriously affected by such an injudicious plan. This man was a rugged fellow of over one hundred and ninety pounds in weight, strong and robust, who, under a physical examination by a physician, had been pronounced absolutely sound. He was trying for the 'Varsity, and, as a new man, had not been taken to training-table, but was boarding at a house where it was afterwards learned the midday meal was served at half past one. At that time the practice began soon after two o'clock. The result was that this man ate very heartily at half past one, and then went on the field at two. In spite of this his play was strong, and it was some days before there was any reason to suspect anything wrong. The man, in some marvelous way, seemed able to retain the food, or there would have been an indication of the difficulty. One day he came over in citizen's clothes, and was asked what was the matter. He said that he had concluded to give it up. Pressed for the reason, he said he thought there was something wrong with his heart. He was taken over at once for another examination, and the physician reported him as showing no signs of any organic trouble; however, there might be some irritability, according to the man's account, and it was decided to watch him. After a few days' observation, the doctor hit upon the trouble when he learned the time of his dinner. This corrected, the man speedily came into shape.

Kind of Food and How Served. As to the kinds of food best suited for the training-table, they are unquestionably, for stand-bys, beef and mutton in the way of meats, toast and stale bread, vegetables and fruits in moderation, and water. Football diet may be far more liberal without error than that of certain other athletes, and the addition of eggs, occasionally, fish, provided it can be secured in an absolutely fresh condition, oatmeal, and plain puddings, are perfectly allowable. It would seem unnecessary to go into further particulars, but

Diagram **M**. — Too early development. Yale team of 1887. A high scoring team, but irregular in defense in November.

experience has satisfied us that it is advisable to take up the detail of this matter with far more care. It is no exaggeration to state that a team fed upon the above foods may go entirely out of condition, owing merely to the cooking or the service of the food. Therefore, let us say at the outset that the food should be well cooked, appetizing, and served in a tempting fashion. The meats are best broiled or roasted. In spite of a prejudice against warmed-over meats for men in training, an occasional *réchauffée* is by no means to be entirely condemned, as it makes an agreeable change when attractively cooked. Boiling is not so satisfactory a method of cooking as roasting, but not to be entirely tabooed. Frying is not well suited as a means of cooking meat or anything else for men in training, although an occasional fried egg, if free from grease, is not likely to be injurious, and is a most agreeable change from the more flabby boiled and poached article.

Vegetables. It is sometimes asked what vegetables may, with advantage, be added to the menu of the training-table. They are as follows: Potatoes, onions, spinach, asparagus, cooked celery, artichokes, French beans, and the like. Unfortunately, in the East it is impossible to get all these fresh in the season of football, and canned food of all kinds should be avoided because it is sometimes in a condition to be injurious. Peas are not to be recommended, because usually "bolted," that is, not sufficiently masticated, by the men. If they are all crushed on the plate with the fork, that difficulty is avoided.

Drinks. Upon the question of drinks there is a wide difference of opinion. As a rule, water is sufficiently satisfying. Milk agrees with some men, but is just as well let alone by the majority when in training. Iced tea is not a good thing, although it is much fancied. Mild hot tea is to be preferred to this, but it is better to bar both tea and coffee. Ale to men "going fine" is quite right, but only once a week to those who are in condition, and then only after a hard day. To return then to water. Oatmeal water is the common form for service at our football training-tables, and it is the best regular beverage. Bearing upon this point of drinks, and showing the advisability of moderation, is the case of a

DIVIDED BY PERIODS, NOT BY WEEKS.						
Yale, 28: Wesleyan, 0.	Yale, 26: Crescent, 0.	Yale, 36: Trinity, 0.	Yale, 46: Williams, 0: Yale, 28: Staggs, 0: Yale, 36: Orange, 0.	Yale, 38: Lehigh, 0: Yale, 70: Crescent, 0: Yale, 76: Wesleyan, 0.	Yale, 27: Amherst, 0: Yale, 48: Univer of Pa, 0.	Yale, 10: Harvard, 0: Yale, 19: Princeton, 0.

Diagram N. — Yale team of 1891. Most successful and steady development.

centre rusher in one of our crack 'Varsity teams, whose weight was altogether too great, and who was, therefore, put through a rather severe course to reduce his avoirdupois. He weighed close to two hundred and forty pounds, and only a little of it would come off, in spite of his daily work on the field, followed by long runs and evening work in the gymnasium. Those who had the case in charge would put him on the scales in the evening after his day's work was done, and show a reduction of perhaps six or seven pounds. But by noon of the following day he would have made up the waste and tip the old amount. Many were the sighs heaved over this incorrigible mountain, until at last one of the suspicious coaches arranged to have the man watched. Then the cat came out of the bag, for it was discovered that, nightly, before retiring, the youth had a huge pitcher of milk brought up to his room, from which he appeased that thirst which the banting process made severe.

Novel Ideas and Emergency Suggestions. In this chapter on training it is well to speak of certain novel ideas that have not yet received sufficient test in a practical way to be set down as reliable, but which are well worth further trial, especially in cases where the ordinary methods fail.

Reduction of Flesh. First is that regarding the reduction of superfluous flesh in obstinate cases. The following system has had a fair amount of trial, and has not apparently resulted in anything that could be called objectionable, although in this, as well as in other experiments, it is well to submit the treatment and patient to the physician, and watch the experiment with care. The method consists in a strict diet of lean meat and hot water. Only moderate exercise should be indulged in during the first week. After that the exercise may be, and should be, up to its regular limits. The hot water is to be taken four times a day, one hour before each meal, and a half hour before retiring, and the quantity should be two ordinary glasses at a time. This makes eight glasses a day. The man will, almost from the outset, exhibit a good appetite, and he can be allowed to eat as much of the meat as he cares for. Beef and mutton only should be given. The treatment need not be as severe as the above in ordinary cases, but

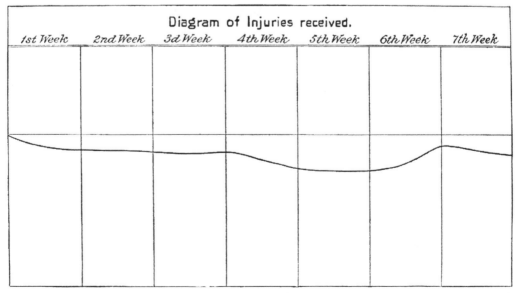

Diagram O. — This curve shows the usual physical condition so far as injuries are concerned ; not the general condition, but merely number of men laid off with injuries.

the man should be allowed a few vegetables — not potatoes — and toast. He should, however, be kept upon a two thirds meat diet.

Increase in Nitrogenous Ratio. A good authority on food stuffs, after following the diet of a team for two years, and making some experiments, is strongly of the opinion that, as a rule, it is advisable to give the men more sugar than is usually believed in during the week or so before a game. The usual experience in this line has been against much sweet, but it is probable that a slight increase of the sugar allowed would not prove harmful in the case of those who craved it, and whose stomachs were not upset by it. Of course, this does not mean to displace the ordinary food with candy or sweets, but merely the addition of ice cream, sweet desserts of plain character, such as prunes, etc.

To Steady a Nervous Team. Another theory that has met with some success in practice is that of putting the men to bed after an early luncheon on the day of a big match. This experiment tried upon a team that had always been nervous and unsteady in the first five minutes had a markedly favorable effect. The men were put in separate rooms, — darkened as far as possible, — and given over half an hour between the sheets. The majority said they actually went to sleep, although it was hardly supposed that they would.

Over-Training. This chapter would be incomplete without a thorough consideration of that bugbear of all coaches,—over-training. At the outset it is well to state that there is no fancy that can creep into the head of a player that will do more to mar his performance than that he is overtrained, or "too fine," or going "stale." When a man acquires such a notion, it is often mere imagination, but if it becomes a fixed idea he is as badly off as though it were real. Coaches and captains should, therefore, be particularly careful not to set up the notion by directing their inquiries of the man with such form as to let him suspect that he is in danger.

The theory of over-training is that a man does not repair the waste.

More Mental than Physical. Now, as strength depends upon newness of muscle, that is, the constant waste and repair, it is the exception that a good

RECAPITULATION OF EIGHT ENGLISH TRAINING SYSTEMS.

SYS-TEM No.	SLEEP Hrs.	Kds.	EXERCISE Hrs.	Meat Kds.	Fish Kds.	Raw Kds.	Cooked Kds.	Puddings and Jellies Kds.	Fresh Kds.	Dry Kds.	Bread	Toast	Water	Beer Pts.	Tea Cups.	Wine Glasses.	Tobacco	Gruel Pinta.
1	9	2	1	2	0	1	1-5	1-3	0-1	0	Stl.	Dry.	0	2	1-2		0	0
2	9	2	1	2	0	1	1-5	1-3	0-1	0	"	"	0	1	1-2	"	0	0
3	9	2	1½	2	0	2	2	3-d	1	1	"	"	0	2	1½ or 2	2	0	0
4	9	2	1½	2	0	2	2	3-d	1	1	"	"	0	1½	1½ or 2	1	0	0
5	8 or 9	3	4 or 5	2	0	0	c	1	0	0	"	"	0	½	h	0	0	½
6	8	3	4 or 5	2	0	0	1	0	0	0	"	"	0	1½ or 2	½	0	0	½
7	10 or 11	3	4	6-d	2-b	0	3	1	0	0	"	"	"	3 or 4	0	3	0	L
8	8	3	3 or 4	a	0	3	12	2	e	f	Brown	"	ad lib g	1 or 1½	2	2 or 3	k	L

(Meat, systems 3–6: Underdone; systems 7–8: Well done.)

(a) Any kind of wholesome meat. (b) Conditionally. (c) Not stated. (d) Allowed. (e) Condemned. (f) Allowed. (g) At night. (h) Quantity not stated. (i) Some colleges allowed. (k) Allowed. (L) Quantity not stated.

healthy subject of the age of most of our football players becomes over-trained in the sense of physically over-worked. The chances are usually that some other factor enters into the equation. But if a man be set at a task until he loathes it, or until he dreads the time of its return, then we bring in mental worry, and with it speedily over-training. This suggests the best way to avoid the occurrence of such a condition, as well as indicating the remedy. A player should be given something new to think of every few days, not crammed all in a day with all the possibilities of his position, and then found fault with for neglecting half of them. He should be carried along by gradual steps, and should see some new opportunity often enough to encourage him. Then, when he begins to show indication of having too much on his mind, send him over to coach the freshmen, or anything else that will amuse and distract him. Just as an instance of what an injudicious coach will do: There was at one of our large universities a coach who had a substitute quarter playing occasion-ally upon the 'Varsity, but more frequently on the scrub, or second eleven side. The sides had separate signals. It occurred to this coach, late in the season, to give each team an entirely new set of signals in addition to the set it already possessed. The substitute quarter was given both new sets, — he already had mastered the first two. Three days later, in the first ten minutes of a match, the regular quarter was laid up, and the substitute quarter went in. He was told which of the four sets the team was using, and for a few minutes did well. Then suddenly he stopped, rushed over to the captain, and said, "I can't remember a single signal; I'm no use," and it was two weeks before the boy was really himself again. This was simply a case of mental worry. A conscientious man will go fine much more easily than the stolid, indifferent player, for the former takes all fault-finding to heart, and treasures it up until he becomes discouraged, and fairly on edge with nervousness. A coach should bear this in mind, and when he wants to make an example he will be wise if he select one of the stolid kind who can stand it, and not use the whip too freely in public upon some high-strung chap, who frets under even a light rein.

How to Diagnose. The first indication of over-training usually appears in a dullness in the eye and manner, while the nerves are still very sensitive. Then there is a loss of appetite and inability to sleep or even to rest, and the man begins to go off rapidly in his play. A loss of weight is usually a very early symptom, too, and for this reason the men should be put on the scales twice a week regularly, and suspicious cases oftener. As soon as the case is diagnosed as even doubtful, the man should be given a rest and freedom from care and worry, just as indicated later in this chapter for sleeplessness. A day or two may set him straight, and if so, the coach is fortunate. If not, then his place should be at once filled for a week, if the time of the season admits. If it be on the eve of an important game, compromise measures are, of course, necessary. If the man must play, he may have his appetite pampered, — may have a little champagne with his meals, and be given as little to do as is consistent with the absolute needs of the team. When he is not in uniform, get him away from the men and give him all the outside entertainment possible. Send him to the theatre, or anywhere else that will divert him.

The Agent of Repair. Sleep, the agent of repair, is one of the most important needs of the football player. And attention to the proper securing of undisturbed rest is one of the most serious problems that sometimes, late in the season, faces the coach. During the early weeks of training sleep comes naturally and easily to the player, and usually throughout the season to the majority, with, perhaps, the exception of the night before the big game. But there are occasionally cases of over-work, or more properly over-worry; for the captain and some important player like the quarter-back have too much on their minds in the way of responsibility to be free from trouble of this nature. It is a fair criticism against the game that so much should devolve upon the captain or quarter, but the strain is temporary and is surely a strong developer of character. But the coach must consider, not the question of sparing the man the worry, but of keeping him in as good physical condition as possible under it. As to the team in general, the law must be laid down with decision that during the period of training the men must keep regular hours. Some believe in nine hours sleep at least, but eight hours will answer if it be always secured. From ten o'clock to seven o'clock are good limits, and no football man should be seen out of his room after ten. The night before a game the team can be allowed to stay up a little longer, to insure their speedy sleep.

Care of the Over-Trained.

Now for the men who are over-trained or over-worried. It is not always easy to know whether a man is getting his proper sleep. Many a captain and conscientious player has answered up cheerily as to his sleep, rather than to allow any one to suppose that he is not all right. This spirit is a good one, but the player should remember that if the coach can help him, he ought to confess to him privately all his troubles. It is not difficult for the coach to secure such an understanding in confidence with his men. There is no necessity that the whole team shall know if a man is not sleeping well, but there is a great necessity of the coach's knowing it and acting upon that knowledge. As to the remedy or rather remedies. In the first place, drugs, although they have been resorted to by some teams under urgent necessity, are never to be countenanced until the man is in such a condition that he passes from the hands of the

TABLE SHOWING THE DIGESTIBILITY OF CERTAIN ARTICLES OF FOOD.

Article of Food.	Mode of Preparation.	Time of Digestion.	
		Hours.	Minutes.
MEAT.			
Beef	Boiled.	2	45
Beefsteak	Broiled.	3	0
Beef, lean	Roasted.	3	30
Beef, with mustard and vegetables	Boiled.	3	30
Beef and vegetables	Fried.	4	0
Beef, hard salt	Boiled.	4	15
Lamb	Broiled.	2	30
Mutton	Boiled.	3	0
Mutton	Broiled.	3	0
Mutton	Roasted.	3	15
Veal	Broiled.	4	0
Veal	Fried.	4	30
Pig, sucking	Roasted.	2	30
Pork, steak	Broiled.	3	15
Pork, salted	Broiled.	3	15
Pork, salted	Boiled.	4	30
Pork, salted	Fried.	5	15
Venison	Broiled.	1	35
Tripe	Boiled.	1	0
Liver	Broiled.	2	0
Gelatine	Boiled.	2	30
Heart	Fried.	4	0
POULTRY.			
Turkey	Boiled.	2	25
Turkey	Roasted.	2	30
Goose	Roasted.	2	30
Chicken	Fricasseed.	2	45
Fowls	Broiled.	4	0
Fowls	Roasted.	4	0
Ducks	Roasted.	4	0
Ducks, wild	Roasted.	4	30
FISH.			
Trout	Boiled.	1	30
Trout	Fried.	1	30
Cod	Boiled.	2	0
Oysters	Raw.	2	55
Oysters	Roasted.	3	15
Oysters	Stewed.	3	30
Flounders	Fried.	3	30
Salmon, salted	Boiled.	4	0
EGGS, ETC.			
Eggs	Raw.	2	0
Eggs	Roasted.	2	15
Eggs	Soft boiled.	3	0
Eggs	Hard boiled.	3	30
Milk	Raw.	2	15
Milk	Boiled.	2	0
Butter	Melted.	3	30
Cheese	Raw.	3	30
SOUPS, ETC.			
Barley broth		1	30
Hash (meat and vegetables)	Warmed.	2	30
Soup (chicken)	Boiled.	3	0
Soup (mutton)	Boiled.	3	0
Soup (beef)	Boiled.	3	0
FARINACEOUS SUBSTANCES.			
Bread (wheaten)	Baked.	3	30
Beans	Boiled.	2	30
Rice	Boiled.	1	0
Sago	Boiled.	1	45
Tapioca	Boiled.	2	0
VEGETABLES.			
Potatoes	Roasted.	2	30
Potatoes	Baked.	2	30
Potatoes	Boiled.	3	30
Parsnips	Boiled.	2	30
Carrots	Boiled.	3	15
Turnips	Boiled.	3	30
Cabbage	Boiled.	4	30
FRUITS.			
Apples (sweet)	Raw.	2	0
Apples (sour)	Raw.	2	0

coach into those of the physician. Hence drugs will have no part in this chapter. The first thing to be attempted is the removal of the cause for worry. If this be impossible, it can almost always be greatly lessened by judicious moves. If it be the case of the captain, an especial effort should be made in a private conference between him and the coaches, to show him that his fears are groundless. The truth of the matter is that by the time this trouble of sleeplessness comes upon a captain, the season is usually so near its end that the coaches are justified in assuming the entire burden of responsibility, and so encouraging the captain, even at a slight stretching of their consciences, in the expression of belief in the team's probable success. Having done everything possible so far as the mental condition of the man is concerned, it is well to try one or two simple methods of inducing sleep. Beer or ale before retiring, in the case of a man who has been accustomed to it when out of training, will often bring about the desired result. Another very efficacious plan is to have the man eat nothing but meat at his evening meal, and then half an hour before bedtime drink a glass of hot water. Light work in the afternoon and an evening walk of half an hour or so will sometimes serve when everything else fails. Above all, no evening football talk or football reading, but some entertaining book or conversation with people not interested in football.

Cleanliness. Cleanliness comes next for our consideration. It may seem a strange term to apply to the condition of men who literally wallow in the mud upon occasion, but it is, nevertheless, thoroughly applicable, for the man in training should especially keep his skin in good condition. Too much tubbing is a mistake, but with a good sponge bath and a single tub, the football man can daily be as pink and glowing as possible. There is no need to dwell upon methods. All sorts of showers are common nowadays, and with the sole caution not to overdo the pleasure, we can leave this agent of health, and the final consideration of the subject.

CHAPTER XI

SUGGESTIONS OF POSSIBLE FAKES AND BLUFFS: HOW AND WHERE THEY MAY BE EMPLOYED

The Plan Explained. It is not intended in this chapter to give a complete scheme for the employment of different fakes, nor is it intended to furnish diagrams of plays. The object of the chapter is, as its name implies, merely to give suggestions to the coach of the various lines along which he can successfully conduct strategic operations. The ingenuity of the coach, and his knowledge of the capacities of his team, will enable him to select the right suggestion and clothe it with the proper movement.

As to the Value of Different Ideas. It must not be understood that these suggestions are offered as novel movements, or that they are especially commended. Many of them are of doubtful value, and some of them might easily be conducted in such a manner as to jeopard the safety of the ball. They should only be regarded as possibilities which may, in some cases and in certain directions, be found to be peculiarly adapted to the abilities of the team.

The doubtful value of many of these suggestions makes it unnecessary to caution the coach against using too many fakes and bluffs in the work of his team. If one or two of them are employed, it is usually all that the team will need, or that it would be wise to give them. Their value lies not alone in themselves, but in the train of thought which they stimulate. Ideas in football are always at a premium, and some new ideas may come to the coach from a hasty perusal of the following suggestions:

A Line Man Brought Back. (1) *Calling a line man back, with the apparent intention of heading an interference, and letting the play eventuate in a totally different manner*

For example, if a guard was called back to head a heavy interference around either end of the line, the positions being taken exactly as if the play was to move around the farther end from the side from which the guard was withdrawn, it might then be a wise plan to start the play in that direction, and have it eventuate in a double pass, and a sharp dive through some part of the line.

An Accidental Start. (2) *Make an apparently accidental start of the entire interference before the ball is snapped, and have a reprimand from the quarter; then, without any change of signal, let the ball come back, and a totally different play eventuate.*

The value of such a bluff lies in the readiness of the average player to follow his instinct as against his coaching. The fact that the play has already started toward a certain point in the line, and that the quarter-back has reprimanded the players and moved them back to their original positions, without any change of signal, leaves the inference reasonably sure that the same movement is to take place as soon as the ball is snapped. This interference might be strengthened by the quarter-back, immediately after his reprimand (which need consist of nothing more than "Steady, fellows, don't give the play away!"), calling out to the team, "Same signal." This might emphasize the inference in the minds of the opponents, and more effectually lead them astray.

An excellent play to embody this suggestion would be a double pass, or any play with a bluff movement, or demonstration toward a part of the line where the runner does not go. In that case the demonstration would be all the more deceptive, in view of the accidental start-off.

The Quarter-Back Changed. **(3)** *Have some man change with quarter-back for a single play, and let it appear that quarter is to do some special thing.*

For example, if near enough to the opponents' goal to make a drop-kick possible, let the quarter-back go up the field on the first down, as if to make the trial. Let the formation be for the protection of a drop-kick, but let the ball be passed quickly to a half-back on the side for a quick dive through the line. The sending of the quarter-back up the field might be a useful adjunct to a good "fake kick" which had worked well two or three times, but which was now being stopped by the opponents becoming familiar with the movement.

Quick Scrimmage Kick. (4) *Study the possibilities of an unexpected scrimmage kick.*

There are various ways in which this might be employed. The centre rush, on some word signal from the quarter-back, might rise from his stooping position, as if disgusted at something, and kick the ball between his opponent's legs, or on either side of his opponent where a favorable opening may occur. The ball must go ten yards unless stopped by an opponent. The entire team would then be on-side, and should make an instant rush for the ball. Such a play should only be tried, of course, when the attendant risk of the loss of the ball may be wisely entertained.

Another method would be to practise an easy short snap back toward the quarter, which would not move the ball more than a foot; the quarter, being ready upon the instant, could then kick the ball directly against the leg or body of an opponent. Properly, the ball would then belong to any one of the twenty-two men who first dropped upon it. In other words, it would have been put in play according to the rules, having touched a third man, as provided in Rule 21. The opponents would have lost their prior claim to drop on the ball by virtue of its having already touched one of their number. A play of this nature might easily be worked up so as to be tolerably effective on a third down, when the distance to gain was difficult, or when the regular punts had, in two or three instances, been blocked by opponents. Care should be taken in the event of the first or second method of putting the ball in play, to caution the centre rush not to fall on the ball in a scrimmage, as he is prevented from touching it until it has touched some other player of his side.

Ball Put in Play by a Guard. (5) *Have the ball put down unexpectedly by the guard, who puts it in play without signal on a quick line-up.*

If the opponents are caught napping in this, you may be able to put the ball in play one point nearer the end of the line, and so bring off a round-the-end play without having to travel so far to circle the line. If the opponents move over, the play should then be quickly sent to the long side of the line, where you will have one extra man at your disposal to pocket the end or tackle.

An Unexpected Punt. (6) *Study the possibilities of an unexpected kick from an ordinary running line-up, the player kicking the ball immediately behind the line with a sideways kick, and at least one man going down the field on-side.*

A very effective way of making this kick is to have it ordered from the side of the field, and the punt directed on an oblique toward the other side. The on-side runner can then be well started across the field before the punt is delivered, and the moment he sees the punt made he can start immediately forward toward the point where the ball is to drop. The value of these unexpected kicks is not alone in themselves, but in the added value which they often give to the rushing game by reason of the uncertainty of the opponents as to whether the play is to be a run or a kick.

Second Pass and Kick. (7) *Try a second pass, with the last receiver kicking the ball well over to the side of the field five or ten yards ahead of the line of scrimmage; the entire team to follow the ball quickly, and the kicker to put his team on-side.*

The probabilities in this manoeuvre would be that the unexpectedness of the second pass, followed by the unusual feature of a kick, would so far disconcert the opponents that the kicker would be enabled to go straight down the field on the opposite side from which the ball was kicked, and with such a slight advance of the ball as five or ten yards he would be able to put his team on-side. The play could only properly be attempted on the side of the field (say ten yards from the side lines), and the kicker should then go down the short side of the field, while the rest of the team move as rapidly as possible toward the point where the ball will drop.

Making Exchanges when on the Offensive. (8) *Remember that exchanges on the offensive are always wise.*

For example, if by sending your full-back ten or twelve yards up the field for a kick, you can compel your opponents to send an extra back up the field to receive the expected kick, the advantage is clearly with you in any subsequent running play. The idea may be more clearly grasped by assuming that the teams are composed of only one man each, and that your one man who has the ball is trying to carry it down to the goal posts. It would be a comparatively easy matter for him to dodge his opponent. Now, by enlarging the teams to two men, it might still be easy, although the danger that the second man may fail in blocking his opponent increases the difficulty of the runner passing the line of two men. This same difficulty is increased by the addition of every extra man to the team. Hence the rule is that as every man who fails to block his opponent jeopardizes the play, it follows that the greater number of men in the game on each side, the greater the difficulty of advancing the ball by running. Hence when you have the ball, you can always afford to make exchanges, or "pair men off," if they keep each other out of the play.

Furthermore, by sending your kicker ten or twelve yards up the field (on a pretense of kicking), it is often possible to bring him into the play at some later point in its development, where he can do effective service. The opposing back, however, who was sent up the field to receive the punt, is too far removed from the point of action to be of any service until the runner has made a substantial gain.

Diagonal Blocking. (9) *Diagonal blocking is the most effective of all methods for making an opening in the line.*

Hence make your assignments in every play, not on the basis of the man taking the opponent whom he can first reach in the line, but rather the opponent whom he can strike on the most obtuse angle from a line at right angles with the rush-line.

Shifting Positions. (10) *Wherever you can find a man who can play two positions, see whether it is not possible to emphasise some bluff by shifting him especially for this play.*

In other words, if the runner were to go through the right side of the line, but the demonstration were to be made toward the left side of the line, it might be possible to shift some player from the right to the left side of the line, under pretense of making the left side a trifle stronger, and this slight movement would make the opponents more ready to start to the defense of that side of the line when the bluff demonstration was made.

As to Unexpected Kicks. (11) *Remember that unexpected kicks should not be ordered when an extra back has been sent up the field.*

One point of advantage about an unexpected kick is that it can be directed to a part of the field where there is no man located to receive it. It is a well-attested fact that a full-back who cannot get under the ball before it touches the ground is in more or less danger of having the ball touch some part of his person, in which case he stands a good chance of losing it altogether, or of being jostled by the opposing players while the ball is bounding along the ground, during which time the opposing kicker may be coming down the field to put his team on-side. An unexpected kick should, therefore, never be played from a running line-up on the third down, when an extra back has been sent up the field. It may always be played on a second down; or on a third down where the running line-up so far deceives the opponents that the extra back is not sent away from the line.

A Long First Pass on First Down. (12) *When the ball is secured from opponents on a fourth down, near the side lines, let your full-back advance slowly, as if doubtful whether the ball had been regained or not; on a quick line-up let the quarter make a long pass to the full-back, who will be out toward the centre of the field and five yards behind the quarter.*

A very good play can be drawn up on this suggestion. It would be wise to arrange some signal on the third down between the quarter and full back, whereby there is a mutual understanding that the play is to be ordered immediately if opponents lose it upon the next down. There should then be a quick line-up, and the ball snapped before any one could have time to notice that the full-back was not in his place. The full-back, in the mean time, would be feigning unusual dullness, and advancing in a hesitating manner, as if uncertain as to whether his side had regained possession of the ball or not. The team being on the side of the field, the full-back would naturally be a little toward the centre, and in coming down to rejoin the team he might move down more directly toward the centre of the field, as if about to question one of the officials.

In the event of an extra back having been sent down the field, this extra back might be used as a principal interferer, or he might immediately rejoin the team as soon as it was seen that the opponents had trusted to gain their distance and had not resorted to a kick.

Side Line Possibilities. (13) *Study up the strategic possibilities of the side line.*

When the ball is near the side line is a possible time to play a long criss-cross, the runner going down the short side of the field, but the first movement being toward the long side. It is well to have a special play to use when advantageously near the side line, the ball criss-crossing toward the line.

A Quarter-Back Kick. (14) *Have a quarter-back kick to side of field.*

There are situations during the game (as, for example, when inside opponents' thirty-five-yard line) when it is most desirable to retain possession of the ball on a third down, and when the distance to gain is too great to make it prudent to attempt to rush the ball. At such times, the line-up being for a running play, it is possible for the quarter-back, working from a position near one side of the field, to kick toward the other side with an advance of ten yards, and the whole eleven, moving rapidly after the ball, will often be able to secure it from the opposing full-back. It must be remembered that the three backs behind the quarter are all on-side when he kicks, and if the tackle or end can come sharply round behind the quarter, as if to join an interference around the other end, he will be in just such a position as will make him on-side when the kick is made, while not retarding in any way his arrival at the other side of the field. The movement of the three backs should be across the field, without advancing forward until the kick has been delivered. A sharp oblique may then be made toward the probable locality where the ball will descend. Care should be taken that the end or tackle should circle well out so as not to disconcert the kicker. Of course, in this play the quarter-back would endeavor immediately to put his team on-side.

Fake Kick and Dive Play. (15) *Work up a good fake kick with the runner going on a quick dive through the tackle-guard hole.*

This is always an easy play to devise and a very successful one to work against some teams. It is astonishing to note with what success fake kicks are often operated against even the strongest opponents. One such play should be in the category of every eleven. It should be thoroughly rehearsed, and given a simple, plain signal, and one which does not seemingly indicate any unusual play. It would be much better if the signal could be the same as for a punt, with some slight disguise or accompanying hand or arm signal on the part of the quarter-back, which should indicate that it was not a punt in reality.

Fake Kick and Full-Back Run. (16) *Send the full-back up for a punt, and let him, instead of kicking, rush the ball, moving well out on a wide circle around the end of the line, and passing on either side of the opposing end, if he has drawn the end well out.*

This is always an easy play to work up, the only important point being the interference given to the runner. It might be a wise plan, if the run was to be attempted around the right end of your line, to draw your left tackle back to join the immediate body guard in front of the full-back, who are supposed to protect

him from any man who has broken through the line. Your left end would then
come in from his extreme position and stand where he could slightly body-check
the opposing tackle before going down the field under the supposed kick. This
arrangement would give your full-back a direct interference of at least three men,
with the quarter-back as a possible fourth.

Overhead Pass. (17) *Work up an overhead pass: — the quarter pretending to
pass to the half-back, but throwing the ball over his head to an end rush who has
sneaked well out.*

It may be claimed for this play that when successful it is almost worth a
touch-down; when not successful it need not be attended with great risk or loss.
The assignments should be so made that all protection may be afforded to the
ball in the event of the end rush failing to catch it.

A Pretended Fumble. (18) *Let the full-back make a pretended fumble of the
ball.*

This is a "last resort" play, to be used near the end of a game when five points
extra would not win the match, but six points would. The full-back goes up for a
drop-kick, and on receiving the ball holds it just long enough to draw the
opposing end and tackle on his left side well down upon him. The guards and
other side of line are blocked, as usual. The end and tackle come straight down.
Your own right end, starting sharply on the snap, circles behind the full-back
and receives the ball from him by a short backward pass, just as the end and
tackle have reached him. They will naturally be in front of him in order to reach
his kicking side and block the path of the ball. The end on receiving the ball
circles the other unguarded end.

The Concealed Ball. (19) *The trick of the concealed ball.*

This is a suggestion which offers some little field for the ingenuity of the
strategist. It is a trick which has been worked very successfully on one or two
occasions in the past. It was a favorite line of operations with a well-known Yale
player less than a dozen years ago. By his ingenuity he had planned two or three
successful mass movements where the opponents, unless exceptionally sharp-
sighted, completely lose the direction of the ball, and the play, which was
usually quite a slow one, was worked with deadly effect against even the
strongest opponents.

Pocketing an End. (20) *In a formation for a close attack against tackle on one
side of the line, let the pass be made unexpectedly to a runner who swings out
from his position on the other side of the centre and circles behind the mass and
around the end.*

The success of this play is wholly dependent upon drawing in the end by the
repeated attacks at the tackle hole. The formation may be of a nature which
makes it quite difficult for the end to readily see what is transpiring beyond the
centre of the line; the runner coming around very sharply and receiving the ball
almost at full speed, is under such headway that, unless the end has kept well
out of the pretended attack, he will not be in a position to successfully tackle the
rapidly moving runner. The possibilities of work along this line are unusually
promising.

Right-Angling an End. (21) *Work up a series with a formation having your
right end never less than five yards outside his opponent.*

Several interesting plays may be made from this formation. A round-the-end
play may be attempted, in which you would be able to direct an attack upon the
opposing end from exactly opposite directions at the same time. In other words,
he would have to look out for the on-coming interference and the runner, and
also keep track of the movement of his opponent, who is five yards outside of his

position and moving towards him from the opposite direction. The best result would probably be effected if the outside end met his opponent just before the interference reached him. He could then disconcert him just at the decisive moment, when the end was preparing to smash the interference.

Another Outlet. Another outlet in such a series would be a long pass to the right end rush, either by the quarter-back direct, or by the left half-back receiving the ball from the quarter and starting around behind the right side of his own line to make the long pass. In this case the full-back and right half-back would be assisting the right guard and tackle in blocking for the left half-back when he turned to make his pass.

In the event of the opposing end rush following your right end out to the side of the field, this series of plays could not be worked, but you could then successfully effect other operations, and the withdrawal of these two men, as you are acting on the offensive, would be to your, and not your opponents' advantage.

A Quarter-Turned Attack. (22) *Try a line-up with all the men facing in a wrong direction, and with a sharp quarter turn to the right or left the instant the ball is put in play.*

This is of minor value, but there are a few movements in which it may be effectively employed with no risk.

A Quarter-Back Run. (23) *Let the quarter run with the ball.*

In a play of this sort the ball should be passed immediately to one of the backs who is advancing toward one side of the line as he receives it. Immediately upon receiving it, he swings round upon one foot with his back to the line, using the foot which is nearest to the quarter-back, which thus enables him to face the quarter-back the entire time. The quarter-back has followed up his pass by advancing himself, and as the half-back turns, he takes the ball from him and tries to circle the end, keeping well out on a long turning.

Another Way. There are two ways in which this play may be tried with perhaps equal success. The ball may be passed to the left half-back, and the other two backs may make a bluff attack upon the right side of the centre of the line, the left half-back moving almost forward, and with a very little movement toward the centre from his position. Another method is for all three of the backs to move rapidly toward the tackle-guard hole on the left side of the line; the right half-back, being the last man, receives the ball, and turns in the same manner as described, passing to the quarter-back, who circles the left end of the line.

Second Pass in a Moving Interference. (24) *Work a double pass from one man to another in a heavy interference just before it reaches the end of the line.*

This is always a deceptive manoeuvre, unless the opposing end rush is exceedingly watchful. He has clearly seen the first pass and located the runner. He finds this runner is well inside of his interferers, and running behind them. Naturally the end rush is tempted to keep inside of the interference group, and seize the runner from the side. The runner should make the pass to the man on the farthest outside edge of the group of interferers, and the pass can be made just before he is to be tackled by the end rush. The man who receives the pass, and who is moving at the full speed of the interference, is then protected by the interfering group from the end rush, and if a wide circle of the field is made, and he is a good runner, the chances are that he will be able to pass the half-back, who is moving out rapidly to support the end.

Two Operations in One. (25) *Combine two styles of play in one operation.*

Or, in other words, under cover of one familiar form of attack make another familiar form of attack. For example, if you have a strong interference around the end, which is headed by some heavy rusher who is drawn back from the line, let there be a criss-cross incorporated with this play, by which the back who is nearest to the end which is circled shall receive the ball from the runner, and with the interference still moving on around the end, let him make a quick dive directly through the line in front of him. This is one of the most successful methods of bringing off a criss-cross. It seems to combine in one play the advantages of the quick dive and the criss-cross proper, and although less brilliant than the long criss-cross, with the runner circling the opposite end, it is more productive of gains in the long run, and may be repeated many times during a game.

A Running Kick. (26) *Practise running kicking and study its possibilities.*

There is really a great opportunity in this direction, and a mine of unused wealth awaits the enterprising coach who will develop running kicking to its fullest extent. There are a great many times when a runner has passed the critical point in the line, and is sufficiently free to enable him to kick the ball. At such times it may be questioned whether it would not be an excellent policy to do this, and endeavor either himself to regain it, or to put his team on-side. A good opportunity for such a play would be where an end rush had been circled on a very long movement out toward the side of the field, and an opposing line back was rapidly moving across the field with every possibility of intercepting the runner when he turned in circling. It might be easily possible at such a time for the runner to make a running kick over the head of the half-back and also of the full-back, who would probably have advanced to a point very close to the runner's position. The runner, with his interference, might then, keeping straight on, have an excellent opportunity of regaining the ball.

Deceptive Line-Up Attitudes. (27) *Encourage the players to certain deceptive false motions, calculated to deceive the opponents as to the direction of the play, or as to the moment when the ball is to be snapped.*

The effect of this will often be to slow up or rattle the opponents. Very much may be accomplished by taking advantage of an opponent's weakness and inducing him to start before the ball is put in play. It is easily possible for clever players to cultivate such deceptive movements as shall greatly mislead the opponents at critical times.

A Fake Kick Criss-Cross. (28) *Work up a fake kick criss-cross.*

This is a comparatively unused and very promising style of play. It will be necessary to work the fake kick two or three times before trying the fake kick criss-cross. Make the interference as heavy as possible for the second runner, and let this interference go to its work at the very beginning of the movement. There need be no special demonstration to help the first runner.

CHAPTER XII

WHEN ACTING AS AN OFFICIAL

Future of the Sport in Hands of the Officials. The very existence of a sport like football is dependent upon satisfactory rulings by officials. The future of the game is really almost as much in their hands as in the hands of the legislators and the players. It requires a man of the highest character, having a special knowledge of the game, to make a satisfactory referee or umpire. In fact, the way in which an important match is conducted, and the effect upon both players and spectators, depends upon a judicious selection of these two arbiters. The linesman is, of course, an important man, but has far less of the game in his hands than the other two.

Learn the Rules. A referee or umpire should thoroughly learn the rules. He must not only be familiar with the wording, but he should also be posted upon the derivation of the rules and (in a measure) their history, in order that his interpretation of them may be based upon a correct knowledge of the reasons why the rules were made. He should also be familiar with the location of the rules in the book, as often in a game a captain may demand a reference to the rule, and an official who can turn at once to any rule without hesitation has made a long step towards securing the confidence and respect of the players whose game he is conducting.

Learn the History of the Rules. An official should acquire his knowledge not alone from the rule-book and the watching of games, but he should also read up the history of the sport and make himself master of that history. He should then practise with his knowledge, just as a player practises to acquire skill. An official should act in the daily play frequently, and from this learn the following points.

Learn the Players' Interpretation. He should learn the players' interpretation of rules, for the players' interpretation may differ from the interpretation of the legislator and of the official. It may be a hard thing to say, but it is nevertheless true, that players learn various ways of coming very close to an infringement of a rule without — in their minds, at least — actually breaking it. A referee or umpire who is not familiar with this feature will find himself wholly incompetent to pass judgment when, in an important match, he is called upon to follow the play closely.

He should find out, also, what the natural action of the player is. That is, what he will do under certain set conditions. He will learn, also, what fouls are most apt to occur, and the points at which these take place.

The Referee. The duties of the referee are comparatively simple. Not but that he has enough to attend to (the additional duty of watching the play in the centre, looking out for runs by the quarter, or forward passes, having added somewhat to his work), but, as a rule, all the decisions that he has to make are questions of fact regarding the position or the progress of the ball itself, while the duties of the umpire involve a much more difficult element because there is but one ball, and there are twenty-two players, and the umpire has the duty of judging the actions of these twenty-two players.

Cannot Deliberate when on the Field. The umpire or referee who is not thoroughly familiar with all the constructions that may be placed upon the rules is not competent to decide clearly upon the merits of the case on the field. No matter what his interpretation of the rule may be originally, he should have had all the various constructions brought before him, and should not be obliged to deliberate when on the field.

Position to Occupy when Watching the Play. The referee can stand in almost any position and satisfactorily follow the ball. But he should make it a point to give the umpire the preference, that is, to allow the umpire to stand where he can best see the ball, while he (the referee) takes up a position which will assist the umpire to thoroughly cover the field. The best umpires find it advantageous to stand facing the side which has the ball, and approximately in front of the man putting the ball in play. From this position the umpire can see the work in the centre in the way of holding, and can also move quickly out to the point where the line is assailed, and be in a fair position to judge of the effect as well as the making of any fouls which occur in the line of the progress of the ball.

Pay no Attention to Remarks and Never Try to Even Up. An umpire should thoroughly disassociate himself from any consideration of the two sides so far as personal feeling goes. He should never, under any circumstances, allow himself to be affected by what the players or the spectators say, and he should, under no circumstances, endeavor to even up any decisions. He should have but one thought, and that the strict fulfillment of his duty, no matter which side it affects.

Don't be too Technical. But no umpire should enter a game or should conduct a game, under the impression that every technical violation of rule should be penalized. As one of the best umpires in this country has said, there is probably never a play made on the field without some violation of a rule which could be discovered by a too particular official. A man's foot may be a half inch off-side. The centre rush is very apt to have his head over the ball. A thousand and one things which make no difference whatever in the result and are wholly without intent to defraud or take advantage, may occur; they would allow ample opportunities for calling fouls to an umpire whose business was not to conduct the game, but to find fault. Hypercritical officials do more harm than good.

Despise and Disgrace the Foul Players. But the man who has the interest of the game at heart, who wants to see fair play, who hates the foul player as he hates poison, and who goes even farther than the rule provides if it is necessary for the prevention of unfair tactics, is the kind of man to bring the game up, and the man who will see that both sides get justice. Such men are hard to find, but everything should be done to encourage them to act. The effect of such men upon the education of players in this country cannot be too highly estimated.

Difficulties. The most difficult duty of the referee is undoubtedly to discover who has the ball when in a fumble a number of men drop on it and the pile is so dense that he cannot see the man in possession. The wise act for him in this emergency is to take away the men one by one, beginning with those whom he can see have no hands on the ball. In this way he will bring it down to two or three, and it is not then difficult to tell from the position of the arms of these men, after he has reached the bottom of the heap, to which man the ball belongs.

It is also the duty of the referee to tell whether the kick is a punt or a drop-kick when a try-at-goal is tried and is successful. Some kickers in attempting a drop-kick catch the ball with the toe before it hits the ground, and this must be closely watched by the referee.

Both the referee and umpire must not only cultivate, but actually acquire, a total indifference to remarks made while they are on the field. Among the present day teams it is seldom that much is said in comment upon decisions. The practice of trying to bulldoze the umpire and referee has largely gone by. But there are persons in the crowd, and sometimes, we regret to say, on the teams, who, in the heat of excitement, express too forcibly their difference of opinion from that of the umpire or referee. The official should take no note of this, and remember that in times gone by, when he was a player, he had something of the same feelings, and possibly at times he expressed them.

Never Leave the Game without a Decision. But above all things, no matter what the provocation, an official should never leave a game until it is finished or forfeited. If there is a dispute over one of his decisions, he has not the right to throw up the place, but before he leaves the field he must decide the game, so that there can be no further claims of any kind save in the case of an

Association game, where, by the constitution, an appeal is permitted regarding the interpretation of the rule.

There is never any appeal, however, from a decision of the referee upon a question of fact, and this should be thoroughly borne in mind by both officials and players.

Ground Rules. It is the duty of the officials to call the two captains together as long a time as possible before the game, and bring up the question of ground rules. It often happens that neither of the captains has reflected upon this matter, and the official has to make suggestions. This he should be fully competent to do, for he should have gone out on the field and looked it over, and know the necessity for each ground rule which may be proposed.

Proximity of Fence or Grand Stand. For instance, a grand stand or fence may be so near the goal line as to make a kick-out from behind the goal impossible. In that case a ground rule should be agreed upon making it perfectly fair for both sides, but insuring that the play will be carried on as it would be in an open field. The easiest way to adjust this is to determine a certain distance, say, for instance, five yards, and when the defending side secure the ball, or have the ball in their possession inside their own five-yard line, they are privileged to take the ball out to the ten-yard line and have it down there.

Out of Bounds. Again, it may be that the sides of the field are so arranged that it is not easily possible or wholly safe for the players to follow the ball when it goes out of bounds. In that case a ground rule should be made giving the ball to the opponents of the side that made the kick when the ball goes beyond the boundary. There is some question as to whether a ground rule should be made in this case providing that the ball shall become the property of the opposing side when it is kicked out of bounds as soon as it crosses the side line, whether it go into the crowd or not. Usually a rule is made that the ball is the property of the man securing it (provided he is on-side), so long as it does not actually pass the fence, or the line of the crowd, or strike an outsider. It is better, however, and less open to dispute, if the rule gives the ball to opponents the instant it goes out of bounds from a kick.

The referee must be sure to raise the question whether a blocked kick is to be governed by the same rules if the ball goes out of bounds before it is secured. It may be decided either way, but must be settled always in advance.

Interpretations and Points Made by Captains. After all matters of ground rules have been gone over, the referee should bring up any questions likely to produce a misunderstanding in the rules, and should advise the two captains of his interpretation of these obscure points. He should also ask the captains to bring up to him any points that they wish to have discussed, and should notify them that on any questions not brought up at that meeting he will decide according to his own interpretation, without regard to any later discussions, that is, unless both captains are present at the later discussion, and it takes place before the players go on the field.

The reason for this is that it is always an awkward thing for a referee to hold anything like confidential relations with either captain. All points should be brought up and discussed *with both captains present*, or else they must be satisfied with the interpretation of the referee when the actual play happens.

Warning by the Umpire. When the referee has gone over his part of the work in this way, the umpire should discuss all matters likely to fall under his province, and finally the umpire should give the captains definite and decided warning regarding anything like unfair play or brutality. It is the duty of the umpire to make this talk a sound one, that shall impress the captains with the fact that nothing in the nature of foul tactics will be for a minute countenanced by him; and that he will go even beyond the letter of the rules to see that offenses of this nature are promptly punished.

When the players come upon the field, the referee and umpire should call the two captains together, and the ground rules should be stated as they have been agreed upon before the play is started. The umpire should take occasion once more to reiterate what he has said about unfair play, and should ask the captains if they thoroughly understand, and have made their teams thoroughly understand, his attitude.

All this may seem like going to great lengths to eliminate possible later discussions, but it is well worth while, and the game will be far more satisfactory not only to the players, but to the officials, if this line of policy is strictly carried out.

Linesman. Marking Distances. The linesman acts under the referee, and marks the distance gained or lost. It is customary for him to have an assistant, and one of the easiest ways to keep track of the distance is to have two canes joined together with a five-yard cord, and, when a first down is made, set one cane opposite the down, and stretch the cord tight in a straight line by the side line, and the other cane will mark the distance which must be made in the three attempts.

Bearing Testimony. All officials are obliged to do their best to see that all the rules are enforced, and whenever one official is asked to bear testimony in another official's province, he should be ready with a frank statement, and should not hesitate a moment to give his views.

Extraordinary Occurrences. There are some extraordinary occurrences which have happened in sections of the country where football has only just begun to make for itself a sound foothold, and which perhaps ought to be noted. There is no danger of such things happening where the game is understood and appreciated, as the public feeling is too strong to tolerate such exhibitions for a moment.

A case has arisen where a player has been disqualified by the umpire, and refused to leave the field. Fortunately, such an occurrence cannot happen on a team that has any appreciation for the sport, but an official who is likely to act in some of the remote parts of the country may have such a thing brought before him. There is but one thing for the umpire to do, and that is to give the captain of the offending side, even if he be the disqualified player himself, a certain limit of time for the player to leave the field, say three minutes, or less time if he prefers. If the player does not leave the field inside of that time, the umpire should advise the referee, and the referee should at once declare the game forfeited to the other side.

There is nothing specifically stated in the rules to cover this point, and there are several other points which it would be superfluous to put into rules, which are made for gentlemen in the conduct of sport as gentlemen. All questions of this kind are covered by a point in the rules which makes the referee absolute in all cases not covered by the umpire, and the umpire is the judge of the conduct of the players. At such a time the referee must uphold the umpire strongly. In point of fact, the umpire would probably be upheld in himself declaring a game forfeited, but such a declaration is more in the province of the referee, and if he is a man of any character, he will see that every decision of the umpire is respected.

Calling the Game on Account of Darkness. Another point that may arise is the question of calling a game. A football game should not be called for any condition of the weather, but should be played, rain or shine. In the event, however, of a game having been started so late, or through accidents having been so prolonged as to make it impossible to finish it by daylight, it is the duty of the referee to call the game an unfinished game, unless some previous agreement has been entered into by the two captains. Every game, however, should be started so early as to make any chance of this event occurring impossible; there can be nothing more unsatisfactory than an unfinished match. For all this a referee ought not to let a game continue after it is so dark that he and the umpire cannot, by their inability to follow the operations on the field, be reasonably sure to make all their decisions correctly.

CHAPTER XIII

DIAGRAMS OF PLAYS

Explanation of the Diagrams. Before presenting the diagrams of the plays in this chapter, there must be a few words of explanation.

The team executing the play is drawn in outline, and the opponents by shaded figures. To avoid multiplication of detail, one or two of the opponents are omitted in each diagram, their positions being so far removed from the seat of action that they could not reasonably be counted upon to take any part in the immediate checking of the play before the line is pierced. None of these plays are carried beyond the passage of the line. The primary object is to get the runner through the opponents' line free and clear, with one or more interferers, if possible, to help him down the field. Those opponents who are omitted from the diagram would be the ones who might check his progress after he had pierced the line and started down the field.

The path of each player directly concerned in the interference is indicated by a dotted line. Where there is no dotted line the player blocks in his position in the line. The pass of the ball from the quarter-back to the runner is indicated by a feathered line. The dark, arrow-like strokes at the end of a dotted line indicate the direction in which the player applies his blocking.

Positions of the Players. The players in each case are lettered as follows: c., centre-rush; R.G., right guard; L.G., left guard; R.T., right tackle; L.T., left tackle; R.E., right end; L.E., left end; Q., quarter-back; R.H.B., right half-back; L.H.B., left half-back; F.B. full-back.

The positions in which they stand are indicated as clearly as possible upon the diagram, and it is intended that these diagrams shall be relatively accurate. A single distance, therefore, on one of these diagrams, should furnish a sufficient key to the position of each player, since the diagrams are supposed to be projected on one general scale, the scale being a quarter of an inch to one foot.

In arranging the positions of the men acting upon the defensive, the attempt has been made to place them in as advantageous positions for checking the play as they would be likely to assume. If there arose any doubt or question, the side acting on the defensive has been given the benefit of the doubt, and have then always been placed in the better position of the two for checking the play. It is believed that in no case has any diagram been arranged with an unduly unfavorable situation of the players on the defense.

The two opponents usually omitted from the diagrams are the full-back and the rush-line half-back on the side farthest from the play.

Reversing the Movement. It will be noticed that in nearly every case the same play can be executed upon the other side of the centre. The choice of sides is purely arbitrary, and had better be decided according to the ability of the runner to execute the movement to best advantage. Some runners prefer to dodge upon the right foot, while others will prefer the left foot. The same element of choice or preference exists on many other points, and if it is desired to change the play from one side to the other, these minor points should be considered.

Each Play Practical. No one of the plays presented in this chapter is purely theoretical. Each has been thoroughly tested against an experienced eleven. There is not one of them which cannot be advantageously worked if properly directed. If the play is found to work bunglingly, or with poor success, the reason should be sought and the fault corrected. It may exist in the slowness of some member of the interference, the failure of some player to do his complete work, or more probably a slight deviation in the path of some one of the players, by which he interferes with, or slows down, the successful execution of the movement. No play can be successful unless all of these minor details have close attention.

The coach should never discard a play from his repertory until he is satisfied, not merely that it is not proving successful, but that it cannot be made to prove successful. In other words, he must know not merely that it is stopped, but the reason why it is stopped. It may often happen that that reason is a neglect of duty on the part of some one player which may be easily corrected. Some man in the rush-line has not, perhaps, been taught the art of long blocking, and his failure to obstruct his opponent a sufficient interval of time may be the root of the whole difficulty, and be easily remediable. A very good method of judging a play is to make use of some of the tests enumerated in the chapter on "Accessories of Coaching."

Making the Dispositions. The assignments of the men to the work should be, in each case, the result of careful study, but changes may be tried if desired. No change, however, should be attempted which will interfere with the quick line-up. In some cases a change might be made where an interferer, instead of preceding the runner, is directed to follow him. These are really questions of personal preference, to be determined by the captain or coach, who knows the peculiar ability of his players, and will recognize where such a change as this would be wise.

In making the dispositions of players in different plays, it is always a mooted point whether an extra man can be of more service by going through the line ahead of the runner and "cleaning out the hole," as the expression is, or whether he is of more value as a pusher behind the runner, where the full force of his strength may be applied to force the runner past any point where he is temporarily obstructed. It is not possible to lay down any arbitrary rule on this matter, as it must depend, not alone upon the play, but upon the system of defense of the opponents, and often upon the peculiar ability of the runner or the assisting player. This is a point, however, which will constantly arise, and in each case it can, perhaps, best be settled by trying both methods in practice.

The Play on the Blackboard. In presenting one of these plays to a team, the best plan will be to assemble the players and have the movement carefully drawn out upon the blackboard, making such slight changes in the dispositions or in the minor details as may be desired. The coach should then be prepared to answer any inquiries, and after every point has been cleared up, the players should go out upon the field, and taking their positions as provided in the diagram, walk through the play two or three times before attempting to execute it in the regular way. The players can thus familiarize themselves with the appearance of the movement, and get a better idea of the path over which each man travels. After walking through the play three or four times, let the pace be gradually quickened until the men execute the movement at a slow trot. From this the pace can be steadily quickened until the greatest possible speed is attained.

It may be questioned why a play requires to be interpreted upon the blackboard, when it is already in the hands of each one of the players. There is a reason, however, for this, and it is a valid one. Team play, as we have previously stated, is only possible in its highest efficiency when the players study the principles involved in every movement, so that they understand their own relative importance in each play, and realize wherein the success of the play may be obstructed through their negligence. A blackboard explanation, accompanied by questions and discussion, will give to many players a much clearer idea of the principle involved in the movement than they would have if this feature of the instruction was omitted.

Special Instructions to the Leading Players. After the first day of practice of the play, the coach or captain being then fairly familiar with the movements of each man, a sheet of special instructions should be prepared for the important players. These instructions should emphasize the points which must be borne in mind, thereby saving the coach much repetition, beside expediting the time when the play shall be smoothly executed.

In order to show more clearly the nature of these instructions to the players, we present the draft of possible instructions to the six players who take the most important parts in a single series of plays here offered. A similar set of instructions may easily be prepared for any of the plays here shown, if the plays themselves are studied a little more closely by the captain or coach, and the various contingencies and critical points carefully noted. It is not necessary that such instructions should be prepared for each player, but only for the men who fill the most important positions in the movement.

FORMATION OF SMALL WEDGES
(See Diagrams)

Instructions To Right End.

26. The rush-line half is the dangerous man. You should help the right tackle block his man, but one or the other of you (whichever is free first) should go to the rush-line half. This is imperative. Arrange it between you.

27. Your tackle goes through line instantly inside of his opponent; you remain and block his opponent or any one else who tries to come through on your side.

28. Push behind runner.

29. Look out for your opposing end; keep him out of the play if he gets into it. It is not probable that he will get into it for the first two or three times, and you can at first afford to let him go, and take the rush-line back, if you can get him. Otherwise the quarter-back, if you can get him.

30. Get into this play very cautiously, foxing your own end if you can, so as to get on the outside of him by some quick movement. *Under no circumstances must you be drawn beyond him.* Your work in the play is to block off the end, as the play is around this end.

31. This play is the reverse of No. 30. Follow instructions given to left end for No. 30.

32. Get down the field as quickly as possible under the kick.

33. You are the runner. Follow the exact path shown on the diagram, which must be parallel to the path of the first runner, and in an exactly opposite direction. Then make your dodge and find your hole just inside of the tackle-guard hole, close to guard. You should receive the ball by a hand pass, not by a toss. If the play does not work well, it is probably because you are not going far enough back before receiving the ball.

Instructions To Right Tackle.

26. The rush-line half is the dangerous man. You and the right end block your man. Whichever one of you finds himself least effective should instantly go on to the rush-line half. This is imperative. Help runner all you can after he is through the line.

27. Go through instantly inside your man, and get across and help pull runner through hole.

28. Do just the same as in 27, but block an instant.

29. Block your man hard in the line. Your work in this play is more important than in any other. Quarter will help you with your man immediately after first pass; make your man go outside of you. Special Note. If any opponent blocks in the line between tackle and guard, leave your own man and take this inside opponent and throw him in. Notify your right end that he must take your man.

30. Block your man in the line, and throw him in (just the opposite of heretofore); a second later, if possible, block opposing rush-line back, getting him on the outside. Special Note. If an opponent blocks in the line between tackle and guard, leave your own man and take the inside opponent. In this case notify right end that he must take your man and throw him in.

31. This play is the reverse of No. 30. Follow instructions given to left tackle in No. 30.

32. Get down the field quickly under the kick.

33. Block your man hard and long. Right half-back will block the hole on your left. Make your man go well outside of you.

Instructions To Right Half-back.

26. You are wholly responsible for the hole in this play. If any opponent blocks in the line between tackle and guard, take him and throw him in. Otherwise quarter-back, if he is where you can get at him. Otherwise take guard, striking him hard and low, and keep on for quarter.

27. Go across inside of quarter and take tackle, not the end. If tackle is out of the play take either end or rush-line back, as seems best in practice.

28. You are the runner. *The hole is farther out than you would naturally expect. Go through close to tackle.*

29. You receive the ball as in 28, but make the second pass and keep on exactly as in 28. Give the ball to runner in the pit of his stomach.

30. You receive the ball in this play exactly as in Nos. 28 and 29, but instead of passing it to the full-back as in No. 29, you pass it to the left half-back, who will cross from his position and receive the ball from you on your left side. Full-back "fakes" the play and does exactly the same as in 29, but you do not pass to him.

31. This play is the reverse of No. 30. Read the instructions given in No. 30 to the left half-back.

32. Block hard in the line between tackle and guard. Special Note. In Nos. 26, 27, 32, and 33 you are solely responsible for any inside man between tackle and guard, and must keep him out of the play without regard to anything else.

33. You are responsible for the tackle-guard hole. Be sure that no one comes through that hole and obstructs the second pass in this play.

Instructions To Left End.

26. Get over quickly and push behind runner. Once or twice try going straight through the line and go over to meet runner as he comes through hole and help pull him through. After careful practice of both methods, report to quarter-back which you think most effective, and do that one only.

27. Help the tackle with his man. *You must make a good hole!* The quarter and left half-back are both coming ahead of the runner to block off tackle and end. Therefore, after your first moment of blocking the tackle, you may find yourself free to go on to rush-line back or quarter-back.

28. Help your tackle block his man. If possible throw tackle back into the rush-line back. If this is not possible, throw the tackle outward; make no mistake on this last point.

29. With the left half-back you cross inside of the quarter. Try and arrive just in time to push behind the second runner.

30. Go across as in No. 29 (inside quarter), and with the quarter and right end block off the opposing left end. The play is around that end.

31. This play is the reverse of No. 30. Follow instructions given to right end in No. 30.

32. Get down the field under the kick.

33. Do just the same as in 27.

Instructions To Left Tackle.

26. Block your man in the line, and then go through and help the runner as he emerges.

27. Block your man and make him go outside of you. Left end helps you in this play.

28. Block your man. Left half-back helps you. If possible try and throw him back on to the rush-line back. If this is not possible, throw him outward.

29. Block an instant, and then come quickly around behind to drop on ball in case of a fumble on the second pass. If rarely fumbled in practice, follow the path shown in diagram.

30. Block hard in the line, and with the left guard keep any one from coming through the tackle-guard hole on your side, while also attending to your own man. The latter is more important.

31. This play is the reverse of No. 30. Read the instructions given to right tackle for No. 30.

32. Get down the field quickly under the kick.

33. Do just the same as in 27.

Instructions To Left Half-back.

26. Go across quickly and push behind runner. Be very careful, however, not to obstruct the pass. If opposing left end gets runner, arrange with quarter-back to start on signal for the snap and take the left end. It might be well to act similarly if the rush-line back stops the play, as he perhaps will. If the change does not work, however, go back to the first instructions to push behind runner. Notify the quarter of any change in your play.

27. You are solely responsible for the hole in this play. Take the inside man, if there is any, and throw him in. If there is no inside man, take the half-back as he starts toward the other side of the line. He is the dangerous man to the play. If there is an inside man, with half-back and quarter-back all in around the hole, call on left end to help you. Otherwise not.

28. Do just the same as in 27. You are responsible for the hole. Take the inside man (if there is one) above everything else. On every play at this hole, in this series,

you are absolutely responsible for any opponent who blocks in the line between opposing tackle and guard.

29. Get off quickly and go across inside quarter. Take care, however, not to obstruct his work. If you reach hole ahead of runner, go through ahead of him. Otherwise help him through. If you have a chance to go through ahead of runner, take tackle, end, or rush-line back.

30. You are the runner. Get away very quickly and receive ball on a criss-cross from right half-back. The play is around the opposite end, and your blockers are the left end, quarter-back, and right end. You will probably find it easier to circle the end than go inside of it.

31. This play is the reverse of No. 30. Read the special instructions to right half-back in that play.

32. Get down the field under the kick.

33. The danger in this play is that opposing right guard will not be put out of the play. Get into him hard and low, and shove him back as much as possible and over on to centre. Stay with him.

Instructions To Full-back.

26. You are the runner. The hole is just inside your right tackle. You have a strong pushing force behind you, so keep your feet as long as possible.

27. The success of this movement depends on your ability to make the dodge. Practise it continually. Let your dodging step be made with the right foot and spring backward sharply from it. The first path (before the dodge) must be maintained long enough to draw over the opposing backs. Get the ball always before you dodge. For the line-up stand a trifle farther to the left than usual. There is a good wide hole in this play. Keep your feet, and play it as if for a long run. Run low after you dodge.

28. Go on left side of runner, and push him hard and low. You can meet and steady him on his turn into the line. Try in practice going through once or twice ahead of runner, and taking the opposing rush-line back. Change if it proves better.

29. You advance slowly so as to be in the correct position for right half-back to simply transfer the ball from the quarter to you. He should not himself carry it forward a foot; after receiving it, he passes it to you on a level with the pit of your stomach, so that there can be little danger of your fumbling. This play should be executed at lightning speed, and is entirely safe on a wet day. You pass behind right half-back, not in front of him.

30. Do just as you do in No. 29, but pass behind the right half-back, and go into the same hole in the line. Try and execute the play so that opponents shall think the second pass is to you. Keep out of runner's way. When through line, go straight for opposing rush-line half or quarter.

31. This play is the reverse of No. 30. Do the same thing on the other side of line.

32. A quick side kick. It ought to be placed out of reach of opposing full-back. It should be a long, low punt that will roll. Or it may be a short punt of twenty yards with good height.

33. You cannot make this play quite as rapidly as No. 29. Your pass to the right end must be a short hand pass, not a toss. Start from a little to the left of your usual place. The play will need practice more than any other of this series.

With these few words of general explanation we will proceed immediately to the presentation of the diagrams, accompanying each diagram with a brief description of so much of the movement as is not clearly interpreted by the engraving, giving the precedence of different players traversing the same track, stating our own preference in certain cases for an interference ahead or behind the runner, and giving one or two hints as to the times and occasions when the play may be most successfully employed.

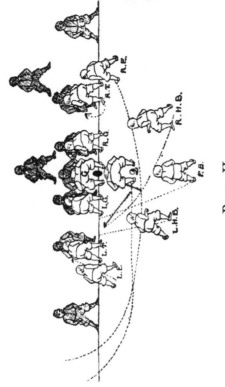

Play II

Ordinary Formation: Outlet No. 2

This is a good play for a team having an extra strong quarter-back, but in no other case should it be attempted. Few plays are more completely dependent upon the effort of a single individual, and the quarter alone can make this movement successful.

The play is a fake at the tackle-guard hole. The ball is passed to the right half-back, who turns half round after receiving it, and blocking himself backward against his own line and interferers, passes the ball to the quarter-back, who circles the left end. If the play is successfully executed, the opposing right end will be drawn in and should miss the runner by about three feet.

Right end interferes for the quarter-back down the field.

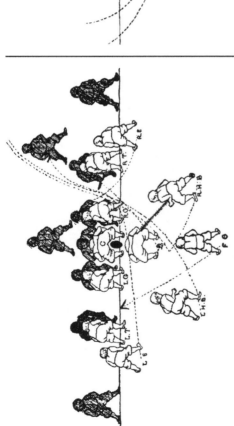

Play I

Ordinary Formation: Outlet No. 1

[Plays I. to IX. inclusive are offered as suggestions for indirect attacks to supplement the usual direct attacks from this primary formation.]

A dodge by the right half-back after receiving the ball. He should keep on his original path for an appreciable moment of time after the pass. The left half-back steadies him on his reverse, and then pushes from behind. The nearer the dodge is made to the line, without danger of contact with the centre, the more effective it will be. Full-back crosses in front of left half-back.

The ability of different players to execute a sharp dodge varies greatly, but in the hands of a light, quick-moving back this play should be very effective.

In an important match on a rainy day this play should not be attempted.

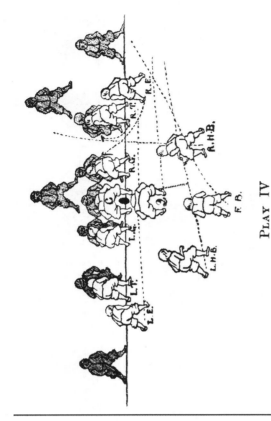

PLAY IV

ORDINARY FORMATION: OUTLET No. 4

This play is based on a double pass, and is a fairly strong attack. With practice, it is entirely safe for a wet day.

The first pass is to the left half-back, who passes again to the right half-back for a run through the tackle-guard hole. The pass should be a hand-pass, — not a throw, — and the ball should be delivered to the second runner directly in the pit of the stomach. The right half-back does not move until he gets the ball, unless to take one step backward. The play is ostensibly a round-the-end attack. The left tackle blocks an instant, and then comes around in a position to drop on the ball if it should be fumbled in the second pass. Full-back goes *ahead* of the left half-back.

PLAY III

ORDINARY FORMATION: OUTLET No. 3

Ball to the left half-back, who dodges behind his interferers. The play starts as if the interference was to go around the end.

In an important match on a rainy day this play should not be attempted.

PLAY VI

ORDINARY FORMATION: OUTLET No. 6

Ball to left end.

The full-back steadies the left end, and helps to turn him into the line. Left half-back goes ahead of full-back.

PLAY V

ORDINARY FORMATION: OUTLET No. 5

This play is a little dangerous, but can be successfully worked with a clever end.

The ball goes to the left half-back, and the entire interference starts as if to circle the end. The left end gets away *instantly* on the snap, and circles quickly to a position one and a half yards outside of runner, and one yard behind him.

The second pass must be made when the left half-back is opposite the opposing left tackle, *and not a moment later.* It should be a slightly backward toss of the ball, and the left end should be held responsible for being in the position where he can receive this toss at the moment it is made, which must be just before the opposing left end hits the interference. Practically the left half-back passes as soon as he can transfer the ball from one side to the other. The left tackle must block an instant, and come around quickly to fall on the ball in case the second pass is fumbled.

This play need not be discarded on a rainy day.

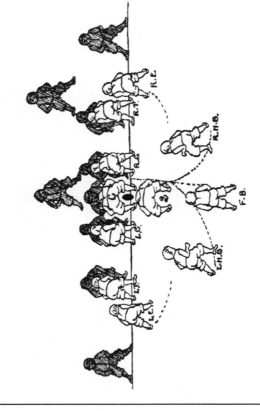

PLAY VIII

ORDINARY FORMATION: OUTLET No. 8

Ball to the full-back, with the right half-back as the principal pusher. Left half-back and quarter-back should get immediately into the push, reinforced by the two ends. The play can also be made on the other side of the centre.

PLAY VII

ORDINARY FORMATION: OUTLET No. 7

Ball to the right half-back.

This must be played as a dive play, and not as a regular run with interference. The full-back should push immediately behind the runner, with the quarter-back pushing behind the full-back.

The same play can be operated on the other side of the line.

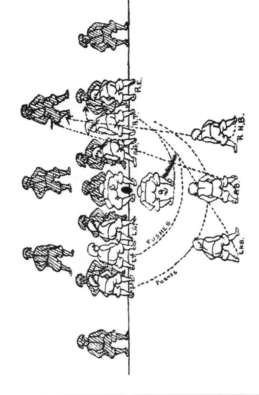

PLAY X

CLOSE FORMATION: OUTLET No. 1

Ball to left half-back. Right tackle and right end engage opposing tackle, and throw him outward. Right half-back and full-back go straight through the hole ahead of the runner, and engage opposing rush-line back. Left end and tackle, with quarter-back, push the runner.

Try also letting right half-back help right guard with his man instead of going straight through.

PLAY IX

ORDINARY FORMATION: OUTLET No. 9

Ball to left half-back, who goes outside end. Form the interference carefully, and do not attempt speed at the beginning of the practice. The same play can be directed around the other end if desired.

Right half-back and full-back must get off instantly, and put the opposing end out of the play, or it will inevitably fail. Strike him low and hard.

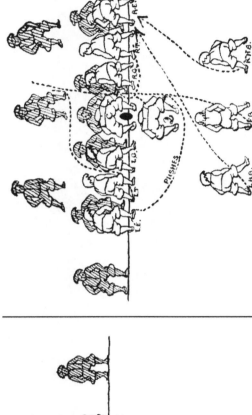

PLAY XI

CLOSE FORMATION: OUTLET NO. 2

Ball to right tackle.

This is a difficult manoeuvre, and will require very careful rehearsing. The paths of several players cross each other at a point just outside the position of left end. The order of precedence of these players should be as follows: left half-back (who, with left end, engages opposing tackle and throws him in); left guard (who engages opposing end, blocking him out); right half-back (who engages opposing rush-line back, blocking him in); right end (who, circling outside runner, engages opposing end, blocking him outward); the runner (who goes between end and tackle).

Quarter-back blocks off opposing left tackle, or any opponent following behind runner. Left tackle and full-back instantly engage opposing right guard, the full-back crossing ahead of runner, right end, and right half-back.

PLAY XII

CLOSE FORMATION: OUTLET NO. 3

A centre dive by the full-back. Right guard and right tackle engage opposing left guard and throw him out. Left half-back and right half-back make a feint attack against opposing left tackle; left end, with quarter-back, pushes behind runner.

When properly worked, this is one of the most effective of plays at the centre of the line. Another disposition of the labor is to let centre and right guard throw opposing left guard outwards, while right half-back, from a position a little to the right of his ordinary place, strikes the opposing centre without an instant's delay, and throws him to the left. The attack must be quick, and the more he can strike from the side the better. Left half pushes behind.

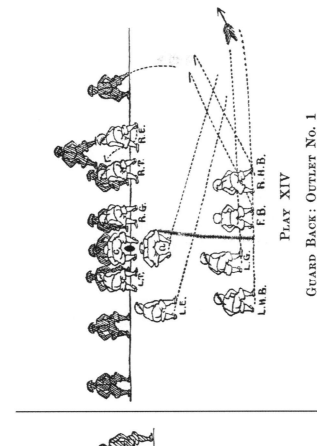

Play XIV

Guard Back: Outlet No. 1

The guard should line up half a yard in advance of the line of the backs, who should be five yards back; any nearer distance will seriously hinder the effectiveness of the play. Ball to left half-back. The play is a simple round-the-end attack, but cannot possibly succeed unless the interference is directed straight out across the field for some little distance after it starts. If allowed to work up toward the line of scrimmage in order to meet the opposing end, it will undoubtedly fail as often as it succeeds.

Full-back and right half-back are the only players to go straight for the end.

Play XIII

Close Formation: Outlet No. 4

Ball to right half-back.

With a good dodging half-back this is, perhaps, the most effective play in this volume. The dodge must be sharp and quick, but it must not be executed so soon as to fail to draw off the opposing backs toward the left side of line. The left half-back steps backward a trifle, timing his movement so as to grasp the runner strongly around the waist, and help him forward after his dodge. Left tackle and left end cross inside the quarter, and with the quarter and right end all engage the opposing left tackle and throw him outward. Right tackle, with right guard, blocks opposing left guard inwards. Full-back aids in the feint first attack toward the left side of line.

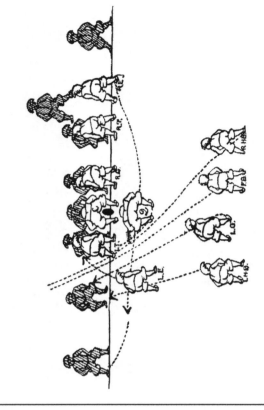

PLAY XVI

GUARD BACK: OUTLET No. 3

A short backward pass to the right half-back. Left end helps left tackle against opposing guard. Left half-back and left guard engage opposing right tackle. Full-back precedes the runner through the hole; right end crosses sharply behind the interference, and prevents opposing right end from following runner and overtaking him from behind.

Guard against a forward pass in this play.

PLAY XV

GUARD BACK: OUTLET No. 2

The pass is to the guard. Right tackle helps block opposing left guard. Right end engages rush-line back; right half-back and full-back take the tackle; left half-back, left end, and quarter push behind runner.

This same movement should also be tried with the ball passed to the left half-back, who in this case is preceded by the guard.

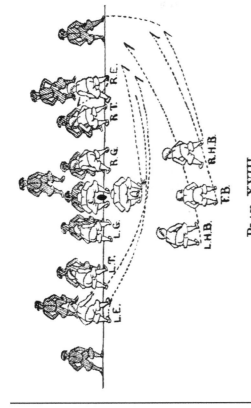

Play XVIII

Ends In: Outlet No. 1

Left end receives the ball from quarter, leaving his position in the line and coming close behind the quarter. In doing this he should get off as quickly as does the tackle when he runs from his position in the line. The pass from the quarter should be very short, and the quarter should go on with the runner. In the diagram, the right end and right tackle box the opposing tackle, and the quarter, as he comes with the runner, disposes of the rush-line back. Should the quarter, either from being too slow, or from the fact of the runner being an especially fast man, find that he cannot take this rush-line back, then the half-back may be sent against him instead of in the mass of interference at the end. The left tackle follows left end and makes the play safe from behind.

Play XVII

Guard Back: Outlet No. 4

Ball to left half-back for a side kick. Right tackle goes down field; also left end, after a moment's blocking. The kick should be a high one, and not too long to prevent the assembling of two men around the opposing full-back when he receives the ball.

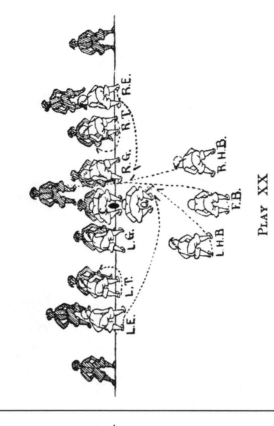

PLAY XX

ENDS IN: OUTLET No. 3

Full-back receives the ball on a hand pass from quarter, and plunges directly through between centre and right guard, who open a hole for him. Both halves go in from behind and push while both ends follow the halves and add their weight and strength to the mass. Both tackles crowd their men out in order that they may be unable to help stop the push.

PLAY XIX

ENDS IN: OUTLET No. 2

Left half-back under full headway gets the ball on a short pass from the quarter. Right end helps right guard to crowd his man in. Right half-back aids right tackle in forcing his man out, while full-back precedes left half through the opening. Left end and left tackle follow behind and push while quarter goes in directly behind left half and practically attached to him.

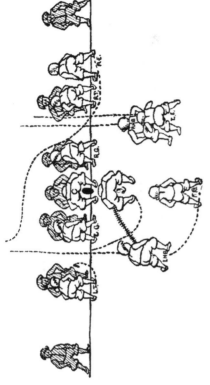

PLAY XXII

TANDEM ON TACKLE: OUTLET NO. 1

The four plays from this line-up (Nos. XXII., XXIII., XXIV., and XXV.) will be found to be good ground gainers, and well adapted for use inside the opponents' twenty-five-yard line. They will be much more effective if the left end is a strong player. He takes his position at each line-up with his arms extended, and resting his hands upon the hips of the right half-back. In all the attacks at the right tackle-guard hole, the right half-back is the apex of the movement. The formation should be very close to the line, and the manœuvres should be executed as straight dive plays, without an instant's delay for the formation of interference.

In the above play the attack at the right side of the line is a fake, but should be strongly made. Ball to left half-back; full-back pushes.

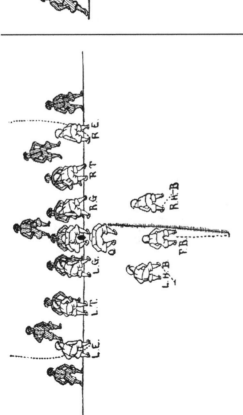

PLAY XXI

ENDS IN: OUTLOOK NO. 4

As this play is intended to appear to the opponents similar in its formation to XVIII., XIX., and XX., the ends should, upon the line-up, take their positions close to the tackles, but may, and should, as soon as the play is started, slightly body-check the man most likely to interfere with the kick, and then make all haste down the field. Full-back and the two halves take the same positions as in the former plays, but full-back starts upon a backward run just before the snap, which should be properly timed, so that the ball is put in play and passed by the quarter to reach the full-back just as he has come to a standstill at the proper distance for a kick. After the ball is snapped, and not till then, the two halves take a step or two backward and out, and then protect the kicker in the usual way.

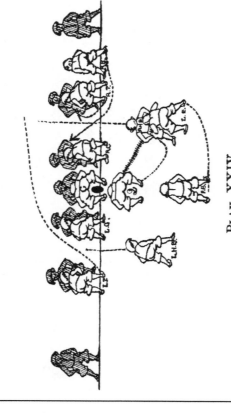

Play XXIII

TANDEM ON TACKLE: OUTLET No. 2

Ball to left end. This play will be found to be the strongest play in the series, if left end is a strong player. The right half-back pushes on the left side of the runner, and the quarter-back on the right side.

Play XXIV

TANDEM ON TACKLE: OUTLET No. 3

If this is executed strictly as a dive play, it will be found to be a very strong attack. The pass is to the right half-back. Left end is the principal pusher, reinforced by the quarter-back and full-back. The left half-back executes a fake attack on the other side of the centre. Right end goes in *ahead* of the tandem, and must keep out of its way.

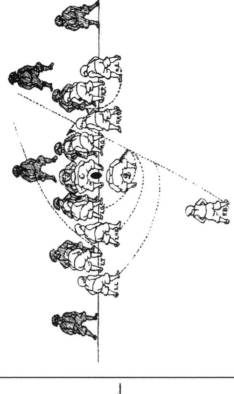

PLAY XXVI

SMALL WEDGES: OUTLET No. 1

(See fuller instructions upon this series in an earlier part of this chapter.)

Ball to full-back.

Opposing rush-line half is the dangerous man to this play. Right end or right tackle should take him *instantly,* whichever one is free first. This is imperative. As rush-line back can only meet runner, however, at or behind the line, the pushers behind runner are valuable. Left half-back must be careful not to obstruct the pass. If opposing left end interferes with runner, let the left half-back cross ahead of the pass and take this end.

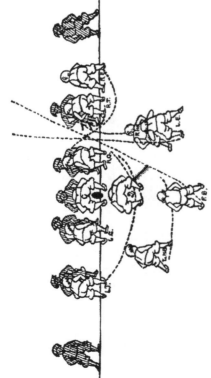

PLAY XXV

TANDEM ON TACKLE: OUTLET No. 4

The pass is to the full-back. Right half-back and left end go through the line ahead of the full-back, and clear the opponents out of the path. Left half-back is the principal pusher, reinforced by quarter-back and left tackle. Right end goes in ahead of the tandem.

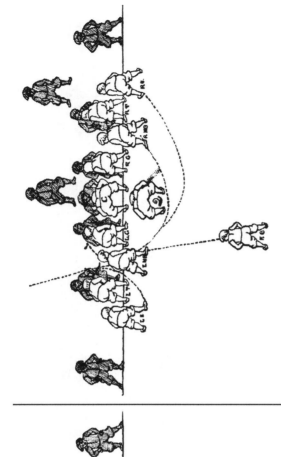

PLAY XXVII

SMALL WEDGES: OUTLET No. 2

(See fuller instructions upon this series in an earlier part of this chapter.)

Ball to full-back.

The left-hand wedge *must* make the hole, and left half-back is responsible for this. Let him call on the left end if needed. Right half-back should go inside the quarter and push opposing tackle outwards.

If the dodge is well executed and sufficiently pronounced, the runner will find a large hole awaiting him. Let him bear this in mind and keep his feet at all hazards, executing the movement as if it was to be a long run and not a mere dive attack. This play need not be abandoned on a wet day.

PLAY XXVIII

SMALL WEDGES: OUTLET No. 3

(See fuller instructions upon this series in an earlier part of this chapter.)

Ball to right half-back.

The full-back goes on the left side of runner, and engages opposing right half-back. The tackle should be thrown back on to the opposing rush-line back, if possible; otherwise throw him outward. Opposing right guard must be blocked hard and long; left guard must not be thrown back so as to block the runner's path.

The runner should remember that the hole is farther out than he would naturally expect.

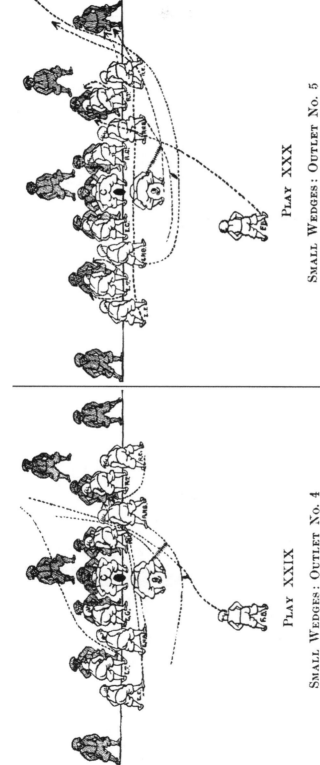

PLAY XXIX

SMALL WEDGES: OUTLET NO. 4

(See fuller instructions upon this series in an earlier part of this chapter.)

Criss-cross from right half-back to full-back.

This play should be executed at full speed. Left end and left half-back cross inside of quarter. Quarter helps right tackle on his man. The runner follows after quarter; left end and left half-back follow behind runner and push him. This play need not be abandoned on a wet day.

PLAY XXX

SMALL WEDGES: OUTLET NO. 5

(See fuller instructions upon this series in an earlier part of this chapter.)

Criss-cross from right half-back to left half-back.

The runner goes inside the end, but otherwise as far out from the centre as possible. The three centre men must block hard and long, and not yield an inch, thus enabling the criss-cross to be executed as close to the line as possible. This play need not be abandoned on a wet day.

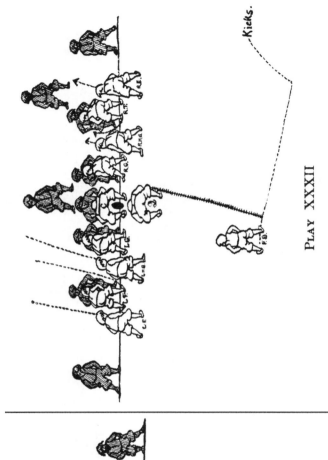

Play XXXII

Small Wedges : Outlet No. 7

(See fuller instructions upon this series in an earlier part of this chapter.)

Quick punt by full-back.

The kick should be toward the left side of field, and a low, long-rolling punt. Being unexpected, it should prove effective. *Every man down the field on this kick!* Left half-back and left end go down field immediately, without blocking opponents in the passage through the line. Not less than four men should be gathered about the opposing full-back when he reaches the ball.

Play XXXI

Small Wedges : Outlet No. 6

(See fuller instructions upon this series in an earlier part of this chapter.)

Criss-cross from left half-back to right half-back.

This play is a reversing of the previous movement, and should be brought off in the same manner, the attack being directed at the other side of the line. This play need not be abandoned on a wet day.

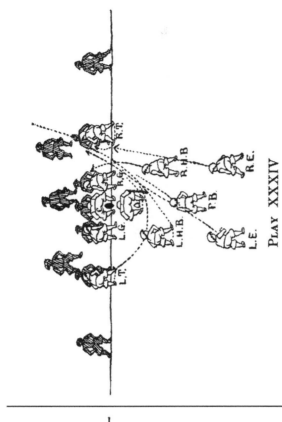

PLAY XXXIV

FIVE-SQUARE FORMATION: OUTLET No. 1

Ball to left half-back, who falls in behind the full-back, and in advance of left end and tackle. Right half-back blocks opposing guard. Right end assists right tackle against tackle. Full-back goes ahead of runner to clear the path of opponents.

PLAY XXXIII

SMALL WEDGES: OUTLET No. 8

(See fuller instructions upon this series in an earlier part of this chapter.)

Criss-cross from full-back to right end.

Follow paths exactly as drawn on diagram for second pass. The danger in this play is of having the centre thrown back. Left half-back must be sure that his side of the line is firmly blocked, to prevent a fumbled second pass. This movement should not be attempted on a wet day.

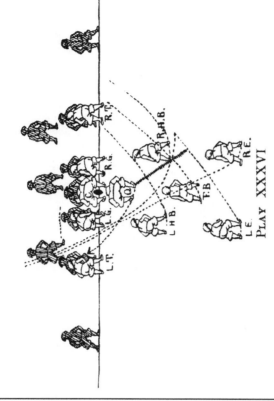

PLAY XXXV

FIVE-SQUARE FORMATION: OUTLET No. 2

Ball to left half-back, who receives it on his left side, and transfers it to his right side, half turning, and passing the ball (by a hand or "short" pass) to the left tackle, who circles the end. Full-back and right end should engage the opposing left end, getting outside of him if possible, and pocketing him. Right tackle blocks the guard. Right half-back instantly engages tackle.

It will be better for the left tackle to keep close in to the mass and break away just before reaching the passing of the end.

PLAY XXXVI

FIVE-SQUARE FORMATION: OUTLET No. 3

This is the strongest play of this series, and should be repeatedly successful for average gains of two or three yards. The ball is passed to the left end while he is going forward with the interference toward the *right* of line. He dodges at the point shown on diagram, and, assisted by right end (who has held his place), goes through between left tackle and left guard. Quarter-back, after the pass, helps left tackle block his opponent outward. Left half-back, right half-back, and full-back feint an attack on the right side of line, getting away instantly.

The pass is made behind the full-back and left half-back, and not in front of them.

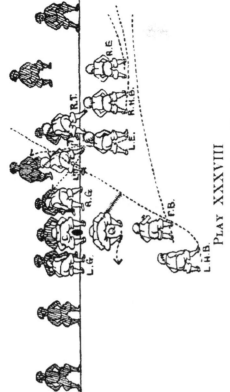

PLAY XXXVIII

TACKLE FORCE: OUTLET No. 1.

This is an effective series, both outlets being unusually strong. Right tackle blocks his opponent on the inside. Left tackle plunges into opposing left guard, opening a wide hole. Left end engages quarter-back; full-back, right half-back, and right end make a dash toward the end to draw out opposing rush-line back. The left half-back receives the ball on his left side, and until he has it he keeps on (for a step or two) with the full-back as if to circle the end; then makes a straight rush toward the line, going through close to the guard's position. The hole is midway between tackle and guard. The relative paths of runner and full-back are as drawn in diagram.

The play will be more effective if the runner is a small man, who will keep on until he cannot gain another inch.

PLAY XXXVII

FIVE-SQUARE FORMATION: OUTLET No. 4.

This is an attempt to introduce an unexpected kick by the full-back. Right end should instantly advance, keeping out of the way of the full-back as the latter drops back and to the right for a kick. Left and right tackle go down the field after a moment's blocking.

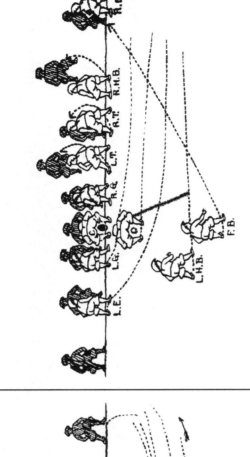

PLAY XXXIX

TACKLE FORCE: OUTLET No. 2

An unusually strong play around the end of the line. Ball to left half-back. The play should be started as quick as a flash. Its especial effectiveness lies in the fact that the runner is wholly protected except at the passage of the end. The space between tackle and end is amply covered; a body of four interferers should accompany runner as he circles the end.

Right-end must get off on the instant of the snap and engage opposing half-back. If the play is started with snap and dash, opposing right tackle cannot reach runner from behind.

PLAY XL

TWO-PLAY FORMATION: OUTLET No. 1

This is not in itself a movement of special value, but will serve to introduce the following play, which, in a critical situation, may be used with really surprising results.

In the attack here shown the full-back helps the right end with his opponent; left guard and left end, with the quarter-back, form the interference for the runner. Right half-back engages opposing left half-back; right tackle engages opposing tackle; left tackle engages quarter. Ball to left half-back.

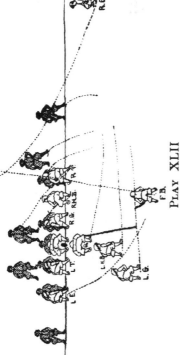

PLAY XLII

TRICK SERIES: OUTLET NO. 1 — DOUBLE PASS

This play is effective and not dangerous, but will need much practice. It may be played in either one of two ways. The pass may be to the left guard, who repasses it to the full-back. Or the pass may be made directly to the full-back, between the left half-back and the left guard. In the latter case the left guard must slow up slightly, and the left half-back get away instantly. This latter pass makes the play a trifle quicker.

Let opposing left end, tackle, and rush-line back *straight through the line*. Block all other opponents strongly on a line with the position of the guard. The runner can then go straight to the line, piercing it at about the position of tackle. Left end should come around in time to fall on the ball if fumbled in the second pass. Right end is principal interferer for the runner after the passage of the line. This attack is very deceptive when well executed.

The runner's path is protected by left guard, left half-back, and quarter on the right; by right guard, right half-back, and right tackle on the left.

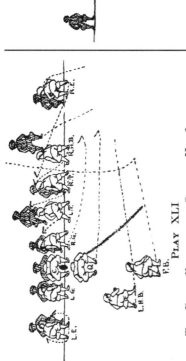

PLAY XLI

TWO-PLAY FORMATION: OUTLET NO. 2

Ball to full-back, who starts as if to circle right end, but, on a sharp quarter-turn dodge, goes through line at the tackle's position.

This will be found an unusually strong play. Right end blocks his opponent a moment, and then helps right tackle with his man. He must be careful not to detain opposing rush-line back; but let him through outside the interference. This player is really the dangerous opponent. The hole may be a little farther out than is expected. Runner can place his hand on left half-back to aid him in the dodge.

Block the tackle *in* : let the end and rush-line back through on the outside of the play. If the runner is caught from behind, it will be the fault of the left end, and he must stay longer with his man. Right half-back and right end must keep clear of right guard. If they collide with him they must change their path, giving him the shortest route. Left tackle must get off very quickly, striking the opposing guard hard and low, and blocking him long.

If opposing left guard catches runner on his dodge, let right guard stay with him and keep out of the interference.

In the interference as here formed the work of the right guard and quarter is to engage opposing left half-back and prevent him from reaching the runner.

Do not be discouraged if, in a first attempt, this movement seems of little value. It is a play which will improve every time it is played, and should be good for a gain of three to five yards on repeated occasions.

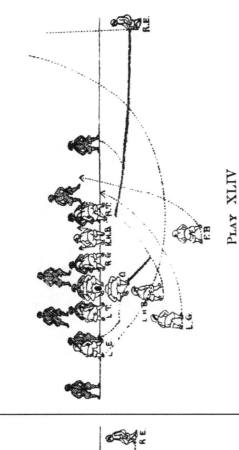

PLAY XLIV

TRICK SERIES: OUTLET No. 3 — LONG PASS

A long second pass from left half-back to right end, who stays out as far as possible. Right half-back and right tackle block close and hard. Left half-back delays his pass as long as possible to draw opposing left end well in. Left end circles wide out as main interferer for the runner. He must be careful not to obstruct the pass.

It may be necessary in this play for the left end to slightly change his position in order to reach the runner in time to be of any service. He must arrive in time to engage the opposing end, and prevent him, if possible, from reaching the runner. It may be well for him to slightly shift his position toward the centre, if necessary, to enable him to do this.

PLAY XLIII

TRICK SERIES: OUTLET No. 2 — RIGHT-ANGLING THE END

Ball to left guard.

An attempt to circle the end, with interference against the opposing end from diametrically opposite directions. Right end should endeavor to reach his opponent an appreciable instant before the main interference reaches him, striking him hard enough to unsettle him and prevent his breaking the interference. Full-back blocks the end for an instant, but keeps on immediately against rush-line back. Left end must get into the interference.

The position of the right end should be *never less than five yards* outside his opponent.

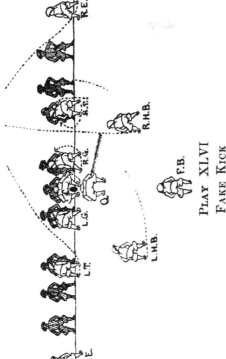

Play XLVI
Fake Kick

This is the simplest form of a fake kick, in which the ball may be passed to either the right or left half-back for a sharp dash through the tackle-guard hole. The tackle should find it easy to get his opponent in such a position that it will be impossible for him to go through inside of his position. As he starts to go through on the outside, the tackle can effectively block him off from the runner.

The guard will have the more difficult task of blocking his opponent and keeping him away from the runner. He should have the immediate assistance of the centre as soon as the latter can safely render that assistance. The guard should block his opponent on the outside, and be prepared to render the centre sufficient assistance to enable them mutually to block the man on the inside.

The half-back should stand very close to the line for this play, and right end and left tackle should go sharply through to render him assistance as he emerges from the line.

Be careful not to have a forward pass.

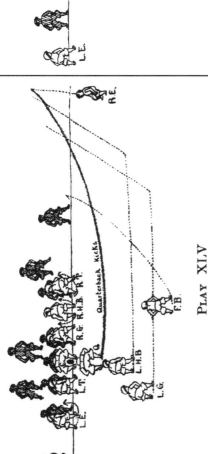

Play XLIV

Trick Series: Outlet No. 4 — Quarter-Back Kick

A quick kick by the quarter. The ball is to be recovered by the right end, who must keep on-side until the kick is delivered. Left half-back and left guard follow the paths indicated in the diagram, keeping well on-side until they know that the kick has been made. Full-back goes straight to the opposing end.

This play can only be executed from the left side of the field, and the kick should be high enough to enable the right end to get under it and capture it if possible before it reaches the ground. Failing to do this, if close pressed by the opposing end, he should leave the ball to be secured by his own left guard or half-back, and himself vigorously engage the end.

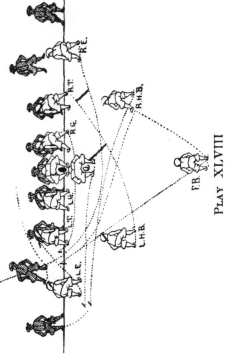

PLAY XLVII

FAKE KICK CRISS-CROSS: OUTLET No. 1

This is the first of a series of two plays in each of which the line-up is for a kick, while the play terminates in a run.

In the first movement, as shown above, the full-back has dropped back for a kick, but the ball is passed to the left half-back, and. aided by strong interference, he carries it through the hole between right tackle and end. The dispositions are as follows: Right half-back and full-back take opposing end. Right tackle blocks his own man inwards. Right end goes through immediately and engages opposing half-back. Left guard, left tackle, and quarter-back form an interference for the runner as he circles into the line. Left end goes sharply through to assist runner as he emerges.

This movement should be tried once or twice before disclosing the nature of the second attack, contained in diagram XLVIII, which is the criss-cross.

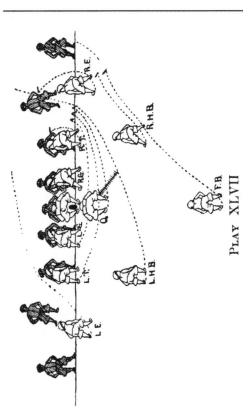

PLAY XLVIII

FAKE KICK CRISS-CROSS: OUTLET No. 2

As soon as the opponents have become a little familiar with the movement in the preceding diagram, this criss-cross form of attack should be tried. The line-up is the same, and the ball, as before, is passed to the left half-back, who, as he rushes forward into the line, repasses it to the right end. Left end and left tackle box the opposing tackle. Quarter-back and right half-back engage the opposing right end. Right guard and full-back act as immediate interferers for the second runner.

The full-back should notice that his first movement is the same as in the preceding play. His dodge should take place immediately after the first pass to the left half-back, and *not before this pass*. This will be in ample time for him to precede the runner in the interference. Right guard should not leave his opponent until he has successfully blocked him for a short interval, to prevent his interfering with the second pass.

Right tackle blocks hard and long.

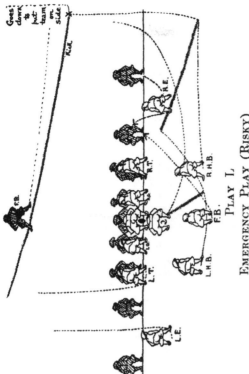

PLAY XLIX
MASS AT TACKLE

This is a single play; but if successfully mastered it will be found very easy to develop a round-the-end attack from the same line-up. The pass is to the left half-back. The path of the runner is just over the spot where opposing left tackle stands, or slightly inside of that place. Left tackle is forced in by the combined attacks of the four players directed against him. Full-back engages opposing end; left end pushes behind runner; quarter-back (after the pass) keeps opposing right tackle out of the play. Opposing left half-back will undoubtedly misjudge the nature of the attack on the first trial, and be found outside the path of the runner.

Right end and right half-back cross ahead of the full-back.

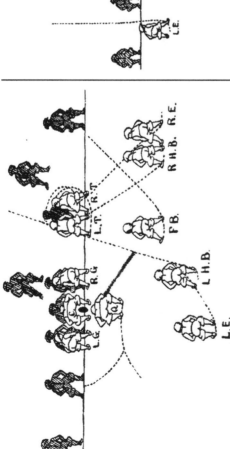

PLAY L
EMERGENCY PLAY (RISKY)

Special play for the last five minutes of a match, with a slightly adverse score.

The pass is to the left half-back. Right end and full-back block the opponent who is next inside of the end. Left half-back, on nearing the line, repasses the ball over the head of opposing left end, to right half-back, who has gone as far as possible toward the side of the field. The play will require careful rehearsing in the matter of this double pass.

Right half-back should not undertake to pass the full-back, but just before meeting him should make a running kick to the farther side of the field, where left tackle and left end must be already located. Right half-back should then dodge the full-back and go straight down the field to put his team on-side. The ball can then be secured by either left end or left tackle, with a good possibility of a touch-down, if the movement has been successful up to this point.

CHAPTER XIV

RULES OF THE SEASON OF 1896

Rule 1. (a) The game shall be played upon a rectangular field 330 feet in length and 160 feet in width, inclosed by heavy white lines marked in lime upon the ground. The two end lines shall be termed goal lines. The goal lines and the side lines shall extend beyond their points of intersection, and the spaces lying behind the goal lines and outside of the side lines shall be termed touch-in-goal. The goal shall be placed in the middle of each goal line, and shall consist of two upright posts exceeding 20 feet in height and placed 18 feet 6 inches apart, with a cross-bar 10 feet from the ground.

(b) The game shall be played by two teams of eleven men each.

(c) The football used shall be of heavy leather inclosing an inflated rubber bladder. The ball shall have the shape of a prolate spheroid.

Compare corresponding rules in old code, namely, 12 and 13, as follows:

Rule 12. The grounds must be 330 feet in length and 160 feet in width, with a goal placed in the middle of each goal line, composed of two upright posts, exceeding 20 feet in height, and placed 18 feet 6 inches apart, with a cross-bar 10 feet from the ground.

Rule 13. The game shall be played by teams of eleven men each, and in case of a disqualified or injured player, a substitute shall take his place. Nor shall the disqualified or injured player return to further participation in the game.

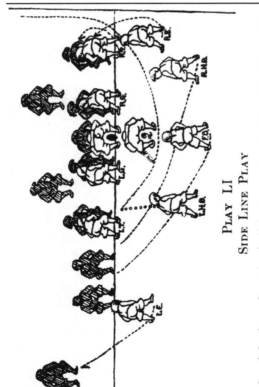

PLAY LI
SIDE LINE PLAY

Special play when the ball is down close to the side line. The position of the ball should be close enough to the line to prevent the right end taking his customary place beside the tackle, and he takes position as shown on diagram. The play begins with a false start by the left half-back. He goes straight to the line, stopping there abruptly, as if discovering his error. *Immediately* upon his stopping in this position, the ball is snapped. The attack is apparently directed toward the long side of field, but under cover of this diversion a "short," or hand, pass is made to the left half-back, who starts from his attained position in the line and circles close behind the quarter and around the right end. Opposing left tackle (who is the outside man of opponents) is blocked inward by right tackle and right end.

The runner must be careful, in the excitement of the play, not to swerve over the side line.

Rule 2. (a) A drop-kick is made by letting the ball fall from the hands and kicking it the very instant it rises from the ground.

(b) A place-kick is made by kicking the ball after it has been placed upon the ground.

(c) A punt is made by letting the ball fall from the hands and kicking it before it touches the ground.

(d) Kick-off is a place-kick from the centre of the field of play, and cannot score a goal.

(e) A kick-out is a drop-kick, place-kick, or punt made by a player of the side which has touched the ball down in its own goal, or into whose touch-in-goal the ball has gone.

(f) A free kick is a term used to designate any kick where the opponents are restrained by rule from advancing beyond a certain point. If a side obtain a free kick they may put the ball in play by a punt, drop-kick, or place-kick, and their opponents cannot come within ten yards of the line on which the free catch was made. The kicker may kick the ball from any point directly behind the spot where the catch was made, on a line parallel to the side line.

Compare Rules 1 and 22 of old code, which read as follows: —

Rule 1. (a) A drop-kick is made by letting the ball fall from the hands and kicking it at the very instant it rises from the ground.

(b) A place-kick is made by kicking the ball after it has been placed on the ground.

(c) A punt is made by letting the ball fall from the hands and kicking it before it touches the ground.

(d) Kick-off is a place-kick from the centre of the field of play, and cannot score a goal.

(e) Kick-out is a drop-kick, place-kick, or punt made by a player of the side which has touched the ball down in its own goal, or into whose touch-in-goal the ball has gone.

As amended by Yale and Princeton: —

Rule 1. (e) Leave out "or into whose touch-in-goal the ball has gone." Otherwise unchanged.

(f) A free kick is a term used to designate any kick where the opponents are restrained by rule from advancing beyond a certain point.

As amended by Harvard, Pennsylvania, and Cornell: —

Rule. (f) "A free kick is a term used to designate any kick where the opponents are restrained by rule from advancing beyond a certain point. If a side obtain a free kick they may put the ball in play by a punt, drop or place kick, and their opponents cannot come within ten yards of the line on which the free kick was made."

Rule 22. A player who has made and claimed a fair catch shall take a drop-kick, or a punt, or place the ball for a place-kick. The opponents may come up to the catcher's mark, and the ball must be kicked from some spot behind that mark on a parallel to touch line.

As amended by Yale and Princeton: —

Rule 22. Substitute the following: "After a fair catch, the ball may be put in play by any player of the side having made the catch. It may be put in play either by a free kick or by a scrimmage, the point of scrimmage being at the catcher's mark. If by a free kick, the opponents must not advance beyond the catcher's mark, and the ball must be kicked from some point behind that mark on a parallel with the touch line."

As amended by Harvard, Pennsylvania, and Cornell: —

Rule 22. This rule is stricken out by Harvard, Pennsylvania, and Cornell, and is supplied by Rule 1, section *f*, and Rule 8, *supra*.

As will be noted, the principal alteration lies in the free kick clause. A player may — see later rules — heel the ball or run with it. If he heel it, the opponents retire ten yards.

Rule 3. The ball goes out of bounds when it crosses the side line, or when the holder puts part of either foot across or on that line. The side line is out of bounds, and the goal line is in goal.

Compare Rule 2 of the old code.

Rule 2. (a) In touch means out of bounds.

(b) A fair is putting the ball in play from touch.

Rule 18. The ball goes in touch when it crosses the side line, or when the holder puts part of either foot across or on that line. The touch line is in touch, and the goal line is in goal.

The term "out of bounds" is used throughout the new code in place of "in touch."

Rule 4. A foul is any violation of a rule. This is identical with Rule 3 of the old code.

Rule 3. A foul is any violation of a rule.

Rule 5. (a) A touch-down is made when the ball is carried, kicked, or passed across the goal line and there held either in goal or touch-in-goal. The point where the touch-down is marked, however, is not where the ball is carried across the line, but where the ball is fairly held or called "down."

(b) A safety is made when a player guarding his goal receives the ball from a player of his own side, either by a pass, a kick, or a snap-back, and then touches it down behind his goal line; or when he himself carries the ball across his own goal line and touches it down; or when he puts the ball into his own touch-in-goal; or when the ball, being kicked by one of his own side, bounds back from an opponent across the goal line, and he then touches it down.

(c) A touch-back is made when a player touches the ball to the ground behind his own goal, the impetus which sent the ball across the line having been received from an opponent.

The old code Rule 4 is the same.

Rule 4. (a) A touch-down is made when the ball is carried, kicked, or passed across the goal line and there held either in goal or touch-in-goal. The point where the touch-down is marked, however, is not necessarily where the ball is carried across the line, but where the ball is fairly held or called "down."

(b) A safety is made when a player, guarding his goal, receives the ball from a player of his own side, either by a pass, a kick, or a snap-back, and then touches it down behind his goal line, or when he himself carries the ball across his own goal line and touches it down, or when he puts the ball into his own touch-in-goal, or when the ball, being kicked by one of his own side, bounds back from an opponent across the goal line, and he then touches it down.

(c) A touch-back is made when a player touches the ball to the ground behind his own goal, the impetus which sent the ball across the line having been received from an opponent.

Rule 6. A punt-out is a punt made by a player of the side which has made a touch-down to one of his own side for a fair catch.

Identical with old Rule 5.

Rule 5. A punt-out is a punt made by a player of the side which has made a touch-down in its opponents goal, to another of his own side for a fair catch.

Rule 7. A scrimmage takes place when the holder of the ball places it upon the ground and puts it in play by kicking it forward or snapping it back.

Identical with old Rule 7.

Rule 7. A scrimmage takes place when the holder of the ball puts it down on the ground, and puts it in play by kicking it forward or snapping it back.

Rule 8. A fair catch is a catch made direct from a kick by one of the opponents, or from a punt-out by one of the same side, provided the man while making the catch makes a mark with his heel, and no other of his side has touched the ball. If he be interfered with by an opponent who is offside, or if he be thrown after catching the ball, unless he has advanced beyond his mark, he shall be given fifteen yards.

See Rule 8 (also Rule 29) of the old code, which reads as follows: —

Rule 8. A fair catch is a catch made direct from a kick by one of the opponents (or a punt-out by one of the same side), provided the man intending to make the catch indicates that intention by holding up his hand when running for the ball, and also makes a mark with his heel upon catching it, and no other of his side touches the ball. If he be interfered with by an opponent who is offside, or if he be thrown after catching the ball, he shall be given fifteen yards, unless this carry the ball across the goal line. In that case he shall be given but half the intervening distance. After having raised his hand he cannot run with the ball, but must take his fair catch if he succeed in making one.

As amended by Yale and Princeton: —

Rule 8. Substitute the following: "A fair catch is a catch made direct from a kick by one of the opponents, or from a punt-out by one of the same side, provided the man making the catch makes a mark with his heel and does not advance beyond that mark, and no other of his side has touched the ball. If he be interfered with by an opponent who is off-side, or if he be thrown after catching the ball, he shall be given fifteen yards, unless this carry the ball across the goal line; in that case he shall be given but half the intervening distance."

As amended by Harvard, Pennsylvania, and Cornell: —

Rule 8. "A fair catch is a catch made direct from a kick by one of the opponents (or a punt-out by one of the same side), provided no other of the catcher's side touches the ball. If the player be interfered with while attempting to catch the ball by an opponent who is off-side, or if he be thrown after catching the ball, he shall be given fifteen yards. After having caught the ball, he cannot run with it, but may pass it to one of his own side who can run with it or kick it, otherwise it must be put in play at the spot where the fair catch is made, either from a scrimmage, as provided in Rules 7 and 30, or by a free kick, as provided in Rule 1(f). In case the ball is muffed, the opponents shall have an equal chance at the ball."

Rule 29. If a player when off-side interferes with an opponent trying for a fair catch by touching him or the ball, or waving his hat or hands, or deliberately getting in his way, the opponent may have an advance of fifteen yards and a free kick, or down, from where the interference occurred.

As noted earlier, a player may exercise his judgment as to heeling the ball, but if he does heel it, the opponents are subject to a penalty of fifteen yards if they throw him. They are also subject to the same penalty if they interfere with him when trying to make his catch.

Rule 9. A goal consists in kicking the ball in any way except by a punt from the field of play over the cross-bar of the opponents' goal. If the ball pass directly over one of the uprights it shall count a goal.

See Rule 6 of the old code.

Rule 6. A goal is obtained by kicking the ball, in any way except a punt, from the field of play, over the cross-bar or post of the opponents' goal.

The change is merely in the wording. Rule 10. Charging is rushing forward to seize the ball or tackle a player.

The same as Rule 9 of the old.

Rule 9. Charging is rushing forward to seize the ball or tackle a player.

Rule 11. Off-side.

(a) If a player be in the opponents' territory when the ball is put in play he is off-side.

(b) A player is put off-side if the ball in play has last been touched by one of his own side behind him. No player when off-side shall touch the ball except on a fumble in a scrimmage, nor with his hands or arms interrupt or obstruct an opponent until again on-side. No player can, however, be called off-side in his own goal.

(c) A player being put off-side is put on-side when the ball has touched an opponent, or when one of his own side has run in front of him, either with the ball or having been the last player to touch it when behind him.

(d) If a player when off-side touch the ball inside the opponents' ten-yard line, the ball shall go as a touch-back to the opponents.

This covers Rule 24 of the old set.

Rule, 24. (a) A player is put off-side if, during a scrimmage, he get in front of the ball, or if the ball has been last touched by one of his own side behind him. No player can, however, be called off-side in his own goal. No player when off-side shall touch the ball, or with his hands or arms interrupt or obstruct an opponent until again on-side.

As amended by Yale and Princeton: —

Rule 24. (a) Substitute the following: "A player is put off-side if, during a scrimmage, he get in front of the ball, or if the ball has been last touched by one of his own side behind him. No player can, however, be called off-side in his own goal. No player, when off-side, shall touch the ball, except on fumble in scrimmage, nor with his hands or arms interrupt or obstruct an opponent, until again on-side."

Sections b and c of Rule 24 remain unchanged.

(b) A player being off-side is put on-side when the ball has touched an opponent, or when one of his own side has run in front of him, either with the ball or having been the last player to touch it when behind him.

(c) If a player when off-side touch the ball inside the opponents' ten-yard line, the ball shall go as a touch-back to the opponents.

The two rules amount to the same thing, the alteration being in the wording, in order to make on and off side play more clear.

Rule 12. The ball is dead.

(a) Whenever the umpire or referee blows his whistle or declares a down.

(b) When a goal has been obtained.

(c) When a touch-down, safety, or touch-back has been made.

(d) When a fair catch has been heeled.

(e) When it has been downed after going out of bounds or into touch-in-goal.

No play can be made while the ball is dead, except to put it in play by rule. See old Rule 11.

Rule 11. The ball is dead —

I. When the holder has cried down, or when the referee has called a down, or when the umpire has called foul.

II. When a goal has been obtained.

III. When it has been downed after going into touch or touch-in-goal.

IV. When a touch-down or safety has been made.

V. When a fair catch has been made.

VI. When time has been called by the umpire or referee. No play can be made while the ball is dead, except to put it in play by rule.

Here, again, the force of the rule is the same as of old.

Rule 13. (a) The officials of the game shall be an umpire, a referee, and a linesman.

(b) The umpire is the judge of the conduct of the players, and his decision is final regarding fouls and unfair tactics, except in the cases mentioned in (d). The umpire may appeal to both the referee and linesman for testimony in all cases of fouls seen by them, and it shall be their duty to volunteer their testimony in all cases prescribed in 30(a); but they cannot be appealed to upon these points by the captains or players.

(c) The umpire shall permit no coaching, either by substitutes, coaches, or any one inside the ropes. If such coaching occur, he shall warn the offender, and upon the second offense must have him sent behind the ropes for the remainder of the game.

(d) The referee shall see that the ball is put in play properly, and he shall be judge of its position and progress. He is also the judge of forward passes, and of running with the ball by the quarter-back. His decision is final in all points not covered by the umpire.

The referee may appeal to both the umpire and linesman for testimony upon all points within his jurisdiction.

(e) Both umpire and referee shall use whistles to indicate the cessation of play on fouls and downs.

(f) The linesman shall, under the supervision of the referee, mark the distance gained or lost in the progress of the play, and he shall give testimony as prescribed above. He shall also, under direction of the referee, keep the time, and shall use a stop-watch for so doing.

(g) Only one official representative for each side shall come upon the field of play in case of an accident to a player.

This corresponds to Rules 14 and 15 of the old code.

Rule 14. There shall be an umpire, a referee, and a linesman.

As amended by Yale and Princeton: —

Rule 14. Substitute the following:

"(a) The officials of the game shall be an umpire, a referee, and a linesman. The linesman shall have an assistant.

"(b) Any official may disqualify a player under the rules, subject to the approval of the umpire.

"(c) The umpire alone can be appealed to by the captains regarding fouls and unfair tactics.

"(d) No appeal can be made except through the captain.

"(e) The three officials shall formulate ground rules, prior to each game, governing the disposition of the ball in case it touch or be obstructed by some person or object surrounding the field of play. The referee shall announce such rules to the captains before calling play."

As amended by Harvard, Pennsylvania, and Cornell: —

Rule 14. "There shall be two umpires, a referee, and a linesman, who shall be nominated by the captains and confirmed by the Faculty Athletic Committees of the respective universities."

Rule 15. (a) The umpire is the judge of the conduct of the players, and his decision is final regarding fouls and unfair tactics. The umpire may appeal to both the linesman and referee for testimony in cases of unnecessary roughness, off-side play, or holding; but they shall not volunteer their opinion, nor can they be appealed to upon these points by the captains or players.

(b) The referee is judge of the position and progress of the ball, and his decision is final in all points not covered by the umpire.

(c) Both umpire and referee shall use whistles to indicate cessation of play on fouls and downs. The linesman shall use a stop-watch in timing the game.

(d) The umpire shall permit no coaching, either by substitutes, coaches, or any one inside the ropes. If such coaching occur, he shall warn the offender, and upon the second offense must have him sent behind the ropes for the remainder of the game.

(e) The linesman shall, under the advice of the referee, mark the distance gained or lost in the progress of the play, and upon request of the umpire shall give testimony upon any unnecessary roughness or side-play, or holding; but he may not be appealed to by any player or captain. He shall also, under the direction of the referee, keep the time.

(f) Only one official representative for each side shall come upon the field of play in case of an accident to a player.

As amended by Yale and Princeton: —

Rule 15. Substitute the following:

"(a) The umpire is the judge of the conduct of the players, and his decision is final regarding fouls and unfair tactics. The umpire may appeal to both the referee and the linesman for testimony regarding cases of unnecessary roughness and unfair tactics.

"(b) The referee is judge of the position and progress of the ball, and his decision is final in all points not governed by the umpire. He shall have power as in Rule 14, clause b.

"(c) Both umpire and referee shall use whistles to indicate cessation of play on fouls and downs. The linesman shall use a stop-watch in timing the game.

"(d) The umpire shall permit no coaching, either by substitutes, coaches, or any one inside the ropes. If such coaching occur, he shall warn the offender, and upon the second offense must have him sent behind the ropes for the remainder of the game.

"(e) The linesman shall, under the advice of the referee, mark the distance lost or gained in the progress of the play, and upon request of the umpire shall give testimony upon any unnecessary roughness or unfair tactics. He shall, under direction of the referee, keep the time. He shall have power, as in Rule 14, clause b. He cannot be appealed to by the captains on any point whatever.

"(f) Only one official representative for each side shall come upon the field of play in case of an accident to a player."

As amended by Harvard, Pennsylvania, and Cornell: —

Rule 15. "(a) The umpires are the judges of the conduct of the players, and the decision of either is final regarding fouls and unfair tactics. Either umpire may appeal to both linesman and referee for testimony in all cases of fouls or violations of the rules.

"(b) The referee is judge of the position and progress of the ball, and his decision is final in all points not covered by the umpire. He may appeal both to the linesman and umpires for testimony on all points within his jurisdiction. It shall be his duty to give testimony in all cases of fouls or violations of the rules seen by him to either of the umpires, who shall accept such testimony as conclusive, and forthwith impose the penalty for the offense committed prescribed by these rules.

"(c) The linesman shall, under the advice of the referee, mark the distance gained or lost in the progress of the play, and it shall be his duty to give testimony in all cases of fouls or violations of the rules seen by him to either of the umpires, who shall accept such testimony as conclusive, and forthwith impose the penalty for the offense committed prescribed by these rules. He shall also, under the direction of the referee, keep the time.

"(d) Both umpires and referee shall use whistles to indicate cessation of play on fouls and downs. The linesman shall use a stop-watch to time the game. The linesman shall notify the referee, who shall announce the close of the play in the first half and at the conclusion of the game by blowing his whistle.

"(e) The umpires shall permit no coaching, either by substitutes, coachers, or any one inside the rope; if such coaching occur, he shall warn the offender, and upon the second offense must have him sent behind the ropes the remainder of the game.

"(f) After the game all questions of disqualification shall go before a committee of four, to be chosen by the faculty or athletic committee of the two competing universities—two from each. The committee shall have power to disqualify for the remainder of the season, for a year, or for any longer time, according to its discretion. In case of a tie vote the committee shall choose a fifth member, and the decision of the majority shall be final.

"(g) Only one official representative from each side shall come upon the field of play in case of accident to a player."

Here a few of the duties of the umpire have been given to the referee.

Rule 14. (a) The time of the game shall be seventy minutes, each side playing thirty-five minutes from each goal. There shall be ten minutes' intermission between the two halves. The game shall be decided by the final score at the end of even halves. Either side refusing to play after being ordered to do so by the referee shall forfeit the game. This shall also apply to refusing to begin a game when ordered to do so by the referee. The linesman shall notify the captains of the time remaining for play not more than ten nor less than five minutes before the end of each half.

(b) The time shall not be called for the end of a half until the ball is dead, and in case of a try-at-goal from a touch-down, the try shall be allowed. Time shall be taken out, while the ball is being brought out either for a try, kick-out or kick-off, and when play is, for any reason, suspended.

Is identical with the old version as in Rule 16.

Rule 16. (a) The time of game is seventy minutes, each side playing thirty-five minutes from each goal. There shall be ten minutes' intermission between the two halves. The game shall be decided by the final score at the end of even halves. Either side refusing to play after being ordered to by the referee shall forfeit the game. This shall also apply to refusing to commence the game when ordered to by the referee. The linesman shall notify the captains of the time remaining not more than ten nor less than five minutes from the end of each half.

(b) Time shall not be called for the end of a half until the ball is dead; and in the case of a try-at-goal from a touch-down, the try shall be allowed. Time shall be taken out while the ball is being brought out either for a try, kick-out, or kick-off, and when play is for any reason suspended.

Rule 15. No one wearing projecting nails or iron plates on his shoes, or any metal upon his person, shall be allowed to play in a match. No sticky or greasy substance shall be used on the persons of the players.

Corresponds to Rule 17.

Rule 17. No one wearing projecting nails or iron plates on his shoes, or any metal substance upon his person, shall be allowed to play in a match. No sticky or greasy substance shall be used on the person of players.

Rule 16. The captains shall toss up before the beginning of the game, and the winner of the toss shall have his choice of goal or of kick-off. The same side shall not kick off in two successive halves. The ball shall be kicked off at the beginning of each half, and whenever a goal has been obtained the side which has lost the goal shall kick off. In the case of kick-off, kick-out, and kick from a fair catch, the ball must be kicked a distance of at least ten yards into the opponents' territory, unless stopped by an opponent.

Practically the same as Rule 19.

Rule 19. The captains shall toss up before the commencement of the match, and the winner of the toss shall have his choice of goal or of kick-off. The same side shall not kick off in two successive halves. In all cases where the rules provide for a kick, the ball must be actually kicked a distance of at least ten yards into the opponents' territory, unless stopped by the opponents.

The word "actually" is omitted.

Rule 17. At kick-off if the ball go out of bounds before it is touched by an opponent, it shall be brought back and kicked off again. If it be kicked out of bounds a second time, it shall go as a kick-off to the opponents. If either side thus forfeit the ball twice, it shall go as first down at the centre of the field to their opponents.

Corresponds to Rule 20 of the old code.

Rule 20. The ball shall be kicked off at the beginning of each half; and whenever a goal has been obtained, the side which has lost the goal shall kick off. If the ball go into touch before it is touched by an opponent, it shall be brought back and kicked off over again. If it be kicked into touch a second time, it shall go as a kick-off to the opponents.

As amended by Yale and Princeton: —

Rule 20. Substitute the following: "The ball shall be kicked off at the beginning of each half; and whenever a goal has been obtained, the side which has lost the goal shall kick off. If the ball go into touch before it is touched by an opponent, it shall be brought back and kicked off over again. If it be kicked into touch a second time, it shall go as a kick-off to the opponents. If either side thus forfeit the ball twice without it going into the field of play, it shall go as first down at centre of field to opponents."

The clause which was added in the Yale-Princeton amendation has been adopted here to prevent such delay of the game as would occur from repeated kicking into touch.

Rule 18. The side which has a free kick must be behind the ball when it is kicked. At kick-off the opposite side must stand at least ten yards in front of the ball until it is kicked.

Identical with Rule 21 of the old code.

Rule 21. The side which has a free kick must be behind the ball when it is kicked. At kick-off the opposite side must stand at least ten yards in front of the ball until it is kicked.

Rule 19. Charging is lawful for the opponents if the punter advances beyond his line, or, in case of a place-kick, as soon as the ball is put in play by touching the ground.

In case of a punt-out or kick-off, however, the opponents must not charge until the ball is kicked. If opponents charge before the ball is put in play, they shall be put back five yards for every such offense.

Corresponds to Rule 23 of the old code.

Rule 23. Charging is lawful for the opponents if a punter advance beyond his line, or, in case of a place-kick, as soon as the ball is put in play by touching the ground. In the case of a punt-out, however, not until the ball is kicked.

A penalty, it will be seen, is added, directed at unfair or premature charging.

Rule 20. A player may throw or pass the ball in any direction except toward the opponents' goal. If the ball be batted in any direction or thrown forward, it shall go down on the spot to the opponents.

Identical with Rule 28 of the old code.

Rule 28. A player may throw or pass the ball in any direction except toward the opponents' goal. If the ball be batted in any direction, or thrown forward, it shall go down on the spot to the opponents.

Rule 21. (a) If a player having the ball be tackled and the movement of the ball stopped, or if the player cry "down," the referee shall blow his whistle and the side holding the ball shall put it down for a scrimmage. As soon as a runner attempting to go through is tackled and goes down, or whenever a runner having the ball in his possession cries "down," the referee shall blow his whistle and the ball shall be considered down at that spot. Any piling up on the man after that shall be punished by giving him fifteen yards.

(b) The snapper-back is entitled to full and undisturbed possession of the ball. The opponents cannot interfere with the snapper-back nor touch the ball until it is actually put in play. Infringement of this nature shall give the side having the ball five yards at every such offense.

(c) If in snapping the ball the player so doing be offside, the ball must be snapped again, and if this occur three times on the same down, the ball shall go to the opponents. The man who first receives the ball when snapped back from the down shall not carry the ball forward unless he has regained it after it has been passed to and touched another player.

(d) The man who puts the ball in play in a scrimmage, and the opponent opposite him, cannot pick up the ball until it has touched some third man. "Third man" means any other player than the one putting the ball in play and the opponent opposite him.

(e) If in three consecutive downs (unless the ball cross the goal line) a team shall not have advanced the ball five yards or taken it back twenty yards, it shall go to the opponents on the spot of the fourth down. "Consecutive" means without going out of the possession of the side holding it, except that by having kicked the ball they have given their opponents fair and equal chance of gaining possession of it. No kick, however, provided it be not stopped by an opponent, shall be considered as giving the opponents a fair and equal chance of possession unless the ball go beyond the line of scrimmage.

(f) If the snapper-back kick the ball, no player of his side can pick it up until it has gone ten yards into the opponents' territory, unless it be stopped by an opponent.

(g) When the referee or umpire has given a team a distance penalty, the resulting down shall be counted the first down.

Corresponds to Rule 30 of the old code.

Rule 30. (a) If a player having the ball be tackled and the ball fairly held, the man so tackling shall cry "held," the one so tackled must cry "down," and some player of his side put it down for a scrimmage. As soon as a runner attempting to go through is tackled and goes down, the referee shall blow his whistle, and the ball shall be considered down at that spot. Any piling up on the man after that shall be punished by giving him fifteen yards, unless this carry the ball across the goal line, when he shall have only half the intervening distance. The snapper-back and the man opposite him cannot pick out the ball with the hand until it touch a third hand; nor can the opponents interfere with the snapper-back by touching the ball until it is actually put in play. Infringement of this nature shall give the side having the ball five yards at every such offense. The snapper-back is entitled to full and undisturbed possession of the ball. If the snapper-back be off-side in the act of snapping back, the ball must be snapped again, and if this occur three times on the same down, the ball goes to the opponents. The man who first receives the ball when snapped back from a down shall not carry the ball forward under any circumstances whatever. If, in three consecutive fairs and downs, unless the ball cross the goal line, a team shall not have advanced the ball five, or taken it back twenty, yards, it shall go to the opponents on the spot of the fourth down. "Consecutive" means without going out of the possession of the side holding it, and by a kick giving the opponents fair and equal chance of gaining possession of it. When the referee or umpire has given a side a distance penalty, the resulting down shall be counted the first down.

(b) The man who puts the ball in play in a scrimmage cannot pick it up until it has touched some third man. "Third man" means any other player than the one putting the ball in play and the man opposite him.

(c) No momentum-mass plays shall be allowed. A momentum-mass play is one where more than three men start before the ball is put in play. Nor shall more than three men group for that purpose more than five yards back of the point where the ball is put in play.

As amended by Yale and Princeton: —

Rule 30. (c) Substitute the following: "In scrimmage, not more than one man shall start forward before the ball is in play. Not more than three men shall group themselves at a point behind the line of scrimmage before the ball is in play. Seven men or more shall be on the line of scrimmage until the ball is in play, except that the man playing the position of either end rusher may drop back, provided he does not pass inside the position occupied by the man playing adjacent tackle before the ball is put in play." Other sections of Rule 30 remain unchanged.

As will be seen, a necessary distinction has been made regarding what kicks give the opponents fair and equal chance of possession, and a provision has been made as to the centre-rush kicking the ball forward, stating how far it must go before his side can take it up. The next rule treats of momentum and mass plays.

Rule 22. (a) Before the ball is put in play in a scrimmage, should any player of the side which has the ball take more than one step in any direction he must come to a full stop before the ball is put in play.

Exception: One man of the side having the ball may be in motion toward his own goal without coming to a stop before the ball is put in play.

(b) When the ball is put in play, at least five players must be on the line of scrimmage.

(c) If, when the ball is put in play, five players, not including the quarter-back, be behind the line of scrimmage and inside of the positions occupied by the players at the ends of said line, then two of these players must be at least five yards back of this line. But all of these players may be nearer than five yards to the line of scrimmage if two of them are outside of the positions occupied by the players at the ends of said line.

See Rule 30 of the old code, printed above.

Rule 23. If the ball goes out of bounds, whether it bound back or not, a player of the side which touches it down must bring it to the spot where the line was crossed, and there either:

I. Touch it in with both hands, at right angles to the side line, and then kick it; or,

II. Walk out with it at right angles to the side line, any distance not less than five nor more than fifteen yards, and there put it down for a scrimmage, first declaring how far he intends walking. The man who puts the ball in must face the field or the opponents' goal, and he alone can have his foot outside the side line. Any one, except him, who puts his hands or feet between the ball and his opponents' goal is off-side.

Is identical with Rule 31 of the old code.

> *Rule* 31. If the ball goes into touch, whether It bounds back or not, a player of the side which touches it down must bring it to the spot where the line was crossed, and there either
> I. Touch it in with both hands, at right angles to the touch line, and then kick it; or,
> II. Walk out with it at right angles to the touch line, any distance not less than five nor more than fifteen yards, and there put it down for a scrimmage, first declaring how far he intends walking. The man who puts the ball in must face the field or the opponents' goal, and he alone can have his foot outside touch line. Any one, except him, who puts his hands or feet between the ball and his opponents' goal is off-side.

Rule 24. A side which has made a touch-down in their opponents' goal must try-at-goal, either by a place-kick or a punt-out. If the goal be missed, the ball shall go as a kick-off at the centre of the field to the defenders of the goal.

Is identical with Rule 32 of the old code.

> *Rule* 32. A side which has made a touch-down in their opponents' goal must try-at-goal, either by a place-kick or punt-out. If the goal be missed, the ball shall go as a kick-off at the centre of the field to the defenders of the goal.

Rule 25. (a) If the try be a place-kick, a player of the side which has touched the ball down shall bring it up to the goal line, and, making a mark opposite the spot where the ball was touched down, shall bring it out at right angles to the goal line any desired distance, and there place it for another of his side to kick. The opponents must remain behind their goal line until the ball has been placed upon the ground.

(b) The placer in a try-at-goal may be off-side or out of bounds without vitiating the kick.

Corresponds to Rule 33 of the old code.

> *Rule* 33. (a) If the try be by a place-kick, a player of the side which has touched the ball down shall bring it up to the goal line, and, making a mark opposite the spot where it was touched down, bring it out at right angles to the goal line such distance as he thinks proper, and there place it for another of his side to kick. The opponents must remain behind their goal line until the ball has been placed on the ground.
> (b) The placer in a try-at-goal may be off-side or in touch without vitiating the kick.

Very slight change in wording only.

Rule 26. If the trial be by a punt-out, the punter shall bring the ball up to the goal line, and, making a mark opposite the spot where it was touched down, punt out to another of his own side from any spot behind the line of goal and not nearer goal than such mark. The players of his side must stand in the field of play not less than fifteen feet from the goal line. If the touch-down be made in touch-in-goal, the punt-out shall be made from the intersection of the goal line and the side line. The opponents may line up anywhere on the goal line except in the space of five feet on each side of the punter's mark, but they cannot interfere with the punter. The punter cannot touch the ball after kicking it until it strikes or is touched by some other player. If a fair catch be made from a punt-out, the mark shall serve to determine the position as a mark of any fair catch. If a fair catch be not made on the first attempt, the ball shall go as a kick-off at the centre of the field to the defenders of the goal.

Corresponds to Rule 34 of the old code.

Rule 34. If the try be by a punt-out, the punter shall bring the ball up to the goal line, and, making a mark opposite the spot where it was touched down, punt out from any spot behind the line of goal, and not nearer the goal post than such mark, to another of his own side, who must all stand in the field of play not less than fifteen feet from the goal line. If the touch-down be made in touch-in-goal, the punt-out shall be made from the intersection of the goal and the touch lines. The opponents may line up anywhere on the goal line except the space of five feet on each side of punter's mark, but cannot interfere with the punter, nor can he touch the ball after kicking it until it strikes or is touched by some other player. If a fair catch be made from a punt-out, the mark shall serve to determine positions as the mark of any fair catch. If a fair catch be not made on the first attempt, the ball shall go as a kick-off at the centre of the field to the defenders of the goal.

An immaterial alteration in the wording.

Rule 27. A side which has made a touch-back or a safety must kick out, except as otherwise provided, from not more than twenty-five yards outside the kicker's goal. If the ball go out of bounds before striking a player, it must be kicked out again, and if this occur twice in succession it shall be given to the opponents as out of bounds on the twenty-five-yard line on the side where it went out. At kick-out, the opponents must be on the twenty-five-yard line or nearer their own goal, and the kicker's side must be behind the ball when it is kicked, or be adjudged off-side. Should a second touch-back occur before four downs have been played, the side defending the goal may have the choice of a down at the twenty-five-yard line or a kick-out.

Exception: Whenever a side has tried a drop-kick at the goal upon a first down inside the twenty-five-yard line, and the result has been a touch-back, the line of kick-out shall be the ten-yard instead of the twenty-five-yard line, in determining the position of the opponents, and the kicker's side must be behind the ball when it is kicked.

Corresponds to Rule 35 of the old code.

Rule 35. A side which has made a touch-back or a safety must kick out, except as otherwise provided, from not more than twenty-five yards outside the kicker's goal. If the ball go into touch before striking a player, it must be kicked out again; and if this occur twice in succession it shall be given to the opponents as in touch on the twenty-five-yard line on the side where it went out. At kick-out, the opponents must be on the twenty-five-yard line or nearer their own goal, and the kicker's side must be behind the ball when kicked, or be adjudged off-side. Should a second touch-back occur before four downs have been played, the side defending the goal may have the choice of a down at the twenty-five-yard line or a kick-out.

Exception. . . . Whenever a side has tried a drop-kick at the goal upon a first down inside the twenty-five-yard line, and the result has been a touch-back, the line of kick-out shall be the ten-yard instead of the twenty-five-yard line, in determining the positions of the opponents, and the kicker's side must be behind the ball when it is kicked.

"In touch" changed to "out of bounds."

Rule 28. The following shall be the value of each point in the scoring: —

Goal obtained by touch-down - 6

Goal from field-kick - 5

Touch-down, failing goal - 4

Safety by opponents - 2

Identical with Rule 36 of the old code.

Rule 36. The following shall be the value of each point in the scoring: —
Goal obtained by touch-down - 6
Goal from field-kick - 5
Touch-down, failing goal - 4
Safety by opponents - 2

Rule 29. Before the ball is put in play no player shall lay his hands upon, or, by the use of his hands or arms, interfere with an opponent in such a way as to delay putting the ball in play. After the ball is put in play, the players of the side that has possession of the ball can obstruct the opponents with the body only, except the player who runs with the ball. But the players of the side not having the ball can use their hands and arms to push their opponents out of the way.

Corresponds to Rules 25 and 10 of the old code.

Rule 25. No player shall lay his hands upon, or, by the use of his hands or arms, interfere with an opponent, unless he himself or that opponent has the ball. That is, the players of the side which has possession of the ball can obstruct the opponents with the body only. But the players of the side which has not the ball can use the hands and arms, as heretofore; that is, to push their opponents out of the way in breaking through when the ball is snapped.

As amended by Harvard, Pennsylvania, and Cornell: —

Rule 25. "No player shall lay his hands upon, or by the use of his hands or arms interfere with, an opponent before the ball is put in play. After the ball is put in play, the players of the side that have possession of the ball can obstruct the opponents with the body only, except the player who runs with the ball. But the players of the side which has not the ball can use hands and arms to push the opponents out of the way in breaking through."

Rule 10. Foul interference is using the hands or arms in any way to obstruct or hold a player who has not the ball. This does not apply to the man running with the ball; that is, the runner may push off his adversaries.

In effect, the rule prevents any pulling of men off-side or other "scrapping" in the line, of such a nature as would cause the centre to wait and not put the ball in play.

Rule 30. (a) A player shall be disqualified for unnecessary roughness, hacking, or striking with the closed fist.

(b) If a player be disqualified or injured, a substitute shall take his place. The player thus replaced cannot return to further participation in the game.

(c) For the offenses of throttling, tripping, or tackling below the knees, the opponents shall receive fifteen yards, or a free kick, at their option. In case, however, the fifteen yards will carry the ball across the goal line, they may have half the distance from the spot of the offense to the goal line, but shall not be allowed a free kick.

Corresponds to Rules 27 and 13 of the old code.

Rule 27. (a) A player shall be disqualified for unnecessary roughness, hacking, or striking with closed fist.

(b) For the offenses of throttling, tripping up, or intentional tackling below the knees, the opponents shall receive twenty-five yards, or a free kick, at their option. In case, however, the twenty-five yards would carry the ball across the goal line, they can have half the distance from the spot of the offense to the goal line, and shall not be allowed a free kick.

Rule 13. The game shall be played by teams of eleven men each, and in case of a disqualified or injured player, a substitute shall take his place. Nor shall the disqualified or injured player return to further participation in the game.

The wording is slightly altered, but the intent and effect are the same.

Rule 31. (a) A foul shall be granted for any violation of the rules, unnecessary delay of the game, off-side play, or holding an opponent, unless he has the ball. No delay arising from any cause whatsoever shall continue more than three minutes.

(b) The penalty for fouls, except where otherwise provided, shall be, when the offending side has the ball, the immediate surrender of it to the opponents for a down; or, when the offending side has not the ball, the advance of the ball ten yards.

(c) The offended side may refuse to accept the penalty where it is to its disadvantage. But in the case of a run resulting, should it be over fifteen yards, that distance shall be the limit allowed.

(d) Whenever the rules provide for a distance penalty, if the distance prescribed would carry the ball across the goal line, one half the intervening distance shall be given.

Corresponds to Rules 26 and 3 of the old code.

Rule 26. (a) A foul shall be granted for intentional delay of the game, offside play, or holding an opponent, unless he has the ball. No delay arising from any cause whatsoever shall continue more than three minutes.

(b) The penalty for fouls or violations of rules, except where otherwise provided, shall be, when the offending side has the ball, the immediate surrender of it to the opponents for a down, or, when the offending side has not the ball, the advance of the ball ten yards. In this, as in other penalties of a similar nature, if the distance given would carry the ball across the goal line, only half the intervening distance shall be given.

(c) The offended side may refuse to accept the penalty where it is to its disadvantage; but in the case of a run resulting, should it be over fifteen yards that distance shall be the limit allowed.

Rule 3. A foul is a violation of any rule.

The order and wording slightly altered.

INDEX

TRILOGY INDEX

FUNDAMENTALS

POSITIONS

Linemen (forwards, rushers)

KICKING & SPECIAL TEAMS

GENERAL SUBJECTS

Made in the USA
Las Vegas, NV
13 November 2021